Published under the auspices of
THE CENTER FOR JAPANESE AND KOREAN STUDIES,
University of California, Berkeley

THE FUTURE AND THE PAST

The Future and the Past

A translation and study of the
Gukanshō,
an interpretative history of Japan
written in 1219

by Delmer M. Brown and Ichirō Ishida

UNIVERSITY OF CALIFORNIA PRESS

BERKELEY • LOS ANGELES • LONDON

University of California Press
Berkeley and Los Angeles, California
University of California Press, Ltd.
London, England
Copyright © 1979 by
The Regents of the University of California
ISBN 0-520-03460-0
Library of Congress Catalog Card Number: 77-73493
Printed in the United States of America

123456789

To Mary and Kikuko

Contents

Preface

Our common interest in the intellectual and cultural ferment of Japan's thirteenth century led us to the *Gukanshō,* a study of Japanese history written just before the 1221 outbreak of a decisive war between the aristocratic court in Kyoto and the military government in Kamakura. We were attracted above all by the work's significance as the first known Japanese attempt to construct a pattern of historical change that would explain the disturbed situation of that day and show what could and should be done to restore peace and stability. We were also intrigued by the question of why the author, a Buddhist priest steeped in Buddhist doctrines of spiritual truth and historical decline, was impelled to write a political history that was grounded in, and shaped by, belief in the possibilities (or destiny) of a brighter future. Concluding that a close reading of the book would help us and others to gain a surer grasp of the ideas and beliefs of people living in Japan during those days of social upheaval and impending crisis, we decided to undertake a study and translation of this historical classic.

We also agreed that this should be a joint venture, particularly since the *Gukanshō* is the most difficult of all Japanese historical works to comprehend. Written over 750 years ago and apparently in a hurry, the book is replete with archaic phrases, obsolete terms, and involved sentences that can be worked out only after the reader has become familiar with the subject discussed and with the author's unique view of history. Furthermore, the original text is no longer extant, and recently published editions are based on copies that, although considered authentic, are somewhat defective. But the most serious difficulty arises from the view of the author (Jien, 1155–1225) that Japanese history had taken, and was still taking, its form and direction from a constantly changing pattern of interaction between various unseen forces, deities, and Principles *(dōri)*. Jien believed that some Principles had been pulling Japan's "single course" of history downward toward ultimate destruction while other Principles, when properly understood and followed by persons of ability *(kiryō),* had pulled, and could still pull, it upward toward improvement. Such complex and fluid interaction between spiritual forces and imperatives (Principles) has made it difficult for modern historians, Japanese or non-Japanese, to agree on the basic character of the work's interpretation.

After we decided to make a joint translation and study of the *Gukanshō,* Mr. Ishida first prepared—with the assistance of graduate students at the Tōhoku University—a modern-Japanese version of the original text. Then Mr. Brown drafted an English translation, using the Jirō Maruyama edition of the original, the Etsuji Nakajima commentary, and Mr. Ishida's modern-Japanese version. For about six months during the academic year 1963–64 while we were Senior Research Fellows at the East-West Center in Honolulu, we worked together on the meaning of difficult passages. Mr. Ishida would first read the draft translation, marking places where he thought improvement could be made, and then we would discuss (in Japanese) the questions raised and try to reach an agreement on whether, and if so how, the translation should be changed. During the next three or four years each of us made independent studies of the *Gukanshō* interpretation. Mr. Ishida published one monograph and four articles. Two of the articles have been translated and edited by Mr. Brown for Chapter 10. Mr. Brown wrote several papers that were first discussed at colloquia of the Center for Japanese Studies at Berkeley and then rewritten for the Introduction and Chapters 8 and 9. Since these studies had given us a clearer picture of the *Gukanshō* interpretative pattern, we felt that the translation should be revised once more. When the task was completed, we devoted three more months to daily conferences on such problems as the author's periodization of Japanese history, his conception of Inner and Outer

Cause, his mixture of Buddhist and Shinto belief, and his basic political concerns. The final draft—like the earlier ones—was written by Mr. Brown but was frequently altered in producing a version acceptable to us both.

Certain features of the translation, the scope and nature of the footnotes, as well as the problems selected for treatment in introductory studies arise from our conclusion that the *Gukanshō* is, and was meant to be, a theological interpretation of Japan's past, not an historical source or literary classic. We have therefore added chapter titles, topical headings, and even phrases and words (placed in brackets when we are not sure of our ground) in an attempt to help the reader understand Jien's unique approach to history. Realizing the importance of clan (and house) affiliation in the *Gukanshō* view of the past, we have also decided to place the names of all clans and houses in capital letters; and we have tried to limit footnotes to those that will help the reader grasp the relationship of a particular subject to Jien's conception of the historical process.[1] Finally, our introductory studies are confined to these questions: the evolution and character of Jien's historical thought; how the *Gukanshō* differs from, and is affected by, earlier historical interests and themes; to what extent Jien's own religious beliefs, familial connections, political concerns, and dream revelations figured in his historical consciousness; and how these beliefs, concerns, and revelations were fused into a remarkably coherent thought structure.

Our task has been facilitated enormously by the scholarly endeavors of others. Although Japanese history after 1219 did not follow the course that Jien claimed it should, and although no Japanese government has ever stated that the *Gukanshō* either explained or justified that government's existence, the book has been the subject of investigation for centuries, especially since World War II. These studies have emerged mainly from three types of interest: (1) a political interest of persons who, at times of military government *(bakufu)* weakness, saw merit in Jien's advocacy of a government in which aristocratic leaders would co-operate with military leaders; (2) a textual interest by those who, under the influence of National Learning *(kokugaku)* and Western standards and methods of historical research, saw the *Gukanshō* as a valuable historical source; and (3) an intellectual interest by recent scholars who have appreciated Jien's book as a unique interpretation of Japanese history. Some historians have of course been motivated by more than one of these interests,

1. Information on persons, offices, ceremonies, temples, shrines, customs, and treatments in other historical accounts can be found in the voluminous notes of Masao Okami and Toshihide Akamatsu, eds., *Gukanshō* (vol. 86 of Iwanami Shoten: *Nihon koten bungaku taikei,* 1967).

and no interest can be confined to one period, but these distinctions will be helpful in outlining the contributions that have made our task easier and more exciting.

In the fifteenth century, when endemic civil war had seriously weakened the Ashikaga *bakufu,* an aristocrat by the name of ICHIJŌ Kaneyuki (1402–81) wrote a treatise that was meant for the eyes of the current Shogun and that presented a *Gukanshō*-like case for the establishment of a government in which the major aristocratic house would co-operate with the strongest military clan. It was at about this time that the oldest extant copy of the *Gukanshō,* the Bunmei text, was transcribed. But interest in Jien's work was much deeper during the century or so that preceded the collapse of the Tokugawa *bakufu* in 1868. That was the period when all other twenty known copies of the *Gukanshō* were made, and in 1846 Nobutomo Ban (1773–1846) wrote a commentary entitled the *Doku Gukanshō.* Although Nobutomo was interested mainly in what Jien had actually said and meant, he was certainly aware of the *Gukanshō's* relevance to contemporary interest in the position of the Emperor: "When someone reads the *Gukanshō,* he will become drenched in tears if he is deeply saddened and indignant about the loss of respect for Imperial tombs, and about the world's continuing decline. . . ."[2] Nobutomo seems also to have understood that the *Gukanshō* had an integrated but complex thought structure, and he drew some astute conclusions: that the book was written by Jien (later confirmed); that it was written in 1223 (now we think it was written four years earlier); that it advocated political change and was meant to be read by Retired Emperor Go-Toba (generally accepted); and that Jien did not attach his own name to the manuscript, and referred to himself in the third person, because he was indignant about the current situation (not established).[3]

The textual study begun by Nobutomo Ban was extended and deepened by later Japanese historians who were influenced by the stress of Western scholarship on the importance of having accurate and complete historical evidence objectively assessed. Carefully collating and editing recently discovered copies of the *Gukanshō,* these historians published six editions of the work between 1900 and 1967.[4] Other notable achievements of this type include the publication of Jien's collected works by Munehaya Taga in 1945, the completion of a commentary by Etsuji Nakajima in 1969, and Toshihide

2. "Hikobae," Ban Nobutomozenshū (Tokyo, 1907), 4.356.
3. Ibid., 353–7.
4. For our translation and study, we have followed the earlier Iwanami edition: Jirō Maruyama, ed., *Gukanshō* (Iwanami Shoten, 7th ed., 1960), but have consulted others. The notes of the later Okami edition (see note 1, above) have been especially helpful.

Akamatsu's recent discovery and publication of important documents—especially dream interpretations and prayers—written by
Jien.[5] Probably the first distinguished textual historian was Hiroyuki
Miura (1871–1931). He discovered letters in the archives of the Shōren Cloister that enabled him to prove that Jien was the *Gukanshō's*
author. And he also opened up a long controversy when he wrote
that the *Gukanshō* was composed before the outbreak of the Shōkyū
War of 1221, not afterward as Nobutomo Ban had claimed. Sōkichi
Tsuda (1873–1961) felt, however, that Jien had written his history
after that War but with the intention of causing the reader to think
that it had been written before. Tsunetsugu Muraoka (1884–1946)
sided with Miura, and, after several decades of further research and
writing on this subject, historians are now generally agreed that
Miura and Muraoka were right.

While these textual historians were engaged principally in the
work of identifying, collating, and editing texts and documents—
and in working on questions of authorship, dating, and how many
chapters (fascicles) were included in the *Gukanshō* original—they
were also asking why Jien had written this history and to whom he
was addressing it. But it was Tsunetsugu Muraoka, Japan's eminent
historian of Shinto thought,[6] who made the first significant advances
in the analysis of Jien's view of history. He noted that Jien's interpretation was firmly rooted in kalpic doctrines and pointed out that his
Principles were not merely norms but historical imperatives. Muraoka also saw that Jien's belief in kalpic deterioration was mixed with
belief in the power of Buddhist law "to destroy evil and create
good."[7] A number of post–World War II historians have made further advances in different areas of Jien's thought, and we will cite
studies that have been especially helpful. In general, however, modern scholars have devoted their research primarily to specific problems rather than to the overall pattern and character of Jien's historical interpretation.

Three partial translations have been made by others. Over forty
years ago—before the best editions were published and Nakajima's
commentary was completed—J. Rhader translated the summary
chapter (Chapter 5 of this translation) and published it in the *Acta
Orientalia* (1936) under the title of "Miscellany of the Personal Views
of an Ignorant Fool (Gukwansho)." Those parts of the *Gukanshō* covering events of the Hōgen War of 1156 were translated and ap-

5. Full references to these and other recent studies are found in the Bibliography.

6. Cf. his *Studies in Shinto Thought,* translated by Delmer M. Brown and
James T. Araki (Tokyo, 1966).

7. "Mappō shisō no tenkai to *Gukanshō* no shikan," *Nihon shisōshi kenkyū:
Nihon shisōshi jō sho mondai* (Tokyo, 1964), 2.111–209.

pended to William R. Wilson's *Hōgen monogatari: Tale of the Disorder of Hogen* (Sophia University, 1971). And finally, Charles H. Hambrick's dissertation on the subject of "Gukansho: A Religious View of History" (submitted at the University of Chicago in 1971) contains translations of several other sections. Although we have made an independent translation of the entire work, we have consulted these partial translations and benefited from them.

We also wish to express our appreciation for the institutional support that has enabled us to carry out this project together. The East-West Center of Honolulu awarded us grants that freed us from teaching responsibilities during an entire semester in 1963–64 and provided excellent office and library facilities. The Center for Japanese Studies on the Berkeley campus of the University of California supplied Mr. Ishida with funds that enabled him to come to Berkeley for work on the project during the summer of 1972, and the Center also made grants to Mr. Brown, year after year, for the employment of research assistants. Finally, a Fellowship awarded to Mr. Brown by the Humanities Research Fellowship Program on the Berkeley campus has permitted us to bring this translation and study to completion in Sendai.

We are grateful too for the stimulation, encouragement, and assistance received from fellow historians. Professor Noah Brannen of the International Christian University in Tokyo, and Professors David Keightley, Irwin Scheiner, and William McCullough of Berkeley, have read the manuscript and offered valuable suggestions for improvement. Professor Masao Maruyama of Tokyo University read Chapter 8 and made critical comments that enabled Mr. Brown to tighten his comparative analysis of *Kojiki* and *Nihongi* thought. Chizuko Kawamoto read the whole of an early draft, comparing it with the original and calling attention to errors and omissions. She also prepared an index of names, offices, and special terms. We have been aided greatly by other research assistants, especially Peter Wetzler. Finally, we wish to express our gratitude to Julie Clelland for arranging to have much of the manuscript typed, and related matters handled, while we were both in Japan.

In appreciation for the patient support of our wives we are pleased to dedicate this book to them.

DELMER M. BROWN
ICHIRŌ ISHIDA

Introduction

Jien (1155–1225) wrote the *Gukanshō* in an attempt to convince his readers that Japanese deities had created a divine plan by which KUJŌ Yoritsune (1218–56), a young boy of Jien's own aristocratic KUJŌ house, was to grow up and administer state affairs in behalf of the Emperor. According to the *Gukanshō* delineation of Japan's single course of history, this two-year-old Yoritsune was destined to become not only Regent but Shogun of the military government located in eastern Japan. Although Jien, like most intellectuals of his day, assumed that the universe was moving toward extinction, he was certain that if Yoritsune were permitted to play his preordained role, Japan would enjoy another period of temporary improvement.

One can fathom Jien's historical advocacy of an untried form of political control only by considering the significance of the ties that had been established between KUJŌ aristocrats and MINAMOTO generals. Jien's favorite brother, KUJŌ Kanezane (1149–1207), was appointed Regent in 1186 because his candidacy was supported by MINAMOTO Yoritomo (1147–99), the most powerful general of that day and the head (Shogun) of the new military government. And

Yoritomo's influence can also be detected in Jien's own appointment as Tendai Abbot in 1192. The KUJŌ house had therefore lost much of its aristocratic purity, helping us to see why Jien should have later concluded that the decade between 1186 and 1196—sometimes referred to as the Golden Age of the KUJŌ house—was a time of improvement produced by cooperation between the KUJŌ Regent and the MINAMOTO Shogun.

Jien's preoccupation with KUJŌ fortunes was deepened by the several KUJŌ dismissals of 1196. Having held key positions at the Imperial Court, KUJŌ men and women now found themselves outside the court's inner circles. Although some of their old power and prestige was regained between 1202 and 1206, members of the more purely aristocratic KONOE house received the highest court appointments after the untimely death of KUJŌ Yoshitsune in 1206. And the KONOE continued to overshadow the KUJŌ down to and beyond 1219 when the *Gukanshō* was written. Indeed, until 1218 the prospects for a KUJŌ return to power were becoming increasingly dim as relations between the court and the military government worsened, for the KUJŌ—standing in an isolated position between the two contending camps—seemed not to be fully trusted by either side.

But just a few months before Jien began writing his study of history in 1219, two events aroused high hopes that a KUJŌ man might soon become Regent and that a KUJŌ boy might grow up to become Shogun. The first of the two events was the selection of an Imperial son by a KUJŌ Empress as Crown Prince. If the Prince should ascend the throne, a KUJŌ brother of the Imperial mother would surely be named Regent. The second event, the adoption of the two-year-old KUJŌ Yoritsune into the MINAMOTO clan as its next head, was even more auspicious. These two "incomprehensible" developments made Jien and his relatives hopeful that the KUJŌ house might capture the most prestigious and powerful offices in the land: Regent for the Emperor in Kyoto, and Shogun of the military government in Kamakura. Not long afterward, Jien seems to have dreamed of having KUJO Yoritsune become both Regent and Shogun. And the *Gukanshō* was written under the influence of such hope and belief.

Readers of the present day have difficulty understanding why the leaders of the MINAMOTO clan, as well as Retired Emperor Go-Toba and his advisers, were receptive to the proposal that an aristocratic son be adopted into, and made the head of, the country's strongest military clan. All officials of that day must have been skeptical of Jien's later declaration that KUJŌ Yoritsune's birth, his adoption into the MINAMOTO clan, and his future appointment as Shogun were all willed (or created) by Japan's principal ancestral Kami. But everyone knew that the assassination of MINAMOTO Sanetomo, who had not produced a son, presented the country with a serious succession problem. MINAMOTO advisers—especially the mother of the assassinated Sanetomo—felt that the adoption of a KUJŌ boy as the next MINAMOTO head would add legitimacy and unity to the weakened military government. The true aristocrats of Kyoto, on the other hand, probably thought of the adoption as a harmless concession that would allow the Imperial Court more time to prepare for war against the military regime. Located between the two opposing parties, the KUJŌ were clearly excited by the possibilities of emerging, once again, to the top of an administrative structure supported by both the aristocratic court and the military government. It was then that Jien apparently began to write an historical study that would persuade persons in positions of authority that Yoritsume, as Regent and Shogun, should and would serve the Emperor with the combined strength of learning (from the aristocratic house of KUJŌ) and military might (from the military clan of MINAMOTO).[1]

Why did Jien elect to use a new historical form in attempting to show what was bound to happen? He says nothing directly about the question, merely stating that he had decided to write about the unilinear course of Japanese history in a way that would help able men to understand how events have been, and will continue to be, drawn along that course by unseen Principles. But it seems that Jien and his KUJŌ relatives were no longer able to exert influence in such traditional ways as talking personally with the Retired Emperor or writing memorials and dream interpretations. Even long prayers addressed to Buddhist or Shinto deities may not have been thought of, under the circumstances of that day, as a particularly effective way of altering court policy. Furthermore, as hopeful as Jien had become about the future of his KUJŌ house, he may well have known or guessed that Retired Emperor Go-Toba and his advisers were already making plans to destroy the military government. And Jien was positive that a war would be disastrous for the KUJŌ, regardless of its outcome. Also, Jien had had a number of dreams which he believed to be revelations of ancestral Kami will, and his attempts to understand those revelations led him to conclude that human affairs were being drawn along a single road by unseen powers. Finally, he was undoubtedly aware that, as one of the country's most respected religious leaders, he could speak with authority about the will and purpose of the ancestral Kami. Whatever the reason, he seems to have become confident that by delineating a "single course" of Japanese history he could convince Retired Emperor Go-Toba and other officials that Japan was destined to enter a period of temporary stability and prosperity *if* KUJŌ Yoritsune were permitted to serve the

---

1. See Chapter 9 for a fuller discussion of Jien's life and the evolution of his unique view of history.

Emperor as Regent *and* Shogun. So his decision to make his case by
writing a new kind of history seems to have emerged from feelings
that were mixed with hope, desperation, belief, and self-assurance.

The special character of the *Gukanshō's* historical interpretation is
firmly rooted in Jien's belief that the course of Japanese history had
been, and would continue to be, determined by divine imperatives
called Principles *(dōri)*, a word used throughout his study of history
and also in prayers, poems, and letters written by him during those
troublesome years before the Shōkyū War. Noting the importance of
these Principles to the *Gukanshō* view of history, and reading Jien's
statements that "all phenomena are affected by Principles" and
"nothing lies outside the bounds of Principles," early readers referred to his work as a Tale of Principles *(dōri no monogatari)*. Although Jien made a point of writing "so that even the unlearned
might understand" how Principles interacted with each other, he
admitted that only a few persons of ability *(kiryō)* would be able to see
just how the interaction was driving events of Japanese history along
one definite course. It is therefore not surprising that modern historians, Japanese and non-Japanese, have had difficulty comprehending either the essential meaning of Principles or the general pattern
of their interaction.

The *Gukanshō* interpretation is structured by two types of Principles, pulling the course of human affairs in opposite directions: destructive ones that account for a continuing process of deterioration
over time, and constructive ones that make it possible for "understanding" leaders to achieve partial and temporary improvement.
Principles of the first type, pressing everything toward extinction,
arise from an acceptance of the old Hindu belief[2] that the world is
now passing through the deteriorating half of a small kalpa and that
everything will continue to deteriorate until this half comes to an
end, thousands of years hence. In Jien's day, Buddhism itself was
believed to have entered a third and final age of decay: the age of
Final Law *(mappō)*, which was thought to have begun in A.D. 1052
and to be destined to end only when this deteriorating half of the
present small kalpa has run its course. Deeply influenced by Final
Law belief, Jien outlines seven periods of Japanese history (Chapter
5) and explains that each period, governed by its own destructive
Principle, is another stage of progressive decay.

Principles of the constructive type, on the other hand, include
Shinto and Buddhist Principles which, if understood and adjusted
to, have the power to negate kalpic decline, temporarily and partially. Jien identifies several Buddhist Principles of this type: the
Principle of "destroying evil and creating good," the Principle of

2. Discussed in Chapter 10.

"hindering evil and maintaining good," and Principles associated with "blessings of expediency" bestowed upon the Japanese people by various Buddhas and Bodhisattvas. Blessings-of-expediency Principles occupy an especially important place in Jien's view of the past, as is disclosed in his discussion of four important historical figures who, as Buddhist incarnations, bestowed "blessings" upon Japan at times of significant improvement. Commenting on such blessings, he says: "Alas, if all Emperors and ministers had believed deeply in those 'expedient blessings' and given some thought to the true course of Principles, not deviating one iota from them, I think that the 'time fate' of deterioration from the beginning to the end of the first half of the present small kalpa could not have been avoided, but that for the time being, there would have been no unfortunate or unexpected disasters" (Chapter 1). Constructive Buddhist Principles, especially those associated with Japanese leaders who are depicted as Buddhist incarnations, are used to explain and sanctify two developments of special importance to Jien and his view of Japanese history: the spread of Buddhism in Japan, and the rise of the FUJIWARA clan and its KUJŌ house.

As central as constructive Buddhist Principles are to Jien's historical outlook, constructive Shinto ones—those created or activated by the ancestral Kami of Japan—are even more decisive for periods of improvement in which Jien has the strongest interest. The first period[3] of temporary upturn toward improvement—Jien's third period, which began when Buddhism was first supported by the state in the 6th century and reached its highest point in the glorious days of FUJIWARA Michinaga in the 11th—is presented as a period when constructive Shinto Principles were operative. It was a time, Jien writes, for which the Sun Goddess (the ancestral Kami of the Imperial House and the highest Shinto deity) had decided that the power of Buddhist Law should be brought to the support of Imperial rule by FUJIWARA ministers (Chapter 1). We are told that the "three meritorious acts" of FUJIWARA ministers occurred then because of a Principle created when the Sun Goddess agreed with the ancestral Kami of the FUJIWARA clan that the two of them should join forces in guarding the Imperial House (Chapter 5).

But constructive Shinto Principles are even more decisive in the *Gukanshō* treatment of later periods of improvement. Jien says that the improvement of the fifth period—beginning in 1156 and reaching its highest point when Jien's brother was serving as Regent—was due to the Principle created when the Sun Goddess and the ancestral Kami of the FUJIWARA clan agreed that Imperial rule should now be

3. Figure 4, Chapter 10, shows how Jien related his seven periods of Japanese history to Kami-created Principles for times of improvement.

supported by the cooperative service of an aristocratic Regent and a
military Shogun. Finally, the improvement of the seventh period—
beginning in 1199 and encompassing a future time of partial
recovery—is attributed to a Principle created by a second agreement
between these same three ancestral Kami: that Imperial rule should
now be supported by KUJŌ Yoritsune as Shogun *and* Regent. Thus
the importance of constructive Shinto Principles is revealed not only
in their contributions to the improved character of particular
periods in Japan's past but in their centrality to Jien's belief in a
better future.

Although Jien bases his historical interpretation on belief in Principles with different origins (Buddhist and Shinto), with different
time spans of effectiveness (some for the whole of Japanese history
and some for certain periods), and with different effects on Japanese
life (some destructive and some constructive), he insists that an "understanding" reader will see how continuous interaction between
these Principles has driven the course of Japanese history along one
definite course. Retracing that course—like the task of understanding the character and relationships of Principles—is not easy, mainly
because the course is not straight: it moves generally downhill toward extinction but is marked by short uphill stretches of improvement, somewhat as shown in Figure 1. While the course is irregular,[4]
and interaction between Principles complex, Jien is intent upon convincing his reader that this single course of history makes it inevitable
and desirable that KUJŌ Yoritsune will soon occupy the aristocratic
office of Regent as well as the military post of Shogun.

Jien approaches Japan's past in a new way but does so under the
influence of old historical interests.[5] Especially important is an old
genealogical one. Like the men who ordered and compiled the earliest extant chronicles, Jien values Japan's unbroken line of Imperial
descent from the Sun Goddess. And he is also preoccupied, as were
the authors of earlier Historical Tales, with connections between
Imperial and FUJIWARA lines of descent. The opening paragraph of
the *Gukanshō* contains the statement that no Succession Tale (*yotsugi
no monogatari*) has been written since the outbreak of the Hōgen Rebellion of 1156, leaving the impression that Jien thought of his study
as an up-to-date Succession Tale. Probably because he was bent on
establishing the legitimacy of KUJŌ Yoritsune's future appointments

4. The nature of the irregularity is explained by Jien's analogy of the man
whose supply of paper is being gradually exhausted because each replenishment is less than the amount used since the last replenishment
(Chapter 1).

5. Outlined in Chapter 8.

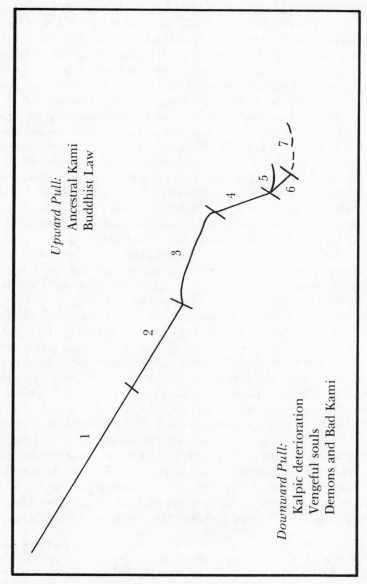

Figure 1.

as Regent and Shogun, and assumed that such legitimacy flows principally from ties between the KUJŌ house and reigning Emperors,
Jien compiled an Imperial chronology (Chapters 6 and 7 of this
translation) before beginning to write the *Gukanshō's* narrative chapters. This chronology is essentially a reign-by-reign delineation of
Imperial succession into which is worked the succession of FUJIWARA
ministers (and Tendai Abbots) who were male relatives of Imperial
mothers. These succession lines are prominent and important
throughout the narrative chapters that follow. Thus the genealogical
core of the *Gukanshō* is not unlike that of a Succession Tale.

But unlike a Succession Tale, the *Gukanshō* presents an interpretation of Japanese history that is rooted in the uniqueness and sacredness of the Imperial line. The uniqueness of that line is commented
on in this way: "China selects its Emperors and Empresses on the
basis of ability, but in this country of Japan there never has been an
Emperor or Empress who has not been in the Imperial line" (Chapter 5). The Imperial line's sacredness, clearly revealed in declarations
that the Sun Goddess had created a special type of Imperial rule for
each of Japan's seven periods of history, is based upon two related
beliefs: that the Imperial line has been created by the Sun Goddess;
and that each Emperor or Empress on that line has ruled Japan in
accordance with an arrangement created by the Sun Goddess for
that particular stage of kalpic deterioration.

While some of the *Gukanshō's* divine Principles are Buddhist in
origin and character, its Shinto Principles—created by the Sun Goddess and calling for specific types of Imperial rule at given periods
of time—elevate the Sun Goddess to a position above all other ancestral Kami and apparently above other unseen forces propelling
the human affairs of Japan along one single course. The primacy of
the Sun Goddess and her Imperial agents is made very clear in what
the *Gukanshō* has to say about the will of the Sun Goddess and the
character of Imperial rule for the immediate future. True, Jien
maintains that Buddhist Principles had a powerful effect on secular
affairs when four famous incarnations of Buddha appeared in Japan,[6] but neither Buddhist Principles nor incarnations of Buddha
figure prominently in those modern periods of Japanese history in
which Jien has the deepest interest. Moreover, the *Gukanshō* carries a

6. Each of the four incarnations has a special position in Jien's view of
Japanese history. The first (Prince Shōtoku, 574–622) is considered to be the
father of Japanese Buddhism; the second (FUJIWARA Kamatari, 614–669) is
honored as the founder of the FUJIWARA clan; the third (SUGAWARA
Michizane, 845–903) is described as an incarnation that wishes to protect
Imperial Law under conditions of the final reigns; and the fourth (Ji'e,
912–985) is said to have made a "firm patron pledge" with FUJIWARA
Morosuke (908–960), the founder (according to Jien) of the KUJŌ house.

heavy accent on the existence of an Imperial line of Emperors and Empresses who have been, and will continue to be, sacred instruments for the implementation of Principles created by the Sun Goddess.

The place of Japan's unbroken Imperial line in the *Gukanshō* thesis is reflected—but not fully explained—in Jien's use of the word Imperial Law *(ōhō)*. In ancient Buddhist writings this word denoted the secular authority of rulers, as distinct from the divine authority of Buddhist Law *(buppō)*. But for Japanese writers, Imperial Law was gradually narrowed to Emperors and Empresses of Japan. And to the extent that these rulers were revered as descendants of the Sun Goddess, the word pointed to sacred origins and functions. In at least one Military Tale (the *Heike Monogatari*) Buddhist priests are made to affirm a special relationship between Buddhist Law and Imperial Law, but in the *Gukanshō* that relationship takes on a divine quality. This is suggested in Chapter 5, where it is stated that a leader should protect both Buddhist Law and Imperial Law and become a "receptacle for the divine blessings of Buddhas and Kami." The author does not search for the religious roots of Imperial Law—nor say that it is divine—but by focusing his study on Japan's unbroken line of Emperors and Empresses descended from the Principle-creating Sun Goddess, he leaves the impression that for him Imperial Law is a divine truth revealed by ancestral Kami, just as Buddhist Law is a divine truth revealed by Buddha. Noting, therefore, the core position of constructive Principles created by the ancestral Kami of the Imperial House, appreciating the primacy of that Kami over other ancestral Kami (and apparently over other unseen powers), and sensing Jien's assumption of a divine quality in Imperial Law, we see that belief in the divine origins of the Imperial line has been transformed into a powerful historical determinant.

Jien inherited other interests from previous historians, and the Buddhist ones have left a deep imprint upon his view of history. Japan's Six National Histories—completed between 720 and 901—include a wealth of information about the spread of Buddhism, and later Historical and Military Tales often refer to Buddhist doctrines of impermanence, karmic retribution, and Final Law decline. But Buddhism in the *Gukanshō* does more than provide subjects for, and leave its mark on, reports and stories of the past: it is a source and transmitter of doctrines about divine powers which, together with the power of Principles created by native Kami, are believed to have driven, and are still driving, Japanese history along one definite course. Although Jien's motives for writing history do not emerge solely from his Buddhist faith, and his convictions about the possibility of future improvement arise mainly from his belief in the relevations and power of Kami, several features of the *Gukanshō* treatment of secular history are truly Buddhist in character: its periodization in terms of Buddhist doctrines of kalpic decline until the end of the first half of the present small kalpa; its view that four important men in Japanese history were incarnations of Buddha; and, above all, its thesis that Buddhist Law is a divine force that can be used to check kalpic decline in this physical world. Such features make the *Gukanshō* more nearly a Buddhist interpretation of Japanese history than any previous chronicle or Tale.

Like earlier Tales of the past, the *Gukanshō* is also the work of an individual—not of some governmental bureau—interested in the activities of eminent men and women. But unlike the authors of the Historical and Military Tales, Jien is not fascinated by an individual's achievements in study, love, art, or war. He focuses his attention instead upon men who have (or can develop) an ability *(kiryō)* to understand unseen Principles and who have (or will) become instruments for constructive change in the affairs of state. Jien believes that such ability cannot be obtained simply by mastering the Confucian classics, gaining familiarity with artistic tastes and techniques, or even studying and reflecting on Buddhist scripture, but by perceiving the nature and interaction of Principles that have been created for a particular time and place. Believing, however, that abilities—as well as divine power and everything else—are subject to kalpic decay, Jien is certain that very few able persons are left. His insists, nevertheless, that the most urgent task of the country's leaders is to find those rare individuals and to use them for the handling of state affairs until KUJŌ Yoritsune grows up and personally assumes the responsibilities of Regent and Shogun.

Jien also implies that these few able persons—presumably he places himself on the list—may even be justified in forcing the Emperor to abdicate, or the Retired Emperor to yield control over the administration of court affairs, if either should be uncooperative. This delicate subject is taken up in Chapter 5, where FUJIWARA Mototsune's part in the abdication of Emperor Yōzei in 884 is discussed. Beginning with the statement that Principles change, and admitting the existence of the ancient Principle that an Emperor should be left on the throne until he wants to step down (no matter how bad he might be), Jien says that no one has ever concluded that Mototsune was engaged in rebellion when he forced Yōzei to abdicate. In fact he claims that Mototsune has been praised for his meritorious service to the throne. Why? Jien's explanation is a bit involved and imprecise, but he seems to be saying that (1) the Kami-created Principle by which the head of the FUJIWARA clan serves the reigning Emperor as a Regent or Chancellor stood, at that time, above the Principle that an Emperor should not be forced to abdicate; (2) FUJIWARA Mototsune was a man of great "ability," comparable to the great FUJIWARA Michinaga, who understood this; and (3) Emperor Yōzei was a very bad Emperor, like the terrible Emperor Buretsu of ancient times. Thus Mototsune's forcing Yōzei to abdicate is rated one of the "three meritorious acts of the FUJIWARA clan." The other two were FUJIWARA Kamatari's assassination of SOGA Iruka in 645 and FUJIWARA Nagate's and FUJIWARA Momokawa's enthronement of Emperor Kōnin in 770. Each was a coup that enabled the FUJIWARA clan, as Jien might have put it, to assume its Kami-created role. In sum, Jien does not merely honor and glorify great men of the past and present, as previous authors of Tales did, but tries to show how men of "ability" have altered, and can still alter, the course of history in deep and even drastic ways.

Jien also gives special attention, as do the authors of Military Tales, to military leaders. Most of his history is devoted to the Military Age that began, he says, in 1156. He certainly realizes that the backing of the victorious MINAMOTO Yoritomo is what made it possible for his brother KUJŌ Kanezane to become Regent and for himself to reach the high post of Tendai Abbot. Moreover, he is painfully aware that every subsequent change in the fortunes of the KUJŌ house has emerged from altered relationships between the Imperial court and the military government. Jien nevertheless has no desire to write *Heike*-like Tales of military heroes and villains. Worried about the political implications of new military developments, he is preoccupied mainly with the conviction that close cooperation between aristocratic and military clans is now required by Japan's single course of history. In his concluding chapter he recommends that Retired Emperor Go-Toba have "ministers who understand Principles" call in military leaders and tell them that the time has come for "soldiers to be used just as at present" and for political improvements to be made by one particular person, the child KUJŌ Yoritsune who is destined to become both an aristocratic Regent and a military Shogun[7] (Chapter 5). Jien therefore does not think of military leaders as simply good subjects for an interesting Tale but as individuals who can and should implement (or be used to implement) Principles for that late period of history.

7. Since Yoritsune was only two years old when the *Gukanshō* was being written, Jien could not say that this child—destined for such an exalted position in the Japanese state—is a person of demonstrated ability. But he does try to convince the reader that Yoritsune is sure *to become* a man of ability who will understand Principles for that late period of history, and who will therefore achieve improvement. We are told that the boy's birth was brought about by ancestral Kami, not by human beings; that he was born at the auspicious hour of the tiger in the tiger month of the tiger year; and finally that he is "an incomparable child" who did not cry at all on his trip from the capital to Kamakura (Chapter 4).

Since the *Gukanshō* is colored by beliefs and assumptions that are prominent in earlier accounts of the past,[8] the reader may conclude that the work's uniqueness as history arises largely from its new stress on, and combination of, old themes. Jien does tie earlier themes more closely to each other and to the process of secular history, creating a rather coherent structure of historical thought.[9] But it is submitted that a more significant aspect of the *Gukanshō's* uniqueness is its articulation of Jien's belief—emerging apparently from his understanding of Buddhist scripture—that periodic changes in Imperial rule, Buddhist Law, and individual leadership (aristocratic or military) have been due, and will continue to be due, to divine powers which are above and external to the secular life of Japan. As far as can be determined, no earlier study of history written in Japan, China, or India is shaped, as the *Gukanshō* is, by a temporal view in which periods of secular deterioration (resulting from kalpic decay that is seen in, or facilitated by, demons and vengeful souls) alternate with periods of secular improvement (resulting from the power of deities and divine truths to negate such decay). Furthermore, no known earlier history written in the Far East depicts the whole of physical change—in the future as well as in the past—as determined by such spiritual polarity *and* by the ability of man to understand how Principles (divine imperatives) of kalpic decay interact with Principles which can check that decay. Therefore the *Gukanshō* is not written—as earlier histories all seem to have been—from conviction concerning the desirability and power of cosmic harmony, Confucian virtue, or past models, but from belief in the way physical events are affected, through the actions of man, by unseen beings (destructive and creative) and divine truths (kalpic and Buddhist/Shinto).

Realizing that the future dimension of Jien's historical consciousness is important to the formation of his unique interpretation, some

8. Because Confucianism was prominent in the education of Japanese aristocrats during the previous five centuries, the reader may well ask why nothing has been said about Confucian themes. At the beginning of Chapter 5, Jien does refer to the thirteen Confucian classics and to Chinese histories and literary works deeply influenced by Confucian principles. But in doing so he is simply making the point that it is now difficult for a Japanese to understand anything written in Chinese, especially if it is a translation of Sanskrit scripture or is a Chinese classic. Consciously or unconsciously, Jien may be reminding his reader that he can understand these Chinese sources. And at times he seems to assess the abilities of a person in terms of Confucian virtue, but it is clear that the *Gukanshō* view of history is not influenced in any fundamental way by Confucian ideas about why or how a history should be written.

9. Analyzed in Chapter 10.

scholars have characterized the *Gukanshō* as a work of prophecy *(miraiki)*. Jien himself seems to have been aware that his study might give that impression, for at the end of Chapter 4 he explains that in writing about the future he deals *only* with "that which has been revealed by the Great Hachiman Bodhisattva" (the ancestral Kami of the Imperial House and of the MINAMOTO clan), and he declares that the incorporation of *more detail* about the future would have made his book unconvincing, even if the prophecies were true. In spite of his efforts to chart a single course of history from the perspective of belief in a Kami plan for the future, he avoids the posture of a prophet and assumes that a stronger case for the existence and power of the Kami plan can be made by an historical study which will show just where that unilinear course is headed. Prayers and other writings by Jien, composed both before and after 1219, indicate that he did have dreams in which features of the Kami plan had been revealed to him. These dreams surely strengthened his faith in the existence of a future extension to Japan's single course of history. But the *Gukanshō* does not even mention them. Instead, Jien tries to convince his reader that the ancestral Kami plan for Imperial rule in Japan is disclosed by the direction which the "single course of history" is taking and by mysterious movements of the heavens and social disasters which portend future developments. Just as a frightening comet and a terrifying epidemic (Chapter 2) preceded and portended the glorious days of FUJIWARA Michinaga, it is implied that another comet and a series of worldly disasters (Chapter 4)—occurring just prior to the writing of the *Gukanshō*—precede and portend improvement for that future time when KUJŌ Yoritsune will become an adult Regent and Shogun.

Reflection on the *Gukanshō's* distinctive and apparently contradictory features (temporal periods of sharp kalpic decline interspersed with temporal periods of partial improvement)[10] leads one to conclude that previous writers who have characterized the *Gukanshō* as a product of Final Law thought *(mappō shisō)* or prophecy *(miraiki)*[11] have obscured the fact that the study has been deeply influenced by both. Indeed it is difficult to understand how Jien could have become interested in writing a future-oriented history if he had been affected by only one or the other. Final Law convictions alone would have produced fatalistic despair likely to make him certain that any attempt to comprehend the past would disclose nothing of sig-

10. By identifying two periods of history for roughly the same span of time (periods five and six for the years between 1156 and 1198), Jien has Japan's bad periods of sharp decline (2, 4, and 6) preceded and followed by periods of considerable improvement (1, 3, 5, and 7). See Figure 1.

11. Tsunetsugu Muraoka is probably the leading exponent of the former, and Toshihide Akamatsu of the latter.

nificance for the future. Belief only in the revelations of Kami will
for the future, on the other hand, would logically have made Jien a
prophet with no special interest in the past. But believing in the inevitability of Final Law decline[12] as well as in a Kami plan for future
betterment, Jien was able to trace a unilinear course of events that
moves from the past into the future, a course that runs generally
downhill toward extinction (Final Law belief) but will soon turn up
toward improvement under a Regent and Shogun of the KUJŌ house
(revelation of Kami will).

   As to which of these two elements has the greater weight, it is felt
that Jien's principal reason for writing the *Gukanshō* was to provide
historical proof for the Kami-created Principle that KUJŌ Yoritsune
should and would serve the Emperor as Regent and Shogun, not to
relate Buddhist doctrines of kalpic decline to the process of secular
change. Jien was a Buddhist priest who had embraced Buddhist doctrines of kalpic deterioration, but his historical study is focused quite
sharply on the origins, rise, and prospects of the FUJIWARA clan and
its KUJŌ house. Moreover, what we know of Jien's thoughts and writings before 1219 suggests that he turned to writing history soon after
Kami plans for the future had been revealed to him, and just when
his revived hopes for the KUJŌ house were being seriously
threatened by an impending war between the Imperial Court and
the military government. Concluding therefore that belief in Kami
plans for the future occupied a central position in Jien's motives for
writing the *Gukanshō*, and that the interpretation's future dimension
accounts for much of its uniqueness, we have decided to entitle our
translation and studies *The Future and the Past*.

   12. Those who play down the influence of Final Law thought point out
that the word *mappō* appears only once in the entire text. But the effects of
belief in kalpic deterioration are more deeply engrained in the *Gukanshō*
interpretation than the single use of that term suggests. As noted, all seven
of Jien's periods of Japanese history are marked by progressive decay. Not
only that, several other terms, reflecting belief in Final Law and pointing
directly to decline in the affairs of this world, are used frequently. These
include: final reigns *(matsudai)*; Final Age *(yo no sue* or *masse)*; and one
hundred reigns *(hyaku-ō)*. Since Jien actually counts how many of the allotted
one hundred reigns are left, it seems that he even believed the Kami-
created Imperial line would end at a later point in the age of Final Law. Cf.
Chapter 1.

Abbreviations

The titles of the most frequently mentioned source collections are abbreviated as follows:

KT	*[Shintei zōho] Kokushi taikei*
NKBT:	*Nihon koten bungaku taikei*
ST:	*Shiryō taisei*
Taishō:	*Taishō [shinshū] daizōkyō*
Zenshū:	*Jien zenshū*

Part I
Gukanshō

1
Ancient Age

Emperor Jimmu to
FUJIWARA Michinaga

Introduction

With the passing of the years and days I think only about the Principles of things. And while seeking diversion from the sleeplessness of old age, I spend more and more time—as I approach the end of life—observing world affairs. Consequently I have become keenly aware of Principles that have been changing since ancient times. I do not know how it was in the age of Kami, but I hear that after the beginning of the age of man and the enthronement of Emperor Jimmu, Japan is to have only one hundred reigns.[1] Now that we are in the 84th reign not many more are left. Meanwhile, no one has

1. The belief that Japan was destined to have only one hundred reigns (*hyaku-ō*) seems not to have emerged until late in the Heian era (794–1185) when an increasingly large number of intellectuals were becoming influenced by the doctrine that Buddhist Law would enter, or had entered, the third and last age of deterioration in the year 1052. By the twelfth century, the belief was being expressed frequently. Some writers seem to have thought of "one hundred" as an indefinite number, but apparently Jien accepted the doctrine literally. Later on (Chapter 4), he writes that only 16 reigns are left.

written Succession Tales[2] for the period after the outbreak of the
Hōgen Rebellion of 1156. I hear that there may be some, but I have
not seen any. Why? I am convinced that because people prefer to
write only about that which is good and everything has been disturbed since the outbreak of the Hōgen Rebellion, they have shied
away from events that are all bad and not written Succession Tales
for this modern period.

Because I have been thinking that I would like to write about Principles that have caused the world to change and deteriorate in a unilinear way, I have become thoroughly convinced that my interpretations are quite reasonable. But people do not agree with me, simply
entertaining ideas and feelings that are in conflict with Principles and
doing precisely that which makes the world more confused and less
peaceful. So I have begun to write, hoping that this will bring peace
to a mind that has been mulling over matters of this kind.

Since an Imperial chronology has been provided, the reader will
obtain a deeper understanding of what is written here by referring
to it as he reads.[3]

The Beginning of Deterioration

During the thirteen reigns from Jimmu to Seimu, Emperors were
succeeded by their sons. But Emperor Chūai, the fourteenth occupant of the throne, was Emperor Keikō's grandson. Seimu had had
no sons, and so Chūai was appointed Crown Prince in the 48th year
of the Seimu reign. Two of Keikō's sons were twins. The first-born
of the twins was Prince Yamato Takeru no Mikoto who died at the
age of thirty and then became a white bird that flew off into the sky.[4]
Emperor Chūai, who was Prince Yamato Takeru no Mikoto's son,

2. Both the *Eiga Monogatari* and the *Ōkagami* were referred to as Succession Tales *(yotsugi ga monogatari)*, but neither deals with events after the
Hōgen Rebellion of 1156. See Chapter 8.

3. The Imperial chronology *(kōtei nendai ki)* precedes the narrative chapters of the *Gukanshō* in all extant texts but is placed at the end of this translation as Chapters 6 and 7.

4. Only a brief reference is made here to the myth which, according to
the *Nihongi,* begins with Prince Yamato Takeru no Mikoto's burial in a tomb
located in Ise and his transformation into a white bird that flies off in the
direction of Yamato. The Prince's retainers open his coffin but find only his
robes. Messengers are then sent to follow the bird, and they find that it had
stopped in Yamato. So a second tomb for the Prince is built in that province.
Then the white bird takes off for Kawachi and lands in the village of
Furuichi, where a third tomb is constructed for the Prince. People then
begin talking about "the white bird tombs," and eventually the bird flies high
into the sky, leaving only the Prince's clothes and headgear in the tombs.
[*Nihon koten bungaku taikei* (hereafter cited as NKBT). 67.310–311.]

made Jingū his Empress. She later became, as the great-great-granddaughter of Emperor Kaika and the daughter of OKINAGA no Sukune, a reigning Empress. Emperor Chūai had died because he failed to comply with instructions received in a Kami oracle. Then Empress Jingū, carrying in her womb the future Emperor Ōjin and dressing herself as a man, postponed the birth of her child and conquered the three kingdoms of Silla, Kōkuli, and Paekché. When she returned to Kyushu, she took hold of a pagoda tree in a parturition house and gave birth to the future Emperor Ōjin.[5]

Empress Jingū had followed Chūai on the throne and made Ōjin the Crown Prince. She then governed the state and acted as Ōjin's regent for 69 years. After her death, Ōjin succeeded to the throne and reigned 41 years, reaching the age of 110. Chūai had gone to Kyushu for the purpose of conquering Silla and other kingdoms of Korea because the Kami had instructed him to do so. But before he had complied with the Kami's instructions, he suddenly died.

In reflecting about these early reigns, I conclude that the earliest Principle was that succession should be correct (from father to son) and that Emperors should govern faultlessly (without the assistance of ministers) through the 13th reign. But the governing Principle for later reigns was that a grandson should be placed on the throne if there was no Imperial son.

Emperor Chūai, Japan's 14th sovereign, received instructions from the Kami but died suddenly before carrying them out. It is said that he died because there had been many instances in which he did not believe in, or act in accord with, what had been revealed to him in a Kami oracle.

Empress Jingū

Why did a reigning Empress, bearing an Imperial son in her womb, become the commanding officer of an expedition to Korea? And why did she rule the country as a reigning Empress for more than 60 years after giving birth to an Imperial son?[6] I conclude that

5. Though Jien devotes considerable space to Empress Jingū's place in history and to her miraculous deeds, he does not include her on his list of persons born on Japan's line of Imperial descent, a list (Chapter 6) containing only the names of Emperors and Imperial sons. The soul of her son, Emperor Ōjin, was later enshrined as Hachiman, a Kami that was honored—along with the Sun Goddess—as an ancestral Kami of the Imperial House. The power, will, and creative acts of these two ancestral Kami are linked to divine Principles that are basic to Jien's theological view of history.

6. Later on in this chapter, Jien gives special attention to two other Empresses, both of whom were associated with male leaders described as Buddhist incarnations: (1) Empress Suiko, who was enthroned after the SOGA

these developments manifested Principles by which nothing remains
fixed. Such fusions of Inner and Outer Causes[7] were meant to reveal the following Principles to people living in these later reigns: the
Principle that the highest priority shall be assigned to ability *(kiryō)*
regardless of sex, and the Principle that an Imperial son shall be
filial to his mother, simply leaving everything in her hands as long as
she is alive. Although these Principles were revealed, no one understands them.

In the reign of Keikō, the 12th Emperor, TAKENOUCHI Sukune
became the first Great Imperial Chieftain. This too manifested the
Principle that the time had come when Emperors should be assisted
by ministers. TAKENOUCHI Sukune was a great-great-grandson of
Kōgen, Japan's 8th Emperor.

The eight Emperors (Ōjin through Seinei) who ascended the
throne after Empress Jingū were sons of the previous Emperor; and
three were sons of Emperor Nintoku. But Emperor Seinei, the
23rd sovereign, was followed by Kenzō, who was Emperor Richū's
grandson.

A Good Emperor: Nintoku

While Ōjin was alive, his son Uji was appointed Crown Prince, and
therefore Uji should have been enthroned after Ōjin's death. But Uji
ordered his brother Nintoku to take the throne, probably because
Nintoku was his elder brother. Nintoku's reaction was: "You were
appointed Crown Prince. Why do you order me to take the throne?"
Instead of competing with each other for the throne, the two
brothers competed in turning it down. Three years passed and then
Crown Prince Uji said: "It is grievous for the people that years pass
without their having a sovereign. I will therefore kill myself." And
he did. When Nintoku heard what his brother had done, he rushed
to Uji's side in a state of agitation and perplexity. Three days later,
Uji suddenly returned to life, talked with Nintoku, and died a sec-

---

military victory of 592 and connected with Prince Shōtoku's support of Buddhism; and (2) Empress Kōgyoku, who was enthroned twice—once before
and once after the Great Reforms of 645—and paired with FUJIWARA
Kamatari, the founder of the FUJIWARA clan.

Ōjin probably reigned at the beginning of the fifth century A.D. Reliable
evidence for the existence of earlier reigns is sparse or non-existent.

7. Jien implies that the divine Principles of history operate in accord with
Buddhist conceptions of causation, but he does not explain the two Causes
(in and *en)* nor show how their "fusion" has affected Japanese history. He
seems to assume that (1) Inner Causes *(in)* are rooted in the process of
kalpic deterioration; (2) Outer Causes *(en)* may be generated by reverence for Kami or the practice of Buddha Law; and (3) Inner and Outer
Causes together produce results *(ka).*

ond and final time. Then Nintoku succeeded to the throne and reigned 87 years.

Developments such as these defy understanding or description. We hear that the real way to be human is to forget self and know others. It is therefore deduced that Uji was made Crown Prince in order to reveal this true way to be human. Ōjin and other early Emperors were succeeded by their sons. This is really the ideal form of succession, the True Law (*shōbō*) of Japan.[8] And Nintoku was succeeded by three sons. TAKENOUCHI Sukune served as Great Imperial Chieftain down through the Nintoku reign, living more than 280 years. The place where he died is not known. The three Nintoku sons (Richū, Hansei, and Ingyō) reigned in the order of their ages, the eldest first and the youngest last.

The Assassination of a Bad Emperor

Emperor Ankō, Ingyō's second son, murdered his elder brother the Crown Prince and ascended the throne. Although he was Emperor Nintoku's grandson, people were painfully aware that he was not like his grandfather. After reigning three years, Ankō was killed by his seven-year-old stepson, Prince Mayuwa. And soon after Ankō's assassination, Prince Mayuwa and Great Imperial Chieftain KATSURAGI Tsubura were both killed in the latter's residence. Did not these disorders and rebellions within the short period of three years portend the coming of the Final Age?[9]

Prince Mayuwa's father, Prince Ōkusaka, was Emperor Ankō's uncle, and we hear that Ankō murdered this uncle and then seized the uncle's wife and made her his Empress. It seems that one day Ankō and his Empress (Prince Mayuwa's mother) were talking together and enjoying themselves in the upstairs room of the palace when Ankō said: "Won't my stepson want to seek revenge for his father's death when he grows up?" Prince Mayuwa overheard the remark, since he was in a room below. He dashed upstairs and saw his stepfather Ankō lying intoxicated in the lap of his mother. Seizing a sword at Ankō's side, he cut off Ankō's head and fled to the residence of the Great Imperial Chieftain. Such events should be thought about carefully and understood.

8. True Law is the first and best of the three ages of Buddhist Law, but here Jien uses the term to point up the ideal form of succession for the first and best of Japan's seven periods of secular history.

9. Embracing the doctrine that Buddhist Law has entered its third and final stage of decline, Jien assumes that Japanese secular history has also entered the third stage of decline: the Final Age (*yo no sue* or *masse*). The previous two secular ages are: the Ancient Age (*jōko*) and the Medieval Age (*chūko*). See Chapter 10.

Improvement under Emperors Ninken and Kenzō

After Emperor Ankō was assassinated, his young brother Yūryaku ascended the throne, and Yūryaku was in turn succeeded by his son Seinei. Seinei was unable to produce an Imperial son and therefore adopted two grandsons of Emperor Richū: Ninken and Kenzō. The elder of the two, Ninken, was appointed Crown Prince and Kenzō became an Imperial Prince. The two brothers had become alarmed by the state's disorder during the Ankō reign and fled to the provinces of Harima and Tamba. But they were tracked down. Crown Prince Ninken should have succeeded to the throne at the time of Seinei's death, but he urged his young brother Kenzō to become Emperor. Kenzō refused. Since the two brothers were unbending in deferring to each other, their young sister followed Seinei on the throne as a reigning Empress in the 2nd month of the year in which Seinei died. But she herself died in the 12th month of that same year. Perhaps this is why we do not find her reign listed in the ordinary Imperial chronologies and why people know nothing at all about her. She was called Empress Iitoyo and it is said that her reign was in the *kinoe-ne* year of the sexegenary cycle.

Prince Kenzō ascended the throne on the 1st day of the 1st month of the following year. This meant that Crown Prince Ninken, the elder brother, had been passed over and that the throne was being occupied by a younger brother who was only an Imperial Prince. But concluding that it was bad for the two brothers to continue deferring to each other, the ministers recommended strongly that Kenzō be enthroned first. Kenzō finally acceded to his brother's order and to the ministers' recommendation, but he died within three years. Meanwhile, Ninken retained the position of Crown Prince, and so he succeeded Kenzō and reigned 11 years.

In reflecting about these reigns, I conclude that the two brothers were living out their Imperial destinies and were placed on the throne in this order because the life of the young brother was to be short and that of the elder brother long. The length of a man's life and his fortune *(kahō)* do not necessarily coincide. This Principle is often manifested, under conditions of these final reigns *(matsudai)*, in the lives of lower-ranking officials.

A Bad Emperor Followed by a Knowledgeable One

Emperor Buretsu—the son of, and Crown Prince under, Emperor Ninken—turned out to be an indescribably bad ruler. He succeeded to the throne at the age of ten and reigned until he was 18. The situation was so bad then that his ministers could only grieve. And since Buretsu died without producing an Imperial son, the people lamented that he had no heir. The ministers and officials assembled to consider the question of succession and·they selected a great-

great-great-grandson of Emperor Ōjin from the province of Echizen. This was Emperor Keitai who reigned 25 years—longer than
his predecessors. Having lived many years in the provinces, he was
familiar with the conditions of the people.[10] He therefore ruled the
country well. He was succeeded by three sons (Ankan, Senka, and
Kimmei) in order of their age, but the eldest did not rule very long.
It was during the reign of the third son, Kimmei, that Buddhist Law
(buppō) was first introduced to Japan. Prince Shōtoku, a grandson of
Kimmei, was born in the last years of Kimmei's rule. We can see that
this country has been protected and preserved by Buddhist Law
since that time.

A Period of Transition

Each of the 12 reigns (from Richū to Senka) which followed the
87-year reign of Emperor Nintoku was very short, although Ingyō
ruled 42 years. Of these 12, the reigns of Ankō and Buretsu were
unusually bad while those of Kenzō and Ninken—who followed the
example set by Nintoku and Uji when they urged each other to take
the throne—were praiseworthy but short. I conclude that these 12
reigns came at a transitional time between the first 13 reigns and the
reign of Kimmei when Buddhist Law was introduced to Japan.[11]
From the beginning of the age of man down through the reign of
Emperor Seimu (the first 13 reigns), Emperors were all succeeded by
their sons—the form of succession referred to as the True Law of
Japan. Chūai (the 14th ruler) was the first to be enthroned as an
Imperial grandson, and Empress Jingū—the great-great-granddaughter of Emperor Kaika—was the first reigning Empress. Then
Ōjin ascended the throne, feeling that "Since our country is no
longer to have the spirit of the age of Kami and the situation is
henceforth destined to deteriorate rapidly, with people having only
bad thoughts and feelings, I will protect the country until the introduction of Buddhist Law." The reigns of all his successors were
short. The Ingyō and Yūryaku line of descent was not continued,
and the descendants of an earlier Emperor had to be sought out.
After that, Buddhist Law and other forms of Chinese learning were
introduced. It was difficult in that period for an Emperor or Empress to reign alone. Empress Suiko (554–628) was placed on the
throne in 592, and she reigned 36 years while Shōtoku (574–622)

10. Keitei is also the first Emperor after Ōjin who is found on Jien's list of
Emperors and Imperial sons born in Japan's line of Imperial descent (Chapter 6).

11. This statement should be read in the light of Jien's delineation of
Japan's first three periods. The second period (Chūai to Kimmei) stands between period one (when Emperors were succeeded by their sons) and period
three (when Buddhism and the FUJIWARA clan prosper). See Figure 1.

was Crown Prince. Although Emperor Sushun had been assassinated in 592, the state was well governed under Suiko. In 587 Prince Shōtoku (at the age of 16) and Great Imperial Chieftain SOGA Umako had agreed that Moriya, who was displeased with the introduction of Buddhist Law, should be attacked and killed. Then Prince Shōtoku and SOGA no Umako began to promote Buddhist Law, which has flourished until this day.

Assassinating Emperors

Why was Emperor Sushun's assassination by Great Imperial Chieftain SOGA Umako in 592 treated as a good deed, warranting not the slightest punishment? People of that day talked about the strangeness of this, and nowadays we too should understand why an Emperor's assassination should have been treated so lightly. Generally, Emperors were not being assassinated then. It was a firmly established rule that such a crime should not be committed. Nevertheless, Emperors Ankō and Sushun were assassinated. But no others.

Ankō's assassination at the hands of the seven-year-old Prince Mayuwa presents no problem since Mayuwa himself was killed soon afterward. Mayuwa was, after all, only a seven-year-old boy who was avenging the murder of his father. So the Principle is clear. Moreover, Ankō had killed his elder brother, the Crown Prince who should have succeeded to the throne, and made himself Emperor. Before a year had passed he also killed Mayuwa's father, took Mayuwa's mother for his Empress, and became involved in other disreputable acts of violence against his allies and clan. Because of such strange behavior, the Principle behind Ankō's assassination is clear.

Concerning the assassination of Emperor Sushun, the current Great Imperial Chieftain (SOGA Umako) had heard that Emperor Sushun was going to kill him, and he therefore proceeded to kill the Emperor first. But was it right to overlook the act, not punishing Umako in the least and allowing him to go free? Since Prince Shōtoku was present, why didn't he do something about the assassination? And why did he quickly ally himself with Umako, the assassin? People really could not understand it. And yet there has been absolutely no inclination, since then, to think that a precedent had been established.

What Principles Were Being Manifested?

In reflecting about these developments, I find the essential point to be this: Imperial Law (ōbō)[12] was henceforth to be protected by Buddhist Law. Those events occurred in order to manifest the Principle that, after the introduction of Buddhist Law to Japan, Imperial

12. Discussed in the Introduction.

Law could no longer be preserved without the help of Buddhist Law. And a second Principle was manifested: that some Principles are important and others less important and that an important Principle shall be embraced and a less important one rejected. Who was to reveal these Principles for that day? Clearly it was Prince Shōtoku, an incarnation of Avalokiteśvara. Such things happened because he was performing his divine role.

Why do I reach such a conclusion? Because people came to realize, after the Prince's death, that he was a magnificent incarnation of Avalokiteśvara.[13] They thought of him as just an ordinary human being while he was alive, but after his death they came to realize that he had been a magnificent incarnation of Avalokiteśvara. When a child, he of course acted like a child. But when he was only 16, he was able to defeat Moriya (who was really destroying Buddhist Law) because he was supported mainly by a close alliance with Great Imperial Chieftain SOGA Umako, an adult with power and prestige. This Umako was clearly a model minister who had been converted to Buddhist Law. When it seemed that Emperor Sushun (who had no virtue whatsoever and succeeded to the throne simply because he was a son of Kimmei) was going to kill Umako, the assassination occurred because Umako (with power that flowed from his belief in Buddhist Law)[14] killed the Emperor before he himself was killed. That was his only purpose. We cannot say that Sushun was assassinated because he was destroying Buddhist Law, as was true of Moriya. To say that Buddhist Law and Imperial Law were in bitter conflict with each other, and that Buddhist Law had emerged victorious, would be defaming Buddhist Law. It was not Buddhist Law that did such things as kill Moriya. Rather, Imperial Law did away with a bad minister who was bad because he was destroying the Three Treasures of Buddhist Law that were to guard Imperial Law. In trying to shed light on the Principles of things, I conclude that the above Principle of Buddhist Law protecting Imperial Law was a true Principle.

In considering the second Principle (some Principles are more important than others), let us turn to Suiko being both the Empress and younger sister of Emperor Bidatsu. Emperor Kimmei was the father of both. Why did Bidatsu marry his sister? Probably such marriages were not frowned upon then. The custom that a brother

13. Cf. note 6 of the Introduction.

14. Umako's support of Buddhist Law is stressed, but no mention is made of SOGA ties with the Imperial House, even though such relationships are given close attention when FUJIWARA ministers are taken up. Umako's involvement in the 592 assassination of Emperor Sushun (Umako's nephew) suggests that the SOGA were moving toward direct control, if not usurpation, of the throne. No SOGA dynasty was founded in 592, but Umako placed on the throne a woman (Empress Suiko) whose Imperial mother was a SOGA.

should not marry his sister came later, after Buddhism and other Chinese ideas and practices were introduced to Japan. Following the precedent set by Empress Jingū, Suiko should have been enthroned immediately after the death of Bidatsu in 585. But Yōmei ascended the throne first because he, the father of Prince Shōtoku, was thought to be the most suitable candidate. But Yōmei did not reign long, dying after a rule of two years. Prince Shōtoku probably had a premonition of this. Then Sushun, another son of Emperor Kimmei, was placed on the throne because there was no way Prince Shōtoku could prevent it. But when the Prince read Sushun's features, he said: "Such-and-such in your eyes indicates that you will not live long and that you will meet with military disaster." Not believing what the Prince had predicted, Sushun had a boar killed and pronounced this curse: "I want the person I hate killed just as this boar has been killed." But the importance of the Principle that Buddhist Law and Imperial Law should be protected by Suiko's ascending the throne after Sushun's assassination in 592, and by Prince Shōtoku's administering state affairs, was so great that its power could not be resisted at that time. So people probably thought that Sushun's assassination was "a good deed performed by this Great Imperial Chieftain of the SOGA clan." I do not know but it may also have been a requirement of Principle that Empress Suiko be involved. Since Buddhist Law and Imperial Law were now firmly joined, the Crown Prince merely looked on, not saying anything and tacitly approving what his minister had done. Because the Principle of Buddhist Law protecting Imperial Law was the most important Principle for that day, Prince Shōtoku seems to have assumed that the assassination of Emperor Sushun was all right. Thereafter, and with events moving along this single course of history, there has been absolutely no conflict between Buddhist Law and Imperial Law. And no one has ever been inclined to attack an Emperor because such a thing had been done before. People have not even spoken of attacking an Emperor, for that is abominable. If anyone had even thought of it, he would have come to a clear realization of the Principle that such an act is abominable. In sum, if Prince Shōtoku had punished Umako for assassinating Emperor Sushun in 592, treating the incident as an ordinary human event, he would have been responding to the assassination in an ordinary way and not been acting in accord with the basic intent of the most important Principle for that time.

Prince Shōtoku as an
Incarnation of Avalokiteśvara

We must reflect deeply about this question: Why did Prince Shōtoku delay funeral arrangements for his father (Emperor Yōmei), have Moriya's head cut off, become engaged in many battles involving the slaughter of people, and only then make arrangements for his father's funeral? Here we have a truly marvelous Principle: since the way of Buddha was being obstructed, the Prince felt he should remove that obstruction before concerning himself with the burial of his father. And how could Prince Shōtoku, an incarnation of Avalokiteśvara, have established a bad precedent? If that sort of thing had been done in the Final Age, or when the Prince was not alive, a bad precedent would have been set. Indeed, it was precisely because these things were done while the Prince was alive that a bad precedent was *not* set. Those events must be understood in this way. In conclusion, if the Prince had inflicted some punishment on Umako for what he did, he would have been handling the matter in accord with an ordinary causal Principle of the age, not in accord with the most important Principle for that particular time. And since the assassination of this bad Emperor was really in conformity with such a Principle, there has been no criticism—from that day to this—of the Prince for not punishing Umako. Times in which such a true Principle becomes fully realized are also times, even now, when people should stand in awe of all developments. It should be understood that such incidents as the assassination of an Emperor have not occurred again because it is the plan of the Sun Goddess that, in the Final Age, bodily weaknesses of Emperors shall prevent them from committing errors of extreme willfulness.

FUJIWARA *Ministers*

Then there came a time when the ministerial house of FUJIWARA was to emerge and administer state affairs. The Sun Goddess had made a divine agreement[15] with the Great Illuminating Kami of the Kasuga Shrine that these two ancestral Kami would guard the Imperial palace together. Because of that agreement, a time had come for the Emperor to be assisted by the ministerial house of FUJIWARA, and for FUJIWARA Kamatari (614–669) to be born to succeed Prince Shōtoku as an administrator of state affairs who would support Buddhist Law.[16] It was also the time of Empress Kōgyoku's reign (642–645) when Tenchi became Crown Prince and worked with the Empress to achieve improvement. After SOGA Iruka's head had been

15. This agreement *(go-ichidaku)* was conceived of as a divine act that created a form of Imperial rule appropriate to Japan's third period of history, one by which Emperors and Empresses were supported by FUJIWARA ministers. Other divine agreements account for other forms of Imperial rule for later periods. Cf. Chapter 10.

16. More recent historians have thought of Prince Naka no Ōe, the future Emperor Tenchi, as Prince Shōtoku's successor, and of FUJIWARA Kamatari as SOGA Umako's. But believing that Kamatari had a Kami-given mission to bring Buddhist Law to the support of Imperial Law at that particular time in the secular history of Japan, Jien sees a special relationship between Prince

cut off by Kamatari in the garden where the Imperial banquet of 645 was being held, it was clearly understood that the Sun Goddess had now begun to feel that

> This country of Japan can no longer be maintained by the prestige and power of the Emperor alone. That would simply add disorder to disorder. The time has come for the power of Buddhist Law to be joined with the power of Imperial Law by FUJIWARA ministers.

So administrative arrangements have been in strict accord with this intention of the Sun Goddess, right down to the present day.

Reigning Empress Kōgyoku—the great-granddaughter of Emperor Bidatsu, and Emperor Jomei's Empress—gave birth to the future Emperor Tenchi in 626. In making Tenchi the Crown Prince and occupying the throne herself soon afterward, Empress Kōgyoku was obviously following a precedent set by Empress Jingū. Tenchi should have succeeded her on the throne, but Kōtoku—Tenchi's maternal uncle and Empress Kōgyoku's younger brother—was enthroned first, probably because he was destined to be Emperor and was virtuous. Kōtoku reigned 10 years after 645. Then Tenchi's mother, the former Empress Kōgyoku, ascended the throne a second time and reigned during seven calendar years (644–661) as Empress Saimei. She was the first Empress to occupy the throne twice. Tenchi did not become Emperor until his Imperial mother died in 661, seven years after the death of Kōtoku, because Tenchi had deep feelings of filial piety. When Tenchi did take the throne, FUJIWARA Kamatari devotedly assisted him in the conduct of state affairs. Kamatari was the first to receive the clan name of FUJIWARA and the first to hold the office of Minister of the Center. Tenchi reigned 10 years (661–671). When Kamatari died in the 8th year of that reign, Tenchi went personally to pay his respects. His Majesty regretfully bade Kamatari a tearful farewell, expressing his feelings in a gracious manner.

The Rebellion of 672 and Its Meaning

Tenchi had made Temmu—his brother who was a son of Empress Saimei—the Crown Prince, intending to make him his successor. But Tenchi also appointed his son, Prince Ōtomo, to the post of Prime Minister. Crown Prince Temmu seems to have thought that Prince Ōtomo did not have a righteous heart. He therefore resigned as Crown Prince, entered the Buddhist priesthood, and went into se-

---

Shōtoku (an administrator of state affairs who supported Buddhism as an incarnation of Avalokiteśvara) and FUJIWARA Kamatari (the first FUJIWARA minister who, as another incarnation of Avalokiteśvara, had the mission to support Imperial Law with Buddhist Law).

clusion on Mt. Yoshino. We are told that after Emperor Tenchi died in 671 in a state of grief over the way things had turned out, Prince Ōtomo[17] took up arms and was about to attack Mt. Yoshino when his consort, who was Temmu's daughter, secretly passed word to Mt. Yoshino that such an attack was to be made. She was probably afraid that her father would be killed. When Temmu heard of the impending attack, he thought: "Why is Ōtomo doing this? I entered the priesthood and secluded myself in these mountains because I did not think that I was qualified to be Emperor." Then Temmu renounced his priestly calling, left Mt. Yoshino, and went to worship at the great Ise Shrine before mobilizing troops in the provinces of Mino and Owari. Then he deployed his forces for an attack on Prince Ōtomo, who was preparing for battle in the province of Ōmi. Temmu's army won and Ōtomo was beheaded. The Minister of the Right was also beheaded and the Minister of the Left was sent into exile, for they had sided with Ōtomo. Temmu then ascended the throne and ruled 15 years (672–686). During those years, a descendant of FUJIWARA Kamatari should have served the Emperor as a devoted assistant, but probably FUJIWARA Fuhito (659–720) was then too young to assume such responsibilities. A person who wants to achieve a broad and deep understanding of history should reflect on these developments in terms of my explication of the true course of Principles, a course that has propelled events along a single path in this way.

Emperor Temmu's disposition was that of a superior man. In thinking that he lacked the ability to be Emperor, he was like Prince Uji. And when he came to deal with this Prince Ōtomo, who had no attitude of this sort, he felt deeply that his country would be ruined if Ōtomo were to occupy the throne. In attacking and defeating such a man, Temmu was acting like T'ai Tsung of T'ang China. Perhaps this was why Tenchi had planned to pass over his son and make Temmu his successor.[18]

17. Neither the *Gukanshō* nor the *Nihongi* calls Prince Ōtomo an Emperor, although modern chronologies list him as Emperor Kōbun (648–672). By having Tenchi succeeded by Temmu, with no intervening reign, Jien is not presented with the necessity of explaining a victorious war against a reigning Emperor.

18. This explanation of the Rebellion of 672 shows with particular clarity how Jien's view of history differs from that of modern historians. Whereas his theological interpretation is based on his conception of the true course of divine Principles and upon his idea of a "superior man" who acted like the great T'ai Tsung of T'ang China, modern historians give their attention to such this-worldly conditions as clan rivalry (especially the restiveness of small clans located in outlying regions), international relations (particularly the deterioration of Japan's position on the Korean peninsula), and a succession dispute (based on rivalry between those supporting Tenchi's son Ōtomo and those backing Tenchi's brother Temmu).

Reigning Empresses and Imperial Mothers

Emperor Tenchi made a deathbed request that his two daughters be placed on the throne. They were the future Empresses Jitō and Genmei. Empress Jitō, who succeeded Temmu in 686, was Tenchi's second daughter and Temmu's Empress. To her and Temmu had been born a son, Prince Kusakabe, who was appointed Crown Prince. But shortly after Jitō was enthroned—in conformity with an earlier precedent—Crown Prince Kusakabe died. In her grief, Empress Jitō had Prince Kusakabe's son, the future Emperor Mommu, appointed Crown Prince. It was during Mommu's reign (697–707) that era names were first used. Beginning with the Taihō era (701–704), era names have been used until the present day.[19]

After Mommu was enthroned in 697, ex-Empress Jitō received the honorary title of Retired Empress *(daijō tennō)*, the first Empress to be so honored. Although Mommu had a son who was later placed on the throne as Emperor Shōmu, he was succeeded by two Empresses: Genmei and Gensei, who reigned from 707 to 724. Shōmu was appointed Crown Prince in 714. His Imperial mother was a daughter of Great Minister FUJIWARA Fubito, Kamatari's grandson, and all later Imperial mothers have been descendants of Kamatari. Women of other clans were Imperial consorts, but, from that time to the present, Imperial mothers have always been women of the FUJIWARA clan.

Emperor Shōmu's Support of Buddhist Law

Shōmu assumed responsibility for the conduct of state affairs while he was Crown Prince. Early in the Genmei reign he had been too young to handle state affairs but was appointed Crown Prince toward the end of that reign, and while Gensei was Empress (715–724) everything was done just as he wanted. It was then that officials were permitted to carry scepters, regulations for women's clothing were instituted, and priests and nuns were first certified.

Shōmu was enthroned in the Imperial Council Hall on the 4th day of the 2nd month of 724, when he was 25 years old. During his reign Buddhist Law flourished, great Minister KIBI and High Priest Genbō went to T'ang China and brought back a 5,000-fascicle collection of Buddhist scripture, the Tōdai Temple was built, and Bodhisattva Gyōgi (668–749) founded provincial temples.[20] As indicated by such

19. In his Imperial chronology (Chapter 6), Jien says that era names were first instituted in the reign of Kōtoku (645–655), and he even provides details about era names after the reign of Temmu (671–686). However, his statement here is rather close to the position taken by modern scholars.

20. No other known source provides support for this claim. Possibly Jien misread a statement found in the *Renchū shō*, which is thought to have been used by him when he compiled his Imperial chronology. [*Shiseki shūran*, 23.20–21.]

developments, Buddhist Law prospered while Shōmu reigned. Because Shōmu had no sons, he passed the throne to his daughter in 749. He lived on for another eight years. It was during his daughter Empress Kōken's reign from 749 to 758 that an oracle message was received from Great Bodhisattva Hachiman, revealing this Kami's desire to be transported from Usa to the capital so that it might honor the great Buddha worshipped at the Tōdai Temple.[21] Retired Emperor Shōmu, Empress Kōken, and Shōmu's Empress all went to worship at the Tōdai Temple. The characters for "world peace" mysteriously appeared at the Imperial Palace around this time.

The Last Reigning Empress

Living on for eight years after abdicating in 749, Retired Emperor Shōmu died in 756. Then Empress Kōken, acting in accord with Shōmu's wishes, had Emperor Temmu's grandson—Prince Funado (Minister of Ceremonies), who was a son of Prince Niitabe First Rank—appointed Crown Prince. But for some reason Prince Funado gave absolutely no thought even to such matters as the memorial services for the late Emperor Shōmu. And in other matters he did not comply with instructions issued by the Empress. He was therefore removed from his position as Crown Prince. After conferring with her officials about his replacement, the Empress appointed Prince Ōi. Then she abdicated in 758 so that Prince Ōi might succeed her. But because Prince Ōi too developed bad feelings and allied himself with EMI Oshikatsu against the Retired Empress Kōken, he was deposed in 764 and exiled to the province of Awaji. Kōken then ascended the throne a second time. Prince Ōi is known as the "deposed Emperor of Awaji."[22]

During her second reign (764–770), Kōken was called Empress Shōtoku. Having fallen in love with Dōkyō, a Buddhist priest, she committed such iniquities as promoting him to the position of Priest Emperor *(hōō)* in 766 and placing other priests in secular positions of

21. This is the first known case of a Kami being enshrined near a Buddhist temple and becoming that temple's guardian Kami. Jien seems not to have been aware of the importance of this event as an early step in the fusion of Shintoism and Buddhism, a process that was well advanced by Jien's time and the results of which are deeply embedded in his theological view of history.

22. Now referred to as Emperor Junnin (733–765), a grandson of Emperor Temmu. Junnin's Imperial mother was not a FUJIWARA woman. He seems to have incurred the disfavor of Empress Kōken by warning her that it was wrong to allow Dōkyō to occupy a position of political power. In 764, FUJIWARA Nakamaro, known also as EMI Oshikatsu, decided to remove Junnin from the throne and to eliminate Dōkyō, but Nakamaro was himself eliminated and the ex-Empress returned to the throne for a second reign.

state. The senior minister, EMI Oshikatsu, was replaced by Dōkyō as the Empress's favorite, creating a bad situation. This Empress was no ordinary person. A story is told of her vow with Amoghapāsa Avalokiteśvara at the Saidai Temple.[23] The things she did were gossiped about, but they were not thought of as precedents. Her actions really should be understood as the actions of a Buddhist incarnation (gonge). The Empress's second reign lasted five years, and she died in 770 at the age of 53.

No one had been selected to succeed Empress Shōtoku, and so the ministers considered various candidates. Among those who participated in the succession conference were two superior noblemen: FUJIWARA Nagate (son of Fusasaki) and FUJIWARA Momokawa (son of Umakai). A grandson of Emperor Tenchi and son of Prince Shiki—a person known as the Senior Counselor Prince Shirakabe —was placed on the throne in 770 as Emperor Kōnin. Before her death, Empress Shōtoku issued an Imperial edict stating that Prince Shirakabe should be the next Crown Prince; and the appointment was arranged by FUJIWARA Momokawa. So Shirakabe succeeded to the throne as Emperor Kōnin and reigned 12 years. Kōnin's son, the future Emperor Kwammu, was appointed Crown Prince in 773.

New Strength for Buddhist Law and the State

Emperor Kwammu, who reigned from 781 to 806, moved the capital to Heian in 794, where it still is. Since then, Japan has had no more reigning Empresses, no Emperor has ascended the throne as an Imperial grandson—because each one has been the son or young brother of his predecessor—and every Imperial mother (kokumo) has been a daughter of some ministerial descendant of FUJIWARA Kamatari. So the state was ruled firmly and the people prospered. It was the intention of the Sun Goddess—and has been down to the present—that there be no deviation from that course.

During the Kwammu reign and the Enryaku era (782–806), two Grand Preceptors crossed the sea to China. Grand Preceptor Dengyō (767–822) brought back the incomparable and unique Tendai teach-

23. The Mizukagami (probably written around 1200) describes the incident as follows: "The Saidai Temple was built in 765, and bronze statues were made of the four Heavenly Kings. Three were successfully cast, but there were seven failures in casting the fourth. Finally the Empress made this vow: 'If I can discard my womanly body and become a Buddha through Buddha's virtue, may the next casting be successful as I put my hand into the molten copper. And may my hand be burned off if my prayer is not to be granted.' Not the slightest injury was found on the Empress's hand, and the fourth statue was then cast successfully." [Nihon bungaku taikei, 12.79.]

ings, the exposition of which was the main reason why Shaka Nyorai (who revealed the teachings) appeared in this world. And Grand Preceptor Kōbō (774–835) introduced Shingon teachings which incorporated in one sect all the Buddhist and worldly truths that had been inwardly understood by all the Buddhas of the past, present, and future. Grand Preceptor Kōbō built a baptismal hall and initiated the Second-Week Mass at the Shingon Hall within the Imperial palace grounds, and Grand Preceptor Dengyō propagated the Bodhisattva precepts. It was certainly because of what these Grand Preceptors did that the state came to be ruled firmly and the people prospered. Later on, Grand Preceptors Jikaku (794–864) and Chishō (814–889) also crossed the sea to China. By introducing to Japan such rites as the Burning Light Mass and the Revered Star Mass, they protected Emperors and brought peace to the country.[24]

Japan was later subjected to various disturbances, but Imperial Law and Buddhist Law jointly protected the state. The ministerial house of FUJIWARA did nothing to destroy its fish-in-water relations with the Imperial House, and the country did extremely well. Deterioration increased, however, and Imperial Law and Buddhist Law have now almost been destroyed. I will write about this in detail.

The Course of History

When trying to understand the course of history in this country of Japan, we should adopt the method used when attempting to follow the way of Buddha: first understand one's situation, move to comprehend the essence of fundamental Buddhist teachings, develop a Bodhisattva heart, and enter upon the way of Buddha. The course of secular history should be understood in exactly the same way. But no one is trying to achieve understanding by adhering strictly to this method. Since there is absolutely no understanding, deterioration continues. Moreover, deterioration, occurring spontaneously and naturally *(hōni)*, cannot be checked by the power of man. But in Buddhist Law there is a way to partially negate *(taiji no hō)* it.

Uneven Deterioration

When worldly affairs are considered temporally, we use the word *bō*, which refers to the sixty years that elapse before any one combination of the twelve zodiac signs and the ten celestial stems is re-

24. These four Grand Preceptors are more generally known as Saichō, Kūkai, En'nin, and En'chin. Saichō departed for China in 804 and returned in 805 to found the Tendai Sect. Kūkai went abroad in 804 and returned in 806 to introduce esoteric teachings known in Japan as the Shingon Sect. En'nin sailed for China in 838 and did not return until 847, becoming Tendai Abbot in 854. See Edwin O. Reischauer's *Ennin's Travels in T'ang China*

peated. When measuring time in terms of this cyclical unit, we see
that deterioration is periodically followed by improvement, and improvement by deterioration. But the improvement is always less than
the deterioration. Both the state and man have been affected—down
to the present—by this uneven process of decay.

In order to help the reader understand the unevenness of deterioration in history during Japan's allotted one hundred reigns, I offer
this analogy. A man has one hundred *jō* of paper. He gradually uses
his paper until one or two *jō* are left, and then builds up the supply
to 90 *jō*. He continues to use the paper, but the next replenishment
restores his supply to only 80 *jō*. In another case he might use his
one hundred *jō* until one *jō*—or even 10 sheets of one *jō*—are left
and then build up his supply to 94 or 95 *jō*. Here great deterioration is followed by remarkable improvement. In still another case he
might start off with 70 or 80 *jō*, and when he has used 60 or 70 *jō*
(leaving him 10 or 20 *jō*), 40 or 50 *jō* are added to the supply. Here
appropriate improvement occurs before the deterioration has been
excessive and before there is a sharp turn for the worse. In sum,
the Principle of deterioration and improvement of the Southern
Continent—and of customs in the three countries of China, India,
and Japan—means that deterioration alternates with improvement
in this way.[25]

This Principle also means that man's life expectancy will decline to
10 years by the end of the deteriorating half of this small kalpa and
then increase to 80,000 years at the end of the improving half.[26]
Within that span of time Principles operate in this same way—even
with respect to Japan's one hundred reigns. The waxing and waning
of the moon, seen every month, also shows how Principles work. In
trying to understand this, we find that all phenomena alternately
deteriorate and improve. The following Principles tell us the same
thing: "What flourishes will certainly deteriorate," and "those who
are united will certainly become separated." By comprehending this,
everyone should achieve an understanding that is deep enough to
place him on the path to Buddhahood. And having achieved such
understanding, His Majesty should proceed to read what is written
here.

(New York, 1955). En'chin travelled in China between 853 and 858 and was
named Tendai Abbot in 868.

25. This analogy suggests that the number of reigns, like the number of
jō, might be replenished. Elsewhere (Chapter 4), however, Jien says that
only 16 reigns are left, leaving the impression that no change was to be
made in the number of reigns allotted to Japan. The analogy is, nevertheless, an accurate reflection of Jien's conception of an uneven process of
kalpic decline during the first half of the present small kalpa.

26. Kalpic cycles are described in Chapter 10. Cf. Figure 3.

The Importance of Women

The True Law of Imperial succession in Japan was manifested during the 13 reigns that began with the accession of Emperor Jimmu. The next 36 reigns (from Chūai through Kōnin) moved this way and that, revealing the operation of other Principles. It was during these 36 reigns that reigning Empresses appeared. Two occupied the throne twice: Kōgyoku, who was Saimei in her second reign; and Kōken, who was Shōtoku in her second reign. The truth of the old saying that women provide "the finishing touches"[27] in this country was revealed by the appearance of these reigning Empresses. In trying to understand the basis for this in Buddhist teachings, I conclude that the phrase "birth of the human world" clearly points to the meaning of the fact that people are all born from the wombs of women. The pain that a mother suffers in childbirth is indescribable. Since causal effects *(inga)* are both good and bad, persons born of women include those who are good as well as those who are bad: Holy Men *(hijiri)* of the Two Vehicles and Bodhisattvas, as well as non-Buddhists like Devadatta and Kokāka. All have received female, mother blessings. So the Principle that a person should try to take care of and revere his mother was followed. Reigning Empresses Jingū and Kōgyoku were placed on the throne because each was the wife of the previous Emperor and also the mother of the Crown Prince. At a time when good ministers were destined to handle the affairs of state, Empresses were enthroned in order that ministers might perform their proper role. This is probably why Great Imperial Chieftain TAKENOUCHI and Empress Jingū, Prince Shōtoku and Empress Suiko, and FUJIWARA Kamatari and Empress Kōgyoku appeared in this world in pairs.

FUJIWARA Regents and FUJIWARA Women

FUJIWARA Kamatari's descendants have served in ministerial posts since the Kwammu reign (781–806), and all Empresses and Imperial mothers since then have been Kamatari's descendants.[28] It should be clearly understood that the state has somehow been preserved during these final reigns because the ancestral Kami decided that as there are to be no more reigning Empresses in these final reigns, Empresses and Imperial mothers shall come from the ministerial house of FUJIWARA, and that the father of the current Imperial mother shall be appointed Imperial Inspector. It should also be un-

27. A metaphorical use of *jugan* (inserting the eye), the last thing done when making a statue or painting a picture of a Buddhist figure.

28. Kwammu's reign stands out in Jien's view of history because Kwammu's Empress (FUJIWARA Otomuro) was a FUJIWARA daughter who was the Imperial mother of Emperors Heizei and Saga.

derstood that the state has been preserved during these final reigns
because the ancestral Kami also decided that the following Principles
should be carried out conjointly: women providing the finishing
touches *(nyonin jugan)*, filial devotion *(kōyō)*, and gratitude for blessings received *(hōon)*.

Later Administrations by Retired Emperors

The True Law of Imperial succession has gradually deteriorated
during these final reigns. Therefore the time came when an Emperor could no longer handle the affairs of state by himself. So Emperor Go Sanjō, who reigned from 1068 to 1072, devised the plan of
administering the state, as a Retired Emperor, after abdicating and
placing his son on the throne. This was a realization of the Principle
that a period of deterioration in Imperial Law would be followed by
a turn toward improvement, when the state would settle down for a
while.

The Reigns of Kwammu's Three Sons (806–833)

Emperor Kwammu (737–806) had three sons, but bad relations
developed between the eldest two: the future Emperors Heizei and
Saga. While the capital was being moved to Heian, and before conditions had really settled down, the two Princes turned against each
other. This is said to have been the doing of FUJIWARA Kusuko (Mistress of Palace Attendants at Heizei's court),[29] indicating that iniqui-
tous behavior is also included in those "finishing touches" provided
by women. Prince Tomohira (964–1009) has told the story that while
Saga was Crown Prince and Heizei was Emperor, Heizei wished to
remove Saga from his position as Crown Prince. Saga's guardian,
FUJIWARA Fuyutsugu (775–826), felt that this was such a serious
matter that he urged Saga to report it to his father's Imperial tomb.
After the Crown Prince made his report at the Kwammu tomb, the
country was reportedly engulfed in darkness. Then Heizei dropped
the idea of dismissing Saga as Crown Prince.

Such developments revealed, for the first time, the meaning of
everything that happens in these final reigns.

Relations between Kwammu's second and third sons (Saga and
Junna) were surprisingly good. After both had abdicated, they

29. Kusuko was Emperor Heizei's favorite consort. When Heizei passed
the throne to his brother in 809, Kusuko and her brother FUJIWARA Nakanari (774–810) plotted to have Saga abdicate so that Heizei might return to
the throne for a second reign. But the plot was uncovered and Kusuko was
dismissed from her positions and removed from the palace. Heizei and
Kusuko fled in the direction of the eastern provinces but were caught and
placed under arrest. Nakanari was executed, Heizei was placed under house
arrest, and Kusuko took poison.

amused themselves together in the Sacred Spring Garden of the palace. Saga's son Nimmyō succeeded Junna in 833. And while Junna's son (Prince Tsunesada) was serving as Nimmyō's Crown Prince, Junna died on the 8th day of the 5th month of 840. Saga also passed away on the 15th day of the 7th month of 842. It seems that people had been dreading the loss of these two Retired Emperors.

Japan's First Regent: FUJIWARA Yoshifusa

Two days after Saga's death on the 17th day of the 7th month of 842, Prince Aho reported to Emperor Nimmyō's Imperial mother that a plot by the backers of Crown Prince Tsunesada had been uncovered. An attendant of the Crown Prince, a man by the name of TOMO Kowamine, had reported this to Prince Aho. Undoubtedly Kowamine thought Prince Aho was on his side. The traitors included TACHIBANA Hayanari (Acting Governor of Tajima), FUJIWARA Yoshimichi (Senior Counselor), and FUJIWARA Yoshino (Middle Counselor). They had conspired to have Crown Prince Tsunesada placed on the throne immediately. The Imperial mother quickly called in Middle Counselor FUJIWARA Yoshifusa (804–872)[30] and, after talking over the matter with him, had several of the conspirators exiled. TACHIBANA Hayanari was sent to the island of Izu, and FUJIWARA Yoshimichi was dismissed from his position as Senior Counselor and replaced by FUJIWARA Yoshifusa. Since Crown Prince Tsunesada was only 16 years old at the time, he probably was not involved in the plot. When he was brought to the Reizei palace for questioning, he said that he had known nothing about it. Nevertheless, the Prince was removed from the office of Crown Prince by an Imperial order handed to Prince Consultant Masami, for it was revealed that the traitors had been conspiring in his behalf. On the 4th day of the 8th month of 842, Prince Michiyasu (the future Emperor Montoku and a son of Yoshifusa's sister) was installed as Crown Prince.

Alas, the sons of Emperor Kwammu probably could not have had the spirit of Emperor Nintoku, who became the Great Illuminating

30. Complicated clan rivalries lie behind this incident. Emperor Nimmyō's Imperial mother, TACHIBANA Kachiko (786–850), was the only Imperial mother for a number of reigns after Saga's who was not a FUJIWARA. While Nimmyō was on the throne, her brother TACHIBANA Otsugu (773–843) seems to have had more influence at court than any member of the FUJIWARA clan. But in 842 this Imperial mother of the TACHIBANA clan called in FUJIWARA Yoshifusa, and together they not only exiled "the traitors" but arranged to have a Crown Prince appointed whose mother was FUJIWARA Yoshifusa's sister. It seems that this Imperial mother was more determined to keep her son on the throne than to retain or strengthen her clan's control over state affairs.

Kami of the Hirano Shrine.[31] But shouldn't they have aspired to the feelings of Kenzō and Ninken? We are told that such intentions were very strong in Emperors Saga and Junna.

Then Seiwa, Emperor Montoku's son, succeeded to the throne in 858. We read that during his reign Priest Eryō of Mt. Hiei did such things as put his head in the *goma* fire when he prayed. Since Seiwa had been appointed Crown Prince at the age of one and placed on the throne at nine, and since the practice of appointing Regents for child Emperors had not yet been adopted in Japan, a Chinese precedent set by the Duke of Chou in the reign of King Ch'eng was followed. Therefore FUJIWARA Yoshifusa (Lord Chūjin), the father of Emperor Seiwa's Imperial mother, was appointed Japan's first Regent. After that it was customary to have a Regent or Chancellor serve the Emperor. But a diary tells us that Yoshifusa was at first given the title of Imperial Inspector and that an Imperial edict appointing him Regent was not issued until the 19th day of the 8th month of 866, seven years later.

During the Seiwa reign, Senior Counselor TOMO Yoshio reportedly set fire to the Ōten Gate of the Imperial Palace and placed the blame on Minister MINAMOTO Makoto (810–868), who was almost sent into exile. Meanwhile Yoshisuke (817–867), Minister of the Right and a young brother of Yoshifusa, had been entrusted with affairs of state following Yoshifusa's retirement. Since the Emperor thought what Senior Counselor TOMO had told him was true and Yoshisuke was not suspicious of what the Emperor told him, Yoshisuke made some terrible blunders. FUJIWARA Mototsune, Director of the Imperial Secretariat, was alarmed when he heard about it, and he rushed off to Yoshifusa's mansion at Shirakawa to report. Thus Yoshio's activities were brought to light. Since everyone knows about the incident, I will not go into detail.

Regent Mototsune Removes Emperor Yōzei in 884

Emperor Seiwa held the throne for 18 years but abdicated in 876 at the age of 26, yielding the throne to the nine-year-old Crown Prince who became Emperor Yōzei. Seiwa entered the Buddhist priesthood in 878 at the age of 29 and died when he was 31. Yōzei succeeded to the throne when he was nine and reigned eight years, until he was 16. He did unspeakably bad things, like Emperor Buretsu in the ancient past. So FUJIWARA Mototsune (836–891), Re-

31. In 794, the Hirano Shrine was moved to Heian from Yamato by Emperor Kwammu. Its four Kami are thought to have been the ancestral Kami of the TAKANO clan, the clan of Kwammu's Imperial mother (TAKANO Niigasa), who died in 789. In later times, three of the Kami were identified with the souls of Prince Yamato Takeru no Mikoto, Emperor Chūai, and Emperor Nintoku.

gent and brother of the Emperor's Imperial mother, consulted with various nobles about the situation. Concluding that the Emperor's bad behavior was due to the rough treatment of an evil spirit, they decided that Yōzei should not continue to govern the country. He was therefore forced to abdicate. Then they picked out Prince To-kiyasu, son of Emperor Nimmyō and Prince-Minister of Ceremonies, and placed him on the throne. This was Emperor Kōkō, who became Emperor in 884 at the age of 55. He reigned for three years and died when he was 58.

Emperor Kōkō was succeeded by his son Uda (known as the Priest-Emperor of the Kanpyō era), who ascended the throne in 887 at the age of 21. When Emperor Kōkō (known as the Emperor of Komatsu) became seriously ill and was about to die, he was unable to come to a decision about his successor, although he had several sons. He seems to have made this comment: "My becoming Emperor was due to steps taken by Minister Mototsune. Therefore I would like to consult him about my successor." Mototsune went to the Emperor's bedside and asked to whom His Majesty wished to transfer the throne. Emperor Kōkō replied: "That is something that should be taken care of. Handle it just as you wish." So Mototsune, thinking of the Emperor's third son, Prince Chamberlain Uda, said: "The throne should be handed over to Uda. He would make a fine sovereign." The Emperor's delight was unbounded and he im-mediately called Uda in and told him what had been decided. The following sentences were written down in the Uda Diary:[32] "Hold-ing Mototsune's hand in his left hand, and mine in his right, my Imperial father Kōkō wept and said: 'The kindnesses that Mototsune has shown to us have been very great. I want you to be aware of this.'" What is written there is only a very small part of what is known, even by those who have not seen the Diary. If those who have read the Diary will compare its contents with what I have writ-ten, they will be moved, just as if they were personally involved.

From the beginning of his reign, Emperor Uda often said that he wanted to step down from the throne as soon as possible because he felt he had "absolutely none of the abilities of a sage ruler." He al-ways consulted with Mototsune on such occasions, but Mototsune would only say: "Why should you do such a thing?" So Uda en-trusted all administrative matters to Mototsune with such words as these: "In that case I would like you to handle all state affairs."

---

32. The *Kampyō no gyoki* (the Imperial diary of the Kampyō Era) was more commonly called the *Uda Tennō gyoki* (Imperial diary of Emperor Uda). Portions of the 20-fascicle work were lost during the Ōnin Wars (1467–77). In the Tokugawa period (1600–1868), extant remnants were assembled and published in the *Zokuzoku Gunsho ruijū*, 5.1–14.

Mototsune died in the 6th year of Uda's ten-year reign. Then his
eldest son Tokihira (871–909) and SUGAWARA Michizane (845–903)
were appointed Imperial Inspectors in 891. After writing out injunctions[33] for his successor, Emperor Uda abdicated in 897 at the age of
31, passing the throne to Emperor Daigo. Daigo was 13 at the time
of his enthronement and had not yet been put through the coming-
of-age ceremony. So the ceremony was carried out on the very day
he ascended the throne. Emperor Daigo consulted with FUJIWARA
Tokihira and SUGAWARA Michizane about state affairs without appointing a Regent, just as had been stipulated in Uda's injunctions.

The SUGAWARA Michizane Incident of 901 and Its Meaning

The Michizane Incident occurred in 901, when Emperor Daigo
was 17 years old. The diaries of the various houses and the documents of the Council of State that dealt with the Incident were all
burned by Imperial command, presumably because the Emperor
was afraid the incident was due to some terrible misdeed he had
committed. Therefore no one really knows what happened. But
some brief references to the Incident have been found in other
places. Moreover, this was such a big affair that details have come
down to us by word of mouth. So we probably know the main points.

Are not such things likely to occur when an incarnation of Buddha
(*gonjya*) is alive? No ordinary person is an incarnation of Buddha. We
can clearly understand that these things happened because SUGA-
WARA Michizane, undoubtedly an incarnation of Avalokiteśvara,
wanted to protect Imperial Law under conditions of the final reigns
and at a position near the Emperor. Certainly Tokihira made a false
accusation against Michizane. This is noted in the biography of the
priest Jōzō. But apparently Michizane's vengeful soul could not obtain its revenge until eight years later.[34] We read that it attached
itself to Tokihira but that Jōzō made incantations and severely tor-
tured Michizane's vengeful soul, making it difficult for the soul to
cope with the miraculous power of Buddhist Law. We also read that
Consultant MIYOSHI Kiyoyuki, Jōzō's father, was still alive then and
that one day he received the following message from Michizane's
soul: "Get that priestly son of yours out of the way!" Even Jōzō was
frightened and stopped reciting incantations. It was only then that
Tokihira died. If the vengeful soul had had its way, it would have
destroyed the entire Imperial Inspector and Regent/Chancellor

33. Addressed to Emperor Daigo at the time of Uda's abdication in 897.
Most of the text has been lost, but extant portions have been published in
the *Gunsho ruijū*, 17.133–134.

34. A reference to FUJIWARA Tokihira's death in 909, eight years after
Michizane's exile. This was only one of the disasters believed to have been
caused by Michizane's vengeful soul.

house of FUJIWARA. But Tokihira's young brother Tadahira (880–947) became head of the Regent/Chancellor house of FUJIWARA immediately afterward and was a surprisingly successful Imperial Inspector and Regent. Thus the line of FUJIWARA descent was not broken, and it has continued brilliantly to the present day.

In reflecting about these developments, I draw these two conclusions: (1) since Japan is a small country, it really is bad to have two Imperial Inspectors at one time; and (2) the divine agreement made between the Sun Goddess and the Great Illuminating Kami worshipped at the Kasuga Shrine[35] was to be respected until the end of Japan's final reigns. Michizane was therefore to lose his life by purposely allowing Tokihira to make a false accusation against him, thereby creating a situation in which Michizane's soul would become a Kami that would protect FUJIWARA Kamatari's descendants and preserve the Regent/Chancellor house of FUJIWARA. Certainly Tokihira's heart was quite evil. But even while Michizane was in Kyushu, Tadahira (Tokihira's young brother) and Michizane kept in personal touch with each other by exchanging letters. So Michizane's vengeful soul did not intend to seek full revenge against the Regent/Chancellor house of FUJIWARA.

I have stated the truth about the above events and pointed out that the sons of wise people are not always wise. It is the way of stupid, sentient beings to think that the entire house of numerous Imperial Inspectors, Regents, and Chancellors would become the object of revenge by Michizane's vengeful soul. No one understands clearly that the soul acted as it did in order to manifest the truths outlined above. But we should understand those developments in this way, relating them carefully to true Principles.

One night Michizane's soul had pine trees grow at Kitano near the Greater Imperial Palace and moved there from Kyushu where Michizane had died, becoming a Kami to whose shrine pilgrimages have been made by Emperors, and a Kami that has continued to check the false charges made by man.[36] It is clearly understood that Michizane's soul appeared as a Kami that was to be deeply revered, and heavily relied upon, by Regents and Chancellors. If it had not been for this incarnate guide with his expedient teachings *(hōben kyōmon),* we would simply have been subjected to the deterioration

35. Cf. note 15, above.
36. An allusion to the enshrinement of Michizane's soul as a Kami at the Kitano Shrine, the main shrine—among thousands scattered about Japan— for the worship of a Kami now commonly referred to as Tenjin (the Heaven Kami). Jien seems to have purposely avoided saying that the enshrinement was meant to pacify Michizane's vengeful soul, stressing instead the point that Michizane's soul appeared as a Kami which was to be revered by Emperors and relied upon by Regents and Chancellors.

that is destined to continue from the beginning to the end of the first half of the present small kalpa. This deterioration continues whether the fortunes of persons in this Southern Continent are good or bad, or whether their lives are long or short. Even if one escapes illusion and achieves Buddhahood by being deeply affected, like this incarnate guide, by the Outer Causes *(en)* of reverence for Kami and conversion of Buddha, he will still be subjected to this process of kalpic decline. On that day when a person understands this interaction between kalpic deterioration and Outer Causes generated by reverence for Kami and conversion to Buddha, he will not be mistaken about any of the various turning points in history.

We are told that ex-Emperor Uda (869–931) became a Buddhist priest in 900 at the age of 31, mastered the Shingon teachings of Grand Preceptor Kōbō's school, and entered Nirvana in 939 [*sic*] at the age of 65. It is also recorded that Uda went to the Imperial palace at the time of the Michizane incident to ask Emperor Daigo why Michizane had been exiled. But Emperor Daigo would not listen, saying that "It has been established that once a sovereign has yielded the throne to his successor, he should have nothing further to say about state affairs." Other reports tell us that Uda was not permitted to speak to the Emperor and that no one would pass along his message. In any case, the matter was handled according to Emperor Daigo's wishes. Since ancient times no Emperor had involved himself in state affairs after he had stepped down from the throne. Presumably Emperor Daigo did not yet understand that administrative matters were destined to be handled in the Final Age by a Retired Emperor—that when the sovereign was having doubts about his ministers, and ministers were currying favor with their sovereign, a Retired Emperor was destined to rule the state at the time of a turn toward improvement.

As for the Michizane incident, no one seems to place any reliance upon Nichizō's dream,[37] even though it was probably true. Emperor Daigo reigned for 33 years, but no successor occupied the throne as long as 30 years.

KUJŌ Morosuke's Pledge with Priest Ji'e

FUJIWARA Tadahira had two sons: Lord Ono no Miya Saneyori (900–970) and Lord KUJŌ Morosuke (908–960). Since events in the

37. According to the *Fusō ryakki*, a young brother of MIYOSHI Kiyoyuki (847–918) went to Mt. Kinbu in 941 to engage in ascetic practices, where he dreamed that he was given the name of Nichizō and led to the Kinpu paradise. There he met Buddhist deities, including one that said it had appeared in the physical world as SUGAWARA Michizane. [*Shiseki shūran*, 1.216–217.]

lives of these two sons have been reported in Succession Tales,[38] only turning points need to be dealt with here. Minister of the Right Morosuke was certain that he would die before his elder brother, and he therefore made this vow: "Although I am destined to have a short life, I will have the Regency passed to my descendants, who will administer state affairs as maternal uncles or maternal grandfathers of Emperors." So he made a firm patron pledge *(shidan no chigiri)* with Grand Preceptor Ji'e[39] of Mt. Hiei, an incarnation of Avalokiteśvara, and had a temple (the Ryōgon Sammai Hall) built on the Yokawa Peak of Mt. Hiei. Only the Lotus Sutra Hall of the new temple was completed before Morosuke's death in 960. One day Morosuke climbed Mt. Hiei and in the midst of a crowd of priests struck a flint while intoning these words: "If my wish is to be granted, a fire will be started within three strikes of this flint." A fire was started with the first strike, and the permanent light of the Lotus Sutra Hall was lit. We are told that the light has not been extinguished to this day. Thus from the reigns of Reizei and Enyū down through the reign of Gō-Reizei, learned Emperors, Imperial Inspectors, and Regents from the wombs of women descended from KUJŌ Morosuke have flourished gloriously.[40] After that, relationships to Emperors through their Imperial mothers shifted to ministers of the KAN'IN line—to descendants of Morosuke's son Kinsue (956–1029). Emperors Shirakawa and Toba were of that line, and they administered state affairs as Retired Emperors—holding the title of Cloistered Emperor—from 1086 to 1156. The current Retired Emperor Go-Toba succeeded Retired Emperor Go-Shirakawa as the administrator of state affairs, but Go-Toba is of the Interim-Chancellor Michitaka line.[41]

38. Probably a reference to the *Ōkagami*, which has sections devoted to each of these Tadahira sons. NKBT, 21.85–90 and 115–132. See Chapter 8.

39. Known as Ryōgen (912–985), founder of Tendai Shugendō and one of the first Tendai Abbots to use armed priests *(sōhei)* for the protection of Tendai interests.

40. Descended, that is, from Yasuko (927–964), who was the Imperial mother of Emperors Reizei and Enyū as well as the daughter of Morosuke. Thenceforth—down through the Go-Reizei reign (1045–68)—every Imperial mother and every Regent and Chancellor was a Morosuke descendant.

41. FUJIWARA Michitaka (957–995), Kaneie's eldest son, was appointed Chancellor at the time of Kaneie's death in 990. But when Michitaka resigned in 995, he was replaced by Kaneie's second son Michikane (961–995), not by Michitaka's son Korechika (974–1010). Then when Michikane died a few days later, another Kaneie son—the famous Michinaga (966–1027)—was placed in charge of administrative affairs. Since it was Michinaga's descendants, not Michitaka's, who were the later heads of the Regent/Chancellor house of FUJIWARA, Michitaka is referred to as the Interim

No one thinks deeply about even the expedient blessings *(rishō hō-ben)* of Avalokiteśvara that have been bestowed upon this country of Japan, first by Prince Shōtoku and then by FUJIWARA Kamatari, SUGAWARA Michizane, and Senior High Priest Ji'e. Alas, if all Emperors and ministers had believed deeply in these expedient blessings and given some thought to the true course of Principle, not deviating one iota from it, I think that the time fate *(jiun)* of deterioration from the beginning to the end of the first half of the present small kalpa could not have been avoided but that, for the time being, there would have been no unfortunate or unexpected disasters. And if Emperors and ministers had believed in these expedient blessings and given some thought to the true course, we would have had only a well-governed state about which it would have been said that "calamity did not prevail over virtue."

It was probably because of KUJŌ Morosuke's unrivalled fame that he was able to steal into Emperor Murakami's palace to woo Daigo's daughter. At first he visited her secretly, but later his visits were found out. Since she was an Imperial princess, she lived in the Koki Hall within the palace. By Morosuke she gave birth to a son who was to become Prime Minister Kinsue, founder of the KAN'IN house. And it is said that this was why members of the KAN'IN were referred to as "persons of the flourishing house."

The appointment of a succession of Regents and Chancellors descended from Morosuke began in 970, when Lord Ono no Miya Saneyori died and Lord KUJŌ Morosuke's heir, Koretada (924–972), was appointed Regent. Since Koretada was a brother of Enyū's Imperial mother and was Minister of the Right, and since Morosuke had died without being appointed Regent or Chancellor, no one had as strong a claim to the post of Regent as Koretada.

FUJIWARA *Headship*

Originally the Emperor did not appoint FUJIWARA heads.[42] The red bowl, tray, and seal—the symbols of FUJIWARA headship—were simply passed from one head to the next. Then the head would be appointed Imperial Inspector but not necessarily Regent or Chancellor. A Regent was appointed only when the Emperor was a minor. After FUJIWARA Yoshifusa (Lord Chūjin) was appointed Imperial Inspector in 858 or 866, the term Number One Man *(ichi no hito)* was applied to a person who was both head of the FUJIWARA clan and Imperial Inspector. An Imperial Inspector was not necessarily ap-

---

Chancellor, the man whose administration fell between the administrations of Kaneie and Michinaga.

42. The first case was that of Jien's father FUJIWARA Tadamichi (1097–1164), who received an Imperial appointment as FUJIWARA head in 1156.

pointed. The position of Chancellor originated with an Imperial edict handed down in 880, after FUJIWARA Mototsune had first served as Regent. Probably a Chinese precedent was followed, the one established during the reign of Emperor Tsuan when, in about 74 B.C., Ho Kuang was entrusted with the affairs of state and permitted to report to the Emperor after action had been taken. FUJIWARA Saneyori was impressed that he was the first to receive an Imperial edict in 967 appointing him Chancellor without his having previously served as Regent. Later on in the Daigo reign and following the death of Tokihira in 909, as well as during the Murakami reign, not even an Imperial Inspector was appointed, much less a Regent or Chancellor. In the post-Tokihira period of the Daigo reign, Lord Teishin Tadahira had simply been head of the FUJIWARA clan and First Minister. However, when Suzaku was placed on the throne in 930 at the age of eight, Tadahira was named Regent. Then he was asked at the beginning of the Murakami reign to continue on as Chancellor. But when Tadahira died in 949, FUJIWARA Saneyori (Minister of the Left) assumed responsibility for the conduct of state affairs. Then when Reizei was enthroned in 967, an Imperial edict was issued appointing Saneyori to the position of Chancellor.

When making such appointments, the ability of the current Emperor had to be considered. No sovereign in this Final Age can be compared to sovereigns of ancient times. Since a true sage ruler is hard to find, Regents and Chancellors are now appointed routinely. Even so, FUJIWARA Michinaga first served as an Imperial Inspector and was not appointed Regent until 1015, toward the end of the Sanjō reign. FUJIWARA Tadazane, too, was first an Imperial Inspector and was not appointed Chancellor until 1105 in the Horikawa reign. That was the best way.

Great FUJIWARA Heads: Tadahira and Saneyori

FUJIWARA Tadahira (880–949) was no ordinary man. At the time of the Masakado Rebellion in 937, and when he was participating in a Benevolent Mass at the Imperial Palace, his voice could be heard but his body could not be seen. We are told that people concluded that he had mastered the art of disappearing.

When FUJIWARA Saneyori (900–970) died in 970, a great number of people assembled at the gate of his mansion to mourn his passing. Whenever a man of virtue died in ancient times, people would gather to express their grief by wailing and crying. But nowadays nobody is worthy of such expressions of grief. So the spontaneous wailing of persons—noble and mean, high and low—assembled outside the gates of Saneyori's mansion at the time of his death was really sad. People claimed that "his death was the saddest thing in the world." Such matters are worthy of reflection.

Rivalry between KUJŌ *Morosuke's Sons*

Two of Lord KUJŌ Morosuke's sons—Lord Horikawa Kanemichi
(925–977) and Lord Hōkō-in Kaneie (929–990)—fell out over a
promotion irregularity in which Kaneie was promoted to a position
higher than that of his elder brother Kanemichi. Probably Kanemichi was passed over for some good reason. People came vaguely
to realize that since both sons were maternal uncles of Emperors
Reizei and Enyū, they were given positions in the Crown Prince's
household. Being the eldest of the two, Kanemichi was the first
to be made Assistant Master of Crown Prince Reizei's household.
But then something happened. Reizei became displeased with
Kanemichi, removed him from the position of Assistant Master, and
gave the position to Kaneie. When Reizei was enthroned in 967,
Kaneie was named Director of the Imperial Secretariat, a position
even further ahead of the one held by his elder brother. Being an
aggressive competitor who was wise to everything, Kaneie rose to the
position of Director of the Imperial Secretariat while holding only
the title of Middle Counselor. When he was later promoted to Senior
Counselor and Senior Commander, Kanemichi was only Middle
Counselor.

Then, in the early years of Enyū's reign (969–984), Kanemichi
heard that Regent Koretada was seriously ill. Kanemichi therefore
handed a letter written in *kana* to the Emperor, who was then standing in the Demon Room of the Imperial Palace. The Emperor un-
rolled the letter and read: "The posts of Regent and Chancellor
should be filled on the basis of seniority." The letter had been written by the deceased Yasuko (927–964), Imperial mother of Emperor
Enyū and Secondary Empress of Emperor Murakami. Everyone
thought it was really crafty of Kanemichi to have had the Imperial
mother write this letter and then to have had it handed to the Emperor while the latter was mourning her death. After reading the
letter, and because the Regent's illness had become serious, the Emperor did not hesitate to appoint Kanemichi Imperial Inspector. So
without even having held the title of Senior Counselor, Kanemichi
was now given an accelerated promotion to Minister of the Center,
outranking his young brother who was still Senior Counselor and
Senior Commander. Then, by an Imperial edict of 974, Kanemichi
was appointed Chancellor.

In 977, while Kaneie was still feeling uneasy about this turn of
fortune, Kanemichi became quite sick and was heard to be at the
point of death. So Kaneie straightened out his robes and went to the
Imperial Palace. People thought that Kaneie was going to call on his
ailing elder brother. Kanemichi himself probably thought that was
what Kaneie had in mind. But when Kanemichi heard that Kaneie
had actually gone to the Imperial Palace, he suddenly got up out of

bed and left his mansion saying that he too was going to the palace. Even his aides felt that this was strange behavior and asked themselves what the Chancellor was up to. Intent upon his mission, he hurried off, carried by four attendants. People at the palace clamored: "The Lord Chancellor will soon be here!" Kaneie could not believe that a man who was said to be dying would now be coming to the palace, but when he realized that his ailing elder brother had indeed arrived, he departed in confusion. Kanemichi went before the Emperor and said: "I have come to conduct the installation ceremony for the last time." And he issued such commands as these: "Hey, come here! Call in the nobles who are nearby! Let's get on with the installation ceremony!" People assembled, thinking that these were strange doings. Kanemichi first chatted with the Emperor about some trivial matters and then said: "Senior-Commander-of-the-Right Kaneie is an impudent fellow! His Majesty ought to dismiss him!" And in a loud voice he addressed the nobles: "Does someone want to be Senior Commander? If so, don't hesitate to speak up!" Not wishing to cross the Chancellor, no one said anything. One person present was Middle Counselor Naritoki, son of Minister Morotada of Kochijō. (Morotada was a younger brother of Lord KUJŌ Morosuke.) Naritoki's thoughts went like this: "I had better speak up. If I am not appointed Senior Commander now, I probably never will be." So when Kanemichi said once more: "Doesn't anyone want to be Senior Commander? If so, just say so!" Naritoki loudly proclaimed his own candidacy. Kanemichi said: "Fine! Fine! Hurry up with the arrangements!" Naritoki was listed as a Senior Commander of the Imperial Guards. But who was the secretary at the time? Are there no diary entries about this matter? Was the formal installation ceremony actually held in the guest quarters of the palace?

Kanemichi then stated: "Yoritada's personality makes him an appropriate person for the position of Chancellor. He is a Minister and so there should be no objection to his candidacy. Therefore I yield the Chancellorship to him." An Imperial edict was handed down in 977 appointing Yoritada (924–989) to the office of Chancellor. Emperor Enyū was quite frightened and thought: "Why does he do this?"[43] But the Emperor did just as Kanemichi wished, probably thinking that this would not be a serious mistake. While he had not complied precisely with the wishes expressed in the letter written by his deceased Imperial mother, he probably intended to do so at the next opportunity. The deceased Imperial mother of Emperors Reizei and Enyū, known as Secondary Empress Yasuko, was a daughter of Lord KUJŌ Morosuke.

43. Emperor Enyū was apparently puzzled because Yoritada was neither a brother nor father of the Imperial mother.

It is generally known that while Regent Koretada was ill, Kanemichi and Kaneie went before the Emperor and argued about who
should be the next Regent. In the diary of Senior Commander
Naritoki,[44] we read such things as this: "They got to the point of
using unguarded language." Although we are not certain about the
circumstances of Kanemichi's last installation ceremony, it was certainly held. Such a grudge as the one Kaneie and Kanemichi held
against each other was not in accord with Principle. It was not good
for state or man and contributed to the ruination of the country. But
this yielding of the chancellorship to Yoritada of Sanjō, a good man
who was the son of Lord Ono no Miya Saneyori, was destined to
occur. Was not this course of action, required by a fusion of Inner
and Outer causes, also a working out of Principle? So Yoritada was
appointed Chancellor by an Imperial edict handed down on the 11th
day of the 10th month of 977. He continued to hold the position for
about ten years, until Ichijō succeeded to the throne in 986. But
when Ichijō was enthroned, Kaneie was appointed Regent in accordance with an indisputable Principle.[45]

The Regency Question of 984

Emperor Enyū yielded the throne to Kazan in 984. In those days
Emperors and their young brothers were all grandsons of a Regent
or Chancellor; and when an Emperor passed the throne to his
younger brother, a son of the abdicated elder brother was immediately appointed Crown Prince. Many successions were of this
type. So when Reizei stepped down from the throne in 969 to be
succeeded by his young brother Enyū, Reizei's son Kazan was appointed Crown Prince. Then when Enyū yielded the throne to
Kazan in 984, Enyū's son Ichijō became Crown Prince.

Being pushed into the background by his elder brother Kanemichi, Kaneie was only Minister of Civil Affairs. But since Emperor Kazan's Imperial mother was FUJIWARA Koretada's daughter
(and Reizei's Empress), she was Kaneie's niece. Therefore when
Kazan was enthroned in 984, Kaneie hoped that he would be named
Regent. Kaneie—then Minister of the Right—was strengthening the

44. No such diary is now extant.
45. The indisputable Principle was that the father of an Imperial mother
should be appointed Regent or Chancellor. Kaneie's discontent arose from
the fact that although he was a brother of Enyū's Imperial mother and an
uncle of Kazan's Imperial mother, Yoritada—a more distant relative of both
Emperors—was made Chancellor in the middle of the Enyū reign and continued to hold that post during the Kazan reign. Only in 986 was Kaneie,
the father of Ichijō's Imperial mother, appointed Regent. Yoritada had
given daughters to both Enyū and Kazan, but Ichijō was an Enyū son by
Kaneie's daughter Akiko.

barriers[46] on the day when the decision about the Chancellorship was being made, but when he heard that FUJIWARA Yoritada would be asked to remain on as Chancellor, he stopped attending court and even refused to serve as master of ceremonies at the Imperial banquet. The next highest official should then have become master of ceremonies, but Masanobu (Minister of the Left) and his young brother Shigenobu (Senior Counselor) were in mourning and could not perform that function. And the other two Senior Counselors, Tamemitsu and Asamitsu, made excuses and left the palace. The duty was therefore performed by Naritoki, only a Middle Counselor. This Naritoki was not afraid of Kaneie. Because this too was a working out of Principle, we should not criticize Naritoki for what he did.

FUJIWARA Yoshifusa was the first man who was, as the maternal uncle of the reigning Emperor, appointed Regent. He became Regent in 858 for Emperor Seiwa, Japan's first child Emperor. After that, there was not a single violation of the Principle—definitely created by the ancestral Kami of the Imperial House and the FUJIWARA clan—that a man from the Regent/Chancellor house of FUJIWARA who is both a Minister and a maternal uncle or grandfather of the reigning Emperor should become the Minister who handles state affairs. Therefore when Kazan ascended the throne in 984, Middle Counselor Yoshichika (957–1008) should have taken over the affairs of state, since he was Emperor Kazan's maternal uncle. At the time of Kazan's enthronement, Yoshichika was Director of the Imperial Secretariat. At first he was appointed Imperial Attendant Fourth Rank but was given an accelerated promotion to Middle Counselor not long afterward. He was also handed the responsibility for administering state affairs. But within two years an unspeakable situation arose because incomprehensible things were occurring.

Although Kaneie felt that the enthronement of Kazan afforded him an opportunity to wipe out his long-standing disappointment over not being appointed Regent or Chancellor, he was neither a maternal uncle nor maternal grandfather of Emperor Kazan. As the son of Lord KUJŌ Morosuke, he stood in exactly the same relationship to the Emperor as Yoritada, Saneyori's son. So Kaneie abandoned the hope of reaching his goal at this time, for it was also in accord with Principle for him to realize that Yoritada was to continue on as Prime Minister and Chancellor.

46. Barriers *(seki)* were highway stations that were military posts as well as places for the collection of tolls on the transport of goods. The barriers in Omi, Mino, and Ise were particularly important. Cf. Curtis A. Manchester, "The Development and Distribution of *sekisho* in Japan" (Ph.D. dissertation, University of Michigan, 1946).

In 986, Emperor Kazan's beloved Empress, Tamemitsu's daughter, died at the age of 19, and thereafter the Emperor was interested only in practicing the teachings of Buddha. Having decided that he would not remain in this secular world, he immersed himself in reflection. Meanwhile Kaneie's son Michikane—later known as the Lord of Awata and as the Seven Day Chancellor—was lamenting the slowness with which his father's destiny to become a Regent or Chancellor was being realized. And since Michikane was then a Fifth Rank official of the Imperial Secretariat and a Minor Controller of the Left Division (the Imperial Secretary of that day), he was serving near the Emperor and kept hearing His Majesty say that he was bored with the world and wanted to follow the path of Buddha. Michikane must therefore have felt that he could further his father's cause by encouraging the Emperor to yield the throne to his successor.[47] In ancient times as well as at present, a person who makes plots does things that even he considers incomprehensible. Since the Emperor felt strongly about entering the priesthood, it was thought that he and Michikane, being young, had developed an immature urge to practice Buddhist Law. Have not the feelings of people always been the same? And yet it was probably the moment for such things to happen. Certainly they can not happen now.

Japan's Three Ages

The final years of the Ancient Age (*jōko*) and of [Japan's age of] True Law came in the final years of the Kampyō era (889–898). The reigns of Emperor Daigo (898–931) and Murakami (947–967) came at the tag end of that Ancient Age and at the beginning of the Medieval Age (*chūko*). Fine and noble things occurred then, but from the reigns of Reizei and Enyū (967–984) down through the Shirakawa and Toba [administrations as Retired Emperors from 1086 to 1156] the hearts and minds of people only seemed to be the same. But since the close of the Go-Shirakawa reign (1155–58), there has been extreme deterioration; and the last 20 years [from the close of Go-Toba's reign in 1198] have been terrible.[48]

47. Michikane undoubtedly realized that Kaneie's prospects were poor so long as Kazan remained on the throne, for neither of Kazan's principal consorts was a Kaneie daughter. So if Kazan should produce a son by one of these consorts, Kaneie would not be entitled to the position of Regent or Chancellor when that son ascended the throne. But if Kazan could be induced to abdicate before producing a son, Ichijō—an Enyū son by Kaneie's daughter—would be the next Emperor, and Kaneie could then expect an appointment as Regent.

48. Discussed in Chapter 10.

Emperor Kazan's Urge to Enter the Priesthood

Because [Kazan's reign came long after the Ancient Age], we can clearly understand why this Emperor should have developed a youthful urge to follow the path of Buddha and why, when everyone was making guesses about His Majesty's feelings, Michikane developed the same urge and recommended that Emperor Kazan abdicate and enter the Buddhist priesthood. Although I have not heard that Kazan was spoken to as suggested below, such would have been a realization of the Principle for that age. The words addressed to His Majesty would have been like those used by a priest who explains what has happened in India or China. Although he does not speak the languages of those countries, his explanations are praised and described as true explanations if there is no conflict with the essence of Principles for that period of time. Kazan's abdication came in the days of Vicar General Eshin's conversion; and disciples of Eshin (such as Vicar General Genkyū) were called in and asked questions about His Majesty entering the priesthood. They probably made such points as these:

In the sutras it is written that when a ruler dies his wife, children, and treasures can not be taken with him.

Do we not find this quotation in the introductory chapter of the Lotus Sutra: "They all abdicated, entered the priesthood, developed a desire to follow the great Buddha way, and constantly practiced the Buddhist discipline."

In the Devadatta Section of the Lotus Sutra it is written that "at that time a Seer came and said: 'Noble king, I have a wondrous Law which is a rare thing in this world.' So I followed the Seer and served Him."

Shakyamuni said of himself: "Now after I left home, I arrived at supreme, perfect enlightenment."

When such feelings about Buddhism have been aroused, you should follow the Buddha path that is so difficult for men to follow.

Although you may change your mind, your desire for supreme enlightenment will not die. There is no Buddha way superior to that expounded in the Lotus Sutra.

Even if there is only the Outer Cause of Fugyō Bodhisattva, people will achieve enlightenment.

The Bodhisattva precepts are the essence of Buddhism for this age. Even if the precepts are broken, you may still maintain them.

Since it is said that one can not actually throw away the Law once it has been received, and since you have now really made up your mind to enter the priesthood, you should do so right away.

Those who advised the Emperor probably made such points from morning till night. And Michikane made this promise: "If your Majesty really enters the priesthood, I will immediately join you in the practice of Buddhist Law. Since the bonds between us are really strong, I offer my service to Your Majesty today in a way that a subject should serve his sovereign." As a result of such urging, Emperor Kazan became more deeply interested in entering the priesthood. And in the middle of the night of the 22nd day of the 6th month of 986 he left the Greater Imperial Palace with Genkyū and Michikane (Minor Controller of the Left and official of the Imperial Secretariat) riding at the rear of the Imperial carriage. We are told that they left from the Sewing-Hall Guard Gate. In the Succession Tales it is written that, as they were approaching one of the halls, the Emperor said: "This seems hasty! Shouldn't we think it over a bit?" But Michikane replied: "Haven't the Jewel and the Sword already been handed over to the Crown Prince? We can not turn back now." Whereupon the Emperor said: "You are right! You are right!" And they went on.

When the Emperor had decided to leave, Michikane placed Michikata and Michitsuna on the alert and said to the Emperor: "Shouldn't the Jewel and the Sword be handed over to the Crown Prince now?" So Michikata and Michitsuna took the Imperial Treasures to the Luxuriant Flower Hall where the Crown Prince (the future Emperor Ichijō) was residing. Then the Minister of the Right came and closed all the gates, sending FUJIWARA Michinaga, who was the Colonel of the Imperial Guards, to report to Yoritada. Michinaga told Yoritada what a momentous event had occurred.

Kaneie Appointed Regent in 986

Following the enthronement of Ichijō in 986, incomprehensible things happened. Since Ichijō was seven years old at that time, a Regent had to be appointed. And because Kaneie (then Minister of the Right) was the father of Emperor Ichijō's Imperial mother, he was made Regent and Yoritada was removed, to his surprise, from his position as Chancellor. Then the state really settled down.

After Kazan's Abdication

Now when Emperor Kazan was cutting off his hair to enter the priesthood at the Gangyō Temple, he thought that Michikane would soon do likewise. But Michikane tearfully said:

I should like to see my parents once more. And I want them to see me. If I do not go to see them, I will be unfilial. And if I am unfilial, will not even the Three Treasures of the Buddhist Law conclude that I have acted in an unpardonable way? When my parents hear of Your Highness's entrance into the priesthood, they will probably not prevent me from following you. I will return here in a short while.

Then as Michikane stood up to leave, Kazan said, "How you have deceived me!" But Michikane replied: "Why should I do such a thing?" Taking up his whip, he headed for the palace. Would he ever return to the temple again?

When Yoshichika (Middle Counselor) and Koreshige (Middle Controller of the Left) heard of Kazan's abdication and entrance into the priesthood, they immediately joined him, following the path of Buddha without doing anything shameful. It is said that Yoshichika became a priest who resided at the Anraku Temple of Iimuro and that Koreshige got so deeply into Buddhism that he actually became the Holy Man who carried the sacred wand during the Kamo Festival. Although Priest-Emperor Kazan later had an unseemly change of heart, at first—and again in later years—he practiced Buddhism well. Consequently, I think he surely entered upon the path of Buddha.

FUJIWARA *Prosperity: Kaneie to Yorimichi*

After Ichijō's enthronement in 986, Kaneie controlled the state firmly. In looking back at his administration and those that followed—down through the administration of Lord Uji Yorimichi which ended in 1068—one sees that the situation was indescribably good. The FUJIWARA house of the Number One Man was prosperous and the state was peaceful. In a situation in which even the hearts of men were free, nothing bad occurred. Because the true course of Principles was being followed and the state was well governed, one good FUJIWARA man after another appeared, just as if that had been purposely arranged by the ancestral Kami. Three of the famous "four Counselors" were members of the FUJIWARA clan.[49] The state was governed well under FUJIWARA ministers until 1068.

KUJŌ *Kaneie's Daughter and Sons*

Lord Great Lay Priest KUJŌ Kaneie entered the Buddhist priesthood on the 4th day of the 5th month of 990 and yielded the position of Chancellor to his son and heir Michitaka, then Minister of the Center. Kaneie died on the 2nd day of the 7th month of that same year. (Michitaka was known as the Interim Chancellor; and his son Korechika was referred to as the Provisional Minister of the Center and, after his exile, as Honorary Minister.) In 995, Michitaka had his son Korechika appointed Imperial Inspector, but since Korechika's

49. Taken up in Chapter 2.

uncle Michikane was Minister of the Right, and Korechika was only Minister of the Center, Michikane was appointed Chancellor.

Emperor Ichijō's Imperial mother, Higashi Sanjō In (966–1001), was the first person to receive the Cloistered Empress title *(nyō in)*. She received it because she was Kaneie's daughter and Enyū's Empress. We hear that while she was alive the state was governed just as she wanted.

Both Michitaka and Michikane were elder brothers of Higashi Sanjō In, but somehow Michikane had not done well by himself in the Kazan affair. At the right time he would have been a credit to his father Kaneie. Although Minister of the Center Korechika (974–1010), Michitaka's son and Michikane's nephew, was deficient in personality and in ability to handle administrative affairs, he was accomplished in Chinese learning and very good at composing Chinese poems. But because Michikane (Minister of the Right) was senior to Korechika (Minister of the Center), Michikane was appointed Chancellor on the 27th day of the 4th month of 995. But he died on the 8th day of the 5th month of that same year. So people speak of him as the Seven Day Chancellor.

FUJIWARA *Michinaga and Ichijō's Imperial Mother*

After the death of Michikane in 995, Korechika should have been named Imperial Inspector.[50] But his uncle Michinaga (966–1027), Senior Counselor and young brother of Michitaka and Michikane, could not be overlooked. Michinaga's superior ability was recognized by the nobility and the public at large. He confidently and openly stated that "The state will become confused and ruined if Korechika conducts state affairs but will become tranquil if I receive the assignment." Higashi Sanjō In, Ichijō's Imperial mother and Michinaga's sister, also felt that Michinaga should be placed in charge of administrative affairs. But the Emperor, having his own views about the matter, did not agree. His Majesty seems to have become irritated by his mother's pleas in Michinaga's behalf. One day as the Emperor was leaving his royal seat in the breakfast room to perform his official functions, he beckoned to MINAMOTO Toshikata, Director of the Imperial Secretariat. While the two of them were talking together, the Imperial mother opened the door of the Imperial bedroom and, with an odd look in her eyes, said: "Why will you not listen to my request? What I propose will be good for

50. Michitaka wanted his son Korechika to be the next Chancellor, but it seems that Emperor Ichijō's Imperial mother (Higashi Sanjō In) did not like Korechika. It was therefore not Korechika but his uncles—first Michikane and then Michinaga—who obtained appointments that placed them in charge of administrative affairs.

the state and for you. If you don't listen, I will never speak of such things again. This is really a sad and regrettable matter." When the Emperor heard his mother make these comments, he sat up and soberly replied: "How can I refuse a request made so emphatically? Let's hand down the order right away!" Toshikata had left when he saw the Imperial mother enter, but when the Emperor gave his approval, the Imperial mother said: "Toshikata is probably around. Have him called in right away. I will tell him what has been decided." The Emperor ordered Toshikata to return and to issue an order stating that "documents of the Supreme Council of State are henceforth to be presented to the Emperor by Senior Counselor Michinaga." Toshikata said that he understood, and withdrew. Since the order was issued immediately, the Imperial mother returned to the breakfast room where Michinaga was waiting to hear what had transpired. The Imperial mother, wiping away tears with her sleeve and smiling, said: "The order has already been issued!" Michinaga took his leave after expressing his gratitude. For a time he served as Imperial Inspector while continuing to hold the title of Senior Counselor, but before a year had elapsed he was promoted to Minister of the Right. Because he was appointed Imperial Inspector and promoted to Minister of the Right, he moved ahead of Korechika who was Minister of the Center.

The 996 Incident

Korechika and his younger brother Takaie, sons of Michinaga's elder brother Michitaka, were both demoted during the 4th month of 996: Korechika from Minister of the Center to Acting Governor General at Daizaifu, and Takaie from Middle Counselor to Acting Governor of the Province of Izumo. Both were banished from the capital because they had shot at Retired Emperor Kazan. The circumstances were as follows. Prime Minister Tamemitsu—called Lord Kōtoku of the Hōjū Temple—had three daughters. The first was the one whose death had aroused Emperor Kazan's desire to enter the priesthood. Some time after her death, Kazan's interest in Buddhism cooled and he began to call on the second daughter. Meanwhile, Minister Korechika had begun to call on the third daughter. Then people began to say that Retired Emperor Kazan had taken to calling on none other than this same third daughter. Upset by these rumors, Korechika said to his 16-year-old brother Takaie: "What should I do? I am uneasy!" Because Takaie was young and rash, he waited for his chance and, armed with a bow and arrow, shot an arrow that pinned His Majesty's sleeve to a wall. Although it was a close call, the Retired Emperor was able to flee. The affair was hushed up, but gradually information about it leaked out. The above-mentioned punishments were meted out because something had to be done about such a serious offense. Although we are told that this was the way it happened, the FUJIWARA Saneyori Diary[51] states that information about the incident was reported immediately, on the very night it occurred, that Korechika was removed from his position as Minister of the Center at the time of the installation ceremony held on the 13th day of the 1st month of 996, and that people insisted that "of course the right and proper sentences were handed down." Since the Diary deals with this matter in detail, it should be read.

Such crimes had been committed, but people thought that Korechika and Takaie had been exiled because Michinaga was hostile toward them, which was a great embarrassment to Michinaga. Later on, both men were called back to the capital, and Korechika was granted the title of Honorary Minister. It is said that after Takaie was appointed Acting Governor General and went to Daizaifu, he became wealthy. He did pile up an unknown amount of wealth. When he returned to the capital, he went to call on Michinaga. But there was nothing for them to talk about, and so Takaie took from his sleeve a card on which he had written his name. He handed it to Michinaga and withdrew. We hear that Takaie was very clever.

Michinaga and Emperor Ichijō

On a day following the death of Emperor Ichijō in 1011 when Michinaga was disposing of the deceased Emperor's belongings, Michinaga looked into a box and found something that looked like an Imperial Mandate written in the deceased Emperor's hand. At the beginning of the document were these words: "The sun, moon, and stars wish to lighten the world, but they are hidden by great banks of clouds and the sky is dark."[52] Without reading further, Michinaga rolled up the document and burned it. Lord Uji Yorimichi, Michinaga's son, told MINAMOTO Takakuni (Senior Counselor of Uji) this story, and Takakuni wrote it down.

Michinaga was generally like T'ai Tsung of China (founder of the T'ang Dynasty of China) who said: "I think I am the equal of Yao and Shun." Michinaga really was the equal of FUJIWARA Kamatari and FUJIWARA Mototsune. Apparently he had no feelings that were not in accord with Principles for the true course of Japanese history. Not thinking of himself, he once said: "What is called my prestige

51. No such diary is now extant. Saneyori died in 970, years before these events took place.
52. These comments suggest that Emperor Ichijō did not really want to put Michinaga in charge but did so because of pressure exerted by his Imperial mother.

and power is the sovereign's prestige and power." Proof of his style was provided just before his death on the 4th day of the 12th month of 1027. He had entered the Buddhist priesthood and decided, some years before, that he would close his eyes for the last time in front of the central object of worship (a 16-foot statue of nine Amitābha Buddhas) of the Muryōju Cloister of the Hōjō Temple. I doubt whether there has been another person in ancient or modern times who has matched the style of his death behind a folding screen, where he sat properly dressed in Buddhist robes, leaning on an arm-rest.

The end came on the 4th day of the 12th month; and the 12th month was a time for the strict observance of rites connected with the Kami Food Tasting Festival. Purification rites were customarily carried out with great care after the 1st day of that month. The Chancellor/Regent and other nobles respected the taboos of the month. Nevertheless, in the 12th month of 1027, Buddhist priests of the old and new capitals (Nara and Heian) held doctrinal discussions and the Eight Expoundings at the Hōjō Temple as a memorial for Michinaga. The Chancellor, accompanied of course by other high-ranking nobles, was present for the rites held in front of the Buddha statue of the great temple, feeling absolutely no scruples about listening to the doctrinal discussions and the traditional Eight Expoundings. It is thought that the Sun Goddess enshrined at Ise had permitted this violation of the taboos against holding memorial services during the 12th month. This is an example in human affairs of what is meant by the phrase "the virtue of that man." Would such virtue have existed in one who had been the least bit defiled by selfishness or by disloyalty to the Imperial House? His life was truly spendid!

Since Emperor Ichijō had not seen Michinaga as he really was, His Majesty wrote out what appeared to be an Imperial Mandate and died immediately afterward. But Michinaga lived long after that. His descendants prospered, and he died in an incomparable way with a "correct mind" at the moment of death. Because he had felt deep in his heart that this was his destiny, he wished to live on—not developing ill will toward the deceased Emperor and not raising questions about why the Emperor had written the Mandate—in order to conduct memorial services for the deceased Emperor Ichijō. His feelings were unlike those of other people under similar circumstances, high or low. He had rolled up the document that looked like an Imperial Mandate and burned it, feeling that he should not ask why the Emperor had written it or whether the things written were true.

It is clearly understood that the Sun Goddess and the Great Hachiman Bodhisattva really wished to protect Michinaga and that he therefore lived long—until 1027—and came to be admired for the splended way he lived and died.

2
Medieval Age

Emperor Ichijō to
Hōgen Rebellion of 1156

FUJIWARA Michinaga: Brother of Two Imperial Mothers

Emperor Ichijō ascended the throne in 986 at the age of seven, reigned 25 years, and died on the 22nd day of the 6th month of 1011 at the age of 32. He had relinquished the throne on the 13th day of the 6th month of 1011 and entered the Buddhist priesthood on the 19th day of that same month. Tendai Abbot Kyōen was the ordaining priest. Then Sanjō ascended the throne at the age of 36. Since Sanjō's Imperial mother was Kaneie's daughter and Michinaga's sister, there was no doubt but that Michinaga was Emperor Sanjō's maternal uncle and entitled to administer state affairs in Sanjō's behalf.[1]

1. In Chapter 1, Jien states that the Medieval Age began in 967, when Emperor Reizei was enthroned. In thinking of this year as the beginning point of the Medieval Age, he was undoubtedly influenced by the realization that Reizei and his successor Enyū were both sons of KUJŌ Morosuke's daughter Yasuko. But Enyū was succeeded by Kazan, who was not the son of a KUJŌ daughter. After Kazan, however, the throne became firmly tied to Morosuke descendants, for the Imperial mothers of Ichijō and Sanjō were

Why had Sanjō been appointed Crown Prince at the time of Ichijō's enthronement? Ichijō was seven when he ascended the throne on the 22nd day of the 6th month of 986, before he had celebrated his coming of age. Soon after Ichijō became Emperor— on the 16th day of the 7th month of 986—Sanjō, at the age of 11, celebrated his coming of age and was appointed Crown Prince. So when Emperor Ichijō died in 1011 at the age of 32, he had reigned 25 years and Sanjō had been Crown Prince for almost the same length of time.

Having waited until he was 36 years old, Sanjō finally ascended the throne in 1011; but within five years he developed eye trouble and

---

Morosuke's granddaughters and Michinaga's sisters. This may be why Jien begins his second chapter with the Ichijō and Sanjō reigns. At any rate, this chapter covers roughly the period of Jien's Medieval Age, whereas the previous one deals with his Ancient Age, and Chapters 3 and 4 with his Military Age.

As the next several pages reveal, Jien considers the Ichijō reign to have been a time of transition, when a comet was followed by disasters that portend temporary improvement under the great FUJIWARA Michinaga.

The relationships of Emperors, from Reizei to Sanjō, to KUJŌ Morosuke's descendants were as follows (the numbers in brackets are the reign numbers assigned in the *Gukanshō's* Imperial chronology):

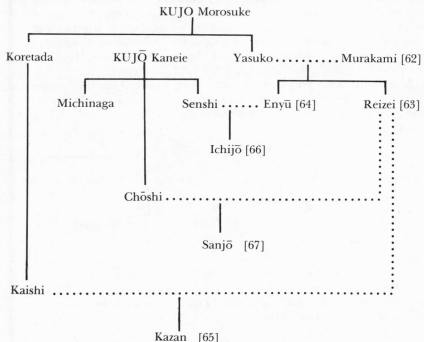

abdicated, entering the Buddhist priesthood the following year. These developments are very difficult to understand. But people agreed that the Great Lay Priest Kaneie, Michinaga's father, had planned things magnificently and unselfishly.[2]

Emperor Sanjō and the Motokata Curse

Emperor Reizei had been placed on the throne back in 967 in response to prayers made by Lord KUJŌ Morosuke, even though Senior Counselor FUJIWARA Motokata (888–953), maternal grandfather of Emperor Murakami's son Prince Hirohira, had wanted Prince Hirohira rather than Reizei to succeed Murakami.[3] Because of the pressure exerted by Murakami's Empress (Yasuko), who was Morosuke's daughter, her sons Reizei and Enyū were enthroned instead.[4] Motokata's soul became vengeful because Motokata had died in disappointment over Prince Hirohira's failure to reach the throne. And due to the curse of Motokata's vengeful soul, Emperor Reizei abdicated in 969, after a reign of two years. Emperor Enyū's reign

2. For Jien, Kaneie had apparently acted "unselfishly" when devoting his energies fully to the interests of the FUJIWARA's regental house and had handled things "magnificently" by arranging marital ties by which two of his daughters became the Imperial mothers of Emperors Ichijō and Sanjō. Such preoccupation with Imperial-FUJIWARA lineage connections is central to Jien's interpretation of Japanese history, just as it stands clearly revealed in the earlier Historical Tales—especially in the *Eiga Monogatari* and the *Ōkagami*—which are focused on FUJIWARA ministers whose daughters were married to, and/or became mothers of, Emperors. As noted, these Historical Tales were also called Succession Tales. Cf. Chapter 8.

3. Both KUJŌ Morosuke and FUJIWARA Motokata had married a daughter to Emperor Murakami, but it was the sons and grandsons of Morosuke's daughter Yasuko that became Emperors:

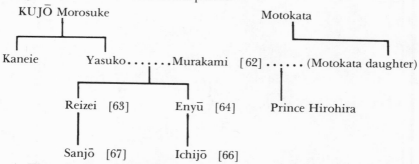

4. The selection of Morosuke's grandson Reizei, rather than Motokata's grandson Prince Hirohira, as the next Emperor was made in 950 when Reizei was appointed Crown Prince.

(969–984) went well, but the affairs of his successor, Emperor Kazan, were indescribably bad. Did not Sanjō's misfortunes occur because Motokata's vengeful soul also wished to destroy him, a young
brother of Kazan? Only the lives—not the reigns—of Reizei and
Kazan were rather long.

During the Sanjō reign and at a time when ex-Emperor Reizei was
62 and about to die, the Emperor planned to call on his ailing father.
Michinaga said that he would go first to see how the ex-Emperor
was. Reizei was so ill that he could not recognize Michinaga, and
therefore Michinaga returned with this advice: "There is no point in
calling on him now. Moreover, I am afraid of what the curse will do
next." So the Imperial visit was cancelled. But Sanjō had certainly
not acted contrary to the Heaven Way *(tendō)* by following his elder
brother Kazan—after the Ichijō reign—on the throne.

FUJIWARA Michinaga: Father of an Imperial Mother

Having reigned five years, Emperor Sanjō abdicated in 1016 to be
succeeded by Go-Ichijō; and Michinaga's son, Lord Uji Yorimichi
(922–1074), was appointed Regent in the following year. Go-Ichijō's
Imperial mother, the future Jōtō-mon In (988–1074), was Michinaga's eldest daughter. When Yorimichi was given the post of Regent,
Michinaga became a lay priest and did the inexpressibly fine thing of
continuing to stand by the throne until his death in 1027.

Dedication of *FUJIWARA* Michinaga's Temple

On the occasion of the 1022 dedication of the Hōjō Temple built
by Michinaga, it would have been boring to have had too much
sameness. Therefore Prime Minister Kinsue (956–1029) of the
KAN'IN house, the white-haired old son of Lord KUJŌ Morosuke, was
invited to attend. Michinaga, as lay priest, was properly dressed in
Buddhist robes and sat in the seat of honor. Prime Minister Kinsue
was in the seat above Lord Uji Yorimichi, the Regent. So Kinsue was
treated with great respect. Because he turned his back on Michinaga
and faced Lord Uji—not sitting formally—people said that he acted
in a really self-effacing, admirable way.[5]

The Four Senior Counselors

During the Ichijō reign (989–1011), four faultless noblemen were
known as "the four Senior Counselors": FUJIWARA Tadanobu (957–
1035), FUJIWARA Kintō (966–1041), MINAMOTO Toshikata (960–

---

5. Jien seems to be reminding his readers that even the founder of the
KAN'IN house had acted deferentially to the descendants of his elder brother
Kaneie.

1027), and FUJIWARA Yukinari (971–1027). All four became Senior
Counselors, but not one was promoted to a ministerial post. Since
MINAMOTO Toshikata was the distinguished son of MINAMOTO
Takaakira (914–982)—the Emperor Daigo son who became an ordi-
nary nobleman and founded the MINAMOTO clan—and Takaakira's
exile in 969 was a momentous event, I will write first about Toshikata.

MINAMOTO Toshikata and FUJIWARA Michinaga

Emperor Murakami had had three sons by KUJŌ Morosuke's
daughter, Secondary Empress Yasuko (927–964). The first was the
future Emperor Reizei, the second was Prince Tamehira, and the
third was the future Emperor Enyū. Another Morosuke daughter
became the principal wife of MINAMOTO Takaakira, Emperor
Daigo's son. Because of such relationships, MINAMOTO Takaakira
married his own daughter to Prince Tamehira, making the Prince
his son-in-law. But upon Reizei's enthronement in 967, Enyū was
appointed Crown Prince, passing over his elder brother, Prince
Tamehira. We are told that this occurred on the 1st day of the 9th
month of 967. Then, in about the 3rd month of 969, MINAMOTO
Takaakira became rebellious, probably wanting to have his son-in-
law (Prince Tamehira) made Crown Prince. Didn't he become rebellious at about the time that state affairs were becoming disturbed
because Emperor Reizei, subjected to the curse of Motokata's vengeful soul, was taking medicine?

Apparently MINAMOTO Takaakira's rebellious plans were disclosed
by two famous soldiers of that day: MINAMOTO Mitsunaka (Assistant
Director of the Imperial Stables of the Left) and FUJIWARA Yoshitoki
(Deputy Governor of Musashi). Because MINAMOTO Takaakira was
demoted, given the position of Acting Governor General at Dazaifu,
and sent into exile on the 26th day of the 3rd month of 969, he
entered the Buddhist priesthood soon afterward. It is recorded that
Priest Renmo, TACHIBANA Toshinobu (Vice Minister of Civil Affairs), MINAMOTO Tsuranaru (Senior Captain of the Imperial Bodyguards of the Left), and FUJIWARA Chiharu (former Deputy Governor of Sagami) were also exiled to distant places. The plot was
disclosed either because MINAMOTO Mitsunaka had been frequently
associated with members of the rebellious group or because he, a
man connected with soldiers, had deduced what the group was planning and reported his deductions. But in the 5th month of 972,
MINAMOTO Takaakira was recalled to the capital. It was popular gossip that such people as Minister of the Left FUJIWARA Morotada, the
three sons of KUJŌ Morosuke, and the sons of FUJIWARA Saneyori
had been trying to discredit him. Why should a person who had
committed no crime have been treated in such a way? Whatever the
reason, MINAMOTO Takaakira had immediately and voluntarily en-

tered the priesthood. Probably he was recalled to the capital because of the gossip that members of the FUJIWARA clan were trying to engineer his fall and because he had been unable to consummate his plot.

MINAMOTO Takaakira's son Toshikata was on very friendly terms with FUJIWARA Michinaga. Absolutely no feelings of resentment existed between them. Being a good man, Michinaga would soon rectify his mistakes. And he held no useless, bad grudges. Everyone said that Michinaga was following "the peaceful and correct course" by being friendly to Toshikata. This must be what is referred to in this quotation from the classics: "No good is higher than that of correcting mistakes." It seems generally clear that everyone in Michinaga's day deferred to him and listened to what he had to say, for he was earnest and unselfish and did not try to do anything that was inappropriate for that particular time.

Probably there is now no Number One Man worthy of that high position, and probably there is no member of a ministerial house who would recognize or make use of such a man. I can only regret that we do not live in an age when men with that kind of ability are gathered together and employed by the state. But there is absolutely no point in dwelling on the subject, since we are in the Final Age and have no way of thinking our way out of this wretched situation.

The Three Other Senior Counselors

Besides MINAMOTO Toshikata, "the four Senior Counselors" included FUJIWARA Tadanobu (son of Prime Minister Tamemitsu), FUJIWARA Kintō (son of Chancellor Yoritada), and FUJIWARA Yukinari (grandson of Regent Koretada and son of Senior Commander Noritaka). All three had gained distinction in both Japanese and Chinese learning and were outstanding in other fields. But not one of them was promoted to the position of minister, because Yorimichi (Minister of the Left), Sanesuke (Minister of the Right), and Norimichi (Minister of the Center) lived long and left no ministerial vacancies.

Two Famous Commanders:
MINAMOTO Narinobu and FUJIWARA Shigeie

Two other distinguished noblemen lived in the days of "the four Senior Counselors": MINAMOTO Narinobu, referred to as "the shining Middle Commander"; and FUJIWARA Shigeie, known as "the sparkling Junior Commander." Since MINAMOTO Narinobu's father was Prince Munehira (Minister of the Department of Military Affairs) and his mother was the elder sister of Michinaga's wife (Lady Takatsukasa), Michinaga adopted Narinobu and gave him the name of Narinobu. The other famous Commander, the "sparkling Junior

Commander" FUJIWARA Shigeie, was the son of FUJIWARA Akimitsu, who had preceded Yorimichi as Minister of the Left.

One day these two Commanders were listening to a court conference in which "the four" Senior Counselors were vying with each other, arguing and displaying their talents and knowledge. The two Commanders thought: "We would like to perform in that way when we are promoted, but since we have no ability, it is useless to continue on in public life. So let's follow the path of Buddha." They did enter the priesthood—without taking Buddhist orders—on the 3rd day of the 2nd month of 1001. FUJIWARA Shigeie was thenceforth referred to as the Junior Commander Lay Priest Jakugen of Ōhara,[6] becoming a famous disciple of Master Kōkei (977–1049) of Ikegami. MINAMOTO Narinobu, on the other hand, entered the Miidera Temple and was reportedly at FUJIWARA Michinaga's side, as spiritual adviser, when Michinaga died. This was an age in which only such fine things happened.

FUJIWARA Yukinari Thwarts Emperor Ichijō

Emperor Ichijō's most beloved consort and his first Empress was Sadako (977–1000), a sister of FUJIWARA Korechika. In about 999, when the Emperor was 20 years old, Sadako gave birth to an Imperial son: Prince Atsuyasu. But since Sanjō was then an adult Crown Prince—the one who was 36 years old when Ichijō became sick and was about to die at the age of 32—and was older than the Emperor and was waiting for the Emperor's illness to take its course, there was no question but that Sanjō was to become the next Emperor. Therefore, Emperor Ichijō wanted Prince Atsuyasu to succeed Sanjō as Crown Prince. But Ichijō was also intimate with FUJIWARA Michinaga's daughter, the future Jōtō-mon In (988–1074), who gave birth to the future Emperors Go-Ichijō and Go-Suzaku.[7] Worrying about whom he should appoint as the next Crown Prince, Emperor Ichijō

6. Jakugen's secular name was Tokinobu. [NKBT, 86.182, note 4.]
7. Ichijō's two Empresses were daughters of different Kaneie sons:

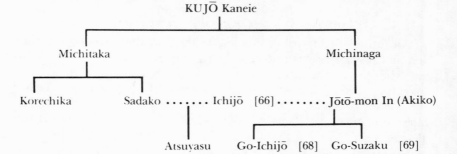

asked FUJIWARA Yukinari (Middle Counselor and Imperial-appointed Commissioner of Prince Atsuyasu's household) to come to his bedside for consultation. His Majesty asked, in a state of deep anxiety, who should be selected, and Yukinari responded as follows: "Don't keep worrying about it. You should select Go-Ichijō. Anyone else would be bad." When details of this consultation were made known, people said that Yukinari was a sincere and fine man.

But Emperor Ichijō was deeply disappointed that Prince Atsuyasu had not been selected as the next Crown Prince. Although he had sat by when Michinaga—rather than Korechika—was appointed Imperial Inspector in 995, and although he had been unable to do anything about Korechika's exile in 996 because Korechika had committed a crime, only bad things had happened. So he could not shake off his feelings of resentment. Was it not because of this resentment that he wrote out the above-mentioned Imperial decree?[8] And would it not have been a really dangerous time if the truly wise Michinaga had not been on hand?

Emperor Ichijō's Transitional Reign

The Ichijō reign (986–1011) was a transitional time *(histosugime)* in the history of state affairs. Was this not really due to the passing of a 60-year cycle?[9] Following Ichijō's enthronement in 986 at the age of seven, a comet streaked across the sky in the last third of the 6th month of 989. The era name was changed to Eiso in the 8th month of that year. Then came the incomparable disaster known as the Eiso typhoon. And in the following year the era name was changed to Shōryaku. A bitter struggle developed on Mt. Hiei in 993 between the followers of Chishō and those of Jikaku,[10] when the Senkō Hall was completely burned by the former. And the years 994 and 995 were marked by a terrible epidemic that caused many deaths in and around the capital. Because eight high-ranking nobles died in 995, and nothing like that had ever occurred before, or has occurred since, it is appropriate to list the eight who died then:

Senior Counselor FUJIWARA Asamitsu (951–995), formerly Senior Commander of the Imperial Bodyguards of the Left, who died on the 28th day of the 3rd month at the age of 45;

8. Cf. Chapter 1.
9. The current 60-year cycle began in 964 and ended in 1024.
10. The conflict led to the establishment of two rival orders within the Tendai Sect: the Mountain Order *(sammon)* based on Mt. Hiei, and the Church Order *(jimon)* at Miidera.

Chancellor FUJIWARA Michitaka (957–999),[11] who died on the
19th day of the 4th month at the age of 43;

Senior Counselor and Senior Commander of the Imperial
Bodyguards of the Left FUJIWARA Naritoki (941–995), who
died on the 23rd day of the same month at the age of 55;

Chancellor and Minister of the Right FUJIWARA Michikane
(961–995), Senior Commander of the Inner Palace Guards
of the Right, who died on the 8th day of the 5th month at
the age of 34, still holding the post of Senior Commander,
etc.;

Minister of the Left MINAMOTO Shigenobu (922–995), who
died on that same day at the age of 74;

Middle Counselor MINAMOTO Yasumitsu (924–995), who died
on the same day at the age of 73; he was called Middle
Counselor Momozono and was the son of Prince Shiroaki
(Minister of Civil Affairs);

Senior Counselor FUJIWARA Michiyori, who died on the 11th
day of the 6th month at the age of 20, who was the second
son of Chancellor Michitaka, and who was called the Great
Counselor of YAMA-NO-I; and

Middle Counselor and Commander of the Palace Gate Guards
of the Right MINAMOTO Koretaka, who died in the 11th
month at the age of 50.

All these prominent persons died within a single year. Then the era
name was changed to Chōhō (long preservation) in 999 and to
Kankō (quiet and broad) in 1004. After Michinaga's daughter
Jōto-mon In entered the palace in 999 as Emperor Ichijō's consort,
and the ceremony for expounding the Saishō Sutra was initiated
during the Kankō era (1104–12), Michinaga administered the state
without mishap and the state seemed definitely to settle down.

Not one of the above eight victims of the epidemic was a good
man for that period. Since MINAMOTO Shigenobu was well beyond
the age of 70, the meaning of his death need not be considered. And
FUJIWARA Michitaka, the Interim Chancellor, liked to do nothing but
drink sake day and night with FUJIWARA Asamitsu and FUJIWARA
Naritoki (Senior Commanders of the Left and Right Imperial Bodyguards). It is said that when a priest was describing the glories of the
Pure Land paradise, Michitaka remarked: "No matter how wonderful paradise is, Asamitsu and Naritoku are not apt to be there; and
without them paradise would be a tedious place indeed."

The Meaning of Comets and Disasters

It is my general understanding that when there is to be improvement in state affairs, a comet (a heavenly change) reveals that disas-

11. Although Jien lists Michitaka as having died in the epidemic of 995,
modern dictionaries state that he died in 999.

ters will occur, signifying future improvement. People whose understanding of changes in the heavens—and everything else—is deep
will be those who think and plan well [about connections between
comets and subsequent disasters and improvements].¹² Many tales
like those told above are neither fabrications of clever men nor
lies. Tales about "the four Senior Counselors" competing with each
other are interesting, but it is difficult to deal with them fully. And it
would be useless to do so. Only events at turning points in history
are to be taken seriously. Having been alert to the truth of events
that stand at turning points in history, I wish to write about that
which, as Outer Causes *(en)*, will broaden and deepen my understanding of those events.

Emperor Go-Ichijō (who reigned for 20 years after 1016) and
Emperor Go-Suzaku (who reigned for the next nine) were both from
the womb of Michinaga's daughter, Jōtō-mon In; and so there were
no objections to their enthronements [or to Jōtō-mon In's brother
Yorimichi serving as their Regent or Chancellor].

Vengeful Soul of FUJIWARA Akimitsu

In 996, FUJIWARA Akimitsu (944–1021), the son of Kaneie's elder
brother Kanemichi, had placed a daughter in the palace as Emperor
Ichijō's consort, but she was unable to produce an Imperial son.
Then when Prince Atsuaki, son of Emperor Sanjō, was appointed
Crown Prince in 1016, Akimitsu placed another daughter in the
palace as this Prince's consort. But the Prince, feeling that his position was inferior to that of such Ichijō sons as Go-Ichijō and Go-
Suzaku, resigned from his position as Crown Prince and received the
title of Cloistered Prince Koichijō. Since the Prince was an understanding man and Michinaga felt sorry for him, the Prince was made
Michinaga's son-in-law. And since the Prince had now become
Michinaga's son-in-law, he could no longer call on his former consort (Akimitsu's daughter), who became very unhappy. Akimitsu
tried to console her by saying: "This is the way of the world. Do not
grieve." But without answering, she would simply stare into the
brazier and make the coals sizzle with the flow of her tears. This
made Akimitsu terribly sad, and it is concluded that his soul soon

12. Here Jien is implying that the appearance of a comet, and subsequent
disasters, portended the improvement that was to come under Michinaga. In
Chapter 4, he tells of later changes in the heavens, and of disastrous developments both in the Imperial capital and in Kamakura, that carry a parallel implication: the coming of another time of significant but temporary improvement if and when KUJŌ Yoritsune becomes both Regent and Shogun.

became vengeful. It was something that was destined to happen.[13] And because Akimitsu's soul became vengeful, various things happened to people around Michinaga. Even so, probably Michinaga calmly thought that he had not made the slightest mistake and that the affairs of state had simply developed in this way because the situation was to improve. Akimitsu's soul seems to have become vengeful because Akimitsu had considered Michinaga's actions superficially.

FUJIWARA Yorimichi's Regency

Emperor Go-Reizei was placed on the throne in 1045 and reigned 23 years. FUJIWARA Yorimichi (992–1074) was his Chancellor and therefore held the positions of Regent or Chancellor more than 50 years, having been the brother of the Imperial mothers of Emperors Go-Ichijō, Go-Suzaku, and Go-Reizei.

FUJIWARA Norimichi's Regency

FUJIWARA Yorimichi's young brother, the Great Lord Nijō Norimichi (997–1076), was named Chancellor in 1068 at the beginning of Emperor Go-Sanjō's reign. Michinaga had considered Norimichi to be a good son and was just as fond of this younger son as he was of his older son Yorimichi. Norimichi had been appointed

13. Jien doubtedly felt that this was destined to happen not simply because Akimitsu did not like to see his daughter's misery but because Akimitsu had been moved farther from the throne:

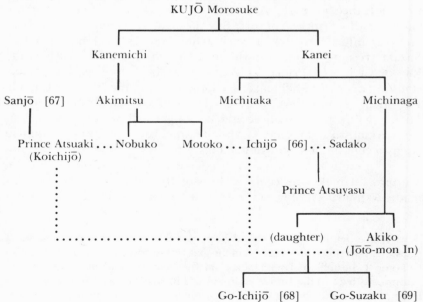

Minister of the Left in 1060 when Yorimichi was 70. Yorimichi's son Michifusa (Senior Commander) had been a fine and highly regarded young man, but he died in 1044 at the age of 20. And Yorimichi's adopted son Morozane (1042–1101), known as Great Lord of Kyōgoku, was too young in 1068 to be appointed Chancellor. Furthermore, Norimichi had so much ability that he could not be passed over. Therefore Yorimichi yielded the position of Chancellor to him. People felt that this decision added to Yorimichi's fame and revealed his excellent qualities as an administrator.

A Turning Point in History: Go-Sanjō (1068–72)

Although Emperor Go-Sanjō was the elder brother of Emperor Go-Reizei (both were sons of Emperor Go-Suzaku), their Imperial mothers were different. Emperor Go-Reizei's Imperial mother had been Michinaga's daughter, but Go-Sanjō's Imperial mother— known as Yōmei-mon In (1013–94)—was Emperor Sanjō's daughter. To be sure, Yōmei-mon In's own mother was Michinaga's second daughter Yoshiko, but this made Emperor Go-Sanjō's maternal relationship to the Regent/Chancellor house of FUJIWARA a bit remote. Yorimichi had married a daughter to Emperor Go-Reizei, but she did not produce an Imperial son. And Norimichi had made one of his daughters Go-Reizei's Empress, but she too had no Imperial son. Therefore the long line of Imperial mothers who were daughters of FUJIWARA ministers was broken at the time of Go-Sanjō's succession to the throne in 1068.

FUJIWARA Yoshinobu's Part in
Go-Sanjō's Appointment as Crown Prince

When Emperor Go-Suzaku became seriously ill back in 1045, Chancellor Yorimichi went to speak to His Majesty about passing the throne to Go-Reizei. But Yorimichi said nothing about the appointment of Go-Sanjō as Crown Prince.

Another Michinaga son, Senior Counselor Yoshinobu (995–1065), had married his adopted daughter Shigeko—the real daughter of Middle Counselor Kinnari of the KAN'IN house of FUJIWARA— to Prince Go-Sanjō. She was the one who later became Go-Sanjō's Empress. So when Yorimichi left the palace without having said anything about the appointment of Go-Sanjō as Crown Prince, Yoshinobu approached the Emperor and spoke as follows: "We still have the matter of naming a priest to preside over Go-Sanjō's entrance into the Buddhist priesthood. Isn't it proper that a decision about this be made now?" The Emperor was startled. "What is this? Go-Sanjō is to be appointed Crown Prince." Hearing the Emperor's words, Yoshinobu asked: "Well, if the order is not issued now, when will it be?" The Emperor replied: "I really forgot about it.

I have been ill." And then His Majesty called Yorimichi back to the
palace and asked him to add Go-Sanjō's appointment as Crown Prince
to the Imperial decree ordering the transfer of the throne to Go-
Reizei. And Yoshinobu became "the KAN'IN Master of the Crown
Prince's Household." People felt this was really strange. The future
Emperor Shirakawa, Go-Sanjō's son by Shigeko, never failed to speak
of the deceased Yoshinobu as "Lord," saying that if it had not been
for the late Lord Master of the Crown Prince's Household, he would
never have become Emperor. This was something that he couldn't
help saying.

The Final Age and the Handling of
State Affairs by Retired Emperors

Emperor Go-Sanjō's reign came at the time of a sharp turn into
the Final Age. Go-Sanjō had come to think and feel that people
would no longer be at peace if ministers continued to do just as they
pleased, if Regents and Chancellors continued to dominate the state,
and if Emperors concerned themselves only with that which was
elegant. He therefore concluded that it would be bad if an Emperor
did not, after abdicating, administer state affairs as Retired Emperor. He probably throught that this would be acting in accord with
various Principles. While I do not know the details of what Go-Sanjō
thought, I conclude, after examining the working out of Principles,
that he thought about everything of importance. In ancient times
sovereigns were wise about administrative matters, and the men who
conducted state affairs for them acted without any selfishness whatsoever. But during the Final Age, Emperors have been young—
tending to be child Emperors—and we do not hear of them reigning
until they have passed the age of 40. Probably Emperor Go-Sanjō
had observed that Chancellor Yorimichi and others were doing some
selfish things. Desiring to govern the state as a Retired Emperor, and
realizing that henceforth all Emperors would be his descendants,
Emperor Go-Sanjō soon relinquished the throne—on the 8th day of
the 12th month of 1072—to Shirakawa. Then, on the 20th day of
that month, His Majesty took his Imperial mother (Yōmei-mon In)
and Chancellor Norimichi with him on a pilgrimage to the
Sumiyoshi Shrine, returning by way of the Tennō Temple and the
Hachiman Shrine. At Sumiyoshi there was a *waka*-composing party
at which Retired Emperor Go-Sanjō composed the following poem:

How happy the Kami must be
Since I have come here
Rowing an empty boat.[14]

14. The metaphor of an "empty boat" pointed to Go-Sanjō's new free-
dom from the concerns and duties of a reigning Emperor, [NKBT, 86.435,
note 48.]

Among the *waka* composed at this time was this one by Tsunenobu:

> Offshore winds seem to blow
>   near here;
> White waves lash the lower limbs
>   of pines
> At the Sumiyoshi seashore.

After the 21st day of the 4th month of 1073 Go-Sanjō's illness worsened, and on the 7th day of the 5th month of that same year he passed away at the age of 42.

Retired Emperor Go-Sanjō had intended to administer state affairs after abdicating, but he probably had some selfishness in him, for he was unable to do so, even for a short time. But because it was appropriate, according to the Principles of things, for affairs to be handled in this way during the Final Age, Shirakawa accepted this role and governed the state, after abdicating, until he reached the age of 77.[15]

Go-Sanjō's Grudge against FUJIWARA Takakata

While Go-Sanjō was on the throne, he personally wrote out an Imperial order that was to be handed to an Imperial messenger [for transmittal to the Ise Shrine]. His Majesty showed the order to his tutor, Middle Counselor ŌE Masafusa (1041–1111). When Masafusa read the words "I have made no mistakes," he stopped reading. The Emperor asked: "What's the matter? Have I done something wrong?" Since Masafusa, out of respect for the Emperor, did not reply, the sovereign pressed him for an answer: "Speak up! Speak up!" Then Masafusa asked: "Why did you appoint Sanemasa and pass over Takakata? You have probably forgotten about that." The Emperor's face turned red and, taking back the order, retreated to his quarters.

The background of the affair was this. While Go-Sanjō was Crown Prince, Sanemasa (the Crown Prince's tutor) was sent as an Imperial messenger to the Kamo festival. While sitting on a high platform and

---

15. Jien's reading of Go-Sanjō's intentions is not accepted by modern scholars. While Jien is advancing the thesis that Kami-created Principles now called for a new form of Imperial rule, recent historians find convincing evidence that Go-Sanjō's main reason for abdicating was to make certain that he would be succeeded by his sons: Shirakawa and two sons by MINAMOTO Motoko (1049–1134). This divergence is discussed in G. Cameron Hurst III's *Insei, Abdicated Sovereigns in the Politics of Late Heian Japan, 1086–1185* (New York, 1976), pp. 110–124. Although Michinaga's son Norimichi was Chancellor during the first three years of the Shirakawa reign, and Yorimichi's adopted son Morozane held this post for the remainder of that reign, the fact that Shirakawa's Imperial mother was not the real sister of either Chancellor made it easier for Shirakawa to control state affairs (and succession) after his own abdication in 1086.

watching the festival procession, FUJIWARA Takakata made the following remark in a loud voice: "It is a truly ugly sight to see grey-haired old men waiting around for a turn of fortune!"[16] Having heard the remark, Sanemasa went immediately to the Crown Prince when the festival was over to report what Takakata had said. Go-Sanjō did not forget, and when he succeeded to the throne in 1068 he gave Sanemasa an accelerated promotion to Middle Controller of the Left as soon as that position fell vacant, although Takakata was Middle Controller of the Right and should have received the appointment. People said that it was not good to have Takakata passed over.[17]

Go-Sanjō and Another Case of Accelerated Promotion

Emperor Go-Sanjō himself told another story of accelerated promotion. When MINAMOTO Takatsuna (1043–74), Takakuni's second son, was still quite young, he was promoted to the positions of Consultant and Middle Commander, passing over men old enough to be his father. The Emperor thought that Yorimichi had made a serious administrative mistake in doing this. But when the Great Ise Shrine filed a suit based on the charge that a fox had been killed in the neighborhood of the Shrine, and when the decision had been made, Takatsuna—the lowest-ranking Consultant—was asked to write up the decision. Some had claimed that although an arrow was shot, it was not clear that a fox was killed or a crime committed. But Takatsuna wrote: "Although we hear that the fox swallowed the feathers of an arrow, we do not really know that it used a hill for its pillow at the time of death." When Emperor Go-Sanjō saw what Takatsuna had written, he thought he had never seen anything like it and realized he had been wrong to think Yorimichi had erred in giving Takatsuna an accelerated promotion. Saying that he had not known Takatsuna was a man of such ability, he stated that acceleration had

16. Both Go-Sanjō and Sanemasa were getting along in years.

17. The above story and the following one reveal some ambivalence about Go-Sanjō. While Jien deplored the disappearance of able Regents and Chancellors, he argues that the process of deterioration now required administrative control by Retired Emperors *(insei)*. The deterioration of the later Military Age, on the other hand, was a time for which the ancestral Kami had created still another type of Imperial rule: co-operative support by the FUJIWARA and MINAMOTO clans. Since the *Gukanshō* was written in order to make Retired Emperor Go-Toba, who had abdicated in 1198, understand and accept the Kami plan for the future, Jien is careful to square comments about a particular Retired Emperor with Principles for the period in which that Retired Emperor lived. Thus Go-Sanjō, the first Emperor to think of administering state affairs as a Retired Emperor, comes off rather well, whereas Shirakawa, Toba, Go-Shirakawa, and finally Go-Toba are given qualities appropriate to later stages of deterioration.

been a requirement of Principle. Generally a sovereign who is not blind to what is required by Principle, and to what is not, will say this sort of thing when he realizes that he has been wrong. In the *Book of Rites* we read about a fox having used a hill as its pillow at the time of death, and about a general who was so strong that when he shot an arrow it pierced the target so deeply that its feathers disappeared. People of Go-Sanjō's day thought it marvelous that a scholar could easily write something in which quotations from the classics were used to express his views.

Go-Sanjō's Relations with Yorimichi

People generally came to wonder if Go-Sanjō did not feel deep resentment against Yorimichi. The reasons are as follows. Go-Sanjō's Imperial mother was Yōmei-mon In (Go-Suzaku's Empress), Emperor Sanjō's daughter—not Yorimichi's. Yōmei-mon In's own mother was Michinaga's second daughter [but this made Go-Sanjō's maternal relationship to Yorimichi rather remote]. Moreover, after Go-Suzaku was enthroned in 1036 [Yorimichi's adopted daughter Genshi became Go-Suzaku's Secondary Empress]. Genshi's father was Prince Atsuyasu (son of Emperor Ichijō and Minister of Ceremonies), and her mother was a daughter of Prince Tomohira.[18]

Yorimichi's Adopted Son: Morozane

Now Yorimichi was also Prince Tomohira's son-in-law, having taken the Prince's daughter Takahime as his principal wife. But since Takahime was barren, Yorimichi came to favor MINAMOTO Teishi (d. 1053), a Lady-in-Waiting known as Shin no Myōbu. By her Yorimichi had several sons. Takahime was very jealous and had the first three adopted out. The first, Sadatsuna, was adopted by Tsuneie and came to be known as "the great Governor of Harima." The second, Tadatsuna, was adopted by Senior Counselor Nobuie and rose to the position of Assistant Master of the Empress's Household. The third, Toshitsuna, was adopted by the Governor of Sanuki, TACHIBANA Toshitō, and became the famous Master of the Palace Repairs Office of Fushimi.

Sadatsuna later married a daughter of Minister Ietada (1062–1136) of the Kazan'in Mansion [and founder of the KAZAN'IN house]. Sadatsuna inherited this mansion, which had belonged to Ietada's

18. Yorimichi was undoubtedly hoping that Genshi would produce an Imperial son by Go-Suzaku and that this Imperial son would then be named Crown Prince and placed on the throne, making Yorimichi the adoptive father of an Imperial mother. As later comments reveal, Genshi's early death and her failure to produce an Imperial son are important in Jien's view of the historical decline that occurred after the death of the great Michinaga.

father Morozane but was given to Sadatsuna instead of having a new one built for him. This is the only old mansion that still stands, and it is the one for which the spirit-quieting rite *(yō-e)* was performed by Vicar General Chōen of Ōhara.

After the death of Yorimichi's adopted son (Senior Counselor Michifusa) in 1044, Yorimichi's principal wife Takahime heard about another Yorimichi son from the womb of Shin no Myōbu: Morozane (1042–1101), who was later known as Great Lord Kyō-goku. Because Takahime said that she wanted this child brought to her, Yorimichi welcomed Morozane to his mansion, openly treated him as a son, and made him heir to the headship of his house.

The mother of the deceased Michifusa had been a daughter of MINAMOTO Norisada, Colonel of the Imperial Guards of the Right Third Rank and a son of Prince Tamehira. And since Yorimichi's principal wife Takahime had had no sons of her own, she had approved the adoption of Michifusa as Yorimichi's heir. This Michifusa had been extraordinarily good-looking and was well treated, but he died at an early age.

Morozane, the Great Lord of Kyōgoku, was a person of destiny endowed with superior ability, and it was a matter for rejoicing that he was on hand as Chancellor when Emperor Shirakawa stepped down from the throne in 1086 to be the first Retired Emperor to assume the responsibility of administering state affairs.

Why Yorimichi Had Remained Silent about Go-Sanjō's Appointment as Crown Prince in 1045

Let us return to Yorimichi's adopted daughter Genshi (1016–39), the real daughter of Prince Atsuyasu and the woman who became Go-Suzaku's Secondary Empress in 1037.

Michinaga's fourth daughter Kishi (1007–25), Yorimichi's sister, had been made Go-Suzaku's consort while he was Crown Prince, but Kishi died in 1025—at the age of 19—after she had given birth to the future Emperor Go-Reizei and while Michinaga was still alive.

After Go-Suzaku was enthroned in 1036, Yōmei-mon In became his Secondary Empress and was promoted to Principal Empress in the following year. But then Prince Atsuyasu's daughter Genshi, who was Yorimichi's adopted daughter, became Secondary Empress; and Empress Yōmei-mon In was no longer permitted to enter the Imperial palace. Emperor Go-Suzaku loved Genshi and had two daughters by her. But Genshi died within two years. Then Yōmei-mon In, called Teishi, was allowed to return to the palace.

Why was Genshi adopted by Yorimichi? The mother of Prince Atsuyasu (Genshi's real father) was Chancellor Michitaka's daughter. But since Atsuyasu was an ordinary Prince, it was inconceivable that he would succeed to the throne. But Prince Atsuyasu's consort was

Prince Tomohira's daughter as well as the young sister of Yorimichi's principal wife Takahime, the woman known as "the principal wife of Takakura" and who lived long enough, seeming to live on forever. Since Secondary Empress Genshi was a daughter of Prince Atsuyasu by this younger sister of Takahime, Genshi was adopted as Yorimichi's daughter and placed in the palace—and advanced to the position of Go-Suzaku's Principal Empress—as a FUJIWARA woman. This is why Yorimichi had said nothing about Go-Sanjō being appointed Crown Prince in 1045, even though Go-Sanjō's Imperial mother was Yōmei-mon In.

Imperial Mothers Now Come from the KAN'IN House

But it was then that Yoshinobu calmly approached Emperor Go-Suzaku, when the throne was being passed to Go-Reizei in 1045, to ask about the priest who was to arrange for Go-Sanjō's entrance into the Buddhist priesthood. Why did he do this and what did it mean?

Being another Michinaga son, Yoshinobu had been made guardian of Go-Sanjō's mother, Yōmei-mon In. And because Yōmei-mon In's own mother was a Michinaga daughter, Yoshinobu was made Master of the Empress's Household when Yōmei-mon In became Empress. When she gave birth to Go-Sanjō in 1034, Yoshinobu was made the Prince's guardian.

Then, after Go-Sanjō was appointed Crown Prince in 1045 and celebrated his coming of age—without the benefit of a secular aide—in 1046, Yoshinobu had his adopted daughter Shigeko made Go-Sanjō's consort. [Since Shigeko was KAN'IN Kinnari's (999–1043) real daughter and was to become Emperor Shirakawa's Imperial mother], the line of Emperors born to the daughters of Regents and Chancellors descended from Lord KUJŌ Morosuke was now broken, and a line of Emperors born to KAN'IN daughters was started. This is why Yoshinobu spoke to Emperor Go-Suzaku as he did, and how it was that the Imperial mothers of later Emperors were from the KAN'IN—rather than the KUJŌ Morosuke—line.

Tension between Yorimichi and Yoshinobu

Yorimichi had received many favors from his father Michinaga, but Yoshinobu (Yorimichi's young brother) was treated generously. Once when Yorimichi found it a bit difficult to obtain a promotion for Yoshinobu, he went to Michinaga and in Yoshinobu's hearing said: "Such difficulties are bound to come up when you bestow favors on a son simply because he is a son." They say that Michinaga made no reply, because the remark had been made in Yoshinobu's presence. Developments of this sort provided strong undercurrents for the complications attending the appointment of Go-Sanjō as Crown Prince in 1045. Nevertheless, relations between Yorimichi and Yoshinobu were not carelessly strained again.

Morozane's Daughter Becomes Shirakawa's Empress

Giving close attention to the abilities of people, Emperor Go-Sanjō eventually had Morozane (Yorimichi's adopted son) give his adopted daughter Kenshi (1057–84) to Crown Prince Shirakawa; and this had a really quieting effect. Shirakawa loved this Kenshi—later his Secondary Empress—from the time he was made Crown Prince; and his love for her was unmatched. He loved only her and showed her a wonderful affection. Meanwhile, people wondered if Go-Sanjō might not come to favor a daughter of such a person as Prime Minister Nobunaga (Yorimichi's brother), but that did not happen.

New Developments during the Go-Sanjō Reign

While Go-Sanjō was on the throne, standards of volume measurement were established by an Imperial decree issued in the Enkyū era (1069–74). Those standards are still used. When they were presented to the Emperor in the garden of the Seiryō Hall, he put sand into the measures and experimented with them. Some people praised him, saying: "Isn't that wonderful!" Others declared that such unusual activity was dazzling. Probably people reacted in this way because they were accustomed to thinking that activities within the Seiryō Hall of the Imperial Palace were limited to that which was quiet and elegant.

The Records Office *(kirokujo)* was also first established in the Enkyū era because the Emperor had come to feel strongly that private estates *(shōen)* not sanctioned by either Imperial decree or official order were encroaching upon public lands in all provinces and had become a serious evil. He had heard it said that during Yorimichi's Chancellorship the entire country seemed to be Yorimichi's estate and that various provinces had so many estates that it was difficult for provincial governors to function. So an Imperial decree was handed down establishing the Records Office and requiring that validations of estate ownership be submitted. Yorimichi reacted as follows:

> Does Your Majesty think that all my estates are improperly held? I have been serving as Imperial guardian for more than 50 years, and during this time people have presented their lands to me, thinking that I would be a strong patron. And I have agreed to accept them, merely saying: "Is that what you want?" What kind of documents would I have under such circumstances? But if Your Majesty hears that any of my estates are held improperly or irregularly, you should not hesitate to confiscate them all, especially since I am the one who should be speaking to you about such matters and handling them for you.

Because Yorimichi spoke out forthrightly, the Emperor's plans came to naught. After reconsidering the matter for a long time, the Emperor issued another Imperial decree which stated: "When ordering landholders to submit validating documents to the Records Office, you are not to send such an order to former Prime Minister Yorimichi." So the decree was not applied to Yorimichi's estates. People said: "Wasn't that an amazing development?"[19]

Yorimichi Favors His Adopted Son Morozane
over His Brother Norimichi

During this same Enkyū era, and after Yorimichi's young brother Norimichi (997–1076) became head of the FUJIWARA clan and was appointed Chancellor in 1068, a dispute arose between the FUJIWARA clan and the provincial governor of Yamato over estates held by the FUJIWARA temple, the Kōfuku-ji. This became a serious incident. When the dispute was brought before the Emperor for settlement, the nobles were at first inclined to decide in favor of the governor. Whereupon Norimichi said: "As head of the FUJIWARA clan, I will be disgraced if you hand down such a decision. Furthermore, it is difficult to ascertain what the Kami will think. I respectfully request the Emperor's sacred judgement, humbly awaiting an expression of Kami will." Then Norimichi quickly left his seat. The nobles of the FUJIWARA clan were dumbfounded by what Norimichi had said and done, but kept quiet. Later on, a Middle Counselor by the name of Chikatsune, a clever Confucian scholar, heard that the nobles had decided the case in favor of Kōfuku Temple and that the priests of the Temple had resumed their long expoundings on the sutras, praying for the state. A Holy Man by the name of Gedatsubō seems to have reported this while expounding the sutra. Since Yorimichi had yielded the position of Chancellor to Norimichi, probably Norimichi wanted to attract Yorimichi's attention by making a strong stand in defense of Kōfuku claims. A certain diary also tells us that: "Toward the end of his installation ceremony held in the 1st month of 1070, Chancellor Norimichi became irritated, left his seat, and went to the Imperial waiting-room. The ceremony was therefore discontinued. After several hours and in response to repeated requests by the Emperor, the Chancellor returned." Although the Diary does not give us reasons for Norimichi's behavior, he may have become upset by FUJIWARA Suetsuna's appointment as Major of the Quiver Bearers.

Having heard such rumors about Chancellor Norimichi's behavior, Yorimichi—now 80 years old and secluded in his Uji Mansion—advised his adopted son Morozane, Minister of the Left, as follows: "Call daily at the Imperial Palace. Even if there is nothing to be done, you should accumulate merit by not missing a single day." So Morozane went to the palace as he had been advised to do, going to the Imperial waiting-room regularly. Emperor Go-Sanjō would routinely call in the Imperial Secretary and say: "Who has

19. Go-Sanjō's attempt to standardize measurements, and to limit the spread of private estates, are analyzed in Hurst, *Insei,* pp. 11–19.

come to the waiting-room?" Even if the question were asked two or three times a day, the answer was always the same: "The Minister of the Left is there." After several days and months had passed, and when the Emperor had asked the same question one evening and received the same reply, he said: "Ask him to come here." Whereupon the Imperial Secretary went to Morozane and said: "You have been ordered into the Imperial presence." Morozane thought: "This is strange. I wonder what the Emperor will say." Having braced himself for going into His Majesty's presence, and straightened out his robes, he went before the Emperor who, after asking Morozane to come closer, proceeded to talk about trivial matters. As the night wore on and the chat was coming to a close, the Emperor asked: "Do you have a daughter?" Morozane replied: "I have an unusual one. She is still a child."

FUJIWARA Morozane and the MINAMOTO Clan

FUJIWARA Morozane did not have a daughter of his own but had taken care of—since childhood—a girl by the name of Kenshi (1057–84). Kenshi was the real daughter of Minister MINAMOTO Morofusa's son, MINAMOTO Akifusa (1026–94). Yorimichi, a son-in-law of Prince Tomohira, had adopted the Prince's son: this same MINAMOTO Morofusa. Furthermore, Yorimichi had seen to it that Morofusa's son, High Priest Ninkaku who became Tendai Abbot, was made Master Teacher for life. FUJIWARA Morozane had also made MINAMOTO Morofusa's daughter his principal wife and then adopted Kenshi, his wife's niece. Through such relationships, the FUJIWARA clan was being tied to the MINAMOTO clan. And Morozane treated Kenshi as his own daughter.[20]

20. Kenshi tied the MINAMOTO to the KUJŌ in this way:

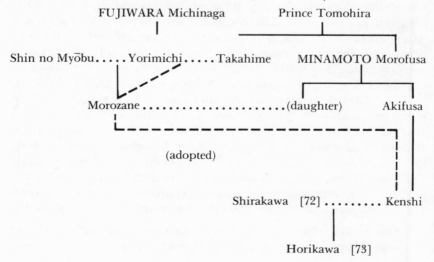

Morozane's Adopted Daughter Becomes Shirakawa's Empress

Therefore when Emperor Go-Sanjō heard Morozane say that he had a daughter, His Majesty said: "In that case she should be given in marriage to Crown Prince Shirakawa right away." Morozane respectfully accepted the command and promptly withdrew from the Imperial presence. Although late at night, he went directly from the Imperial Palace to Yorimichi's mansion in Uji, thinking that he would like to let Yorimichi know right away that although the situation had been uncertain, it now definitely looked better. Morozane ordered someone to notify the post stations that changes of oxen should be made ready, and he started off for Uji, wondering about his father's health and state of mind.

Yorimichi, residing then at a place in Uji called the Small Pine Villa, was inexplicably awake. Feeling uneasy, he had some torches lighted and said that maybe something was happening at the capital. Not many people were living in the neighborhood of Uji in those days, and one could see as far away as the villages of Kowata and Okanoya. A man came to report that he could see a large number of torches coming into view from the direction of the capital. Thinking that this was strange, Yorimichi ordered a close watch. Before long he received a report that "More lights can be seen, and they are coming toward Uji." Yorimichi said: "Maybe the Minister of the Left Morozane is coming. And yet it is very strange that he should be coming in the middle of the night. Watch closely and listen carefully." Shortly after he had placed his guards on the alert, the yelling of attendants at the front of the approaching procession could be faintly heard. Having received a report of this, Yorimichi concluded that his surmise had been correct and issued orders that lanterns be brought out and the wicks lit. Attendants at the front of the procession were clearing the way on horseback, as was the custom on such occasions. Apparently people habitually felt that the yelling out of attendants at the front of a procession would frighten away evil spirits.

Noting Morozane's arrival, and seeing him come forward to pay his respects still dressed in formal court attire, Yorimichi felt that something was up and asked: "What's happened? What's happened?" Morozane replied:

> I have been calling at the Imperial Palace daily, just as you advised me to do. And this evening the Imperial Secretary came to say that I had been ordered into the Imperial presence. When I approached the Emperor, he spoke at length of unimportant matters and then said: "If you have a daughter, marry her to the Crown Prince right away." Having personally heard this Imperial order, I came immediately to report.

Yorimichi could not but weep for joy on hearing this good news. He said: "I have been uneasy about the situation, and now this! What a

glorious sovereign the Emperor is!" And then he gave strict orders
that Kenshi be made ready, right away, for the wedding.

The Crown Prince to whom Kenshi was given was the future Emperor Shirakawa (1053–1129). So Morozane's adopted daughter became the Crown Prince's consort; and after the Crown Prince was
enthroned as Emperor Shirakawa, she was made his Secondary Empress, becoming known as Secondary Empress Kenshi. Finally she
became the future Emperor Horikawa's Imperial mother. Although
she has been thought of—right down to the present—as a model
Imperial mother who was a daughter of the head of the FUJIWARA
clan (the Number One Man), she was also a MINAMOTO daughter.
Many members of the MINAMOTO clan therefore served in positions
close to the throne during the Horikawa reign (1086–1107).

Situation in Go-Sanjō's Day
Compared with that of the Present

An Emperor who was as much of a sage ruler as Go-Sanjō really
knew, down to the finest point, the importance of things, how they
would work out, and what the results would be. And he governed
accordingly. So what reasons would he have had for needlessly hating or destroying the FUJIWARA house or a FUJIWARA Chancellor or
Regent? He did things while considering only whether the abilities of
a man were superior or inferior, and whether a Principle for that
time and place was important or unimportant.

But in this Final Age foolish ministers who presently serve near
Retired Emperor Go-Toba are constantly doing things that worsen
relations between the sovereign and his Chancellor or Regent. So the
state is headed for destruction. Not merely the sovereign, his Chancellor or Regent, and the officials serving near the Retired Emperor,
but everyone else—men and women, priests and laymen—should
understand this well. The same thing can be said about the man-
agement of affairs in the houses of commoners, for deteriorated
conditions exist at all levels of society. Until the present day, there
has been no deviation from this general trend. Specific actions are
taken by everyone in response only to feelings. Even the Seventeen
Article Constitution has become ineffective during these final reigns
because "Principles of things" exist only faintly and unfamiliarly in
the hearts of men. Persons of high position have no sympathy for
those below, and those below have no respect for those above. Turning against the civil and penal codes (and their supplements) compiled long ago—with the Seventeen Article Constitution as their
source—the state is simply going to ruin. It is sad to be thinking
only of what can be done about such deterioration. All that can be
done until the 100th reign is to rely upon the blessings of the Kami
worshipped at the Imperial shrines of Ise and Iwashimizu, and

Kashima and Kasuga, and upon the divine grace of the Three Buddhist Treasures and the deities of the various Heavens. The blessings of these divine beings work through the hearts and minds of human individuals; and they are realized when individual ability *(ki)* is harmonized with Outer Causes *(en)*, causing strange developments that are hard to understand.

Prayers that Kenshi Give Birth to an Imperial Son

Among these strange developments that are hard to understand was the birth of an Imperial son to Morozane's adopted daughter Kenshi. After Shirakawa was enthroned in 1072, His Majesty wanted very much to have an Imperial son by Kenshi; and he therefore asked a famous priest of Miidera, Master Teacher Raigō (1002–84), to pray for an Imperial son. The Emperor promised to give Raigō anything he wished if the prayers were answered. Raigō therefore exerted himself in prayer, and after a time an Imperial son was born to Kenshi, just as the Emperor had wanted. Raigō was delighted and announced that as a reward for his efforts he would like to realize his long-standing desire to have an ordination hall built at Miidera. The Emperor was astounded:

> How can you ask for that? That sort of award did not occur to me. I had in mind something like an accelerated promotion to the rank of High Priest. If I were to grant your request, Mt. Hiei would object and the members of the two monasteries of Mt. Hiei and Miidera would start fighting against each other. And this would destroy Buddhist Law. So how can I grant such a request?

Whereupon Raigō said: "I was praying with this request in mind. If it is not granted, I will die in disappointment. And when I die, the Imperial son which was born in response to my prayers will also die." Raigō then returned to Miidera and secluded himself in his Buddha-Statue Hall. When the Emperor heard about this, he thought: "ŌE Masafusa seems to have been closely associated with Raigō as a patron. So I will have him go to console Raigō." Masafusa was called in and sent immediately to Raigō's Buddha-Statue Hall at Miidera. Masafusa announced himself, said that he had come as an Imperial envoy, and sat down on the veranda. The sliding door of the Hall was black from the smoke of *goma* fires, and for some strange reason Masafusa felt so frightened that his hair stood on end. After a little while the sliding door opened and Raigō emerged. His eyes were sunken, his face was unrecognizable, and he had let his white hair grow long. Raigō grumbled: "Why has the Emperor sent you? I have had my say. Why should there be such a vexatious matter as this?" Then he went back into the Hall and Masafusa could do nothing but return to the Imperial Palace to report what had happened. Not long afterward Raigō died, and soon the Imperial son also

died, at the age of three. Because of these events, the Emperor—
feeling that there was nothing else he could do—called in Ryōshin
(1022–96), the Tendai Abbot, and spoke to him as follows: "This
sort of thing has happened. What can we do? Be sure to offer
up prayers for another Imperial son." Ryōshin replied: "I understand. I think we can rely on the power of the Three Buddhist Treasures of our Tendai monastery at Mt. Hiei and on the Kings of the
Mountain."[21] The future Emperor Horikawa was born in 1079 and
enthroned in 1086. And Emperor Horikawa's son became the future
Emperor Toba. So the Imperial line of descent was not broken. Because of these events—not presented here with any embellishment—the thoughts of the Hiei Priests must be really deep.

Rivalry between the KAN'IN and KUJŌ Houses over the Regency

With the enthronement of Emperor Toba in 1107, the Imperial
mother was the daughter of KAN'IN Sanesue.[22] Therefore her
brother KAN'IN Kinzane, the Emperor's maternal uncle who had
been Master of Crown Prince Toba's Household, had his heart set
on becoming Emperor Toba's Regent. He spoke to Retired Emperor

21. The *sannō daishi* were Kami worshipped at the Hie Shrine on Mt. Hiei
and were considered the guardian Kami of Mt. Hiei and its great temple,
and Enryaku-ji.

22. Emperor Toba's ties with the two houses were:

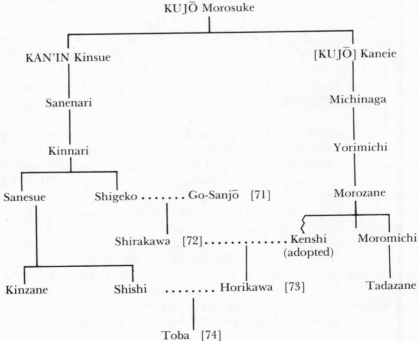

Shirakawa as follows:

> My house goes back to the house of Minister of the Right KUJŌ
> Morosuke. I myself am a Senior Counselor. Only persons who
> have been either a maternal uncle or maternal grandfather of the
> Emperor at the time of that Emperor's enthronement have been
> appointed to the position of Regent or Chancellor. Moreover, the
> position has never been given to a maternal uncle or maternal
> grandfather who does not hold the rank of Senior Counselor or
> Minister.

Since Retired Emperor Shirakawa was himself a son of KAN'IN Kinnari's daughter Shigeko (and Kinzane's cousin), he probably was well
aware of Kinzane's relationship to Toba and felt deeply about it.
Being troubled by the question of who should be appointed Regent
and wondering what to do, he had the corridors leading to his quarters closed off and secluded himself in his rooms.

Thinking that the day for making the decision had arrived and
being surprised and curious that no conference had as yet been held,
Senior Counselor MINAMOTO Toshiaki (1044–1114)—then Retired
Emperor Shirakawa's guardian, and distinguished Commissioner of
the Retired Emperor's Household—put on his formal court robes,
adjusted his clothing, and proceeded to the Retired Emperor's quarters. Since all of the corridors had been closed off, Toshiaki shouted:
"What is the reason for this?" Hearing the doors being tugged at, the
persons who had closed them came out and explained what had
happened. Whereupon Toshiaki said: "I am Toshiaki and have
come to speak to His Majesty on an important matter of state. He
would not have ordered the doors closed for a mission such as mine.
Open them up immediately." And they were. Approaching the Retired Emperor, Toshiaki cleared his throat to indicate his presence,
and then His Majesty asked: "Who is it?" When Shirakawa heard
that it was Toshiaki, he said: "What do you want?" Then Toshiaki
inquired: "What do you intend to do about the accession ceremony?
Since the sun is high, I have come to receive your instructions. What
have you decided?" The Retired Emperor replied: "That is a problem. What do you think I should do about the Regency?" And then
His Majesty added: "Of course there would be no difficulty if a
change was not made."[23] Upon hearing this, Toshiaki responded
loudly and without hesitation: "Yes, Your Majesty!" Then he hur-
riedly rustled his robes and stood up to leave, making it impossible
for the Retired Emperor to say anything more. Toshiaki went directly to KUJŌ Tadazane's mansion to report that the Retired Em-

23. Toshiaki interpreted Shirakawa's remark to mean not only that the
enthronement ceremonies were to be conducted as before but by the same
Regent, Tadazane.

peror wished the enthronement ceremonies conducted according to precedent. And they were conducted in just that way.

Retired Emperor Shirakawa had implied that the succession ceremonies should be conducted by KUJŌ Tadazane and that KAN'IN Kinzane's request should not be granted. Perceiving that this request by Kinzane was contrary to Principle, Toshiaki's thoughts probably ran like this:

> Kinzane should not be appointed Regent. He is a descendant of KUJŌ Morosuke, but even Morosuke's own son KAN'IN Kinsue was not considered suitable for the position of Regent or Chancellor. This was also true of Kinsue's son (Sanenari), his grandson (Kinnari), and his great-grandson (Sanesuke), making Kinzane the fifth person in the KAN'IN line who has not been appointed Regent or Chancellor and who has been treated simply as a commoner. Is Kinzane therefore the sort of person to be appointed Regent? The intimate and estranged, the close and distant, the old, middle-aged, and young, the noble and mean, as well as the high and low all have felt, in the past and the present, that the office of Regent or Chancellor should not be held by a person of the KAN'IN line and that it is deplorable for the Retired Emperor to be the least bit troubled by Kinzane's request.

But if KAN'IN Kinzane had been talented in Chinese and Japanese learning like SUGAWARA Michizane, or if he had been superior to KUJŌ Tadazane in character and in ability to manage state affairs, or if he had been an intelligent man like FUJIWARA Sanesuke, he might have been a suitable man for the post of Regent. But since he was simply a maternal uncle of the reigning Emperor, and many true sons and grandsons of former Regents and Chancellors had not acquired that high position, why did he think he should have such an appointment? Because the matter was serious enough to trouble the Retired Emperor, it was kept secret and confidential, and people did not generally know or gossip about it. Nevertheless, Kinzane did recommend his own candidacy. Thinking only of one thing and wondering how to advance the fortunes of his house, his thoughts may have run like this: "I should be appointed Regent because there has never been a single case of a person not being appointed Regent or Chancellor if he holds a position as high as Senior Counselor or Minister and, as a descendant of a former Regent or Chancellor, is a brother of the Imperial mother." He did think in this way, although that is not generally known.[24]

24. Jien's explanation of Retired Emperor Shirakawa's decision to let Tadazane stay on as Toba's Regent, even though Kinzane was the brother of Toba's Imperial mother, stresses the prestige of the KUJŌ house and Kinzane's lack of ability. Although Tadazane was retained, Shirakawa was still the dominant political figure at court. Since the house of Shirakawa's Imperial mother (and of Tobo's) was the KAN'IN, Shirakawa may well have

After Shirakawa had yielded the throne to Horikawa in 1086, and after Great Lord Kyōgku Morozane had passed the administration of state affairs to his son Moromichi (1062–99) in 1094 (subsequent to Horikawa's becoming an adult), Moromichi turned out to be an obstinate man. It is said that there were actually times when, in handling the affairs of state, he would take action without having consulted at all with either the Retired Emperor or with his father, the Great Lord KUJŌ Morozane.

Retired Emperor Shirakawa Cursed
by the Vengeful Soul of Raigō

Retired Emperor Shirakawa had been extremely fond of his daughter, an Imperial Lady known as Yūhō-mon In, but the vengeful soul of Raigō attached itself to her and cursed her. Although Zōyō and Ryūmei of Miidera prayed that the curse be removed, their prayers were not answered. So Shirakawa called in Ryōshin of Mt. Hiei, who arrived at the palace with 20 priests that had resided at the Central Hall of Mt. Hiei for long periods of time. They prayed earnestly that the curse be removed; and their prayers were answered. Retired Emperor Shirakawa was delighted. But then his daughter suddenly died in 1096. Astounded and saddened by her death, Shirakawa entered the Buddhist priesthood that same year.

Shirakawa Considers Occupying
the Throne for a Second Reign

When Emperor Horikawa died in 1107, Retired Emperor Shirakawa seems to have wanted to ascend the throne a second time; but since he had already entered the priesthood, he placed his son Toba on the throne and handled the affairs of state from the Retired Emperor's office *(sentō)* within the headquarters of the Imperial Guards. It is said that three members of the Imperial Police (MINAMOTO Mitsunobu, MINAMOTO Tameyoshi, and MINAMOTO Yasukiyo) were on duty day and night at the palace. We have some wonderful stories for that period, but since they are not important I will not write them down.

We are told that while Toba was on the throne, he was afraid of Prince Sukehito.[25] Whenever Toba left the palace, he had

---

kept Tadazane on as Regent in order to keep the KAN'IN from amassing the kind of power that had been enjoyed by previous Regents.

25. Prince Sukehito (1073–1119) was the 5th son of Go-Sanjō, the first Emperor—Jien says—to think of administering state affairs as a Retired Emperor. The Imperial mother of Go-Sanjō's son Shirakawa was from the KAN'IN house, but the Imperial mother of Go-Sanjō's 4th and 5th sons (Sanehito and Sukehito) was MINAMOTO Motoko. When Go-Sanjō passed the throne to Shirakawa in 1072, he arranged to have Prince Sanehito made Crown Prince and seems to have requested that Prince Sukehito be named

MINAMOTO Yoshiie and MINAMOTO Yoshitsuna secretly assigned to positions near or behind the Imperial palanquin. Because he was given such assignments, Yoshiie reportedly stayed close to the Emperor, wearing his armor with dignity.

Chancellor Moromichi Cursed for Attacking Priests

During the Horikawa reign (1086–1107), the priestly horde at Mt. Hiei had come down to the capital carrying a portable shrine[26] in order to make demands on the Imperial court. Chancellor Moromichi, feeling that this was an impudent thing for them to do, issued orders against such activity and had the priests attacked. Some arrows struck the portable shrine itself, and an Assistant Head Shinto Priest by the name of Tomozane was injured. Consequently Moromichi was cursed [by the Kami of the Hie Shrine] and soon died.

Crown Prince when Sanehito ascended the throne. Although Shirakawa shared his father's desire to have administrative affairs conducted by a Retired Emperor, he was ambivalent about his father's wishes on the question of succession. Shirakawa did not oppose his father's plan, however, until after Sanehito's death in 1085. Then he had his own son Horikawa—not his half-brother Prince Sukehito—made Crown Prince. And on the following day, Shirakawa abdicated to govern as a Retired Emperor, making Horikawa his successor.

In order to retain control over the throne through the mother of the reigning Emperor, Shirakawa arranged in 1092 to have his sister, aged 32, married to his son Horikawa, who was only thirteen. The sister did not produce an Imperial son, but in 1103, Horikawa obtained an Imperial son by a consort of the KAN'IN house. This son, Toba, was named Crown Prince. But some noblemen felt that Go-Sanjō's wishes should not have been flaunted and therefore continued to support Prince Sukehito's candidacy. The situation was further aggravated in 1107 when Toba ascended the throne at the age of six.

The Senjumaru incident broke in 1113 when supporters of Prince Sukehito arranged to have Senjumaru kill the young Emperor Toba. But the plot was uncovered and Senjumaru was arrested and exiled to Sado, and Prince Sukehito was placed under house arrest. The Prince was soon released, for it seems that Shirakawa either was fond of this half-brother or was uneasy about disregarding the wishes of his father, Go-Sanjō. Prince Sukehito finally entered the Buddhist priesthood in 1119 and died a few days later at the age of 37.

26. The portable shrine (*mikoshi*) was believed to contain one or more of the Kings of the Mountain honored as guardian Kami on Mt. Hiei (cf. note 20, above). By taking the Kami directly to the gate of the palace, the priests were reminding everyone there that these guardian Kami might be displeased if the request was not granted.

Ningen, a Tendai Abbot who was Moromichi's brother, had crossed Mt. Ōmine and was therefore a person endowed with miraculous power. He was asked to pray that the curse be removed from his brother. A medium *(yorimashi)* said: "I will now disclose the arrow wound!" And then blood began to drip from the chest of the medium. This was such a miraculous sight that the Abbot became frightened and stopped praying. And Moromichi finally died in 1099. This is a story that has come down to us by word of mouth.

Moromichi's Son Becomes Chancellor

After Moromichi's death, Morozane should have been re-appointed to the post of Chancellor, but an Imperial decree was handed down appointing Moromichi's son, Senior Counselor KUJŌ Tadazane (1078–1162), to the office of Imperial Inspector. Tadazane was also made head of the FUJIWARA clan, but not Chancellor. He finally received an Imperial appointment as Chancellor in 1105.

After Emperor Toba had reigned 16 years, the throne was passed to Sutoku in 1123. Therefore Retired Emperor Shirakawa had lived to see the enthronement of his grandson and died in 1129 at the advanced age of 77.

The Six Superiority Temples

The Temple of Buddha Superiority (Hōshō-ji) built by Emperor Shirakawa in 1077 has been called an Imperial temple *(koku-ō no ujidera)*, and a succession of later Emperors built such temples as Imperial prayers: the six Superiority Temples built in the great Shirakawa Temple compound. After the Hōshō-ji by Emperor Shirakawa, the Temple of Revered Superiority (Sonshō-ji) was erected by Emperor Horikawa, the Temple of Ultimate Superiority (Saishō-ji) by Emperor Toba, the Temple of Consummate Superiority (Jōshō-ji) by Emperor Sutoku, and the Temple of Prolonged Superiority (Enshō-ji) by Emperor Konoe. That was the last of the Superiority Temples built by Emperors. The sixth one, the Temple of Complete Superiority (Enshō-ji), was constructed in 1128 by Taiken-mon In, Sutoku's Imperial mother.

Toba's Administration as Retired Emperor and the Coming of the Military Age

As Retired Emperor Shirakawa's successor, Retired Emperor Toba administered the affairs of state from 1129 to 1156. And when he died on the 2nd day of the 7th month of 1156, the rebellions of the country of Japan *(Nihonkoku no rangeki)* broke out and the country's Military Age *(musa no yo)* began.

Having thought about the Principles of these developments and concentrated on what is important thereto, I write the following. Many rebellions and battles were fought outside the capital before 1156. For example, rebellions had erupted in the days of Emperor Ankō and Prince Ōtomo, but nothing appears in diaries about these upheavals. Rebellions also occurred after the Taihō era (701–704) and subsequent to the removal of the capital to Heian in 794. But the TAIRA Masakado uprising in the Tengyō era (938–947) of the Suzaku reign, the 12-year war which broke out in 1151 (when MINAMOTO Yoriyoshi attacked ABE Sadato), as well as Governor General Takaie's subjugation of Tōi invaders in 1019 were all fought in the Kantō region or on the island of Kyushu. Absolutely none was fought within the capital, requiring the direct attention of Emperors and their ministers, until after Retired Emperor Toba's administration came to an end in 1156. Rebellions since then have been disgraceful.

Roots of the Military Age:
Shift to Imperial Mothers from the KAN'IN Line

The troubles of the Military Age began back when Emperor Go-Sanjō came to feel that he did not understand Chancellor Yorimichi. But there was then no basis for estrangement between Emperor and Minister—the Emperor above and the Minister below still had a fine understanding and planned accordingly.

Then when the time came, at the beginning of the Toba reign in 1107, for Retired Emperor Shirakawa to select a consort for Toba, and when an order was handed down that a daughter of KUJŌ Tadazane (Lord Chisoku-in) be given to Toba, Tadazane flatly refused; and the wedding did not take place. People could not understand this and, in reflecting about it, wondered if Tadazane had not become worried about the report that Toba had been mischievous in his youth, doing such things as shoot an arrow at the face of a palace guard. Retired Emperor Shirakawa had also been thinking of making Tadazane's son Tadamichi his son-in-law by having him marry his adopted daughter (the real daughter of KAN'IN Kinzane). Arrangements for this marriage were already being made and had progressed up to the point of selecting the wedding date when a number of difficulties emerged.[27] The ceremony had not yet been performed when Shirakawa heard that Tadazane would not marry his daughter to Toba. His Majesty became violently angry, changing his mind about marrying his adopted daughter (the future Taiken-mon In) to Tadamichi. Instead he placed her in the palace as Crown Prince Toba's consort.

When Toba grew up, he became a surprisingly gentle and good-hearted sovereign. KAN'IN Kinzane's daughter, adopted by Shira-

27. There were rumors of a love affair.

kawa, was made Toba's Empress, becoming Taiken-mon In. She gave birth to several Imperial sons and daughters. The eldest son was Sutoku. The next two sons (Naemiya and Memiya) died before they grew up, but Sutoku was enthroned in 1123. The fourth son was enthroned in 1155 as Go-Shirakawa, and the fifth became known as Princely Priest Kakushō (1129–69). All were from the womb of Empress Taiken-mon In of the KAN'IN house.

Final Split between Shirakawa and Tadazane

It was during Shirakawa's day that Imperial pilgrimages were first made to the Kumano Shrines. Shirakawa made several. On one of these and at a time when there was an outpouring of faith in the Kami worshipped at Kumano, Shirakawa was standing in front of the Kumano Sacred Hall when a beautiful hand emerged from below the bamboo curtain of the Hall. It turned over two or three times and then disappeared behind the curtain. Such a thing had occurred in dreams but not in real life. Shirakawa thought it strange to see such a sight and casually asked several female mediums *(mikō)* and shrine attendants what it meant. But none had a reasonable answer. One person present was a well-known seven-year-old medium by the name of Yoka no Ita who had come from the province of Mimasaka. She suddenly became possessed by the Kami and reported that the appearance of the hand showed that in the Final Age one would see conditions that were changing like a hand being turned upside down. Shirakawa was a sovereign who saw strange things of this sort.

Shirakawa made another pilgrimage to Kumano in the 10th month of 1120, toward the end of the Toba reign. Someone at Kumano maliciously insinuated that Chancellor Tadazane was now receptive to Emperor Toba's wish to have Tadazane's daughter (the future Empress Kaya no In) enter the Imperial Palace and that preparations for the wedding were under way. Upon hearing this, Shirakawa became very angry. He thought to himself: "When I suggested that Tadazane give his daughter to Toba, he shrugged it off. Now without my knowledge he does this." So after returning to the capital he quickly arranged to have Tadazane subjected to Imperial censure and had him removed from the Office of Chancellor. And on the 13th day of the 11th month of 1120 Tadazane was also removed from the office of Imperial Inspector and confined to his mansion.

Tadamichi Succeeds Tadazane as Chancellor

Retired Emperor Shirakawa thought of giving the Chancellorship to a minister who was not a relative of Tadazane but found no suitable candidate. He considered Minister of the Left KAZAN'IN Ietada (1061–1136), Morozane's second son who was currently Senior

Counselor and Senior Commander, but when Shirakawa consulted
with Akitaka, the latter said: "How about the incident on the observation platform during the Inari festival?" The incident referred to
involved Ietada's son, Middle Counselor Tadamune, who was a son-
in-law of a Consultant son of FUJIWARA Akisue. Having family connections, Akisue, Ieyasu, and others had gathered for a drinking
party on one of the observation platforms, where they began exchanging drinks, arousing criticism. I do not know exactly what
happened, but the Retired Emperor seems to have concluded that
the position should not be given to such persons.

Except for [my father] Minister-of-the Center KUJŌ Tadamichi
(1097–1164), there was absolutely no suitable candidate for the position of Regent or Chancellor. Retired Emperor Shirakawa was therefore forced to make this announcement: "Since even common
people say that a parent is a parent, and a son a son,[28] have
Tadamichi made Chancellor." Tadamichi responded as follows:

> If I am to succeed to this position, I request that you have the
> Imperial censure against my father Tadazane rescinded for one
> day and allow him to leave his mansion on that day. I ask this
> because it has been a long-standing precedent, followed genera-
> tion after generation, that when the office of Regent or Chancel-
> lor is passed from father to son, both go to pay their respects at
> the Imperial Court on the evening of that day. I would like to
> follow that precedent. If I simply take office without making any
> attempt to have the Imperial censure rescinded, I will be unfilial;
> and I will probably be condemned by the Kami and the Buddhas.

Retired Emperor Shirakawa felt that what Tadamichi said was quite
right, and so the appointment ceremony was conducted just as
Tadamichi had wanted, without any deviation whatsoever from established precedent. And Tadamichi became Chancellor in 1121.

Since Tadamichi had rented and was living in another man's
house located in the guard area of the Retired Emperor's palace,
whenever he went to the Imperial Palace he would first call on Retired Emperor Shirakawa. And when Tadamichi was consulted by
Shirakawa about precedents and other matters of state, he would
always speak forthrightly and without hesitation, giving Shirakawa
the feeling that Tadamichi was looking into a clear mirror. Action
would be taken only after such consultations, and Shirakawa came to
think that no other man was as great as [my father] Tadamichi. Toba
yielded the throne to Sutoku during the 1st month of 1123, when
Sutoku was five years old. So Retired Emperor Shirakawa lived to
see his great-grandson placed on the throne. Then, on the 9th day of

28. Meaning that Tadamichi might well be better than his father
Tadazane, who was disliked by Shirakawa.

the 1st month of 1129, Regent Tadamichi's daughter was placed in the palace, and she was designated Emperor Sutoku's consort on the 16th of that same month. She was the one who became Empress Kōka-mon In (1121–81). Then, on the 7th day of the 7th month of that same year, Shirakawa died, having reached the age of 77. Kōka-mon In had been appointed Sutoku's Empress on the 9th day of the 2nd month of the same year.

Retired Emperor Toba's Administration and KUJŌ Tadazane

Now we come to the years of Retired Emperor Toba's administration from 1129 to 1156. Tadazane was particularly well treated by Toba. Soon after Toba's abdication in 1126, His Imperial Majesty—moving to gratify an old desire—had Kanezane's daughter (the future Empress Kaya no In, 1095–1155) brought to him. She entered the Retired Emperor's palace on the 29th day of the 6th month of 1133, and on the 19th day of the 3rd month of the following year she was advanced to the position of Empress, five years after the death of Shirakawa in 1129. But Empress Kaya no In produced no royal sons.

Empress Taiken-mon In, Emperor Toba's Empress from the KAN'IN house, died on the 26th day of the 8th month of 1145. She probably was present at the celebration of Shirakawa's 60th birthday on the 16th day of the 3rd month of 1112, although she was young. And she died before the celebration of Toba's 50th birthday on the 7th day of the 3rd month of 1152. The influence of Taiken-mon In caused the KAN'IN house to prosper. She had entered Toba's Imperial palace on the 13th day of the 12th month of 1117, was made an Imperial consort on the 17th of that month, and was appointed Empress on the 26th day of the 1st month of 1118.

While these events were taking place, Tadazane made this request:

> Although I was confined to my mansion because of an unexpected break in relations with Retired Emperor Shirakawa, my son Tadamichi has fallen heir to the office of Chancellor. So I am content. But now I would like to go to the Imperial Court once more to pay my New Year respects and to occupy a seat above that of my son, the Chancellor.

And on the 3rd day of the 1st month of 1132 he did pay his New Year respects once more. People tell how Tadazane's second son, Middle Commander Yorinaga, carried the long train of his father's robe on that day. Those who participated in the ceremony included Regent and Prime Minister Tadamichi, followed by Minister of the Right Arihito who was known as Minister of the Left Hanazono and as the son of Emperor Go-Sanjō's third son (Prince Sukehito). Arihito was followed in turn by Minister of the Center Munetada of the Regental house of FUJIWARA. While noble after noble was participating in the ceremony and acting in strict accord with house etiquette, only Minister of the Right Arihito smiled, bowed, and stood erect. People said that his behavior was magnificent.

Tadazane was tenacious in everything he did. At the ceremony and before the various nobles had formed a line to pay their respects, he used his age and poor health to make this excuse: "I have been afflicted with beriberi for some time, and it is painful for me to stand for long periods of time." So he paid his respects to the Emperor quickly, saying: "Please excuse me for offering my compliments first." Because Tadazane had difficulty standing, he was helped by his son Tadamichi, the Regent and Prime Minister. And then Tadazane left before other nobles had paid their respects. People wondered if he was not trying to call attention to the presence of many nobles—from Minister of the Center Munetada on down—who belonged to his Regental house. Tadazane did have great prestige and power in those days, and he therefore acted in a grand way. Because he had such an air about him, even his soul was awesome [and later became awesomely vengeful].

Tension between Tadazane's Two Sons:
Tadamichi and Yorinaga

At about this time, the above-mentioned FUJIWARA Yorinaga (1120–56) had become recognized as Japan's leading scholar, one who was exceptionally able in both Japanese and Chinese learning. Although he was excitable and extreme in everything he did, he was the favorite of his father Tadazane. Yorinaga persisted in saying that he would like to be appointed Regent or Imperial Inspector, even if the appointment were only for a single day. And so Tadazane came to feel that Yorinaga should have the position. He repeatedly and earnestly pled with his eldest son Tadamichi: "What Yorinaga says is reasonable. Since the office of Regent or Chancellor will go to your descendants, let him have what he wants." But Tadamichi never responded to these requests. Finally, Tadazane became uneasy about Tadamichi's failure to take a definite position and spoke about the matter to Retired Emperor Toba: "Whether Yorinaga's wish is realized is, I feel, a matter of secondary importance. I would like Tadamichi to say what he thinks." Toba spoke to Tadamichi, who replied as follows:

> I think Yorinaga is a mediocre administrator. If he were to become the Emperor's guardian, the empire would certainly suffer. But if I were to speak in this way to my father, he would become very angry. And this would mean that I had been unfilial. On the

other hand, if I were to agree to the request on the grounds that this was what my father wants, I would be disloyal to the state. So I am on the horns of a dilemma.

When the Retired Emperor reported back, Tadazane thought: "He responded to the Retired Emperor. Why didn't he respond to me?" Feeling more and more deeply about the matter, Tadazane took the headship of the FUJIWARA clan away from Tadamichi on the 25th day of the 9th month of 1150, declaring that the FUJIWARA headship was not something to be bestowed by the sovereign. And at his mansion on East Sanjō, Tadazane transferred to Yorinaga the symbols of FUJIWARA headship: the red bowl and tray. Because Retired Emperor Toba had been wheedled by Tadazane about this matter in various ways, His Majesty secretly assembled high-ranking nobles for a ceremony and then, in the 1st month of 1151, had an Imperial decree issued appointing Yorinaga only to the position of Imperial Inspector. The action was justified by an earlier precedent of two persons holding that office concurrently.[29] People throughout Japan thought this a strange affair, declaring it to be truly amazing.[30]

Tension between Two Former Emperors: Toba and Sutoku

Relations between Toba and Sutoku became strained in the following way. While Sutoku was still on the throne between 1123 and 1141, Retired Emperor Toba became extremely fond of Middle Counselor Nagazane's daughter, the future Empress Bifuku-mon In (1117–60); and her son Konoe (1139–55) was advanced to Third Rank and immediately appointed Crown Prince. Konoe was also adopted by Empress Kōka-mon In (1121–81), Tadamichi's daughter and Sutoku's Empress. Toba said to Tadamichi: "As Konoe's maternal grandfather, you should take good care of him." Tadamichi did give special attention to being Konoe's true maternal grandfather. Then when Retired Emperor Toba advised Sutoku to yield the throne to his successor, Sutoku obediently passed the crown to Konoe in the 12th month of 1141, announcing that he wished to abdicate.

Konoe had been named Crown Prince in the 8th month of 1139. In the Imperial Mandate drafted by Toba, Sutoku thought that the

29. A reference to the appointments of FUJIWARA Tokihira and SUGA-WARA Michizane as Imperial Inspectors in 899 (cf. Chapter 1). In this case, however, Tadamichi was Chancellor and Yorinaga was Imperial Inspector.

30. It was amazing that Tadamichi, at the age of 25, should be Chancellor while his younger brother Yorinaga was Imperial Inspector. These offices were customarily held by the same man.

words "Imperial son" would be used, but Toba inserted the words "younger brother of the Emperor." Sutoku was upset about this and came to harbor resentment against Toba.[31]

Konoe grew up while occupying the throne, and Yorinaga (Imperial Inspector and First Minister) served superbly as Master of Imperial Banquets, reminding people of the glorious days of Michinaga. But the Emperor never appeared before the Imperial curtain at any of these banquets and remained in his quarters sleeping. Such behavior was quite unconventional. No matter how Toba spoke to him, Konoe paid no attention. Furthermore, Chancellor Tadamichi said again and again: "I will be blamed if you do not attend the banquet." But Emperor Konoe would not listen even to the Chancellor. Retired Emperor Toba thought: "This too is the Chancellor's doing." And his mood worsened. But Tadamichi was not the least bit aware of His Majesty's resentment. Possessing only an estate in the province of Bizen,[32] he continued to wait upon the Emperor, since there was no one who could dismiss him from his position as Chancellor or Imperial Inspector.

At a later date, Tadamichi and Yorinaga accidentally met twice at the Imperial Palace. Yorinaga bowed to Tadamichi as he used to, because the latter was his elder brother, under whom he had grown up as a member of the Regent-Chancellor house. Long before, Yorinaga had become an adopted son of Tadamichi, and Yorinaga remembered this. People said that Yorinaga's behavior was praiseworthy. Tadazane, the father of the two ministers, asked Yorinaga why he had shown such deference to Tadamichi, a member of the FUJIWARA house of which Yorinaga was head, and Yorinaga replied: "The *Book of Rites* states that 'one should not disregard etiquette.'

31. Emperor Sutoku had been forced to legitimize the position of Retired Emperor Toba's favorite son, Konoe:

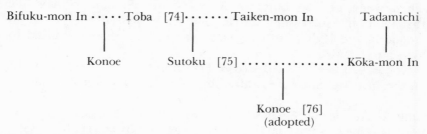

Bifuku-mon In · · · · · Toba [74]· · · · · · · Taiken-mon In   Tadamichi

          Konoe   Sutoku [75] · · · · · · · · · · · · · · · Kōka-mon In

                              Konoe [76]
                              (adopted)

Now Retired Emperor Sutoku had another reason to be angry with Toba. Since his adopted son Konoe had been identified as a young brother (not a son), Sutoku would not be entitled to succeed Toba as the Retired Emperor administering state affairs in behalf of the next Emperor.

32. Not being head of the FUJIWARA clan, Tadamichi held only the Shikada estate in the province of Bizen. All others were held by Yorinaga.

How could I be disrespectful just because we were on bad terms with each other?" People of that day clamored about this.

Toba Turns against Yorinaga

While these things were happening, various people of the country were calling Yorinaga "the irascible Minister of the Left." And signs of his irascibility appeared day and night. For example, he wrecked the carriage of Middle Counselor Sanehira at the time of Retired Emperor Toba's visit to Hōshō-ji. On another occasion he had one of his men run into the house of Middle Counselor Ienari, Toba's favorite. Because of these incidents, Toba came to dislike Yorinaga. And although Tadamichi considered the phrase "irascible Left Minister" an appropriate way to refer to his young brother, he did nothing about Yorinaga's behavior. According to what people have said, Yorinaga overheard his father Tadazane ask why Yorinaga had done such a thing as wreck Sanehira's carriage. Then Tadazane went on to state angrily: "Even if he was angry, he should not have had one of his men run into Ienari's house." Yorinaga felt that this was being too critical, even for a father. In the company of his most favored bodyguard (a person named Kimiharu), Yorinaga had been passing in front of Ienari's house when a servant, who had been ordered to stand by the gate, failed to remove his high clogs as Yorinaga passed. So Yorinaga had one of his men go after the culprit, who was chased into Ienari's house and caught. Being naturally hot-tempered, Yorinaga would do rash things that damaged his reputation.

Meanwhile, people were saying that Emperor Konoe's death in the 7th month of 1155 at the age of 17 was due to a Yorinaga curse. Retired Emperor Toba came to feel that this was true. Was there any proof of such a charge? Because Emperor Konoe had died in this way, Yorinaga thought: "Now I will become Chancellor and Imperial Inspector." As was the custom, he resigned his posts as Minister of the Left and Imperial Inspector; but the court surprised him by accepting his resignation as Imperial Inspector. So in the 1st month of the following year Yorinaga was, once more, only Minister of the Left.[33]

33. The acceptance of Yorinaga's resignation as Imperial Inspector was soon followed by rebelliousness. Having been appointed head of the FUJI-WARA clan in 1150, and named Imperial Inspector in 1151, Yorinaga hoped that the 1155 enthronement of Go-Shirakawa would make it possible for him to reach the post of Chancellor. But Retired Emperor Toba had become displeased with him—probably for reasons more complex than the rumor that Yorinaga had put a curse on the deceased Emperor Konoe. So Yorinaga soon associated himself with the cause of Retired Emperor Sutoku

The Question of Konoe's Successor

Retired Emperor Toba was troubled by the question of who should succeed Emperor Konoe. He thought of his fourth son, later enthroned as Emperor Go-Shirakawa (1127–92), who was born from the womb of Empress Taiken-mon In and who was living with her older son, the junior Retired Emperor Sutoku. But Go-Shirakawa had been playing around so much that he had become the subject of horrendous rumors. Toba therefore did not think that Go-Shirakawa had enough ability to be Emperor. He also considered placing Konoe's elder sister, Princess Hachijō In, on the throne as a reigning Empress. And he thought of the junior Retired Emperor Sutoku's eldest son, Prince Shigehito. Finally he wondered about the son of Go-Shirakawa, a child not yet grown up and the prince who was to become the future Emperor Nijō. Neither Tadazane nor Yorinaga was consulted, for Retired Emperor Toba conferred only with Tadamichi. And Tadamichi took this position: "A minister should have nothing to say about Imperial succession. This is something that should be decided by the sovereign alone." But when Toba asked Tadamichi for advice a fourth time, he pressed for a definite recommendation, saying: "Tell me just what you think. I will consider your answer to be the command of the Sun Goddess." Whereupon Tadamichi replied: "In complying with your royal command, I point out that your fourth son (Go-Shirakawa) is now 29 years old. You should think first of placing him on the throne and then plan for the future." Toba said: "Fine! Fine! Arrange matters accordingly." While grieving over the death of Emperor Konoe and following precedents, Tadamichi went to meet Go-Shirakawa, who was living in the junior Retired Emperor Sutoku's palace. The enthronement ceremony was carried out in magnificent style at the Takamatsu mansion on South Street, located to the south of East Sanjō. Toba (administrator of state affairs as a Retired Emperor) and Tadazane (former Chancellor and father of a Regent) had both come to look with disfavor on their eldest sons (Sutoku and Tadamichi) and to favor their younger sons (Go-Shirakawa and Yorinaga). Between them they handled the most important matters. Since this was in accord with a time fate (*jiun*) which required that things should turn out this way during the Final Age, the two men managed affairs for a short while in full agreement with each other. But in the end the colossal harms that were done by them caused the

---

who, as noted, was also disgruntled. And steps were taken that led to the outbreak of the Hōgen Rebellion of 1156. The complex interaction between tensions and rivalries within the Imperial family and the regental house of FUJIWARA is trace 1 in the first part of the *Hōgen Monogatari*. Cf. Chapter 8.

state to deteriorate. Nevertheless, while Toba was alive, no rebellions or wars broke out.[34]

Death of Retired Emperor Toba

On the 24th day of the 4th month of 1156, Retired Emperor Toba had the current era name of Kyūju changed to Hōgen. Then he died on the 2nd day of the 7th month of that same year. During his illness the noble and the mean, as well as the young and the old, were all mumbling: "What is going to happen when the Retired Emperor is no longer alive?" Minister of the Center Muneyoshi—maybe he was then Senior Counselor—had been thinking deeply about this question, although he was not among Toba's close retainers. He wrote a letter to Toba in which he seems to have said something like this: "What do you think is going to happen to this country after you have passed away? It is likely to fall rapidly into confusion and to be ruined. You should therefore leave detailed instructions about what should be done." Even if Muneyoshi did not write these words, Toba was undoubtedly giving the matter some thought. So His Majesty had about ten soldiers of his northern guard—including MINAMOTO Tameyoshi and TAIRA Kiyomori—swear an oath *(saimon)* which was then handed over to Empress Bifuku-mon In [Emperor Konoe's Imperial mother]. A scholar of some prominence during the Shirakawa reign (1155–58)—a man referred to as Junior Counselor Lay Priest Shinzei—had a wife (Ki Second Rank) who had been Shirakawa's nurse for some years. Considering this Shinzei a trustworthy person, Retired Emperor Toba asked him to have Tadamichi and other ministers and nobles cooperate with each other in respecting Empress Bifuku-mon In as the Imperial mother.[35]

Retired Emperor Toba died on the 2nd day of the 7th month of 1156 at the Imperial Hall which had had built for his last days and which had been erected on the Toba palace grounds: the Anraku Hall.

34. Jien emphasizes Retired Emperor Toba's attempts to find an able person for the throne in 1155; but in selecting his young son Go-Shirakawa, Toba made his elder son Sutoku more discontented than ever. Sutoku's son (Prince Shigehito) was a logical candidate; and if Shigehito had been selected, Sutoku would have been entitled to succeed Toba as the next Retired Emperor administering state affairs in his son's behalf. But Sutoku's hopes were again dashed. He therefore allied himself with the disappointed young brother (Yorinaga) of Chancellor Tadamichi and rebelled against his own young half-brother (Emperor Go-Shirakawa).

35. Toba wanted Bifuku-mon In to be honored as the Imperial mother not only because she was his favorite Empress, and the mother of the deceased Emperor Konoe, but because Go-Shirakawa's Imperial mother (Taiken-mon In) had died in 1145.

Although the junior Retired Emperor Sutoku came to the Toba palace at the time of Toba's death, there was no one there to welcome him. This made Sutoku angry and he caused a disturbance among the Imperial carriages at the Southern Hall of the palace, where no one was present. Retired Emperor Toba was dying while this was going on. And as the horse carriages were being thrown into disorder, a 17- or 18-year-old young man by the name of TAIRA Chikanori (son of TAIRA Noriie and Assistant Head of the Gubernatorial Inspectors) was near the front of the Shōkōmyō Cloister. When he approached the scene, he was attacked. He is said to have shouted: "My eye has been knocked out!" Toba was already at the point of death. His favorite Lady-in-Waiting (Lady Tosa, the daughter of Mitsuyasu) is said to have exclaimed: "People are saying that the junior Retired Emperor has knocked out Chikanori's eye." Hearing this, Toba opened his eyes and looked up. Then, so the story goes, he breathed his last.

Chikanori lived on until the age of 80, coming to be known as the Lay Priest Minister of Civil Affairs. When asked about this story, he said:

> My eye wasn't knocked out. But, as the story has it, when I approached the scene, I was wondering why the carriages should be in such disarray on the occasion of an Imperial visitor. Then suddenly a rock thrown by a servant crashed against a window of the carriage in which I was riding. Someone yelled: "This is a visit of the new Retired Emperor." I immediately ordered my carriage to stop and jumped down. Then, somehow or other, a piece of bamboo from the curtain of the carriage struck the thin part of my lower eyelid, and pierced it like a stitching needle. When the servants saw blood on the front of my patterned light blue gossamer robe, they stopped their attack. If they had not stopped, I suppose they would have knocked me down. I felt that the flow of blood indicated that I was receiving the protection of the Kami and Buddhas.

The Hōgen Rebellion of 1156:
Sotuku and Yorinaga Defeated

Retired Emperor Sutoku, who had been staying at his palace on the Tanaka estate, seems to have consulted with Yorinaga and then suddenly left his palace on the 9th day of the 7th month. He moved to the Sajiki Palace, which is referred to as "the palace of the Amida Hall with the 1,000 statues" and is located on the Nakamikado River bank in Shirakawa. It was not his own palace, but he pushed his way into it and settled down. Feeling that the situation was developing as expected, Chancellor Tadamichi, TOKUDAIJI Saneyoshi (Minister of the Left), and many others assembled at the Imperial Palace. The soldiers who had sworn the oath that was handed to Empress

Bifuku-mon In also came to guard the Imperial Palace.

Yorinaga, the "irascible Minister of the Left," was in Uji at the time. Since it was reported that Yorinaga would probably be going to the Nakamikado Palace of Sutoku, a soldier by the name of Nobukanu was ordered to intercept and kill Yorinaga at the River Hitsu. But because the order was issued hastily, Nobukanu was slow in leaving. Meanwhile, Yorinaga had left Uji in the middle of the night and had reached the Nakamikado Palace.

Now Middle Commander and Consultant FUJIWARA Norinaga, who had served near Sutoku for years, was sent several times to get MINAMOTO Tameyoshi (1096–1156) to come to Nakamikado. Finally word was received that Tameyoshi would come soon. He arrived with two sons: Shirōzaemon Yorikata (d. 1156) and Gempachi Tametomo (1139–77). His eldest son Yoshitomo had allied himself with the group supporting Emperor Go-Shirakawa. For several years Yoshitomo had not been on good terms with his father Tameyoshi, but this is a long story which will be omitted here. Then on the 11th day of that 7th month a conference was held at the Nakamikado Palace and, as people from all over the country were getting excited about what was going to happen, MINAMOTO Tameyoshi spoke out as follows:

> We have absolutely no strength. All my house retainers have attached themselves to Yoshitomo and are at the Imperial Palace. Only my two young sons are with me. What can we possibly do with such a weak force? We certainly will not realize our objectives by waiting here to engage the enemy in battle. I think we should go directly and immediately to Uji and check the enemy's advance temporarily by pulling up the planks of the Uji Bridge. An alternative course of action is to go directly to the province of Ōmi and, with Mt. Kōka at our rear, wait for soldiers from the east to come to our assistance. If such support is late in coming, His Majesty could proceed on to the Kantō. And if we cut off the road that goes to the east over Mt. Ashigara and defend our position there, probably the Imperial forces at the capital will gradually find it impossible to subdue us. In the eastern provinces the MINAMOTO house has been getting stronger ever since the days of Yoriyoshi and Yoshiie (1041–1108), and now every military man there is a follower of mine. As for the Imperial forces at the capital, everyone is likely to be studying the situation. If none of these plans is feasible, maybe we should at least move against the Imperial Palace for a showdown.

But Yorinaga, in the presence of His Majesty, advocated caution: "We should not act too hastily. What is going to happen this moment? At present we seem to have absolutely no strength: There is a man in the province of Yamato by the name of Higaki no Kaza. I have ordered him to mobilize the forces of Yoshino and to come here immediately. He is probably on the way now. Wait a while." In the face of this unexpected recommendation, Tameyoshi withdrew to the garden. Others present, besides MINAMOTO Tameyoshi, were such military figures as TAIRA Masahiro, TAIRA Iehiro, TAIRA Tadamasa, and TAIRA Yorinori. But their strength was slight.

At the Imperial Palace, MINAMOTO Yoshitomo (1123–60) was fretfully advancing this view:

> What is the point of planning a defense if there is no fixed time for the attack? This is no way to fight battles. The first thing to do is to make a direct attack and rout the enemy. After that we can plan. MINAMOTO Tameyoshi, accompanied by Yorikata and Tametomo, has already gone to the new Retired Emperor's palace at Nakamikado. Even though Tameyoshi is my father, I have joined the Imperial forces. If I advance to meet the enemy, he will probably retreat. So let us move directly to the attack.

But no decision was reached during the day of the 10th. While Shinzei was in the garden saying "Well! Well!," Tadamichi remained close to the Emperor, not saying a word. TOKUDAIJI Saneyoshi (Minister of the Center), his son Kimiyoshi, and others looked on. Then at daybreak on the 11th, the Emperor issued this order: "Have the enemy pursued and routed immediately." MINAMOTO Yoshitomo (Governor of Shimotsuke) was delighted. Cheerfully waving his fan with a red sun on it, he said:

> I have gone into battle many times, and I have always been in awe of the Imperial House. In my heart I have been most fearful of committing some crime against the Emperor. Today I have received an Imperial order to pursue and attack the enemy. The refreshed feeling I have, as I move to engage the enemy, cannot be expressed.

Separating his forces from those of TAIRA Kiyomori (Governor of Aki), Yoshitomo left the Imperial Palace in Sanjō to advance against Sutoku's palace at Nakamikado, supported by other MINAMOTO clansmen: Yorimasa, Shigenari, and Mitsuyasu. After a short while and as the day broke, their forces attacked. Although MINAMOTO Yorikata and MINAMOTO Tametomo had an inferior force, they put up a strong defense. In the face of this resistance MINAMOTO Yoshitomo's leading retainer (KAMADA Jirō Masakiyo) was driven back several times. But since the Imperial force was large, it surrounded the Nakamikado palace and set it on fire. Then Retired Emperor Sutoku, wearing his everyday robe, was put on a horse and sent off to the Princely priest Kakushō at the Ninna Temple, with Nobuzane (Assistant Director of the Imperial Stables of the Right) riding behind him. Yorinaga seems to have fled while still wearing his armor. But since he was hit in the face by an arrow that had been shot by someone, his cheek was badly wounded and he fell from his horse and had to be carried into the house of a commoner.

On that same day an Imperial decree was handed down ordering the headship of the FUJIWARA clan returned to Tadamichi. This was the first time that the head of the FUJIWARA clan had been appointed by an Emperor.

A soldier by the name of Shigesada (a former official of Chikugo) was the son of Genta Shigezane of Tosa. He is now an 80-year-old lay priest who says: "I shot the arrow that made a direct hit on Yorinaga." Sticking out his arms to illustrate his point, he says: "I have seven moles on my arms which I call 'the seven stars.'[36] Because of them, I have had supernatural protection in war, and I have never missed a shot." In any case, Yorinaga was put into a small boat that departed from a place called Umetsu on the Katsura River. Accompanied by his elder brother Tsunemori, Yorinaga went to see his father Tadazane at Uji. But Tadazane would not see him, even this once. Then Tsunemori took Yorinaga to a place called Hannyamichi in the province of Yamato. A day or two after their arrival there, Yorinaga died. When Nakayuki's son was asked about the details of Yorinaga's death, he said:

> I have heard that Yorinaga was unable to ride a horse. In the heat of battle he was standing by a sliding door at the Buddha Hall at the Ōimikado Palace, directing his forces, when an arrow hit him below the ear. And so he was put into a carriage parked near the gate and was taken off with Tsunemori (Master of the Imperial Secretariat). They went to the River Katsura, got aboard a cormorant fishing boat, and went downstream to the mouth of the Kotsu River. When Yorinaga announced that he wanted to see his father, Tadazane sent back this message: "From the beginning I thought this would happen. I don't want to see you."[37] After that, Yorinaga died in a boat. Three men—the above-mentioned Tsunemori, Toshinari (Secretary of the Bureau of Books and Drawings), and Nobuyori (an Inspector)—took Yorinaga's body to a place 100 feet above the main road leading to the Hannya Temple, and had it cremated.

What people say among themselves about a matter of this kind differs from what one finds when he asks someone who was directly involved. By comparing various accounts, one can probably learn what really happened.

36. A reference to the seven stars of the Big Dipper, which figure prominently in Chinese and Japanese astrology.

37. Yorinaga had been Tadazane's favorite son, but Tadazane seems to have had no desire to associate himself with his son's lost cause. When the war was over, Tadazane was nevertheless placed under house arrest by his victorious elder son, Chancellor Tadamichi (Jien's father).

As a result of this defeat of Retired Emperor Sutoku's forces, Tameyoshi fled to Yoshitomo's mansion, but when Yoshitomo told the Emperor what had happened, an Imperial decree was handed down ordering Tameyoshi's head cut off immediately. So Yoshitomo put his father in a palanquin and sent him to Yotsuzuka where he was beheaded. There was some commotion around the country about Yoshitomo having beheaded his own father.

Another result of the defeat was that Retired Emperor Sutoku was exiled to the province of Sanuki. And because of steps taken by Tadamichi, his father Tadazane was [only] confined to his Chisoku-in Mansion.

A Trace of the Past

I have had the unexpected opportunity of seeing a diary that was officially written by Middle Counselor MINAMOTO Masayori, Imperial Secretary Fifth Rank and Vice Minister of Civil Affairs. In it I find the following quotation:

> From the beginning of the battle at dawn until it subsided and the troops had returned, we received hourly reports that were detailed and unequivocal. They stated, "Now thus and so is happening." The messengers dispatched by Yoshitomo went back and forth between the battleground and the Imperial Palace, providing such detailed reports that we felt the battle was being fought before our very eyes. Yoshitomo was a great man.

Later on, Norinaga was arrested and questioned about various matters. He was brought to the office of the Council of State and interrogated by the Imperial Secretary and the Controllers in the presence of the head of the Council of State, Master Scribes, and Major Secretaries. Here we have a trace of the ancient past, a past that was still marvelous. Nowadays, we are not destined to have such a marvelous course of events.

3
Military Age I

Emperor Go-Shirakawa to
MINAMOTO Yoritomo

Go-Shirakawa's Reign (1155–58)

The Rebellion of 1156 broke out suddenly, but Emperor Go-Shirakawa's forces crushed it easily and every rebel was punished according to the seriousness of his crime. Although capital punishment had been abandoned many years earlier,[1] it was now revived—probably because the crimes were so serious. Apparently some people were critical [of the authorities for having the rebel leaders executed].

Emperor Go-Shirakawa was devoted to the practice of Buddhist Law. While he was on the throne, Repentance Rites *(senbō)* were held at the Compassion and Long-Life Hall within the Imperial Palace grounds.

Because Shinzei[2] was in full control of state affairs during the Go-Shirakawa reign, he had the Imperial Palace rebuilt. For years his heart had been set on having this done. Back in the Shirakawa

1. Capital punishment was discontinued in 810.
2. Before entering the priesthood, Shinzei's name was FUJIWARA Michinori. He had a MINAMOTO mother. Known as a scholar with considerable ability in a number of fields, he was a provincial governor when he decided to

and Toba reigns (1072–86 and 1107–23) the Imperial Palace had become virtually non-existent, though knowledgeable persons realized that it was originally and essentially the place for performing state ceremonies and functions *(kuji)*. Since people were unhappy that the palace had been neglected during these two reigns, Lord Hōshō-ji Tadamichi planned, as soon as he was ordered (toward the end of the Toba reign) to take full charge of state affairs as Chancellor, to make palace reconstruction his first order of business. But this was not to the liking of Retired Emperor Shirakawa, who said: "This man Tadamichi is really an old-fashioned man!" Shinzei, being quick to seize an opportunity, carried out the rebuilding of the palace in a magnificent way [after the Rebellion of 1156 had been crushed]. Without causing any difficulty for the people in the various provinces and the seven regions, he handled the reconstruction smoothly and finished it within just two years. People said that while Shinzei was working on the project he had his abacus in hand all night and that the sound of it, as well as the sound of reading off the results of his calculations, could be heard from midnight to dawn, arousing respect. By giving close attention to his schedule, he finished the task in a truly fine way. Then he held a banquet at the new palace where female entertainers danced. People wondered about the propriety of such festivities.

Shinzei was also planning to have another Repentance Rite held at the newly constructed Imperial Palace, explaining that since this was the place where the Emperor normally lived, it was a proper place for such a rite. But then Emperor Go-Shirakawa stepped down from the throne on the 11th day of the 8th month of 1158 to be succeeded by Emperor Nijō.

Go-Shirakawa Begins to Administer
State Affairs as a Retired Emperor

After Go-Shirakawa began to administer state affairs in the manner of Retired Emperors Shirakawa and Toba, he became shockingly fond of a high-ranking nobleman by the name of FUJIWARA Nobuyori (1133–59), a son of Lord Tadataka. While low-ranking

---

enter the priesthood. His wife, Lady Ki Second Rank, had been Go-Shirakawa's nurse and was quite influential at court. After Go-Shirakawa's enthronement in 1155, Shinzei served the young Emperor as a "priestly minister," attempting to strengthen court administration and to revive ancient court ceremonies. At the time of the Rebellion in 1156, Shinzei seems to have obtained the backing of MINAMOTO Yoshitomo and was therefore given much credit for putting down the rebellion. He was subsequently criticized for recommending the execution of defeated rebel leaders but was probably the most powerful person at court until his death in 1159.

persons of the Retired Emperor's military guard such as the TAIRA brothers Nobunari and Nobutada, and Tameyuki and Tameyasu, were becoming prominent, FUJIWARA Nobuyori was rising to positions as high as Middle Counselor and Commander of the Palace Gate Guards of the Right. And Shinzei was having his sons promoted: Toshinori to Middle Controller of the Right, and Narinori to a position in the Imperial Bodyguards. Toshinori and his brother Narinori were really superior in intelligence and in their ability to write. They therefore distinguished themselves in reestablishing the Records Office[3] along lines laid down during the Enkyū era (1069–74).

Jealousies and Grudges before the Rebellion of 1159

While all of Shinzei's sons—including an unknown number of those who had become Buddhist priests—were gaining prominence, FUJIWARA Nobuyori developed feelings of jealousy toward Shinzei. Having noted rivalry between MINAMOTO Yoshitomo and TAIRA Kiyomori and having assumed that the victor in a war between them would seize control of the state, he allied himself with MINAMOTO Yoshitomo (1123–60) and began immediately to plot a rebellion.[4]

Another element in the rebellious situation of that day was MINAMOTO Yoshitomo's deep grudge against Shinzei. Since Shinzei was then a person of incomparable influence, and MINAMOTO Yoshitomo and TAIRA Kiyomori were now competing against each other, Yoshitomo decided to make Shinzei's son Korenori his son-in-law. This Korenori (known as the Lay Priest of Shinano) was the one who later became the Holy Man (*hijiri*) believed everywhere to have actually achieved rebirth in the Pureland paradise at the Ōjō Hall on the Yoshi Peak of Nishiyama by repeating the sacred name of Amitābha ten times in the final moments of life. Yoshitomo made his proposal of a marriage alliance when Korenori was in the prime of life, but Shinzei did not accept the proposal and bluntly said: "My son is a scholar and cannot be made your son-in-law." Shortly afterward, Shinzei made his son Shigenori—born from the womb of Shinzei's wife Lady Ki Second Rank—the son-in-law of TAIRA Kiyomori. This was why Yoshitomo could not but bear a bitter grudge against Shinzei. Even great men make such blunders. It is something that cannot be avoided by relying only on human power.

3. Cf. Chapter 2.
4. The rivalries that led to the Heiji Rebellion of 1159 and 1160—when MINAMOTO Yoshitomo and FUJIWARA Nobuyori (supporting Emperor Nijō) were defeated by TAIRA Kiyomori and Shinzei (supporting Retired Emperor Go-Shirakawa)—are subjects of tales that make up the first third of the *Heiji Monogatari*. [NKBT, 31.186–221.] Cf. Chapter 8.

In any case, all that we can do to avoid wrong action is to know, quite well, the relative importance of the various Principles of things. Anyone can do just what he wants once in a while if it is only an isolated case, but when two or three such wrong actions converge, a time comes for sharp distinctions between good and bad. Just when Shinzei had become fully satisfied with the advancement of his sons and with his authority over the affairs of state, why should he have become involved in a grudge against a military man as strong as Yoshitomo? It was because the final hour for retribution had arrived. Furthermore, anger is the worst of all faults—one which destroys the individual—and Shinzei was one to become angry easily.

The Rebellion of 1159

Not long afterward—on the night of the 9th day of the 12th month of 1159—the palace at Karasuma and Sanjō was surrounded. This was where Retired Emperor Go-Shirakawa resided and where Shinzei, attended by his sons, usually waited upon his Majesty. Wishing to kill everyone in the palace, MINAMOTO Yoshitomo and FUJIWARA Nobuyori surrounded it with their troops and set it on fire.

Then an Imperial carriage was drawn up to the central gate of the palace by an ally (Middle Counselor MINAMOTO Moronaka) and the Retired Emperor and Empress Jōsai-mon In were both placed in it. Shinzei's wife (Ki Second Rank, who was the mother of Shigenori) was so small that she was able to hide herself in Empress Jōsai-mon In's robe; and no one noticed that she too entered the carriage. Empress Jōsai-mon In (1126–89) had been advanced to the position of Empress because she and Go-Shirakawa were both from the womb of Empress Taiken-mon In and because Jōsai-mon In was granted the assimilated rank of Imperial mother. She and Go-Shirakawa thought alike on various matters and usually lived in the same palace. MINAMOTO Shigenari, MINAMOTO Mitsumoto, and MINAMOTO Suezane were ordered to accompany the carriage that took the royal party to the Imperial Library. MINAMOTO Shigenari was later praised as a person whose place of death was not known.

Shinzei's son Toshinori and Sadanori, who had served the Retired Emperor, fled. Thinking that he was about to be burned to death, Toshinori climbed under the veranda of the northern section of the palace. Looking around, he concluded that he might still escape; so he dashed through the flaming fire and got out.

Sensing impending defeat, Shinzei took FUJIWARA Moromitsu (Captain of the Palace Gate Guards of the Left), FUJIWARA Narikage (Captain of the Palace Gate Guards of the Right), TAGUCHI Shirō Kanemitsu, and SAITŌ Kiyozane (Secretary of the Imperial Stables Right Division) with him and, commandeering some palanquin bearers that people would not recognize, went to a place called Tawara in the province of Yamato. There they dug a pit and had Shinzei covered up. Because the four who accompanied Shinzei had entered the Buddhist priesthood, they were then called by their Buddhist names: Saikō, Saikei, Saijitsu, and Sai'in.[5] Saikō and Saikei later re-entered the service of Go-Shirakawa. Saikō said to Shinzei: "Please set sail immediately for China. I will go with you." But Shinzei rejected the proposal: "When I left the capital, the position of the stars was the same as at the time of my birth. I definitely should not flee."

FUJIWARA Nobuyori, who had caused Retired Emperor Go-Shirakawa and his supporters to disperse, took Emperor Nijō to the Imperial Palace. Giving his support to Nijō (the current Emperor), Nobuyori took over the conduct of state affairs, confined Retired Emperor Go-Shirakawa to the Imperial Library, and immediately carried out an installation ceremony at which MINAMOTO Yoshitomo was made Governor of Harima (and advanced to Fourth Rank) and Yoshitomo's thirteen-year-old son Yoritomo was appointed Colonel of the Imperial Guards of the Right.

Shinzei's Death

Now Shinzei thought he had hidden himself well, but the palanquin bearers talked and a soldier by the name of MINAMOTO Mitsuyasu overheard them. Since Mitsuyasu was on Yoshitomo's side, the information was passed on; and an order was issued that Shinzei be found and brought in. Consequently a search party headed for Tawara. Meanwhile, FUJIWARA Moromitsu (Saikō) had climbed to the top of a big tree and, while waiting for dawn to break, faintly heard the voice of Shinzei inside the pit calling out the name of Amitābha. When Moromitsu saw a large number of lights, he got down out of the tree and yelled into the pit: "I see suspicious lights! Be careful!" Then he climbed back up the tree and saw soldiers quickly approaching. Shinzei thought that he had hidden himself well, but Nobuyori's soldiers, after looking around, found the board that had been placed over the entrance to their pit and removed Shinzei, who had died from a thrust of his own dagger in the upper part of his breast. They cut off Shinzei's head and took it triumphantly to the capital and paraded it through the streets. Shinzei's sons, including those who had become Buddhist priests, were exiled to various provinces.

5. The character for *sai* in each of these four priestly names is the second character used in writing Shinzei, and the second character (with one exception) is the second character in that person's original name.

TAIRA Kiyomori Returns to the Capital

TAIRA Kiyomori (1118–81), Deputy Governor General of Dazaifu, was on a pilgrimage to the Kumano Shrines when these events were taking place. Before he arrived and while he was stopping over at the Tanobe Inn (also called Futagawa Inn), a messenger ran in to report developments at the capital. Kiyomori was puzzled as to what he should do. He was accompanied by two sons—Motomori (Governor of Echizen) and his thirteen-year-old son Munemori (Governor of Awaji)—and 15 retainers. Although he was advised to retreat immediately to some such place as Kyushu in order to build up his forces, a warrior from the province of Kii by the name of YUASA Muneshige (Acting Governor) came forward with 37 mounted soldiers—a strong force for that day—and advised Kiyomori as follows: "I think you should enter the capital immediately." Tankai of Kumano[6] was not counted among Kiyomori's retainers, but this man dutifully took out seven suits of armor and all his military gear, including bows and arrows, and without hesitation entrusted them all to Kiyomori. Muneshige's thirteen-year-old son put his own small purple-colored leather belt on Munemori, Kiyomori's thirteen-year-old son. This son of Muneshige's was probably the one that later became the Holy Man Jōkaku who was closely associated with Mongaku.[7] Appointing someone to go on to Kumano in his place, Kiyomori set out immediately for the capital, arriving on the 17th day of the 12th month of 1159.

Logically, MINAMOTO Yoshitomo should have attacked TAIRA Kiyomori, but he did not—probably because his reinforcements from the eastern provinces had not arrived. While Yoshitomo was doing nothing about Kiyomori's presence in the capital, Minister of the Center Kinnori of Sanjō,[8] the former Prime Minister Saneyuki of Haichijō, and other officials of lower rank were consulting together about the general state of affairs, making such comments as these: "With the situation developing in this way, what shall we do? Neither FUJIWARA Nobuyori, MINAMOTO Yoshitomo, nor MINAMOTO Moronaka is a man who can govern the state well." Both Senior Counselor Tsunemune (brother of Emperor Nijō's Imperial mother, and Commissioner of Imperial Police) and FUJIWARA Korekata (a

6. Tankai was Intendant *(bettō)* of the Kumano Shrines.
7. Cf. Chapter 4.
8. Kinnori was the eldest son of Saneyuki (1079–1162), the SANJŌ house founder who was appointed Prime Minister in 1150 and who resigned in 1157. Kinnori became prominent after the Rebellion of 1156 and was appointed Minister of the Center in 1157, on the same day that his father resigned as Prime Minister.

person who had been particularly close to Retired Emperor Toba) were near the Emperor and were said to be on good terms with Nobuyori. But as rumors were flying, they consulted with Kinnori and decided that since TAIRA Kiyomori had had no trouble entering the capital and had taken up his residence at Rokuhara, they would have the Emperor moved to Kiyomori's residence at Rokuhara.

Emperor Nijō Moved to Kiyomori's Mansion in Rokuhara

The person selected to move the Emperor was Imperial Secretary Koreaki, a son of the Doctor Tomomichi who had been the Crown Prince's tutor. Because FUJIWARA Korekata (Superintendent of Imperial Police) was Tomomichi's son-in-law, Korekata and Koreaki were on intimate terms with each other. Having selected this clever Koreaki to be their messenger, [Tsunemune and Korekata] then consulted together about other matters. Because Koreaki was then under Imperial censure and had not been allowed to enter the Imperial Palace, it was deemed convenient to use him for moving the Emperor since most people at court would not recognize him. So at about 2:00 A.M. on the 25th day of the 12th month of 1159, Emperor Nijō was moved in accordance with a plan spelled out to Koreaki by Kiyomori as follows:

> During the day you will have a screened carriage attended only by ox-drivers brought out and made to look as though preparations are being made for an excursion by Ladies-in-Waiting. Then at night you will have a fire started near the intersection of Nijō and Ōmiya that will cause the soldiers to rush out. At that moment you will take the Emperor to the carriage and have him driven to Rokuhara.

Koreaki agreed to the plan.

Persons who knew about the plan consulted among themselves and decided to make this recommendation to Kiyomori:

> Since your return from Kumano, time has been passing without anything being done. Therefore Yoshitomo and Nobuyori are probably expecting you to attack any day. Because they will be taking strict precautions, they will be suspicious even of loud noises. So it would be good to do something that would throw them off guard. We suggest sending a card to Nobuyori. Let us know what you think of the idea.

Kiyomori quickly replied: "It's a good idea. Handle it as you think best." So Minister-of-the-Center Kinnori wrote out an appropriate message in Kiyomori's name. What he wrote on the card taken to Nobuyori by Iesada (Kiyomori's leading retainer) was:

Since the situation is like this, you should of course be careful. Even if I had not sent you a card, it would not have been considered rude. But I send this to express my regards and to let you know that I will not oppose your plans or wishes in any way.

The card was sent by Kiyomori to Nobuyori early on the very day the Emperor was moved to Rokuhara. Nobuyori's response was: "I am very happy to hear from you. Knowing your intentions, I would like to consult with you about everything. I am most grateful." Upon reading this, Kiyomori said: "Good! Good!" And the removal of the Emperor was carried out according to plan.

Superintendent of Imperial Police Korekata went after dark to the Imperial Library where Retired Emperor Go-Shirakawa was staying. Being a small man who had tucked up the skirts of his everyday robe, he proceeded unnoticed to the Imperial Library, talked privately with the Retired Emperor, and departed. Since a carriage had been prepared for Go-Shirakawa's use, no one knew that His Majesty [was talking with Korekata]. And since no one was suspicious, no one was worried [about the possibility of the Emperor being moved to Rokuhara].

As for Emperor Nijō's movements at the Imperial Palace, two mats had been provided by Koreaki, who was accustomed to the way things were done at the palace. He had the mats used for an Imperial matted walkway as His Majesty passed through the corridors of the Southern Hall. While the Emperor was walking on one mat, the other was spread out in front of him. Two handmaids, Iyo and Shōsuke, knew what was going on and went ahead to place the Imperial seal box and the Imperial sword in the carriage. As planned, the Emperor was sent off as if nothing unusual was occurring and while the fire was burning. After the fire had been extinguished, Nobuyori asked the handmaid Iyo, through the Imperial Secretary, to report to the Emperor that the fire had not been serious. She said: "I have already told His Majesty." These two handmaids departed, wearing only informal robes and with their hair informally parted in the middle and tied on both sides. Koreaki quietly took out a long chest and put these personal belongings of the Emperor into it: a Chinese lute *(genjō)*, a Japanese lute *(suzuke)*, a box containing the Imperial fife *(fue)*, a Chinese box containing the Imperial sword and bell, a sword that the Emperor kept by his side during the day, and a chair for the Imperial waiting-room. When Koreaki was following the Emperor to Rokuhara, he was intercepted by some Kiyomori soldiers who, drawing their bows and long swords and blocking the road, yelled out: "Who goes there?" Koreaki replied firmly: "Tell the Emperor that I am Koreaki, Bachelor of Literature and Imperial Secretary, and that I bear some items belonging to His Imperial Majesty." The message was relayed to the Emperor, and Koreaki was allowed to proceed after His Majesty quickly ordered him to do so. It was then about dawn. Retired Emperor Go-Shirakawa, Empress Jōsai-mon In, and Empress Bifuku-mon In went to Rokuhara; and the Great Lord Tadamichi and Chancellor Motozane went with them. The "Great Lord" was [my father] Lord Hōshō-ji Tadamichi.

The former Chancellor Tadamichi had yielded the position of Chancellor and the headship of the FUJIWARA clan to his sixteen-year-old son [KONOE Motozane] on the 11th day of the 8th month of 1158—on the same day that Nijō was placed on the throne. Everyone felt that Motozane was extremely young to hold such a high post. He was called "the interim Lord."[9] He was also referred to as "the Regent of Rokujō" and "the interim cloistered Regent." Was it not because Motozane had been married to the young sister of Nobuyori that people said Kiyomori had to pay some attention to the wishes of Lord Hōsho-ji Tadamichi?[10]

Among those in attendance on Retired Emperor Go-Shirakawa and Emperor Nijō at Rokuhara was Minister of the Center Kinnori of Sanjō, who looked at Kiyomori and said: "They say that Chancellor Motozane has arrived. How should he be treated?" Without hesitation, Kiyomori replied as follows: "The Chancellor is not a subject for discussion. If the Chancellor had not come to the Emperor, he should have been called. His coming here now should be considered praiseworthy." When people heard Kiyomori say this, they thought: "How well he has spoken!"

That night there was a stir in the capital about the Emperor having been moved to Rokuhara. In the middle of the night an Imperial messenger was sent to the Shirakawa Cloister where Princely Priest Kakukai (1134–81), known as the First Grade Abbot of Hōshō-ji, was

9. Motozane (1143–66) was only sixteen at the time. By drawing the reader's attention to Motozane's youth, and to the interim character of his terms as Chancellor and Regent, Jien seems to be pointing out that this eldest Tadamichi son, the founder of the KONOE house, deserved a position below that of Tadamichi's younger son Kanezane (1149–1207) of the KUJŌ house. Motozane was appointed Chancellor for Nijō (enthroned in 1158 at the age of 16) and was named Regent for Rokujō (enthroned in 1165 at the age of two).

10. Tadamichi's marital ties with Nobuyori, the person favored by Go-Shirakawa, were as follows:

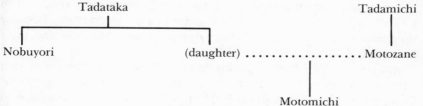

conducting a Buddhist Eye Mass *(butsugen-hō)* in response to a request that he had received from the court. Probably he had been requested to conduct this Mass because, as the seventh son of Retired Emperor Toba and a disciple of Tendai Abbot Gyōgen, he was familiar with esoteric rites. The Imperial messenger said to the Princely Priest: "The Emperor has gone to Rokuhara! Pray earnestly!"

Disarray at the Palace

Meanwhile, at the Imperial Palace FUJIWARA Nobuyori, MINAMOTO Yoshitomo, and MINAMOTO Moronaka were dashing about the Southern Hall like horseflies with their eyes removed. According to later reports by Middle Counselor Moronaka, Yoshitomo said to Nobuyori: "This happened because I relied upon the most stupid man in all Japan." And Nobuyori could say nothing in reply. As Nobuyori was putting on his armor, standing on the open floor of the Ceremonial Hall, he started to attach to his sword the small key of the Chinese chest that contained the Imperial sword and bell. But Moronaka, having placed the Sacred Mirror in his bosom, said: "Please give the key to me. I want to keep it with the Sacred Mirror. There is no point in attaching it to your sword." Nobuyori said: "You are right," and handed it over. Having taken possession of the key, and putting on an indigo-colored military uniform, Moronaka said: "I will never permit either one of these to be separated from me." Yoshitomo quickly tied the strings of his helmet and rushed from the palace. Although his retainers were behind him, they became separated from him when they entered the narrow streets of the capital.

TAIRA Kiyomori Attacks

The forces of Rokuhara soon advanced toward the Imperial Palace. MINAMOTO Yoshitomo declared: "I earnestly hope to leave my corpse to rot at Rokuhara! I will fight it out there!" Then he advanced to meet the attack from Rokuhara. On the TAIRA side, two Supreme Commanders fought like great commanders: Shigemori (Colonel of the Palace Gate Guards of the Left) and Yorimori (Governor of Mikawa and young brother of Kiyomori). After his horse was shot, Shigemori was seen standing on a pile of logs on the bank of the Hori River, using his bow as a cane and mounting another horse. It was a magnificent sight! The two Commanders returned to Rokuhara with broken arrows still penetrating their armor. Because they had won, the hearts of those watching were relieved and their hopes were raised.

MINAMOTO Yoshitomo quickly advanced as far as the fence that surrounded Rokuhara. In the confusion that followed, Supreme Commander TAIRA Kiyomori rode up to the central-gate corridor of Rokuhara on a black horse. He was dressed in black, carried black-lacquered arrows, and wore a deep indigo-colored military uniform over which there was a suit of armor laced with black straps. Putting on his large hoe-shaped helmet and tying it fast, he rushed out. Twenty or thirty men ran alongside his horse and, as he moved out amidst the clatter of hoofs, he said: "There's a commotion here. Let's see what's going on." He aroused confidence among those present.

The Defeat of MINAMOTO Yoshitomo and FUJIWARA Nobuyori

Since Yoshitomo had less than ten retainers left, he could do nothing and soon retreated. Thinking of how he might get to the eastern provinces and how he might wipe out the shame of his defeat by engaging the enemy once more, Yoshitomo passed the Chizuka Cliff of Ōhara and retreated toward the province of Ōmi. KAMADA Masakiyo went with Yoshitomo, never leaving his lord's side.

High Priest Jūyu of the Tendai Sect was serving as the Emperor's guardian priest *(gojisō)* at the time.[11] He went to Rokuhara and, wearing a pale reddish-yellow robe and facing northeast toward Mt. Hiei, alternately stood erect and bowed low while piously chanting, "Praise be to the Three Buddhist Treasures." This too was something that inspired confidence. It was necessary to have such a person at such a time.

Kiyomori laughed as he remarked: "I have taken back today the same card that was written and sent to Nobuyori's residence in the Imperial Palace grounds yesterday."

FUJIWARA Nobuyori fled to the quarters of Kakushō (the princely priest of Ninna Temple), but on the following day the prince forced Nobuyori to leave. Then TAIRA Kiyomori, having assembled his retainers, had Nobuyori—accompanied by Middle Commander FUJIWARA Narichika—captured and taken to a place behind Rokuhara where there was a spring and where a tent had been set up. Nobuyori said, in a really disgraceful way, that he had done nothing wrong. How could he have helped his cause by speaking in that way about such a serious matter? Kiyomori shook his head and said: "How can you say that?" Whereupon Kiyomori's retainers, understanding what their Lord's feelings were, had Nobuyori stand up; and they took him to the Rokujō riverbed where he was beheaded. Narichika, the son of Middle Counselor Ienari and a young, useless high-ranking nobleman, had been associated with Nobuyori, but since he had not been deeply involved in the affair, his crime was not considered particularly serious. Other soldiers allied with Nobuyori were all punished with varying degrees of severity.

So MINAMOTO Yoshitomo, being unable to get a horse, fled barefooted to the province of Owari. His feet had become swollen and tired, and he therefore went for help to the house of TAIRA

11. He was appointed Tendai Abbot in 1162.

Tadamune (manager of the Utsumi estate), who was a descendant
of ŌYA Munetsune of the Palace Gate Guards of the Left and the
father-in-law of Yoshitomo's retainer KAMADA Jirō Masakiyo. Because of such connections, Tadamune took Yoshitomo in. But while
Tadamune was politely saying that he was glad to be of service, and
was heating up the water and leading Yoshitomo to the bath,
Masakiyo became suspicious. Realizing that they might be killed in
this very house, he said to his lord: "Defeat probably cannot be
avoided much longer. The situation is bad." Yoshitomo's reply was: I
agree. I know everything." So Masakiyo beheaded his master and
immediately took his own life. Then MINAMOTO Yoshitomo's head
was seized by the TAIRA soldiers, taken to the capital, paraded
through the streets, and hung up in an ordinary tree at the eastern
entrance to the prison. Beside the head could be seen a poem which
someone had composed:

> The Shimotsuke Governor
> Has also become Governor of Kii;
> Such a dual appointment
> Does not seem fortunate.[12]

People who saw the poem were excited, since it did not contain a
single meaningless word. In those days it was thought that Prime
Minister Koremichi of Kujō was composing many poems like this
and dropping them anonymously along the roadside.

Tsunemune and Korekata Exiled

On the 29th day of the 12th month of 1159, Emperor Nijō
(1143–65) was moved to the Hachijō Palace where Empress
Bifuku-mon In resided, and on the 6th day of the 1st month of the
following year Retired Emperor Go-Shirakawa (1127–92) took up
his residence at Lord Akinaga's mansion at Horikawa and Hachijō.
From a viewing platform which had been built in front of Lord
Akinaga's mansion, Go-Shirakawa would look down on the street
and call commoners into his presence. In order to keep the Retired
Emperor from indulging himself in this way, Tsunemune and
Korekata[13] arranged to have the viewing platform boarded up. And
because Go-Shirakawa was doing such things, the two men were
broadcasting the view that state affairs should be administered by
the Emperor, not by the Retired Emperor. When Go-Shirakawa
heard what they were saying, he called in TAIRA Kiyomori and tear-

12. The poem contains three puns: (1) *ki no kami* means both "Governor
of Ki" and "his head has been hung up on the scaffold"; (2) *Yoshitomo*
means both "Yoshitomo" and "fortunate"; and (3) *kakezukasa* means both
"holding two titles" and "hanging there."

13. The activities of these two men during the Heiji Rebellion of 1159 are
touched upon above.

fully complained: "I can not administer affairs of state so long as these two men are around. Have them seized and brought here." Lord Hōshō-ji Tadamichi may have been in Go-Shirakawa's presence at the time, and Kiyomori too may have had his own thoughts about the matter. Using two retainers (Tadakage and Tamenaga), Kiyomori had Tsunemune and Korekata tied up; and when Go-Shirakawa was proceeding to a palace guard station, the prisoners were brought to his carriage. Word got around that the two men were forced to scream out. Since this was an odious affair, I will not write about it in detail. Anyway, probably everyone knows all about it. Tsunemune was immediately exiled to the province of Awa, and Korekata to the province of Nagato. Shinzei's children were all returned from exile. The arrest of Tsunemune and Korekata occurred on the 20th day of the 2nd month of 1160, and MINAMOTO Yoshitomo's son Yoritomo was exiled to the province of Izu on the 11th day of the 3rd month of that same year. After that, people came to speak of Korekata as "the interim small Superintendent."

Tension between Retired Emperor
Go-Shirakawa and Emperor Nijō

Relations between Retired Emperor Go-Shirakawa and Emperor Nijō had been good during the period from 1159 to 1162. They consulted together and agreed with each other. But then it was heard that the Emperor had been subjected to a curse. Lord Sanenaga reported that because an effigy of the Emperor had been drawn at the Upper Kamo Shrine, the effects of a curse were being manifested. By tying up and questioning one of the male mediums at the Shrine, it was disclosed that the curse had been inflicted upon the Emperor by such Go-Shirakawa aides as MINAMOTO Sukekata. So on the 2nd day of the 6th month of 1162, Sukekata was relieved of his position as Director of the Palace Repairs Office.

Another development that worsened relations between the Retired Emperor and the Emperor was the report that TAIRA Tokitada[14] had made a serious slip of the tongue when the future Emperor Takakura was born to his sister, Lady Koben. Therefore Tokitada was removed from his office in 1161, the year before Sukekata lost his position. Since each of these two incidents had increased the seriousness of the other, Sukekata and Tokitada were both ordered into exile on the 23rd day of the 6th month of 1162.

On the 10th day of the 4th month of 1164, TAIRA Kiyomori made Chancellor Motozane his son-in-law by giving his daughter Moriko,

14. Tokitada's prominence was connected with his marriage ties to powerful persons of that day. One sister (Tokiko) was married to TAIRA Kiyomori, and another (Lady Koben) was a consort of Retired Emperor Go-Shirakawa.

not yet grown, to Motozane in marriage. She was to become Motozane's principal wife.[15]

Kiyomori was having all state affairs handled directly by the Emperor.[16] He had built a palace for the Emperor at Oshikōji and East Tōin, and the Emperor had taken up his residence there [in 1162]. Kiyomori also had ordered members of his own house to construct mansions near the Imperial Palace, where they served the Emperor day and night. Kiyomori and others were deeply concerned about having the Emperor handle state affairs because a Retired Emperor had customarily borne that responsibility, but Kiyomori was very cautious and managed things magnificently, giving his attention to both the Emperor and the Retired Emperor. Because Lady Koben, the young sister of Kiyomori's wife Tokiko, and Go-Shirakawa's favorite, had produced an Imperial son, Kiyomori secretly hoped [that this Prince would be enthroned].

Retired Emperor Go-Shirakawa had long cherished the desire to build a Buddhist hall for a thousand statutes of the One-thousand-armed Kwannon, and Kiyomori gratified that desire by having the cost covered by assessments levied on the province of Bizen. The Retired Emperor wanted Emperor Nijō to attend the dedication ceremony held on the 17th day of the 12th month of 1164, but the Emperor was not the least bit interested. And the Emperor did nothing about Go-Shirakawa's request that awards be granted to officials of the new hall. An Imperial messenger was sent to the Emperor by Imperial Secretary Chikamori; and the hall was named the Renge-ō Cloister.[17] When Chikamori was called into Go-Shirakawa's presence at the latter's palace and asked whether the request had been granted, Chikamori reported that it had not. Tears welled up in Go-Shirakawa's eyes as he said: "Why does he hate me so?" Chikamori

15. By marrying his daughter Moriko (then nine years old) to Motozane, Kiyomori was trying to gain control over the FUJIWARA house in the same way that the FUJIWARA had gained (or legitimized) control over the Imperial House. As the *Gukanshō* states later on in this chapter, Kiyomori also came to entertain the ambition of becoming the minister who, as the maternal grandfather of a Chancellor or Regent, would be made responsible for handling state affairs. When Motozane died in 1166, Kiyomori claimed that much of Motozane's land should be retained by Moriko, Motazane's widow and Kiyomori's daughter.

16. The phrase "had all the affairs of state handled" *(yo no koto wo ba ikkō ni okonawase mairasete)* by the Emperor should not be taken literally. What Jien was saying, and what Kiyomori undoubtedly had in mind, was that the Emperor should take back some of the power and prestige that had been monopolized by the Retired Emperor. As is indicated later on in the *Gukanshō*, Kiyomori was moving to seize control of state affairs.

17. Now popularly referred to as the Sanjūsangen-dō (the hall of the 33 spaces between its 34 pillars).

said that he was afraid the Retired Emperor was blaming him for not obtaining Imperial approval. In building the Cloister, the Retired Emperor had relied mainly on Gyōkei (1105–65)—a son of Retired Emperor Shirakawa who became a priest of esoteric Buddhism and was referred to as the Korean High Priest—since Gyōkei was a fine priest who was affiliated with the Church Order of Miidera. Gyōkei gave special attention to the construction of the Cloister and, with his own hands, touched up the face of the sixteen-foot statue that became the Cloister's central object of worship. This Gyōkei was said to have been careful about everything he did. He was the guardian priest of Princely-Priest Dōkei, Retired Emperor Toba's sixth son.

At an early age, Nijō was sent to the Ninna Temple for training as a Buddhist priest; and he was placed under Princely-Priest Kakushō (1129–69), Retired Emperor Toba's fifth son. But since Nijō's Imperial lineage was deemed more important than training for the priesthood, he was returned to secular life in 1155 and appointed Crown Prince. Nijō and Kakushō continued to be closely associated. When Nijō ascended the throne in 1158, Kakushō built a place for Buddhist worship at Sanjō Bōmon and Karasuma, near Nijō's palace. And because Kakushō was with the Emperor day and night, he expressed his views to His Imperial Majesty on many matters of state. And when the position of Intendant of the Shitennō Temple was taken from Gyōkei and given to Kakushō, people gossiped [about this new sign of strained relations between the Retired Emperor and the Emperor].

Then, on the 7th day of the 3rd month of 1162, Tsunemune was brought back from exile, and on the 22nd day of the 1st month of 1164 he was reinstated as Senior Counselor. In 1166 he was promoted to Minister of the Left (First Minister) and for years was highly respected as a person well versed in traditional court practices and ceremonies. He was a true grandson of Great Lord Morozane. Since his personality was not like that of his father Tsunezane (Senior Counselor Second Rank), and since he devoted himself to public affairs and was destined to become familiar with traditional court practices and ceremonies, he had been sending messengers to Tadazane (who was confined to the Chisoku Hall and was crippled) and was constantly learning about state affairs. So people around Tadamichi became increasingly suspicious of him. In political circles there were even slanderous charges that because he was the maternal uncle of Emperor Nijō, he probably wanted to become Regent or Chancellor. But he had not yet reached the point of such a fault. In general the odiousness of popular gossip lies in things being said with the implication that there is supporting evidence when there is none whatsoever. This too is something that should be well understood. Then, in the 3rd month of 1166, Korekata too was returned from exile, [which was further evidence of Retired Emperor Go-Shirakawa's loss of influence at court].

Former Chancellor Tadamichi's Daughter Becomes Empress

Meanwhile, Tadamichi's young daughter Ikushi (1146–73)[18] was placed in the Imperial Palace and made Emperor Nijō's Empress. She was appointed his Secondary Empress. The Emperor loved her more than any other woman, but she conceived no children. The Emperor became seriously ill during the 6th month of 1165 and relinquished the throne to his two-year-old son Rokujō. We have not heard who Rokujō's mother was. Ex-Emperor Nijō died, at the age of 23, on the 22nd day of the 7th month of that year.

TAIRA Kiyomori's Rise at Court

Kiyomori was appointed Senior Counselor on the 17th day of the 8th month of 1165 and, having Interim Lord Motozane as his son-in-law, entertained a desire to control all affairs of state. Not long afterward—on the 13th day of the 11th month of 1166—Kiyomori was appointed Minister of the Center, and he was made Prime Minister on the 11th day of the 2nd month of 1167.

Meanwhile, Regent Motozane had died on the 26th day of the 7th month of 1166. Kiyomori was stricken with grief over Motozane's death and could only say: "How can this be?" Then he was approached by FUJIWARA Kunitsuna, a person favored above all others by Tadamichi and a noble who had been promoted to such positions as Governor of Iyo, Governor of Harima, and Assistant Master of the Secondary Empress's Household. This Kunitsuna, a useful man, spoke to Kiyomori as follows:

> Not all of Lord Morozane's legacy should necessarily go to his successor, Regent Motofusa. Actually the FUJIWARA holdings used to be divided but were consolidated at the end of Tadazane's life. So only Tadamichi possessed everything. But Motozane's principal wife [who is your daughter Moriko] is still alive. Furthermore, the young son Motomichi of the deceased Motozane (although not from the womb of his principal wife) is also alive. Therefore it probably would not be improper [for your daughter] to assume personal responsibility for disposing of [her deceased husband's property].

Suddenly Kiyomori brightened up, for he was delighted with what he had heard. Agreeing with what Kunitsuna had said, he arranged to have only a portion of the property passed to Motofusa (Minister of the Left), who was then appointed Regent without any questions being raised. But only the estates of Kōfuku Temple, Hōjō Temple,

18. Actually an adopted daughter.

Byōdō Cloister,[19] and the Academy for the Promotion of Learning
(*kangaku-in*)—together with estates called Shikada and Katagami—
were given to him. The remainder—from the Shimazu estate in
Kyushu on down, plus the diaries and treasures in the Kamoi Mansion that had been passed down from previous generations, and the
East Sanjō Mansion—all became the possessions of Motozane's
widow Moriko. Kunitsuna, Moriko's guardian, was asked to take
care of the young Lord KONOE Motomichi (1160–1233); and while
Motomichi was growing up, all administrative matters were to be
handled by Retired Emperor Go-Shirakawa.

Empress Kenshun-mon In (1142–76), then called Lady Koben,
was the daughter of TAIRA Tokinobu, the sister of TAIRA Kiyomori's
wife and the consort of Retired Emperor Go-Shirakawa. So
Kiyomori gave her special attention. When she gave birth to an Imperial son (the future Emperor Takakura) by the Retired Emperor,
Kiyomori immediately had her son Takakura moved to the East
Sanjō Mansion; and on the 10th day of the 10th month of 1167 he
was appointed Crown Prince. During that year Kiyomori became
seriously ill. He entered the Buddhist priesthood on the 11th day of
the 2nd month of 1168, but he recovered. It was in this same year
that the four-year-old Emperor Rokujō was removed from the
throne and replaced by the eight-year-old Crown Prince Takakura.
The young ex-Emperor Rokujō died at the age of thirteen, even
before he had celebrated his coming of age.

Kunitsuna's eldest daughter, the Mistress Third Rank who was the
wife of FUJIWARA Nariyori, had been Emperor Rokujō's nurse. (An
interesting story has been told about Nariyori entering the Buddhist
priesthood, but there is no point in relating it here.) Kunitsuna's
second daughter, Superintendent Third Rank, had also been Takakura's nurse when he was Crown Prince. Because Kunitsuna had
cleverly planned such associations with Rokujō and Takakura, he
soon became Director of the Imperial Secretariat, Consultant Third
Rank, and Acting Master of the Crown Prince's Household, even
though Lord Hōshō-ji Tadamichi had had no intention of seeing
him advanced as high as Third Rank. After his second daughter
became Takakura's nurse, Kunitsuna was advanced even further: to
Senior Counselor, Senior Grade Second Rank.

TAIRA Kiyomori's sons Shigemori (1138–79) and Munemori
(1147–85) were made Senior Commanders of the Imperial Bodyguards of the Left and Right, and Kiyomori himself was promoted

19. These three temples had been erected and supported by the FUJI-
WARA. The Kōfuku-ji in Nara was the FUJIWARA clan temple; the Hōshō-ji
in Kyoto was built by FUJIWARA Michinaga; and the Byōdō Cloister in Uji
was built by FUJIWARA Yorimichi.

to Prime Minister [in 1167]. Shigemori eventually became Minister
of the Center as well as Senior Commander of the Imperial Bodyguards of the Left. Meanwhile, Retired Emperor Go-Shirakawa had
returned his affections to Empress Kenshun-mon In. Even if we
consider just her case, we will see the truth of the statement that
women are "the finishing touches" of Japan. At first she was Retired
Emperor Go-Shirakawa's consort but was later given the Cloistered
Empress title of an Imperial mother. And she also adopted
Kiyomori's son, Munemori.

Then, on the 14th day of the 12th month of 1171, Lay-Priest
Prime Minister Kiyomori placed his own daughter, the future Empress Kenrei-mon In (1155–1213), in the Imperial Palace; and she
was appointed Emperor Takakura's Secondary Empress on the 10th
day of the 2nd month of 1172.[20] Kiyomori wanted this daughter to
give birth to an Imperial son who could be named Crown Prince and
placed on the throne, enabling Kiyomori—as maternal grandfather
of the reigning Emperor—to handle state affairs in his own way.
Various prayers were offered up for an Imperial grandson. First, a
100-day prayer was made at the Hie Shrine by the Empress's
mother. But because this and other prayers did not have the desired
effect, Kiyomori said, "There are no signs that your prayers will be
answered. Now watch! I will pray and get results!" Having deep faith
in the [ancestral Kami of the TAIRA clan worshipped at] the Itsukushima Shrine in the province of Aki, he had a boat built and
started out on a first-on-the-month pilgrimage from Fukuhara in
order to pray at this ancestral shrine. Only 60 days later Kiyomori
heard that his daughter was pregnant. And on the 11th day of the
11th month of 1178 an Imperial grandson was born at Rokuhara,
just as Kiyomori had wanted. In 1180 this grandson was enthroned
as Emperor Antoku, making Kiyomori the maternal grandfather of
a reigning Emperor.

Retired Emperor Go-Shirakawa
and the Disturbance of 1177

Before the birth of Kiyomori's Imperial grandson, Empress
Kenshun-mon In had caught smallpox and died on the 8th day of

---

20. By arranging this marriage, Kiyomori was moving beyond his earlier
ambition to become the guardian of a FUJIWARA Regent. Now he was aiming
at becoming the guardian of an Emperor—not merely controlling the
FUJIWARA but replacing them. His daughter was placed in the palace when
she was seventeen and when Emperor Takakura was eleven. Six years later,
the daughter gave birth to a child who occupied the throne as Emperor
Antoku from 1180 to 1183.

the 7th month of 1176. Then conditions at the Retired Emperor's palace seem to deteriorate, and the Retired Emperor came to love a man named FUJIWARA Narichika (1138–77).[21] Although this Narichika had gotten into trouble at the time of the Nobuyori incident in 1159 and been exiled, he and all others involved—including Moronaka—had been recalled to the capital because they had demonstrated their loyalty by returning the Sacred Mirror and the small key that Nobuyori had been asked to hand over. Go-Shirakawa favored this Narichika above all others. His Majesty was also served by FUJIWARA Moromitsu and FUJIWARA Narikage, the men who had taken the Buddhist names of Saikō and Saikei at the time of the Shinzei incident. The Retired Emperor gaily called in such comic-play buffs as TAIRA Yasuyori and elevated Shunkan (Superintendent of the Hōshō Temple) to the rank of Vicar General. Possibly because the Retired Emperor hated, and was envious of, the TAIRA for handling state affairs just as they pleased, or because he was uncertain about the Emperor's feelings, he frequently went to Deer Valley in the mountains to the east of the capital where a First Grade priest by the name of Jōken had built a small mountain hut. This Jōken was a Shinzei son who had once been the Superintendent of the Hōshō Temple. Now he was Superintendent of the new Renge-ō Cloister and was a priest in whom the Retired Emperor had great confidence. Because Jōken was a knowledgeable and sincere man who kept things to himself, both the Retired Emperor and the TAIRA Prime Minister used him and talked over matters with him. It was rumored that whenever Go-Shirakawa made a visit to Jōken's secluded hut, Narichika, Saikō, and Shunkan would assemble there to consult with him.

I do not know about the accuracy of the following story, but we are told that [in 1177] the Retired Emperor called in TADA Yukitsuna (an Imperial Secretary descended from MINAMOTO Mitsunaka) and ordered him to make preparations for war [against the TAIRA]. The Retired Emperor also gave him, as the story goes, 30 *tan* of Uji cloth with which to make white MINAMOTO banners. But Yukitsuna took the cloth, instead, to Fukuhara in the province of Settsu where the TAIRA Prime Minister usually stayed after his 1168 entrance into the priesthood—after he had come to feel that his worldly tasks were completed. When Yukitsuna [showed the cloth to Kiyomori] and told him what was being done and said, Kiyomori made no reply but simply seized the cloth, took it to the courtyard, and burned it. Then

21. In 1159, Narichika apparently was saved from exile (or worse) by this Go-Shirakawa attachment and/or the marriage of his sister to TAIRA Shigemori.

he went to the capital and called in and arrested the priest Saikō, one of the Shinzei sons who was serving the Retired Emperor. That seems to have been on the 2nd day of the 6th month of 1177. When Saikō was thoroughly questioned at the Hachijō Mansion, and prodded with bamboo sticks, he confessed everything. And after Saikō was forced to write out a confession and affix his seal, Kiyomori had him taken to the Sujaku highway and beheaded. On that same day, Abbot Myōun of Mt. Hiei brought his priests down the western slope of the mountain as far as Nishi Sakamoto, saying that he had come to support Kiyomori. People were amazed and perplexed.

The day before Saikō was beheaded, Senior Counselor Narichika had been called into the presence of Kiyomori, where he was suddenly grabbed, thrown down, tied up, and placed in confinement by a strong Kiyomori retainer, TAIRA Morikumi's son Moritoshi. Narichika had come to the noblemen's waiting-room where he met TAIRA Shigemori and TAIRA Yorinori; and he said to them: "I was ordered to come here and do something or other." Since this was a time of state mourning over the death of Empress Kenshun-mon In, Narichika was dressed in mourning clothes. Shigemori said, "When you come out, let us talk things over." But since Narichika was grabbed and tied up, Shigemori was taken by surprise; but he went to the room where Narichika was confined and spoke to him, probably because they were brothers-in-law: "This time too I will at least save your life." Apparently that was why Narichika was exiled to the province of Bizen [and not executed]. But after he had been deprived of food for seven days and then given some incomparably strong sake, he suddenly died. Shunkan and TAIRA Yasuyori (an official of the Imperial Police) were exiled to the island of Yuō, where Shunkan died.

An Imperial decree was handed down on the 29th day of the 7th month of 1177 ordering that ex-Emperor Sutoku, who had been exiled to the province of Sanuki in 1156, be given the Cloistered Emperor title *(in)*. Such things were being done because people had become frightened by the activities of Sutoku's vengeful soul. Another Imperial decree ordered that the Imperial Eight Expoundings *(gohakkō)* be held at the Jōshō Temple and that Yorinaga be posthumously promoted to the office of Prime Minister (Senior Grade First Rank).

In that same year the capital suffered from a terrible fire. The flames spread to the Imperial Council Hall, which was burned down. Because of that disaster the era name was changed to Jishō.

Having done the things recounted above, Kiyomori took Saikō's confession and went to Retired Emperor Go-Shirakawa's palace, where he summoned Lord Mitsuyoshi (Commander of the Imperial

Bodyguards of the Right) and made this statement: "I took such measures because of the situation. What I have done was solely for the good of the state and of the sovereign. My own personal concerns were secondary." Then Kiyomori returned immediately to Fukuhara, wearing the same clothes that he had worn when calling at the Retired Emperor's palace.

Death of TAIRA Shigemori in 1179

After that, and while Go-Shirakawa and Mitsuyoshi were wondering how these events would affect the state, Shigemori (Minister of the Center of Komatsu) died on the 1st day of the 8th month of 1179. We hear that Shigemori, being an extremely fine man, had said that he wanted to die soon, when he realized that his father had developed a rebellious heart. For some reason he had not acted in accord with his father's instructions and had done one strange thing: made his son Sukemori a son-in-law of Middle Counselor FUJIWARA Motoie. One day when Sukemori (known as Middle Commander of the Jimyō Cloister, Third Rank) was very young, he slipped out of his mansion when Regent Motofusa was leaving his. Unfortunately their carriages met. Sukemori's carriage was roughed up [by the Regent's retainers] and its bamboo curtain torn. Shigemori deeply resented this. So he placed his soldiers on the alert, and when the Regent was on his way to a coming-of-age ceremony on the 21st day of the 10th month of 1170, Shigemori's soldiers cut off the topknots of the Regent's advance guards. Because of this incident, the coming-of-age ceremony was postponed. There were other strange happenings, and yet there was no criticism of Shigemori for what he did. The Regent resumed his official functions the next day. This was the beginning of a succession of strange events [leading to the downfall of the TAIRA clan].

Rivalry between the SANJŌ and KAZAN'IN Houses

Motofusa was the son-in-law of SANJŌ Kinnori (Minister of the Center), since his principle wife of some years had been Kinnori's daughter. Therefore Kinnori's sons, Sanefusa and Sanekuni, would carry Motofusa's shoes and roll up the curtain of his carriage. They had treated Motofusa very well ever since the days when Tadamichi had been alive. But after Motofusa became Regent in 1166, Prime Minister KAZAN'IN Tadamasa wanted his own daughter to become Motofusa's principal wife. This led to some terrible gossip, for Tadamasa's daughter did become Motofusa's favorite. To them was born Moroie, who was appointed Middle Counselor at the age of eight. After that, SANJŌ Sanefusa behaved only in unlovely ways,

doing such things as merely showing the sleeve of his robe at the
door of a corridor leading to the central gate when Motofusa left his
mansion. But KAZAN'IN Kanemasa acted differently, for his group
followed house etiquette. Alas, ability is singularly important!

Go-Shirakawa and Motofusa Challenge Kiyomori

Lady Shirakawa (TAIRA Moriko and the widow of the deceased
Regent KONOE Motozane) had built a fine house to the west of the
Enshō Temple, but she died on the 17th day of the 6th month of
1179. And within two years of the 1177 incident—on the 1st day of
the 8th month of 1179—TAIRA Shigemori (Minister of the Center of
Komatsu) also died. Whereupon Retired Emperor Go-Shirakawa,
without saying anything to Kiyomori, seized the province of Bizen,
the income from which had for years gone to Shigemori. And after
Lady Shirakawa's death, the property and documents of the
Regent/Chancellor house that had been retained by her were transferred to Regent Motofusa [with no consultation with Kiyomori].
Hearing that the Retired Emperor had taken such steps, and thinking that these actions were connected somehow with what had occurred two years before, Kiyomori immediately mobilized his troops
and left Fukuhara for the capital. It was said that he never removed
his armor again after that.

A cancellation-of-appointments ceremony was held on the 19th
day of the 11th month of 1179, and a new-appointments ceremony
was held on the 21st day of that same month. KONOE Motomichi
(previously Middle Commander Second Rank, and then twenty years
old) was given an accelerated promotion to Minister of the Center,
the position vacated by Shigemori's death and not yet filled. Soon
afterward, Motomichi was appointed Chancellor and Imperial Inspector. Although KUJŌ Kanezane (1147–1207), Minister of the
Right and Tadamichi's third son, had been routinely consulted on
Imperial matters and given a bodyguard, he was passed over when
the Motomichi appointment was made. Moreover, Kanezane was
told to be particularly helpful to the new Chancellor; and Kanezane's
twelve-year-old son Yoshimichi (previously Middle Commander Second Rank) was advanced, in one leap, to Middle Counselor and
Senior Commander of the Imperial Bodyguards of the Right.
Motofusa was not exiled immediately to the province of Bizen, for,
due to Kunitsuna's intercession, he was permitted to call in the priest
Honkaku of Ōhara and to enter the priesthood at the Toba palace.
Those who had served near the Retired Emperor were sent off to
different provinces, and Retired Emperor Go-Shirakawa himself was
moved to the Toba palace on the 20th. Not a single person was assigned to him. Only the priest Rōkei was with the Retired Emperor.

Later on, His Majesty was attended only by his beloved Lady Jōdo-ji Second Rank (Tango).²²

The Prince Mochihito Incident of 1180

Prince Mochihito (1151–80), son of Retired Emperor Go-Shira-kawa by his beloved Lady Takakura Third Rank, had made studies in various fields of learning and was thought to have had his heart set on occupying the throne.²³ Therefore it was ordered, on the 15th day of the 5th month of 1180, that the Prince be sent into exile immediately. An Imperial Police officer named Kanetsuna (son of Third Rank MINAMOTO Yorimasa) was dispatched to execute the order, but when he arrived at the Prince's mansion at Sanjō and Takakura he found that the Prince had fled to Miidera, where the priests had taken the Prince in and closed off the roads leading to the Temple. MINAMOTO Yorimasa had already entered the priest-hood, but now he burned down his house at Konoe and Kawara and, accompanied by his sons Nakatsuna (Governor of Izu) and Kane-tsuna, went to the support of the Prince. People wondered if he had not purposely arranged the Prince's escape. A hubbub erupted and comments such as these were made: "What does this mean? Now is the time for the empire [to crumble]."

Since Prince Mochihito could not stay on at Miidera, he departed for Nara, intending to go on to Mt. Yoshino. MINAMOTO Yorimasa arrived at Miidera on the 22nd and then left for a night attack on Kiyomori's headquarters at Rokuhara. But since he started late and did not arrive at Matsuzaka before daybreak, he was unable to make a night attack. On the 24th he retreated to Uji where he spent the night, and on the 25th the TAIRA advanced to engage him in battle. The Prince's military force was not strong, consisting only of Yorimasa's soldiers. So when the TAIRA crossed the Uji River—using their horses as rafts—what could the Prince and his men do? MINAMOTO Nakatsuna rushed into a corridor of the main hall of the Byōdō Cloister and committed suicide. Then the TAIRA chased the Prince to a place behind the Nieno Lake where they caught and killed him. And MINAMOTO Yorimasa was also killed.

22. She is known as TAKASHINA Eishi (d. 1216), who was first married to a supporter of Go-Shirakawa named TAIRA Narifusa. Narifusa was executed in 1174 for his part in challenging TAIRA control, and soon afterward his wife Eishi became Go-Shirakawa's consort. In 1181, she became the mother, by Go-Shirakawa, of the future Empress Senyō-mon In.

23. Although Retired Emperor Go-Shirakawa was the father of both Takakura (the current Emperor) and Prince Mochihito, TAIRA Kiyomori was the maternal uncle of the former and would have lost his familial ties to the throne if Prince Mochihito had become Emperor.

Not knowing whether the head they had taken was really that of the Prince, the TAIRA showed it to various people who had known him. When the Prince's tutor (Munenari) was called in and asked if he could identify it, he said that it was definitely the Prince's head. But later on some people claimed that the Prince was still alive and that strange things were happening. Others insisted, however, that anyone who believed he was still alive was stupid. And the rumors died out. The TAIRA then attacked Miidera and burned many priestly huts *(bō)*, leaving the halls and houses.

KUJŌ Kanezane Opposes Revenge against Nara

When Prince Mochihito left Miidera, people in Nara and on Mt. Yoshino had made preparations for taking him in. TAIRA Kiyomori resented this. Stating that he wanted to chastise Nara, he called a conference of nobles. Officials such as FUJIWARA Takasue and MINAMOTO Michichika lined up with Kiyomori, and they therefore insisted that Nara should be punished. But ŌIMIKADO Tsunemune and KUJŌ Kanezane, who had been Ministers of the Left and Right for several years, were present; and Kanezane resolutely spoke out against punishment:

> Since there is no definite proof of a plot, we should not recklessly chastise those incomparable temples. Moreover, the Great Il-luminating Kami of the Kasuga Shrine in Nara is Japan's most important guardian Kami. Imperial Law and Buddhist Law are like the two horns of an ox: neither should be destroyed.

When Kanezane spoke in this way, people thought that Tsunemune, a man who stood in awe of ancient customs, would never take such a position. But Tsunemune said: "I do not disagree with a single word spoken by the Minister of the Right. I hold exactly the same view." So in spite of TAIRA pressure, the nobles agreed that the Ministers of the Left and Right were probably right, and the proposal was temporarily dropped.

Capital Moved Twice

The capital was suddenly moved to Fukuhara on the 2nd day of the 6th month of 1180, and Emperor Antoku took up his residence there, creating indescribable confusion. Since matters could not be left as they were, a conference of nobles was held, and on the 23rd day of the 11th month the capital was moved back to Heian. The feelings of the people had settled down a little when, on the 28th day of the 12th month, TAIRA forces invaded Nara and burned down [the temples of Kōfuku and Tōdai]. The Supreme Commander of the operation was TAIRA Shigehira (1157–85), Middle Commander Third Rank. "Disgusting" is not a sufficiently strong word to describe what happened. Middle Counselor Nagakata has said:

When we were thinking that the situation was bad [after the capital was moved to Fukuhara], and it was announced that there would be another conference of nobles, I assumed that Kiyomori would like to have the capital moved back to Heian, and so I said that that would be a proper thing to do.

Rise of MINAMOTO Yoritomo

While these events were taking place, the situation was changing. During the seven or eight days that Prince Mochihito was at Miidera, copies of the Prince's edict were distributed to all provinces and regions of the country. The exiled MINAMOTO Yoritomo (1147–99), Colonel of the Imperial Guards and son of MINAMOTO Yoshitomo, was then in Izu, and he had been thinking deeply about world affairs.

At the time of the Heiji Rebellion of 1159 and 1160, MINAMOTO Yoritomo had been a thirteen-year-old Major of the Imperial Guards. The Rebellion had broken out in the 12th month of 1159, and in the 1st month of 1160 the era name was changed to Eiryaku. On the 19th day of the 2nd month of that year, TAIRA Munekiyo (Major of the Imperial Guards of the Right and a retainer of Yorimori) found Yoritomo and brought him in. Yorimori's mother, Ike no Zen-ni, was a daughter of FUJIWARA Munekane, Provisional Master of the Palace Repairs Office. She was an indescribably beautiful Lady-in-Waiting who had given considerable assistance to her husband TAIRA Tadamori. At the time of the earlier Rebellion of 1156, Yorimori should have allied himself with Retired Emperor Sutoku's cause, for his mother Ike no Zen-ni had been the nurse of Sutoku's eldest son. But Ike no Zen-ni said: "Sutoku will certainly lose! The situation is one in which there is no reason for him to win!" She therefore urged her son Yorimori to support his elder brother Kiyomori. Though she was this kind of a woman, when she saw that Yoritomo was very young and cute, she said weepingly: "Why should his head be cut off? For my sake let him go!" Her request was granted and Yoritomo was exiled to Izu. The course of things is indeed interesting and strange! Did not Yoritomo's reemergence after 1180 occur because he was a man destined to become master of the state? He had a deep trust in Ike no Zen-ni's son TAIRA Yorimori.

Upon seeing a copy of Prince Mochihito's edict, MINAMOTO Yoritomo's hopes were raised: "It's happened! I thought the affairs of this world would turn out like this!" Another account has it that FUJIWARA Mitsuyoshi, realizing what the Retired Emperor had in mind, sent priest Mongaku to tell Yoritomo what the Retired Emperor wanted. Mongaku was the Saint *(shōnin)* who had been exiled to Izu because of going too far in requesting estates for Takao, but he was not an emissary for Mitsuyoshi. Mongaku and his disciples, Jōgaku and

Sengaku, were among the Holy Men *(hijiri)* who had been sent into exile. While Mongaku was close to Yoritomo day and night during the four years the two men were in exile on the Izu peninsula, Mongaku did not receive crafty ideas [from Mitsuyoshi] but made deductions about the inner feelings of people, high and low, and then told Yoritomo what had been deduced.

After Yoritomo mobilized his forces in 1180 and moved to the attack, he was accompanied by KAJIWARA Heizō Kagetoki, DOI Jirō Sanehira, and his father-in-law HŌJŌ Shirō Tokimasa of Izu. With the backing of these men Yoritomo intended to subjugate the eastern provinces, but because the TAIRA had been in control of the state for a long time, the TAIRA had a large number of retainers even in these eastern provinces, including the two HATAKEYAMA brothers (Shigenori and Arishige). Since the HATAKEYAMA brothers were then at the capital, Shigenori's son Shigetada came to engage Yoritomo's forces in battle, chasing Yoritomo into the Hakone mountains and bottling him up. Because Yoritomo had become discouraged enough to take off his armor, DOI Sanehira—an old man—said: "There is a proper way for a great Shogun to remove his armor." He took a pine limb, placed it under the armor, and then put the helmet on the limb. We are told that Sanehira's behavior was magnificent. After that, Yoritomo boarded a boat with his retainers, proceeded to the stronghold of Hachirō Hirotsune (Deputy Governor of Kazusa), and received Hirotsune's support. Then everyone in the eastern provinces placed himself under Yoritomo. The MIURA group, on its way to Yoritomo's base, fought and conquered the HATAKEYAMA. Thenceforth Yoritomo's forces were concentrated in one area.

In the northern provinces, MINAMOTO Yoshinaka (1154–84)—the "peerless man of Kiso" who was the son of MINAMOTO Yoshikata (Master of the Crown Prince's Household)—mobilized troops and allied himself with Yoritomo. Others, such as the Prince Mochihito's son, also joined Yoritomo. TAIRA Kiyomori, on the other hand, had captured and killed Prince Mochihito and, feeling increasingly confident, did the things recounted above. But after the MINAMOTO assembled their forces in the eastern provinces, creating a national crisis, Kiyomori dispatched an expeditionary force under the command of TAIRA Koremori (Shigemori's eldest son and a Middle Counselor Third Rank) and had an "attack-and-kill" edict handed down. When Koremori left the capital on the 21st day of the 9th month of 1180 saying that he would destroy Yoritomo, people came out to see him off. But without even participating in the battle of Ukishimabara of Suruga, Koremori's troops—accompanied by soldiers from the eastern provinces—defected to the enemy. Those who did not defect entered the capital in a state of flight and confusion. Then Lay-Priest Prime Minister TAIRA Kiyomori became seriously ill with a fever and died shortly afterward—on the 5th day of the intercalary 2nd month of 1181. The conduct of state affairs reverted, after Kiyomori's death, to the Retired Emperor Go-Shirakawa; and TAIRA Munemori, Minister of the Center, fell heir to the headship of the TAIRA house.

Before this, on the 14th day of the 1st month of 1181, ex-Emperor Takakura had also died. As days passed, the eastern provinces and the northern region were occupied by MINAMOTO forces. The TAIRA were reportedly making preparations that would insure victory, but the sympathies of all—high and low—were with the MINAMOTO. Then it was heard that the MINAMOTO were gradually gaining the upper hand. It was, however, not until the 7th month of 1183—in the third year after Kiyomori's death—that MINAMOTO troops from the northern region first advanced toward the capital, filling the province of Ōmi. Some TAIRA had been sent to Echizen to oppose the MINAMOTO, but they were repulsed and dispersed, having been stopped at the battle of Tonami. Meanwhile, Emperor Antoku was moved—since the situation had become so serious—to the TAIRA headquarters in Rokuhara on the 24th day of the 7th month of 1183; and TAIRA leaders assembled there. TAIRA Yorimori (Senior Counselor) was asked to guard the Yamashina entrance to the capital, but he begged off several times, saying:

> In the winter of 1179 I heard some bad things [about my siding with Motofusa], and so I told Kiyomori that I would never again become engaged in battle. And when I heard about the order that the capital was to be moved to Fukuhara, I said that I would not serve under such circumstances.

But because Munemori (Minister of the Center) would not listen to Yorimori, and pressed him to take the assignment, Yorimori was forced to leave for Yamashina.

The Retired Emperor Leaves the Capital

Since it was felt that MINAMOTO Yoshinaka, TAKEDA of the eastern provinces, and others would be entering the capital any day, people were afraid that a great battle was going to be fought within the capital. So, in the middle of the night of the 24th day [of the 7th month of 1183], Retired Emperor Go-Shirakawa secretly left his Hōjū-ji palace and went to Yokawa of Mt. Hiei by way of Kurama. This was reported to the MINAMOTO forces of Ōmi. A low-ranking soldier of the Retired Emperor's guard—a person named Tomoyasu but nicknamed "the Imperial guard drummer"—was said to have been in attendance upon Go-Shirakawa at the time, doing such things as helping to carry His Majesty's palanquin. At dawn of the night in which the Retired Emperor left his palace in the capital, Rokuhara was in turmoil, since the TAIRA had noticed that strange things were going on. And within a few hours TAIRA Munemori and his entire group could do nothing but take the Emperor and flee to Toba, where they boarded boats and departed for Shikoku. Because the houses of Rokuhara were burned, thieves appeared in the capital, dashing into the burning houses to steal.

The TAIRA Escape

Meanwhile, reports of the TAIRA escape had reached the ears of TAIRA Yorimori at Yamashina. Learning of what had happened, he sent his eldest son Tamemori (Colonel of the Imperial Guards) to contact the fleeing TAIRA. When Tamemori caught up with them at Toba and asked why they were fleeing, they could not even reply. Noting that they had lost heart, Tamemori ran back to report. Although Yorimori left the capital intending to overtake his fellow clansmen, he did not really want to leave. One other member of the TAIRA clan, Sukemori (Middle Counselor Third Rank), had prospered because of favors extended to him by the Retired Emperor and therefore decided to ask the Retired Emperor for help. When he and Yorimori returned to the capital from Toba and entered the Retired Emperor's palace, they found the uproar there earthshaking. When their return was reported to the Retired Emperor on Mt. Hiei, His Majesty had this word sent to Yorimori: "I have received your message. I have long felt that you would decide to stay. Go unobtrusively to Empress Hachijō In's palace." Since Empress Hachijō In's original nurse Saishō (wife of Senior High Priest Kanga) was also the mother of Yorimori's wife, and Yorimori had become Empress Hachijō In's guardian, the Retired Emperor decided that Yorimori should now stay with the Empress. Sukemori, on the other hand, had no one to intercede for him. He did not even receive a reply to the message that he had sent the Retired Emperor. He therefore fled with the TAIRA.

The Retired Emperor and His Supporters

When Retired Emperor Go-Shirakawa had gone to the Enyū hut within the eastern section of Mt. Hiei on the 25th, people said that it would be bad for Tendai Abbot Myōun to remain on, since he had for years been the guardian priest of the TAIRA clan. But instead of fleeing with the TAIRA, he returned to Mt. Hiei. He did not, however, approach the Retired Emperor. Even though the people at the capital also felt that Motomichi (Lord KONOE who was then Regent) would surely flee with the TAIRA, they were wrong. He stayed on and went up to Mt. Hiei. Motofusa (the Lord Lay Priest of Matsu), Minister KUJŌ Kanezane, and others joined the Retired Emperor's supporters on Mt. Hiei.

Within the capital there was so much pillage that it seemed that nothing of value would be left. But since all members of the TAIRA clan had fled, removing the fear [that battles would be fought within the capital], the Retired Emperor returned to the capital early in the morning of the 26th. TAKEDA, who had fought his way into Ōmi, was the first to call on His Majesty. Next came MINAMOTO Yoshinaka who also entered the capital on the 26th. Yoshinaka was given the house of "the nun of Hahaki" (a Lady-in-Waiting who served Empress Hachijō In), a house located at Rokujō and Horikawa.

Emperor Antoku's Successor

At the time of this confusion at the capital, Emperor Antoku— along with the Imperial Jewel, the Imperial Sword, and the Sacred Mirror—was retreating toward the western provinces. People wondered if it was right not to have an emperor in the capital, causing them to express such views as this: "Since the Retired Emperor—an Imperial father—is alive, shouldn't we wait and take up the question of succession when it is learned whether the Emperor, who has been taken off to the western provinces, is safe." Meanwhile, the Retired Emperor was consulting with such officials as the Ministers of the Left and Right (Tsunemune and Kanezane), the Lord Lay Priest of Matsu (Motofusa), and others. But His Majesty claimed that what the Minister of the Right (KUJŌ Kanezane) told him was particularly clear. The Retired Emperor was really making use of him.

Realizing that a new emperor had to be selected, Go-Shirakawa considered three sons of ex-Emperor Takakura. One of them (Prince Morisada) had been taken on the boat with the retreating TAIRA, since he had been brought up by Kiyomori's wife Tokiko (Rokuhara Second Rank). The other two (Prince Koreakira and Prince Takanari) were still in the capital, and so the Retired Emperor called them in for an interview. When ex-Emperor Takakura's fourth son, Prince Takanari, came forward, he did so without any shyness. Moreover, the diviners said that this Prince would be a good choice.[24] Therefore Prince Takanari was enthroned as Emperor Go-Toba on the 20th day of the 8th month of 1183. Many new precedents were established then, but Retired Emperor Go-Shirakawa, consulting with various nobles, paid special attention to what the Minister of the Right (KUJŌ Kanezane) had to say.[25] Thus did a new emperor appear.

24. Prince Koreakira had a TAIRA mother, but Prince Takanari's mother was a FUJIWARA.

25. Kanezane's diary (the *Gyokuyō*) suggests that Kanezane did not have much to do with the selection of Go-Toba in 1183. In an entry for the 30th day of the 7th month, Kanezane wrote that he had urged the immediate enthronement of a new Emperor. On the 6th day of the 8th month, a decision had not yet been made. Go-Shirakawa was still wondering whether it would

KONOE *Motomichi Reappointed Regent*

Knowing that the state would somehow settle down, and that events in Japan would develop in this way, this [Kanezane] sort of man should have been appointed Regent. But as soon as the Retired Emperor came down from Mt. Hiei, he issued an order that Lord KONOE Motomichi (1160–1223) be reappointed Regent. Whether Lord KONOE was selected because he had stayed on in the capital when he should have fled with the TAIRA, or for some other reason, he was not a man who could handle that kind of a situation.[26] Whenever there was a matter with which he was the least bit unfamiliar, he would deal with it in consultation with the Minister of the Right (Kanezane). So Motomichi was only Regent in name. TAIRA Kiyomori had appointed him Regent, and then Chancellor, [simply] because he had received title to the estates of his stepmother: TAIRA Moriko, who was younger than he was. The

---

not be best to wait for the return of Antoku and the Imperial Regalia. On the 10th of that month, Kanezane reported that there was another meeting at Go-Shirakawa's palace. Only then was it finally decided that a new Emperor should be placed on the throne. But Go-Shirakawa and the victorious MINAMOTO Yoshinaka proposed different candidates. Go-Shirakawa wanted one of the two Takakura sons still in the capital, but Yoshinaka pressed the candidacy of Prince Mochihito's son, Prince Kiso. In an entry for the 14th of that month, the diary reports that Go-Shirakawa sent a messenger to ask for Kanezane's advice and that Kanezane refused to express his views on the matter, preferring to leave the decision to Go-Shirakawa. On the 18th, Kanezane said that another conference had been held but that he did not attend. Other consultations are mentioned and references are made to the use of diviners, but nothing is said about Go-Shirakawa's calling in the two boys for an interview—this is mentioned, however, in the *Heiki monogatari*. [*Gyokuyō*, 2.612–618 and *Heike monogatari*, NKBT, 33.621–622.]

Why did Jien not include any of the details found in his brother's diary when he was writing about the selection of Go-Toba in 1183? Since it is thought that Jien was addressing the *Gukanshō*, first of all, to Go-Toba, it is deduced that Jien was not averse to leaving the impression that KUJŌ Kanezane had been largely responsible for Go-Toba's enthronement. [NKBT, 86.499–500.]

26. MATSU Motofusa's son Moroie was appointed Regent shortly after Go-Toba's enthronement in 1183, but KONOE Motomichi was reappointed Regent on the 22nd day of the 1st month of 1184. In a *Gyokuyō* entry for the 2nd day of the 8th month of 1183, KUJŌ Kanezane gives two reasons why Go-Shirakawa did not reject Motomichi, who had been Regent under the TAIRA and under MINAMOTO Yoshinaka: (1) Motomichi heard, around the 20th of the previous month, that TAIRA Munemori and TAIRA Shigehira were secretly thinking of taking Go-Shirakawa with them when they retreated from the capital, and Motomichi had passed this information on to Go-Shirakawa; and (2) Go-Shirakawa had feelings of love for the charming Motomichi. [*Gyokuyō*, 2.613.]

more that came to light, the more everyone realized that this Moto-michi was a man with absolutely no understanding. The state had reached this level of disorder because it was a time (*jisetsu*) when nothing good would happen. Not since Regents and Chancellors had first been appointed had there been a Regent or Chancellor who had such useless abilities as Motomichi. In such a way was the state being ruined.

FUJIWARA *Norisue and the Throne*

FUJIWARA Norisue (d. 1205)—posthumously appointed Minister of the Left—has told this story:

At the time when the MINAMOTO were pouring into the province of Ōmi and the TAIRA headquarters at Rokuhara were in a state of confusion, the Retired Emperor secluded himself in the Ima Kumano Shrine. Since I had been called in to serve as his aide, I found a time when he was not busy to speak to him as follows: "No matter what the TAIRA do, they are no match for the MINAMOTO. This is because all MINAMOTO soldiers in the eastern provinces—down to the ordinary recruits—are well trained in the use of bows and arrows. Shouldn't you therefore take steps to drop the TAIRA?" Whereupon the Retired Emperor smiled and said: "Now is the time to do just that."

That had been the Retired Emperor's plan from the start.

This FUJIWARA Norisue, having been in charge of Go-Toba's up-bringing, was given the responsibility for handling court affairs after Go-Toba was enthroned in 1183. Although Norisue had risen as high as Second Rank, he later became father of the present Emperor [Juntoku's][27] Imperial mother Shigeko. That was why he was post-humously appointed Minister of the Left.

FUJIWARA Norisue also had a niece by the name of Noriko (Lady Gyōbu Third Rank) who was the wife of Priest Nōen. This Nōen became the father of Empress Shōmei-mon In (1171–1257), Emperor Tsuchimikado's Imperial mother, and Noriko was the mother of that Imperial mother. Noriko was also Go-Toba's nurse. But since Nōen was the adopted son of TAIRA Kiyomori's wife (Rokuhara Second Rank), he fled from the capital with the TAIRA, forcing his wife Noriko to turn to her uncle (FUJIWARA Norisue) for support. Later, Minister of the Center MINAMOTO Michichika (1145–1202) took an interest in Noriko, and by him she gave birth to several children. And since Noriko was also the elder sister of Kaneko (Lady Second

27. Since "the present Emperor" obviously refers to Juntoku, and Jun-toku's reign ended in 1221, this is one of the many *Gukanshō* references which suggest that this work was written while Juntoku was on the throne.

Rank),[28] she was very close to Retired Emperor Go-Toba. Noriko was a woman of such good fortune![29]

Conflict between MINAMOTO *Yoshinaka and Retired Emperor Go-Shirakawa*

Meanwhile, MINAMOTO Yoshinaka of Kiso [who had entered the capital in the 7th month of 1183] came to regard his cousin Yoritomo as his enemy. The TAIRA clan, based in the western seas, was intent then upon reentering the capital. Rumor had it that TAIRA leaders and Yoshinaka were exchanging views, joining forces, and planning to move against Yoritomo in the eastern provinces. While people were whispering among themselves and saying that there was no truth to these rumors, Tomoyasu and Kimitomo (low-ranking guards at Retired Emperor Go-Shirakawa's palace) were earnestly cultivating their warrior spirit. Convinced that Yoritomo was the man of the future—a person with a truly fine personality— they placed their confidence in him and waited for his entrance into the capital. Feeling too that Yoshinaka had a doubtful future, they made Go-Shirakawa's Hōjū-ji Palace into a fortress and filled it with soldiers collected from the MINAMOTO clan and from various temples and monasteries. Abbot Myōun of Mt. Hiei also came to the Retired Emperor's palace, bringing the armed priests of Mt. Hiei. The Hōjū-ji defenses were therefore greatly strengthened.

Yoshinaka was also feeling that the time had come for a showdown. He was served by four groups of retainers (YAMADA, HIGUCHI,

28. The name Kaneko is preceded in the text by the character for "deceased," although Kaneko did not die until 1229 and the *Gukanshō* is thought to have been written in 1219. Mr. Ishida concludes that the character was added later when the text was being edited or copied. [*Kenkyū Nempō*, pp. 2–28.]

29. Noriko's change of husbands was connected with the shift of control from the TAIRA to the MINAMOTO:

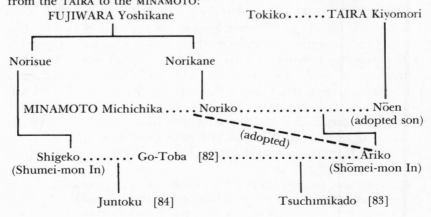

TATE, and NENOI) but apparently felt that he would eventually be forced to retreat from the capital and that he had better do something before that became necessary. So, on the 19th day of the 11th month of 1183, he made a sudden attack upon the Retired Emperor's Hōjū-ji Palace with a force reportedly made up of 500 horsemen from a total of 1,000. On his side was a MINAMOTO clansman named Chief Saburō. The fact that Yoshinaka's position had become so [uncertain], and everybody was going over to the Retired Emperor's side, made Chief Saburō more devoted to Yoshinaka than ever. This loyal retainer had a heavy barrage of arrows shot at some of Abbot Myōun's priestly soldiers who were defending the Saishōkō Cloister, forcing the Abbot's men to retreat in confusion. Chief Saburō pursued and scattered these forces and captured all the high-ranking nobles and princes [who had sided with the Retired Emperor]. One noble above the Fifth rank, FUJIWARA Nobuyuki (Governor of Mino), was killed in that battle, but no other high-ranking nobleman lost his life. All the rather prominent soldiers supporting the Retired Emperor fled, and Go-Shirakawa himself secluded himself in the Shōjōkō Cloister. [Chief Saburō's] soldiers came to Go-Shirakawa and respectfully made arrangements for him to reside at Nobunari's house, which was located beside Yoshinaka's mansion on the Rokujō. That is now called the Rokujō Palace.

Fate of the Priests Who Supported Go-Shirakawa

Abbott Myōun of Mt. Hiei and Prince Hachijō of Miidera (son of Retired Emperor Go-Shirakawa) were both killed at that time. Myōun's head was found at the West Tōin River and claimed by priest Kenshin.[30] A man who was with Myōun at the time, and who saw his defeat, has described what transpired:

> Myōun was at Go-Shirakawa's palace when he heard that soldiers defending the palace had fled. Wearing a yellow Buddhist surplice over his long silk robe and not being able to find anyone to carry his palanquin, he mounted a horse and, accompanied by only a few disciples, fled southward along the western wall of the Renge-ō Cloister. An arrow struck him on the hip above the rim of the saddle. When it was pulled from his back, blood flowed from the area where his *obi* had been tied. At a well in a field toward the southern end of the Cloister, Myōun fell from his horse, and soldiers chased him with drawn bows.

Among the disciples fleeing with him was the fifteen- or sixteen-year-old Go-Shirakawa son who was later known as Prince Kajii and who (as Princely Priest Shōnin) held the position of Tendai Abbot

30. Kenshin (1131–92) was appointed Tendai Abbot in 1190, and Jien received that same post after Kenshin's death in 1192.

for a time. Because the young Prince cleverly said: "I am a Prince," he was taken alive. He was reportedly placed on a Chinese chest in the small house of a soldier. Someone has also told this story:

> A man accompanying Princely Priest En'e (1152–83)[31] at the time made the mistake of advising him to remove his Buddhist surplice and to put on a simple blue garment. Therefore when Yoshinaka's soldiers overtook him, they moved to kill him. But behind the Prince was a priest called Junior Commander Priest who had served near the Prince and was the elder brother of MINAMOTO Toshimitsu, Director of the Imperial Stables at the Retired Emperor's palace. I heard the priest say, "I am the priestly elder brother of Toshimitsu," and I saw him spread his arms to protect the Prince and get his arms cut off.

When the soldiers who had taken Myōun's head made their report to Yoshinaka, Yoshinaka seems to have said: "I don't care what is done with such a man!" Myōun's head was then thrown into the West Tōin River.

People also say that Princely Priest Shukaku (1150–1202)[32] of Ninna Temple, who was in Go-Shirakawa's presence at the time, was the first to flee and that what he did was despicable.

Myōun had fought with Kaishū[33] over the position of Abbot at Mt. Hiei [in 1167], and as a result of the struggle between them the bodies of 48 dead men were strewn over the snow between the Gobutsu Cloister and the Western Pagoda of Mt. Hiei. Myōun was a person who did one evil thing after another. We hear that on the day Saikō's head was taken [in 1177], Myōun led his priests down to the western slope (Nishi Sakamoto) of Mt. Hiei, saying that he had come to the support of Kiyomori.[34] We also hear that Lay Priest TAIRA Kiyomori spread mats in his garden and offered prayers [to the guardian Kami of Mt. Hiei] until he could see the torches of Myōun's priests climbing back up the mountain. Since Myōun had acted in such a way, many people were naturally very critical, even though they lived in the Final Age. And they declared [in 1183] that "His taking up arms again today is not right."

31. En'e (referred to here as Prince Hachijō) was a Go-Shirakawa son who was appointed Intendant of the Shitennō Temple in 1168. When his brother Prince Mochihito agreed to head a move against the TAIRA in 1180, En'e tried but failed to dissuade him. Because of Prince Mochihito's opposition, En'e lost his position at the Shitennō-ji. Then when MINAMOTO Yoshinaka attacked Go-Shirakawa in 1183, En'e joined Myōun in supporting the Retired Emperor.

32. Another Go-Shirakawa son.

33. Kaishū was Tendai Abbot before, and Myōun after, the battle of 1167.

34. The incident is discussed earlier in this chapter.

Princely Priest En'e of Miidera had carried out the Revered Star Mass [before the 1183 battle between the forces of Yoshinaka and Go-Shirakawa], and it is said that he swore an oath that "If something is destined to happen [to my father] the Retired Emperor, I want to take that misfortune upon myself." It was also reported that En'e was among those who had flushed Prince Mochihito from Miidera Temple [in 1180]. There is absolutely no doubt but that the later conflict between Go-Shirakawa and MINAMOTO Yoshinaka was the work of demons *(tengu)*. Since the hearts of men had become extremely bad, no man was a divine-grace vessel—even for Buddhist Law—that could be used to quiet those demons. Not a thing could be done about it!

Moroie Appointed Regent

MINAMOTO Yoshinaka soon made MATSU Motofusa's (1144–1230) twelve-year-old son Moroie (1172–1238) Minister of the Center, Regent, and head of the FUJIWARA clan. This was the boy who was called the "eight-year-old Middle Counselor," since he was appointed to that position at the age of eight. [In 1183] there had been no ministerial vacancy, and so Yoshinaka asked FUJIWARA Sanesada (1139–91) to lend his Minister-of-the-Center position to Moroie temporarily. Thus Moroie was referred to in official circles as "the holder of the borrowed post of Minister." [Because Moroie was so young, his father] Lord MATSU Motofusa had to administer state affairs in his behalf. Motofusa probably wished to assume those responsibilities just this once, since he had been under the TAIRA shadow for several years.

Motofusa carried out the installation ceremony, considered what would be "good administration," and appointed Toshitsune to the position of Consultant. Because such a situation had developed and all estate documents of the FUJIWARA house were being handled now by Lord MATSU Motofusa, Lord KONOE Motomichi became despondent. Feeling that Motomichi was a fine man, the Retired Emperor asked Motofusa to let Motomichi have at least the Empress Kaya no In estates that had been inherited by Motomichi's father Motozane (the adopted son of Empress Kaya no In). Even in that age, the Retired Emperor made such requests. Motofusa's reply that it was improper to do such a thing was resented by Go-Shirakawa. It was truly despicable that a man like Motofusa should have desired, in Yoshinaka's day, to govern the state indefinitely. Fortunately, Lord KUJŌ Kanezane had not been selected—at that time—to assume this role. Instead, the responsibility was given to MATSU Motofusa by the wretched device of appointing his twelve-year-old son Moroie to the position of Regent and allowing Motofusa to take over the duties of that office in his son's behalf. Declaring this to be a "very serious matter," KUJŌ Kanezane was delighted that the Buddhas and the Kami had helped him to avoid [such shame].³⁵

MINAMOTO *Yoshitsune Occupies the Capital*

Not long afterward, and while Yoritomo was hearing reports of what was going on at the capital, he assigned DOI Sanehira, KAJI-WARA Kagetoki, and NAKAHARA Chikayoshi (Deputy Director) to his young brother Yoshitsune (1159–91). These generals moved their troops toward the capital and fought their way into it without difficulty on the 20th day of the 1st month of 1184. They defeated Yoshinaka's forces and took his head on that same day. Having previously heard that soldiers of the eastern provinces were advancing toward the capital, Yoshinaka made extensive plans and deployed his retainers for the defense of Seta, Uji, and Yodo. But when he heard that Yoshitsune and Chikayoshi were pressing toward the capital from Uji and had taken up positions along the banks of the Kamo River, he left the capital accompanied by only four horsemen. After this precipitate retreat, Yoshinaka fell back toward Ōtsu, intending to join his forces at Seta. But Yoshitsune pursued him and chased him into the rice fields of Ōtsu. Then a report was received that a retainer by the name of Saburō of Ise had killed Yoshinaka.³⁶ When the head was brought in, Retired Emperor Go-Shirakawa went by carriage to the gate of his palace to see it.

35. Jien again favors his brother Kanezane, although two older brothers had also held the post of Regent/Chancellor and headed a FUJIWARA house:

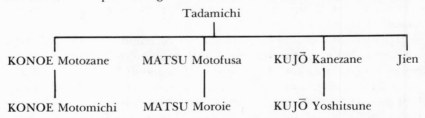

Tadamichi

KONOE Motozane   MATSU Motofusa   KUJŌ Kanezane   Jien

KONOE Motomichi   MATSU Moroie   KUJŌ Yoshitsune

Since Motozane, Motofusa, and Motomichi had served as Regent or Chancellor while the TAIRA were in power between 1158 and 1183—and Moroie and Motomichi were Regents between 1183 and 1186—Kanezane was left uncontaminated, as Jien might have put it, by associations with defeated military leaders. Kanezane, on the other hand, was elevated to the highest ministerial position after 1186 by MINAMOTO Yoritomo. Because Jien's preeminence as a Buddhist priest, reaching a high point with an appointment as Tendai Abbot in 1192, was due largely to the backing of Kanezane and MINAMOTO Yoritomo, Jien identified himself with the KUJŌ house and was very critical of his half-brothers and their sons.

36. Both the *Azuma Kagami* and the *Heike Monogatari* state that ISHIDA Tamehisa was the one who beheaded Yoshinaka. No other known source corroborates the *Gukanshō* statement that this was done by Yoshitsune's retainer ISE Saburō. [NKBT, 86.503, note 206.]

TAIRA Munemori (1147–85),[37] Minister of the Center, was then moving toward the capital from the western provinces accompanied by his sovereign [Emperor Antoku]. His purpose was to join forces with Yoshinaka. When he arrived at Fukuhara, Yoritomo's retainers advanced immediately to engage him in a battle that was fought on the 6th day of the 2nd month of 1184. At a place called Ichi no Tani, Munemori was attacked from the rear by MINAMOTO Yoshitsune. (Because this Yoshitsune had the same name as Kanezane's son Yoshitsune,[38] the name of the former was later changed to Yoshiaki.) From Ichi no Tani, MINAMOTO Yoshitsune moved against the TAIRA and captured TAIRA Shigehira, the Supreme Commander who had burned the Tōdai Temple of Nara [in 1180].[39] About ten other TAIRA leaders were killed that day, including Michimori (son of Middle Counselor Norimori) and Tadanori Third Rank. TAIRA Munemori stumbled into a boat and escaped.[40]

Quieting the Vengeful Souls of Emperor Sutoku and Yorinaga

Not long afterward, on the 16th day of the 4th month of 1184, a shrine was built for quieting the vengeful souls of the deceased Emperor Sutoku and Yorinaga. Yorinaga had already been posthumously appointed Prime Minister.[41] The buildings of the shrine were placed on the bank of the Kasuga River where the battle of 1156 had been fought. FUJIWARA Norisue carried out the building of the shrine, and as a result the "soul snakes" [of Sutoku and Yorinaga] came out. It was also rumored that URABE Kanetomo, Vice Minister of the Department of Religion and the official in charge of the shrine, had a dream in which messages from [Sutoku and Yorinaga] were received. One reason for deciding to build this shrine was that people had come to feel that Yoshinaka's attack against Retired Em-

37. TAIRA Kiyomori's second son.
38. Yoshitsune (1169–1206) was KUJŌ Kanezane's heir and was appointed Regent in 1202.
39. TAIRA Shigehira's execution is discussed in a later section of this chapter.
40. These TAIRA men were related to each other as follows:

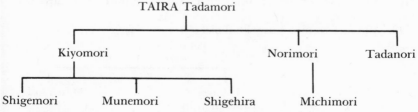

41. Cf. Chapter 2 for comments about Yorinaga's defeat in the Hōgen Rebellion of 1156.

peror Go-Shirakawa's Hōjū-ji Palace had been the work of demons [and vengeful souls], but the building of the shrine was rushed because people were saying that the vengeful soul of ex-Emperor Sutoku was terrifying. Since Lady Karasuma (Sutoku's favorite consort) was still alive, she also erected a place at her mansion near the Kamo River—at Aya no Kōgi—where a likeness of Sutoku was enshrined and where it was rumored that various signs [of soul vengeance] had been seen.

TAIRA Defeat and the Imperial Regalia

As such things were occurring, the TAIRA clan—now in boats on the seas of the western provinces—was still in possession of several provinces in that region. In the eastern provinces there was a lull in the fighting, but the situation had not yet settled down. And at the capital people were quite distraught. Then reports were heard that because preparations were being made for a naval engagement, the time for a showdown was at hand. Yoritomo's soldiers poured into the capital on their way to the western provinces, and on the 24th day of the 3rd month of 1185 a naval battle was fought at Dan no Ura, near the Moji barrier of the Nagato Province. Carrying Emperor Antoku in her arms and holding the Sacred Jewel and the Imperial Sword, the Imperial Grandmother Second Rank Tokiko,[42] Munemori's mother, jumped into the sea. She was indeed a fine Lady-in-Waiting! Minister of the Center Munemori and all TAIRA clansmen went overboard. But Munemori, being an able swimmer and wanting to live, remained afloat and was eventually captured.

Antoku's Imperial mother, Empress Kenrei-mon In, was removed from the sea and saved. The Sacred Jewel and the Imperial Mirror were returned to the capital on the 25th day of the 4th month of that year. The Imperial Sword, on the other hand, sank into the sea. The box containing the Sacred Jewel had floated on the water and was picked up by a soldier who brought it to FUJIWARA Koreaki's daughter of the Handmaids' Office. The Imperial Mirror was removed from the water by a Senior Counselor by the name of TAIRA Tokitada, an elder brother of the Imperial Grandmother. TAIRA Tokinobu's son Tokitada was one of those who had accompanied Munemori and served the Emperor. Since he had done only crafty

42. Antoku's connections with Tokiko were:

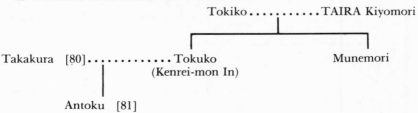

things, he had been exiled several times.[43] Taking all these prisoners and Imperial Regalia with them, the MINAMOTO returned to the capital. Having also captured Prince Morisada (second son of Emperor Takakura), they placed him in the care of Empress Jōsai-mon In. Rumors circulated about the Imperial Sword but it was never found, even though female divers were used to look for it.[44] The situation then was something that cannot be written about exhaustively, no matter how hard one tries. It is probably something only for the exercise of one's imagination. Since events not crucial to an incident are unimportant, I will simply drop the subject.

Why Emperor Antoku Was Drowned

The sovereign at that time was subsequently called Emperor Antoku. How do we explain his drowning? The birth of this sovereign was an act of divine grace performed by the Great Shining Kami of Itsukushima Shrine in the province of Aki, an act brought about by the prayers of TAIRA Kiyomori.[45] Word has come down to us that the Kami of this Itsukushima Shrine was a daughter of the Dragon King.[46] In response to Kiyomori's faith, this Kami was incarnated as Emperor Antoku. People acquainted with the situation said: "At last she has returned to the sea!"[47] It is thought that that is what happened.

43. Cf. note 14, above.

44. Kanezane's diary states that the court sent offerings to 22 of the most important shrines in 1185 and requested that the priests pray for the return of the Imperial Sword. [*Gyokuyō*, 5–6–1185, 3.81.]

45. Discussed earlier in this chapter.

46. A reference to the old myth that the Imperial Sword had been taken from the tail of a dragon by Susa no Ō no Mikoto.

47. The *Heike Monogatari* section on the loss of the Imperial Sword in 1185 closes in this vein:

Learned men of that day have this to say:
The Sun Goddess vowed to protect the one hundred sovereigns of Japan, a vow that has not been altered. As long as the blessings of Hachiman (worshipped at the Iwashimizu Hachiman Shrine) continue to flow, the light of the Sun Goddess will not cease to shine on this land. Although we live in the deteriorated days of the final reigns, we probably have not come to the end of the Imperial destiny.

Then one of these learned men added this comment:
The great dragon that was killed by Susa no Ō no Mikoto on the upper Hino River in the province of Izuma must have felt deep resentment over the loss of the Sacred Sword [which Susa no Ō no Mikoto had taken from its tail]. As is suggested by the dragon's eight heads and eight tails, the dragon was to take back the Sacred Sword after the 80th reign, when the new Emperor was eight years old, and return to the bottom of the sea.

Since the Sacred Sword has again become the divine dragon's treasure, it is understood that the Sacred Sword is not to be possessed by man a second time. [NKBT, 33.348–349.]

Why the Imperial Sword Was Lost

The loss of the Imperial Sword was a really sad thing for Imperial Law. In turning over the thought that a Principle had probably been created which would enable us to understand this event, I have come to the conclusion that since present conditions have taken such a form, and soldiers have emerged for the purpose of protecting the sovereign, the Imperial Sword turned its protective function over to soldiers and disappeared into the sea. One reason for reaching this conclusion is that a sword called the long sword *(tachi)* was a soldier's original military weapon, and so the Imperial Sword became the Emperor's military protective talisman. The nation's sovereign rules the state by following two ways: the way of military might *(bu)*, and the way of learning *(bun)*. The way of learning is associated with the Emperor in the phrase: "He inherits the throne and protects learning," and so a Confucian scholar is customarily attached to the Emperor. (This scholar is called a tutor [*gakushi*] when attached to a Crown Prince, and a reader [*jitoku*] when attached to the Emperor.) With respect to the military way of ruling the state, the two ancestral Kami of the Imperial House have provided protection—until these final reigns—with this Imperial talisman. But then the Sun Goddess and the Great Hachiman Bodhisattva reached this agreement: "Clearly there is now a time fate *(jiun)* which makes it impossible, since great military Shoguns have definitely gained control of the state, for the country's ruler to survive if he openly opposes the wishes of the great military Shoguns." Consequently, the Imperial Sword no longer has a function to perform. Emperor Takakura was placed on the throne by the TAIRA clan in 1168, and the Imperial military talisman was finally lost in 1185. Understanding clearly why the Imperial military talisman was lost, I have come to feel deeply about conditions of the present age.

Deterioration and Improvement

In general the destiny of man (high and low) and the time fate *(jiun)* of the three ages (past, present, and future) move spontaneously and naturally *(hōni jinen)* [toward deterioration]. Consequently some will think that there is no reason to accept what I have written here, even though I have thought about and fitted things together carefully in this way. But Principles of cause and effect in the past, present, and future have definitely been created. These Principles, and the time fate of the three ages moving toward deterioration spontaneously and naturally, were created together from the beginning. So although there is deterioration, there is also improvement.

When a truly wise man really comprehends the great power of these Principles, he will know developments before they occur and without the slightest mistake—like one who is able to know the feelings of others and to predict the future. By such comprehension, all wise men—beginning with Confucius and Lao Tsu (the "sages" of China)—have spoken of events before they took place. Even in this deteriorated age a slightly intelligent person will be able to do likewise if he thinks and reflects about things. We hear that a state in which such men are used will be governed well, but that when the state is taken over by persons who are not like that, and who only handle matters with which they are immediately confronted, the state will simply be subjected to deterioration that leads to destruction.

The Execution of TAIRA Shigehira

On the 7th day of the 5th month [of 1185], MINAMOTO Yoshitsune (who had been appointed to the positions of Master and Captain) took his prisoners, TAIRA Munemori and TAIRA Shigehira, to Yoritomo's headquarters at Kamakura. Later on, the two prisoners were sent back to the capital, and on the 23rd day of the 6th month TAIRA Munemori (Minister of the Center) was decapitated at a place near Seta. TAIRA Shigehira definitely was the Supreme Commander who had burned the great Buddha statue at Tōdai Temple. Having explained that "we want to indicate, in this way, that Buddha's enemies are destroyed," Yorimoto purposely had Shigehira beheaded in the neighborhood of Kotsu of Izumi and then had his head displayed on Nara Hill. Since the head of Munemori, formerly Minister of the Center, was handed over to the Office of Imperial Police, even Retired Emperor Go-Shirakawa went to see it.

A man named FUJIWARA Yorikane, son of Lay Priest Yorimasa, was the messenger sent to take TAIRA Shigehira back to the capital, and then to the Tōdai Temple for execution. The party left Ōtsu, passed Daigo, came to the Hitsu River, crossed the Uji Bridge, and moved on toward Nara. On the way, Shigehira was pleased to be taking a road convenient for [a side trip] to the place where his former wife was staying. Shigehira had married FUJIWARA Kunitsuna's daughter, a woman called "Senior Counselor Suke" who had served ex-Emperor Takakura and had been Emperor Antoku's nurse. She was now living with her elder sister (Mistress Third Rank), who had built a house between Hino and Daigo. [At a point where the road led to his wife's place] Yorikane allowed Shigehira to get out of his palanquin and, because he was about to die, to pass some time weepingly doing such things as change his clothes. In general, people hate a person while he is vigorously adding one evil deed to another; but at a time like this, people who hear what is happening become drenched in tears of sorrow.

First Grade Priest Hangen, son of Lay Priest Suemichi and a distinguished scholar of the Tendai Sect, was on a trip to Mt. Yoshino when Shigehira was being taken to Nara. He was noted as a physiognomist. On his way back to Mt. Hiei from Mt. Yoshino, he met the Shigehira party at a place near Kunugihara and asked what was going on. Upon being told about the mission, and not having become familiar with the physiognomy of a man who was about to die, Hangen got out of his palanquin, wishing to see Shigehira. He approached the place where the soldiers were giving their horses a rest and eating their lunches. But when he took a look at Shigehira, he saw nothing at all that suggested Shigehira was a man about to die. Wondering why this was so, he walked around Shigehira, studying his features, but was unable to find anything that suggested the approach of death. He said: "Isn't that strange?" What is this thing called physiognomy?

People of that day marvelled at the things Yoritomo did, such as ordering this [execution of Shigehira near the Temple he had burned].

A Severe Earthquake

FUJIWARA Yorikane, Yorimasa's heir, was of course on guard at the Imperial Palace grounds, but before long he unexpectedly died. So his son Yorishige succeeded him and took up guard duties at the palace. While the situation was developing in this way, and people were wondering if the world was now settling down, an unusually severe earthquake was felt at about noon on the 9th day of the 7th month of 1185. There was no old Buddhist hall that did not collapse, no earthen wall that did not crumble, no house with any weakness that was not damaged, and no Buddhist building—from the Main Hall of Mt. Hiei on down—that was not wrenched askew. People said: "This too is due to unusual activity by the Dragon Kings." And others claimed that TAIRA Kiyomori had become a dragon and was shaking. The nine-storied pagoda at Hōshō Temple leaned crazily, without actually falling, and all the tips of its eaves on all nine stories fell off.

Yoshitsune Develops Bad Feelings toward Yoritomo

After the earthquake, MINAMOTO Yoshitsune was appointed to such positions as Captain of the Imperial Police (Fifth Rank) and Governor of the province of Iyo. Following the trip to his Kamakura mansion in the eastern provinces, and his return to the capital, he developed bad feelings [toward his brother Yoritomo]. While staying on in the eastern provinces, Yoritomo gradually obtained high positions at court, rising as high as Senior Second Rank. And while the fiefs and possessions of the TAIRA house were being registered [by court officials], Yoritomo had more than 500 pieces of property declared "confiscated" and seized. So Yoritomo received just what he wanted, including—above all—the eastern provinces of Musashi and Sagami.

When MINAMOTO Yoshinaka had first entered the capital [in 1183] with the intention of capturing and beheading the TAIRA leaders, TAIRA Yorimori[48] (Senior Counselor) fled to Yoritomo's headquarters in Kamakura. Yoritomo went two-days' distance from Kamakura to welcome him, treating him like a father. Some years earlier Yoritomo had married his sister to FUJIWARA Yoshiyasu (1147–97), Acting Assistant Master of the Empress Dowager's Household. Because of this marriage tie, Yoshiyasu and his wife also went to Kamakura after Yoshinaka entered the capital in 1183. For such reasons, several people went to Kamakura and gathered around Yoritomo. He was therefore quite familiar with what was going on in the capital and with what people were doing who stayed on there.

Then MINAMOTO Yoshitsune, who was Yoritomo's representative at the capital, suddenly turned against his brother Yoritomo and, on the 3rd day of the 11th month of 1185, had an Imperial edict issued [by Retired Emperor Go-Shirakawa] calling for Yoritomo's chastisement. When the Retired Emperor consulted with people about issuing such an edict, nearly everyone—being afraid of Yoshitsune—had said: "That is a proper thing to do." Only one person, Minister-of-the-Right KUJŌ Kanezane, spoke out against the proposal. His position was this: "An edict of chastisement should be based upon a crime committed. What crime has Yoritomo committed? Since we do not yet know that there has been a crime, it is difficult to say that such an edict should be issued." After the edict was handed down, a Yoritomo retainer (a Master of Buddhist Law called "the priest of Tosa") unhesitatingly forced his way into Yoshitsune's residence one night. Yoshitsune was awakened and a fierce fight ensued. Although Yoshitsune escaped death, he was injured. Not having a superior force, he hung the Imperial edict around his neck and, on the 3rd day of the 11th month of 1185, boarded a boat saying that he was leaving for the western provinces. Word of Yoshitsune's retreat from the capital was followed that night by a great clamor. It was thought that Yoshitsune might have taken the Emperor as a hostage, but Yoshitsune had simply fled. Yoritomo's retainers overtook Yoshitsune at Kawajiri and scattered his forces. A man named MINAMOTO Yukiie[49] (Jurō of the Imperial Secretariat who had previously been associated with Yoshinaka) had joined Yoshitsune's forces. But now he became separated from Yoshitsune and was killed at Kita Iwa-

48. A brother of TAIRA Kiyomori.
49. MINAMOTO Yoshitsune's uncle.

kura. After hearing that Yukiie's head had been taken, Yoshitsune went underground for a time. Later on it was reported that he was put up for a short while at the hut of a Mudō Temple custodian by the name of Zaishū. But eventually he fled to FUJIWARA Yasuhira's (1155–89)[50] headquarters in the province of Mutsu. Yasuhira killed Yoshitsune, even though he was told that this was a terrible thing to do, and reported what he had done to Yoritomo. Even in the province of Mutsu, people said: "He should not have gone that far! An evil thing has been done!"

Yoritomo Has Kanezane Appointed Imperial Inspector

On the 25th day of the 12th month of 1185, an Imperial edict was issued appointing KUJŌ Kanezane (Minister of the Right) to the office of Imperial Inspector. Yoritomo also asked that all persons who had supported the handing down of the Imperial edict of chastisement be subjected to Imperial censure. FUJIWARA Mitsumasa (Director of the Imperial Secretariat) and OTSUKI Takamoto (Fifth Rank Secretary of the Council of State) were removed from office. ŌIMIKADO Tsunemune (Minister of the Left and a high-ranking nobleman) [had favored the edict], but Yoritomo did not say anything about [removing him from office]. However, when Yoritomo was having his say about "those high-ranking noblemen who were to be consulted before making reports to the throne," he did not mention Tsunemune. By this non-action, people understood Tsunemune's position. They said: "That is the kind of man Yoritomo is!" Yoritomo seems to have planned things brilliantly, even in such matters as this. In addition, TAKASHINA Yasutsune (Third Rank) and all others who had been aides of Retired Emperor Go-Shirakawa were placed under house arrest. Then, on the 26th day of the 11th month of 1186, an Imperial edict was issued for the arrest of MINAMOTO Yoshitsune. These were astonishing developments indeed!

Yoritomo Subjugates Mutsu

Later, on the 19th day of the 7th month of 1189, Shogun Yoritomo left Kamakura saying that he was going to enter the province of Mutsu. He wanted finally to destroy FUJIWARA Yasuhira, the man who had succeeded Hidehira of Mutsu. That was said to be a reasonable thing for Yoritomo to do. Since Yasuhira had taken possession of a province as large as Mutsu, and acted as if he would not follow anyone, Yoritomo must have thought he would like to make that province his own private possession. He left with an imposing

50. Son of the famous FUJIWARA Hidehira (d. 1187), who had developed a virtually independent kingdom in the province of Mutsu.

force, quickly invaded the province, and easily subjugated it on the 3rd day of the 9th month of 1189. Then he divided the entire province among his retainers, reported what he had done to the Emperor, and formally took the position of provincial governor. Being unlike other governors who had held the post in past years, Yoritomo did good things even in that office.

FUJIWARA Hidehira had had two sons: Yasuhira ("mother's eldest son") and Kunihira ("father's eldest son"). Kunihira—who had received only a small, separate estate because Yasuhira was Hidehira's heir—was an impressive soldier. He was considered a charming man who stood out on a day of battle. Among those Yoritomo soldiers who had the urge to kill Kunihira was HATAKEYAMA Jirō Shigetada, an estate manager. Shigetada cut his way into the enemy, quickly engaged Kunihira in battle, cut off his head, and took it to Yoritomo. After that, Yoritomo always had Shigetada take the lead when an attack was being made. Shigetada was a magnificent soldier! We hear that he was [such an austere] man that, until the very end, fellow soldiers would not cross their legs when sitting near him, even at times of relaxation.

Because Yoritomo did not once remove the bowstring from his bow—or permit his bow to be taken from him—after he left Kamakura to engage the enemy in battle, even his retainers stood in great awe of him. As for Yoritomo's physical strength, when hunting he would have his horse run alongside a big deer, and then he would grab the deer's horns and bring it down with his bare hands. Everyone had also heard that the physical strength of his son Yoriie was extraordinary, in terms of either past or present standards.

4
Military Age II

KUJŌ Kanezane to KUJŌ Yoritsune

KUJŌ Kanezane Appointed Regent

An Imperial decree was finally issued on the 12th day of the 3rd month of 1186 appointing Minister-of-the-Right KUJŌ Kanezane (1149–1207) to the position of Regent. He was also made head of the FUJIWARA clan. Because he had held only the office of Imperial Inspector since the 29th day of the 12th month of the previous year, neither he nor anyone else knew what to think. But when the decision was made, everyone felt that a really fine Regent had been named. Kanezane said:

> Because I had not known since the winter of 1179 what was going to happen, I prayed to the Kami and the Buddhas. They revealed to me that I certainly would obtain the position of Regent at some point in the future. And now—after waiting ten years—I have obtained it.

Soon afterward, on the 16th day of the same month, Kanezane went to the Imperial Palace to express his gratitude to Emperor Go-Toba for the appointment. A very heavy rain fell that night. Then when Kanezane went to call on Retired Emperor Go-Shirakawa, His

Majesty said: "I have arrived at this ambiguous position, but I have ruled the world for a long time. You should simply conduct the affairs of state without paying any deference to me, and in just those ways that you think will be best." Go-Shirakawa also had Lady Jōdo-ji Second Rank,[1] his favorite and the mother of the future Empress Senyō-mon In,[2] come out to meet Kanezane. And MINAMOTO Yoritomo of the eastern provinces made promises to Kanezane about various matters. So time passed with people thinking that the state had really settled down.

Kanezane's Son and Daughter

A great state dinner was held on the 28th day of the 10th month of 1186 to celebrate the appointment of Kanezane's son and heir (Senior Counselor Yoshimichi, 1167–88) as Minister of the Center. Then, in the 1st month of 1188, Kanezane went on a pilgrimage to the Kasuga Shrine.[3] Because he took his son Yoshimichi with him, it was an occasion for which precedents were rare. An official of the Imperial Bodyguards, accompanied by a lead escort, was attached to Yoshimichi just as if he had already become head of the FUJIWARA clan. The lead escorts—made up of a Major Secretary, a Master

1. Listed in modern dictionaries as TAKASHINA Eishi (d. 1216), Lady Jōdo-ji was first married to TAIRA Narifusa, a Go-Shirakawa supporter who was killed in the disturbance of 1179. After that she was loved by Go-Shirakawa, and in 1181 she had a daughter (Senyō-mon In) upon whom Go-Shirakawa doted. In those years Lady Jōdo-ji may well have been the most influential person at Go-Shirakawa's palace. She carried out negotiations with NAKAHARA Hiromoto, who was sent from Kamakura to the capital in 1186 to obtain the court's backing for a proposed Land Steward (*jitō*) system. She apparently rejected many of Hiromoto's suggestions. She was also prominent in Yoritomo's welcome to the capital in 1189. Even after Go-Shirakawa's death in 1192, her influence was considerable. She continued to hold property, and her daughter by Go-Shirakawa was popular. Jien assigned great importance to her role in the plot that led to Kanezane's dismissal in 1196. She continued to reside at her first husband's mansion, the Jōdo-ji, and was therefore known as Lady Jōdo-ji.
2. This was Go-Shirakawa's favorite daughter (1181–1252) by his beloved Lady Jōdo-ji. At the age of nine she was given the assimilated rank of Empress and was granted, in 1191, the *in* title and called Senyō-mon In, even though she had never been a true Empress. Before Go-Shirakawa died, he gave her a mansion and a large estate that was managed by MINAMOTO Michichika. She and her mother were particularly influential after 1196, when MINAMOTO Michichika's group is said to have engineered Kanezane's dismissal As a supporter of Go-Toba and Juntoku, she seems to have been involved in decisions that led to the outbreak of the Shōkyū War of 1221.
3. The principal shrine for the worship of the ancestral Kami of the FUJIWARA clan.

Scribe, a Controller, and a Junior Counselor—rode by the entrance to the house-shaped carriages. It was really magnificent! When two nobles make such a pilgrimage together, the escort usually consists of an ordinary Scribe and Secretary of the Sixth Rank. But on this occasion each of the two had a Scribe and Secretary of the Fifth Rank. So the pilgrimage was a bit formal.

Then Yoshimichi suddenly died in his sleep at dawn on the 20th day of the 2nd month of 1188. He could have boarded any one of the "three boats"[4] and was an intelligent scholar with remarkable ability in both Chinese and Japanese literature. So Yoshimichi was not thought of as being only 21 years old. Although rather short, his manners and bearing were praised. Kanezane therefore thought of him as an unusually fine son. Immediately after the untimely death of Yoshimichi—who was to have become Kanezane's successor and who had been brought up by Empress Kōka-mon In[5]—Kanezane went into mourning, reporting this to the Retired Emperor and thinking:

> There is nothing I can do about it. Because I have been born a man for whom it was difficult to be born a man, my sole desire now is to follow the way of Buddha. Having achieved the highest office for which a member of my house is entitled, I now wish to enter the Buddhist priesthood.

But Kanezane also had a daughter Ninshi (1173–1238), Yoshimichi's young sister, whom he was equally fond of. Kanezane wanted to have her placed in the Imperial Palace—following a precedent established when Empress Jōtō-mon In was placed there long ago—and made the Empress of Go-Toba (then eight years old) when His Majesty celebrated his coming-of-age [in 1190]. But Kanezane didn't think he would be able to realize this desire because Retired Emperor Go-Shirakawa had similar plans—even though he had already become a priest—for his daughter by Lady Jōdo-ji. Furthermore, MINAMOTO Yoritomo had a daughter that he wanted to place in the palace. Since Kanezane did not think that he would succeed in getting Ninshi into the palace, he thought he would enter the priesthood when the 49 days of mourning for Yoshimichi had passed. But while praying earnestly, he received a miraculous revelation that his hopes for Ninshi would be realized. So he stopped thinking about becoming a priest. Devoting himself to good government *(zensei)* and reviving

---

4. On Imperial outings three boats were often set aside for three different cultural activities: composing Japanese poems, composing Chinese poems, and playing instrumental music. A nobleman usually chose to board the boat for that activity in which he excelled. Therefore a man who could select any one of the three was truly cultured.

5. Sutoku's Empress (1121–81) and Jien's sister.

court ceremonies, he solicited views from various nobles at the beginning of his term as Regent and gave special attention to the Records Office. Then, after Emperor Go-Toba celebrated his coming-
of-age on the 3rd day of the 1st month of 1190, Kanezane
realized—as he expected—his desire to place his daughter Ninshi in
the palace as Go-Toba's consort (in accordance with the precedent
established by Empress Jōtō-mon In) on the 11th day of that same
month.[6]

MINAMOTO Yoritomo Enters the Capital

Not long afterward, on the 11th day of the 4th month of 1190, the
era name was changed to Kenkyū (Building Permanently), and on
the 7th day of the 11th month of that year MINAMOTO Yoritomo
came up to the capital. Everyone had waited expectantly for his arrival. He had a mansion built—on about five acres of land—at the site
of TAIRA Kiyomori's Rokuhara Mansion. Because it was raining on
the day Yoritomo planned to enter the capital, he stopped over at a
place near Seta. Then when he entered the capital on the 7th—the
rain having stopped just as he had wanted—his soldiers came riding
into the city three abreast. Over 700 horsemen preceded him and
more than 300 were grouped behind him. Riding a black horse and
wearing an apron of deer's summer fur over a glossy tri-colored
robe (dark blue, blue, and red), he was an impressive figure. After
entering the capital, he paid his respects to Retired Emperor Go-
Shirakawa and called at the Imperial Palace. In the eyes of Go-
Shirakawa no one was the equal of Yoritomo. Therefore Yoritomo
was soon appointed Senior Commander of the Imperial Bodyguards
of the Right. On the 9th day of the 11th month of 1190, he was
given an accelerated promotion to Acting Senior Counselor without
ever having been a Consultant or Middle Counselor. He was appointed Senior Commander of the Imperial Bodyguards of the
Right on the 24th day of that month and, on the same day,[7] went to
the palace to express his gratitude for the appointment. Then he
resigned from both positions on the 3rd day of the 12th month of
1190, having risen step by step to Senior Second Rank. He might
have had any position, even that of a minister, but he reflected on
the meaning of such appointments and conducted himself in a

6. Kanezane's daughter, like Jōtō-mon In (988–1074), was placed in the
palace and immediately promoted to Secondary Empress. But while Jōtō-
mon In was 12 at the time, Ninshi was 18 and Go-Toba 11. Ninshi was
forced to leave the palace after the 1196 crisis. A few years later, she and
her father Kanezane were converted to the Pure Land faith by Hōnen.

7. Again Jien is not following his brother's diary, which states that
Yoritomo went to the palace to pay his respects on the 1st day of the 12th
month of 1190. [Gyokuyō, 3.639.]

praiseworthy manner [by not accepting them]. He was really a rare man to be Shogun in the final reigns and a man of superior ability! Even when expressing his pleasure at being appointed Senior Commander, he devised a fine and unusual ceremony. The ten lead marshals were all men from the Retired Emperor's military guard, and his attendant was HATA Kanehira, Keneyori's son. Yoritomo was accompanied by the following nobles: (1) FUJIWARA Yoshiyasu, the husband of Yoritomo's sister and a man who later rose rapidly, by a succession of promotions, to the position of Middle Counselor; (2) SAIONJI Kintsune, a Middle Commander who had become Yoshiyasu's son-in-law by marrying Yoshiyasu's daughter (who in turn was a daughter of Yoritomo's sister); and (3) FUJIWARA Yasuie, a Junior Commander who was the son of Middle Counselor Motoie (Yoshiyasu's cousin and adopted son of Yoshiyasu). Behind Yoritomo's carriage rode only seven horsemen wearing armor and no helmets. Since their names are not definitely known, I do not list them here.[8] Those who saw the ceremony have said that it was an impressive spectacle. Then Yoritomo proceeded to the palace, where he talked earnestly with KUJŌ Kanezane about governing the state.

Yoritomo also went frequently to call on Retired Emperor Go-Shirakawa. It had been decided, at the outset, that Senior Counselor FUJIWARA Tsunefusa was to be Yoritomo's liaison officer at the capital. Therefore when Yoritomo went first to call on the Retired Emperor—surprisingly soon after going to his mansion at Roku-hara—Tsunefusa expected that he would be asked to serve as Yoritomo's guide. Tsunefusa was familiar with the plans for the Rokujō Palace, which had been rebuilt soon [after the fire of 1188]. He had handled matters down to such details as plans for rooms inside and outside the threshold, and he had been praised by people for acting as if he had been calling on the Retired Emperor from the very beginning. But Yoritomo moved on ahead of Tsunefusa without saying anything about a guide. So Tsunefusa walked behind. Even though Yoritomo could see everything, since it was daylight, Tsunefusa kept making such explanations as "This is the place inside the threshold, and this is the place outside," talking incessantly like a born chatterer. Later, Yoritomo remarked that Tsunefusa was not an understanding man.[9]

After having been praised by people while he was at the capital, Yoritomo took some time to pay his respects at such religious institutions as the Iwashimizu Hachiman Shrine, the Tōdai Temple, and

8. The names are listed in the *Azuma kagami*, 12–1–1190, 1.357–359.

9. Both the *Azuma kagami* (9–18–1185, 1.139) and the *Heike monogatari* (3.539) give the impression that Yoritomo placed great trust in Tsunefusa.

the Tennō Temple.[10] Then, quite early on the 18th day of the 12th month of 1190, he returned to the capital and departed for Kamakura. The day before he left, Yoritomo was awarded 100 *chō* of rice land in perpetuity;[11] and he spoke to the Retired Emperor as follows:

As an indication of the way I have been unselfishly taking upon myself the concerns of the Emperor for the sake of the Imperial House, I would like to tell you about a man named TAIRA Hachirō Hirotsune, Assistant Governor [of Kazusa]. When I first started my campaigns to repel the enemies of the Emperor, I enlisted the support of this Hirotsune, a man of influence in the eastern provinces. With such military backing I was able to subdue the Emperor's enemies, and Hirotsune proved to be a meritorious soldier. But he said such things as this: "Why do you painfully think only of the Imperial House? If you were just to stay in the eastern provinces, who could dislodge you?" After turning this over in my mind, I concluded that because Hirotsune was a man with rebellious feelings, divine favors *(myōga)* would be withheld from even me if I kept him as a retainer. So I had him eliminated.

KAJIWARA Kagetoki was therefore ordered to do away with Hirotsune. While playing a game of Japanese backgammon,[12] and giving no sign of what he intended to do, Kagetoki leaped over the backgammon board, quickly cut off Hirotsune's head, and took it to Yoritomo. It was truly an unthinkable affair! If this were written up in detail, errors would creep in. Therefore it is probably best to stop here. If this report of what Yoritomo told the Retired Emperor is true, Yoritomo was really a jewel for the Imperial House.

Death of Go-Shirakawa

Retired Emperor Go-Shirakawa died on the 13th day of the 3rd month of 1192. He had been ill for some years, but improvement had been reported. His illness was described as "an enlarged abdo-

10. Kanezane's diary states that Yoritomo visited the Hachiman Shrine on the 11th day of the 11th month of 1190, but nothing is said about his having gone to the Tōdai-ji or the Tennō-ji. [*Gyokuyō*, 3.636.] The editors of the NKBT text wonder if Jien did not confuse the visit made in 1190 with the one made in 1195. [NKBT, 86.277, notes 49–50.]

11. Kanezane says he recommended the award. [*Gyokuyō*, 12–12–1190, 3.640.]

12. *Suguroku*, a game in which one player uses twelve white stones and the other twelve black ones. The players take turns in moving their stones forward according to the throw of two dice. The player who first gets his stones into the enemy camp wins.

men and painful urination." Although his legs had become emaciated, he continued to perform the *goma* rite until the day before his death. Nowadays we do not hear of such splendid rites as those that were held during the taboo period following Go-Shirakawa's death. In fact we hear that they were excessive.

Go-Shirakawa had made a practice of wearing the Buddhist surplice and participating in *goma* rites before he entered the priesthood. And after he became a priest, he was increasingly preoccupied with the practice of Buddhism. The tens of thousands of volumes of Buddhist scripture that he read included two hundred readings of the Lotus Sutra. He was always fond of dances and comic plays and went to see performances that he had ordered. His younger sister Jōsai-mon In (1126–89) was also a reader of sutras, and because she read them somewhat faster than His Majesty did, he insisted that they read in unison. During the period of his illness, and whenever Emperor Go-Toba went to call on him, Go-Shirakawa would provide the Emperor with a full report on state affairs. Go-Shirakawa had been the third Retired Emperor—after Shirakawa and Toba—to administer state affairs as a Retired Emperor. It was therefore now strange to have no Retired Emperor performing such functions. Even the *sonshō darani* Mass, which had been performed at Retired Emperor Go-Shirakawa's palace, was now held at the Hosshō Temple. Henceforth the Lord (Kanezane) and the Kamakura Shogun (Yoritomo) conducted state affairs in consultation with each other.

New Support for Buddhist Temples

The first thing done after Retired Emperor Go-Shirakawa's death was to have estates in the provinces of Harima and Bizen that had belonged to the Retired Emperor presented to two Buddhist Saints *(shōnin)*: Mongaku and Sunjō. The Harima income was given to Mongaku of Tōdai-ji and the Bizen income to Shunjō of Tō-ji, with these instructions:

> Construction work on Tōdai Temple shall be completed quickly. The Tō Temple, founded by Grand Preceptor Kōbō and the temple where incomparable rites have been held for the protection of the state *(chingo kokka)*, has all but disappeared; and so it shall be rebuilt. Can a more superior memorial rite be performed than having such reconstruction work done?

Income from the province of Suwō had been granted to the Tōdai Temple some years before, but now income from the province of Bizen was added, since construction work at the Temple had not been completed.

After Mongaku had been exiled to the province of Izu,[13] he and Yoritomo—also in exile there—were together from morning until night. And in those days Mongaku told Yoritomo that he should believe in Buddhist Law and carefully protect Imperial Law. Since Yoritomo did not think state affairs would continue unchanged, he made promises about what he would do when he fought his way out of exile. And since events occurred just as he had thought they would, the Takao and Tō temples were made to prosper in an extraordinary way. Mongaku's practice of Buddhism was superb, but he was no scholarly saint. He was criticized for slandering and abusing people excessively—some said that he even worshipped demons *(tengu)*. Nevertheless, during the seven years that he received income from the province of Harima, he made the Tōdai Temple prosper, probably because he had a sincere heart *(makoto no kokoro)*.

Lord KUJŌ Kanezane, now that he had realized his desire to become Chancellor, had the great temple compound of Kōfuku-ji [the FUJIWARA's clan temple] constructed alongside the Tōdai-ji. Prior to this, the former had become virtually non-existent.[14] The new compound included the Nan'en Hall with its sacred object of worship, a 16-foot statue of Amoghapāsa. The mass for the dedication of the reconstructed Kōfuku Temple was held on the 22nd day of the 9th month of 1194. A heavy rain fell that day. Kanezane had worshipped at Kasuga Shrine the previous day. Hearing that officials of the rank of Middle Counselor and below rode horses in the procession, people considered this something beyond belief. It was the first time such a pilgrimage had been made to Kasuga since the days of Michinaga.

Then, on the 13th day of the 3rd month of 1195, a dedication ceremony was held at the Tōdai Temple. Emperor Go-Toba attended, accompanied by his Imperial mother (Empress Shichijō). A strong wind blew and a heavy rain fell. Stating that he wanted to be present for the ceremony, Shogun Yoritomo arrived at the capital on the 4th day of that month for another short visit, and on the day of the ceremony he went to the temple surrounded by soldiers. Even though it was raining hard, his soldiers maintained strict order and seemed not to realize they were getting wet. Because of this, understanding persons were really surprised.

MINAMOTO Yoritomo and KUJŌ Kanezane met each other several times. Not long afterward, on the 25th day of the 6th month of 1195, Yoritomo returned to Kamakura, probably because he was uneasy about various developments there.

13. Cf. Chapter 3.
14. It was burned by the TAIRA in 1180.

Kujō Kanezane's Granddaughter

Great excitement was caused by the report, received on the 8th day of the 8th month of 1195, that Emperor Go-Toba's Secondary Empress Ninshi had given birth to a child. Probably more prayers had been made that an Empress give birth to an Imperial son than had been made during any previous reign. And yet, because the child was a girl, Kanezane was disappointed. She was given to Hachijō In for upbringing. People everywhere claimed that "Whether the princess is standing or sitting, her beauty is unmatched by that of any Lady-in-Waiting (high or low, mean or noble) in these final reigns. How long and thick her hair is!" Even Emperor Go-Toba thought she was truly an unusual daughter and took pleasure in having her brought into his presence so that he could see her. In later years she was given the title of *in* and called Shunkamon In (1195–1211), but people really objected to her name [because *shunka*, spring flower, suggested that her life would be short].

KUJŌ Kanezane Dismissed as Chancellor

The following events occurred in the winter of 1196: Chancellor KUJŌ Kanezane was placed under house arrest; Lord KONOE Motomichi (1160–1233) was appointed Chancellor in Kanezane's place; and Kanezane's daughter, Secondary Empress Ninshi, was forced to leave the palace. Why did these things occur? MINAMOTO Yoritomo wanted very much to have his daughter placed in the palace as Go-Toba's consort, but Senior Counselor MINAMOTO Michichika (1145–1202) wrote that he had hidden away a daughter[15] whom he also wanted to place in the palace. Michichika's [adopted] daughter was the real daughter of his wife Noriko (Lady Gyōbu Third Rank), who had served as Go-Toba's nurse.

Princely Priest Shōnin (1169–97), a Myōun disciple captured at the time of Yoshinaka's attack on Retired Emperor Go-Shirakawa's palace in 1183, had grown up and was going to the palace daily.[16] It was rumored that Shōnin was in secret contact with Go-Shirakawa's favorite consort, Lady Jōdo-ji Second Rank. While these people were consulting together after Retired Emperor Go-Shirakawa's death in 1192, large estates that had been held by Go-Shirakawa in the provinces of Harima and Bizen were suddenly confiscated by Kanezane;

15. This was Ariko, later known as Shōmei-mon In (1171–1257), an adopted Michichika daughter who became a Go-Toba consort and gave birth to the future Emperor Tsuchimikado. She was a niece of the powerful Lady Second Rank.

The political upheaval of 1196 is discussed in Chapter 9.

16. Shōnin was a Go-Shirakawa son who had been brought up by Kenshun-mon In of the TAIRA clan. He was trained under Myōun for the priesthood and replaced Jien as Tendai Abbot in 1196.

and FUJIWARA Naritsune and FUJIWARA Sanenori, members of houses traditionally entitled to appointments at the Master level, were dismissed from their positions as Consultant and Middle Commander. Kanezane felt that these were good administrative acts that had been tacitly approved by Yoritomo. But Lady Jōdo-ji was critical. Conspiring with Princely Priest Shōnin, she urged Michichika [to move against Kanezane]. Whenever they would inquire about the Retired Emperor's feelings, they would find his personal pleasures a source of embarrassment to him, especially since [Kanezane] was talking only of correct administrative action. Therefore, they would tell His Majesty, here in Kyoto, that Yoritomo's feelings were so and so but tell Yoritomo, in Kamakura, that the Retired Emperor had bad feelings [toward Kanezane], acting as if they were doing nothing wrong. And if they were asked something definite, they planned to give plausible [but different] explanations to Yoritomo and Go-Toba. Because this was a time when ingenious plots were common and even the protection of Kami and Buddhas was to no avail, Secondary Empress Ninshi was moved from the Imperial Palace to the residence of Hachijō In on the 23rd day of the 11th month of 1196.

An Imperial edict was handed down on the 25th day of that month appointing former Regent KONOE Motomichi to the office of Chancellor and making him head of the FUJIWARA clan. We hear that MINAMOTO Michichika was then in charge of court ceremonies, TAIRA Chikakuni was Controller, and FUJIWARA Tomotsune was Imperial Secretary. These men soon urged that Kanezane be sent into exile. Although charges were made against the Chancellor, the Emperor had absolutely no desire to exile him. Kanezane's enemies claimed that he had committed a crime, but since there was no proof, the charges were dropped.

Because of such developments, Kanezane's young brother Jien[17] was forced to resign from his position as Tendai Abbot. He was replaced by Prince Kajii whose priestly name was Shōnin. But soon after his installation in the 4th month of 1197, the Prince became sick and died. People felt that these were strange developments indeed. Even MINAMOTO Yoritomo deeply regretted Jien's resignation as Tendai Abbot.

Emperor Go-Toba's Abdication

Suddenly, on the 11th day of the 1st month of 1198, MINAMOTO Michichika had Go-Toba yield the throne to his four-year-old son Tsuchimikado who was from the womb of Shōmei-mon In (daughter of priest Nōen by the above-mentioned Lady Gyōbu Third Rank).

17. Jien never refers to himself in the first person.

Go-Toba himself wanted to abdicate because he wished to conduct state affairs in his own way [like Retired Emperor Go-Shirakawa]. MINAMOTO Yoritomo of the eastern provinces did not definitely approve Go-Toba's abdication. He may have thought it was a matter beyond his control. Such events take place in a world in which there are no understanding persons. Senior High Priest Nōen (father of Tsuchimikado's Imperial mother) was still alive, and so people wondered if it was proper [for a priest to be the father of an Imperial mother]. But Nōen soon became ill and died, and persons associated with the state thought that his death was a good thing.

The Deaths of FUJIWARA Yoshiyasu and His Son Takayoshi

Lord FUJIWARA Yoshiyasu (1147–97) had been appointed Middle Counselor and Commissioner of Imperial Police [in 1191]. Then he became ill and entered the Buddhist priesthood shortly afterward. He recovered from his illness and resumed his visits to the Imperial Palace but was apparently surprised by [Kanezane's dismissal from the Chancellorship in 1196]. Kanezane's son Yoshitsune, the future Regent, was married to Yoshiyasu's daughter, MINAMOTO Yoritomo's niece. The ceremony by which Yoshitsune became Yoshiyasu's son-in-law was magnificent. Then Lay Priest Yoshiyasu died on the 13th day of the 10th month of 1197.[18]

On the 14th day of the previous 7th month, the daughter that Yoritomo wanted to send up to the capital [to become Emperor Go-Toba's consort] died after a long illness. A miracle-working First Grade Priest by the name of Jitsuzen had gone down to Kamakura

18. FUJIWARA Yoshiyasu and SAIONJI Kintsue linked the MINAMOTO clan to the KUJŌ house in the following way:

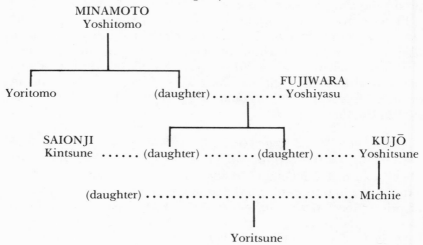

to cure her, but his efforts had absolutely no effect. Yoritomo was very tactful even about this: he had a report issued that his daughter was better and asked Jitsuzen to return to the capital. But before Jitsuzen had arrived there, it was heard that the daughter had died. Since Jitsuzen did not enter the capital until after the girl's death had been reported, the odd impression was given that he had returned after killing her with his incantations.

Yoshiyasu's son Takayoshi had become a high-ranking nobleman at an early age, obtaining appointments as Consultant and Commander of the Imperial Guards. He had gone down to Kamakura amidst a great hubub. After that, Yoritomo—who was now receiving information about developments at the capital—was reportedly more desirous than ever of going up to the capital with his second daughter. Then Takayoshi died on the 17th day of the 9th month of 1198.

Death of MINAMOTO Yoritomo

Meanwhile, an astounding and unthinkable incident occurred. In the 1st month of 1199, while people were blankly saying that the Shogun of the eastern provinces seemed to be ill, it was suddenly reported—after the 15th or 16th of that month—that Yoritomo had entered the priesthood on the 11th and died on the 13th. People wondered whether this was a dream or the real thing. Shogun Yoritomo had sent such messages as these to Lord KUJŌ Kanezane: "I am planning to go up to the capital some time this year in order to take care of some matters of state. Various developments there are not to my liking."

On the 20th day of the 1st month of 1199, a few days after Shogun Yoritomo's death, an installation ceremony was held at which MINAMOTO Michichika was appointed Senior Commander of the Imperial Bodyguards of the Right, and ŌIMIKADO Yorizane (1155–1225)[19]—referred to later as the Lay Priest Prime Minister—was appointed Minister of the Right, passing over Minister of the Center KUJŌ Yoshitsune (the future Regent, now deceased, who came to be

19. The rise of ŌIMIKADO Yorizane to a position of prominence at the Imperial Court was undoubtedly due to his close association with the Michichika group that, according to the *Gukanshō*, brought about the dismissal of KUJŌ Kanezane in 1196. But Yorizane's father Tsunemune had been Minister of the Left from 1166 to 1189, standing just below the men who were then serving as Regent or Chancellor. Yorizane was to become even more prominent after he married Lady Second Rank in 1203. Because of her influence, Yorizane succeeded in making his daughter Tsuchimikado's Empress. Jien is very critical of Yorizane for wanting to rise too high. His critical attitude seems to arise primarily from Yorizane's earlier relations with the hated Michichika.

called Lord Go-Kyōgoku). This Yorizane had resigned as Senior
Commander of the Imperial Bodyguards of the Right, leaving the
position vacant [for the appointment of Michichika]. In that installation ceremony of 1199, MINAMOTO Yoriie (1182–1204), Yoritomo's
son and heir to the headship of the Yoritomo house, was appointed
Middle Commander of the Imperial Bodyguards of the Left.

Strange Rumors

At about this time strange rumors were heard. Because prospects
for the descendants of the Lay Priest Yoshiyasu and his son Takayoshi were quite dismal [as a result of the political changes engineered by Michichika and his collaborators], retainers of the Yoshiyasu house (three Captains of the Palace Gate Guards of the Left
named FUJIWARA Motokiyo, NAKAHARA Masatsune, and ONO Yoshi-
nari) [became discontented]. So when MINAMOTO Yoriie had
achieved a position of influence and KAJIWARA's eldest son had been
promoted to Captain of the Palace Gate Guards of the Left, these
three captains complained about what was being done by Senior
Commander MINAMOTO Michichika. And when word got out that
complaints were being made, the three captains went directly to,
and secluded themselves in, Retired Emperor Go-Toba's palace, saying that they would be killed if they left. Then an extraordinary
thing happened. Michichika had an ally of his (NAKAHARA Hiromoto,
who served with Shogun Yoriie) say certain things [to Yoriie]. So the
three Captains of the Palace Gate Guards of the Left were brought
into the presence of the Retired Emperor, handed over to
Michichika, and sent into exile. SAIONJI Kintsune and FUJIWARA
Yasuie, men who had accompanied Yoritomo when he came to the
capital [in 1190] to express his gratitude for a recent appointment,
were also placed under house arrest. And a man named MINAMOTO
Takayasu, who had been appointed Director of the Imperial Stables
of the Left and was a great favorite of Yoshiyasu, was exiled. These
events are said to have occurred on the 14th day of the 2nd month
of 1199. Although Saint Mongaku had rebuilt the Takao Temple,
just as he had wanted, by using income from the province of
Harima, and had also restored the Tō Temple in a magnificent way,
he was placed under surveillance by officers of the Imperial Police.
But after Michichika died [in 1202], the three Captains of the Palace
Gate Guards of the Left were all recalled from exile and treated well.

The Rise of KUJŌ Yoshitsune

Meanwhile, absolutely no unfairness appeared in the thoughts of
Retired Emperor Go-Toba. It could not be helped that His Majesty
did not know or notice that persons were doing things which he
would not have thought of. Although not aware of what these

people were doing, the Retired Emperor was making plans for KUJŌ Yoshitsune (1169–1206), who still had not been removed from the position of Minister of the Center. So His Majesty promoted Minister of the Left Yorizane to Prime Minister, making the appointment effective on the 22nd day of the 6th month of 1199. Then Yoshitsune was appointed Minister of the Left (filling the vacancy left by the resignation of Kanemasa), KONOE Iezane (Regent Motomichi's heir and the man who is now Chancellor)[20] was made Minister of the Right, and Michichika became Minister of the Center. Yorizane was gossiped about, since he then became very angry, resigned from his position as Prime Minister, and secluded himself in the province of Tosa. He was angry because he thought he had been advanced to the [honorary][21] position of Prime Minister in order that Michichika might be advanced to Minister of the Center. FUJIWARA Muneyori, Lord Kanezane's distinguished guardian, was then a Senior Counselor and the husband of Kaneko, Lady Second Rank. Kanezane had thought very well of him. But Muneyori was simply a good-natured man who was not vigorous.

Meanwhile, Michichika and Yoshitsune, Ministers of the Left and Center respectively, were going frequently to Retired Emperor Go-Toba's Minase Palace for Japanese and Chinese poetry-composing parties. Well along in that year of 1200, on the 13th day of the 7th month, Yoshitsune's principal wife died. Reportedly, she did not recover from the birth of a child on the 10th day of that month. Not long afterward, it was said that Lord MATSU Motofusa wanted to have his daughter replace Yoshitsune's deceased wife, and, on the 3rd day of the 10th month of 1201, Yoshitsune did marry Motofusa's daughter.[22] She is reported to have been 28 years old at that time. Then, on the 9th day of the 12th month of that year, Yoshitsune's mother (the principal wife of Kanezane) also died.

MINAMOTO Michichika died on the 21st day of the 10th month of 1202. People felt that his sudden death was something strange. After his wife Noriko (Lady Gyōbu Third Rank) had died, Michichika doted on his wife's daughter Ariko, who received the *in* name and title of Shōmei-mon In [and who was Tsuchimikado's Imperial mother].

20. Iezane was appointed Regent in 1206 and made Chancellor shortly afterward, continuing on in that position until 1221. Thus the phrase "who is now Chancellor" indicates that this portion of the *Gukanshō* was written before the end of his term.

21. Although a Prime Minister ranked above a Minister of the Left, the former was an honorary post and was not held by a Regent or Chancellor who was responsible for administering the affairs of state.

22. MATSU Motofusa and KUJŌ Kanezane (Yoshitsune's father) were brothers. Thus Yoshitsune married his cousin.

Retired Emperor Go-Toba had come to favor FUJIWARA Norisue's daughter Shigeko,[23] who was advanced to Third Rank following a precedent set by Bifuku-mon In. Shigeko and Go-Toba had several children. Since it seemed that he wanted his eldest son by her to become Crown Prince, Michitaka made arrangements by which this son Juntoku was appointed Crown Prince on the 14th day of the 4th month of 1200. It was while the situation was developing in this way that Kanezane's principal wife, like Yoshitsune's, preceded her husband in death. And then Kanezane entered the Buddhist priesthood [in the 1st month of 1202]. Apparently Go-Toba sincerely wanted people to realize that these developments had not been brought about by his own personal wishes; and so an Imperial edict was handed down on the 27th day of the 11th month of 1202 appointing Kanezane's son, Minister of the Left Yoshitsune, to the positions of Imperial Inspector and head of the FUJIWARA house. Soon after the edict was issued, Go-Toba departed—on the 28th—for a pilgrimage to the Kumano Shrines. Yoshitsune was still in deep mourning for the death of his mother (Kanezane's principal wife) during the 12th month of 1202. After Go-Toba's return to the capital from his pilgrimage to the Kumano Shrines, another Imperial edict was issued on the 27th day of the 12th month appointing Yoshitsune Regent. Because Yoshitsune went to the Imperial Palace to express his gratitude for the appointment before he attended the New Year ceremony held on the 1st day of the 1st month of 1203, people thought this was really an auspicious event.

Lady Second Rank and Her Two Husbands

Senior Counselor Muneyori (1154–1203)[24] should have been in mourning then, since his adoptive father Nariyori, a lay priest at Mt. Kōya for several years, had died. Before that, Muneyori had not gone into mourning when his real father, Senior Counselor Mitsuyori, died. He promised to do so at the time of his adoptive father's death but did not because, being very prominent in state affairs, he could not spare the time. People criticized Muneyori for acting as if he had no parents. He went with Retired Emperor Go-Toba on the latter's pilgrimage to the Kumano Shrines and got his leg burned by a pine torch. The burn was serious, and Muneyori died on the 30th day of the 1st month of 1203. His wife (Lady Second Rank), having lost her husband, was thinking of what she should do when she spoke to Prime Minister ŌIMIKADO Yorizane, a

23. She became Shumei-mon In (1182–1264), Imperial mother of Juntoku who reigned from 1210 to 1221.

24. Muneyori had been manager (*iezukasa*) of Kanezane's household but did not lose his position at court when Kanezane was dismissed in 1196, probably because of the influence of his wife, Lady Second Rank.

man who was on intimate terms with Shichijō In (Go-Toba's Imperial mother). Yorizane took Lady Second Rank as his wife and was immediately made Go-Toba's guardian.

Go-Toba's Relations with Yoshitsune and Jien

Even Retired Emperor Go-Toba thought Lord Go-Kyōgoku Yoritsune was really a fine Regent and that Yoshitsune did good things because he acted in accordance with the Retired Emperor's wishes. The Tendai Abbot, High Priest Jien, was Kanezane's brother [and Yoshitsune's uncle]. The reader will not believe this, but Jien was reputed to be a fine poet, and therefore Go-Toba was disposed to say: "You must come to the palace; and you must come as a person with the same standing as the Regent." Therefore Jien was always calling on Go-Toba. It was reported that Jien, as the Retired Emperor's guardian priest, had for years been the man Go-Toba trusted most.[25] (Go-Toba built a fine palace at Uji where His Majesty resided, but the palace was destroyed by fire soon afterward.)

KUJŌ Yoshitsune's Disappointment and Death

At the time of Emperor Tsuchimikado's coming-of-age [in 1205], Regent Yoshitsune wished to have one of his daughters placed in the Imperial Palace as Tsuchimikado's consort, since this was what his own father had recently done and would be in accord with ancient practice. Lord Yoshitsune had several daughters, but his eldest had been born—at some time or other—to the wife that had made him Yoshiyasu's son-in-law. Therefore Lord Yoshitsune wanted to have this daughter placed in the Imperial Palace as the highest-ranking consort; and he made arrangements for the marriage, keeping the Retired Emperor informed of what was being done. But Lady Second Rank made a strong plea [that her own husband Yorizane's daughter be made the Emperor's consort]. Prime Minister ŌIMIKADO Yorizane's first wife had not produced a male child but had given him a daughter who was made a provisional junior consort to Tsuchimikado. Yorizane had a strong desire to place this daughter in line for promotion to Empress.

Having been forced to take the honorary position of Prime Minister [in 1199], Yorizane wanted to be re-appointed Minister of the Left, making him—like his father ŌIMIKADO Tsunemune—the country's Number One Man.[26] Some time later, when Yorizane was pleased to become Lady Second Rank's husband, he requested an appointment as Minister of the Left. But Retired Emperor Go-Toba felt that it would be irregular to have Yorizane downgraded from

25. The most detailed comment that Jien makes about himself.
26. Tsunemune had not been a Regent or Chancellor but was Minister of the Left from 1166 to 1189.

Prime Minister to Minister of the Left, and that this should not be done. So the request was denied. And now [in 1205] Lady Second Rank asked Lord Kujō Yoshitsune if ŌIMIKADO Yorizane should not be allowed to achieve, for a while, his heart's desire to have his daughter accepted as the Emperor's senior consort. Lady Second Rank argued that whereas Yorizane would not be able to place his daughter in the Imperial Palace after Yoshitsune's daughter had been placed there, it would not be contrary to either precedent or principle for Yoshitsune to marry his daughter to the Emperor after Yorizane's daughter had been extended that privilege. Lord Yoshitsune discussed the matter with the Retired Emperor. Go-Toba concluded that it would be best to have Yoshitsune's daughter placed in the palace after Tsuchimikado's early abdication and after Crown Prince Juntoku (son of Empress Shumei-mon In) had been enthroned. People did not know this was Go-Toba's view. They only surmised that, when Yoshitsune and His Majesty talked together, something like this intent may have been expressed. In any case, ŌIMIKADO Yorizane's daughter was placed in the Imperial Palace as Emperor Tsuchimikado's consort and later promoted to Secondary Empress, just as Yorizane had wished.[27]

Lord KUJŌ Yoshitsune was uneasy about having to wait for a chance to place his own daughter in the palace, and probably felt envious. While avoiding people and telling himself it was best that he had not gotten what he wanted, he built a house—superior to all others—at the intersection of Nakamikado and Kyōgoku.[28] He beautified it with a garden containing well-placed ponds and hills, and people began to look forward with excitement to the "meandering stream party"[29]—one had not been held for some time— scheduled for a date around the 13th day of the 3rd month of 1206 and for which chambered-nautilus shell cups had been made.

27. Lady Second Rank won and Yoshitsune lost, but Jien tries to gloss over his nephew's defeat by writing that Go-Toba had discussed the matter with Yoshitsune and promised to have Prince Juntoku enthroned soon and to have Yoshitsune's daughter made Juntoku's consort. Yoshitsune died in 1206, and Juntoku was not enthroned until 1210. Nevertheless, Yoshitsune's daughter Risshi (Higashi Ichijō In) eventually did become Juntoku's Empress. Go-Toba may have thought that it did not much matter, in 1205, who was made Tsuchimikado's Empress, since Juntoku was already Crown Prince. See note 38, below.

28. Remains of this house are still extant in Matsukage-chō of Kyoto.

29. *Kyokusui no en* were popular among the noblemen of the aristocratic age. For such an occasion a platform was built beside a mountain stream. Cups were set afloat at some point upstream. A guest attempted to compose a poem before the cup passed. Then he drank the wine in the cup, refilled it, and put it back in the stream for the next person.

Meanwhile, the daughter of MATSU Motofusa had become Yoshi-tsune's principal wife. Since it was rare for a Regent, while Regent to be the son-in-law of a former Regent, and since both Lord Yoshi-tsune's father (Kanezane) and father-in-law (Motofusa) had been Regent or Chancellor, and also lay priests, people thought it proper for Yoshitsune—who excelled as an administrator, was an expert on court ceremony, and could compose poems superior to those of ancient times—to hold such a party. As the hearts of people were being stirred, and their eyes and ears opened [in anticipation of the great event], Lord Yoshitsune died in his sleep and without reason on the 7th day of the 3rd month of 1206. The empire was shocked and speechless. The Retired Emperor felt a boundless sorrow, but to no avail. Since this was something beyond the power of man to prevent, and since Iezane (the son of Lord KONOE Motomichi) had been Minister of the Left for some time, he was appointed Chancellor.

The Meeting of the Three Stars

During the spring of that year, a great change had occurred in the heavens, one referred to as "the meeting of the stars." With great fear, astrologers reported this to the throne. High Priest Jien was then at the Itsutsuji Palace, where Retired Emperor Go-Toba was temporarily residing, and was beginning to conduct a carefully arranged Yakushi Mass. The three stars (Venus, Jupiter, and Mars) appeared every evening in the western sky, invading each other's spheres. When it was raining, the stars could not be seen; but when the sky cleared, they would re-appear in strange positions. Again rain would fall and the stars would be hidden. This went on four or five days. People thought it fortunate if the sky did not clear for a while. But when the rain stopped, the stars would be seen still invading each other's spheres. The sky clouded up again on the third day, and from morning until night it looked like rain. After dusk on that day, and while the High Priest was offering up incantations, a light rain fortunately fell, and at dawn a report was sent to the throne that the sky was clearing. Then after this rain stopped, it was observed that the three stars had moved away from each other. Thus the great change in the heavens had finally come to an end. And not long afterward, Lord Yoshitsune suddenly died.

An astrologer by the name of Harumitsu explained the phenomenon in this way: "The confluence of the three stars is connected with a great sovereign crisis. The three stars jostled each other but have finally returned to their normal positions because [Go-Toba's] crisis was transferred to Lord Yoshitsune." Probably the vengeful soul [of Tadazane] was also active at the time. Go-Toba was especially pleased with the Mass that had been conducted by Jien, and he did such things as offer promotions and awards to participating priests.

People expressed such thoughts as these: "No matter how we look at it, the death of Lord Yoshitsune is a regrettable development of the Final Age. How sad it is to have a time fate that such good men are not to remain alive." People felt generally that the deaths of Minister of the Center KUJŌ Yoshimichi and this Regent KUJŌ Yoshitsune showed that the vengeful soul of Tadazane (Lord Chisoku-in) was still taking its revenge against the descendants of Tadamichi (Lord Hōshō-ji). Between and including Tadamichi and Yoshitsune, seven different men had been appointed Regent or Chancellor.[30] If only they had had it in their hearts to earnestly help Tadazane's soul to achieve Buddhahood after death, probably such disasters would not have occurred. Alas, if there had been only two or three officials who had been sincerely thinking about the Principles of things, probably there would have been some confidence [about the future].

As things moved along in this way, and because Retired Emperor Go-Toba was deeply grieved by the death of Regent Yoshitsune, Go-Toba had [Yoshitsune's son] KUJŌ Michiie (Middle Counselor and Middle Commander) appointed Senior Commander of the Imperial Bodyguards of the Left, giving him the position that had been left vacant by KONOE Iezane's appointment as Regent. That was on the 26th day of the 6th month of 1206. (I have written down the names of Regents and Chancellors in this disrespectful way because I am trying purposely to be clear.)[31]

The Vengeful Soul of Go-Shirakawa

Other strange things had happened. Around the year 1196—after Retired Emperor Go-Shirakawa had died—there lived a man by the name of TACHIBANA Kanenaka who had been an aide to Lay Priest FUJIWARA Kimitoki (Second Rank). Word was passed around that the soul of the deceased Go-Shirakawa had attached itself to this

---

30. The seven were: (1) FUJIWARA Tadamichi from 1121 to 1158; (2) KONOE Motozane from 1158 to 1166; (3) MATSU Motofusa from 1166 to 1179; (4) KONOE Motomichi from 1179 to 1183, 1184 to 1186, and 1196 to 1202; (5) MATSU Moroie from 1183 to 1184; (6) KUJŌ Kanezane from 1186 to 1196; and (7) KUJŌ Yoshitsune from 1202 to 1206. The last six were sons or grandsons of Tadamichi:

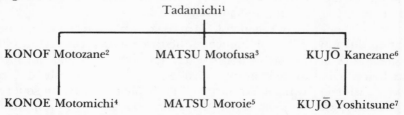

Tadamichi[1]

KONOF Motozane[2]	MATSU Motofusa[3]	KUJŌ Kanezane[6]
KONOE Motomichi[4]	MATSU Moroie[5]	KUJŌ Yoshitsune[7]

31. Apparently the respectful way was to use titles and positions, not personal names.

man's wife and that she was saying: "Build a shrine in my honor! Have the income of a province set aside for its upkeep!" A conference was held about this, and an incident developed when it was decided to exile Kanenaka to the province of Oki and his wife to the province of Awa. For a while people did not believe [that Go-Shirakawa's soul had actually possessed Kanenaka's wife], but when Middle Counselor Yoshiyasu was on the point of death—after having entered the priesthood—he exclaimed, "I am here! I am here!" So it was believed for a time that the deceased Go-Shirakawa's soul really was vengeful. Because Kanenaka's wife spoke in the same way, Lady Jōdo-ji Second Rank said that steps should be taken to gratify the wishes of Go-Shirakawa's soul. But when Kanenaka and his wife were called into the capital for seven days to see whether the wife actually was revealing the will of Go-Shirakawa, and when Lay Priest FUJIWARA Kimitoki was called in [to talk to the former aide and his wife], absolutely no messages from Go-Shirakawa were received. Since nothing happened to prove that the wife was expressing Go-Shirakawa's will, Kanenaka and his wife were declared insane and sent into exile because "she really has not been possessed."

Seven or eight years later—around the year 1206—an incident arose over the report that the soul of Go-Shirakawa had also attached itself to the wife of priest Nakakuni (son of priest Mitsutō but not the famous one by that name), a man who had served the deceased Go-Shirakawa morning and night. Nakakuni's wife was also saying: "Build a shrine in my honor!" Lady Jōdo-ji Second Rank and others were constantly having meetings with this woman, crying over her, and then reporting to Go-Toba. A conference of nobles was held at which it was decided that "the soul of Go-Shirakawa should be honored." While everyone was saying "that is the thing to do," it was heard that Kintsugu, former Minister of the Right, was expressing doubts. Therefore High Priest Jien wisely wrote out a letter—probably because he was really trusted by the Retired Emperor—and sent it to Prime Minister Yorizane, the husband of Lady Second Rank. In it he said:

Why do we do such a thing [as decide to build a shrine] because we hear reports [that a woman has been possessed by Go-Shirakawa's soul]? Certainly there have been many such cases [of shrines being built to pacify a vengeful soul]. But has Go-Shirakawa's soul become vengeful because of something done by Retired Emperor Go-Toba? And should the deceased Go-Shirakawa's soul be considered a manifestation of the Great Hachiman Bodhisattva and honored as an ancestral Kami of the Imperial House? Have there been signs of miraculous power? Have not such things occurred because people have believed what persons—possessed only by foxes (*yakan*) and demons (*tengū*)—

have said? Due to such beliefs, the idea of building a shrine has already been heard by everyone in the capital, and a proposal to build it near the Imperial Palace has been reported. In reflecting about these developments, I have the feeling that I see crazy people—shamans *(miko)*, mediums *(kōnagi)*, dancers *(mai)*, and comic actors *(sarugō)*, as well as coppersmiths and the like, all low-ranking people who served near the deceased Retired Emperor—exerting their influence over this woman [for their own selfish purposes]. The state is now going to ruin! Nevertheless, if it is still felt that such a shrine should be built, we should first ascertain the truth by having Imperial prayers sincerely offered.

When Retired Emperor Go-Toba heard these views, he immediately said: "I too think that way! Jien has made a fine statement!" His Majesty quickly held a serious discussion [with Jien] about the matter. Then when Go-Toba asked whether Nakakuni and his wife should be exiled, High Priest Jien again spoke out:

If Nakakuni and his wife have said what was in their own hearts without being at all possessed by foxes and badgers, they should of course be punished, even with exile. But we should not conclude that they have done this simply because they are strange. At an earlier time, the wife of a man named Kanenaka said strange things [but was judged to be insane]. Because there have always been foxes and demons that will take possession of crazy people, some persons have come to think that, because the state is disturbed, they can realize their heart-felt desire to have themselves worshipped [as Kami]. We have heard stories, in the past as well as at present, of efforts to comfort such crazy persons. And there are cases of actual possession. That is, some have developed the sickness of possession. But since punishment should not be meted out from above simply because a person is ill, we should place Nakakuni and his wife in isolation and pay no attention to what they say. Then the fox or badger will soon remove itself without a sound [if there is no angry soul possession]. Therefore you should simply wait and see what happens.

Retired Emperor Go-Toba said that High Priest Jien had spoken well, and the matter was dealt with as Jien recommended. Nakakuni and his wife were placed in isolation and allowed to reside at a mountain temple, called the Nakayama Temple, in the province of Settsu. While there, they did not again speak as mediums for the soul of Go-Shirakawa; and since they kept quiet, the matter was dropped. Understanding persons all admired [Go-Toba and Jien] for handling the affair in this way. Even Lady Jōdo-ji Second Rank ceased, in embarrassment, to support the proposal to build a shrine. It really was a strange development! Later on, Nakakuni was pardoned and Lady Second Rank apparently used him as a guardian.

Reflecting on the affair, I conclude that the current Retired Emperor is a fine sovereign. In his own mind and heart he seems to have considered the proposal only in terms of what was correct and right *(seigi)*. But since bad people in government were speaking to him, His Majesty may have thought that what he was being told was true. It is really appalling to realize that if, in that situation, such an understanding man [as Jien] had not been on hand, scandalous things would have occurred and, in a single day, this country would have been placed at the mercy of evil demons *(jama)*. The persons possessed by demons at that time were later pardoned and are still living.

Hōnen and Demon Possession

Another case of demon possession was that of the saint with the priestly name of Hōnen (1133–1212)[32] who has lived at the capital in recent years—during the Ken'ei era (1206–07). He established the Invocation-of-Buddha's-Name *(nembutsu)* teaching. Using the slogan "*Nembutsu* is the only teaching," he maintained that people should simply praise one Buddha (Amitābha), not practicing other Buddhist teachings, esoteric or exoteric.[33] This strange teaching was embraced by priests and nuns who lacked wisdom and were foolish. But the teaching was very popular and spread rapidly. Among those who embraced it was Lay Priest Anraku who had served under Lay Priest TAKASHINA Yasutsune. Calling himself a "practitioner of the select discipline," Anraku associated himself with a priest by the name of Jūren. These priests established a "rite of praising Buddha six times a day" *(rokuji raisan)*, claiming it had been performed by Shan-tao (613–681).[34] Some nuns also become ardent believers in this teaching. The *nembutsu* priests went so far as to make such promises as these:

> If you become a practitioner of this teaching, Amitābha Buddha will not consider you the least bit sinful, even if you lust after women and eat fish or fowl. If you follow the select discipline

32. Founder of the Pure Land Sect of Buddhism and the saint who had converted Jien's brother Kanezane to the Pure Land faith.

33. Buddhist teachings in that day were commonly divided into (1) *kengyō*, exoteric teachings that had been written down in sacred scripture and therefore open to all; and (2) *mikkyō*, esoteric teachings that were transmitted, secretly and mysteriously, from one believer to another. The Tendai Sect was generally identified with the first and the Shingon with the second, although the two sects embraced both teachings. It was Hōnen's rejection of these two types of teachings that caused the establishment Buddhist sects, and Jien, to turn against him.

34. A Chinese Pure Land teacher who was thought by Japanese Pure Land believers to have been an incarnation of Amitābha.

single-heartedly, and believe only in [the efficacy of] *nembutsu,* Amitābha will certainly come to welcome you [to Pure Land paradise] at the time of death.

While the movement was spreading throughout the capital and the countryside in this fashion, a Lady-in-Waiting at the Retired Emperor's detached palace, as well as the mother of the princely-priest of Ninna Temple,[35] became believers. These ladies secretly called Anraku and other *nembutsu* priests into their presence to explain their teaching. Anraku seems to have gone with some colleagues to see these ladies, even staying overnight. Because this was an unspeakable affair, Anraku and Jūren were eventually beheaded. Saint Hōnen was banished [in 1207] and not allowed to reside in the capital. Although the matter was disposed of with such [lenience], the movement really seemed to have been checked for a while. But since Hōnen had not been involved [with the visit to the ladies at Go-Toba's palace], he was pardoned, finally dying [in 1212] in the eastern mountains at a place called Ōtani. Even at the time of his death, Hōnen kept saying "Rebirth! Rebirth!" and people gathered round him. But there is no proof he was actually reborn into Pure Land paradise. Even the rites he performed in the final moments of life were not comparable to those performed by such Pure Land believers as Saint Zōga (917–1003). Because of such activities by Hōnen and his disciples, the movement has continued on down to the present day. And because the "select discipline"—with its permissive attitude toward lust for women and the eating of fish and fowl—had not yet been checked, the priests of Mt. Hiei rose up and forced the *nembutsu* priests to flee, exclaiming, "We will chase away Hōnen's *nembutsu* believers." There were such incidents as Shunjō of Todai Temple claiming that he was an incarnation of Amitābha and giving himself the name of "Glorious Amitābha Buddha." Many others received names that were made up of "Amitābha Buddha" preceded by a Chinese character [denoting some Buddhist truth], producing names like Kū Amida Butsu (Void Amitābha Buddha) and Hō Amida Butsu (Law Amitābha Buddha). Many priests and nuns had such names. In time, the activity of persons who called themselves the disciples of Hōnen left no doubt but that Buddhist Law had really reached its "deteriorating phase."[36]

35. A reference to Princely Lay Priest Dōjo (1196–1249), a Go-Toba son who was placed in the Ninna Temple in 1201 and ordained in 1206. His mother was a daughter of Nobukiyo, appointed Minister of the Center in 1211.

36. *Messō,* the last of the four phases *(laksana)* in Buddhist Law: birth, being, change, and deterioration.

According to my understanding of this phenomenon, there are two types of demons: the deceptive *(jumma)* and the antagonistic *(gyakuma)*. Deceptive demons were responsible for such pathetic teaching as Hōnen's. At a time when "the one teaching of Amitābha" will really increase divine grace, people will certainly have their sins and troubles removed and enter paradise. But before that time comes, and while the Shingon and "eliminate-illusion" *(shikan)* teachings of Tendai are still destined to prosper, no one will be able to achieve salvation by following the teachings of deceptive demons. Pathetic things happen when people think they can!

After Lord KUJŌ Kanezane had come to believe the *nembutsu* teaching propagated by Saint Hōnen, and after he had entered the priesthood with Hōnen serving as the ordaining priest, there occurred the wretched affair of Nakakuni's wife and the sad affair of Hōnen's banishment. Then, following a long illness, when he could not get up or sit down without help, Kanezane died blissfully on the 5th day of the 4th month of 1207.

KUJŌ Yoshitsune's Daughter

Since the deceased Regent's daughter Risshi (1192–1247) had become more and more like an abandoned child [following the death of her father in 1206], and various things were not working out as expected, people wondered what was going to happen to her. But when Retired Emperor Go-Toba thought of [making her the consort of Crown Prince Juntoku], both the Great Illuminating Kami worshipped at the Kasuga Shrine and the Great Hachiman Bodhisattva wanted her to give birth to an Imperial son who would come to rule the country well. Furthermore, everyone thought that both the Kami and the Buddhas would sympathetically bestow their blessings upon her because her grandfather Kanezane had immersed himself in the spirit and way of his ancestral Kami *(shashoku)*. Was this not why Yoshitsune's daughter Risshi was married (at the age of 18) to Crown Prince Juntoku on the 10th day of the 3rd month of 1209? Everyone felt that her younger brother KUJŌ Michiie, who was then Senior Commander of the Imperial Bodyguards of the Right, was more able than most adults and superior to his father Yoshitsune in everything he did. Consequently, he handled the marriage preparations magnificently.

The Burning of a Pagoda and the Meaning Thereof

Another unusual thing happened. On the 15th day of the 5th month of 1208, the top of the nine-storied pagoda of the Hosshō Temple was struck by lightning and burned. It was terrible! Fortunately the fire did not spread to other buildings. The Retired Em-

peror had just said to High Priest Jien: "Taboos *(tsutsushimi)* are
heavy upon me! Come and carry out a mass that you think will have
a miraculous effect!" Jien replied that he would conduct a Lotus
Sutra mass and went to Go-Toba's palace with 20 priestly assistants.
Soon after Jien had completed the seven-day mass at Go-Toba's
palace and departed, the pagoda burned down. The High Priest
gave the matter some serious thought and made this statement:

> It would have been regrettable indeed if the pagoda had burned
> down while I was at the Retired Emperor's palace carrying out the
> mass. But I feel that while the Retired Emperor was destined to be
> weighed down with taboos, those taboos were certainly trans-
> ferred to the pagoda. So His Majesty should not grieve! The fire
> was a good thing! His Majesty should simply issue an order, im-
> mediately, that the pagoda be rebuilt quickly. The burning of the
> pagoda at this time came as a substitute for His Majesty's death. If
> the pagoda is rebuilt soon, His Majesty will be "destroying evil and
> creating good."

So the Retired Emperor quickly ordered Senior Counselor SAIONJI
Kintsune to rebuild the pagoda, using income from the province of
Iyo. And preparations for reconstruction were soon started.

Eisai's Contribution to Reconstruction and His Reward

But a serious problem for the state emerged because Iyo was
troubled by this additional assessment. A saint by the name of Eisai
(1141–1215)[37]—a priest who had lived long in China—was said to
have talent for such reconstruction work, and so he was granted income from the province of Suwo [and asked to expedite the rebuilding of the pagoda]. Consultant FUJIWARA Nagafusa was placed in
charge of the project. (First Grade Priest Shōgen, Superintendent of
the Hosshō Temple, had witnessed the burning of the pagoda and
died immediately thereafter. He was over 80 at the time. How
deeply moving this was!) The pagoda was completed in 1213, in the
seventh [*sic*] year following its destruction by fire, and then dedication rites were held.

Eisai requested that he be appointed High Priest [as a reward for
his contribution to the reconstruction of the pagoda]. He had al-

37. Eisai, referred to here as Yōjō, went to China in 1167 and again in
1187, returning from his second trip in 1191. Like Hōnen, he was subjected
to pressure from the Tendai order but went to Kamakura in 1199 where he
obtained support that enabled him to start building, in 1202, the Kennin
Temple of Kyoto. Although he is considered the founder of the Rinzai Sect
of Zen, his willingness to participate in the restoration of the Hosshō-ji
pagoda demonstrated—as did his contributions to the rebuilding of Tōdai-ji
in 1206—his desire to cooperate with the established Buddhist sects.

ready held the rank of First Grade *(hōin)* but was now appointed to the office of High Priest *(sōjō)*. The Retired Emperor came to regret this appointment, saying that it was something he should not have done. Eisai also brashly asked for the title of Grand Preceptor *(daishi)*, but High Priest Jien put a stop to that. Eisai was nevertheless appointed High Priest.

Another Change in the Heavens

Meanwhile, on the 30th day of the 9th month of 1210, a comet—the most significant of all changes in the heavens, and one that had not occurred for a long time—appeared on several successive nights, burning for a prolonged period. The people of the country were afraid of what was going to happen. Imperial prayers were offered up. High Priest Jien and others did such things as carry out the Burning Light Mass, and so the comet disappeared. But while questions were being raised about the Imperial taboo, the comet appeared again on the 11th month of that same year. This time, even the astrologers were greatly surprised, and people said: "Has not this comet appeared because the Retired Emperor, having expressed his faith and offered up Imperial prayers, has received a dream-revelation from divine beings?" It was therefore arranged to have Emperor Tsuchimikado yield the throne immediately to his successor, and the ceremony for the accession of Juntoku was held on the 25th day of the 11th month of 1210. Juntoku's consort, KUJŌ Yoshi-tsune's daughter, was advanced to Secondary Empress shortly afterward—on the 25th day of the 1st month of 1211.

ŌIMIKADO Yorizane's daughter, Tsuchimikado's Secondary Empress while Juntoku was Crown Prince, should have gone to Tsuchimikado's palace after his abdication, but Go-Toba felt that "she should not go there at the present time." She had given the name and title of Onmei-mon In [a few months before Tsuchimikado's abdication in 1210].[38]

38. The mothers and Empresses of Tsuchimikado and of his successor Juntoku (and their maternal fathers and grandfathers) were:

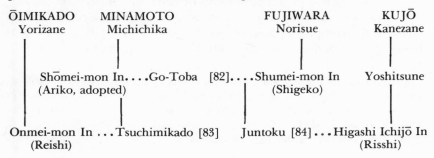

ŌIMIKADO	MINAMOTO		FUJIWARA	KUJŌ
Yorizane	Michichika		Norisue	Kanezane
	Shōmei-mon In....Go-Toba	[82]....	Shumei-mon In	Yoshitsune
	(Ariko, adopted)		(Shigeko)	
Onmei-mon In ...Tsuchimikado [83]			Juntoku [84] ...Higashi Ichijō In	
(Reishi)			(Risshi)	

Collapse of a Palace Gate

At the time the Extraordinary Harvest Festival *(daijō-e)*[39] [of 1211] was to be held, the Suzaku Gate of the palace suddenly collapsed; and then Empress Shunka-mon In[40] died. Since the Emperor was in mourning, the Festival was postponed until the following year. People were startled that the Suzaku Gate should have collapsed on the very day that the Emperor had proceeded [to the Kamo Shrine] to carry out the Imperial Purification Rite for the Festival. The Festival was therefore postponed, following an earlier precedent of calling it off after the Purification Rite alone had been performed. People were anxious about this but nothing untoward happened. The Suzaku Gate was rebuilt the following year, and after that the Extraordinary Harvest Festival was celebrated without misfortune. Probably the comet had portended the transfer of the throne to Juntoku. The taboos of the Retired Emperor had been completely removed.

Yorizane Reaches Too High

At the time when Prime Minister ŌIMIKADO Yorizane's daughter was Emperor Tsuchimikado's Secondary Empress, an incident occurred that has been referred to as "the Empress's visit to the Kasuga Shrine." Although there was not a single precedent for a man in Yorizane's position to accompany an Imperial party on such a visit, Prime Minister Yorizane did just as he wanted. Attended by a personal bodyguard assigned to him by the Emperor, he acted like a Number One Man. After that, Yorizane entered the Buddhist priesthood and came to be known as the Lay Priest Prime Minister. A person may achieve all personal desires that are appropriate to his status but should certainly be very careful to restrain himself from thinking of achieving anything more!

New Appointments

The mother of the current Emperor [Juntoku] was given the *in* title on the 7th day of the 6th month of 1207. She was not promoted to the position of Empress. She was, however, advanced to Second Rank and promptly appointed to the assimilated position of Empress, receiving the name and title of Shumei-mon In. The prece-

---

39. One of the three great ceremonies held at the Imperial Court following the enthronement of an Emperor or Empress. See D. C. Holtom, *The Japanese Enthronement Ceremonies, with an Account of the Imperial Regalia* (Tokyo, 1972), pp. 73–111.

40. Go-Toba's daughter by KUJŌ Kinshi.

dent followed was first established when Hachijō In was so honored [in 1161].[41] The *in* title has been recently granted to the mother of a Crown Prince after her son ascended the throne.[42] So Shumei-mon In's father Norisue (Second Rank) was awarded a posthumous appointment as Minister of the Left [in 1211].[43] He was a man who should certainly have entered the priesthood, but he died thinking about the [possibility of his grandson becoming Emperor] and without having become a priest. It was fortunate for him that things worked out in this way.

KUJŌ Michiie, Senior Commander of the Imperial Bodyguards of the Left [and brother of Juntoku's Empress], was appointed Minister of the Center on the 29th day of the 6th month of 1212.

Death of Shogun Yoriie

Let's turn to the Shogun's affairs in the eastern provinces. MINAMOTO Yoriie (1182–1204) was advanced to Second Rank [*sic*] and made Commander of the Palace Gate Guards of the Left [in 1200]. Because Yoriie was appointed (as Yoritomo's successor) to the office of Shogun, Middle Counselor FUJIWARA Norimitsu (then Controller) was sent to Kamakura as an Imperial messenger to report the appointment.

41. Hachijō In was a Toba daughter born about 14 years after Toba's abdication in 1123. She was given the assimilated rank of Empress in 1146 (at the age of nine), even though she had not been a consort or mother of an Emperor.
42. A reference to Emperor Tsuchimikado's mother Shōmei-mon In (1171–1257), who received the *in* title in 1202. Cf. note 38, above.
43. Although FUJIWARA Norisue does not rate an entry in ordinary biographical dictionaries, and never held a ministerial post until six years after his death, he does occupy a central position in the *Gukanshō* interpretation of recent Japanese history. He is given considerable credit, first of all, for recommending in 1183 that Retired Emperor Go-Shirakawa ally himself with the MINAMOTO rather than the TAIRA, and for bringing up the young Emperor Go-Toba. But that which makes Norisue truly important for Jien is his paternity of Juntoku's Imperial mother. The 1210 enthronement of Juntoku brought to an end the hated Tsuchimikado reign that was associated with the machinations of Michichika and the downfall of KUJŌ Kanezane. Moreover, Juntoku had a KUJŌ Empress whose son (the future Emperor Chūkyō) was destined, according to the *Gukanshō*, to have the joint support of the KUJŌ house and the MINAMOTO clan. Norisue also had two influential nieces: Noriko (Lady Gyōbu Third Rank) who had been Michichika's wife; and Lady Second Rank who, Jien writes, exerted roughly the same sort of influence at the capital that Masako exerted in Kamakura after Sanetomo's assassination in 1219.

In about the 9th month of 1203, Yoriie became seriously ill and was about to die. He had been favoring a daughter of HIKI Yoshikazu, a Fifth Rank Lieutenant of the Imperial Police from the province of Awa; and by her he had a son (Ichiman) to whom he wished to transfer the headship of the MINAMOTO house and all its possessions, intending to have Yoshikazu conduct military-government affairs in his grandson's behalf. But Yoriie's maternal uncle, HŌJŌ Tokimasa (Governor of Tōtōmi), felt that Sanetomo (Yoriie's younger brother and Yoritomo's beloved son) should have been selected. So, on the 20th day of the 9th month of 1203, HŌJŌ Tokimasa had HIKI Yoshikazu called in. Yoshikazu was grabbed by Lay Priest AMANO Tōkage and was stabbed to death by NITTA Shirō. Then HŌJŌ Tokimasa dispatched troops [to destroy Ichiman]. Yoriie, being sick, had been moved to the residence of ŌE Hiromoto. When Ichiman's mother heard that soldiers had been sent to kill her son (who was at a place by the main MINAMOTO house), she took the boy in her arms and escaped through a small gate. The soldiers guarding the house, knowing shame, did not flee and were killed.

Among Yoriie's soldiers on duty at Hiromoto's residence at the time was KASUYA Arisue.[44] Even the enemy thought it a shame to kill a man like that. So they yelled out: "You have no reason to oppose us! Come on out!" But Arisue did not surrender. He was killed only after he had taken the lives of eight enemy soldiers. People really thought it a shame that he was killed.

Other soldiers killed at that time were KASAHARA Jūrō Chika-kage[45] of the Palace Gate Guards of the Left and SHIBUKAWA Kanetada[46] of the Department of Justice. The HIKI sons, HIKI's son-in-law KODAMA, and others associated with Yoriie were all cut down. This engagement was on the 2nd day of the 9th month of 1203. Then, on the 5th day of the 9th month, NITTA Shirō—who had been Yoriie's special aide, and who had killed Yoshikazu without knowing that this would endanger Yoriie himself—fought a stiff battle with HŌJŌ Yoshitoki and was killed. NITTA Shirō and Yoshitoki had been heads of the eastern and western Military Affairs Offices of Yoriie's main house.

On the 10th day of the 9th month, Yoriie was confined to a mountain temple, the Shuzen-ji[47] in the province of Izu. Suffering from the disease of the current epidemic, he had entered the priesthood in the middle of the night on the 30th day of the 8th month of 1203.

44. A son-in-law of Yoshikazu.
45. Another son-in-law of Yoshikazu.
46. Yoshikazu's father-in-law.
47. A temple said to have been founded by a Kūkai disciple in 798.

While staying at the ŌE Hiromoto residence and after entering the priesthood, he had come to feel that his retainers would all be on good terms with each other now that Ichiman would become the next Shogun. He did not know that things were destined to turn out in such a disastrous way. He recovered from his illness shortly after entering the priesthood. Having heard of the attack on Ichiman on the 2nd day of the 9th month, he seized the long sword by his side and said: "Why have they done this?" When he tried to stand, he found that his illness made it impossible for him to do so. He was therefore helped by his mother, who had become a nun.[48] He was taken into custody soon afterward and confined to the Shuzen Temple. That was a sad affair indeed!

HŌJŌ Yoshitoki Kills Ichiman and Yoriie

On the 3rd day of the 11th month of 1203, HŌJŌ Yoshitoki (1162–1224) finally captured the young Ichiman. The boy was then stabbed, killed, and buried by a retainer named Tōma. Then, on the 18th day of the 9th month of the following year, Lay Priest Yoriie was also stabbed to death at the Shuzen Temple. We hear that because Yoriie could not be easily subdued, his enemies killed him by tightening a rope around his neck and pulling out his testicles. This was behavior that cannot even be talked about. Somehow or other, there had to be retribution (*mukui*) for such [cruelty and treachery].[49] No matter how strong and fierce a man may be, he does not have the power [to avoid retribution].

HIKI Yoshikazu's wife was the daughter of Master MISEYA Yukitoki who belonged to the military group (*tō*) in that particular district [of Musashi] that was headed by [Yoshikazu's] father. This wife gave birth to Ichiman's mother. MISEYA Yukitoki had also married a daughter to [a leader of] the KODAMA military group.

KAJIWARA House Destroyed

In about 1199, KAJIWARA Kagetoki—considered the leading MINAMOTO retainer—had been made Yoriie's guardian. But complaints were made against him, probably because he was painfully self-centered and was contemptuous of those under him. When charges were made and he was about to be executed, he left his province for the capital [in 1200] but was killed on the way. Not a single child of his was spared, and all his original Kamakura retain-

---

48. MINAMOTO Yoritomo's widow Masako, who became a nun at the time of Yoritomo's death in 1199.

49. Jien is implying that Sanetomo had to be assassinated in 1219 (by Yoriie's son) as retribution for the treachery that had been inflicted upon Yoriie in 1204.

ers were killed. People thought this would have serious repercussions for Yoriie and, sure enough, Yoriie was eliminated in this cruel way on that particular day [in 1204].⁵⁰

MINAMOTO Sanetomo Appointed Shogun

Messengers were sent to the capital to report these developments, and a coming-of-age ceremony was held for Senman, who received the name of MINAMOTO Sanetomo from the Emperor. Not long afterward, on the 8th day of the 12th month of 1203, an Imperial edict was issued appointing Sanetomo to the office of Shogun; and his mother's father, HŌJŌ Tokimasa (1138–1215), assumed control of affairs in the eastern provinces. While Tokimasa was handling affairs in the name of Sanetomo, who was not yet an adult, the question came up as to who should marry his daughter to the young Shogun. This turned out to be Senior Counselor FUJIWARA Nobukiyo, a young brother of Go-Toba's Imperial mother (Shichijō In).⁵¹ Nobikyo's 13-year-old daughter (one of several) was elegantly prepared for the wedding, and soldiers were dispatched from the eastern provinces to welcome her to Kamakura. She departed from Kyoto on the 3rd day of the 11th month of 1204. An Imperial grandstand had been erected on the narrow road on the west side of the Hosshō Temple, where Retired Emperor Go-Toba viewed the bridal procession. Zōen, First Grade Superintendent of the Enshō Temple, had been ordered to build the grandstand.

FUJIWARA Nobukiyo had been suffering for years from a serious illness that everyone thought would surely kill him. Finally [in 1211] he recovered and was appointed Minister of the Center. But he entered the priesthood on the 18th day of the 2nd month of 1215 and died on the 15th day of the 2nd month of the following year. When writing about the affairs of a man like this, I seem to be writing of things that happened long ago.

50. Here Jien is saying that just as Sanetomo's assassination had been retribution for the cruel way Yoriie had been treated, Yoriie's own death was retribution for the ruthless way he had destroyed his guardian.

51. The marriage of Nobukiyo's daughter to Sanetomo tied the MINAMOTO clan to the Imperial House as follows:

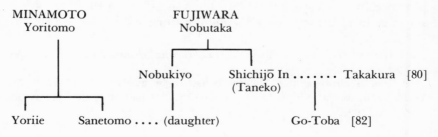

HŌJŌ Tokimasa Opposed by His Daughter Masako

While time was passing in this way, HŌJŌ Tokimasa of the eastern provinces had obtained a young wife who gave birth to many children, including several daughters. She was the daughter of MAKI Munechika, Assistant Director of the Bureau of the Imperial Attendants. The young wife's brother, MAKI Tokichika of Ōoka (an official of the Imperial Police), was made a Fifth Rank Lieutenant; and her father MAKI Munechika, who had served several years with TAIRA Yorimori, was given an estate in the province of Suruga called Ōoka-no-maki. It was indeed strange that such good fortune should have come to persons who were not soldiers.

HŌJŌ Tokimasa sent his son Masanori to the capital [in 1204], where he received such honors as an appointment to the post of Assistant Director of the Imperial Stables. But Masanori soon died. Then Tokimasa sent the husband of his eldest daughter, a man named Tomomasa, to the capital. Apparently Tomomasa was the young brother of [ŌUCHI] Koreyoshi. We hear that he had become a member of the MINAMOTO clan by his adoption as Yoritomo's son. Tomomasa went to call on Retired Emperor Go-Toba and was in attendance upon His Majesty even on such occasions as archery contests.[52] Tokimasa's other daughters all came to be wives of nobles above the Fifth Rank.

When Masako (1156–1225), known as Lady Mother-Nun,[53] heard that her son Sanetomo was going to be killed, and that Tomomasa was to be named Shogun, she created a storm. She called in MIURA Yoshimura and said: "What I have heard is really true! Help me! What shall we do?" Whereupon Yoshimura, who was an able conspirator, placed Sanetomo and Masako in the house of Masako's brother, HŌJŌ Yoshitoki (1162–1224). Then Yoshimura quietly assembled his retainers and, announcing that he had received orders from the Shogun to prepare for battle, summoned Tokimasa (Masako's father and Sanetomo's grandfather) to Kamakura and forced him to return to Izu, his home province. Then Yoshimura ordered soldiers in the capital to kill Tomomasa, reporting his intentions to the Retired Emperor. Tomomasa's house, located at the intersection of Rokkaku and East Tōin, was surrounded. After a brief battle, Tomomasa set fire to his house, fought his way out, and retreated toward Ōtsu. Apparently his rear was purposely kept open for an escape. Because Yoshimura's soldiers were overtaking him, Tomomasa committed suicide at Yamashina. We are told that a man by the name of Kanamochi, a soldier attached to the Constable of

52. *Kasagake* (rush-hat hanging) was a form of target-shooting from horseback that was popular in those days.
53. *Haha no amagimi.* She was also referred to as *ama shōgun* (Nun Shōgun).

Hōki, cut off Tomomasa's head and brought it to the capital, and that Retired Emperor Go-Toba went by carriage to the gate of his palace to see it. This happened on the 26th day of the intercalary 7th month of 1205.

There was nothing wrong in Masako's forcing her father HŌJŌ Tokimasa to return to his home province of Izu, for she was both the widow of MINAMOTO Yoritomo and the mother of MINAMOTO Sanetomo. HŌJŌ Tokimasa was also Yoshitoki's father, but because Tokimasa's young wife had done such things [as try to make Tomomasa Shogun], Yoshitoki joined Masako in confining their father to Izu, explaining that Tokimasa had decided to destroy his own maternal grandson Sanetomo. So Sanetomo was placed firmly at the head of the military government. Masako, daughter of Tokimasa and mother of Yoriie and Sanetomo, was still alive and in control. Yoshitoki reported to the throne as Tokimasa's son and rose to a high position at court, becoming Acting Commissioner of the Capital Office of the Right.

In the eastern provinces, Yoshitoki and his sister Masako administered the affairs of the military government. And at the capital, Lady Second Rank was firmly in control. So this country of Japan really is a state where "women are the finishing touches."

In his day, Tokimasa had been the most powerful figure in the eastern provinces. He had killed all soldiers—from HATAKEYAMA Shigetada on down—who were the least bit troublesome. Shigetada had been a famous soldier who was reported to be "the best." Even after his forces were defeated, no one dared to approach him. In the end he died by his own hand.

The Meaning of These Developments

I can not think that the destruction of all TAIRA descendants or the course of events for the descendants of MINAMOTO Yoritomo— who really pacified the empire and with an ability that was rare for either ancient or modern times—have been the doings of man. The ancestral Kami of the Imperial House *(sōbyō)* have decided that soldiers are to control the state in this visible world *(ken)*. This is now a requirement of, and in line with, Principle. Understanding people should realize, moreover, that there are many TAIRA vengeful souls [whose destructive activities] are simply the working out of causal effect *(inga)* in the realm of the invisible *(myō)*.

MINAMOTO Sanetomo's Devotion to Learning

As days and nights passed in this way, and as people were wondering how affairs in the eastern provinces would turn out, Sanetomo was gradually growing up and saying that he wanted to take personal charge of military affairs. A man by the name of MINAMOTO Nakaaki (son of Mitsutō) improved the position of his house, entered the Confucian house of SUGAWARA, became a disciple of SUGAWARA Nagamori, devoted himself to the study of Confucianism, and served as Shogun Sanetomo's tutor—probably because of an Outer Cause *(en)*. Nakaaki went frequently to Kamakura, and Sanetomo came to devote more time and energy to learning than to military affairs. When Nakaaki was at the capital, he did such things as dispatch messengers to Kamakura. While people were gossiping about the way Nakaaki was teaching the Shogun through various Chinese precedents, they wondered if it was not quite wrong [for Sanetomo to have such interests].

Trouble at Kamakura

Strange things were also occurring in the eastern provinces. Sanetomo's house was completely burned and a dangerous situation developed. The head of the MIURA group (WADA Yoshimori of the Palace Gate Guards of the Left) was intensely jealous of HŌJŌ Yoshitoki and wanted to kill him. Hearing that his plans had been leaked, Yoshimori suddenly forced his way into Yoshitoki's house on the 2nd day of the 5th month of 1213. Since Sanetomo was with Yoshitoki, and the battle was fought with Sanetomo at the front of Yoshitoki's forces, most soldiers were on Yoshitoki's side. After two days of fighting, WADA Yoshimori's head was taken. Persons allied with Yoshimori, including the KODAMA and YOKOYAMA groups, were all killed. After that, the remnants of Yoshimori's force reassembled. They took Yoriie's fourteen-year-old son—the one who had become a Zen priest under Saint Eisai—and planned to fight their way out in his name. But Yoshitoki also heard about this; and the entire reassembled force was destroyed. The fourteen-year-old Zen monk's suicide was carried out with dignity, and the situation in the eastern provinces quieted down somewhat.

KUJŌ Risshi Gives Birth to an Imperial Son

Secondary Empress Risshi also became seriously ill. Her brother, First Grade Priest Ryōson, had been a disciple of Senior High Priest Jikkyō and had, after the deaths of his teacher Jikkyō and his father Yoshitsune, performed ascetic rites at such places as the reedy grotto in the mountains of Ōmine. Whenever this brother would happen to come to his sister's palace to offer up incantations for her recovery, he would pray improperly. Since the effects of a curse were still being manifested, he came to see that he had been praying improperly. So he prayed correctly and his sister recovered miraculously. He had held only the ordinary First Grade *(hōin)* rank but was now appointed to the post of Senior Vicar General *(daisōzu)*.

Then the Secondary Empress suddenly became pregnant and gave birth to an Imperial daughter (the future Meigi-mon In) on the 24th day of the 4th month of 1217. It was more difficult to produce an

Imperial son! While people were thinking that since her father Yoshitsune was not alive and that she really would prefer to have had a son, it was heard—in the first month of 1218—that she was pregnant again. And, at about 4:00 A.M. in the morning of the 10th day of the 10th month of 1218, she gave birth, without complications, to an Imperial son [the future Emperor Chūkyō], just as she had wanted. Retired Emperor Go-Toba was delighted, for this was what he had really wanted, and soon—on the 26th day of the 11th month of 1218—the boy was appointed Crown Prince. Ever since Seiwa's [appointment as Crown Prince in 850] it has been customary to appoint an Imperial son Crown Prince at the age of one. It is indeed a rare thing to have such an auspicious event in the Final Age! People at all levels of society—high, middle, and low—had such thoughts as this: "Will not the Age last a while longer?"

Few Daughters of Regent/Chancellors Have Produced Imperial Sons

Jōtō-mon In (988–1074), Michinaga's daughter and Ichijō's Empress, was the Imperial mother of two Emperors: Go-Ichijō and Go-Suzaku. Her sister Kishi (1007–25), known as Head Mistress of the Imperial Handmaids' Office *(naishi no kami)*, was the Imperial mother of Go-Reizei. After that, other daughters of Regent/Chancellors were placed in the Imperial Palace and promoted to the position of Empress, but not all of them produced Imperial sons. None of the following did:

Name	Daughter of	Empress of
Lady Shijō (1036–1121) (Kanshi)	Lord Uji (Yorimichi)	Go-Reizei
Lady Empress Dowager Ono (1021–1102) (Kanshi)	Lord Ōnijō (Norimichi)	Go-Reizei
Kaya no In (1095–1102) (Yasuko)	Lord Chisoku-in (Tadazane)	Toba, after abdication
Kōka-mon In (1121–81) (Seishi)	Lord Hōshō-ji (Tadamichi)	Sutoku
Lady Empress (1146–73) (Ikushi)	Lord Hōshō-ji (Tadamichi)	Nijō

One gave birth to an Imperial daughter (Shunka-mon In), but I have already written about her.[54]

Gishū-mon In (1173–1238) (Ninshi)	Lord KUJŌ (Kanezane)	Empress of the present Retired Emperor

54. KUJŌ Ninshi's daughter (discussed earlier in this chapter) by Retired Emperor Go-Toba.

So it was indeed a rare thing for Secondary Empress Risshi, the daughter of Lord Kyōgoku Yoshitsune, to give birth to a princess and then to an Imperial son who was appointed Crown Prince.

SAIONJI Kintsune and ŌIMIKADO Yorizane

Senior Counselor SAIONJI Kintsune (1171–1224) was appointed Master of Crown Prince Chūkyō's Household [in 1218]. And he served well.

SAIONJI Kintsune was in a direct line of descent from SAIONJI Michisue (1090–1128), a Middle Counselor and Commander of the Palace Gate Guards of the Left who had obtained the hereditary right to use a carriage decorated with a *tomoe* design. Michisue had in turn been the son and heir of KAN'IN Kinzane (1043–1107), Master of Crown Prince Toba's Household. Because Michisue had died early, while still Middle Counselor, he had not been able to assume the responsibilities of a brother to the Imperial mother (Taiken-mon In) of two Emperors (Sutoku and Go-Shirakawa) when those Emperors were on the throne.[55] KAN'IN Kinzane had two other sons whose descendants rose to the position of Minister or Senior Commander: TOKUDAIJI Saneyoshi (1096–1157) and SANJŌ Saneyuki (1079–1162).[56]

SAIONJI Michisue's son Kinmichi rose as high as Senior Counselor but died before he had become the highest-ranking Senior Counselor. Then Kinmichi's son Sanemune (1145–1210) was appointed Minister of the Center [in 1205]. It was pointed out then that no person in that house had yet risen as high as Minister. But no one

55. Michisue did not die until the 6th year of the Sutoku reign, and yet Tadamichi (Jien's father) was Regent during the whole of that reign.

56. Kizane's sons founded three houses:

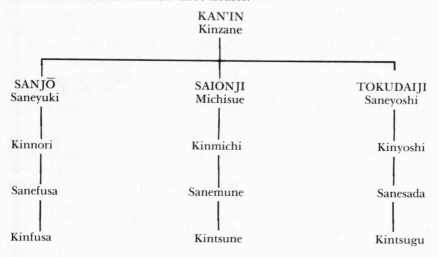

KAN'IN
Kinzane

SANJŌ Saneyuki	SAIONJI Michisue	TOKUDAIJI Saneyoshi
Kinnori	Kinmichi	Kinyoshi
Sanefusa	Sanemune	Sanesada
Kinfusa	Kintsune	Kintsugu

had a stronger claim to the position at that time. He received the appointment for two reasons: his son Kintsune was an aide to Retired Emperor Go-Toba in those years and was consulting with His Majesty about various matters; and Sanemune was then suffering from palsy [and Go-Toba felt sorry for him].

Then SAIONJI Kintsune asked for an appointment as Senior Commander. An earlier precedent for such an appointment had been established when Prime Minister SANJŌ Saneyuki's son Kinnori was named Minister of the Center [in 1157].[57] Because Regent KUJŌ Yoshitsune had said to SAIONJI Kintsune: "The SANJŌ Kinnori appointment as Minister of the Center is certainly a precedent that applies to you," Retired Emperor Go-Toba agreed to promote Kintsune to Senior Commander when the time came for Kintsune's father Sanemune to resign from his ministerial post.

But Lady Second Rank (wife of Lay Priest Prime Minister ŌIMIKADO Yorizane) also recommended that her husband's brother (Senior Counselor Morotsune, who was also Yorizane's adopted son), a man junior to Kintsune, be promoted to Senior Commander. She argued that this was something that had to be done. So both SAIONJI Kintsune and ŌIMIKADO Yorizane were seeking a position that was not yet open, a common practice in the Final Age. People used to wait until an office had been vacated by death before requesting an appointment to that office if the incumbent had committed no crime and wanted to retain the position. But because we have come to this Final Age, office seekers urge incumbents to resign, claiming that administration as a whole will improve if people are given what they want. And because people do this sort of thing, it has become customary to ask for positions before a vacancy occurs. This is why such serious incidents can be expected.

The Retired Emperor had been making use of the services of FUJIWARA Tadatsuna, a member of the Retired Emperor's guard and a man who really had no ability in anything. This Tadatsuna did not even know Chinese characters but was a member of a group that provided guards for officials in various noble houses. Because he had served near Go-Toba ever since His Majesty had occupied the throne, he had risen to be Director of the Bureau of the Treasury. So Go-Toba, residing at the Minase Palace, ordered Tadatsune to go tell Kintsune the following: "Since the Lay Priest Prime Minister Yorizane had made this request, I am undecided as to who should be appointed Senior Commander at this time." The message did not mean that the Retired Emperor had broken his promise. His Majesty went as far as he could. But Tadatsuna said nothing to convey the

57. SANJŌ Kinnori was appointed Minister of the Center on the same day that his father, SANJŌ Saneyuki, resigned as Prime Minister.

Retired Emperor's intentions and left the impression that His Majesty had really broken his promise. So Senior Counselor Kintsune became resentful and bitter, saying such things as this:

> In that case I will become a lay priest in some out-of-the-way place. People in this physical world—high or low—are concerned about their wives and children, and since I have ties [through my wife] with Sanetomo, I will simply send my family to Kamakura and prolong their lives.

Kintsune's son Saneuji (1193–1269), Middle Counselor and Commander of the Palace Gate Guards of the Left, was a sincere man who was adept at composing both Chinese and Japanese poems and who was an aide to the Retired Emperor. Saneuji told Tadatsuna exactly what Kintsune had said. Then Tadatsuna terrified the Retired Emperor by telling him that Kintsune "is going to appeal his case to Sanetomo."[58] Go-Toba became angry and immediately had Senior Counselor Kintsune placed under house arrest. Apparently the affair did not arise simply from competition over the position of Senior Commander. There were, it seems, deep undercurrents. Probably some trouble had been generated by princes who wanted the Retired Emperor's heir to be someone other than the current Emperor Juntoku.[59] I do not know precisely, but Go-Toba may have thought from the beginning—ever since Juntoku was placed on the throne—that he really wanted Juntoku to become his heir and to be the sovereign who would administer affairs of state as a Retired Emperor.

58. SAIONJI Kintsune had this marital connection with MINAMOTO Sanetomo:

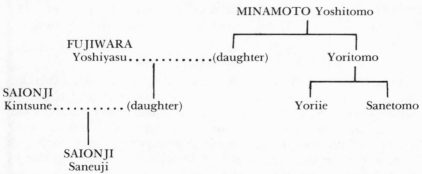

59. Jien was apparently pointing to political rivalry between those who wanted Tsuchimikado and those who wanted Juntoku to succeed Go-Toba as the Retired Emperor who would assume control over court affairs. The implication is that ŌIMIKADO Yorizane (and his influential wife Lady Second Rank) favored Tsuchimikado, whereas SAIONJI Kintsune (and the KUJŌ) favored Juntoku.

MINAMOTO Sanetomo eventually heard about these developments and was greatly surprised. His thoughts ran like this:

> Because Kintsune has close family relations with me, he has—at a time of trouble—entrusted his own wife and children to me, apparently saying to his family that he only wanted them to stay alive. And because of this, he was immediately subjected to Imperial censure. My father-in-law Nobukiyo has been my liaison officer with the Retired Emperor for years, but Senior Counselor Kintsune's reports to me have also been reliable. There is no reason why he should now be placed under house arrest.

Becoming thoroughly convinced that [Yorizane's wife], Lady Second Rank, had turned against him, Sanetomo sent word to the capital that her part in this [action against Kintsune] was regrettable. Lady Second Rank was surprised and upset. She therefore asked that the Retired Emperor pardon Kintsune, and her request was granted on the 18th day of the 2nd month of 1218.[60] These events may be described as "past events that should simply be thought of as dreams, and then forgotten."

Masako Comes to the Capital

On the 21st day of the 2nd month of that year, MINAMOTO Sanetomo's mother Masako arrived at the capital, saying that she wanted to make a pilgrimage to the Kumano Shrines. Lady Second Rank called on her several times and, while they were seeing each other, Masako became the first nun to be advanced to Third Rank. She returned to Kamakura on the 15th day of the 4th month of 1218. Then she was advanced to Second Rank and came to be referred to as the Lady Second Rank of Kamakura. People said: "This is the first time such [a high Rank has been granted to a nun]."

MINAMOTO Sanetomo's Ambitions

Meanwhile, Nakaaki was going back and forth between Kamakura and the capital as a messenger. Earlier on, Sanetomo had requested and received the positions of Middle Counselor and Middle Commander, but now he wanted promotion to Senior Commander. So Minister of the Left KUJŌ Michiie exchanged his post as Senior Commander for the right to have a bodyguard. Explaining that he was following a precedent established by Lord KUJŌ Kanezane, Michiie quickly vacated [the position of Senior Commander], and Sanetomo was then made Senior Commander of the Imperial Body-

---

60. Another example of Lady Second Rank's remarkable influence. No references to Sanetomo's complaints, to Kintsune's pardon, or to Lady Second Rank's request are found in other sources. [NKBT, 86.310, note 3.]

guards of the Left [in 1218].[61] Not long after that, Sanetomo said that he wanted an appointment as Minister. Strange reports were heard that he would not be content with Minister of the Center, since previous appointments to that position had turned out badly —both TAIRA Shigemori and TAIRA Munemori were Ministers of the Center [when they died].

KUJŌ Yoshisuke

Meanwhile, people were thinking of Minister of the Left KUJŌ Yoshisuke (1185–1218), Lord KUJŌ Kanezane's son [and Jien's nephew], as a really important jewel for the Imperial court since, as Minister of the Left and First Minister, he was a scholar unequalled in either ancient or modern Japan.[62] Understanding persons thought he [and his brother Yoshitsune] were really like FUJIWARA Morotada (Minister of the Left) and FUJIWARA Koretada (Regent and Minister of the Right) of earlier times.[63] The Retired Emperor also thought Yoshisuke was a fine minister. His mother, Lady Third Rank, served Hachijō In [Toba's daughter]. Due to such maternal connections, Yoshisuke was the "number one person" at Hachijō In's household and was brought up by her. But in the winter of 1218 he became very sick with what she called smallpox (*mogasa*), then spreading throughout the country, and he died on the 11th day of the 11th month. FUJIWARA Morotada had also died in this way [while still holding the position of Minister], making them that much alike. Since the world was delighted that an Imperial son [the future Emperor Chūkyō] had been born into the KUJŌ house on the 10th day of the 10th month of 1218, and since the fortunes of the KUJŌ house had been restored, Yoshisuke—realizing that his death was at hand—made the following comment on the day before his death: "I will certainly die! Although this is a wretched situation, I have reached this high position. Therefore, I am one about whom it can be said, 'Both grief and joy have come to his gate.'" Because of Yoshisuke's death in 1218, the position of Minister of the Left was now open. So MINAMOTO Sanetomo, Minister of the Center, was appointed Minister of the Right, just as he had wanted.[64]

61. About the time that Michiie gave up his position as Senior Commander, his sister became pregnant, making him hopeful of becoming the maternal uncle of a reigning Emperor.

62. Yoshisuke was KUJŌ Kanezane's third son. The first (Yoshimichi) had died in 1188 and the second (Yoshitsune) in 1206.

63. Morotada and Koretada were respectively appointed Minister of the Left and Minister of the Right in 969 and 970. Yoshisuke and Michiie were given those same posts in 1199 and 1209.

64. When Yoshisuke died in 1218, his nephew Michiie was promoted from Minister of the Right to Minister of the Left, leaving the former position open for Sanetomo.

Sanetomo's Assassination

Sanetomo had not gone up to the capital to celebrate his earlier appointment as Senior Commander, and now his appointment as Minister of the Right was also celebrated at Kamakura in a grand way. Five noblemen went from the capital, taking the palm-leaf carriage with them; and they assembled for the ceremony on the 28th day of the 1st month of 1219. The five were:

Name	Office or Rank	Comment
FUJIWARA Tadanobu	Senior Counselor	Son of Minister of the Center Nobukiyo
SAIONJI Saneuji	Middle Counselor	Son of SAIONJI Kintsune, Master of the Crown Prince Chūkyō's Household
FUJIWARA Kunimichi	Consultant and Middle Commander	Son of the late Senior Counselor Yasumichi, whose wife was formerly the wife of HIRAGA Tomomasa
TAIRA Mitsumori	Senior Third Rank	Son of Senior Counselor Yorimori
FUJIWARA Munenaga	Minister of Justice, Third Rank	Said to have gone down to Kamakura earlier for football (*kemari*)

On the night of the 28th, when the celebration—for which fine preparations had been made—was being held and the Imperial offering (*hōhei*) was being presented to the Tsurugaoka Hachiman Shrine, Sanetomo descended the stone bridge in front of the main hall of the shrine and greeted those at the front of the procession. As he was walking along carrying his scepter and pulling the train of his robe behind him, a hooded monk ran up, stepped on Sanetomo's train, and slashed at Sanetomo's head with a single thrust of the sword. When Sanetomo fell to the ground, his head was cut off. The assassin picked up the head and fled. Three or four men dressed like the assassin emerged from the rear and dispersed the procession. They attacked and killed Nakaaki, who was at the front of the procession and was mistaken for HŌJŌ Yoshitoki. Then the assassins disappeared. Yoshitoki, with a sword at his side, had stayed behind because he was ordered to remain at the middle gate of the shrine. [Sanetomo] had been generally careless. With everyone fluttering about like baby spiders, every nobleman fled. Fortunately TAIRA Mitsumori had not gone to the place where the attack was made but had waited at the *torii* of the shrine. So he got into the palm-leaf carriage and returned to his quarters. Since everyone had scattered, the tens of thousands of soldiers stationed outside the *torii* did not know what had happened.

The Assassin and His Death

The man who killed Sanetomo was Yoriie's son, Priest Kugyō (1192–1219), who had been appointed Intendant of the Tsurugaoka Hachiman Shrine.[65] On that day, Kugyō satisfied his deep-seated urge—harbored for years—to kill Sanetomo. When he first swung his sword at Sanetomo's head, all noblemen present clearly heard him yell: "This is for my father's enemy!" Having caused everybody to flee in this way, Kugyō sent the following message to the head-quarters of MIURA Yoshimura (an officer of the Palace Gate Guards of the Left) and a man who was considered to be Sanetomo's leading retainer: "I have taken revenge against my father's enemy! Now I am the Shogun! I will come to your headquarters!" Yoshimura re-layed the message to HŌJŌ Yoshitoki. Kugyō took Sanetomo's head with him, and he quickly crossed the mountains of Okayama alone during a blizzard and in deep snow. Soldiers were sent to intercept him on his way to Yoshimura's headquarters, but he was not killed easily, for he slashed away at his attackers, scattered them, fled, and was about to climb over a fence and enter Yoshimura's headquarters when he was caught and killed.

MINAMOTO Yoritomo was a truly unusual Shogun! He had such a grandson as Kugyō, a man with warrior spirit *(bushi no kokorogiwa)*. But Yoritomo also had a son (Sanetomo) who was foolishly careless, indulging himself in learning and disgracing the offices of Minister and Senior Counselor. And he died without leaving an heir.

MINAMOTO Sanetomo's head was dug out of the snow of Oka-yama. Soldiers then advanced to the house where Kugyō had been staying—a house built in the neighborhood of the shrine called Wakamiya—and killed all those who had been allied with him. They also burned down the house. So, once more, a dreamlike event had occurred.

Repercussions at the Capital

Early in the morning of the 2nd day of the 2nd month, a report of the incident was received at the capital, and word passed among the people. Retired Emperor Go-Toba was then staying at the Minase Palace. Since SAIONJI Saneuji had sent letters to his father Kintsune, Kintsune went to the Retired Emperor's palace and, upset and

65. According to the *Azuma kagami* (2.120), Kugyō had been made Inten-dant of the Tsurugaoka Hachiman Shrine on the 20th day of the 6th month of 1217.

perplexed, reported what had happened in Kamakura. Lady Second Rank was on a pilgrimage to the Kumano Shrines at that time and had arrived at the Tennō Temple. When she was told what had occurred in Kamakura, she wanted to return to the capital; but three Imperial messengers came, one after the other, from the Retired Emperor to tell her that it would be irreverent to break off the pilgrimage and that she should not return. So she went on to Kumano. While rumors were being bruited about that the assassination of Sanetomo was very mysterious, the nobles who had gone to Kamakura for the installation ceremony gradually returned to the capital.

HŌJŌ Yoshitoki and Masako in Control at Kamakura

Reports were received that a conference had been held in Kamakura and that it had been decided to have Masako (Sanetomo's mother who was known as Lady Nun Second Rank) take over all the Shogun's property and to have her brother HŌJŌ Yoshitoki (Acting Commissioner of the Capital Office of the Right) handle military-government affairs. During that night and the following day, 70 or 80 Sanetomo retainers entered the Buddhist priesthood. This was really deplorable!

ŌE Hiromoto, Master of the Palace Table Office and a man who had been around for a long time, had been having eye trouble. Because his illness had worsened, he went blind. He was told that he might regain a little of his eyesight, and so he entered the priesthood [in 1217]. But it seems that he is not like he once was. Even his sons, who were all young at the time, entered the priesthood. The large number of men who became lay priests at that time is too terrible for words.

Emperor Reports Deaths of KUJŌ Yoshisuke and MINAMOTO Sanetomo

Because such things had happened, a noble was sent [to the Ise Shrine in 1219] with an Imperial decree (written in the Emperor's own hand) which reported, when referring to prominent civil and military leaders, the shocking news that Minister of the Left KUJŌ Yoshisuke had died during the winter of the previous year and that in the spring of the current year MINAMOTO Sanetomo had also died. Thus KUJŌ Yoshisuke was a Minister who definitely could not be disregarded.

Masako Arranges for an Aristocrat to Become Shogun

Meanwhile, Masako, Lady Nun Second Rank, sent a messenger to Retired Emperor Go-Toba. The messenger was FUJIWARA Yuki-mitsu, a fine person who had for years been conducting the affairs of the military government's Supreme Military Council. Having made a gift to the Imperial Court, Yukimitsu was appointed Governor of Shinano. He had also gone to the capital to manage matters for Masako's pilgrimage to the Kumano Shrines [in 1218].[66] Masako had him take this message to the Retired Emperor:

> Please send a suitable son of Your Majesty to Kamakura. He will be made Shogun. The soldiers who follow the Shogun number several tens of thousands, but since they have lost their leader, diverse feelings will certainly arise. [Having one of your sons appointed Shogun] will surely quiet them down.

Probably this message was sent because, when Masako had gone to the capital on her way to the Kumano Shrines when Sanetomo was still alive, she had heard Lady Second Rank ask whether such an arrangement might not be made, since Sanetomo had no children.

Now Nishi no Onkata, a daughter of FUJIWARA Nobukiyo, had been serving Retired Emperor Go-Toba and was the adopted daughter of Lady Second Rank. By Nishi no Onkata, Go-Toba had a son called Suguru Gozen, a child who was brought up by Lady Second Rank. At first, it was planned to make Suguru Gozen a Miidera priest, but he was put through the coming-of-age ceremony and named Prince Yorihito. Because he was so well treated, people probably thought that Lady Second Rank was determined to have him placed on the throne or, failing that, appointed Shogun. People who disliked her actually made such deductions! Why should a person with a sincere heart have had thoughts like those? We hear that there have been succession disputes since ancient times, but no one should have such ideas today. Knowing how the Retired Emperor felt, how could anyone have thought of placing Prince Yorihito on the throne or sending him off to Kamakura to be the next Shogun?

When Go-Toba heard of the proposal that one of his sons be sent to Kamakura, he objected: "That would divide the country of Japan in two! What is this all about?" So he turned down the proposal. In his reply to Masako he made this straightforward statement: "If you had proposed an ordinary person, even the son of a Regent or Chancellor, I would have approved." Because Masako accepted the Retired Emperor's suggestion, and because Yoshimura[67] had previously thought that choosing the son of a Regent or Chancellor was a good idea, Masako concluded that this was the course she would have to take; and it was decided to send someone to the capital to wel-

---

66. She was on this pilgrimage when she heard of Sanetomo's assassination.

67. Probably Jien meant to write Yoshitoki, Masako's brother.

come Minister-of-the-Left KUJŌ Michiie's son Norizane (Junior Commander Third Rank). So she wrote as follows to Go-Toba:

> The son of the Minister of the Left has familial ties with the MINAMOTO house, since he is the great-grandson of Yoritomo's sister. Therefore, if you cannot accede to our request to send a prince, I recommend that this son Norizane be sent to Kamakura for upbringing and that he guard the sovereign as Shogun.

After that message was dispatched, various conferences were held at the capital, and FUJIWARA Tadatsuna was sent to Kamakura as an Imperial messenger. (He had previously been sent there in that same capacity.) Tadatsuna came back with this message:

> After all, the main point of our original request was simply that the person sent to Kamakura to become the next Shogun should be a son of the Minister of the Left. Since the Minister of the Left has several sons, any one of them will do.

Whereupon the Retired Emperor replied: "In that case, your proposal is quite acceptable." So Michiie's two-year-old son Yoritsune—the one being brought up by his mother's father (Senior Counselor SAIONJI Kintsune)—was selected. This son had been born at the tiger hour of the tiger month of the tiger year.[68] Since he was also a really unusual and incomparable child, and both diviners and astrologers had declared him to be a fortunate choice, soldiers were sent to welcome him to Kamakura. Michiie's young son and his escort finally left the capital for Kamakura on the 25th day of the 6th month [of 1219]. People said this was a really wondrous event, as was shown by the boy's not crying one bit during the trip from the capital to Kamakura.

SAIONJI Kintsune Promoted

Then, in the winter of that same year, on the 13th day of the 10th month of 1219, Senior Counselor SAIONJI Kintsune (1171–1224) received this Imperial order: "Prepare yourself to express your delight, because you are going to be advanced to Senior Commander of the Imperial Bodyguards of the Right." At the installation ceremony held on the 13th day of the 11th month [of 1219]—after Go-Toba had returned from his pilgrimage to the Kumano Shrines—Kintsune finally became Senior Commander of the Imperial Body-

68. The year 1218 was *tsuchinoe-tora* (the fifth stem and the tiger branch), and Yoritsune's birth was also in the tiger hour (about 4:00 A.M.) and in the tiger month (the 1st). Such a concurrence of tiger points in time was considered propitious.

guards of the Right.⁶⁹ And on the 19th of that month, he expressed in a superb way his gratitude to the Emperor for the appointment. He was praised by all.

Rebelliousness of MINAMOTO *Yorishige*

Meanwhile, MINAMOTO Yorishige (grandson of MINAMOTO Yorimasa), a man who served at the Imperial Palace, had become rebellious. It came out that he thought he should have been ap-

69. Jien does not explain why SAIONJI Kintsune was suddenly promoted in the 11th month of 1219 to an office that he had sought several years before. Nor does he explain why Kintsune figures so prominently in this 4th chapter of the *Gukanshō*. But the 13th-century Japanese reader needed no such explanations. As shown in note 58 above, SAIONJI Kintsune linked the MINAMOTO clan with the KUJŌ house. More importantly, just before Kintsune's promotion to Senior Commander, he was placed at the very pinnacle of the aristocratic order and at a position of great importance in Jien's hopes for the future. First, he was appointed Master of Crown Prince Chūkyo's Household in the 11th month of 1218. Second, his daughter's son Yoritsune had been sent off to Kamakura to be the next MINAMOTO Shogun in the 6th month of 1219. Thus SAIONJI Kintsune had just become the guardian of the next Emperor and the new Shogun, the two boys on whom Jien's hopes for the future were pinned.

Being the son of a Senior Counselor, Kintsune was born to high aristocratic position. But in the early 1190s, when Go-Toba was on the throne, he was also married to a daughter of MINAMOTO Yoritomo's brother-in-law. This marital connection with the Shogun certainly enhanced his position at court. Kintsune even benefitted from the political upheaval that led to the downfall of KUJŌ Kanezane (and Jien) in 1196 and to the enthronement of Tsuchimikado in 1198, for he was then appointed to a high office in Retired Emperor Go-Toba's household. And Kintsune's position was not damaged by the later eclipse of Michichika's power, because Kintsune and allies of his deceased father-in-law had joined a plot to destroy Michichika. The plot was leaked and Kintsune was dismissed from office, but was soon pardoned. By 1202, he had gained the confidence of Go-Toba and in 1208 was made Master of the Secondary Empress's Household.

SAIONJI Kintsune wanted, at the time of Sanemune's resignation as Minister of the Center in 1206, an appointment as Senior Commander of the Imperial Bodyguards of the Right. Some time after Sanemune's death in 1210, Go-Toba was disposed to accede to Kintsune's request. But ŌIMIKADO Yorizane wanted the same position for his brother. And since Yorizane had the backing of an influential wife (Lady Second Rank), Go-Toba was forced to renege on his earlier promise to Kintsune, who became resentful and turned to MINAMOTO Sanetomo for help. This caused Kintsune to be censured in 1217, but he was soon pardoned, apparently because of pressure exerted by Sanetomo. So Kintsune had considerable influence in both the military government at Kamakura and in the Retired Emperor's palace at the capital, but it was only after he became a guardian of both the new

pointed Shogun. Since a soldier residing in the capital informed on him, Yorishige was ordered to come to the Retired Emperor's palace. But Yorishige would not comply with the order, and so the Imperial Palace was surrounded with soldiers. During the fighting that ensued, fires were started and the Imperial Palace was burned down on the 13th day of the 7th month of 1219. TAIRA Moritoki

---

Crown Prince and the new Shogun that he was finally promoted to Senior Commander, reaching a position of vital importance to Jien's hopes for the future.

That Jien was deeply aware of Kintsune's importance to his future plans is vividly revealed in a letter that Jien wrote to Kintsune sometime between 1219 and 1221, after the *Gukanshō* was written but before the outbreak of the Shōkyū War. The long letter begins with a request that Kintsune restore Jien's temple, the Sammai Cloister. The request is reinforced with a detailed reminder that the Cloister had been built by FUJIWARA Morosuke (908–960) and Grand Preceptor Ji'e, that the offices of Regent and Chancellor had been occupied—right down to Jien's own day and without a break—by Morosuke descendants, that many Emperors were descended from Morosuke, and that Jien himself belonged to the Ji'e school of Buddhism. The second request was that Kintsune do his best to keep Go-Toba from moving toward a showdown with the military government in Kamakura. In supporting this request, Jien reiterates the central thesis of the *Gukanshō:* the ancestral Kami have decided that the time has come for Emperors to be supported jointly by the FUJIWARA and MINAMOTO clans. Then Jien urges Kintsune to stop toadying to Yoshitoki and Masako and write a memorial to Go-Toba assuring His Majesty that "the soldiers of the eastern provinces" are not to be feared, that Yoritsune's becoming Shogun is in accord with the will of ancestral Kami, and that Kintsune himself has no desire to seize control of state affairs. In closing the letter, Jien states that if Kintsune memorializes Go-Toba in this way, "the blessings of the Heaven Way, Buddha, and the Kami—as well as the blessings arising from my own prayers—will surely be your reward." Jien's final sentence carries a reaffirmation of the belief that must have motivated him to write both the letter and the *Gukanshō:* "I also am fully aware that the Great Boddhisattva Hachiman—in not abandoning this [Japanese] state—has prepared the way, in consultation with the Great Illuminating Kami of Kasuga, for the emergence of this Crown Prince Chūkyō and this Shogun Yoritsune, and has inflicted the death penalty on MINAMOTO Sanetomo [because he did not act in accord with the will of those Kami]." [*Zenshū*, 881–886.]

But apparently SAIONJI Kintsune paid little or no attention to Jien's recommendations, for he seems to have kept the military government apprised of everything Go-Toba was doing. So when the Imperial forces were defeated by the armies of the *bakufu*, HŌJŌ Yoshitoki saw to it that Kintsune was properly rewarded. By 1222, Kintsune had been promoted to Prime Minister and had received enough wealth to make his temple, and Saion-ji, truly prosperous. Jien, on the other hand, had become a disappointed and disillusioned man.

(Captain of the Palace Gate Guards of the Left)[70] cut off Yorishige's head and took it to the Retired Emperor. It is said that a soldier by the name of KŌNO from the province of Iyo had been persuaded to become Yorishige's ally but had leaked the plot.

The Dismissal of FUJIWARA Tadatsuna

During the 8th month of 1219, when Retired Emperor Go-Toba was ill, he dismissed FUJIWARA Tadatsuna from his positions, confiscated his holdings in provinces possessed by Go-Toba, and threw him out. The explanation was this:

> As I think calmly about things, I come to realize that it was a mistake to appoint this fellow Tadatsuna to positions as high as Fifth Rank Director of the Treasury. No matter how I look at it, I now realize that it was a mistake without any redeeming features.

Go-Toba's illness was then completely cured, probably because—as a person with any understanding would realize—the firing of Tadatsuna was a superb act. We hear that even when Tadatsuna was serving as an Imperial messenger to the eastern provinces, he made several mistakes and instigated several weird plots.

Motoie (1203–80), young brother of Minister of the Left Michiie and son of the deceased Lord Go-Kyōgoku Yoshitsune, was born from the womb of Yoshitsune's principal wife (daughter of Lord MATSU Motofusa). Wishing to make Motoie his adopted son, Go-Toba ordered the boy brought to him and handed over to Tadatsuna for upbringing. As the boy was growing up, it was heard that Tadatsuna was planning to send him to Kamakura as the next Shogun and that Tadatsuna was doing nothing but telling lies at the capital and in Kamakura.

Tadatsuna was particularly close to Yorishige; and while people were thinking about these strange goings-on, Yorishige's guardian priest was arrested and forced to reveal various things [about Yorishige's plot]. But without disclosing what the priest had said, Tadatsuna sent off a messenger to the eastern provinces. Considering various events in their relationships to each other, understanding people concluded that "the firing of Tadatsuna was a fortunate result of the destiny and plans of an extraordinary sovereign." And they felt that such action was definitely auspicious. People were certainly critical of Lady Second Rank for still recommending that Tadatsuna be pardoned.

Concluding Reflections

The process of change in the lives of the rulers, ministers, and soldiers of this country of Japan has gradually become clear to me as

70. It could not have been Moritoki, for he died in 1204.

I write about past conditions. Thinking about this process and these conditions, and relating them to the Principles for particular periods of time, I have also come to understand, and give attention to, mistakes that are confusing the state. People of later generations should be careful to administer the state well, make distinction between wrong and right (and good and evil) Principles, act in accord with Principles for these final reigns, become receptacles for the blessings of Buddhas and Kami, and continue to protect Buddhist Law and Imperial Law during the remaining 16 of the allotted one hundred reigns. Because such is the basic intent *(hon-i)* of the limitless Buddha and Kami blessings produced in the realm of the invisible, I have made that the main point of what is written here.

Although I have written broadly about past conditions, I intend to write details later on. Because I have been drawn to the meaning *(omobuki)* of them, everyone will become sleepy and stop reading. [In later treatments] I will keep the reader awake with good stories about those conditions. I regret that much has been left out, but nothing can be done about that. Because I have written incompletely, people will want to add stories that they have heard. When they do, they should be able to understand the truth and falseness of those stories [as a result of reading this historical study]. The Buddhas and Kami will see that not one word of embellishment or fabrication is written here. As for points which may be unclear, the reader will soon grasp their meaning. I still regret that much has been left out.

Now in considering the conditions of the future, I conclude that they will be inexpressibly dangerous while there is retribution for the [wrong] administration and [poor] understanding of these last 20 years—down to the year of the Shōkyū era (1219–21). Because a detailed account of future conditions would become a prophecy *(miraiki)*, even that which will turn out to be true would not be accepted as true. Therefore what I write concerning the future will be only that which has been revealed by the Great Hachiman Bodhisattva. When understanding persons write of future conditions at a later time, they will add to what has been said here.

5
Summary and Conclusions

Why I Write in Japanese

It will appear condescending for me to write in Japanese [rather than in Chinese], but I do so in order to make it possible for the reader to comprehend the changing conditions of the world. Generally speaking, both priests and laymen display a serious lack of ability to understand *(chige)* when they look at the world of today, and they are producing nothing that can be called scholarship *(gakumon)*. Whether a priest is studying exoteric or esoteric teachings, or a layman is familiarizing himself with Chinese histories or classics, his work will be interesting and scholarship will be produced only if he grasps the meaning of what he studies by making use, as he studies, of an ability to understand. But in these final reigns no one understands anything. Everyone is like a "Dog watching the stars [without knowing what it sees]."

Buddhist writings are particularly difficult to comprehend and therefore require greater ability to understand when they are being studied by a Japanese—even if he is using easy-to-read Japanese translations—because the scriptures have been translated from Sanskrit into Chinese. Such Japanese translations are also useless for those who try to achieve understanding by reading (1) the "thirteen classics"¹ that include, first of all, the *Book on Filial Piety* and the *Book of Rites,* as well as the Tso, Kung-yang, and Ku-liang commentaries on the *Spring and Autumn Annals* of Confucius; or (2) the Chinese historical and literary works that range from the "three histories"² and the "eight dynastic histories"³ to the *Anthology of Literature,* the *Literary Collection,* and *The Collection of Correct Views on Politics.*⁴

As for materials written in Japan, all documents in the house of Minister SOGA Emishi were burned at the time of SOGA Iruka's assassination [in 645]. Nevertheless, Prince Toneri and KI Kiyohito compiled the Chronicles of Japan [in 720]. (One view is that the *Chronicles of Japan* were compiled by Ō no Yasumaro⁵ et al.) That work

1. According to Burton Watson, the term "thirteen classics" seems to have been used first in the thirteenth century [*Early Chinese Literature* (New York, 1962), p. 148n.]. It would appear, then, that Jien was keeping abreast of recent literary developments in China. The common listing of the thirteen is: (1) *I ching* (Book of Changes); (2) *Shu ching* (Book of History); (3) *Shih ching* (Book of Odes); (4) *Chou i* (Chou Changes); (5) *I li* (Book of Ritual); (6) *Li chi* (Book of Rites); (7) *Ch'un ch'iu Tso chuan* (*Tso* commentary on *Spring and Autumn Annals*); (8) *Ch'un ch'iu Kung yang chuan* (*Kung yang* commentary on the *Spring and Autumn Annals*); (9) *Ch'un ch'iu Ku liang chuan* (*Ku liang* commentary on the *Spring and Autumn Annals*); (10) *Lun yü* (Analects); (11) *Hsiao ching* (Classic of Filial Piety); (12) *Erh ya* (Dictionary); and (13) *Meng Tsu* (Mencius).

2. These were: (1) *Shi chi* (Records of the Historian) by Ssuma Ch'ien (d. about 85 B.C.) and translated in Burton Watson, *Records of the Grand Historian of China: Translated from the Shi Chi of Ssu-ma Ch'ien,* 2 vols. (New York, 1961); (2) *Han shu* (History of the Former Han Dynasty) by Pan Ku (A.D. 32–92) and translated by H. H. Dubs, *History of the Former Han Dynasty,* 2 vols. (Baltimore, 1938–44); and (3) *Hou Han shu* (History of the Later Han Dynasty) by Fan Yeh (A.D. 398–445).

3. The eight were: (1) *Chin shu* (History of the Chin Dynasty [(about) A.D. 265–420]); (2) *Sung shu* (History of the [Liu] Sung Dynasty [(about) 420–479]); (3) *Ch'i shu* (History of the [Southern] Ch'i Dynasty [479–502]); (4) *Liang shu* (History of the Liang Dynasty [502–557]); (5) *Ch'en shu* (History of the Ch'en Dynasty [557–589]); (6) *Chou shu* (History of the Northern Chou Dynasty [556–581]); (7) *Sui shu* (History of the Sui Dynasty [581–619]); and (8) *T'ang shu* (History of the T'ang Dynasty [618–907]).

4. These three titles were: (1) the *Wen hsüan,* a famous Chinese anthology compiled by Hsiao T'ung (501–531); (2) the *Wen chi* by the great T'ang poet, Po Chü-i (772–846); and (3) the *Chen-kuan chêng-yao,* instructions issued by T'ang T'ai Tsung (who reigned from 627 to 649) and compiled by Wu Ching.

5. Ō no Yasumaro is known as the author of the *Kojiki,* Japan's oldest chronicle, presented to Empress Gemmei in A.D. 712. As noted in Chapter 8, the genealogical preoccupation of the *Kojiki* (and of later works like it or influenced by it) was strong in the *Gukanshō.* But Jien does not cite the work here, nor is there any evidence that he used it.

was followed by the *Continuation of the Chronicles of Japan* in 50 chapters. The first 20 chapters were compiled by Middle Counselor ISHIKAWA Nataru, the next 14 by Minister of the Right FUJIWARA Tsuginawa, and the last 16 by Assistant Minister of Civil Affairs SUGANO Mamichi. These three were the core of a group responsible for the project, and they did the work in compliance with an order received from the Emperor. Then we have: (1) the *Later Chronicles of Japan* by FUJIWARA Otsugu; (2) the *Continuation of the Later Chronicles of Japan* by FUJIWARA Yoshifusa; (3) the *Journal of Emperor Montoku* by FUJIWARA Mototsune; and (4) the *Journal of the Three Emperors* by Minister of the Left FUJIWARA Tokihira.[6] In addition, there were [these legal works]: (1) the *Administrative and Penal [Code]*[7] by FUJIWARA Fuhito; (2) the *Kōnin Era [810–824] Amendments and Procedures* by Minister of the Left FUJIWARA Fuyutsugu; (3) the *Jōgan Era (859–877) Amendments* by Senior Counselor FUJIWARA Ujimune; and (4) the *Engi Era (901–923) Amendments and Procedures* begun by FUJIWARA Tokihira and finished by FUJIWARA Tadahira. And there was a work with a title something like *Encyclopedia for Officials*,[8] but it seems that no one has a copy. I have heard that one was deposited in the treasure house of the Renge-ō Cloister, but no one has even tried to take the copy out and read it.

We still have all these excellent Buddhist and non-Buddhist writings, including the complete compendium of Buddhist scripture, but no one is studying them. Everyone is like "the siskin that picks up a walnut [and does not know what to do with it]," or is "counting his neighbor's riches [without knowing their worth]." Persons born into houses [known for scholarship] think they are working hard, but they have no awareness of right Principles *(giri)*. When considering the descendants of present-day scholars and what will happen from here on, one concludes that no individual will be the least bit able to succeed his father.

In reflecting about this, I suppose that because I have written in this funny way, wise-looking students—feeling that what has been written here is easy to understand—will quote assiduously from the sources and, smiling to themselves, will look wise. But that will be a farce. Indeed, it is because they do not know anything at all that,

6. The four Chronicles and two Journals listed here are Japan's Six National Histories. Cf. Chapter 8 and the Bibliography.

7. Jien is apparently referring to the *Taihō ritsuryō* (the civil and penal codes of the Taihō era [701–704]) and the *Yōrō ritsuryō* (the civil and penal codes of the Yōrō era [717–724], although there were earlier ones. For a review of early Japanese codifications, see Felicia Gressitt Boch, *Engi-Shiki; Procedures of the Engi Era* (Tokyo, 1970), 1.8–11.

8. The *Kansō jirui,* a compilation of precedents for the use of officials that is not now extant. It has been referred to in old catalogues as a 30-*kan* work submitted to the throne in 803 by SUGANO Mamichi et al.

having come to understand man for myself, I have set to work on this book, thinking that I might leave something of slight value for posterity as a result of my having identified and understood the Principles of things.

Since this book has been written in Japanese, it will sound common. But meaning may be deeply embedded in Japanese words. Writing what I have to say in this unusual way, and wanting the reader to identify and understand Principles and the true intent [of invisible beings], I have written only about the unilinear course of history, purposely explaining Principles without the use of unfamiliar words and showing how the Principles of world affairs have been created for each successive period and how those Principles have protected the state and man. If even one person in ten thousand is attracted to what I have written, or if someone thinks that what is written here is really terrible and wants to look at a few of the sources, my main desire will have been fully realized. Because there are both Buddhist and non-Buddhist writings that deal with these matters, such a person should certainly consult them. He should refer to the following non-Buddhist writings: the injunctions left by Emperor Uda (869–931);[9] the chronicles of the two reigns [of Daigo and Murakami, 897–930 and 946–967];[10] the injunctions left by Lord KUJŌ Morosuke (908–960);[11] and the house diaries of famous, knowledgeable men. As for Buddhist writings, such materials as commentaries by former meritorious priests of both the exoteric and esoteric persuasions will have some value. Only if a person reads these sources as if they were his own, and sees what lies behind them, will he be able to understand their meaning. Certainly a person will not be able to pick up Principles from the sources by dipping into them haphazardly.

I have used a large number of frivolous words—like *hatato, muzuto, kito, shakuto,* and *kyoto*—because it is realized that they lie at the core of the Japanese language. Even if I had tried, in my pursuit of meaning, to spell out Japanese words with Chinese characters, the meaning would have been expressed less fully. Japanese words seem

9. *Kampyō yuikai* (injunctions of the Kampyō era [889–898]). These were passed on to Emperor Daigo by Uda in 897.

10. *Nidai gyoki,* a chronicle of the reigns of Emperors Daigo and Murakami. The source had several other titles. The extant portions appear under the title *Engi Tenryaku gyoki shō* (Selections from the Imperial Chronicles of the Engi (901–923) and Tenryaku (947–957) Emperors). This deals with events from 949 to 957 and has been published in *Zokuzoku Gunsho Ruijū* (Tokyo, 1909), 5.15–125.

11. *Kujō dono no yuikai* (Injunctions of Lord Kujō). These are injunctions that Morosuke passed on to his descendants and that have been published in the *Gunsho Ruijū* (Toyko, 1904), 17.135–138.

to be inferior to Chinese words written in characters, and to be very common, but they are basic to the Japanese language. Therefore when I try to say something, I find that these words, loaded with meaning, permit me to speak clearly about the conditions of a particular period. The view that those words are absurd, appropriate only to the chatter of children and women, is valid if one is using them to compose true Chinese or Japanese poems in an original style. But by writing in Japanese for the purpose of communicating an understanding of Principles to the minds of the unlearned, I have simply followed a truly important method of achieving that objective. One should read these funny words and, through them, try simply and earnestly to understand [the Principles of things].

Purpose of This Chapter

In [previous chapters of] this book I have written only what has come to mind about Principles that change from reign to reign, but I would also like to summarize those Principles and to point up the essence of their meaning. I have [already] written about developments from the time of Emperor Jimmu to the Shōkyū era (1219–21) in accordance with my understanding [of Principles], dealing with their importance.

Rulership in China

As for broad distinctions between different sorts of rule, we find that three Ways have been followed by the ruling houses of China: the Sovereign Way *(huang-tao);* the Imperial Way *(ti-tao);* and the Kingly Way *(wang-tao).* I would like to relate Japanese Emperors and Empresses to these three Ways, but in Japan the standards for compiling chronicles (from the *Chronicles of Japan* on) have been inferior—actually non-existent. Therefore I do not think that such an attempt would turn out well. If a person would like to know how Japanese rule has been related to these three Ways, certainly everything written here—even that expressed in common Japanese words —will have to be considered and thought about.

In China a man by the name of Shang Yang[12] emerged as a minister who conducted the affairs of state [in about the 4th century B.C.]. There is a good story about his way of ascertaining the abilities of men. In the Ch'in period, the Duke of Hsiao[13] was looking for a good minister; and so a man named Ching Chien found and

12. Shang Yang, more commonly known as Lord Shang, died in 338 B.C. To him are attributed many of the "legalistic" reforms associated with the centralized Ch'in state. See J. J. L. Duyvendak, *The Book of Lord Shang, A Classic of the Chinese School of Law* (Chicago, 1963).

13. Said to be the 13th ruler of Ch'in. With Wei Yang's help, the Duke of Hsiao instituted reforms and brought six states under his rule.

brought in Shang Yang. At the first interview with the Duke, Shang Yang expounded on the conditions under which the empire would be well governed. The Duke listened but seemed not to agree with what had been said. Shang Yang went to the Duke a second time, and the Duke did not listen and went to sleep. At the third meeting, when Shang Yang went to the Duke saying that he would like— distasteful as it was—to have another interview, the Duke moved closer and closer and accepted Shang Yang's ideas enthusiastically. Thenceforth the Duke governed his empire well.

At the first interview Shang Yang had expounded the Imperial Way and admonished the Duke, and at the second one he had expounded the Kingly Way and taught the Duke. On both occasions what Shang Yang said was not acceptable. But at the third interview, when Shang Yang had come with the conviction that none of the three Ways was appropriate for this sovereign, he expounded on the policy of achieving control through the use of military might *(pa-yeh)*,[14] and the Duke accepted it. A sovereign called Shih Huang Ti of the Ch'in Dynasty (221–209 B.C.) was also said to have ruled in accordance with this military policy.

There is another story about Shang Yang at the time of Prince Ch'i in the Wei Dynasty.[15] A minister named Fan Shu had taken over the administration of the state affairs. He claimed that Shang Yang was a great man. But a person by the name of Ts'ai Tse emerged and argued: "Shang Yang was great, and yet it is said that he was eventually killed by 'cart ripping.'[16] Even rulers and ministers should spend their entire lives doing nothing[17] and being at peace." Fan Shu lost the debate and, having been taken in by the Ts'ai Tse argument, yielded responsibilities for state affairs to Ts'ai Tse and went into seclusion. Ts'ai Tse accepted those responsibilities; and he and his sovereign spent the rest of their lives in peace. Were not these charming men? Fan Shu had been a fine man, but what made

14. This Chinese theory that a person had the right to seize control of the state by military force when a ruler is not virtuous was not popular in Japan, since an Emperor was believed to be virtuous because he was an Emperor. Jien refers to the theory here in an apparent attempt to show that China, like Japan, had been subjected to a process of deterioration that culminated in something like a Military Age.

15. The editors of the NKBT text of the *Gukanshō* conclude that Jien made a mistake: that he should have written "Prince Chao of Ch'in," the fourth Ch'in ruler after the Duke of Hsiao and one whose minister had fled from Wei.

16. Punishment inflicted by tying the arms of the culprit to two separate carts and then having the carts driven off in different directions.

17. *Wu-wei (mui* in Japanese), a Taoist-Legalist concept of inactivity. For a discussion of *wu-wei* at that time, see Fung Yu-lan, *A Short History of Chinese Philosophy* (Glencoe, Ill., 1966), pp. 162–164.

him really unusual was the feeling that led him to yield to Principle, resign his positions, and go into seclusion. By this story we will understand fully those qualities that the Chinese assign to the words "sage" *(seijin)* and "wise man" *(kenjin)*. The affairs of T'ai Tsung of the T'ang Dynasty were disclosed in *The Collection of Correct Views on Politics* written during the Chen-kuan era (627–649 A.D.). Even in Buddhist enlightenment, and in the 42 stages of achieving Buddhahood,[18] we are made to realize fully that there are good and bad stages in the development of enlightenment [as well as in the history of states].

Early Periods of Japanese Imperial Rule

As I continue to think of the present-day world, while considering what has happened from the reign of Jimmu down through the reigns of Daigo and Murakami [which came to a close in 967 A.D.], I find that the situation is beyond the reach of thought or word. But as I look back over those earlier reigns from the perspective of the present, I conclude that the first 13 reigns, from Jimmu through Seimu, were a time when only Imperial Law and the secular aspect of truth *(zokutai)* existed, a period of 846 years when the throne was being passed, without any difficulty whatsoever, from Imperial son to Imperial son. The next 17 reigns, from Chūai to Kimmei, were a time when the deterioration was relieved now and then by improvement. The terrible reigns of Ankō and Buretsu came then, as did the good reigns of Nintoku and Ninken. This second period of 17 reigns lasted 394 years and was therefore shorter than the first one of 13 reigns.

Then, during the reign of Kimmei, Buddhist Law was introduced to Japan. Prince Shōtoku was a child during the Bidatsu reign [which came at the beginning of the third period]. After the Prince was five or six years old, Buddhist sutras and commentaries brought to Japan from the continent were all entrusted to him; and he read them with understanding and lectured before the Emperor. During the reign of Empress Suiko—following the reigns of Bidatsu, Yōmei, and Sushun—Crown Prince Shōtoku was placed in firm control of the state as Regent *(sesshō)*. And Imperial Law was maintained by Buddhist Law. If we consider the 20 reigns from Bidatsu to Kwammu—down to the time when the capital was moved to its present site in Heian—as a single stage *(ichidan)*,[19] we have one that

18. Several sutras refer to stages in the achievement of enlightenment, but they do not give the same number. The most common number is 52. [NKBT, 86,520, note 4.]

19. This unit of 20 reigns runs through only a part of period three, as that period is described below. Just why Jien thinks of this as a distinct segment of Japanese history is not clear, although Kwammu's reign is obviously

lasted 236[20] years, less than the number of years that had elapsed during the previous 17 reigns.

Nothing Lies Outside the Bounds of Principle

In making this attempt to explain that Principles have been changing, I conclude that all phenomena *(hō)* are definitely affected by "Principle," a word written with two Chinese characters. Nothing lies outside the bounds of Principle. It is of utmost importance to know and identify wrongdoing *(higa)* as Principle. The world of man moves down the path of these Principles of wrongdoing from the beginning to the end of the first half of the present small kalpa, and up the path toward improvement from the beginning to the end of the second half. Furthermore, both large and small states follow this path toward deterioration from the beginning to the end of a small kalpa's first half.

Different Principles for Successive Stages of Deterioration in Japanese History

Although I have written about various developments of the past in order to explain Principles of continuous deterioration, I would like—for the purpose of helping those who still do not understand—to summarize those Principles in a way that will be easy to comprehend:

1. The beginning [of Japanese history] when the invisible was fused with the visible and when [visible] Principles were penetrated by [invisible] Principles.

Was not this the situation from the beginning of the reign of Emperor Jimmu down through the 13th reign [of Seimu]?

2. The period of the Principle by which people of this visible world could not see historical change as the working out of Principles [created in the realm] of the invisible. It was a time when people did not understand that beginnings differ from ends, that heads differ from tails, that good does not continue to be good, and that bad does not end up as [totally] bad.

Was this not the situation from the beginning of the reign of Chūai down to the end of the Kimmei reign [in 571 A.D.]?

3. The period of the Principle by which people of the visible world did not act in accord with the will of invisible beings *(myōshū),* although everyone felt that what he was doing was actually a re-

---

important. After Kwammu ascended the throne, Japan had no more reigning Empresses, and Emperors were again succeeded by their sons. Moreover, Kwammu was Japan's 50th ruler (half of the allotted one hundred), and this may be why his reign ends the first half of the Imperial chronology in the Shimabara text of the *Gukanshō.*

20. The reign lengths given in the Imperial chronology (Chapter 6) add up to 234.

quirement of a Principle [created by invisible beings]. This was a situation in which something that was thought to be good would certainly be regretted later on. In this period people who thought of something as a requirement of Principle came to realize, later on and upon reflection, [that it was not in accord with the will of invisible beings].

Was not this the situation from the beginning of the Bidatsu reign [in 571] down through the time of FUJIWARA Michinaga [who died in 1027] in the Go-Ichijō reign?

4. The period of the Principle by which all people first thought that what they were doing was in accord with a Principle [created by invisible beings], but when a wise man[21] emerged and said that such things should not be done, they changed their minds and said: "He is right!"

This is a Principle for a situation that people in the Final Age *(yo no sue)* should be keenly aware of.[22]

Was not this the situation from FUJIWARA Yorimichi down through Toba's administration as Retired Emperor [which ended in 1156]?

5. The period of the Principle by which people would first divide up into two groups[23] and contend bitterly against each other but then, because there was still one Principle [for this period of history], the group which was drawn to that Principle would win out and act accordingly. The Principle for this period was one that people did not originally understand, but it was one which required that when leaders with prestige and virtue *(itoku)* appeared in accordance with that Principle,[24] those leaders would be used.

Was not this the situation on the military side *(bushi no yo)* down through the time of MINAMOTO Yoritomo [who died in 1199]?

6. The period of the Principle by which people could not make distinctions in the fifth-period way, contending against each other and letting the time pass without settling anything. Eventually

21. Apparently a reference to Go-Sanjō (1034–73) who "had come to feel that the hearts of people would not be at peace in these final reigns if ministers continued to do just as they pleased, Regents and Chancellors continued to dominate the state, and Emperors concerned themselves only with that which was elegant" (Chapter 2).

22. This sentence suggests that Jien thought of the Final Age as beginning with period four. Since period four starts after the death of FUJIWARA Michinaga in 1027, and the Japanese believed that the age of Final Law had begun in 1052, we see that Jien's conception of the Final Age reflects contemporary thinking on when the age of Final Law began. Cf. Chapter 10.

23. A reference to the two contending military clans: the TAIRA and the MINAMOTO.

24. Here Jien is undoubtedly referring to his brother KUJŌ Kanezane's supporter, MINAMOTO Yoritomo.

they would move toward a certain position and take action, having
been pulled along by bad ideas and feelings and making the mistake
of considering non-way *(mūdo)* as Principle. This was a period-
Principle in which wrongdoing *(higagoto)* was Principle. It was for
a time when all historical change, being affected by wrongdoing as
Principle, got worse as one stage of deterioration was followed by
one that was even more deteriorated.

Was not this also the situation from the beginning of Go-
Shirakawa's administration as Retired Emperor [in 1158] down to
the end of the reign of the sovereign [Go-Toba] who is now administering state affairs as a Retired Emperor [and who abdicated in
1198]?[25]

7. The period of the Principle by which people, when thinking
and planning from the first about anything, simply react to the existing situation without looking ahead to the future, for this is a time
when no one knows anything at all about Principle. This is the Principle by which people act like a person with tapeworms: when his
affliction is causing no pain, he drinks water because he is thirsty and
therefore gets sick again and begins to die.

This is the Principle of the present age *(yo)*. Is not the present a
time when there is nothing that can be called Principle?[26]

Ever since the beginning of the Japanese state, Principles have
been created to replace Principles—and political life has changed—
in this way because there has been continuous deterioration in the
abilities *(kiryō)* and fortunes *(kahō)* of rulers and ministers. Buddhist
Law and Imperial Law, the Ancient Age and the Medieval Age, and
the abilities of rulers, ministers, and commoners have certainly been
made to decline together in this way, and in conformity with Principles, from the beginning to the end of the first half of the present
small kalpa. Therefore a person cannot check this process, no matter what he thinks. And since the process cannot be checked, deterioration continues.

25. It will be noted that periods five and six cover roughly the same
years. By resorting to this type of periodization, Jien seems to be consciously relating his conception of a down-and-up course of history to his
seven periods. Although the emphasis of this outline is on continuous deterioration, period five was a time of improvement when "leaders of prestige and virtue" appeared, and period six was a time when "wrongdoing
was Principle."

26. Although the destiny of future improvement is basic to the *Gukanshō*
interpretation, that dimension of his periodization is not touched upon in
these statements about period seven, where the stress is upon an advanced
stage of deterioration in which "there is nothing that can be called Principle."

Principles That Counteract Deterioration

Nevertheless, [counteracting Principles] are definitely revealed in Buddhist and non-Buddhist literature: the Principle of "destroying evil and creating good" *(metsuzai shōzen);* the Principle of "hindering evil and maintaining good" *(shaaku jizen);* the Buddhist commandments "Do no evil! Do only good!"; and the expedient blessings *(rishō hōben)* received from various Buddhas and Bodhisattvas. One should join an understanding of these [Principles that can bring about improvement] with an understanding of the above-mentioned Principles [that account for deterioration]. How can one really do this? An ordinary person certainly cannot teach such understanding, but a wise man will know, through an understanding achieved by the exercise of his wisdom, how to do so. Thinking that I may be able to help others to achieve such understanding, I attempt to explain—to the extent that thought and words make this possible—[the interaction between these two types of Principles].

Scope of This Treatment

People who made a record of events in the ancient past were generally understanding men who, after hearing only one thing, knew all. And they wrote very little. If I were to write about those times after reading what these people have written, what I wrote would seem like pure guesswork. And because people of today would have no confidence in such guesswork, I find it difficult to write in detail about those times. I therefore touch very briefly on what seems to have been the situation in the ancient past.

Conditions in the Final Age *(yo no sue)* are complex and difficult to treat exhaustively, but I will take up developments after FUJIWARA Yoshifusa became the first Regent [in 866] during the Seiwa reign, and after FUJIWARA Mototsune (Yoshifusa's adopted son) forced his nephew Emperor Yōzei to step down from the throne [in 884] to make room for Kōkō.

Principles Affecting Enthronements

First of all, people should be made to understand, well and fundamentally, the replacement of one Principle by another. First, there was a Principle that an Emperor should never be a child under the age of ten, since a country's ruler should administer and pacify the state and be compassionate to the people. Then there had to be another Principle that after an Emperor had been placed on the throne, he should be left there no matter how bad he was—that so long as His Majesty did not voluntarily say that he wanted to step down from the throne, no one would be justified in forcing him to abdicate. Doing so would constitute "rebellion." And yet, has anyone ever said that FUJIWARA Mototsune was engaged in an unjustifiable rebellion when he forced Yōzei to abdicate [in 884]? No one has said, or even thought of, such a thing! Word has even come down to us that Mototsune was exceedingly meritorious in serving the Emperor. And has anyone really said that it is [now] wrong to place a "child Emperor" on the throne when he is only four or five years old? Or that he should be placed on the throne only when he is old enough to handle the affairs of state? Since no person has ever, in ancient or modern times, been made Emperor who should not have been placed on the throne, and since Imperial rule would have been destroyed if the enthronement of children had been abhorred, it is in accord with this [later] Principle that children are now made Emperors. By noting that these two Principles [were for different periods], one should understand that Principles change.

The State and Man

I conclude that what is of central importance to Principles is adopting methods that will be good for the state and man. "State" *(yo)* and "man" *(hito)* are not completely disassociated from each other. "State" encompasses "man." The "state" side of "man" refers to the administration of the country—to the making of distinctions between what is good and what is bad—in terms of "public Principle" *(ōyake dōri)*. The "man" side of "state," on the other hand, refers not to the administration of the state [in the public sense] but to [private] administration which is concerned with gently exercising compassion for everyone in all houses. "Man" includes everyone from the country's ruler on down to mean commoners *(ayashi no tami)*.

Good and Bad Emperors

It is desirable to have an Emperor whose behavior as an Emperor is good, but Japan is a country that has had the tradition, since the age of Kami, that no person should become Emperor who is not in the Imperial line of descent. It is also the tradition of the country to want an Emperor from that line who will be a good Emperor. But since it has necessarily become difficult for an Emperor to govern the state well by himself, it was established that a Great Imperial Chieftain would be appointed and used as Imperial guardian, and that the state would be governed in consultation with this minister. According to this Principle, if an Emperor is excessively bad, he will be oppressed by the fortunes *(kahō)* of state and man and will be unable to retain possession of the throne. There are various ways by which the destiny *(un)* of a bad Emperor is worked out.

Role of Imperial Guardian Determined by Ancestral Kami

An instruction from the Sun Goddess and the Great Hachiman Bodhisattva created an arrangement—referred to as the "fish-and-water propriety"—by which it would be deemed improper for an Emperor to be the least bit estranged from his guardian. Whether the empire is governed well or becomes chaotic depends on whether that instruction is respected. Long ago, the Sun Goddess made a divine agreement *(ichidaku)* with Ama no Koyane no Mikoto [the ancestral Kami of the FUJIWARA clan] that the latter was to reside in, and guard, the Imperial Palace.[27] The descendants of Ama no Koyane no Mikoto grasped the implications of this Principle, which was not to be violated one iota; and consequently "the three meritorious acts of the FUJIWARA clan" were performed: (1) the death penalty was inflicted by FUJIWARA Kamatari on SOGA Iruka [in 645]; (2) Emperor Kōnin was enthroned by Minister FUJIWARA Nagate and Consultant FUJIWARA Momokawa [in 770]; and (3) Emperor Kōkō was enthroned by FUJIWARA Mototsune [in 884]. The first two occurred long ago, but Mototsune's came after the Seiwa reign (858–876).

The Shortness of Imperial Reigns after the Beginning of the Medieval Age

The shortness of Imperial reigns after Seiwa is indescribable. Not one Emperor reached the age of 50 while occupying the throne. But they all seemed to live long after retirement. Everyone knows about these Emperors from Seiwa to Go-Reizei, but because the shortness of their reigns will not have been brought to the reader's attention all at once, I will list them, even though this is a tiresome thing to do:

1. Seiwa (850–880) died at the early age of 31, having reigned 18 years (858–876).

2. Yōzei (868–949) abdicated in the 8th year of his reign (876–884) and lived until he was 81. But he did not administer the state after abdication.

3. Kōkō (830–887) reigned only three years (884–887). Moreover, because of an incident, he did not occupy the throne until he was 55.

4. Uda (867–931) abdicated in the 30th [*sic*] year of his reign (887–897) and then entered the Buddhist priesthood, living until he was 65.

5. Daigo (885–930) reigned for the long period of 33 years (897–930) and died at the age of 46. His reign alone was excellent.

6. Suzaku (923–952) reigned 16 years (930–946) but died when he was 30.

27. Jien's belief in such an agreement is apparently based on his acceptance of the following sentence in the "age of Kami" section of the *Nihongi*: "The Sun Goddess also addressed this order to Ama no Koyane no Mikoto and Futotama no Mikoto: 'You two august Kami are asked also to serve together at the Imperial Palace and to guard it well.' " [NKBT, 67.153.] The second Kami was the IMBE ancestral Kami.

7. Murakami (926–967) reigned 21 years (946–967) and lived to the age of 42. This Emperor, one of the two Emperors referred to as "Engi Tenryaku,"[28] really reigned quite long.

8. Reizei (950–1011) abdicated in the 2nd year of his reign (967–969) and lived to be 62, but his life after abdication was just like Yōzei's.

9. Enyū (959–991) reigned 15 years (969–984) and died at the age of 34.

10. Kazan (968–1008) abdicated in the 2nd year of his reign (984–986) and lived to the age of 41. But he was bad beyond description.

11. Ichijō (980–1011) died in the 25th year of his reign (986–1011) at the age of 32. He reigned only as a child Emperor. Although his reign was long, nothing good was accomplished.

12. Sanjō (976–1017) reigned five years (1011–16). He was Crown Prince for a long time, but nothing good was accomplished while he was Crown Prince or Emperor.

13. Go-Ichijō (1008–36) reigned 20 years (1016–36) but died at the age of 29. He also reigned long as a child Emperor.

14. Go-Suzaku (1009–45) reigned nine years as an adult (1036–45) but died at the age of 37. His reign too was not long.

15. Go-Reizei (1025–68) reigned 23 years (1045–68) and died at the age of 42. He actually reigned rather long, but simply did what FUJIWARA Yorimichi (Lord Uji) wanted.

One will gain a deep understanding of the situation at that time by noting that one Emperor after another died early. Probably nothing reveals how one Principle has been created to replace another more clearly than how long people (high or low) live. Principles that created for Japan one form of administration after another probably would not have called for the conduct of state affairs by Regents and Chancellors (before deterioration had reached the point at which Retired Emperors were to govern the state) if Emperors had continued to live to the age of 60 or 70. If Emperors had still been serving as true sovereigns and had not abdicated until the age of 50 or 60, they would have been ruling just as they did in the Ancient Age. Instead, an Emperor was placed on the throne while young, and at the beginning of his reign as a child Emperor he would have a Regent administer state affairs in his behalf. Although he would gradually grow up, he would never gain enough understanding to consider governing the state directly.

---

28. Engi (901–923) referred to the reign of Daigo (897–930); and Tenryaku (947–957) to the reign of Murakami (946–976).

Sun Goddess Decided that FUJIWARA
Regents Should Support Imperial Rule

But nothing was amiss in governmental affairs during this Medieval Age, because the abilities of FUJIWARA regents were superb and because they assisted Imperial rule and had the state governed well. Meanwhile, all [*sic*] Emperors died around the age of 30. The reason why governmental affairs came to be handled in this way was that in the age of Kami the Sun Goddess had said to the ancestral Kami of the FUJIWARA clan: "You will guard the Imperial Palace well." She did so because she realized that Emperors in the Medieval Age would not be like sovereigns in the Ancient Age. Therefore one descendant of the ancestral Kami of the FUJIWARA clan after another was born with appropriate ability, and descendants of the Minister of the Right KUJŌ Morosuke (908–960) emerged to assist Imperial rule. [The Principle that Emperors would not be able to rule unassisted and the Principle that the descendants of the ancestral Kami of the FUJIWARA clan were to assist Emperors] were created together.

Sun Goddess Decided that Retired
Emperors Should Administer the State

Then the Sun Goddess made another decision: the state is henceforth to be administered by Retired Emperors (*dajō tennō*). Therefore three Retired Emperors handled the affairs of state in succession: Shirakawa (1086–1129), Toba (1129–56), and Go-Shirakawa (1158–79 and 1181–92). Each was destined to administer the state for a long time—Shirakawa until he was over 70, Toba until he was more than 50, and Go-Shirakawa until he had lived beyond the age of 60. Hence it was understood that a Principle had been created which required a Retired Emperor to administer state affairs.

Go-Sanjō (1034–73) should have lived long after assuming the responsibility for conducting state affairs as a Retired Emperor, but he died at the age of 40, just as he was beginning his administration as a Retired Emperor. This was strange, but it seems to have revealed the Principle that the state would now deteriorate rapidly. What Retired Emperor Go-Sanjō intended to do was probably something very fortunate [for Japanese secular history].

Bad Relations between Retired Emperors and Regents

In any case, there should have been absolutely no disagreement— only singleness of mind—between the sovereigns (*kimi*) who were administering state affairs as Retired Emperors and the Regent/ Chancellors (*setsuroku*). But because men and women who served the Retired Emperors as personal ministers (*kinshin*) rose to positions of influence, they stood between the sovereign and his Regent/Chancellor, doing much to worsen relations between them. Alas, fine people as high as MINAMOTO Toshiaki (1044–1114) were included among these personal ministers! The [present] sovereign [Retired Emperor Go-Toba] should know that the presence of these personal ministers is an important feature of deterioration in these final reigns.

Rise of Soldiers in the Military Age

Now soldiers have also emerged and, as Shoguns, have [further] isolated sovereigns and their Regent/Chancellors. After the passing of a period during which soldiers controlled the state, all military leaders were destroyed; and soldiers were simply retainers of anyone who came along. The appointment of the young Lord Yoritsune of the regental house as the next Shogun has occurred because the Sun Goddess and Hachiman (sōbyō) felt that the state should now be governed for a while by returning to the ancient model of unity between the sovereign and his Regent or Chancellor. I intend to write fully about this process by which the will of those ancestral Kami is, and will be, carried out. I will write in some detail about events after the 4th year of the Go-Sanjō reign (1068–72).

Summary of Administrations by Retired Emperors

Things changed and Go-Sanjō (1034–73) planned to step down from the throne and to administer state affairs as a Retired Emperor. But he soon died. His son Shirakawa (1053–1129) did administer state affairs as Retired Emperor until he reached the age of 77. And it was because Shirakawa abdicated to assume the role of a minister that he lived long. After his death, Emperor Toba (1103–56) was destined to administer state affairs as a Retired Emperor until age 54. Then Go-Shirakawa (1127–92), who was the grandfather of five Emperors, ruled as a Retired Emperor until he was 66. (Since it would be useless to write about the length of the reigns of the sons and grandsons of Retired Emperors who were placed on the throne after Retired Emperors took to administering the state, such details will be omitted. Emperors were removed from the throne after they had occupied it a short time, just as if that was being done on purpose.) Then came the administration of the present Retired Emperor Go-Toba (1180–1239), an administration that has existed during 28 calendar years—beginning with the year in which Go-Shirakawa died [in 1192] and running on through [1219], the [first] year of the Shōkyū era.[29]

---

29. This is one of the supports for Ishida's conclusion that the *Gukanshō* was written in 1219. It will be noted, however, that Go-Toba's administration as a Retired Emperor did not begin at the time of Retired Emperor Go-Shirakawa's death in 1192, but after Go-Toba's abdication in 1198.

Deterioration of Relations between Emperor and Regent

The "fish and water" relationship between a sovereign and his Regent or Chancellor appears to have been really fine down through the reigns of Daigo and Murakami (897–930 and 946–967).[30] Even the SUGAWARA Michizane incident [of 901] provides proof that there was no serious disagreement between Emperor Daigo and FUJIWARA Tokihira.[31] Then the empire seems to have been placed firmly in the hands of ministers who were Regents or Chancellors after the Reizei reign (967–969).[32] Until the time of FUJIWARA Michinaga (966–1027), Regents or Chancellors were not the least bit inclined to look down on an Emperor, and they pointed out and corrected an Emperor's mistakes in a fine way. But after the reigns of Enyū and Ichijō (969–984 and 986–1011), Emperors misunderstood their ministers and had such thoughts as these: "Doesn't he despise me? He will not govern the state in the way I think he should." I conclude that all such thoughts were mistakes. There was a tendency for FUJIWARA Yorimichi (992–1074) to despise the Emperor and to think of the state as his own personal property after he had taken firm control of state affairs during the Go-Reizei reign (1045–68). Emperor Go-Sanjō noted this and, feeling that ministers really had come to despise the Emperor, thought: "Now when I abdicate, I will simply govern the state directly." Even though Yorimichi and Go-Sanjō felt this way about each other, it seems that they realized this was very bad and corrected their ways; and that because the Emperor and his minister had placed themselves squarely on the correct path, state affairs really settled down.

After Shirakawa took to administering state affairs [in 1086], a Retired Emperor did just as he pleased and considered a Regent or Chancellor unimportant.[33] At the beginning of Shirakawa's administration as Retired Emperor, such persons as MINAMOTO Toshiaki —and at the end of this administration, FUJIWARA Akitaka and FUJIWARA Akiyori—emerged as very important "personal ministers" for the Retired Emperor. Although these personal ministers looked down on a true Regent or Chancellor and made him fearfully reticent—oppressing him in a pitiful way—some remnants of the ancient spirit were still strong [in some Regents and Chancellors]. This seems to have been so down to the time of Lord Hōshō-ji Tadamichi

30. Through the Ancient Age.

31. Cf. Chapter 1.

32. Here Jien is calling attention to the emergence of a form of Imperial rule appropriate for the Medieval Age: firm control of state affairs by FUJIWARA Regents and Chancellors.

33. Conditions in the following Final Age are now taken up. Cf. note 22, above.

who was Regent or Chancellor during Toba's administration and the first part of Go-Shirakawa's.

Retired Emperor Shirakawa certainly damaged the state with his mistake of treating Tadamichi's father, Lord Chisoku-in Tadazane, so badly: placing him under house arrest and dealing with his son in ways that would estrange father from son. It seems that differences between the invisible *(myō)* and the visible *(ken),* and between good and bad Kami, were really being manifested externally and internally. But toward the end of Toba's administration, His Majesty appears to have thought about the matter and understood that it had been a mistake to treat a Regent in such a way. So Toba consulted with Tadamichi, followed Tadamichi's advice, and had Go-Shirakawa placed on the throne [in 1155]. This should have corrected the situation, but since history was moving along toward deterioration in this way, the political conditions could not be corrected. Therefore the destiny of the Japanese state continued to work itself out: a great rebellion broke out [in 1156], and we came definitely to the Military Age *(bushi no yo).*[34]

Regents and Chancellors in the Military Age

After the beginning of the Military Age, Regents and Chancellors lost their éclat, since their prestige and power to handle state affairs had now fallen to the level of third- or fourth-class officials. Henceforth there were only two persons who seemed to be like a Number One Man: Lord MATSU Motofusa (1144–1230) and Lord KUJŌ Kanezane (1149–1207). It is really sad that the situation evolved as it did. Lord MATSU was destroyed along with the TAIRA house. And because Lord KUJŌ Kanezane was elevated to the position of Regent by a MINAMOTO Shogun, the ruler of our country really lost sight of the path by which he, yielding to the sacred will *(mikokoro),* trusts and hates a Regent or Chancellor as his own personal property. Under such circumstances we have now come to a situation in which it is absurd to say that a Regent or Chancellor is good or bad. And yet the present Retired Emperor [Go-Toba] did appoint Lord Go-Kyōgoku Yoshitsune to the position of Regent [in 1202]. That seems to have been a fortunate development indeed. But after a very short time, Yoshitsune died, as if in a nightmare.

While Lord KONOE Motomichi (1160–1233) and Lord KONOE Iezane (d. 1242)—father and son—were born into a regental house

---

34. For Jien, the Military Age does not follow the Final Age—the former starts later but falls within the latter. Therefore when we come to "this Age" in subsequent pages, we cannot be sure whether Jien is referring to the Final Age (which began sometime after the death of Michinaga in 1027) or to the Military Age (which began in 1156). He seems not to have made a clear distinction between the two when discussing events after 1156.

and held the position of Regent or Chancellor, they knew, heard, saw, or learned absolutely nothing about either state administration or house customs. Furthermore, they gained possession of deeds to the land of the regental house but lost, and never recovered, most of them. Because these two KONOE lords have not yet been destroyed and are still living, it seems clear that we are in an age when the fish and water relationship between the sovereign and his Regent or Chancellor has really disappeared.

And yet the powerful and correct way by which Lord KUJŌ Kanezane—recently known to both sovereigns and ministers—considered state affairs was willed by the ancestral Kami of the Imperial House and of the FUJIWARA and MINAMOTO clans. Should we not therefore continue to follow that way? The recent selection of Minister of the Left KUJŌ Michiie's son Yoritsune as the next great military Shogun was certainly made by the Great Hachiman Bodhisattva.[35] It is a mysterious development that seems certainly to have been an act of Kami, not the doing of man.

The Ridiculous Views of KONOE Motomichi

I hear that Lord KONOE Motomichi and other unspeakable fellows are saying: "There is no precedent in our house for sending a son off to Kamakura to be Shogun! Isn't it disgraceful?" And I hear that there are those who think that what Motomichi says is right.[36] This is

35. The connection between KUJŌ Kanezane and his grandson KUJŌ Yoritsune is expressed somewhat differently in the letter that Jien wrote to SAIONJI Kintsune just before the outbreak of the Shōkyū War in 1221: "The appearance of this Crown Prince [Chūkyō] and this Shogun [Yoritsune] is probably a causal (*in'en*) result of the fact that some of the power of Lord Kujō [Kanezane's] prayers was still left." [*Zenshū*, 882.]

36. Jien is more explicit about Go-Toba's views in his letter to SAIONJI Kintsune: "There is another very important matter that I would like to speak about. No one knows as well as I do the really important points in the sovereign's [Go-Toba's] thoughts and feelings. They are very bad. His Majesty does not really agree that this Shogun [Yoritsune] should have been sent down to Kamakura. And he accepts KONOE [Motomichi's] view that this was a truly shameful thing for the Minister of the Left to have done. The sovereign really believes that sending Yoritsune was an underhanded act based upon a plot and that it is regrettable and distasteful that soldiers are to be placed under Yoritsune's personal control. It would be a fatal mistake for you to to think that this is not a serious matter. You probably could commit no more serious act of negligence [than to think otherwise]. In the dream of High Priest Chōgin, the Great Hachiman Bodhisattva appeared and said to him: 'Although I have not planned the administration of state affairs badly, the sovereign has little faith in me.' Since the will of the ancestral Kami is something that exists deep within the invisible world, there is nothing we can do about our sovereign's lack of trust and comprehension.

simply ridiculous! Something like that might have been said, even if
foolish, by a person who had fallen heir to the headship of his house
in a fine way. But KONOE Motomichi was a man who, knowing nothing at all and being childishly foolish, was promoted from Middle
Commander (Second Rank) to the nominal position of Chancellor
[in 1179] as a result of the rebellion by which the TAIRA Shogun
really threw the state into turmoil. Is it in accord with the will of the
Great Hachiman Bodhisattva that the question of "house disgrace" is
raised by a man who is so stupid that he does not know that he is
being purposefully protected by a vengeful soul and allowed to live
long in order to destroy his own house? It is a situation beyond the
reach of words!

What Should Be Done?

Since it is difficult for persons to see how periods and Principles of
things change, I have written this book. But even those who read
what I have written will still not get what I am driving at if they do
not immerse themselves in thought. What can I do about that?

It seems, in this connection, that we have come to a time when the
state should be protected, and the sovereign guarded, by uniting the
Regent/Chancellor house of FUJIWARA with the military house of
MINAMOTO, thereby combining learning with military might. Certainly the time has come to really understand the way to return to
what is correct by thinking about the ancient past, reflecting on the
present, subjecting onself to the correct will [of the Kami], and rejecting evil. In understanding this way, the first thing to do is to
probe deeply into the question of whether this appointment of the
next Shogun from the Regent/Chancellor house was in accord with
the plan of the Great Hachiman Bodhisattva or was the doing of
heavenly or earthly demons *(tengu* or *chigu).*

Power and Nature of Vengeful Souls

Since ancient times, there has been the Principle that vengeful
souls *(onryō)* ruin the state and destroy man. The first thing to do
about this is to pray to Buddhas and Kami.

It is said that Consultant FUJIWARA Momokawa did the fine thing
of enthroning Kōnin [in 770] and, amidst a debate over who should
be Kōnin's successor, had Kwammu installed as Crown Prince. But
he went too far. He had a pit dug out for a jail and had Princess

---

His Majesty's thoughts are not brought to the surface, and therefore they
have not yet become critical. But they are getting stronger. Therefore a serious incident will probably occur soon. But since the Great Hachiman
Bodhisattva has spoken in this way, if the sovereign's lack of understanding
is to be manifested in some great incident, he will certainly meet his destiny
before that incident takes place." [*Zenshū*, 883.]

Ikami incarcerated therein. Because of that, as the story goes, the Princess took the form of a dragon and eventually kicked Momo-kawa to death.

We also are told that Regent FUJIWARA Koretada (924–972) of Ichijō became possessed by the vengeful soul of a Middle Counselor named FUJIWARA Asahira, while Asahira was still alive, and that the vengeful soul killed persons as close to Koretada as his son, Junior Counselor Noritaka. (Ashahira was the son of Sadakata, Minister of the Right.) At a time when he was Consultant and ranked above Koretada, and when the two were competing for a promotion, Asa-hira said some slanderous things about Koretada. Later on, Asahira, hoping for promotion to Senior Counselor, went to see Koretada, who had meanwhile become Regent. In those ancient times it was not easy to gain access to a Regent, and so Asahira was kept standing in the garden rather long. When Asahira was finally admitted, Koretada listened to him argue the Principle by which he should be promoted to Senior Counselor, and then said: "A few years ago when we were both hoping to be promoted to Middle Counselor, I was insulted by you. Now your promotion depends on what I think and feel. The affairs of this world really are hard to foresee!" Then Koretada suddenly returned to his quarters, causing Asahira to be-come so angry that he threw his scepter into his carriage with such force that he broke it in two. In telling about this, ŌE Masafusa (1041–1111), Acting Governor General at Dazaifu, also said that Asahira's soul became vengeful while Asahira was still alive. Asa-hira's house stands at the intersection of Sanjō and East Tōin. It is said that the descendants of Regent Koretada will not go near the place.

The vengeful soul of Senior Counselor FUJIWARA Motokata (the maternal grandfather of Prince Hirohira who was Emperor Mura-kami's eldest son) likewise took possession of and tormented Em-peror Reizei (959–1011).[37] And it is said that FUJIWARA Michi-naga (966–1027) was possessed by the vengeful soul of Minister FUJIWARA Akimitsu, because Akimitsu was the father-in-law of Prince Atsuaki [who was named Crown Prince but not enthroned].[38] Nevertheless, Regents did not suffer from excessive destruction by such soul possession, since Buddha Law was prospering and many Buddhist priests were wise and well-trained in austerities. By sin-cerely trusting honored priests, people received the blessings of the Three Treasures of Buddhism. We hear that there was such trust by Lord KUJŌ FUJIWARA Morosuke in Grand Preceptor Ji'e, by FUJI-WARA Michinaga in Kyōen (Abbot of the Sammai Hall) and Kyōmyō

37. Cf. Chapter 2.
38. Also discussed in Chapter 2.

(Abbot of Mudō Temple),and by FUJIWARA Yorimichi in Myōson (High Priest Shiga).[39]

If we look closely at state affairs, we see that Lord Hōshō-ji Tadamichi's house was on the verge of being destroyed, since nothing was being done to appease the souls of Retired Emperor Sutoku (1119–64) and Lord Uji Tadazane (1078–1162). But it seems that nothing horrible happened, probably because Lord Hōshō-ji had a superior ability that made it impossible for the resentful soul of his father to affect him. But the early death of the "interim lord" KONOE Motozane [in 1166], the things that happened to Lord MATSU Motofusa and Lord KUJŌ Kanezane, the frequent dismissals of Lord KONOE Motomichi, the destruction of Motomichi's house by his living on and playing around until the present day, and the things that were continuing to happen during the Go-Shirakawa administration were all certainly brought about by vengeful souls that were simply responding to, and bringing about the realization of, destructive Principles in these various ways. At first each incident seems to have been something quite ordinary but became serious later on. If Sutoku had been called back from exile, allowed to live on in the capital, granted a province, and permitted to compose poems and do good deeds, probably such incidents would not have occurred. Likewise, if Tadamichi had asked to take care of his father and then had him placed in the Jōraku Cloister at Uji, given him some estates, and let him—like Sutoku—enjoy himself playing musical instruments, such things might not have happened. But Tadamichi undoubtedly thought it had been a real achievement to keep his father Tadazane from being exiled. That was a proper conclusion to draw, and so Tadazane's curse did not affect Tadamichi. But such terrible things happened later on because Tadamichi, in his handling of things, did not think deeply about the ways to quiet his father's vengeful soul.

In this human world there is necessarily the misery of resentment and hatred.[40] Therefore, if a person abuses a superior excessively— even with a single word—he will be killed then and there by some powerful blow. The main point about a vengeful soul is that it bears a deep grudge and makes those who caused the grudge objects of its revenge even while the resentful person is still alive. When the vengeful soul is seeking to destroy the objects of its resentment—all the way from small houses to the state as a whole—the state is thrown into disorder by the slanders and lies it generates. The de-

39. All four priests were Tendai Abbots: Ji'e from 966 to 985; Kyōen from 1014 to 1019; Kyōmyō from 1028 to 1038; and Myōson in 1048.

40. *Onzō eku,* one of the eight miseries of human existence listed in Buddhist scripture.

struction of people is brought about in exactly the same way. And if the vengeful soul is unable to obtain its revenge while in this visible world, it will do so from the realm of the invisible.

Prince Shōtoku's Injunctions Disregarded

In his Seventeen Article Constitution [of 604], Prince Shōtoku wrote these injunctions:

1. "Be not envious! The evils of envy know no bounds."
2. "Wisdom and ignorance are like a bracelet that has no end. Let us therefore not think that we alone have achieved wisdom."
3. "It is easy for persons of wealth to win suits, like throwing stones into water. But it is hard for the poor, like crushing stones with water."[41]

These three injunctions are important, but in the world affairs of today—under conditions of the Final Age—people do not even think about them. Therefore if someone knowingly thinks well of these injunctions, and has some administrative talent, he will still be envious, conceited, and corrupt. And if such a man seizes control of the state, disasters will occur. This has become quite clear!

The Evils of Office Seeking

There is a saying that "in a well-governed state the government seeks men to fill its offices, but that in a chaotic state men seek offices."[42] At the present time there are 10 Senior Counselors. And we have 50 or 60 Third Rank officials, although there were only about 10 until the death of Retired Emperor Go-Shirakawa [in 1192]. The number of Captains of the Palace Gate Guards and Imperial Police is not now fixed. If we look at the lists of appointments made at installation ceremonies, we will find no list with less than 40 new Captains of the Palace Gate Guards or Imperial Police. The total number holding such appointments has reached 1,000.

A person seeking an office will make inquiries of an attendant (*wakizashi*) and present him with a bribe. In case he approaches a man or woman who serves the Retired Emperor as a "personal

41. These are taken from Articles 14, 10, and 5 of Prince Shōtoku's Seventeen Article Constitution. [NKBT, 68.182–185.]

42. This is Jien's interpretation of the last part of Article 7: "Few are born into this world with knowledge. A sage is produced by deep reflection. Whether a matter is large or small, it will necessarily be well managed if one finds an able man. Whether the time is critical or peaceful, it will be improved by encounters with a wise man. Because of the [endeavors of sages and men of ability and wisdom], the state will last and the shrines will be kept free of danger. This is why a sage ruler of the ancient past has said that a man should be sought for an office, not an office for a man." [NKBT, 68.182–183.]

minister," he will have no trouble getting what he wants. It is unthinkable that the practice has gone so far.

What Should Be Done?

Since we have really entered the age of Final Law *(mappō)*[43]—a bad age in the final reigns when soldiers have risen to positions of power in the state—my only wishes are: (1) that Retired Emperor [Go-Toba], remembering a little of Principles, will rouse himself and ask why these things have happened and then consider this question: "Why should we fall into the hands of these evil spirits and vengeful souls so easily?"; and (2) that the men and women serving the Retired Emperor as "personal ministers" will rouse themselves a little.

Another problem is that soldiers, who have lost their Shogun and have nothing to fear, are collecting—as land stewards *(jitō)*[44]—all the taxes of Japan. Every "personal minister" serving near the Retired Emperor is pleased when he or she is titillated by the gift of a portion of the land steward's take. Because soldiers have military power and glare at anyone who displeases them—saying: "Hey, you!"—no one raises a hand against them. Nowadays it seems that soldiers really think they can do just as they please.

A great rebellion will be caused by this accumulation of mistakes; and the state, man, and we ourselves will be destroyed. But the horrendous three disasters *(sansai)*[45] have not yet struck. We still seem to have some remnants of Buddhist-Law activity, and the ancestral Kami of the Imperial House and of the major clans still seem to have some spark. I wish that His Majesty would discern just a little of the true intent [of the ancestral Kami], slightly weaken the forces of the non-way *(mudō)* and the non-visible *(muken)*, call in the two or three (maybe four or five) priests and laymen who still have some understanding, and place them in the service of the empire. The important point is this: there are now no true sages or wise men who

43. This is the only place where Final Law *(mappō)* appears in the *Gukanshō*. But the way it is used here, and the general tenor of the work's historical interpretation, indicate that this Buddhist idea of a final stage of deterioration in Buddhist Law (beginning in A.D. 1052) influenced Jien's ideas of continuous deterioration in the secular affairs of state. Such influence is clearly reflected in his use of the terms Final Age *(yo no sue)* and final reigns *(matsudai)*.

44. These were military officials sent to local districts by the *bakufu*. For a recent study of related institutional developments at the beginning of the Kamakura era, see Jeffrey P. Mass, *Warrior Government in Early Medieval Japan: A Study of the Kamakura Bakufu, Shugo, and Jitō* (New Haven, 1974).

45. Sometimes the term refers to flood, fire, and typhoon, but at other times to famine, epidemic, and war.

understand everything. For those who would become leaders, beginning with the ruler of the country and including leaders of even the smallest groups, the important requirement for maintaining peace is that they, having made distinctions between the good and bad of man, be of one mind with the good men they have called in and employed. But because crows are being brought in to do the work of cormorants—just as if this was being done on purpose—the state is being ruined.

Dealing with the Military

Principles are easy [for an understanding man to see and follow]. I wish His Majesty would order ministers who understand such Principles to assemble persons with military power and speak to them as follows:

It seems clear, to begin with, that we have come to the Final Age when soldiers *(bushi)* should be used just as at present. Therefore the present position of soldiers is not to be questioned. Even if His Majesty thinks soldiers are bad, he realizes that persons superior to them will not emerge. Under conditions of this Final Age, we have come gradually to a time when only bad persons emerge. Counter-rebellions organized to destroy such bad fellows will fail. Aside from what will be done by Heaven Way *(tendō)* in the invisible realm, the Retired Emperor will have no doubts about, or hate, you soldiers in this visible world.

The problem of land stewards is very serious! In dealing with it, the Retired Emperor will consult calmly and carefully with soldiers and then make his plans. The Imperial House will not be threatened by those who set fires[46] in order to force the court to drop demands that land stewards be dismissed. The Imperial House will not be frightened by such threats. Certainly we have now arrived at an age when all soldiers should simply know the correct way *(shōdō)*.

The present Crown Prince Chūkyō and Shogun Yoritsune are only two-year-old boys.[47] Clearly they were created by the ancestral Kami of the Imperial House and the MINAMOTO clan *(sōbyō no Kami)*. The Crown Prince's mother KUJŌ Risshi was an orphan and had no one to pray [for her son's appointment as Crown Prince]. We do not know whether [the Crown Prince's appointment] was a response to the request power *(ganriki)* of the Crown Prince's maternal grandfather, KUJŌ Yoshitsune, but it certainly

46. *Mukaebi* (inviting fires) were lit when inviting souls back home at the time of an All Souls Festival *(obon)*. But in this case they were lit by persons exerting pressure on the authorities, suggesting that if their demands were not met, souls of the dead might return and cause trouble.

47. In 1219, both boys were two years old (by Japanese count). This sentence therefore provides additional support for the conclusion that the main body of the *Gukanshō* was written in 1219.

would not have occurred [without the intercession of ancestral Kami]. The assassination of Shoguns, the complete destruction of the TAIRA and MINAMOTO clans, and the selection of this child to be the next Shogun have not been ordinary events.

If we look back over the ages that have come and gone since ancient times, we will see that now—after a long period of precipitous deterioration—we have come to another time of improvement. If deterioration were to become worse, what deterioration it would be! There remain a few who study Chinese historical and literary works and the Confucian classics. And it seems that a few are studying law. We hear that there are also some Buddhist priests of both the esoteric and exoteric persuasions who have no faults. In calculating where we stand with respect to the allotted one hundred reigns, we see that sixteen are now left.[48] When these two-year-old boys grow up, they will either destroy the state completely or bring about substantial improvement. So you soldiers should not make mistakes during the next 20 years. If you do not, it will be easy to keep others from doing so.

Other Advice, and Reflections

After generous new grants of estates have been made to Buddhist temples and Shinto shrines, and to Buddhist and Shinto priests, strict orders should be handed down asking that these institutions and priests "pray that evil spirits ruining the state be suppressed by the power of Buddhas and Kami, and that if evil persons are inclined to rebel, they be arrested before such inclinations develop." Thus will bribery and corruption be checked. It is really an easy thing to do at this time. If we reflect about events from the time of Emperor Jimmu to the present, we will come to realize that there are still remnants of [constructive] Principles.

Alas, there is much that should be written, and I have written only a small part. It would be good to have these children [Chūkyō and Yoritsune] read this book when they grow up. What will they think about it? I have merely written about the "single course of Principle" without including any falsifications whatsoever, knowing that no one else has written in this way about the most true of all true aspects of temporal change.

Good and Bad Men

Another important point is revealed in this quotation: "The essential thing about man is that he becomes a friend of persons like himself." Therefore, bad persons have seized control in this Final Age by being of one mind with each other and by joining forces. Good per-

48. Juntoku was the 84th Emperor and he reigned until the 4th month of 1221.

sons should also talk together and be like-minded. And if there were good men, they would join forces. But there are no such men now. Feeling sad about this, we can only pray for some slight Buddha and Kami blessing. There are still some persons who might become "tigers"[49] if given an appointment, but when good men take a look at the conditions of the state, they decide not to come forward.

Telling Lies

While we are being subjected to this process of deterioration, the Retired Emperor and his personal ministers seem to govern by telling lies *(soragoto)*. There is absolutely no place for lies in Imperial conferences! In a situation in which lies are resorted to, good men will not be able to retain positions of influence in the affairs of state.

The New Shogun and Retired Emperor Go-Toba

Under the conditions of this Age, the [mistakes] of people *(tami)* will not be rectified unless an honest Shogun emerges. But such a Shogun *has* emerged, because the Great Hachiman Bodhisattva planned to produce a person from the regental house who would protect the state and guard the sovereign *(kimi)*[50] with the prestige and power of both learning and military might. And yet the sovereign does not understand that Yoritsune was born for the benefit of the state, man, and the sovereign. A very serious matter indeed! It was definitely a divine decision that it would be good for the sovereign to have the same person serve as Shogun and Regent. The reason for this decision has been made clear. The ancestral Kami decided to provide the sovereign with a guardian who would have no desire to follow a course of rebellion and who would also be powerful and prestigious. It would be best if His Majesty understood that Yoritsune's birth and appointment were brought about in this way. And it would be better still if His Majesty, through such understanding, were to avoid the sort of thing that happened to Emperor Yōzei [in 884].[51] By rejecting the plan for Yoritsune to be both Sho-

49. A Chinese way of referring to a strong man.
50. Throughout this section and elsewhere in this concluding chapter, *kimi* (sovereign) refers to Retired Emperor Go-Toba (1180–1239). By using this word, instead of the title *in* (Cloistered Emperor), Jien was being extremely respectful, adding weight to the view that he hoped Go-Toba would read the *Gukanshō*.
51. Yōzei, who did "unspeakably bad things," was removed from the throne by FUJIWARA Mototsune (Chapter 1). Thus Jien is warning Go-Toba that he might also be removed from his position of control over state affairs if he does not accept the will of the Sun Goddess and Hachiman. Not long afterward, following the defeat of Imperial forces during the Shōkyū War of 1221, Go-Toba was sent into exile.

gun and Regent, the sovereign will be acting contrary to the will of the Sun Goddess and Hachiman. But by accepting it, he will become enlightened.

The Sun Goddess and Hachiman have decided that for the sake of the sovereign the [next] Regent of the FUJIWARA clan will have absolutely no inclination to rebel. Moreover, the next Regent will have been instructed to provide the sovereign with strong protection against doing something bad. And because the sovereign will be protected from straying from the Imperial way *(ōdō)*, he will be prevented from harming himself—and from being left in an unclear position—when and if he is inclined to think as Retired Emperor Yōzei did. And of course such a sovereign will not be acting in accord with the sacred will of the Sun Goddess and Hachiman if he is jealous of a good Regent. This Principle [of a FUJIWARA son becoming the next Shogun and Regent] should not be opposed even a little. This is something definitely established [by the ancestral Kami].

It has come to my attention that the sovereign is making short-sighted plans [to oppose the *bakufu*] because he does not understand either the Principle of deterioration alternating with improvement from the beginning to the end of the present small kalpa, nor the Principle—granted by the ancestral Kami of the Imperial House and of the FUJIWARA and MINAMOTO clans—for this Final Age, a Principle that has come down to us from the ancient past. The Principles of things, and the history of our country, will surely be stabilized if the sovereign acts according to these Principles.

The Power of Buddhist Principles

With respect even to the "ten aspects of Buddhism,"[52] it is said that the first and the last are the same. Indeed, the ancient past comes around to meet the present. Even though conditions of both the past and the present change, they return to the same course. FUJIWARA Kamatari (Tai Shokkan) assassinated SOGA Iruka [in 645], and world affairs were then made to evolve in accordance with the constructive Buddhist Principle of "hindering evil and maintaining good."[53] Today, too, world affairs certainly will be made to improve in this same way. It really will be wonderful to have the sovereign [Go-Toba] united with his minister [Michiie].

52. The ten aspects *(hōmon no jū nyoze)* were: (1) form *(sō)*; (2) nature *(sei)*; (3) substance *(tai)*; (4) power *(riki)*; (5) action *(sa)*; (6) Inner Cause *(in)*; (7) External Cause *(en)*; (8) result *(ka)*; (9) the result of interaction between *en* and *ka (hō)*; and (10) the beginning and end are the same *(honmatsu kukyōtō)*.

53. *Shaaku jizen* is one of the Buddhist Principles which Jien said had the power to temporarily check the process of kalpic decline. Since the assassination of SOGA Iruka was listed as one of "the three meritorious acts of the FUJIWARA clan," Jien is consistent in relating Iruka's assassination to a Buddhist Principle that could bring about improvement.

An Unspeakable Mistake

Having gained a general understanding of the present political situation, I have come to the conclusion that it is an unspeakable, state-destroying mistake for the Retired Emperor to superficially use KUJŌ Michiie as his Regent while secretly thinking of him as a damnable nuisance, and also for the Retired Emperor's personal ministers to know that when they slander the Regent they are acting in accordance with His Majesty's feelings. The same sort of mistake is being made in relations between the heads of small private houses and their particular guardians. Good governance exists in a house where the master and his guardian of appropriate status really see eye to eye. Can we therefore say that it is at all in accord with Principle—in either the visible or invisible worlds, at the head or tail of things, at the beginning, middle, or end of events, or in the past, present, or future—for FUJIWARA Kamatari's descendants (who possess both the power of learning and military might) to have disturbed relations with the country's ruler *(koku-ō)* and for the two of them to be estranged from each other? Alas! Alas! Some time ago I came to fully understand that we are somehow to yield to this Principle [of harmonious relations between the sovereign and that Kamatari descendant who will have the power of learning and military might], a Principle that was definitely created for the Final Age. No matter what we may say, we must act in accordance with its requirements.

During this Final Age we have been moved inexorably toward the Principle that state affairs are not to be peaceful. And since it is the destiny of the times that we come to a point at which evil demons and bad Kami are purposely and definitely making things worse, even the beneficial power *(keyaku)* of the Three Treasures of Buddhism, and of the good Kami, is ineffective. Therefore the rise of each incident precipitates further deterioration, and we come in this way to what is called the Final Age. Under conditions of the Final Age the present Retired Emperor has come to feel more and more strongly that there should be no strong, bothersome Regent. This is a really serious mistake. It seems that His Majesty would be displeased with the appearance of a Regent or Chancellor who, as a strong man enjoying both the power of learning and military might, could not be moved one bit [from doing what he thought he should do]. So now the state is being ruined. The Retired Emperor should become deeply aware of this Principle [of unity between a sovereign and such a Regent or Chancellor] and desist, once and for all, from making mistakes.

There definitely is another Principle: a sovereign selects his minister and a minister selects his sovereign. It would be a fine thing if this Principle could be fully understood by considering the following: the relationship of these two selections to each other; how this Principle and this country of Japan have existed since ancient times;

and how there have been notable examples [of ministers selecting their sovereign as well as sovereigns selecting their ministers] in accordance with this Principle.

Arrangements Made by Ancestral Kami

The Sun Goddess enshrined at Ise Shrine and the Great Illuminating Kami enshrined at Kasuga certainly consulted together and decided *(gijō)* [how Imperial rule was to be supported] in the distant past. And the Great Hachiman Bodhisattva and the Great Illuminating Kami of Kasuga consulted together and decided [how Imperial rule is to be supported] in the present.[54] Thus the state was and is to be maintained. It is clear that the decision for the present, made after the state had been buffeted this way and that, has been made for these final reigns and requires that the sovereign have a guardian who has the power of both learning and military might.

Succession in China and Japan

In China it has been important, when considering the question of dynastic succession, to select a person who is superior in terms of one thing only: his ability *(kiryō)*. It has therefore been established that a man becomes Emperor in China because he has fought and defeated [the ruling house of the previous dynasty]. But in this country of Japan, there never has been—from the beginning—an Emperor who has not been in the Imperial line of descent *(ōin)*. The heads of noble houses below the Imperial House have also been selected according to the principle of head descent. Because we have held strictly to that way of dealing with the question of succession, there had been—down to the present—no deviation from that custom, no matter what kind of situation has arisen. And during the remaining sixteen of the allotted one hundred reigns, there certainly will never be the slightest departure from it. The present sovereign [Go-Toba] probably will not be able to maintain his position as sovereign if he now hates, or is jealous of, the man [Yoritsune] that the ancestral Kami of the Imperial House, and of the FUJIWARA and MINAMOTO clans *(sōbyō shasoku)*,[55] brought forth as a Regent who would have the combined strength of learning and military might.

54. In this passage the Great Illuminating Kami (the ancestral Kami of the FUJIWARA clan) is a party to both agreements (the one for the past and the one for the present), but a few pages back the Sun Goddess tied the two agreements together. In any case, the Imperial House is involved in both, for Hachiman was not only the ancestral Kami of the MINAMOTO clan but one of the two ancestral Kami of the Imperial House.

55. *Sōbyō* referred, in those days, to the two ancestral Kami of the Imperial House: the Sun Goddess enshrined at Ise and Hachiman enshrined at the Iwashimizu Hachiman. The meaning of *shashoku* is less clear. Sometimes

Two Ways of Selecting a New Sovereign

In Japan there are two ways by which a minister selects a new sovereign *(kimi)*. The first way was followed by TAIRA Kiyomori who, having taken a dislike to Retired Emperor Go-Shirakawa, sought to set himself up as a sovereign who would administer state affairs, first by placing Go-Shirakawa's son [Takakura] and then Go-Shirakawa's grandson [Antoku] on the throne [in 1168 and 1180]. MINAMOTO Yoshinaka also followed this course when, having won a military victory, he had the sovereign [Go-Shirakawa] placed under house arrest [in 1183]. Although one cannot say that Yoshinaka actually selected a new sovereign by doing what he did, this soldier had it in his heart to select a different sovereign, one who would administer state affairs [in the place of Go-Shirakawa]. So this is one way to select a new sovereign, a way that disrupts the state. But there is a second way, one that pacifies the state. The disruptive way is the way of rebellion and will not be successful.

Now the second way to select a new sovereign *(kimi)*, the way by which the state is pacified, was followed by: (1) FUJIWARA Mototsune when he forced the abdication of Emperor Yōzei and enthroned Kōkō [in 884]; (2) Minister FUJIWARA Nagate and Consultant FUJI-WARA Momokawa when they had Kōnin enthroned [in 770]; and (3) those ministers that searched out and enthroned Keitai, following the death of Emperor Buretsu [in about 510]. This second way was established by the Principle that "because these sovereigns were bad, they had to be removed for the good of both the sovereign and the state."[56] A Principle had been definitely established that their successors would emerge and bring good fortune to this country of Japan during the remainder of this first half of the present small kalpa, and so ministers selected Imperial successors in response to acts of Kami grace performed in the realm of the invisible. And because of what was done, descendants of those successors have been enthroned without mishap. And thus the state *(yo)* has been maintained until the present day. Clearly, these are the two ways to select a new sovereign.

---

it seems to refer to all other ancestral Kami, but, as used in the *Gukanshō*, it frequently (if not exclusively) stands for ancestral Kami of the FUJIWARA and MINAMOTO clans.

56. When discussing the reigns of Buretsu and Yōzei in Chapter 1, Jien tells us how bad these two Emperors had been; but we detect some ambivalence about Empress Shōtoku. Here he implies that the Empress was one of the three bad sovereigns, but in Chapter 1 she is identified as a person who achieved Buddhahood, leaving the impression that she was removed from the throne mainly because of Dōkyō's improper political ambitions, not because she was a bad sovereign.

Advice to Go-Toba

And yet, it is a sad thing indeed that because the present sovereign
[Go-Toba] has developed feelings of enmity toward this person
[Yoritsune]—who has attained a position from which he might become a Regent with the combined strength of learning and military
power—Japan is being brought to the end of her destiny (*unmei*).
This future Regent will not oppose the sovereign in any way, nor
develop feelings of rebelliousness toward him. Being a bit tough, he
will simply be difficult to ridicule. Considering these points, the Retired Emperor should handle everything in strict accord with Principle. If he does not yield[57] completely to Heaven Way, and does
things according to non-Way, he will be subjected to the punishment
of invisible beings (*myōbatsu*). Under conditions of these final reigns,
if the sovereign comes to conduct the affairs of state just as he
pleases, and then incidents break out, the state will be thrown into
disorder even before the advent of the 100th reign. He should simply look on as the Regent handles the affairs of state, yielding to
Principle without reserve and issuing orders carefully. It is clearly
understood that it is the plan of the several Kami to have the state
temporarily governed well during this next reign, and that this is
why such things [as the adoption of Yoritsune into the MINAMOTO
clan] have occurred. His Majesty should therefore be careful to govern the state by thinking and planning in ways that are in accord
with the sacred Kami plan.

At extremely miserable times, people resentfully say such things
as: "Invisible beings (*myōshū*) do not really exist!" But in truth there
is not a single moment—even at the end of this deteriorating half of
the present small kalpa—when invisible beings do not exist.
Moreover, we are aware—even now—that particularly miraculous
events occur when people think and plan in accordance with [con-
structive] Principles.

With respect to these miraculous events, I have written narrowly
about the appearance of this new Shogun, but my only reason for
doing so was that this event has occurred recently. I would em-
phasize the point that at any time—even when there is a different
Shogun—the sovereign should have the state governed by understanding the purport [of Kami-created Principles]. Whenever a Shogun develops a rebellious heart and comes to the end of his destiny,
he will be easily destroyed. The truth of this has been demonstrated
by the circumstances of Shogun MINAMOTO Sanetomo's assassination

57. All published editions of the *Gukanshō* leave this verb in its positive
form: *makase mairasete*. But Ishida concludes that Jien meant to make it
negative: *makase mairasede*. [*Rekishi shisō shū* (Tokyo, 1972), p. 139, note 4.]

[in 1219] and by the destruction of the TAIRA house [in 1185]. This is why I have written in detail about this wrongheadedness of hating, without reason, this new Shogun even though the Shogun will make no mistakes in either the internal or external affairs of the state. This course of opposition to the new Shogun has been taken because of influence exerted by bad men and women who are serving the Retired Emperor as his personal ministers. It is important that this be understood.

I have really written some surprising things here! Although I am the writer, I have not been the least bit aware that these things were being written by me.[58] This is something that cannot be expressed! Alas, if this were a time when Kami and Buddhas were speaking, I would like to ask them some questions.

Disappearance of Good Men

Having been born at the beginning point *(kawari no tsugime)* of this Military Age,[59] I have become greatly saddened and disgusted to see, so vividly, changes that have taken place before my eyes. A person is a child until the age of 13 or 14. Only at the age of 15 or 16 does an individual of understanding become discriminating. While I have been observing and hearing things during these 5[0][60] years that have elapsed since I was 15 or 16, understanding persons have continued to disappear everywhere at a rapid rate. There really is no way to write adequately about the beginning point of the disappearance of those understanding persons, but since there are no opportunities for people of this Age to understand, I have written down a general outline of what I remember.

In considering the style *(fūgi)* of the present age, should I not first write about events that followed the days of FUJIWARA Yoshifusa [804–872]? Those years were still within the Ancient Age *(jōdai)*. But the days of the "four Senior Counselors"[61] of the Ichijō reign [986–1011] were still splendid. At that time, these priests of the Kōbō,

58. Jien seems to be implying that he has not been writing his own personal ideas and interpretations but transmitting what was revealed to him about the will and actions of invisible beings *(myōshū)* and about the power and meaning of Principles.

59. Jien was born in the year before the outbreak of the Hōgen Rebellion of 1156, which he places at the beginning of Japan's Military Age.

60. All texts say "five," not "fifty." But MURAOKA Tsunetsugu's studies lead him to conclude that Jien had written (or had intended to write) "fifty." In 1219, the year in which the *Gukanshō* is thought to have been written, Jien was 65 years old by Japanese count, and thus 1219 was the 50th year since he had reached the age of 15.

61. Cf. Chapter 2.

Jikaku, and Chishō schools were still alive: Ninkai (951–1046), Kōkei (977–1049), and Kyōsō (955–1019).[62] When a person of this present Age asks people in various houses—first individual Regents and Chancellors and then descendants from the regental house who have not been appointed to the position of Regent or Chancellor, and also members of houses in the MINAMOTO clan and persons in the various houses entitled to appointments at the Master's level—how long just a little of that old style lasted, he comes to assign the Shirakawa reign (1072–86) to the time when Japan's True Law of Imperial succession[63] still existed. And indeed that is true. The beginning point of the period when Emperors were to administer the affairs of state after abdicating came then. Since persons who served Shirakawa while he was administering state affairs have lived on until recent times, we should know what the situation was like in those days. Even the descendants of the "four Counselors" of the Ichijō reign were still alive at the beginning of the Shirakawa reign, but by then the old style had all but disappeared. Successive stages of deterioration followed Shirakawa's abdication [in 1086].

Vestiges of the Old Style

But without doubt, vestiges of that old style were still left. In the days of Go-Shirakawa those vestiges could be found in the following persons:

Regent and Chancellor:

    FUJIWARA Tadamichi or Lord Hōshō-ji [who was Regent twice and Chancellor three times between 1150 and 1158].

Descendants of Regents and Chancellors Other than Heirs:

    KAZAN'IN Tadamasa [who was Prime Minister from 1168 to 1170];
    ŌIMIKADO Tsunemune [who was Prime Minister of the Right from 1164 to 1166, and Minister of the Left from 1166 to 1189]; and
    FUJIWARA Koremichi [who was Prime Minister from 1160 to 1165].

---

62. The three schools were founded by priests who lived in Jien's Ancient Age, and the three successors lived in his Medieval Age. We are being told that while the Ichijō reign was within the deteriorated Medieval Age, it was a time when there were still some priests of ability.

63. True Law (*shōbō*) was originally and essentially a Buddhist concept, but since the *Gukanshō* is deeply concerned with political change, and influenced by beliefs embedded in the concept of Imperial Law (*ōbō*), Jien gives the term a Japanese, genealogical, and political connotation.

Descendants of FUJIWARA *Kinsue who have lived until recent times:*
  Sons of TOKUDAIJI Kinyoshi:
      Sanesada [who was Minister of the Left from 1189 to 1190];
      Saneie [Senior Counselor, who died in 1193]; and
      Sanemori [Provisional Middle Counselor, who died in 1185];
  Three sons of SANJŌ Kinnori:
      Sanefusa [Minister of the Left from 1190 to 1196];
      Sanekuni [Provisional Senior Counselor, who died in 1183];
      and
      Sanetsuna [Provisional Middle Counselor, who died in 1180].

  In addition, vestiges of the old style could be found in the following persons of the

MINAMOTO *house:*
  Masamichi [Minister of the Center, who died in 1175].

Houses at the Master's Level:
  Descendants of FUJIWARA *Akisue:*
      Takasue [Provisional Senior Counselor]; and
      Shigeie [Deputy Governor General at Dazaifu, who died in 1180].
  KANJŪ-JI *House:*
      Tomokata [Provisional Senior Counselor, who died in 1201]; and
      Tsunefusa [Provisional Senior Counselor, who died in 1200].
  HINO *House (father and son):*
      Sukenaga [Provisional Middle Counselor, who died in 1195]; and
      Kanemitsu [Provisional Middle Counselor, who died in 1196].

Those who have observed and heard about persons on the above list are aware that at least these men had just a little of the ancient style and ability of their houses, and they therefore see no point in discussing their deficiencies.

FUJIWARA Mitsuyori (1124–73), a Senior Counselor later known as the Lay Priest of Katsura, was praised by people as an outstanding person in these final reigns. During the Nijō reign (1158–65), he was ordered to handle all state affairs in his own way. But wasn't it really good that he resigned from all his positions and entered the Buddhist priesthood [in 1164]? People did not think that his appointment as Senior Counselor [in 1160] had been proper. They went so far as to say that Mitsuyori was the first member of any Master House to be appointed Senior Counselor. Probably they thought it would have been better if he had not received such a high position. In ancient times an official of the third rank *(shi)* would not have been appointed at the Master level, even if he had had some ability. And of course an able official from a Master house would not have been appointed Senior Counselor. The ranking of houses for official appointments and stipends was established long ago, and a wise man of high rank would not have done anything to cause people to make such a comment as "Mitsuyori is the first member of any Master House to be appointed Senior Counselor." But to criticize Mitsuyori in such a way in these final reigns is going too far. He was, in any case, well regarded.

In the days when the children of the persons listed above were alive, the ability and spirit of their fathers were non-existent from the time of birth. And at present—the days of their grandchildren—the situation has become so bad that there is no sense in saying that one person is good and another bad.

Deterioration in the Regent/Chancellor House

We have also come to a stage of deterioration when four or five former Regents are alive at the same time. These Regents were all sons or grandsons of [my father] Lord Hōsho-ji Tadamichi: Lord Middle [Motozane] and his son Lord KONOE Motomichi; Lord MATSU Motofusa and his son Moroie; and Lord KUJŌ Kanezane and his son Yoshitsune.[64] Not one son of Tadamichi's two eldest sons (Motozane and Motofusa) had enough ability for one to think of him as a man. We hear that Motofusa's son Iefusa (Middle Counselor) may have been a good man, but he died before reaching the age of 30.

KUJŌ Kanezane and His Sons Have Been Able

On the other hand, Lord KUJŌ Kanezane, the youngest of Tadamichi's three sons, seems to have been touched with the spirit of his ancestral Kami *(shashoku)*. His sons appear to have inherited the ancient style, and three have been praised by people of the present age as extraordinary: (1) Minister of the Center Yoshimichi (1167–88), who died at the age of 22 but whose good name was on people's lips; (2) Yoshitsune (1169–1206), who came to conduct the affairs of state as Regent [between 1202 and 1206] and who was prominent among the able and cultured; he was not inferior to anyone, even the ancients, as a poet or calligrapher, and inherited the abilities of his father and grandfather in the handling of administrative and

64. Those who held the post to Regent or Chancellor after Tadamichi, down to 1206, were: Motozane (1158–66); Motofusa (1166–79); Motomichi (1179–83); Moroie (1183–84); Motomichi again (1184–86); Kanezane (1186–96); Motomichi for a third term (1196–1202); and Yoshitsune (1202–06). Between 1202 and 1206, one Regent and four former Regents were alive.

ceremonial affairs; and (3) Minister of the Left Yoshisuke (1185–1218), who was thought to have had no equal, past or present, in Chinese learning and who died at the age of 35. By the early deaths of these three able sons of Lord KUJŌ Kanezane we know that the affairs of state were to deteriorate in this way. How sad! How sad! Now the only son of Yoshitsune still alive is the Minister of the Left Michiie (1193–1252).

A Hopeless Situation

Are not the sons of Lord KUJŌ Kanezane's elder brothers simply confused, only looking like men? No one of ability can be found in any house other than the KUJŌ, not even in the Master Houses. As in earlier times, we still have Imperial Secretaries and Controllers, but they are like non-existent officials. We hear that even if someone of ability is discovered, he will be sure to have entered the Buddhist priesthood and become a lay priest. If a careful search is made, three or four able persons might be found. But if found, we will be sure to hear that they have all been rejected [as suitable candidates for high office]. So what can be done?

SANJŌ Sanefusa (1147–1225) is among the persons listed above who still has some vestiges of the old style, and he is still alive, but isn't he simply accommodating himself to the ideas and feelings of people living in this Age?

Disappearance of Able Priests

No priest with any style whatsoever has appeared at Mt. Hiei since the time of Gyōgen (Abbot of the Shōren Cloister). And more than 60 years have elapsed since his death [in 1155]. Furthermore, we have heard of absolutely no able priests at Miidera since the time of Gyōkei (1105–65) and Kakuchū (1118–77). And as for the Tōji temples, able priests of royal blood existed at Ninna Temple down through the time of Kakushō (1129–69), the fifth son of Emperor Toba. We have heard that the Abbots of Tōji included such good priests as Kanjo (1057–1125) and Kanshin (1084–1153); and when Tōji was prospering, Rishō and Sanmitsu were famous. At temples in the southern capital of Nara there has been no priest of any worth since the exile of Buddhist Judge Eshin.[65] We have heard that Kakuchin (d. 1175) was not bad.

And yet, former Senior High Priest Shin'en (1153–1224), one of Lord Hōshō-ji Tadamichi's sons, should have the ability of a high-

65. The text says "Chūshin," but Nakajima concludes that Jien must have written (or intended to write) "Eshin," who was Jien's brother by a different mother and was appointed Superintendent of Kōfuku-ji in 1157. [Nakajima, 650.]

ranking man. And is not Shin'en's young brother, Senior High Priest Jien, still living at Mt. Hiei?[66]

So what should be done in this age? In reflecting about the deficiencies of man, I simply become depressed and have no confidence that my expectations will be realized. So I now wish only for an immediate and quick death and for correct thoughts in these last moments of life.

Too Many Regents

As an indication that conditions in this Final Age are clearly miserable, and that people realize "we have come to this sorry state because such things have happened," do we not have three or four Regents alive at one time, sitting idly by? It used to seem odd when even one former Regent was alive, but when Lord KUJŌ Kanezane was Regent, children were dancing around singing: "His Lordship the Lay Priest [Motofusa]! His Junior Lordship [Moroie]! His Lordship KONOE [Motomichi]! His Lordship the present Regent [Kanezane]!" And when Yoshitsune became Regent [in 1202], four former Regents—in addition to the current one—were still alive.[67]

Too Many Abbots and Superintendents of Temples

And it seems that four former Tendai Abbots—in addition to the current Abbot—are now alive: Jien [the author], Jitsuzen [who died in 1221], Shinshō [who died in 1229], Jōen [who died in 1236], and Kōen [who died in 1235].[68] At [the Kōfukuji Temple of] Nara four former Intendants, plus the current one, have been alive at one time: Shin'en (d. 1224), Gaen (d. 1223), Kakuken (d. 1211), Shinken (d. 1225), and Ryōen (d. 1220). Shinken had probably been appointed when Kakuken was still alive.[69]

Too Many Officials

And don't we now have 10 Senior Counselors, 10 Middle Counselors, and as many as 50 people of Third Rank who have no position?

---

66. Although stressing the disappearance of able priests, Jien suggests that he and his elder brother were exceptions.

67. Cf. note 64, above.

68. Jien had been appointed Tendai Abbot four times: in 1192, 1201, 1212, and 1213. Jitsuzen was appointed to that office in 1202, Shinshō in 1203, Jōen in 1205 and 1214, and Kōen in 1213. Two points about this statement support the view that the *Gukanshō* was written before the outbreak of the Shōkyū War of 1221: (1) Abbot Engi was not mentioned, and he was appointed Tendai Abbot in the 8th month of 1221; and (2) Jitsuzen was included and he died in the 5th month of 1221.

69. Jien is wrong: Shinken was not appointed until the 5th day of the 12th month of 1213, and Kakuken died in 1211. [Ichirō Ishida, *Gukanshō no seiritsu to sono shisō* (Sendai, 1967), p. 26.]

As for Buddhist officials, we probably have 150 or 160 Preceptors. In the [reign] of Go-Shirakawa [1155–58], people said that having "100 Third Grade priests"[70] was disgraceful, [but the situation is much worse now]. Up through the [reign] of the deceased Go-Shirakawa, there were no more than five High Priests, but now as many as five High Priests are appointed at a single time, and probably as many as 13 priests now hold that office. We also have more than 10 former High Priests. And since there are numberless officers in the Headquarters of the Six Guards,[71] nothing I could say would be sufficient to express [my disgust]. It is now a situation in which no one says that "an office seeks the man." Even the phrase "a man seeks the office" is not heard. Whenever the court has a position to sell (*jōgō*), it has no takers. Court nobles probably would be pleased to sell less than half of the positions and ranks up for sale. Although such corruption exists, nothing can be done about it. That too is a characteristic of the Final Age. It is sad to be saying, over and over, that there are in general no understanding persons.

Too Many Sons of Regents Have Become Priests

Because conditions have worsened in this way, the sons of Regents are also numerous. Up until High Priest Jien's first appointment as Tendai Abbot [in 1192], one could easily count all the sons of Regents who had served as Tendai Abbot: High Priest Jinzen (943–990) of Iimuro; Ningen (d. 1109); Gyōgen (d. 1155); and Jien (1155–1225).[72] But now, probably more than 10 sons of Regents are living at Mt. Hiei alone. And probably 40 or 50 more sons of Regents are at Miidera, Kōfuku-ji in Nara, Ninna-ji, and Daigo-ji. Because the current Regent and three or four former Regents have been alive at one time, it is in accord with Principle [that so many of their sons are now priests at leading temples].

Too Many Imperial Sons Have Become Priests

It was once a rare thing for an Imperial son to become a Lay-Priest Prince, even at Ninna-ji, but now it seems that there are two Lay-Priest Princes even at Mt. Hiei. Numberless sons of Retired Em-

70. Third Grade was held by Preceptors, Second Grade by Vicars General, and First Grade by High Priests.

71. The six were: (1) Imperial Bodyguards of the Left (*sakon efu*); (2) Imperial Bodyguards of the Right (*ukon efu*); (3) Imperial Guards of the Left (*sahyō efu*); (4) Imperial Guards of the Right (*uhyō efu*); (5) Palace Gate Guards of the Left (*saemon efu*); and (6) Palace Gate Guards of the Right (*uemon efu*).

72. Jinzen (son of Morosuke) was Tendai Abbot from 985 to 990; Ningen (son of Morozane) from 1105 to 1109; Gyōgen (another son of Morozane) from 1138 to 1155; and Jien (son of Tadamichi) four times: 1192 to 1196, 1201 to 1202, 1212 to 1213, and 1213 to 1214.

peror [Tsuchimikado], of the present Emperor [Juntoku], and of the
second and third Imperial sons [of Retired Emperor Takakura] have
been sent—when they were children and knew nothing about the
teachings [of Buddha]—to study under a priestly teacher and to become Masters of the Buddhist Law *(hōshi)*. This development seems,
sadly but surely, to be in accord with what Prince Shotoku predicted
in the *Phases of the World's Deterioration.*[73]

Probably there will be many skeptical readers who will ask: "Did
not people have many children in the ancient past?" This brings up
something that should be well understood. In the ancient past, Emperors did have many sons; but most of them were given surnames,
simply appointed to ministerial posts, and given noble rank. The
sons of Imperial sons were treated the same way. And the sons of
Regents who were not heirs to the headship of the regental house,
and not slated to become Regent or Chancellor, were treated as
commoners and ordered to serve in the Imperial Household. Sons
of lower-ranking houses who showed some promise were picked out
for official appointments, and all others were left to fend for themselves. Therefore, those who did receive appointments were all good
men. Not one was a source of embarrassment. But today, princes
and sons of Regents are all treated like princes and heirs to the regental house. And the sons of lower-ranking nobles are treated in
ways that would enable them to reach the positions held by their
fathers. Probably this [bureaucratic topheaviness] has developed because weak sons have been adopted out and their adoptive parents
have tried to get advancements for them.

Worldly Priests

Furthermore, many priests have their own schools *(tachiwake)*, because a priest develops his own following *(montō)* after becoming the
head of a temple. Priests who have left the secular world have therefore developed secular, father-son relationships with each other.

What Does This Mean?

Therefore, when I say that there are no men, I mean that there
really are many of poor ability. Alas! Alas! It is precisely because of
this that people make critical comments such as: "He has things that
are nothing, and a reputation that is false." So priests and laymen
are all resentful and hostile toward each other; and we are in the last

73. *Yo-metsu-shō* (world destruction pine). No such work is now extant.
"Pine" does not seem to fit. The editors of the NKBT of the *Gukanshō* are
inclined to think that the last character in the title should have been the one
for *sō* (phases or aspects). [NKBT, 86.523, note 21.]

and final stage of deterioration: the "stage of conflict."[74] Noblemen and commoners alike have no ability, and there is no way to say [how serious] this is.

What Can and Should Be Done?

My heart and mind will be comforted by raising and answering some questions here at the close of this book:

Question: So now we have a situation that man has no power to alter. Does this mean that the state has absolutely no possibility of improvement?

Answer: It will be easy to make some improvement.

Question: The state has already been ruined, and we are now destined to have no men of ability. And vestiges of the old style have disappeared. How can you say that it is easy to make improvement?

Answer: I said: "Some improvement." It will certainly be easy to make some improvement.

Question: How can some improvement be made?

Answer: Even though able persons have disappeared, the sovereign [Go-Toba] and his Regent should be of one mind. And even though there are bad people among those who are now alive, priests and laymen should be sifted and resifted. The number of promising men who held office during [the reigns of] Shirakawa and Toba [from 1072–86 and 1107–23] should be called in and employed. And others should be completely rejected. If useless persons are really rejected and ignored, there will be some improvement. This is what I mean when I say "some improvement." Since there are now no persons like those who lived in ancient times, the situation can not be restored to what it was then. But it is an age when, even though the situation is bad, improvement can be made if proper selections are made.

Question: How can large numbers of these officials be rejected?

Answer: When I say "rejected," I really mean not calling them in or employing them—that is, not acknowledging their existence even though they are holding governmental posts. Although various sorts of bad things were done while Yōzei (868–949) was alive, the state was well governed during the reigns of Uda and Daigo (from 887–930) because these later Emperors did not talk or listen to Retired Emperor Yōzei. One should not go so far as to

74. Cf. Chapter 10.

dismiss people who lack ability. What I mean by "rejecting" them is that the selected persons should be instructed
to have absolutely no dealings with those who are useless.

Question: Will not serious incidents arise because the rejected
people will be numerous and will get together and con-
coct plots?

Answer: But that is why large numbers of soldiers are maintained.
If there is the slightest disposition to rebel, word will leak
out. Those who have such feelings will not be rebellious
again if two or three are exiled to some distant place.

Question: That is right *(gi)* and excellent! But who will be the proper
persons to make the selections?

Answer: This is very important! Certainly there will be four or five
upright individuals who can be called on to choose the
most able men. They should meet together, make their
selections, and submit their recommendations to the Retired Emperor. And if those selected are really used,
without even the Retired Emperor acting high-handedly
[to alter the selections], the state will be improved easily.

Question: Why shouldn't officials be dismissed?

Answer: Since persons selected for service will require positions as
Consultants, Controllers, and Imperial Secretaries,[75] individuals holding those positions will of course have to be
dismissed. But no others. It is very important to limit the
number of Buddhist and secular office-holders. A good
number for these final reigns is the number that held
office in the middle of the Toba reign [1107–23].

75. These were by no means the highest offices at court. The Consultants
(sangi)—referred to here as the *hachiza* (the eight seats)—were included in
the Council of State but ranked below ministers *(daijin)* and Counselors *(na-
gon)*. The Controllers *(benkan)* were also in the Council of State but ranked
below Consultants. The Imperial Secretaries *(kurodō no tō)*—referred to here
as *shikiji*—were members of an office (the *kurōdo-dokoro* or Imperial Secretariat) that was set up after the Kusuko Incident of 810. This office stood
outside the formal bureaucratic structure and was apparently meant to give
current holders of power direct access to the throne. Imperial Secretaries
therefore came to exercise more power than many officials of higher rank.

Part II
Gukanshō's
Imperial Chronology

6
Chronology I:

Emperor Jimmu to
Emperor Daigo

Chinese Dynasties

P'AN KU (First sovereign after the formation of heaven, earth, and man).

THREE SOVEREIGNS: Celestial Sovereigns; Terrestrial Sovereigns; and Human Sovereigns.

THREE OTHER SOVEREIGNS: Fu Hsi; Shen Nung; and Huang Ti.

FIVE EMPERORS: Shao Hao; Chuan Hsu; Kao Hsin; Yao; and Shun.

THREE KINGLY [DYNASTIES]: HSIA: 17 kings, 432 years; YIN or SHANG: 30 kings, 618 years;[1] and CHOU: 37 kings, 867 years.[2]

TWELVE PRINCIPALITIES: Cheng, Ts'ao, Sung, Chin, Wei, Ch'in, Ch'i, Yen, Lu, Ts'ai, Ch'u, and Ch'en. (Wu is not included among these principalities.)[3]

1. The traditional dates for the Shang Dynasty are 1176–1122 B.C.
2. Usually said to have begun in 1122 B.C. and ended in 256 B.C.
3. These principalities or feudal states figured in a gradual deterioration of Chou that began with the establishment of the Eastern Chou (when the

SIX [WARRING] STATES (States which existed at the time of King Yüan)[4]: Han, Wei, Chao, Ch'i, Yen, and Ch'u.

CH'IN [DYNASTY]: 6 Emperors, 56 years.[5]

HAN [DYNASTY]: 12 Emperors, 214 years. Wang Mang: 14 years. Keng Shih: 3 years.[6]

LATER HAN [DYNASTY]: 12 Emperors, 195 years [A.D. 25–220].

THREE KINGDOMS: WEI: 5 Emperors, 45 years; WU: 4 Emperors, 49 years; and SHU: 2 Emperors, 43 years [221–265].

CHIN KINGDOMS: 15 Emperors, 155 years.[7] After Liu Yüan[8] usurped the throne there were these kingdoms: SOUTHERN YEN; LATER LIANG; LATER CH'IN; LATER SHU; LATER HSIA; WESTERN CH'IN; SOUTHERN LIANG; FORMER CH'IN; FORMER LIANG; LATER CHAO; TAI-WEI; NORTHERN LIANG; NORTHERN YEN; and LATER YEN.

NORTHERN AND SOUTHERN COURTS [420–589][9]: SUNG: 8 Emperors, 59 years; LATER WEI: 14 Emperors, 139 years; SOUTHERN CH'I: 7 Emperors, 33 years; WESTERN WEI: 3 Emperors, 23 years; EASTERN WEI: 1 Emperor, 16 years; LIANG: 4 Emperors, 55 years; LATER CHOU: 5 Emperors, 24 years; CH'EN: 5 Emperors, 33 years; and NORTHERN CH'I: 7 Emperors, 28 years.

SUI DYNASTY: 3 Emperors, 37 years [589–618].

T'ANG DYNASTY: 20 Emperors, 289 years [618–906].

FIVE DYNASTIES [907–959]: LIANG: 3 Emperors, 16 years; T'ANG:

---

capital was moved eastward) and coincided roughly with what is known as the Spring and Autumn Period (722–481 B.C.).

4. The 27th king of Chou, who reigned from 475 to 469 B.C. [NBKT, 86.41, note 12.]

5. The Ch'in did not destroy all rival states until 221 B.C., and the Dynasty lasted only until 206 B.C. Therefore Jien, in concluding that it lasted 56 years, assumed that the Dynasty began before 221 when a Ch'in ruler adopted the title of Shih Huang-Ti (First Sovereign Emperor).

6. The Former Han Dynasty (China's second empire) was founded in 206 B.C. and was destroyed by Wang Mang in A.D. 8. The new dynasty established by Wang Mang in A.D. 8 lasted until A.D. 23. Keng Shih followed Wang Mang and preceded the establishment of the Later Han Dynasty in A.D. 25.

7. There were two Chin Dynasties: the Western Chin (265–317), which united most of China; and the Eastern Chin (317–420), which existed only in South China.

8. Liu Yüan was a ruler of a Turkic people called the Hsiung-nu. He declared himself to be the King of Han in A.D. 306.

9. The Southern Courts included (after the collapse of the Eastern Chin in 420): Sung, Southern Ch'i, Liang, and Ch'en. The Northern Courts were: Northern Wei, Western Wei, Eastern Wei, Northern Ch'i, and Northern Chou. [NKBT, 86.42, note 7.] Jien called the Northern Wei the Later Wei.

4 Emperors, 13 years; CHIN: 3 Emperors, 12 years; HAN: 2 Emperors, 3 years; and CHOU: 3 Emperors, 9 years.

GREAT SUNG DYNASTY: 13 Emperors down to the present, and 263 years down to the present.[10]

The above was written in Shōkyū 2 [1220].[11]

Terms, and the Way I Have Counted the Number of Years in a Reign

JUZEN: receiving the throne when it has been handed over by [the previous Emperor or Empress].

SENSO: accession to the throne.

The first character is read *fumu* in Japanese and means "step," and the second is *hajime* or "first." Thus the term may be rendered literally "the first step" *(senso)*.

DASSHI: abdication.

The Yellow Emperor (Huang Ti) wanted to follow the way of Buddha,[12] and therefore his abdication was referred to as "taking off his sandals *(dasshi)*. . . ."

THE NUMBER OF YEARS IN A REIGN has been calculated by skipping the year in which the throne was received and beginning with the following year, the "skipping-a-year" method.

10. The Sung Dynasty was established in 960, and therefore the lapse of 263 years places "the present" at 1222. This calculation supports the Tsuda thesis that the *Gukanshō* was written after the Shōkyū War of 1221. But Ishida points out that Jien, like the Chinese of that day, undoubtedly thought of the Sung as having had two dynastic breaks: one in 976 when the throne was seized by T'ai Tsung, and another in 1127 when the Southern Sung court was established. At such times, the Chinese customarily concluded that a new Mandate of Heaven had been handed down and that a new era name should be proclaimed immediately, not in the following year. Thus the same calendar year would be counted twice. Since there were two breaks of this kind, "the present" in this passage would be 1220, the date given at the end of this section. [Ichirō Ishida, *Gukanshō no seiritsu to sono shisō* (Sendai, 1967), pp. 4–6.]

11. Ishida's textual study has led him to conclude that the above section on *Chinese Dynasties* was attached to an earlier draft of the CHRONOLOGY. Jien may have added this section in order to provide further support for his belief in the uniqueness of Imperial succession in Japan and also to suggest that Chinese history, as well as Japanese history, had been subjected to continuous deterioration, making later dynasties shorter than the SHANG or the CHOU.

12. Probably Jien meant to say that the Yellow Emperor wanted to follow "the way of a hermit" *(sendō)*, not of Buddha. [NKBT, 86.361, note 13.]

Japan's Direct Line of Imperial Descent[13]

[1] Jimmu;

[2] Suizei [3rd son of Jimmu];

[3] Annei [son and heir of Suizei];

[4] Itoku [2nd son of Annei];

[5] Kōshō [son and heir of Itoku];

[6] Kōan [2nd son of Kōshō];

[7] Kōrei [son and heir of Kōan];

[8] Kōgen [son and heir of Kōrei];

[9] Kaika [2nd son of Kōgen];

[10] Sujin [2nd son of Kaika];

[11] Suinin [3rd son of Sujin];

[12] Keikō [3rd son of Suinin];

Yamato Takeru no Mikoto [son of Keikō];

[14] Chūai [2nd son of Yamato Takeru no Mikoto];

[16] Ōjin [4th son of Chūai]

Prince Hayabusa [son of Ōjin];

Prince Oto [son of Prince Hayabusa];

Prince Shihi [son of Prince Ōto];

Prince Hiko Aruji [son of Prince Shihi];

[27] Keitai [5th generation descendant of Ōjin];

[30] Kimmei [3rd son of Keitai];

[31] Bidatsu [2nd son of Kimmei];

Prince Oshisaka no Ōe [son of Bidatsu];

[35] Jomei [grandson of Bidatsu];

[39] Tenchi [1st son of Jomei];

Prince Shiki [son of Tenchi];

[49] Kōnin [6th son of Prince Shiki];

[50] Kwammu [son of Kōnin];

[52] Saga [2nd son of Kwammu];

[54] Nimmyō [2nd son of Saga];

[58] Kōkō [3rd son of Nimmyō];

[59] Uda [3rd son of Kōkō];

[60] Daigo [1st son of Uda];

[62] Murakami [14th son of Daigo];

[64] Enyū [5th son of Murakami];

[66] Ichijō [1st son of Enyū];

[69] Go-Suzaku [3rd son of Ichijō];

[71] Go-Sanjō [2nd son of Go-Suzaku];

[72] Shirakawa [1st son of Go-Sanjō]; and

[73] Horikawa [2nd son of Shirakawa].

13. This list has no heading or explanation in any known *Gukanshō* text. A study of the way each individual on the list is treated in the CHRONOLOGY and in narrative chapters suggests that Jien listed persons who would have been enthroned if the True Law of Japan (Imperial succession from father to son) had been followed consistently. Every name after that of Emperor Jimmu is the son of the previous man on the list. No names after Horikawa were included, probably because those later Emperors were all sons of previous Emperors.

Numbers in brackets are reign numbers assigned in the CHRONOLOGY. Those persons without numbers did not occupy the throne. The relationship of a man to the previous man on the list, also in brackets, is the relationship shown in the CHRONOLOGY.

Chronology of Japanese Reigns

(1) Emperor Jimmu. A reign of 76 years.
(The first year was *kanoto-tori* [660 B.C.]. Jimmu was enthroned at the age of 52 and lived to the age of 127.)[14]

Jimmu was the fourth son of U no Ha Fukiawasezu no Mikoto and was born on the 1st day *(kanoe-tatsu)* of the 1st month. . . .[15] His mother was Tamayori Hime (eldest daughter of the Sea Kami). One version says he was the third son of the seventh-generation Kami. Another version says his mother entered the sea and that Tamayori Hime was his adoptive mother. . . .

Soon after [the beginning of] this reign, a Master of Ceremonies *(saishu)*[16] was appointed and the myriad Kami worshipped. This country was called the Akizu Islands. The Imperial Palace was at Kashiwara in the province of Yamato. *Kanoto-tori* was the first year of this reign, the 290th year after the death of Shakyamuni. . . .[17] It is also said that this [first year of Jimmu's reign] was the 3rd year in the reign of Hsi Wang, the 16th ruler of the Chou Dynasty. . . . Another view is that *kanoto-tori* was the 17th year of the Hui Wang reign of Chou. Isn't it because [the 17th year of Huei Wang's reign] was propitious that—until the present day—this [second] view has not been questioned?[18]

14. Words and sentences within parentheses are translations of small characters written beside or after the large characters of the text. These were probably added sometime later, either by Jien or an editor. The dates placed in brackets after particular years of the sexagenary cycle are those traditionally assigned, counting backward from 604 when the sexagenary cycle was adopted and when, according to the Chinese, a new cycle (starting with *kinoe-ne*) had begun.
15. A source is quoted but not completed. Such incomplete quotations will be indicated by inserting four dots.
16. This office was regularly held by a member of the NAKATOMI clan after the eighth century. Cf. Felicia Bock, *Engi-Shiki* (Tokyo, 1970), I. 36.
17. This calculation, consistent with the contemporary belief that the Final Law of Buddhism had begun in the year A.D. 1052, is based on the Chinese view that Buddha died in 949 B.C.
18. These two paragraphs seem to have been based upon information taken from the *Renchū shō*, but probably other sources were also used. If Jien had simply copied the *Renchū shō* at this point, he would have written: "Jimmu was the fourth son of U no Ha Fukiawasezu no Mikoto. His mother was Tamayori Hime, eldest daughter of the Sea Kami. [This son] was called Kami Yamato Iwarehiko no Mikoto. He resided in the Kashiwara palace in the province of Yamato. He had two Empresses and four children. At this time the Master of Ceremonies was first appointed and the myriad Kami worshipped. From this time on, the country was called the Akizu Islands." [*Kaitei: Shiseki shūran*, 23, Section 20, p. 7.]

(2) Emperor Suizei. A reign of 33 years.

(The first year was *kanoe-tatsu* [581 B.C.]. Suizei was enthroned at the age of 52 and lived to the age of 84.)

Suizei was the third son of Emperor Jimmu and had been appointed Crown Prince (at the age of 19) on the *kinoe-tora* day of the 1st month of the 42nd year of the Jimmu reign. His mother was Tatara Isuzu Hime, daughter of Kotoshiro-nushi no Kami.[19] He was enthroned four years after the death of Emperor Jimmu. His palace was the Takaoka no Miya in Katsuragi of the province of Yamato. He had one Empress and one Imperial son.

Three Imperial sons had been born to Emperor Jimmu. The first was Tagishi Mimi no Mikoto, the second was Kamu-ya-i Mimi no Mikoto, and the third was the Crown Prince who became Emperor Suizei. After the death of Emperor Jimmu, and during the period of mourning, affairs of state were handled by the eldest Imperial son; but he soon developed feelings of malice toward his two younger brothers. Being aware of his eldest brother's feelings, the Crown Prince urged the middle brother to kill the eldest brother. But when the second son took up the bow and arrow, his hands shook and he could not shoot. Then the Crown Prince seized the bow and shot an arrow that did not miss, killing his eldest brother. The middle brother said: "I do not have enough ability to receive the throne." While the Crown Prince was arguing that his remaining elder brother should take the throne "because you are the elder," and each of the two brothers was deferring to each other, four years passed without the throne being occupied. Finally, in the fourth year, the Crown Prince yielded to the urging of his elder brother and ascended the throne as Emperor Suizei.

In reflecting about this affair, I conclude that it showed everything was to be fortunate at the beginning [of Japanese history]. The killing of the eldest brother seemed bad, but the Crown Prince did not kill his eldest brother in order to place himself on the throne. His purpose was to have an evil destroyed. Then he urged his middle brother to take the throne. So in thinking about this development, I conclude that Principle was simply being made the governing factor *sen*). The Imperial father [Jimmu] had assessed abilities and appointed his third son Crown Prince. If we look at what happened later from the point of view of what occurred here at the beginning [of Japanese history], we see that a precedent—one followed later by Nintoku [17] and the eldest son Prince Uji—was first established by this middle son and Crown Prince Suizei deferring to each other

19. This Kami was not associated directly with the Imperial clan, according to the *Kojiki*, but identified as the son of Ōkuni-nushi no Mikoto, the chief deity of the Izumo clan. [Donald Philippi, *Kojiki* (Princeton, 1969), pp. 636 and 543.]

with correct-way *(shōdō)* feelings. The precedent of Suizei yielding to his elder brother's urgings and occupying the throne was followed well by Kenzō [24] and Ninken [25]. It was a precedent in which things were done in conformity with a human assessment [of ability]. The killing of the eldest Imperial brother was carried out with the idea that all evil should be rejected and that good should be embraced. This precedent was followed when Emperor Sushun [33] was killed in the time of Prince Shōtoku, when Prince Ōtomo was killed by Emperor Temmu [40], and on many later occasions. The precedent for all these cases was first [manifested during this reign].

(3) Emperor Annei. A reign of 38 years.
(The first year was *mizunoto-ushi* [548 B.C.]. Emperor Annei was enthroned at the age of 20 and lived to the age of 57.)

Annei was the eldest son of Emperor Suizei and had been appointed Crown Prince on the *tsuchinoe-ne* day of the 1st month of the 25th year of the Suizei reign (when Annei was 11 years old). His mother was Empress Dowager Isuzu-yori Hime (younger daughter of Kotoshiro-nushi no Kami). His palace was Ukena no Miya in Katashio of the province of Yamato. He had three Empresses and four Imperial sons.

(4) Emperor Itoku. A reign of 34 years.
(The first year was *kanoto-u* [510 B.C.]. Emperor Itoku was enthroned at the age of 34 and lived to the age of 77.)

Itoku was the second (or third) son of Emperor Annei and had been appointed Crown Prince in the 11th year of the Annei reign. His mother was Empress Dowager Nuna-soko-nakatsu Hime (granddaughter of Kotoshiro-nushi no Kami). His palace was the Magario no Miya in Karu of the province of Yamato. Confucius died in the 32nd year of this reign (or in the 7th year of the Kōshō reign). . . . Itoku had three Empresses and one Imperial son.

(5) Emperor Kōshō. A reign of 83 years.
(The first year was *hinoe-tora* [475 B.C.]. Emperor Kōshō was enthroned at the age of 32 and lived to the age of 120.)

Kōshō was the eldest son of Emperor Itoku and had been appointed Crown Prince in the 22nd year of the Itoku reign. His mother was Empress Dowager Ama-toyotsu Hime (daughter of Okishi Mimi no Mikoto). His palace was the Ikekokoro no Miya in Wakinokami of the province of Yamato. He had three Empresses and two Imperial sons.

(6) Emperor Kōan. A reign of 102 years.
(The first year was *tsuchinoto-ushi* [392 B.C.]. Emperor Kōan was enthroned at the age of 36 and lived to the age of 137.)

Kōan was the second son of Emperor Kōshō and had been appointed Crown Prince in the 68th year of the Kōshō reign. His mother was Empress Dowager Yoso-tarashi Hime (younger sister of Okitsu Yoso, distant ancestor of the Deity-Chieftain of Owari). Emperor Kōan's palace was the Akitsushima no Miya of Muro in the province of Yamato. He had three Empresses and one Imperial son.

(7) Emperor Kōrei. A reign of 76 years.
(The first year was *kanoe-uma* [291 B.C.].[20] Emperor Kōrei was enthroned at the age of 53 and lived to the age of 128.)

Kōrei was the eldest son of Emperor Kōan and had been appointed Crown Prince in the 76th year of the Kōan reign. His mother was Empress Dowager Ane-oshi Hime (daughter of Ama-tarashi-hiko-kuni-oshi-hito no Mikoto). His palace was the Ihoto no Miya in Kuroda of the province of Yamato. He had five Empresses and six Imperial sons and daughters.

(8) Emperor Kōgen. A reign of 57 years.
(The first year was *hinoto-i* [214 B.C.]. Emperor Kōgen was enthroned at the age of 60 and lived to the age of 117.)

Kōgen was the eldest son of Emperor Kōrei and had been appointed Crown Prince in the 36th year of the Kōrei reign. His mother was Empress Dowager Kuwashi Hime (daughter of Ōme, head [*agatanushi*] of the Shiki District). His palace was the Sakaihara no Miya of Karu in the province of Yamato. He had three Empresses and five Imperial sons and daughters.

(9) Emperor Kaika. A reign of 60 years.
(The first year was *kanoto-hitsuji* [170 B.C.].[21] Emperor Kaika was enthroned at the age of 51 and lived to the age of 115.)

Kaika was the second son of Emperor Kōgen and had been appointed Crown Prince in the 22nd year of the Kōgen reign. His mother was Empress Dowager Uchi-shiko-me no Mikoto (young sister of Utsu-shiko-o no Mikoto, distant ancestor of the Hozumi no Omi). His palace was Isakawa no Miya of Kasuga in the province of Yamato. He had four Empresses and five Imperial sons and daughters.

No Ministers are recorded for the above nine reigns.

20. The *Nihongi* states that the first year of Kōrei's reign was *kanoto-hitsuji* (290 B.C.), which would give Kōan a reign of 102 years and Kōrei one of 76, just as Jien wrote. In this case at least, Jien was closer to the *Nihongi* than was the editor whose dating is translated within parentheses.

21. In this case too, Jien's calculations are based on the *Nihongi* and are not in accord with what was added later.

(10) Emperor Sujin. A reign of 68 years.
(The first year was *kinoe-saru* [97 B.C.]. Emperor Sujin was enthroned at the age of 52 and lived to the age of 108.)

Sujin was the second son of Emperor Kaika and was appointed Crown Prince in the 28th year of the Kaika reign. His mother was Empress Dowager Ika-shiko-me no Mikoto (daughter of Ō Hesoki). His palace was the Mizogaki no Miya of Shiki in the province of Yamato.

After the enthronement of Emperor Sujin, many people got sick and died. Consequently the Sun Goddess was worshipped at the village of Kasanui. Shrines were set up in the various provinces, and the several Kami were honored. Then the state was well governed and the people prospered. It was during this reign that tribute (*mitsugimono*) was paid to the Imperial Court, that ponds were dug in various provinces, and that boats were built. Imperial envoys were dispatched to the four regions, and thus the people who had not been subjected to the authority of the Emperor were pacified. But there was [as yet] no one who held the title of Imperial Chieftain (*omi*) or Deity Chieftain (*muraji*). Emperor Sujin had four Empresses and 11 Imperial sons and daughters.

(11) Emperor Suinin. A reign of 99 years.
(The first year was *mizunoe-tatsu* [29 B.C.]. Emperor Suinin was enthroned at the age of 43 and lived to the age of 130—or 101, or 151.)

Suinin was the third son of Emperor Sujin and had been appointed Crown Prince in the 48th year of the Sujin reign. His mother was Empress Dowager Mimaki Hime (daughter of Ōhiko no Mikoto). His palace was the Tamaki no Miya at Makimuku in the province of Yamato. He had four Empresses and 11 Imperial sons and daughters.

During this reign, the Ise Shrine—located on the bank of the Isuzu River in the province of Ise—was dedicated. This was done in response to instructions received from the Sun Goddess. Also a High Priestess (*saigū*)[22] for the Ise Shrine was first appointed during this reign. In ancient times, when [an important] person died, his retainers were buried alive with him. But because that practice was stopped during this reign, figurines [of retainers] were made and placed in the tomb [of a deceased master]. During this reign, fruit from the land of Tokoyo was presented to the court—it was the orange (*tachibana*) of today. Persons were first sent to T'ang [China], and envoys first came from Silla [in Korea].

The ancestors of the five clans, including the Imperial-Chieftain

22. Cf. Felicia Bock, *Engi-Shiki* (Tokyo, 1970), 1.151–185.

clan of ABE, received an Imperial edict *(mikotonori)* to consult [with the Emperor] about administrative affairs. But all [heads of these five clans] were called high retainers *(mōchigimi)*—the title of Imperial Chieftain *(omi)* was not yet being used.

(12) Emperor Keikō. A reign of 60 years.
(The first year was *kanoto-hitsuji* [A.D. 71]. Emperor Keikō was enthroned at the age of 44 or 31, and lived to the age of 106—or 133, or 120.)

Keikō was the third son of Emperor Suinin and had been appointed Crown Prince in the 37th year of the Suinin reign. His mother was Empress Dowager Hihasu Hime no Mikoto (daughter of Prince Michinushi of Tamba). His palace was the Hishiro no Miya of Makimuku in the province of Yamato. He had eight Empresses and 80 Imperial sons and daughters.

TAKENOUCHI Sukune was first appointed Great Imperial Chieftain *(Ō-omi)* in this reign. People of various provinces were given [hereditary] titles *(kabane)*.

Chief Minister (tōryō no shin): TAKENOUCHI Sukune.
(From this time on, a Chief Minister was appointed.)

(13) Emperor Seimu. A reign of 61 years.
(The first year was *kanoto-hitsuji* [A.D. 131]. Emperor Seimu was enthroned at the age of 49 and lived to the age of 107.)

Seimu was the fourth son of Emperor Keikō and had been appointed Crown Prince in the 51st year of the Keikō reign. His mother was Empress Dowager Yasaka-iri Hime no Mikoto (daughter of Prince Yasaka-iri Hiko). His palace was the Taka-ana-ho no Miya at Shiga in the province of Ōmi. All previous palaces had been located in the province of Yamato.

During this reign the boundaries of provinces were established. Seimu had one Empress and no children.

Great Imperial Chieftain (Ō-omi): TAKENOUCHI Sukune.
(The title of Great Imperial Chieftain was awarded from this reign on.) Great Imperial Chieftain TAKENOUCHI was treated especially well because his birthday was the same as the Emperor's.

(14) Emperor Chūai. A reign of nine years.
(The first year was *mizunoe-sara* [A.D. 192]. Emperor Chūai was enthroned at the age of 44 and lived to the age of 52.)

Chūai was the grandson of Emperor Keikō and the second son of Yamato Takeru no Mikoto. His mother was Empress Dowager Futamichi-iri-hime no Mikoto (Imperial daughter of Emperor Ikume [Suinin]). He had been appointed Crown Prince in the 48th

year of the Keikō reign, and his palace was the Toyora no Miya in
Anato of the province of Nagato. He had three Empresses and four
Imperial sons.

During this reign the Empress obtained, at the Toyora no Miya, a
Nyoi pearl. It had been found in the sea.

Great Imperial Chieftain: TAKENOUCHI Sukune.

Great Deity Chieftain (ō-muraji): ŌTOMO no Takemotsu no Muraji.
(The title of Great Deity Chieftain was awarded from this reign
on.)

Yamato Takeru no Mikoto, the father of Emperor Chūai, is the
Great Illuminating Kami *(dai myōjin)* now worshipped at the Atsuta
Shrine in the province of Owari.

> (15) Empress Jingū. "Regent" *(sesshō)*[23] for 69 years.
> (The first year was *kanoto-mi* [A.D. 201]. Empress Jingū was
> enthroned at 32 and lived to the age of 100.)

Jingū was Chūai's Empress and the daughter of Okinaga no
Sukune, [the son of Kanime-ikazuchi no Miko, who was, in turn,]
the son of Ōtsutsuki no Mawaka. Ōtsutsuki no Mawaka was the son
of Prince Hiko-imasu no Mikoto, the Imperial son of Emperor Kaika.
Jingū's mother was KATSURAGI Taka-nuka Hime. Her palace was the
Wakasakura no Miya at Iware in the province of Yamato.

Great Imperial Chieftain: TAKENOUCHI Sukune.

Dressed as a man, Empress Jingū conquered the states of Silla,
Kōkuli, and Paikché in Korea. She gave birth to the future Emperor
Ōjin and made TAKENOUCHI the boy's guardian. Ōjin's elder broth-
ers plotted [against the Empress], but Great Imperial Chieftain
TAKENOUCHI defeated them all. It will be difficult to write in detail
about even such matters as these, reign after reign.

> (16) Emperor Ōjin. A reign of 41 years.
> (The first year was *kanoe-tora* [A.D. 270].[24] Emperor Ōjin was
> enthroned at the age of 71 and lived to the age of 101.)

23. Modern chronologies do not list a reign for Empress Jingū, and the
Nihongi does not treat her as a reigning Empress. Furthermore, the above
list of persons in the direct line of Imperial descent does not include her
name. But both the *Gukanshō* and the *Renchū shō* assign her a separate reign.
Therefore the *Gukanshō's* reign numbers after Chūai (14), and down to Tenji
(39), are higher by one than those given in recent Japanese chronologies.
Jien's ambivalence concerning Jingū's position is reflected in his use of the
word *sesshō*, suggesting that he thought of her 69 years as a "regency," not
only as a "reign."

24. Modern scholars are inclined to think that Ōjin's reign began at the
close of the fourth century, about a century later than the traditional date
given here. [Inouye Mitsusada, *Nihon no rekishi I: Shinwa kara rekishi e* (Tokyo, 1965), p. 374.]

Ōjin was the fourth son of Emperor Chūai and had been appointed Crown Prince in the 3rd year of the reign of Empress Jingū. His mother was Empress Jingū, and his palace was the Akari no Miya at Karushima in the province of Yamato. Ōjin had eight Empresses and 19 Imperial sons and daughters.

Emperor Ōjin is the Great Hachiman Bodhisattva[25] of today. Female seamstresses, various artisans, and scholars (*hakase*) were brought from the state of Paikché during this reign. Chinese classics, horses, and other things were presented to the court [from Paikché].[26]

Great Imperial Chieftain: TAKENOUCHI Sukune.

(17) Emperor Nintoku. A reign of 87 years.
(The first year was *mizunoto-tori* [A.D. 313]. Emperor Nintoku was enthroned at the age of 24 and lived to the age of 110.)

Nintoku was the fourth son of Emperor Ōjin and had been made Crown Prince in the 40th year of the Ōjin reign. (There is a variant account that a younger brother was made Crown Prince.) Nintoku's mother was Empress Dowager Nakatsu Hime no Mikoto (granddaughter of Prince Ioki-iri-hiko). His palace was the Takatsu no Miya of Naniwa in the province of Settsu. He had three Empresses and six Imperial sons and daughters.

I have written in detail [in Chapter 1] about how the younger and elder brother urged each other to take the throne, leaving it vacant for three years. Nintoku's young brother was appointed Crown Prince. Probably this version is right.

Great Imperial Chieftain: TAKENOUCHI Sukune.

This Great Imperial Chieftain was Imperial guardian of six Emperors, and he lived to be more than 280 years old. His place of burial is not known.

25. Originally Hachiman seems to have been a guardian Kami worshipped in northern Kyushu and was apparently not identified with the soul of the heroic Ōjin until the last part of the Nara period, when the Iwashimizu Hachiman Shrine was built. During the Heian period, that Shrine—along with the Ise Shrine—was commonly referred to as a *sōbyō* (ancestral shrine of the Imperial House). Archaeological evidence suggests that the worship of Hachiman had been deeply influenced by Buddhist beliefs and practices as early as the sixth century. Hachiman worship at the Iwashimizu Hachiman Shrine was so deeply Buddhist that Hachiman was commonly spoken of, even in the *Gukanshō*, as "Hachiman, the great Bodhisattva." Cf. Nakano Hatayoshi, *Hachiman shinkō shi no kenkyū* (Tokyo, 1967).

26. This short paragraph suggests a realization that Ōjin's reign came at a turning point in early Japanese history, although the reference to a presentation of horses does not mean that he anticipated the recent "horserider" thesis.

During this reign ice houses *(himuro)* first appeared, and falcon hunting emerged then. . . . Emperor Nintoku is the Great Illuminating Kami *(dai myōjin)* now worshipped at the Hirano Shrine.[27]

> (18) Emperor Richū. A reign of six years.
> (The first year was *kanoe-ne* [A.D. 400]. Emperor Richū was enthroned at the age of 62 and lived to the age of 70.)

Richū was the eldest son of Emperor Nintoku and had been appointed Crown Prince in the 31st year of the Nintoku reign. His mother was Empress Dowager Iwa no Hime no Mikoto (daughter of KATSURAGI Sotsu Hiko).[28] Richū's palace was the Wakasakura no Miya of Iware in the province of Yamato, Richū had four Empresses and four Imperial sons and daughters.

During this reign, court waitresses *(uneme)* appeared. Four Great Imperial Chieftains. . . . It was during this reign that storehouses *(kura)* were built in various provinces.

Administrators of State Affairs (shissei):
HEGURI Zuku no Sukune;
SOGA Machi no Sukune; and
MONONOBE no Ikufutsu.
(There was an Administrator of State Affairs from this reign on.)

Great Deity Chieftain: KATSURAGI Tsubura no Omi.
He was the great-grandson of TAKENOUCHI Sukune.

> (19) Emperor Hanshō. A reign of six years.
> (The first year was *hinoe-uma* [A.D. 406]. Emperor Hanshō was enthroned at the age of 55 and lived to the age of 60.)

Hanshō was the third son of Emperor Nintoku and had been appointed Crown Prince in the 2nd year of the Richū reign. His mother was also the mother of Emperor Richū. Hanshō's palace was the Shibagaki no Miya at Tajihi in the province of Kawachi. Hanshō had two Empresses and four Imperial sons and daughters.

Administrator of State Affairs: KATSURAGI Tsubura no Omi.

> (20) Emperor Ingyō. A reign of 42 years.
> (The first year was *mizunoe-ne* [A.D. 412]. Emperor Ingyō was enthroned at the age of 39 and lived to the age of 80.)

Ingyō was the fourth son of Emperor Nintoku, and his mother was the same as Emperor Richū's. His palace was the Tōtsu

27. Cf. Chapter 1, note 31.
28. Inouye concludes that the KATSURAGI clan, located in the southwestern part of the Nara basin, helped the Imperial House after the time of Ōjin to establish the Yamato state. [*Shinwa kara rekishi e,* 378–380.]

Asuka no Miya. Ingyō had two Empresses and nine Imperial sons and daughters. His Empress was Sotōri Hime (said to have been the granddaughter of Emperor Ōjin). . . .

Great Deity Chieftain: ŌTOMO Muroya no Muraji.

(21) Emperor Ankō. A reign of three years.
(The first year was *mizunoto-mi* [A.D. 453]. Emperor Ankō was enthroned at the age of 53 and lived to the age of 56.)

Ankō was the second son of Emperor Ingyō, and his mother was Empress Dowager Osaka no Ōnakatsu Hime (daughter of Prince Wakanuke Futamata). His palace was the Anaho no Miya of Isonokami in the Yamanobe District of the province of Yamato.

Great Imperial Chieftain: KATSURAGI Tsubura no Ō-omi.

In the 8th month of the 3rd year of this reign, Prince Mayuwa killed Emperor Ankō and fled to Tsubura's house. Because of this, [Prince Mayuwa] was killed by Prince Ōhasse.

Great Deity Chieftain: ŌTOMO Muroya no Muraji.

Emperor Ankō killed his elder brother, the Crown Prince, and then succeeded to the throne on the 14th day of the 12th month at the age of 53. He also killed his uncle, Prince Ōkusaka, and took this uncle's wife for his Empress. The above-mentioned Prince Mayuwa was her son, and Mayuwa killed Ankō to avenge the wrong committed against his father. This affair is dealt with in detail in Chapter 1.

(22) Emperor Yūryaku. A reign of 22 years.
(The first year was *hinoe-saru* [A.D. 456]. Emperor Yūryaku was enthroned at the age of 70 and lived to the age of 104.)

Yūryaku was the fourth son of Emperor Ingyō, and his mother was also the mother of Emperor Ankō. His palace was the Asakura no Miya at Hasse in the province of Yamato. He had four Empresses and five Imperial sons and daughters. It was in this reign that the child of Urashima caught a turtle which turned into a woman and went up to heaven.

Great Imperial Chieftains:
HEGURI Matori no Omi; and
MONONOBE Me no Muraji.
(The latter was a son of Ikufutsu, who had been an Administrator of State Affairs.)

(23) Emperor Seinei. A reign of five years.
(The first was *kanoe-saru* [A.D. 480]. Emperor Seinei was enthroned at the age of 35, or 37; and he lived to the age of 39.)

Seinei was the third son of Emperor Yūryaku, and his mother was Imperial Concubine *(kōtai fujin)* Kara Hime (daughter of Great Imperial Chieftain KATSURAGI Tsubura). His palace was the Mikakuri no Miya at Iware in the province of Yamato.

Emperor Seinei was born with white hair and so was called Shiraga (white hair). His Imperial father appointed him Crown Prince because [the white hair seemed] awesome and significant. . . . Emperor Seinei had no Imperial sons, and so two grandsons of Emperor Richū were called in and adopted. Because of the political disturbances of the Ankō reign, they had gone into hiding in the province of Tanba.

Great Imperial Chieftain: Same as in the previous reign.
Great Deity Chieftain: Same as in the previous reign.

(24) Emperor Kenzō. A reign of three years.
(The first year was *kinoto-ushi* [A.D. 485]. Emperor Kenzō was enthroned at the age of 36 and lived to the age of 48.)

Kenzō was a grandson of Emperor Richū and the third son of Prince Ichibe Oshiha. His mother was Hae Hime (granddaughter of Ari no Omi). His palace was the Yatsuri no Miya at Chikaasuka. Kenzō had one Empress and no Imperial sons. Meandering Stream Parties *(kyokusui no en)*[29] were first held during this reign.

Great Imperial Chieftain: Same as in the [Yūryaku] reign.
Great Deity Chieftain: Same as in the [Ankō] reign.

(25) Emperor Ninken. A reign of 11 years.
(The first year was *tsuchinoe-tatsu* [A.D. 488]. Emperor Ninken lived to the age of 50.)

Ninken was the elder brother of Emperor Kenzō, and his mother was the same as Kenzō's. He had been appointed Crown Prince in the 3rd year of the Seinei reign. Ninken's palace was the Hirotaka no Miya at Isonokami in the district of Yamanobe in the province of Yamato. He had two Empresses and eight Imperial sons and daughters.

The affairs of Emperor Ninken and the previous Emperor Kenzō were detailed [in Chapter 1]. While these two brothers were urging each other to take the throne, their sister was enthroned. . . . She was called Empress Iitoyo. . . . She was enthroned in the 2nd month and died in the 11th month. . . . Her reign is not found in the ordinary Imperial chronologies. The state was very well governed during the reigns of these two brothers. Was not their rule good because they had lived in the countryside and were familiar with the people's grievances?

29. Cf. Chapter 4, note 29.

Great Imperial Chieftain: HEGURI Matori no Ō-omi.
(During this reign, HEGURI Matori no Ō-omi was killed by
ŌTOMO Kanamura no Muraji. HEGURI Matori no Ō-omi had
been Great Imperial Chieftain under five Emperors.)
Great Deity Chieftain: ŌTOMO Kanamura no Muraji.

(26) Emperor Buretsu. A reign of eight years.
(The first year was *tsuchinoe-tora* [A.D. 498]. Emperor Buretsu
was enthroned at the age of 10 and lived to the age of 18, or
57. . . .)

Buretsu was the eldest son of Emperor Ninken and had been
appointed Crown Prince in the 7th year of the Ninken reign. His
mother was Empress Kasuga no Ōiratsume. His palace was the
Namiki no Miya of Hasse. Buretsu had one Empress and no Imperial sons or daughters. He was an incomparably bad Emperor and
took pleasure in killing people.[30] Even in the affair in which Matori,
the Great Imperial Chieftain, was killed, Emperor Buretsu had allied
himself with Kanamura, who subsequently was appointed Great
Deity Chieftain.

(27) Emperor Keitai. A reign of 25 years.
(The first year was *hinoto-i* [A.D. 507]. Emperor Keitai was
enthroned at the age of 58 and lived to the age of 82.)

Keitai was a fifth-generation descendant of Emperor Ōjin
and the son of Prince Hiko Aruji. His mother was Furu Hime
(daughter of seventh-generation descendant of Emperor Ikume
[Suinin]). The five generations that followed Emperor Ōjin were:
Prince Hayabusa; Prince Ōto; Prince Shihi; Prince Hiko Aruji; and
Emperor Keitai. But there is a different version that deletes Prince
Shihi. . . . Is that not why, in identifying the five generations, Ōjin's
name is sometimes added and sometimes left out? One version has
it that Empress Jingū was also a fifth-generation descendant of Emperor Kaika, . . . and in that case Emperor Kaika is included as one
of the five. If that is the case, is it not a mistake to include Prince
Shihi [as one of Emperor Ōjin's descendants]? This should certainly
be investigated. Emperor Keitai's palace was the Tamaho no Miya at

30. Cf. Chapter 1. Jien omitted some of the *Renchū shō* details of Buretsu's
wickedness: "This Emperor [Buretsu] did only bad things, nothing good. He
enjoyed killing people. Sometimes he would make a person climb up in a
tree and then shoot him with arrows, or kill him by having the tree cut
down. Sometimes he would subject a person to water torture and stab him
with a halberd. Sometimes he would watch as the abdomen of a pregnant
woman was ripped open. And sometimes he would pull out a man's finger-
nails. . . ." [*Kaitei: Shiseki shūran*, 23, Section 20, p. 14.]

Iware in the province of Yamato. The capital was moved to the province of Yamashiro and then moved back to Yamato. . . .

During this reign, a scholar of the five Confucian classics was sent to the Imperial Court from the state of Paikché in Korea. The line of direct Imperial succession was broken after the reign of Buretsu, and Emperor Keitai was welcomed from the province of Echizen.[31] This was done by the Imperial Chieftains (*omi*) of the Imperial House. This was written up in detail [see Chapter 1]. Emperor Keitai had nine Empresses and 21 Imperial sons and daughters (9 sons and 12 daughters).

Great Imperial Chieftain: KOSE Ohito Ō-omi.
(He was a son of TAKENOUCHI and died in the 9th month of the 20th year of this reign.)
Great Deity Chieftains:
　ŌTOMO Kanamura no Muraji; and
　MONONOBE Arakabi no Ō-muraji.

(28) Emperor Ankan. A reign of two years.
(The first year was *mizunoto-ushi* [A.D. 533]. Emperor Ankan was enthroned at 68 and lived to the age of 70.)

Ankan was the eldest son of Emperor Keitai, and his mother was Menoko Hime (daughter of Kusaka, Deity Chieftain of the province of Owari). His palace was the Kanahashi no Miya of Magari in the province of Yamato. Ankan had four Empresses and no Imperial sons or daughters.

Great Imperial Chieftain: None.
Great Deity Chieftain: Same as in the previous reign.

(29) Emperor Senka. A reign of four years.
(The first year was *kinoto-u* [A.D. 535]. Emperor Senka was enthroned at 69 and lived to the age of 73.)

Senka was the second son of Emperor Keitai. His mother was the same as Emperor Ankan's. His palace was the Hinokuma no Miya in the province of Yamato. Senka had two Empresses and six Imperial sons and daughters.

Great Imperial Chieftain: SOGA Iname no Sukune.
(Son of SOGA Machi no Sukune).
Great Deity Chieftain: Same as in the previous reign.

(30) Emperor Kimmei. A reign of 32 years.
(The first year was *mizunoto-i* [A.D. 543]. How long Emperor Kimmei lived is not recorded—it should be investigated.)

31. It is now generally thought that Keitai's reign, like Ōjin's, was a new beginning in the Imperial line, although the fiction of an unbroken line of Imperial descent has persisted.

Kimmei was the eldest son (or third son) of Emperor Keitai, and his mother was an Empress Dowager called Princess Tashiraka (a daughter of Emperor Ninken). His palace was the Shikishima no Miya. Kimmei had six Empresses and 25 Imperial sons and daughters (16 sons and 9 daughters).

Great Imperial Chieftain: SOGA Iname no Sukune.

(He died in the 3rd month of the 31st year of this reign).

Great Deity Chieftains:

ŌTOMO Kanamura Maro; and

MONONOBE Okoshi no Muraji.

During this reign, a Buddhist statue and some Buddhist scriptures were first brought to Japan from the state of Paikché in Korea. Emperor Kimmei held them in high esteem. Meanwhile, a strange disease broke out in this country. Great Deity Chieftain MONONOBE memoralized the throne as follows: "Since ancient times this country has worshipped Kami. Now the situation is changed and Buddha is revered. Have not the Kami become angered by this?" Because [MONONOBE's views were accepted], Buddhist statues were thrown into the Naniwa canal and Buddhist temples were burned. But then fire fell from the heavens and the Imperial Palace was burned. An object brighter than the sun appeared in the sea. When persons were sent to see what it was, they found a camphor log floating in the sea. The Emperor had this made into a Buddhist statue. It is known as the "shining statue of Yoshino." Prince Shōtoku was born in the final years of this reign.

(31) Emperor Bidatsu. A reign of 14 years.

(The first year was *mizunoe-tatsu* [A.D. 572]. Emperor Bidatsu lived to the age of 24.)

Bidatsu was the second son of Emperor Kimmei and was appointed Crown Prince in the 15th year of the Kimmei reign. His mother was Empress Dowager Princess Ishi Hime (daughter of Emperor Senka). His palace was the Osada no Miya of Iware in the province of Yamato. Bidatsu had four Empresses and 16 Imperial sons and daughters (6 sons and 10 daughters).

Great Imperial Chieftain: SOGA Umako no Sukune.

Great Deity Chieftain: MONONOBE Yuge no Moriya no Muraji [d. 587].

Buddhist statues, as well as Buddhist priests and nuns, were brought to Japan from the state of Paikché during this reign. Great Deity Chieftain Moriya had Buddhist statues burned and Buddhist priests banished. On the day [such things were done] it rained while there were no clouds in the heavens. The Emperor and his ministers contracted a bad skin disease, which spread throughout the country. This was due to the destruction of Buddhist Law. . . . Great Imperial

Chieftain SOGA alone took out a Buddha bone *(shari)* and conducted Buddhist rites, having faith in Buddhist Law. A memorial written on crow's feathers was presented to the Imperial Court from the state of Kōkuli. The document was read by Ō Chin-ni, the first man to hold the [hereditary] title of "recorder of ships" *(fune no fubito).*[32]

(32) Emperor Yōmei [d. 587]. A reign of two years.
(The first year was *hinoe-uma* [A.D. 586].)

Yōmei was the fourth son of Emperor Kimmei, and his mother was Kitashi Hime (daughter of Great Imperial Chieftain SOGA Iname). His palace was the Namitsuki no Miya at Ikebe in the province of Yamato. Yōmei had three Empresses and seven Imperial sons and daughters.
Great Imperial Chieftain: Same as in the previous reign.
Great Deity Chieftain: Moriya (who was killed).
The Emperor died in the 4th month [of 587]. His body was placed in a coffin but not buried. In the 5th month a battle was fought between Moriya and Prince Shōtoku. The Great Imperial Chieftain SOGA Umako and Prince Shōtoku were of one mind [about Moriya]. Moriya was captured and all [his military forces] were destroyed. Buddhist Law prospered after that. Then in the 7th month [of 587] the body of Emperor Yōmei was buried.

(33) Emperor Sushun (Sōshun) [d. 592]. A reign of five years.
(The first year was *tsuchinoe-saru* [A.D. 588]. Emperor Sushun was enthroned at the age of 67.)

Sushun was the 15th son of Emperor Kimmei, and his mother was O'ane no Kimi (daughter of Great Imperial Chieftain SOGA Iname). His palace was the Kurahashi no Miya in the province of Yamato. Sushun had one Empress and two Imperial children.
Great Imperial Chieftain:
SOGA Umako [d. 626], as in previous reigns.
Buddha bones were imported from Paikché. Emperor Sushun was killed by Great Imperial Chieftain SOGA Umako.

(34) Empress Suiko. A reign of 36 years.
(The first year was *mizunoto-ushi* [A.D. 593]. Empress Suiko was enthroned at the age of 40 and lived to the age of 73.)

32. Ō Chin-ni's name suggests that he was an immigrant from Korea or China, and *fubito* was a *kabane* (title) borne by an *uji* (clan or lineage group) which served the Imperial House with bookkeeping and literary skills. See Richard Miller, *Ancient Japanese Nobility* (Berkeley, 1974), p. 2.

Suiko was the middle daughter of Emperor Kimmei (and was Bidatsu's Empress). Her mother was the same as Emperor Yōmei's. Suiko's palace was the Oharida no Miya in the province of Yamato.

Great Imperial Chieftains:

SOGA Umako [d. 626], as in previous reigns.

(He died in the 5th month of the 34th year of the Suiko reign.)

SOGA Emishi no Omi [d. 645].

(He was appointed Great Imperial Chieftain in the same year [that Umako died] and was given the name of Toyora.)

When Emperor Sushun was killed, plans were made and Empress Suiko was placed on the throne. Prince Umayado was appointed Crown Prince and entrusted with the administration of state affairs. This Crown Prince, an Imperial son of Emperor Yōmei, was Prince Shōtoku. He wrote the Seventeen Article Constitution, established cap ranks *(kōburi-kurai)*, and had records[33] kept of developments in state affairs. It is said that after Prince Shōtoku died the state deteriorated and the people became impoverished. Books on the calendar and astronomy were imported from Paikché. High Priests *(sōjō)* and Vicar Generals *(sōzu)* were appointed for the first time during this reign. The affairs of temples, priests, and nuns were regulated.

(35) Emperor Jomei [593–641]. A reign of 13 years [A.D. 629–641].

(The first year was *tsuchinoto-ushi* [A.D. 629]. Emperor Jomei was enthroned at the age of 37 and lived to the age of 49.)

Jomei was a grandson of Emperor Bidatsu and the son of Prince Oshisaka no Ōe, and his mother was Princess Nukate Hime (daughter of Emperor Bidatsu). His palace was the Okamoto no Miya of Takechi in the province of Yamato. His personal name *(imina)* was Tamura. Prior to this, the [personal] names of Emperors were very long and people did not use them. Since the reading of the characters of those earlier names is not certain, they are not recorded here. And since the number of characters in each name decreased after this reign, I will insert names for this and the following reigns. Emperor Jomei had five Empresses and eight Imperial sons and daughters.

Great Imperial Chieftain: SOGA Emishi no Omi [d. 645].

Emperor Jomei went to the Imperial Hot Springs *(yu no miya)* in the province of Iyo. After Empress Suiko died [in 628], and during

33. The *kujiki*, not now extant but apparently available to the compilers of the *Nihongi.*

this reign of Emperor Jomei (Tamura), persons who did not abide by [decisions reached at] conferences became engaged in a battle with the Great Imperial Chieftain, SOGA Emishi (Toyora). After they were defeated, the Great Imperial Chieftain had his son Iruka take over the administration of state affairs. Iruka's prestige and power were superior to that of his father, the Great Imperial Chieftain. . . .

> (36) Empress Kōgyoku [594–661]. A reign of three years [642–645].
> (The first year was *mizunoe-tora* [A.D. 642].)

Kōgyoku was the great-granddaughter of Emperor Bidatsu, and she had been the Empress of the former Emperor, Jomei. Prince Chinu, an Imperial [grand]son of Emperor Bidatsu, was Empress Kōgyoku's father, and her mother was Princess Kibi Hime (granddaughter of Emperor Kimmei). . . .[34] Her palace was the Kawara no Miya of Asuka in the province of Yamato.
Great Imperial Chieftain: SOGA Emishi no Omi [d. 645].
In the 12th month of the 2nd year of this reign, Prince Shōtoku's son committed suicide because of the SOGA Iruka incident. It is said that during the reign of Empress Kōgyoku the offices of Minister of the Left and Minister of the Right were established (but weren't they established during the next reign. . . ?); that SOGA Iruka, the son of the Great Imperial Chieftain SOGA Emishi (Toyora), administered the affairs of state; that his behavior was not good, and that the princes rebelled. It was at this time [in 645] that Prince Naka no Ōe (who became Emperor Tenchi) and NAKATOMI Kamako (who be-

34. Empress Kōgyoku's relations to previous and later sovereigns were:

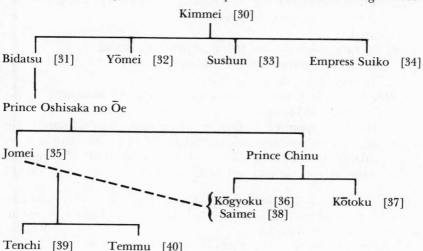

came FUJIWARA Kamatari) made plans together and destroyed SOGA Iruka. Iruka's father, Great Imperial Chieftain Toyora, set fire to his houses and burned himself to death. It is also said that all state documents in that house were burned. This Great Imperial Chieftain became a great demon *(oni)*. In the third year of her reign, Empress Kōgyoku yielded the throne to her young brother [Kōtoku].

> (37) Emperor Kōtoku [596–654]. A reign of 10 years [645–654].
> (The first year was *kinoe-tora* [A.D. 654].[35]

Kōtoku's personal name was Karu, and he was the younger brother of Empress Kōgyoku. His mother was the same as Empress Kōgyoku's. He was enthroned on the 14th day *(kanoe-inu)* of the 6th month of *kinoto-mi* [645], and on the same day Prince Naka no Ōe was appointed Crown Prince. (Prince Naka no Ōe became Emperor Tenchi.) Emperor Kōtoku's palace was the Toyosaki no Miya in Nagara of Naniwa (Namba) in the province of Settsu. He had three Empresses and one Imperial son.

Ministers of the Left:
ABE Kurahashi Maro [d. 649].
(He died on the 7th day of the 3rd month of the 5th year in this reign.)
KOSE Toko no Ō-omi [593–658], Fifth Cap Rank.
(He was appointed Minister on the 20th day of the 4th month of 649.)
Ministers of the Right:
SOGA Yamada Ishikawa Maro [d. 649].
(He was the [grand]son of Umako and the one who committed suicide in the 3rd month of 649 because he was accused of being involved in a plot and was to have been executed.)
ŌTOMO Nagatoko no Muraji, Fifth Cap Rank.
(He was appointed in the 4th month of 649 and died in the 7th month of 651.)
Minister of the Center: NAKATOMI Kamako no Muraji, Seventh Cap Rank [614–669].[36]
(He was appointed in 645. Another name was Kamatari. He was a 21st-generation descendant of Ame no Koyane no Mikoto [the ancestral Kami of the FUJIWARA]. He was the eldest son of NAKATOMI Mikeko, who had a "small virtue"

---

35. Jien or a later editor made a mistake: Emperor Kōtoku was enthroned in *kinoto-mi* [645], as noted two lines later in the Chronology, not in *kinoe-tora* [654], when Kōtoku died.
36. After the Tenchi reign, he was known as FUJIWARA Kamatari.

Cap Rank. On the 3rd day of the 6th month of 645, he killed SOGA Iruka, and for this he received honors and awards. The Imperial edict appointing him Minister of the Center read: "The country has achieved peace, which certainly is due to you. So you are granted the Seventh Cap Rank, appointed Minister of the Center, and given a stipend of 2,000 households. All important military and state affairs are to be administered by you. . . .")

Era names were instituted during this reign. The Taika era was five years long [645–649] and the Hakuchi five [650–654]. The "eight ministries and one hundred bureaus" were established then; and the boundaries of, and tribute from, the various provinces were fixed. Many books and treasures were brought to Japan from T'ang China. Emperor Kōtoku was especially reverent toward Buddhist Law—even more than toward Kami matters. He had the whole compendium of Buddhist scripture *(issai kyō)* read by more than 2,000 Buddhist priests and nuns, and on that same night he had more than 2,000 lanterns lighted at the Imperial Palace. A huge number of rats moved into the province of Yamato in the 1st month of 654. This was said to be a sign that the capital should be moved.

(38) Empress Saimei (Seimei) [594–661].
A reign of seven years [655–661]. (This was the Empress's second reign. The first year was *kinoto-u* [A.D. 655].)

Empress Kōgyoku [36] succeeded to the throne a second time as Empress Saimei. She resided at the palace of Okamoto no Miya in the province of Yamato. (The capital had first been moved to Kawara no Miya at Asuka.) She gave birth to a child by Prince Takamuko, grandson of Emperor Yōmei. Later she became Emperor Jomei's [35] Empress and had three Imperial sons by him. Toward the end of her reign, many people died. It was said that this was due to the vengeful soul of Great Imperial Chieftain [SOGA Emishi] Toyora. That soul was seen flying into the sky on a dragon. On the night that this Empress was buried, [Emishi's vengeful soul] was wearing a big hat, walking around, and observing things.[37]

Minister of the Left: KOSE Toko no Ō-omi [593–658], Fifth Cap Rank.
(He died in the 1st month of the 4th year of this reign.)
Minister of the Center: NAKATOMI Kamako no Muraji, Seventh Cap Rank.

37. In the *Nihongi* we read of a man-like being appearing in the sky riding a dragon, but nothing is there about this being the soul of Imperial Chieftain Toyora. The *Gukanshō* version is almost identical with that of the *Renchū shō*. [*Kaitei: Shiseki shūran*, 23, Section 20, p. 18.]

(39) Emperor Tenchi [626–671]. A reign of 10 years [661–671].
(The first year was *mizunoe-inu* [A.D. 662].)

Tenchi's personal name was Katsuragi. He was the first son of Emperor Jomei [35], and his mother was Empress Kōgyoku [36].[38] His palace was the Ōtsu no Miya in the province of Ōmi. Tenchi had nine Empresses and 14 Imperial sons and daughters.

Prime Minister: Prince Ōtomo.
(He was the eldest son of Emperor Tenchi. A Prime Minister was appointed from this reign on.)

Minister of the Center: FUJIWARA Kamatari [614–669], First Cap Rank *(taishokkan)*.
(He was appointed Minister of the Center on the 15th day of the 10th month of the 8th year of this reign and granted the clan name of FUJIWARA. He died on the 16th day of that same month. He was 56 years old and had held office for 25 years.)

In addition, there were six Ministers of the Left and Right. Since this Emperor had a deep sense of filial devotion, he did not occupy the throne until the 7th year after the death of his mother, Empress Saimei. Prince Ōtomo was appointed Prime Minister; the farmers of the various provinces were investigated; and the [number of] people's hearths *(tami no kamado)* were recorded. While [Tenchi] was Crown Prince, a water clock *(rōkoku)* was made. Kamatari was appointed Minister of the Center and was the first man to receive the clan name of FUJIWARA.

When Empress Saimei succeeded to the throne [in 654], it did not seem likely that she would reign until seven years later. There was, however, no break in Imperial succession. The country had to have a ruler until her death seven years after [she ascended the throne a second time]. During those seven years, Tenchi should have occupied the throne, but since his Imperial mother was reigning a second time, he realized his desire for enthronement after the seven years had elapsed.

(40)[39] Emperor Temmu [d. 686]. A reign of 15 [*sic*] years [673–686].
(The first year was *mizunoe-saru* [672].)[40]

38. Known as Empress Saimei [38] during her second reign.
39. Historians now place the Kōbun (Prince Ōtomo) reign between those of Tenchi and Temmu. But the *Nihongi*, the *Renchū shō*, and the *Gukanshō* do not. Because the *Gukanshō* added a reign for Empress Jingū, and left out the one for Kōbun, its reign numbers coincide with those of recent chronologies after the Temmu reign.
40. The *Nihongi* states that Temmu's reign began in *mizunoe-saru* (672). Temmu destroyed the Ōmi Court in 672, but he was not officially enthroned until the following year *(mizunoto-tori)*.

Temmu's personal name was Ō-ama, and he was the third son of Emperor Jomei. His mother was the same as Tenchi's. His palace was the Kiyomihara no Miya at Asuka in the province of Yamato. He was appointed Crown Prince in the 7th year of the Tenchi reign. Tenchi had said that he wanted the throne passed to Temmu upon his death, but Temmu did not want it. He said that the throne should be passed to either [Tenchi's] Empress or to Prince Ōtomo. In order to show people that he did not want to have the throne, Temmu entered the Buddhist priesthood and secluded himself at Mt. Yoshino. When his daughter (the wife of Prince Ōtomo) secretly informed him that Prince Ōtomo had raised an army for an attack, Temmu probably thought: "Why is he doing that? I thought I had secluded myself [in order to stay out of politics]!" So Temmu fled toward the province of Ise and, after reporting to the Sun Goddess at Ise Shrine, mobilized troops in the provinces of Mino and Owari. He fought and won a battle in the province of Ōmi. Then he occupied the throne and governed the state well. Everyone knows about those military actions.

Prince Ōtsu was Emperor Temmu's son. It is said that this Prince administered the affairs of state, had a liking for Chinese literature, and was the first [Japanese] person to compose Chinese poems (*shifu*).

Minister of the Left: SOGA Akae no Omi, Seventh Cap Rank.
(He was exiled during the 8th month of the 1st year of this reign.)
Minister of the Right: NAKATOMI Kane no Muraji [d. 672], Seventh Cap Rank.
(He was executed in the 8th month of the 1st year of this reign.)
Senior Counselor: SOGA Hatayasu [d. 672].
(He was executed for his part in the incident of the 8th month of the 1st year of this reign. The office of Senior Counselor was created during this reign, and five men held it in those years.)

These era names fell in the Temmu reign: (1) Suzaku, which was one year long [672]. (It began in *mizunoe-saru.)* (2) Hakuhō, which was 13 years long [673–686]. (It began in *mizunoe-saru,* the year Suzaku began. Did both begin in the same year?) And (3) Shuchō, which was eight years long [686–694]. (One year of this era fell within the Temmu reign.)

In the 10th year of Temmu's reign, the Emperor's heir, Prince Kusakabe, was appointed Crown Prince. After the war with Prince Ōtomo, the Ministers of the Right and Left were executed. There were no Ministers during the remainder of this reign.

(41) Empress Jitō [645–702]. A reign of 10 years [686–697]. (The first year was *hinoto-i* [687].)

Jitō's personal name was Uno. She was the second daughter of Emperor Tenchi, and Temmu's Empress. Her mother was Ochi no Iratsume (daughter of Minister SOGA Yamada Ishikawa Maro). Jitō's palace was the Fujiwara no Miya in the province of Yamato.

Prime Minister: Prince Takechi [654–696], First *Jōkō* Rank.

(The third son of Emperor Temmu. He was appointed Prime Minister on the 5th day of the 7th month in the 4th year of the Jitō reign. He died on the 13th day in the 7th month of the 10th year of that reign. The office of Middle Counselor existed from this reign on. . . .)

In addition to Prime Minister, there was also a Minister of the Right and a Senior Counselor. Although the Crown Prince was alive [when Emperor Temmu died], the Crown Prince's mother—and Temmu's Empress—was placed on the throne first. Then the son of this Crown Prince Kusakabe, Prince Karu, was made Crown Prince. It was at the beginning of this reign that Prince Ōtsu rebelled and was killed.

The eras that fell in this reign were: (1) the remaining seven years of Shuchō; and (2) Taika, which was four years long [695–698]. (The first year of this era was *kinoto-hitsuji* [695].)

"Rabbit stick" [rites][41] and "dance poetry" performances[42] were held for the first time. In the 3rd year of the Taika era [697], Empress Jitō yielded the throne to the Crown Prince. She was the first to receive the title of Retired Empress *(daijō tennō)*. She lived on four years after retirement.

(42) Emperor Mommu [683–707]. A reign of 11 years [697–707].

(The first year was *hinoto-tori* [697]. Emperor Mommu lived to the age of 25.)

Mommu's personal name was Karu (and he was enthroned at the age of 15). He was a grandson of Emperor Temmu and the second son of Prince Kusakabe, who was Temmu's Crown Prince. Mommu's mother was the future Empress Gemmei [43]. His palace was the same Fujiwara no Miya that had been occupied by Empress Jitō. He had two Empresses and one Imperial son. He was appointed Crown Prince in the 2nd month of the 3rd year of Taika *(tsuchinoe-inu* [698]).

Acting Prime Minister: Prince Osakabe.

(The ninth son of Emperor Temmu. He was appointed on the

41. *Uzue,* a magic rite held on the day in which the rabbit *(u)* "branch" occurs in the sexagenary cycle.

42. *Tōka,* a dance ritual held at the court during the 1st month of the year. According to the *Fusō Ryakki,* it was introduced by a Chinese. [*Kokushi Taikei,* 12.67.]

20th day of the 1st month of the 3rd year of Taikō [703] and died on the 7th day of the 5th month of Keiun 2 [705].)
Senior Counselor: FUJIWARA Fuhito [659–720].
(The second son of Kamatari. He was appointed in Taihō 1 [701].)
Consultant: ŌTOMO Yasumaro.
(A consultant was appointed from this reign on.)
One year of the Taika era fell in this reign. The following three years had no era name. The Taihō era (which was instituted on the 21st day of the 3rd month of *kanoto-ushi* [701]) was three years long [701–704]. After this there was no break in the continuity of era names. In this reign, penal and civil *(ritsuryō)* codes were compiled;[43] robes were prescribed for the various offices and ranks; the practice of granting caps was abolished; and certificates of Imperial appointments *(iki)* were instituted. The Keiun era was four years long [704–708]. (It began in *kinoe-tatsu* [704].) It began on the 7th day of the 5th month.

(43) Empress Gemmei [661–721]. A reign of seven years [707–715].

Gemmei's personal name was Abe, and she received the throne on the 15th day of the 6th month of Keiun 4 [707]. (She was enthroned at the age of 48 and lived to the age of 61.) Gemmei was the fourth daughter of Emperor Tenchi and the mother of Emperor Mommu. She had been the Imperial consort *(nyōgo)* of crown Prince Kusakabe. Her mother was SOGA Hime (a daughter of SOGA Yamada no Ō-omi). Her palace was the Nara no Miya of the province of Yamato.
Acting Prime Minister: Prince Hozumi [d. 715].
Minister of the Left: ISO Kami Marō.
Minister of the Right: FUJIWARA Fuhito [659–720].
(He was appointed to that post on the 21st day of the 3rd month of 708.)
The Wadō era lasted seven years [708–715] and began on the 11th day of the 1st month (of *tsuchinoe-saru*). Because [the future Emperor] Shōmu was still a child when Emperor Mommu died [in 707], Empress Gemmei was enthroned first.

(44) Empress Gensei [680–748]. A reign of nine years [715–724].
(The first year was _____.)

Gensei's personal name was Hitaka. (She was enthroned at the age of 35.) She was the daughter of Crown Prince Kusakabe (and the elder sister of Emperor Mommu). Gensei's mother was

43. Cf. Felicia Bock, *Engi-Shiki* (Tokyo, 1970), 1.6–16.

Empress Gemmei [43], who was the mother of Emperor Mommu
[42]. Gensei's palace was the Nara no Miya of the province of
Yamato.

Acting Prime Ministers:
    Prince Hozumi [d. 715].
    (He died on the 13th day of the 7th month of 715.)
    Prince Toneri [d. 735].
    (The third son of Emperor Temmu, he was appointed Acting
    Prime Minister on the 1st day of the 8th month of 720.)
Minister of the Left: Same as in the previous reign.
Minister of the Right: Same as in the previous reign.
Middle Counselor: FUJIWARA Muchimaro [677-737].
Consultant: FUJIWARA Fusasaki [681-737].
(Both Muchimaro and Fusasaki were sons of Lord Tankai [FUJI-
WARA Fuhito].)

The era names that fell in this reign were: (1) Reiki, which
lasted two years [715-717] and began on the 3rd day of the 9th
month (of *kinoto-u*). The day the era name was changed was the
same day Empress Gensei was enthroned. And (2) Yōrō, which was
seven years long [717-724] and began on the 17th day of the 11th
month (of *hinoto-mi*).

Minister [FUJIWARA] Fuhito died on the 3rd day of the 8th month
of 720 (at the age of 62). He was given the posthumous name
(okurina) of Lord Tankai. As the maternal grandfather of [the future
Emperor] Shōmu [45], he was treated particularly well after he became ill. He was appointed Prime Minister posthumously. . . .

        (45) Emperor Shōmu [701-756]. A reign of 25 years [724-
        749].
        (The first year was _____.)

Shōmu's personal name is not clearly known. (He was en-
throned at the age of 25.) He was called Emperor Ame-shirushi-kuni
Oshi-hiraki Toyo-sakura Hiko. . . . He was the eldest son of Emperor
Mommu and was appointed Crown Prince in 714. Shōmu's mother
was Imperial concubine *(fujin)* FUJIWARA Miyako (daughter of Lord
Tankai). Shōmu's palace was the same as Empress Gensei's: Nara no
Miya in the province of Yamato. He had four Empresses and six
Imperial sons and daughters.

Acting Prime Minister: Prince Toneri [d. 735].
(The Prince died on the 14th day of the 11th month of 735 at
the age of 60, and he was posthumously appointed Prime Minister on the 22nd day of the month in which he died. In the 6th
month of 758, he was posthumously granted the title *(tsuigo)* of
Emperor Sudō Jinkei.)

Another Acting Prime Minister: Prince Suzuka [d. 745].
(He was the third son of Prince Takechi, Prime Minister, and was appointed Acting Prime Minister in the 9th month of 737. He died on the 3rd day of the 9th month of 745.)
Ministers of the Left:
Prince Nagaya [d. 729].
(This Prince was executed because of his involvement in a plot. Umakai was sent [to arrest him]. . . . He was the eldest son of Prince Takechi.)
TACHIBANA Moroe [684–757].
(Descended from Emperor Bidatsu. His name was changed from Prince Katsuragi to TACHIBANA Moroe.)
Minister of the Right: FUJIWARA Muchimaro [677–737].
(He was appointed Minister of the Right on the 17th day of the 1st month of 734, and he died on the 25th day of the 7th month of 737 at the age of 58. He was posthumously appointed Prime Minister.)
Middle Counselor: FUJIWARA Toyonari [704–765].
(First son of FUJIWARA Muchimaro and Senior Captain of the Middle Bodyguards.)
These eras came in the Shōmu reign: (1) Jinki, which lasted five years [724–729] and began on the 4th day of the 2nd month (of *kinoe-ne*). Emperor Shōmu was enthroned on that same day. And (2) Tempyō, which lasted 20 years [729–749] and began on the 5th day of the 8th month (of *tsuchinoto-mi*).
On the 3rd day of the 7th month of 749, Shōmu stepped down from the throne at the age of 50 and entered the Buddhist priesthood. His Buddhist name *(hōki)* was Shōman. He lived eight years after retirement. He had Tōdai Temple built. Details of this have been written in Chapter 1.
Consultant: FUJIWARA Fusasaki [681–737].
(He was appointed Senior Commander of the Middle Bodyguards in 730 and was the first to receive the title of Senior Commander. He died on the 17th day of the 4th month of 737 at the age of 57.)
It was in these years that four brothers became the founders of four houses: (1) FUJIWARA Muchi (probably an error for Muchimaro, who was the first son of FUJIWARA Fuhito); (2) FUJIWARA Fusasaki (the second son); (3) FUJIWARA Umakai (the third son); and (4) FUJIWARA Maro (the fourth son). Three of them became Consultants. [All four] died in the single year [of 737]. (Umakai on the 5th day of the 8th month, and Maro on the 13th day of the 7th month.) Measles *(akamogasa)* had broken out in the empire, and the number of those who died could not be counted. . . .

(46) Empress Kōken [718–770]. A reign of 10 years [749–758].
(The first year was ____.)

Kōken's personal name was Abe. (She was enthroned at the age of 30.) She was the daughter of Emperor Shōmu, and her mother was Empress Kōmyō (who was in turn a daughter of Lord Tankai [Fuhito]). Kōken's palace was the same Nara no Miya.

Minister of the Left: TACHIBANA Moroe [684–757].

(He submitted his resignation to the throne and retired in the 2nd month of 756.)

Minister of the Right: FUJIWARA Toyonari [703–765].

(He was appointed to this post on the 14th day of the 4th month of 749 and was advanced to Minister of the Left in 757. In the 2nd month of 763, having been implicated in some affair, he was exiled because he had extended favors to his brother Nakamaro. . . .)

Another Minister of the Right: FUJIWARA Emi no Oshikatsu [706–764].

(His original name was FUJIWARA Nakamaro. He was the second son of FUJIWARA Muchimaro and was appointed Minister of the Right on the 19th day of the 2nd month of 757. He continued to hold the original positions of: Supreme Military Official [*shibinaishō*];[44] Vice Minister [*jundaijin*]; and Senior Commander of the Middle Bodyguards. In 758, his title of Minister of the Right was changed to Grand Guardian [*taihō*]—this was on the 25th day of the 8th month. On that day an Imperial rescript was handed down saying: "Emi is to be added to your name and Oshikatsu is to replace Nakamaro. You are to be granted a stipend of 100 *chō* of land. . . .")

On the 2nd day of the 7th month of 749, Empress Kōken was enthroned. [The following eras came during her reign]: (1) Tempyō Shōhō, which lasted eight years [749–757]. (The first year of this era was *tsuchinoto-ushi.*) (2) Tempyō Hōji, two years of which [757–758] fell within the Kōken reign. This era began on the 2nd day (the *Shoku Nihongi* says it was the 18th day) of the 8th month (of the *hinoto-tori* year). It seems that the Tempyō Kanpō era began on the 14th day of the 4th month [of 749], but the era name was changed to Tempyō Shōhō on the 2nd day of the 7th month of that year. Probably this is why Tempyō Kanpō is not found in the ordinary chronologies.

44. An office established during Kōken's reign but abolished after Emi Oshikatsu was killed in 764.

A "10,000 priest" mass was held at the Tōdai Temple during this reign, and at the Imperial Palace the characters "the empire's great peace" *(tenka taihei)* mysteriously appeared. Many things that occurred during this reign were dealt with in [Chapter 1].

> (47) Deposed Emperor of Awaji [733–765].[45] A reign of six years [758–764].
> (The first year was _____.)

His personal name was Ōi. (He was enthroned at the age of 26.) He was a grandson of Emperor Temmu and the seventh son of Prince Toneri. His mother was Imperial concubine Yamashiro (daughter of Taima no Oyu, Governor of Kazusa). His palace was the Nara no Miya.

Prime Minister: FUJIWARA Oshikatsu [706–764].

(On the 11th day of the 1st month of 760, he was promoted from *taihō* to *taishi.* The Emperor called on the residence of the *taihō* and made presents of silk cloth from the Treasury to clerks [*sakan*] and above according to their rank. He then bestowed upon Oshikatsu the title of Prime Minister and allowed him personal bodyguards [*zuijin*]. On the 11th day of the 9th month of 764, a plot [by Oshikatsu] was uncovered and he was stripped of all offices and titles. Oshikatsu lost the clan name of FUJIWARA and was executed.)

Minister: Master of Buddhist Meditation *(zenji)* Dōkyō [d. 772].

(Appointed Minister in 764 and granted the surname of YUGE. Originally he had been a Junior Vicar General.)

Minister of the Right: FUJIWARA Toyonari [703–765].

(He was promoted to Minister of the Left in 760[46] but demoted [to Minister of the Right] in the 4th month of 764. Because he had not committed a crime that warranted punishment, he was called back [from exile to Dazaifu] and treated well.)

On the 2nd day of the 8th month [of 757], the era name was changed to Tempyō Hōji, which was to last eight years [757–765]. (The first year of that era was *hinoto-tori.*) The Deposed Emperor of Awaji had been named Crown Prince in the 1st year of that era, and he was enthroned on the 1st day of the 8th month of the 2nd year in that era [758]. Because he was allied with Minister Oshikatsu in opposition to the former Empress Kōken [46], he was exiled to the province of Awaji, where he died three years later.[47]

45. Usually referred to as Emperor Junnin.
46. Actually appointed Minister of the Left in 757. [NKBT, 72, note 8.]
47. According to the *Shoku Nihongi,* he died the year after he was banished. Jien again follows the *Renchū shō.*

(48) Empress Shōtoku [718-770]. A reign of five years [764-770].
(She was [this time] enthroned at the age of 52.)

This was the second time she [former Empress Kōken] had been enthroned. This enthronement was on the 1st day of the 1st month of 765.

Prime Minister: Master of Buddhist Meditation Dōkyō [d. 772].
(In 766, he was given the title of Priest-Emperor [*hō-ō*].)
Minister of the Right: KIBI Makibi [693-775].
(Son of SHIMOTSU-MICHI Ason Kunikatsu, Junior Captain of the Imperial Bodyguards of the Right. He was also Senior Commander of the Middle Bodyguards.)
Senior Counselor: FUJIWARA Matate [715-766].
(Third son of FUJIWARA Fusasaki. He died on the 16th day of the 3rd month of 766.)

On the 7th day of the 1st month [of 765], the era name was changed to Tempyō Jingo, which was three years long [765-767]. (The first year was *kinoto-mi.*) On the 18th day of the 8th month [of 767], the era name was changed to Jingo Keiun, which also lasted three years [767-770]. (The first year was *hinoto-hitsuji.*)

The Empress died on the 4th day of the 8th month of 769. . . . She had been enthroned at the age of 52, and she died at the age of 57. The appointment of Dōkyō as Priest-Emperor [was in 766], and the oracular messages from the Sun Goddess and the Great Hachiman Bodhisattva to WAKE Kiyomaro [were received in 769].[48] The first year of the Tempyō Shōbō [*sic*] had been *hinoto-tori* [757], and the first year of the reign of the deposed Emperor of Awaji had been *tsuchinoe-inu* [758]. [These matters] can not be written down in detail. Are they not subjects of gossip?

(49) Emperor Kōnin [709-781]. A reign of 12 years [770-781].

Kōnin's personal name was Shirakabe. Originally he was a Senior Counselor. The ministerial group [made their decision] on the 4th day *(mizunoto-mi)* of the 8th month of 770 *(kanoe-inu)*. . . . Prince Shirakabe, Senior Counselor, was appointed Crown Prince and placed in charge of all state affairs (at the age of 62). Empress Takano [Shōtoku] left the following injunction: "Be it here proclaimed that the Senior Counselor Prince Shirakabe is to be Crown

48. A memorial to the throne stated that a message had been received from Hachiman of Usa prophesying that the empire would enjoy peace if Dōkyō were placed on the throne. But WAKE Kiyomaro went as an envoy to the Usa Hachiman Shrine and received another message: no person should be placed on the throne who is not a direct descendant of the Sun Goddess.

Prince. . . ." He was enthroned in the Imperial Council Hall on the 1st day *(tsuninoto-ushi)* of the 10th month of that same year [770]. . . . Kōnin was a grandson of Emperor Tenchi and the sixth son of Prince Shiki. His mother was Tochi Hime (daughter of KI Morohito). His palace was the Nara no Miya. He had five Empresses and seven Imperial sons and daughters.

Minister of the Left: FUJIWARA Nagate [714–771].
(He died on the 21st day of the 2nd month of 771 at the age of 58.)
Minister of the Right: ŌNAKATOMI Kiyomaro [702–788].
Another Minister of the Left: FUJIWARA Uona [721–783].
(The fifth son of FUJIWARA Fusasaki [681–737] and Senior Commander of the Imperial Bodyguards.)
Minister of the Center: FUJIWARA Yoshitsugu [716–777].
(His original name was Sukunamaro, and he was the second son of Umakai, Minister of Ceremonies.)
Consultant: FUJIWARA Momokawa [732–779].
(The eighth son of Umakai. He died on the 9th day of the 7th month of 779 at the age of 48.)

On the 1st day of the 10th month [of 770], the era name was changed to Hōki, an era that lasted 11 years [770–780]. (The first year was *kanoe-inu*.) Then on the 1st day of the 1st month [of 781], the era name was changed to Ten'ō, which was one year long [781–782]. (The first year was *kanoto-tori*.)

Following the death of Empress Takano [Shōtoku], ministers and lower-ranking noblemen made plans and had Kōnin placed on the throne. In the 4th month of 781, the throne was yielded to the Crown Prince. Then in the 12th month Kōnin died at the age of 73.

(50) Emperor Kwammu [737–806]. A reign of 24 years [781–806].

Kwammu's personal name was Yamabe, and he received the throne on the 3rd day of the 4th month of 781 (at the age of 45). He was an Imperial son of Emperor Kōnin. He had been appointed Crown Prince in 773 (at the age of 37). Kwammu's mother was a woman of the TAKANO clan. (Her name was Niikasa and she was a daughter of Otosugi Ason.) He first moved the capital to the Naga-oka no Miya, but later his palace was the Heian no Miya.[49] (This is located in the province of Yamashiro and is the capital today.) He had 16 Empresses and consorts, and 32 Imperial sons and daughters.

49. The capital was moved to Nagaoka in 784 and to Heian (now Kyoto) in 794.

Minister of the Left: FUJIWARA Uona [721–783].

(Uona was exiled for complicity in the incident that occurred on the 14th day of the 6th month of 782. Saying that he was ill, he stopped at Naniwa and returned to the capital in the 5th month of 783. He died on the 25th day of the 7th month [of that year]. His original office was posthumously restored, and the Imperial edict ordering him into exile was withdrawn and burned. . . . He was 63.)

Ministers of the Right:

FUJIWARA Tamaro [722–783].

(Fifth son of Umakai and Senior Commander of the Imperial Bodyguards.)

FUJIWARA Korekimi [727–789].

(A grandson of Muchimaro and son of Consultant Otomaro. He was appointed on the 19th day of the 7th month of 783 and died on the 19th day of the 9th month of 789.)

FUJIWARA Tsuginawa [727–806].

(A son of Toyonari and a Senior Commander of the Middle Bodyguards. He was appointed on the 27th day of the 2nd month of 790. And he died on the 16th day of the 7th month of 796 at the age of 70.)

Prince Miwa [d. 806].

(A grandson of Emperor Tenchi and son of Prince E-no-i. He was appointed in the 8th month of 798.)

Middle Counselor: FUJIWARA Uchimaro [756–812].

(A grandson of Fusasaki. Third son of Senior Counselor Matate. He was appointed on the 16th day of the 8th month of 798.)

On the 19th day of the 8th month [of 782], the era name was changed to Enryaku, which was 24 years long [782–806]. (The first year was *mizunoe-inu.*)

Grand Preceptor Dengyō [767–822].

(Dengyō and Jikaku were [posthumously] given the title of Grand Preceptor on the same day, in response to a memorial submitted by Priest Sōō [831–918], Second Grade, of the Mudō Temple. The Central Hall [of Mt. Hiei] was built in 788 by Grand Preceptor Dengyō, who went to T'ang China in 804 and returned to Japan in 805. He died on the 4th day of the 6th month of 822 at the age of 56.)

During this reign, the capital was moved to Nagaoka in the province of Yamashiro. Not long afterward, it was moved to Heian. Since then, the capital has not been moved. Both Grand Preceptor Dengyō and Grand Preceptor Kōbō went to T'ang China in the closing years of this reign. It is said that Emperor Kwammu had no liking for learning but that he respected military power. Using SAKANOUE no Tamura Maro [758–811] as Supreme Commander [of an expeditionary force], he had the barbarians of the northern provinces *(ebisu)* subjugated. The TAIRA clan of today is descended from Emperor Kwammu.[50]

(51) Emperor Heizei [774–824]. A reign of four years [806–809].

Heizei's personal name was Ate, and he received the throne on the 17th day of the 3rd month of 806 (at the age of 33). Heizei was the eldest son of Emperor Kwammu and had been appointed Crown Prince in the 11th month of 785 (at the age of 12). His mother was Empress Otomuro (daughter of FUJIWARA Yoshitsugu, Minister of the Center). He had three Empresses and seven Imperial sons and daughters.

Ministers of the Right:
Prince Miwa.

50. In the Shimabara text of the *Gukanshō*—the text that has been made the basis of the NKBT edition—the following note has been appended to the entry for the Kwammu reign (probably by an editor):

Enryaku 1 [782], which was *mizunoe-inu*, was the 3rd year of the reign of Emperor Tê-tsung of T'ang [China] in the Chien-chung era. In this year the Yellow River was clear (?). In 788, Grand Preceptor Dengyō built the Basic Central Hall *(kompon chūdō)*. In 794, the capital was moved to Heian. In 796, both the Eastern and Western Temples were founded. In the 7th month of 804, Dengyō and Kōbō went to T'ang [China]. On the 15th day of the 1st month of 793 *(mizunoto-tori)*, the construction of the Heian capital was begun. The Eastern Capital (in the Otagi District) was also called the Left Capital and had the T'ang name of Lo-Yang. The Western Capital (in the Kadano District) was also called the Right Capital and had the T'ang name of Ch'ang-an. From north to south the distance—not counting [the width of] either the broad or narrow streets—was 1,753 *jō* [over 7,000 yards]. From east to west it was—again not including [the width of] either the broad or narrow streets—1,580 *jō* [over 6,500 yards]. (These measurements include both the Eastern and Western Capitals.) In this year [of 793], Grand Preceptor Dengyō built the Enryaku Temple, and in 794 *(kinoe-inu)* the Basic Central Hall was dedicated *(kuyō)*.

On the 21st day *(kanoto-tori)* of the 10th month of that same year [794], the Imperial carriage proceeded to the new capital; and in 795, [it was decided that]Yamashiro of Yamashiro Province should be written with a different character for *shiro*.

The Shimabara text also ends the first chapter of the *Gukanshō's* Imperial chronology with the Kwammu reign. Such a division does not fit Jien's way of periodizing Japanese history, except that the end of the Kwammu reign, Japan's 50th, came at a time when one half of the allotted "100 reigns" had passed. We are inclined to think that Jien himself did not divide his chronology at this point, and we therefore follow the Iwanami text's division of the chronology.

(He died on the 24th day of the 4th month of 806.)

FUJIWARA Uchimaro [756–812].

(He was Senior Commander of the Imperial Bodyguards of the Left. Originally he had been Senior Commander of the Imperial Bodyguards [of the Right], having been appointed on the 19th day of the 5th month of 806; but on the 22nd day of the 4th month of 807, he was made Senior Commander of the Imperial Bodyguards of the Left.)

On the 18th day of the 5th month [of 806], the era name was changed to Daidō, an era that was four years long [806–810]. (The first year was *hinoe-inu.*)

It was during this reign that Senior Commanders of the Imperial Bodyguards of the Right and Left were first appointed. Originally there were Imperial Bodyguards *(kon-e)* and Middle Bodyguards *(chū-e)*, but now the Imperial Bodyguards became the Imperial Bodyguards of the Left, and the Middle Bodyguards the Imperial Bodyguards of the Right. SAKANOUE Tamura Maro [758–811] was appointed Senior Commander of the Imperial Bodyguards of the Right on the same day [that the above change was made]. In the 1st month of 809, Emperor Heizei abdicated and Crown Prince Kamino was enthroned [as Emperor Saga]. On that same day, Prince Taka-oka became the new Crown Prince. Such steps were taken because Heizei was ill. . . . He lived 14 years after stepping down from the throne, and he died at the age of 51 on the 7th day of the 7th month of 824. . . . Since he was still living at Nara [after retirement], he was called "the Emperor of Nara." Junior Commander Narihara was a grandson of this Emperor.

(52) Emperor Saga [786–842]. A reign of 14 years [809–823].

Saga's personal name was Kamino (written with different characters), and he received the throne on the 1st day of the 4th month of 809 (at the age of 24). He had been made Crown Prince in 806 (at the age of 21). Saga was the second son of Emperor Kwammu, and his mother was the same as Emperor Heizei's. He had nine Empresses and consorts and 47 Imperial sons and daughters.

Ministers of the Right:

FUJIWARA Uchimaro [756–812].

(Senior Commander of the Imperial Bodyguards of the Left. He died on the 6th day of the 10th month of 812 at the age of 57.)

FUJIWARA Sonohito [756–818].

(Son of Fusasaki's son, Kaedemaro, who was Consultant and

Minister of the Treasury. He was appointed on the 5th day of the 12th month of 812 and died on the 19th day of the 12th month of 818 at the age of 63.)

FUJIWARA Fuyutsugu [775–826].[51]

(Senior Commander of the Imperial Bodyguards of the Left and the third son of Uchimaro. He was appointed on the 9th day of the 1st month of 821.)

On the 27th day of the 9th month [of 810], the era name was changed to Kōnin, an era that was 14 years long [810–824]. (The first year was *kanoe-tora.*)

Tendai Abbot: Imperial-Palace-Priest Gishin [d. 833].[52] (Practitioner of meditation [*shuzen*]. . . .)

(Gishin was appointed Tendai Abbot by an official order [*kanchō*] issued on the 5th day of the 4th month of 822, when he was 44 years old. He administered the affairs of Mt. Hiei for 11 years. The way to calculate the number of years a Tendai Abbot administers the affairs of Mt. Hiei is not to count the last year of an old Abbot's administration, but to add that year to the number of years in the new Abbot's administration. . . . Gishin died on the 4th day of the 7th month of 833 at the age of 55.)

Imperial Poetry Composing Contests (*naien*) were first held in this reign. Emperor Saga was an accomplished calligrapher, and he also wrote Chinese. He had 16 Imperial sons and 14 Imperial daughters. All received names and became commoners.[53] He had a total of 47 children. . . . He was not on good terms with the former Emperor Heizei, who mobilized troops and proceeded to the eastern provinces. . . . Emperor Saga sent Senior Counselor Tamura Maro and Consultant Watamaro to stop Heizei. They captured and killed FUJIWARA Nakanari, Supreme Commander of the Retired Emperor's forces. FUJIWARA Kusuko, Head Mistress of the Palace Attendants Office [and younger sister of Nakanari], was also killed. The incident occurred because she had urged [the Retired Emperor to rebel]. . . .[54] Heizei then entered the Buddhist priesthood, and

51. In 810—after the Kusuko Incident—Fuyutsugu was appointed Director of the Imperial Secretariat (*kurōdodokoro*), an organ of government that became an important instrument for the establishment of FUJIWARA control.

52. Gishin had gone to China with Saichō. His title (Imperial-Palace-Priest or *naigu*) was held by those (usually ten in number) who accompanied the Emperor at Buddhist rites held at the Shingon Cloister in the Imperial Palace. [NKBT, 86.78, note 10.]

53. They became known as members of the SAGA MINAMOTO clan.

54. This was the Kusuko Incident in which FUJIWARA Kusuko (Head Mistress of the Palace Attendants Office) plotted with her brother (FUJIWARA Nakanari) to have Reizei returned to the throne. Cf. Chapter 1, note 29.

Prince Takaoka was removed from, and Prince Ōtomo appointed to, the office of Crown Prince. Prince Takaoka also entered the priesthood. He became a disciple of Grand Preceptor Kōbō and went to China, where he died. He was called Princely Priest Shinnyo. One source states that he was on his way from T'ang China to India when he died in the Takla Makan desert. A Tendai Abbot was first appointed during this reign. Emperor Saga lived for 19 years after abdicating. (He lived to the age of 57 and died on the 15th day of the 7th month of 842.)

(53) Emperor Junna [786–840]. A reign of 10 years [823–833].

Junna's personal name was Ōtomo. He received the throne (at the age of 38) on the 17th day of the 4th month of 823. He had been named Crown Prince (at the age of 25) in 810. Junna was the third son of Emperor Kwammu; and his mother was Tabiko, posthumously granted the title of Empress Dowager. (She was the daughter of Consultant FUJIWARA Momokawa.) Junna had six Empresses and Imperial consorts and 13 Imperial sons and daughters.

Ministers of the Left:

FUJIWARA Fuyutsugu [775–826].

(Senior Commander of the Imperial Bodyguards of the Left. He was promoted to Minister of the Left in 825, and he died on the 24th day of the 7th month of 826 at the age of 52. He had held office for six years.)

FUJIWARA Otsugu [773–843].

(Eldest son of Momokawa and posthumously appointed Prime Minister.)

Minister of the Right: KIYOHARA Natsuno [782–837].

(Senior Commander of the Imperial Bodyguards of the Left and great-grandson of Prince Toneri, grandson of Prince Mihara, and son of Prince Ogura Senior Fifth Rank Lower Grade. He was appointed to this office on the 2nd day of the 11th month of 832 at the age of 51.)

On the 5th day of the 1st month [of 824], the era name was changed to Tenchō, an era that was 10 years long [824–834]. (The first year was *kinoe-tatsu.*)

Retired Emperor Heizei died on the 7th day of the 7th month of 824. The Rite of Invoking Buddha Names *(butsumyō)*[55] was held for the first time in this reign. During the seven years that Emperor Junna lived after abdication [in 833], two Retired Emperors were alive. Therefore Saga was referred to as the Senior Retired Emperor,

55. A rite held between the 15th and the 17th day of the 12th month.

and Junna, after abdication, as the Junior Retired Emperor. (The latter died on the 8th day of the 5th month of 840.)

(54) Emperor Nimmyō [810–850]. A reign of 17 years [833–850].

His personal name was Masara, and he was called "the Emperor of Fukakusa." Nimmyō received the throne on the 28th day of the 2nd month of 833. He had been appointed Crown Prince on the 19th day *(mizunoe-tora)* of the 4th month of 823 (at the age of 14). He was the second son of Emperor Saga, and his mother was Empress Dowager TACHIBANA Kachiko (daughter of Imperial Attendant Kiyotomo). Nimmyō had nine Empresses, Imperial consorts, and concubines *(kōi)* and 24 Imperial children. Seven were given names and made commoners.[56]

Ministers of the Left:

FUJIWARA Otsugu [773–843].

(He resigned from his official positions on the 18th day of the 1st month of 843.)

MINAMOTO Tokiwa [812–854].[57]

(Senior Commander of the Imperial Bodyguards of the Left and third son of Emperor Saga. He was appointed Minister of the Right on the 7th day of the 8th month of 840 and promoted to Minister of the Left on the 2nd day of the 7th month of 844.)

Ministers of the Right:

KIYOHARA Natsuno [782–837].

(Senior Commander of the Imperial Bodyguards of the Left. He died on the 7th day of the 10th month of 837 at the age of 56.)

FUJIWARA Mimori.

(Grandson of Consultant Kose and son of Masaku, Governor of Awa. He was appointed to this position on the 10th day of the 1st month of 838 and died on the 7th day of the 7th month of 840 at the age of 56.)

TACHIBANA Ujitomo [783–847].

(Third son of Kiyotomo, posthumously appointed Prime Minister. He was appointed to this post on the 2nd day of the 7th month of 844. He was maternal grandfather of the Emperor. He died on the 19th day of the 12th month of 847 at the age of 65.)

56. These became members of the NIMMYŌ MINAMOTO clan.

57. Tokiwa was a young brother of Emperor Nimmyō and one of the sons of Saga who became members of the SAGA MINAMOTO clan.

FUJIWARA Yoshifusa [804–872].[58]
(Son of Fuyutsugu and a Senior Commander of the Imperial
Bodyguards of the Right. He was appointed on the 10th day
of the lst month of 848.)
On the third day of the 1st month [of 834], the era name was
changed to Shōwa, an era that lasted 14 years [834–848]. (The first
year was *kinoe-tora*.) Retired Emperor Junna died on the 8th day of
the 5th month of 840 (at the age of 55), and Retired Emperor Saga
died on the 15th day of the 7th month of 842 (at the age of 57). On
the 13th day of the 6th month [of 848], the era name was changed to
Kashō, an era that was three years long [848–851]. (The first year
was *tsuchinoe-tatsu*.) Emperor Nimmyo died on the 21st day of the
3rd month of 850 (at the age of 41).
    Tendai Abbot: Enchō [771–836].
    (Appointed by an official order issued on the 16th day of the
    3rd month of 834, when he was 61 years old. He administered
    the affairs of Mt. Hiei for three years and died on the 23rd day
    of the 10th month of 836 at the age of 74 [*sic*].)
This Emperor was usually referred to as "the Emperor of
Fukakusa." Fukakusa was the name given to his tomb. After his funeral, a Junior Commander by the name of YOSHIMINE Munesada
[816–890], who had served near the Emperor, entered the Buddhist
priesthood and became High Priest Henjō.
Retired Emperor Saga died on the 15th day of the 7th month of
842. Retired Emperor Junna had died before that, in 840. When
Nimmyō succeeded to the throne [in 833], Junna's son, Prince
Tsunesada, had been appointed Crown Prince. But after both Retired Emperors died, the Prince was removed from his position as
Crown Prince because his supporters were reportedly plotting
[against the Emperor].[59]
Grand Preceptor Kōbō died[60] during this reign, on the 21st day of
the 3rd month of 835 at the age of 62.

58. His daughter Akiko became Montoku's Empress and the mother of
Emperor Seiwa.
59. Prince Tsunesada lost out because FUJIWARA Yoshifusa wanted, and
succeeded in getting, his sister's son (Montoku) made Crown Prince. The
Prince's cause was supported by TOMO Kowamine and TACHIBANA Hayanari.
By defeating these two men and having them sent into exile, Yoshifusa and
the FUJIWARA clan gained firm control over court affairs. This is the Shōwa
Incident of 842.
60. *Nyūjō* (entered meditation). It was believed that Kōbō had not actually
died but entered a meditative state on Mt. Kōya, where he awaited the coming of Maitreya (Miroku in Japanese).

(55) Emperor Montoku [827–858]. A reign of eight years [850–858].

Montoku's personal name was Michiyasu. He received the throne on the 21st day of the 3rd month of 850 (at the age of 24). Montoku had been appointed Crown Prince on the 4th day of the 8th month of 842 (at the age of 16). His coming-of-age ceremony was held on the 16th day of the 2nd month of that same year. . . . Montoku was the eldest son of Emperor Nimmyō, and his mother was Empress Dowager FUJIWARA Junshi (a daughter [*sic*] of Minister of the Left Fuyutsugu, and she was called Empress Gojō). He had six Imperial Consorts and 29 Imperial sons. Fourteen were given names and made commoners.

Prime Minister: FUJIWARA Yoshifusa [804–872].[61]
(Senior Commander of the Imperial Bodyguards of the Left. He was appointed Prime Minister on the 19th day of the 2nd month of 857, retaining his position as Senior Commander of the Imperial Bodyguards of the Left.)

Ministers of the Left:
MINAMOTO Tokiwa [812–854].
(Senior Commander of the Imperial Bodyguards of the Left. He died on the 13th day of the 6th month of 854 at the age of 44.)
MINAMOTO Makoto [810–868].
(First [head of] the MINAMOTO clan [established by] Emperor Saga. He was appointed Minister of the Left on the 19th day of the 2nd month of 857.)

Minister of the Right: FUJIWARA Yoshisuke [813–867].
(Fifth son of Fuyutsugu. On the same day [in the 2nd month of 857], he was made Senior Commander of the Imperial Body-guards of the Right and was advanced to Senior Commander of the Imperial Bodyguards of the Left in the 4th month of that same year.)

On the 28th day of the 4th month [of 851], the era name was changed to Ninju, which lasted three years [851–854]. (The first year was *kanoto-hitsuji.*) On the 29th day of the 11th month [of 854], the era name was changed to Saikō, which lasted three years [854–857]. (The first year was *kinoe-inu.*) And on the 21st day of the 2nd month [of 857], the era name was changed to Ten'an, which was two years long [857–859]. (The first year was *hinoto-ushi.*) Emperor Montoku

---

61. Yoshifusa was the first Minister to be promoted to Prime Minister— the office had been previously held by Imperial Princes—and became head of the FUJIWARA clan in 844.

died on the 27th day of the 8th month of Ten'an 2 [858] (at the age
of 32).

Tendai Abbot: Imperial-Palace-Priest En'nin [794–864]. (Grand
Preceptor Jikaku, posthumously advanced to First Grade.)

(En'nin was appointed Tendai Abbot by an official order *(kan-chō)* issued on the 3rd day of the 4th month of 854, when he was
61 years old. He administered Mt. Hiei for 10 years. He had
sailed for China in 836 with Consultant and Senior Controller of
the Left Tsunetsugu, who was being sent to China as an envoy.
They stayed at Dazaifu for two years awaiting a favorable wind,
and then finally set sail again on the 13th day of the 6th month
of 838. He returned to Japan in 847 and died on the 14th day
of the 1st month of 864.)[62]

During this reign the head of the great statue of Buddha at
the Tōdai Temple suddenly fell to the ground.

(56) Emperor Seiwa [850–880]. A reign of 18 years [858–
876].

Seiwa's personal name was Korehito, and he was called
"the Emperor of Mizu no O." He received the throne on the 27th
day of the 8th month of 858 (at the age of nine). He had been appointed Crown Prince in 850 (when he was one year old). He was
the fourth son of Emperor Montoku. Seiwa's coming-of-age ceremony was held on the 1st day of the 1st month of 864. His mother
was Empress Dowager FUJIWARA Akirakeiko (a daughter of Yoshifusa, Lord Chūjin; and she was called Empress Somedono). He
had 13 Empresses and 18 Imperial sons and daughters. Four received names and became commoners.

Regent and Prime Minister: FUJIWARA Yoshifusa [804–872].

(Called Lord Chūjin and Lord Shirakawa. This was the first time
a Regent was appointed for a child Emperor. He was appointed
on the 7th day of the 11th month of 858, when he was 55. He
received an Imperial edict of appointment as Regent on the
19th day of the 8th month of 866. . . .[63] These dates should be
checked. He died on the 3rd day of the 9th month of 872 at the
age of 69.)

For reigns after this one it will be difficult to list ministers. Apart
from a minister who was Regent, they were unimportant. But those
that were somewhat important will be included.

62. The diary that En'nin kept on his travels in China has been translated
by Edwin O. Reischauer, *Ennin's Travels in T'ang China* (New York, 1955).

63. Yoshifusa was therefore not only the first minister to be named Prime
Minister but the first one to be appointed Regent.

Ministers of the Right:

FUJIWARA Yoshisuke [817-867].

(He died on the 10th day of the 10th month of 867 and was posthumously advanced to Senior First Grade on the 11th day of that month.)

FUJIWARA Mototsune [836-891].

(An adopted son of Yoshifusa,[64] but actually the third son of Middle Counselor Nagara. Nagara was the elder brother of Yoshifusa and the eldest son of Fuyutsugu.)

On the 22nd day of the 9th month of 866, Senior Counselor TOMO Yoshio was exiled to the province of Izu. His crime was that on the 10th day of the 3rd intercalary month [of that year] he had burned the Ōten Gate and the gates to its right and left.[65]

On the 25th day (the *Sandai Jitsuroku* says 15th) of the 4th month of 859, the era name was changed to Jōgan, an era that lasted 18 years [859-877]. (The first year was *tsuchinoto-u.*)

Tendai Abbots:

Imperial-Palace-Priest An'ne [794-868]. (Abbot of Konrin.)

(An'ne received an Imperial Mandate of appointment on the 16th day of the 2nd month of 864, when he was 55. Henceforth Tendai Abbots have been appointed by Imperial Mandate [*semmyō*] rather than by official order [*kanfu*], as a result of a deathbed request submitted to the throne by Grand Preceptor Jikaku. An'ne administered Mt. Hiei for four years. He died on the 3rd day of the 4th month of 868 at the age of 58.)

Imperial-Palace-Priest Enchin [814-891].[66] (Grand Preceptor Chishō, Provisional Junior Vicar General, posthumously advanced to First Grade.)

(Enchin was appointed Tendai Abbot by an Imperial Mandate handed down on the 3rd day of the 6th month of 868, when he was 54. He administered Mt. Hiei 24 years. He had gone to China on the 9th day of the 8th month of 853 and returned to

64. Yoshifusa had no sons of his own.

65. Yoshifusa's position was further strengthened by the exile of Yoshio and his son. The incident was called "the affair of the Ōten gates." For a map of gates to the Imperial Palace grounds, see Jean Reischauer and Robert Karl Reischauer, *Early Japanese History (c. 40 B.C.–A.D. 1167)* (Princeton, 1967), B, 31-32.

66. After returning from China, Enchin built a hall at Mii. This was the beginning of the Miidera Temple which became the center of the Tendai Sect's *ji-mon* (Church Order)—as distinguished from the *sammon* (Mountain Order) that was centered at the Enryaku Temple of Mt. Hiei. The former was associated with the followers of Enchin and the latter with those of En'nin.

Japan on the 17th day of the 6th month of 858. He died on
the 29th day of the 10th month of 891 at the age of 78.)
Regents were appointed from this time on.

Emperor Seiwa abdicated in 876. Three years later, on the 8th day
of the 5th month of 878, he entered the Buddhist priesthood. His
priestly name was Soshin. He died on the 4th day of the 12th month
of that same year (at the age of 31). He resided at the Seiwa Cloister.

During this reign the Great Hachiman Bodhisattva was moved to
Mt. Otoko [where the Iwashimizu Shrine was built]. Hachiman was
moved in response to a prayer made by Priest Gyōkyō of the Taian
Temple. . . .

(57) Emperor Yōzei [868–949]. A reign of eight years
[876–884].

Yōzei's personal name was Sadaakira. He received the
throne on the 29th day of the 11th month of 876 (at the age of
nine). He had been made Crown Prince in 869. Yōzei was the eldest
son of Emperor Seiwa. His coming-of-age ceremony was held on the
2nd day of the 1st month of 882. His mother was Empress Dowager
FUJIWARA Takaiko[67] (the second daughter of Middle Counselor
Nagara). Yōzei had nine Imperial sons, born after he abdicated.[68]

Regent and Prime Minister: FUJIWARA Mototsune [836–891].[69]
(On the day that Emperor Yōzei received the throne, Mototsune
was appointed Regent. Later he was made Chancellor. He received an Imperial Edict of appointment as Regent from Emperor Seiwa in 876. In the 2nd month of 877, he resigned from
his position as Senior Commander. On the 17th day of the 7th
month of 878, he was given a personal bodyguard made up of
two attendants and six guards each from the Imperial Bodyguards of the Left and the Imperial Bodyguards of the Right.
On the 8th day of the 11th month of 880 [*sic*], he was appointed
Chancellor by Imperial edict. On the 14th day of the 12th
month of the same year, he was appointed Prime Minister. Originally he had been Minister of the Right. He was 46 [at the time
of his appointment as Chancellor]. By an Imperial rescript issued on the 1st day of the 2nd month of 882, he was given
emoluments equal to those of the three Empresses [Empress,
Empress Dowager, and the Great Empress Dowager]—like the
deceased Lord Chūjin.)

67. Takako was Yoshifusa's niece.
68. Yōzei had no consort who held the title of Empress.
69. As Yoshifusa's adopted son and Yōzei's maternal uncle, Mototsune
followed his adoptive father as Regent.

On the 16th day of the 4th month of 877, the era name was changed to Gangyō, an era that was eight years long [877–885]. (The first year was *hinoto-tori.*) On the 4th day of the 12th month of Gangyō 2 [878], Retired Emperor Seiwa died (at the age of 31). Emperor Yōzei lived to the advanced age of 81, dying in 949.

(58) Emperor Kōkō [830–887]. A reign of three years [884–887].

Kōkō's personal name was Tokiyasu, and he was called "the Emperor of Komatsu." He received the throne on the 4th day of the 1st month of 884 (at the age of 55). Kōkō was the third son of Emperor Nimmyō. His coming-of-age ceremony had been held on the 2nd day of the 12th month of 836. . . . His mother was FUJIWARA Sawako, posthumously awarded the title of Empress Dowager (daughter of Fusatsugi, Governor of Kii).

Chancellor: Lord Shōsen Mototsune [836–891].

(On the 25th day of the 12th month of 884, the Emperor celebrated Lord Shōsen's 50th birthday in the Imperial Palace. . . .)

On the 21st day of the 2nd month of 885, the era name was changed to Ninna, an era that was four years long [885–889]. (The first year was *kinoto-mi.*)

Emperor Kōkō died (at the age of 58) on the 26th day *(hinoto-u)* of the 8th month of 887 *(hinoto-hitsuji)* at 9:30 A.M. Retired Emperor Yōzei was apparently afflicted with a curse. So everything he did was unspeakable. Lord Shōsen [Mototsune], the maternal uncle [of Yōzei], had consulted with lower-ranking ministers and placed Kōkō on the throne. Emperor Kōkō had four Imperial consorts and 41 Imperial sons and daughters. Thirty-five of them because members of the MINAMOTO clan. . . .

(59) Emperor Uda [867–931]. A reign of 10 years [887–897].

Uda's personal name was Sadami, and he was also called "the Cloistered Emperor of Teiji,"[70] as well as "Priest-Emperor of Kampyō." He received the throne (at the age of 21) on the 26th day of the 8th month of 887. Uda had been appointed Crown Prince in that same year. He was the third son of Emperor Kōkō, and his mother was Empress Dowager Hanshi (daughter of Prince Nakano, Minister of Ceremonies). He had five Imperial consorts and 20 Imperial children. One was given a name and made a commoner.

70. Teiji was the name of the Buddhist hall where he resided after entering the priesthood.

Chancellor and Prime Minister: FUJIWARA Mototsune [836–891].
(Appointed by an Imperial edict handed down on the 19th day
of the 11th month of 887 stating: "All affairs in all the ministries
and bureaus are to be submitted first to the Chancellor and
Prime Minister and only then reported to the Emperor, as has
been done in the past." Mototsune died on the 13th day of the
1st month of 891 at the age of 57. The Emperor was deeply
grieved and handed down an Imperial edict advancing Mototsune posthumously to Senior First Rank and [permitting his
heir to retain] the stipends and attendants previously enjoyed by
Mototsune, as if Mototsune were still alive. This had been done
before. Mototsune also held the office of Prime Minister posthumously. He had been in office 20 years.)

One year of the Ninna era [888] fell within the Uda reign. On the
27th day of the 4th month of 889, the era name was changed to
Kampyō, an era that was nine years long [889–898]. (The first year
was *tsuchinoto-tori*.)

Tendai Abbots:

Imperial-Palace-Priest Ishu [825–893]. (Abbot of Kokū Zō.)
(Ishu was appointed Tendai Abbot by an Imperial Mandate
handed down on the 21st day of the 5th month of 890 [*sic*],
when he was 66 years old. He administered the affairs of Mt.
Hiei for one year and died on the 29th day of the 2nd month
of 893 at the age of 69.)

Imperial-Palace-Priest Yūken [827–893]. (Abbot of Jinen
Dō.)
(Yūken was appointed Tendai Abbot by an Imperial Mandate
handed down on the 25th day of the 3rd month of 893, when
he was 73. He administered the affairs of Mt. Hiei for six
months and died in that same year.)

Master Teacher Kōsai [829–899]. (Abbot of Renge Bō and
provisional Preceptor.)
(Kōsai was appointed Tendai Abbot by an Imperial Mandate
handed down on the 12th day of the 9th month of 894, when
he was 67. He administered the affairs of Mt. Hiei for three
[*sic*] years. He died on the 8th day of the 2nd month of 899 at
the age of 72.)

We have no definite knowledge concerning this Emperor's
coming-of-age ceremony. We know only that it had been held during the Gangyō era [877–885], probably because it was an event of
antiquity. He abdicated (at the age of 31) in 897 and entered the
Buddhist priesthood (at the age of 34) in 900. His Buddhist name
was Kongō Kaku. He died (at the age of 65) in [931]. He lived 30
years as a Retired Emperor. It was during this reign that the Special
Festival of the Kamo Shrine was first held.

(60) Emperor Daigo [885–930]. A reign of 33 years [897–930].

Daigo's personal name was Atsuhito, and he received the throne (at the age of 13) on the 5th day *(tsuchinoe-tora)* of the 7th month of 897. He had been appointed Crown Prince (at the age of nine) on the 2nd day of the 4th month of 893. Daigo was the eldest son of Emperor Uda, and his coming-of-age ceremony had been held (when he was 11) on the 9th day of the 10th month of 895. One source states that it was held on the same day that he received the throne (but that is probably wrong). His mother was FUJIWARA Taneko, posthumously appointed Empress Dowager (and the daughter of Minister of the Center Takafuji. When Daigo received the throne, Takafuji was Middle Counselor; but he was promoted to Senior Counselor in 899).

Minister of the Left: FUJIWARA Tokihara [871–909].

(Imperial Inspector who was given the title of Main Cloistered Minister [*hon'in no otodo*]. He was appointed Minister of the Left on the 14th day of the 2nd month of 899 and died on the 4th day of the 4th month of 909 at the age of 39.)

Minister of the Right: SUGAWARA (Michizane) [845–903].

(Imperial Inspector. The incident of his demotion occurred on the 25th day of the 1st month of 901 *(kanoto-tori)*. He died at Dazaifu on the 25th day of the 2nd month of 903 *(mizunoto-i)*, having lived to the age of 60.)

Minister of the Center: FUJIWARA Takafuji [838–900].

(Grandson of Fuyutsugu and second son of Yoshikado; Imperial Attendant Senior Sixth Rank, Higher Grade. Takafuji was appointed Minister of the Center on the 28th day of the 1st month of 900 and died at the age of 63 on the 13th day of the 3rd month of that same year.)

Minister of the Right: MINAMOTO Hikaru [845–913].

(Third son of Emperor Nimmyō. He was appointed Minister of the Right on the 26th day of the 1st month of 901 and died at the age of 68 on the 13th day of the 3rd month of 913.)

Minister of the Left: FUJIWARA Tadahira [880–949].[71]

(Senior Commander of the Imperial Bodyguards of the Left. He was appointed Minister of the Right on the 25th day of the 8th month of 914 and promoted to Minister of the Left on the 7th day of the 1st month of 924.)

Minister of the Right: FUJIWARA Sadakata [873–932].

(Second son of Takafuji, posthumously appointed Prime Minister. Sadakata was appointed in 924.)

71. Tadahira was a young brother of Tokihira. When Tokihira died in 909, Tadahira was made head of the FUJIWARA clan.

On the 16th day of the 4th month of 898, the era name was changed to Shōtai, an era that was three years long [898–901]. (The first year was *tsuchinoe-uma.*) On the 15th day of the 7th month of 901, the era name was changed to Engi, which was 22 years long [901–923]. (The first year was *kanoto-tori.*) On the 11th day of the intercalary 4th month of 923, the era name was changed to Enchō, which lasted eight years [923–931]. (The first year was *mizunoto-hitsuji.*) Emperor Daigo died (at the age of 46) on the 29th day of the 9th month of Enchō 8 [930].

   Tendai Abbots:
   Master Teacher *(azari)* Chōi [836–906].
   Chōi was a priest of the Third Grade *(hokkyō)*[72] and was posthumously appointed High Priest. He was appointed Tendai Abbot by an Imperial Mandate handed down on the 8th day of the 10th month of 899, when he was 72. He administered the affairs of Mt. Hiei for seven years and died on the 3rd day of the 7th month of 906 at the age of 79. In 908, he was posthumously advanced in grade.)
   Imperial-Palace Priest *(naigu)* Zōmyō [843–927].[73] (Abbot of Tani.)
   (Zōmyō was Buddhist Judge *(hōmu)*[74] and High Priest. He was posthumously given the title of "Jōkan" and appointed Tendai Abbot at the age of 64 by an Imperial Mandate handed down on the 17th day of the 10th month of 906. He administered the affairs of Mt. Hiei for 16 years. He died on the 11th day of the 11th month of 927 at the age of 85. He lived six years after retirement. . . .)
   Imperial-Palace Priest Ryōyū [855–923]. (Abbot of Tani.)
   (Ryōyū was appointed Tendai Abbot by an Imperial Mandate handed down on the 5th day of the 8th month of 922 at the age of 68. He administered the affairs of Mt. Hiei for one

---

72. *Hokkyō* is an abbreviation of *hokkyō shōnin-i,* the lowest of the three grades bestowed upon high-ranking Buddhist priests by the Imperial Court. These grades, and their equivalent positions, were established in 864 as follows [NKBT 86.87, note 27]:

Grades		Positions	
Hōin (daioshō-i) First Grade		Sōjō	High Priest
Hōgen (osho-i, or *Kashō-i)*			
Second Grade		*Sōzu*	Vicar General
Hokkyō (shōnin-i) Third Grade		*Risshi*	Preceptor

73. Zōmyō was credited with having converted Emperors Uda and Daigo to Buddhism and with having miraculously brought rain and cured illnesses through prayer. [NKBT, 86.377, note 49.]

74. Zōmyō is said to be the first Tendai priest to hold this position.

year and died at the age of 69 on the 6th day of the 3rd
month of 923.)

Imperial-Palace Priest Genkan [861–926]. (Abbot of Kazan.)
(Genkan was a Third Grade priest who was posthumously advanced to High Priest. He was appointed Tendai Abbot at the
age of 62 by an Imperial Mandate handed down on the 22nd
day of the 7th month of 923.)

Imperial-Palace Priest Son'i. (Abbot of Hōshō Bō.)
(Son'i was a priest of the First Grade and was posthumously
granted the position of High Priest. He was appointed Tendai
Abbot at the age of 66 by an Imperial Mandate handed down
on the 11th day of the 5th month of 926. He administered the
affairs of Mt. Hiei for 14 years and died at the age of 83 on
the 23rd day of the 2nd month of 940.)

The SUGAWARA Michizane [845–903] incident broke in the 1st
month of 901. The Emperor had the diaries for that period burned.
Lightning struck the Seiryō-den [in the Imperial Palace] on the 26th
day of the 6th month of 930, and both Senior Counselor Kiyotsura
and Middle Controller of the Right Mareyo were killed.[75] The Emperor then moved to the Empress's residence (*jōneiden*). Emperor
Daigo abdicated on the 22nd day of the 9th month of 930, and he
entered the Buddhist priesthood on the 29th day of that same
month at about 2:00 A.M. His Buddhist name was Hō Kongō. He
died shortly thereafter (at the age of 46). He had 21 Empresses, Imperial consorts, and concubines, and 36 Imperial sons and daughters.
Six became members of the MINAMOTO clan.

It is said that comets appeared now and then during this reign,
but since fine acts of administrative benevolence (*tokusei*) were carried out, time passed without a serious incident. This is the only
reign after the beginning of the Taihō era [in 701] to be respected.
Even the SUGAWARA incident is·considered, more and more, to have
been something fine, becoming understood as an incident that was
brought about because an incarnation of Kwannon (*gonja*) had appeared for [the benefit of] the final reigns (*matsudai*).

---

75. The deaths are attributed to the revenge of SUGAWARA Michizane's
vengeful soul.

7
Chronology II:

Emperor Suzaku to
Emperor Go-Horikawa

(61) Emperor Suzaku [923–952]. A reign of 16 years [930–946].

Suzaku's personal name was Yutaakira. He received the throne (at the age of eight) on the 22nd day of the 9th month of 930. Suzaku had been appointed Crown Prince in 925. He was the eleventh son of Emperor Daigo [60], and his coming-of-age had been celebrated on the 4th day of the 1st month of 937 (at the age of 15). His Imperial mother was Empress Dowager FUJIWARA Onshi [885–954], (the fourth daughter of Lord Shōsen [Mototsune]).

Regent and Prime Minister: FUJIWARA Tadahira [880–949].[1]

(The Imperial edict appointing Tadahira to the position of Regent was handed down on the same day that Suzaku received the throne. Tadahira was appointed Prime Minister on the 19th day of the 8th month of 936. He resigned from his position as Regent on the 20th day of the 10th month of 941 and in the 11th month of that same year became Chancellor.)

1. Brother of Suzaku's Imperial mother, Onshi.

Minister of the Right: FUJIWARA Saneyori [900–970].[2]
(Saneyori, the eldest son of Tadahira, was appointed Minister of the Right on the 9th day of the 4th month of 944.)

On the 26th day of the 4th month of 931, the era name was changed to Shōhei, which lasted seven years [931–938]. (The first year was *kanoto-u.*) On the 19th day of the 7th month of Shōhei 1 [931], Retired Emperor Uda [59] died (at the age of 65). And on the 23rd day of the 5th month of 938, the era name was changed to Tengyō, which lasted nine years [938–947]. (The first year was *tsuchinoe-inu.*)

Tendai Abbots:

Provisional Preceptor Gikai [d. 946].
(A Junior Vicar General, Gikai was appointed Tendai Abbot by an Imperial Mandate issued on the 25th day of the 3rd month of 940, when he was 68. He administered Mt. Hiei five years and died on the 10th day of the 5th month of 946 at the age of 74.)

Provisional Preceptor Enshō [880–964]. (Abbot of Byōdō-bō.)
(Enshō became High Priest and was given the posthumous title of Ji'nen. He was appointed Tendai Abbot by an Imperial Mandate issued on the 30th day of the 12th month of 946, when he was 67. He administered the affairs of Mt. Hiei 18 years and died on the 15th day of the 1st month of 964 at the age of 85.)

Imperial visits to the Kamo Shrine were begun during this reign. Also the Special Festival *(rinji no matsuri)* of the Iwashimizu [Hachiman Shrine] was first celebrated.[3] TAIRA Masakado [d. 940] and FUJIWARA Sumitomo [d. 941] rebelled,[4] but they were subjugated by TAIRA Sadamori and TACHIBANA Tōyasu. The Great Fundamental Central Hall *(kompon chūdō)* of Mt. Hiei was burned down [in 935]. Emperor Suzaku abdicated in the 4th month of 946 and died (at the age of 30) on the 15th day of the 8th month of 952. He had two Empresses or consorts and one Imperial daughter.

(62) Emperor Murakami [926–967]. A reign of 21 years [946–967].

Murakami's personal name was Nariakira, and he was called "the Emperor of Tenryaku [era, 947–957]." He received the throne (at the age of 21) on the 13th day of the 4th month of 946.

2. Nephew of the Imperial mother.
3. Held annually after 971.
4. These rebellions in outlying regions—Sumitomo's in the west and Masakado's in the east—are thought to have come at the beginning of a long period of progressive deterioration in central-government control.

Murakami had been appointed Crown Prince in 944 (at the age of 19). He was the fourteenth son of Emperor Daigo, and his coming-of-age ceremony had been held (at the age of 15) on the 1st day of the 10th month of 940. His Imperial mother [Onshi] was the same as Emperor Suzaku's.

Chancellor and Prime Minister: FUJIWARA Tadahira [880–949].

(Tadahira was made Chancellor on the 20th day of the 5th month of 949 and was granted the privileges and emoluments of an Empress [*jusangū*]. On the 21st day of the 1st month of 949, he was awarded 50 ordained priests. Sutras were read at 15 great temples to cure Tadahira's illness. On the 8th day of the 8th month [of 949], he went to bed sick and did not get up again. By an Imperial edict issued on the 14th day, 30 [more] ordained priests were granted to him. And a great Imperial amnesty was declared for the purpose of curing his illness. He died between 7:00 and 9:00 P.M. on that day at the age of 70. By an Imperial edict of the 18th, Senior Counselor Kiyokage, Middle Counselor Motokata, and Consultant Moroaki were sent to pay [the Emperor's] respects before Tadahira's coffin. He was posthumously advanced to Senior First Rank, given the income from the province of Shinano, and called Lord Shinano. The posthumous title of Lord Teishin was also bestowed upon him.)

Minister of the Left: [Ono no Miya] Saneyori [900–970].

(As the eldest son of Tadahira who became Senior Commander of the Imperial Bodyguards of the Left, Saneyori was appointed Minister of the Left on the 26th day of the 4th month of 947. He was appointed Senior Commander on the 21st day of the 3rd month of 957. By an Imperial order of the 5th day of the 4th month [of 957] he was permitted to wear a sword, and in the 3rd month of 959 he received Imperial permission to enter and leave the palace gates by palanquin.)

Minister of the Right: [KUJŌ] Morosuke [908–960].

(As second son of Tadahira and Senior Commander of the Imperial Bodyguards of the Right, Morosuke was appointed Minister of the Right on the 26th day of the 4th month of 947. He resigned from his position as Senior Commander on the 17th day of the 6th month of 955. By an Imperial order of the 22nd day of the 7th month [of 955] he was permitted to wear a sword. On the 2nd day of the 5th month of 960 he entered the Buddhist priesthood at the age of 53 and died on the 4th day of that same month, having held office 14 years.)

On the 24th day of the 4th month of 947, the era name was changed to Tenryaku, which lasted 10 years [947–957]. (The first year was *hinoto-hitsuji.*) Retired Emperor Yōzei died on the 29th day of the 9th month of Tenryaku 3 [949] (at the age of 82). Retired

Emperor Suzaku died (at the age of 30) on the 15th day of the 8th month of Tenryaku 6 [952]. On the 27th day of the 10th month of 957, the era name was changed to Tentoku, which lasted four years [957–961]. (The first year was *hinoto-mi.*) On the 16th day of the 2nd month of 961, the era name was changed to Ōwa, which lasted three years [961–964]. (The first year was *kanoto-tori.*) On the 10th day of the 7th month of 964, the era name was changed to Kōhō, which lasted four years [964–968]. (The first year was *kinoe-ne.*) Emperor Murakami died (at the age of 42) on the 25th day of the 5th month of Kōhō 4 [967].

Tendai Abbots:

Provisional Senior Vicar General Chinchō [d. 964]. (Abbot of Tsuji.)

(Chinchō was a lay priest. . . . His secular name was TACHI-BANA Takakage. He was appointed Tendai Abbot by an Imperial Mandate issued on the 9th day of the 3rd month of 964, when he was 79 years old. He administered the affairs of Mt. Hiei seven months and died on the 5th day of the 10th month of 964.)

Provisional Junior Vicar General Kikyō [d. 966]. (Abbot of Sammai.)

(Kikyō was appointed Tendai Abbot by an Imperial Mandate issued on the 15th day of the 2nd month of 965, when he was 77. He administered the affairs of Mt. Hiei one year and died on the 17th day of the 7th month of 966.)

Provisional Preceptor Ryōgen [912–985].[5] (Abbot of Mimyō.)

(Ryōgen was Buddhist Judge and Senior High Priest, and was posthumously given the title of Ji'e. He was appointed Tendai Abbot by an Imperial Mandate issued on the 27th day of the 8th month of 966, when he was 55. He administered the affairs of Mt. Hiei 19 years and died on the 3rd day of the 1st month of 985 at the age of 74.)

The Imperial Palace burned down on the 23rd day of the 9th month of 960, the first time it had been burned after the capital was moved [to Heian in 794]. . . . Because the Sacred Mirror was found—not the least bit damaged—in the ashes of the Unmei Hall, it was moved to an office of the Empress's Household *(shiki no zōshi)* on the morning of the following day. And the Bureau of the Treasury presented offerings *(hei)* [to thank the Kami for preserving the Sacred Mirror]. Another report has it that [the Sacred Mirror] flew off and hung itself in an aphananthe aspera tree in the Imperial garden. Accounts of what happened on that day are probably not

5. Ryōgen, the priest with whom KUJŌ Morosuke made a "patron pledge," has a prominent place in Jien's interpretation of Japanese history.

accurate. Emperor Murakami died on the 25th day of the 5th month of 967 (at the age of 42). He had 10 Empresses and Imperial consorts and 19 Imperial sons and daughters. There was no Chancellor after 949[6] in the Murakami reign. Lord Ono no Miya [Saneyori] and Lord KUJŌ [Morosuke] administered the affairs of state as Ministers of the Left and Right respectively.[7]

(63) Emperor Reizei [950–1011]. A reign of two years [967–969].

Reizei's personal name was Norihira. He received the throne on the 25th day of the 5th month of 967 (at the age of 18). Reizei had been appointed Crown Prince (at the age of one) in 950 and was the second son of Emperor Murakami. His coming-of-age ceremony was held on the 28th day of the 2nd month of 963 (at the age of 14). His Imperial mother was Empress Dowager FUJIWARA Yasuko [927–964], (daughter of Lord KUJŌ Morosuke, Minister of the Right).

Chancellor and Prime Minister: [Ono no Miya] Saneyori [900–970].[8]

(Saneyori was made Chancellor on the 22nd day of the 6th month of 967. On the 5th day of the 10th month he was granted the privilege of entering the Imperial Palace grounds by an oxdrawn cart, and on the 13th day of the 12th month he was appointed Prime Minister.)

Minister of the Right: FUJIWARA Morotada [920–969].

(Morotada was the fifth son of Lord Teishin [Tadahira], Minister of the Left of Koichijō.)

On the 15th day of the 8th month of 968, the era name was changed to An'na, which lasted two years [968–970]. (The first year was *tsuchinoe-tatsu.*) Emperor Reizei abdicated (at the age of 20) in An'na 2 [969]. He lived 44 years after abdicating.

6. When Tadahira died.

7. Although Saneyori had married one daughter to Emperor Suzaku and another to Emperor Murakami, neither daughter produced an Imperial son. But Morosuke's daughter, a Murakami Empress, had a son who was appointed Crown Prince in 950 and enthroned as Emperor Reizei in 967. Therefore later Regents were of the KUJŌ Morosuke line.

8. Since KUJŌ Morosuke was the father of Reizei's mother Yasuko, Morosuke would have been entitled to the coveted post of Regent when Reizei ascended the throne, but Morosuke died before Reizei's enthronement. Therefore Morosuke's brother Saneyori became Regent. But when Saneyori died in 970 at the beginning of the reign of Enyū, whose mother was also Morosuke's daughter Yasuko, Morosuke's son Koretada was appointed Regent.

(64) Emperor Enyū [959–991]. A reign of 15 years [969–984].

Enyū's personal name was Morihira. He received the throne on the 13th day of the 8th month of 969 (at the age of 11). He had been appointed Crown Prince (at the age of 9) in 967. Enyū was the fifth son of Emperor Murakami. His coming-of-age ceremony had been held on the 3rd day of the 1st month of 972 (when he was 14). His Imperial mother [Yasuko] was the same as Reizei's.

Chancellor and Prime Minister: [Ono no Miya] Saneyori [909–970].[9]

(Known as Lord Seishin, Saneyori became Chancellor on the 13th day of the 8th month of 969 and died on the 18th day of the 5th month of 970 at the age of 71.)

Regent and Minister of the Right: FUJIWARA Koretada [924– 972].

(In the 1st month of 970, Koretada was appointed Minister of the Right, retaining his original position as Senior Commander of the Imperial Bodyguards of the Left. Then on the 21st day of the 5th month of that same year he was made Regent. In the 7th month he resigned his post as Senior Commander and was granted an official bodyguard [*hyōjō*]. On the 2nd day of the 11th month of 971, Koretada was appointed Prime Minister. He died on the 1st day of the 11th month of 972 at the age of 49.)

Chancellor and Prime Minister: FUJIWARA Kanemichi [925–977].

(Kanemichi was appointed Minister of the Center on the 27th day of the 11th month of 972. Originally a Middle Counselor, he never held the position of Senior Counselor. On the 28th day of the 12th month, Kanemichi became Superintendent [*kengyō*] of the Enryaku Temple; on the 28th day of the 2nd month of 974, he was appointed Prime Minister; and on the 26th day of the 3rd month, he became Chancellor. He was given the emoluments and privileges of an Empress on the 4th day of the

9. Emperor Enyū's ministers were related to his Imperial mother Yasuko as follows:

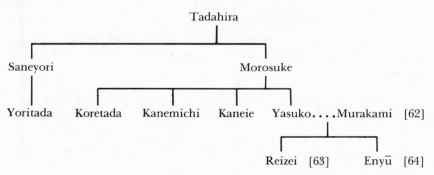

11th month of 977. Then he died on the 8th day of that month at the age of 53. His posthumous name was Lord Chūgi.)

Chancellor and Prime Minister: FUJIWARA Yoritada [924–989].

(Yoritada became Chancellor on the 11th day of the 10th month of 977 and on the 2nd day of the 10th month of 978 was appointed Prime Minister.)

Minister of the Right: FUJIWARA Kaneie [929–990].

(Kaneie was appointed Minister of the Right on the 2nd day of the 10th month of 978.)

On the 25th day of the 3rd month of 970, the era name was changed to Tenroku, an era that lasted three years [970–973]. (The first year was *kanoe-uma.*) Emperor Enyū celebrated his coming-of-age on the 3rd day of the 1st month of Tenroku 3 [972]. On the 20th day of the 12th month of 973, the era name was changed to Ten'en, which was three years long [973–976]. (The first year was *mizunoto-tori.*) On the 13th day of the 7th month of 976, the era name was changed to Jōgen, which was an era of two years [976–978]. (The first year was *hinoe-ne.*) On the 15th day of the 4th month of 978, the era name was changed to Tengen, an era of five years [978–983]. (The first year was *tsuchinoe-tora.*) On the 15th day of the 4th month of 983, the era name was changed to Eikan, which lasted two years [983–985]. (The first year was *mizunoto-hitsuji.*)

Imperial visits were first made to the Hachiman and Hirano Shrines during this reign. Emperor Enyū abdicated (at the age of 26) on the 27th day of the 8th month of 984. He entered the Buddhist priesthood on the 29th day of the 8th month of 985. He became ill (at the age of 27). His Buddhist name was Kongō Hō. He died (at the age of 33) on the 12th day of the 2nd month of 991. He had five Empresses or Imperial consorts and one Imperial son.

During this reign, the Imperial Palace burned down several times. Tradition had it that this was due [to the resentful soul of SUGAWARA Michizane enshrined at] the Kitano Shrine. [At the time of the fire], on the 11th day *(hinoto-ushi)* of the 5th month of 976, the Sacred Mirror was not destroyed but was blackened and reflected no light. . . . It was half destroyed on the 22nd day of the 11th month of 980. . . . Then on the 17th day of the 11th month of 982 it was entirely burned, but the melted metal was collected and presented. It is said that, after this, extraordinary things were done [by the miraculous power of the Sacred Mirror].

(65) Emperor Kazan [968–1008]. A reign of two years [984–986].

Kazan's personal name was Morosada. He received the throne (at the age of 17) on the 27th day of the 8th month of 984. He had been appointed Crown Prince in 969. He was the first son of

Emperor Reizei, and his coming-of-age had been celebrated (at the age of 15) on the 19th day of the 2nd month of 982. His Imperial mother was FUJIWARA Kaishi [945–975], posthumously appointed Empress Dowager. (She was the daughter of Regent Koretada of Ichijō.)

Chancellor and Prime Minister: FUJIWARA Yoritada [924–989].[10]

(The previous Emperor Enyū had requested that Emperor Kazan order Yoritada to remain on as Chancellor.)

Minister of the Left: FUJIWARA Kaneie [929–990].

Middle Counselor: FUJIWARA Yoshichika [957–1008].

(Yoshichika was the fifth son of Regent Koretada of Ichijō. He was advanced to Junior Third rank—a two-step advance—on the 10th day of the 10th month of 984 and to Senior Third Rank on the 14th day of the same month, moving ahead of Michitaka because he was brother of the Imperial mother. He was appointed Consultant on the 14th day of the 9th month of 985; and on the 21st day of the 11th month of that same year, he was advanced to Junior Second Rank. On the 25th day of the 11th month of that year, he was appointed Middle Counselor at the age of 29. Then on the 22nd day of the 6th month of 989, he followed Emperor Kazan into the Buddhist priesthood. Although Prime Minister Yoritada had the title of Chancellor, all matters of state were entrusted to Yoshichika.)

Tendai Abbot: Provisional High Priest Jinzen [943–990].[11]

(Jinzen's posthumous title was Ji'nin. He was appointed Tendai Abbot by an Imperial Mandate issued on the 27th day of the

10. Emperor Kazan's ministers were related to his Imperial mother Kaishi as follows:

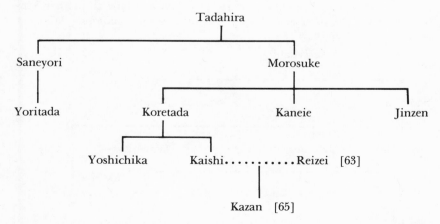

11. Jinzen was not only a brother of the Imperial mother's father but a disciple of Ryōgen, the previous Tendai Abbot.

2nd month of 985, when he was 41. He administered the affairs of Mt. Hiei five years and died on the 27th day of the 2nd month of 990 at the age of 46.)

On the 27th day of the 4th month of 985, the era name was changed to Kanwa, which lasted two years [985–987]. (The first year was *kinoto-tori*.)

Emperor Kazan suddenly developed an urge to follow the way of Buddha during the 6th month of 986;[12] and so he left the Imperial Palace, took up his residence at Kazan, and entered the Buddhist priesthood. His Buddhist name was Nyūkaku. He lived 22 years after that and died in 1008.

(66) Emperor Ichijō [980–1011]. A reign of 25 years [986–1011].

Ichijō's personal name was Kanehito, and he received the throne (at the age of seven) on the 23rd day of the 6th month of 986. He had been appointed Crown Prince on the 27th day of the 8th month of 984. Ichijō was the eldest son of Retired Emperor Enyū. His coming-of-age was celebrated (at the age of 11) on the 5th day of the 1st month of 990. His Imperial mother was Senshi, Empress Higashi Sanjō In [961–1001]. (She was the daughter of Great Lord Lay Priest Kaneie.)

Regent and Prime Minister: FUJIWARA Kaneie [929–990].[13]

12. In Chapter 1, Jien gives considerable attention to the role Michikane played in Kazan's abdication and entrance into the priesthood. Michikane's personal interest is readily apparent when we note that he was only a cousin of Kazan's Imperial mother Kaishi but a brother of the succeeding Emperor Ichijō's Imperial mother Senshi. Cf. note 13, below.

13. Emperor Ichijō's ministers were related to his Imperial mother Senshi as follows (the number following a minister's name indicates the order in which he is listed):

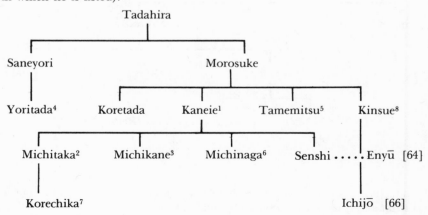

(Kaneie was made Regent on the 23rd day of the 6th month of 986. He resigned his post as Minister of the Right on the 14th day of the 7th month. By an Imperial order issued on the 22nd day of the 8th month, he was extended the right—one enjoyed by an Empress—to make a certain number of appointments of office [*nenkan*], and to award a certain number of court ranks of Junior Fifth Rank and below every year.[14] But Kaneie firmly declined the right and did not receive it. By an Imperial decree of the 25th day of the 3rd month of 988, he was granted permission to enter and leave the Imperial gates, guard stations, and ministries by palanquin. Due to illness, Kaneie requested that he be relieved of his position as Regent on the 5th day of the 5th month of 990, and he was made Chancellor. Kaneie entered the Buddhist priesthood on the 8th day of that same month. His Buddhist name was Nyojitsu. On the 10th day of that same month, he made his house and land at the intersection of Nijō and Kyogōku into a permanent Buddhist temple. The temple was called the Hōkō Cloister. He died on the 2nd day of the 7th month of that year at the age of 62.)

Regent and Minister of the Center: FUJIWARA Michitaka [953–995]. (Michitaka was made Chancellor on the 8th day of the 5th month of 990,[15] and on the 25th day of that month he was permitted "ox-drawn cart" privileges. He became Regent on the 26th.[16] On the 1st day of the 6th month of that year, he resigned from his position as Senior Commander and was awarded an official bodyguard. He resigned as Minister of the Center on the 23rd day of the 7th month of 991, and as Regent on the 27th day of the 4th month of 993, becoming Chancellor. Then, because of illness, he resigned as Chancellor in the 3rd month of 995. On the 6th day of the 4th month of that year he entered the Buddhist priesthood, and he died on the 10th of that month at the age of 43.)

Chancellor and Minister of the Right: FUJIWARA Michikane [961–995].

(Michikane was made Chancellor on the 27th day of the 4th month of 995[17] but died on the 5th day of the 5th month of that same year at the age of 35. He was therefore called "the seven-day Chancellor.")

14. The privilege produced a lucrative income since gifts were received from each appointee.

15. He was made Chancellor on the same day that his father Kaneie resigned as Regent.

16. The appointment was irregular because the Emperor was then of age.

17. He was appointed Chancellor only after his elder brother Michitaka's death earlier that month. Cf. note 13, above.

Prime Ministers:

FUJIWARA Yoritada [924–989].

(Yoritada died on the 26th day of the 6th month of 989 at the age of 66. He was posthumously advanced to Senior First Rank and given the posthumous title of Lord Rengi.)

FUJIWARA Tamemitsu [942–992].

(Tamemitsu was the ninth son of Lord KUJŌ Morosuke. He was appointed Minister of the Right on the 20th day of the 7th month of 986 and Prime Minister on the 7th day of the 9th month of 991. He died on the 16th day of the 6th month of 992 at the age of 51 and was posthumously advanced to Senior First Rank and given the title of Lord Kōtoku.)

Minister of the Left: FUJIWARA Michinaga [966–1027].

(By an Imperial decree issued on the 11th day of the 5th month of 995, Michinaga was named Imperial Inspector.[18] He was then Senior Counselor. He was appointed Minister of the Right on the 19th day of the 6th month of that same year, passing over Koretada who was Minister of the Center. Then he was appointed Minister of the Left on the 20th day of the intercalary 7th month of 996. In the 8th month of that year, he resigned as Senior Commander of the Imperial Bodyguards of the Left and six boys were made his personal bodyguards. By an Imperial order of the 9th day of the 10th month, he was given one guard each from the Headquarters of the Imperial Bodyguards of the Left and the Right. Four [other] men from each of these two Imperial Bodyguards [also] served as his personal bodyguards. But the use of boys as personal bodyguards was discontinued. On the 13th day of the 3rd month of 998, he requested the withdrawal of personal bodyguards and his appointment as Imperial Inspector. By an Imperial order his request was granted. On the 16th day of the 12th month of 999, he was again granted personal bodyguards as before.)

Minister of the Center: FUJIWARA **Korechika** [973–1010].

(Korechika was [appointed Minister of the Center] on the 28th day of the 8th month of 994 at the age of 21, moving ahead of Michinaga. On the 8th day of the 3rd month of 995, an Imperial decree was issued stating: "While the Chancellor is ill, all **documents issued by the Prime Minister or High Nobles [*denjō*] shall all pass, for the time being, through the Minister of the**

18. Michinaga received this position six days after his brother Michikane's death. Jien suggests (Chapter 1) that Michinaga—rather than Michitaka's son Korechika—received the appointment because of influence exerted by Michinaga's sister, Emperor Ichijō's Imperial mother Akiko.

Center." On the 10th day of the 4th month of that year, he was
relieved of his duties because he was in mourning for a deceased
parent. On that same day, he was granted four persons from the
Imperial Bodyguards of the Right and Left to serve as personal bodyguards. Korechika was demoted to Provisional Governor General at Dazaifu on the 24th day of the 4th month of
996,[19] and an Imperial edict was issued stating: "Minister of the
Center FUJIWARA Korechika Ason and Provisional Middle Counselor FUJIWARA Takaie Ason shot arrows at Priest-Emperor
Kazan on the night of the 15th day of the 1st month....
Empress Higashi Sanjō In was ill because she had been cursed
by the use of effigies. ... The laws naturally require punishment for such crimes, but after giving the matter some
thought, it was decided that Minister of the Center Korechika
would be demoted to Provisional General at Dazaifu, and
Takaie to Provisional Governor of Izumo. ...." Korechika was
then 23 years old, and he had been in office three years. On the
16th day of the intercalary 12th month of 998, he was restored
to his original rank because of an amnesty granted on the occasion of Empress Higashi Sanjō In's illness. By an Imperial decree issued on the 25th day of the 2nd month of 1005,
Korechika was ordered to take a seat at conferences immediately
below that occupied by men who were Ministers.)

Minister of the Center: [KAN'IN] Kinsue [956–1029].[20]

On the 5th day of the 4th month of 987, the era name was
changed to Eien, an era that lasted two years [987–989]. (The first
year was *hinoto-i.*) On the 8th day of the 8th month of 989, the era
name was changed to Eiso, which lasted one year [989–990]. (The
first year was *tsuchinoto-ushi.*) On the 7th day of the 11th month of
990, the era name was changed to Shōryaku, which ran for five years
[990–995]. (The first year was *kanoe-tora.*) Retired Emperor Enyū
[64] died on the 12th day of the 2nd month of Shōryaku 2 [991] (at
the age of 33). On the 22nd day of the 2nd month of 995, the era
name was changed to Chōtoku, which was four years long [995–
999]. (The first year was *kinoto-hitsuji.*) On the 13th day of the 1st
month of 999, the era name was changed to Chōhō, which lasted five
years [999–1004]. (The first year was *tsuchinoto-i.*) On the 20th day of
the 7th month of 1004, the era name was changed to Kankō, which

19. Korechika was undoubtedly displeased by Michinaga's appointment as
Imperial Inspector. In any case, he was accused of becoming engaged in a
plot and was therefore demoted and exiled.

20. Kinsue was appointed Minister of the Center in 997, after Korechika's
dismissal.

was eight years long [1004–12]. (The first year was *kinoe-tatsu*.) Emperor Ichijō died (at the age of 32) on the 22nd day of the 6th month of Kankō 8 [1011]. Retired Emperor Kazan [65] died (at the age of 41) on the 8th day of the 2nd month of 1008; and Retired Emperor Reizei [63] died (at the age of 62) on the 24th day of the 10th month of 1011.

Tendai Abbots:

Provisional Senior Vicar General Yokei [919–991]. (Abbot of Kwannon-in.)

(Yokei was given the posthumous title of Chiben and made Provisional High Priest. He was appointed Tendai Abbot by an Imperial Mandate issued on the 29th day of the 9th month of 989, when he was 71 years old. He resigned from that post on the 26th day of the 12th month of that year because the monks of Mt. Hiei would not accept him. After this, followers of Grand Preceptor Chishō were appointed to the position of Tendai Abbot but did not serve long.)[21]

Former Junior Vicar General Yōshō [d. 990]. (Abbot of Chikurin-in.)

(Yōshō became Provisional Senior High Priest. He was appointed Tendai Abbot by an Imperial Mandate issued on the 27th day of the 12th month of 989, when he was 82 years old. He administered the affairs of Mt. Hiei one year, resigned on the 28th day of the 9th month of 990, and died on the 20th day of the 10th month of the same year at the age of 83.)

Provisional Junior Vicar General Senga [917–998]. (Abbot of Hongaku-in.)

(Senga became Provisional High Priest. He was appointed Tendai Abbot by an Imperial Mandate issued on the 20th day of the 12th month of 990, when he was 77. He administered the affairs of Mt. Hiei for eight years and died on the 1st day of the 8th month of 1002 [*sic*] at the age of 85.)

Provisional Senior Vicar General Kakukei [927–1014]. (Abbot of Tōyō-bō.)

(Kakukei became Provisional Senior High Priest. He was appointed Tendai Abbot by an Imperial Mandate of the 29th day of the 10th month of 1002 [*sic*] when he was 71. He administered the affairs of Mt. Hiei 16 years and died on the 23rd day of the 11th month of 1014 at the age of 87.)

21. Yokei was a member of the Church Order of Miidera. His removal from the position of Tendai Abbot in 989 marks the beginning of a long and bitter conflict between that Order and the Mountain Order based on Mt. Hiei. In 993, the followers of En'nin of the Mountain Order drove the priest of the Church Order from Mt. Hiei. [NKBT, 86.384, note 108.]

Imperial visits were first made to the following four shrines: Kasuga; Ōharano; Matsu no O; and Kitano.[22] Minister of the Center Korechika was demoted to Provisional Governor General at Dazaifu. Emperor Ichijō abdicated in 1011. He had five Empresses or Imperial consorts and five Imperial children.

(67) Emperor Sanjō [976–1017]. A reign of five years [1011–16].

Sanjō's personal name was Iyasada. He received the throne (at the age of 36) on the 13th day of the 6th month of 1011. He had been appointed Crown Prince (at the age of 11) on the 16th day of the 7th month of 986. He had celebrated his coming-of-age on that same day. Sanjō was the second son of Emperor Reizei [63], and his Imperial mother was FUJIWARA Chōshi [d. 982], posthumously appointed Empress. (She was the eldest daughter of the Great Lord Lay Priest Kaneie.)

Minister of the Left: FUJIWARA Michinaga [966–1027].[23]

(Michinaga was granted ox-drawn cart privileges on the 23rd day of the 8th month of 1011 and continued on as Imperial Inspector.)

Tendai Abbot: Senior High Priest Kyōen [d. 1019]. (Later Abbot of Sammai.)

(Kyōen was appointed Tendai Abbot by an Imperial Mandate of the 26th day of the 12th month of 1014. He administered the affairs of Mt. Hiei five years and died on the 3rd day of the 9th month of 1019 at the age of 78.)

On the 25th day of the 12th month of 1012, the era name was changed to Chōwa, an era which lasted five years [1012–17]. (The first year was *mizunoe-ne.*) Emperor Sanjō abdicated (at the age of 40) in Chōwa 5 [1016]. He entered the Buddhist priesthood on the 29th day of the 4th month of 1017 and died on the 9th day of the 5th month of that same year.

(68) Emperor Go-Ichijō [1008–36]. A reign of 20 years [1016–36].

Go-Ichijō's personal name was Atsunari. He received the throne (at the age of nine) on the 29th day of the 1st month of 1016.

22. Thenceforth Emperors traditionally made Imperial visits to these four shrines and three others: the Kamo, Iwashimizu Hachiman, and Hirano.

23. Michinaga was a brother of Sanjō's Imperial mother Chōshi as well as a brother of Ichijō's Imperial mother Akiko.

He had been appointed Crown Prince in 1011.²⁴ He was the second son of Emperor Ichijō [66] and celebrated his coming-of-age (at the age of 11) on the 3rd day of the 1st month of 1018. His Imperial mother was FUJIWARA Akikō, Empress Jōtō-mon In [988–1074]. (She was the eldest daughter of Chancellor Michinaga.)

Regent and Minister of the Left: FUJIWARA Michinaga [966–1027].²⁵

(Michinaga was appointed Regent on the 29th day of the 1st month of 1016, and on the 10th day of the 6th month of that same year he was awarded the annual right to make appointments and award ranks, [a right] enjoyed by one of the three ranks of Empresses. Furthermore his wife—MINAMOTO Ason Rinshi, Junior First Rank—was granted households [*fukō*] as well as 30 percent of the annual income received from recommending the bestowal of ranks and appointments to office both inside and outside the capital. On the 7th day of the 11th month, Michinaga resigned as Minister of the Left. On the 16th day of the 3rd month of 1017, he was released upon his own request from the position of Regent.²⁶ In the 12th month of that year he was appointed Prime Minister. On the 3rd day of the 1st month of 1018, he was granted the privilege of entering and leaving the Imperial Palace grounds by palanquin. On the 5th day of the 2nd month of that year he memorialized the throne that he be relieved of all his offices, and on the 21st day of the 3rd month of 1019 he entered the Buddhist priesthood at the

24. Ichijō's eldest son (Prince Atsuyasu) and Sanjō's eldest son (Prince Atsuaki) were in a more direct line of descent, but Go-Ichijō's mother was Michinaga's daughter.

25. Go-Ichijō's ministers were related to his Imperial mother, Jōtō-mon In, as follows:

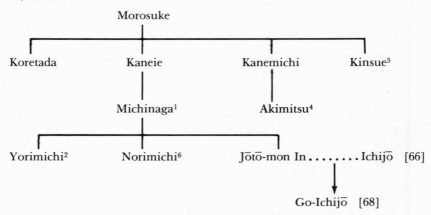

26. His son Yorimichi was appointed Regent on that same day.

age of 54. His Buddhist name was Gyōkan. On the 8th day of the 5th month of that year, an Imperial edict restored to him [the right to make annual appointments, and annual awards of rank, enjoyed by] an Empress. At that time his Buddhist name was changed to Gyōkaku. On the 22nd day of the 3rd month of 1020, the newly built Muryōju Cloister[27] was dedicated. On the 13th day of the 10th month, Michinaga received the Bodhisattva precepts [*bosatsu-kai*] of the Tendai sect. On the 17th day of the 10th month of 1023, he visited the Kongōbu Temple in the province of Kii and on his way paid his respects at the seven great temples in the province of Yamato. He died on the 4th day of the 21st month of 1027 at the age of 62.)

Regent and Minister of the Left: FUJIWARA Yorimichi [992–1074].

(Later Yorimichi became Chancellor. He was appointed Minister of the Center on the 4th day of the 3rd month of 1017 at the age of 26. On the 16th of that same month he was appointed Regent. On the 22nd day of that month he resigned as Senior Commander and was granted an official bodyguard and the privilege of entering and leaving the palace by an ox-drawn cart. On the 22nd day of the 12th month of 1019, he resigned as Regent in order to become Chancellor. He became Minister of the Left in 1021.)

Prime Minister: [KAN'IN] Kinsue [956–1029].

(Kinsue died on the 17th day of the 10th month of 1029 at the age of 73. He was posthumously advanced to Senior First Rank and given the title of Lord Jingi.)

Minister of the Left: FUJIWARA Akimitsu [944–1021].

(Akimitsu died on the 25th day of the 5th month of 1021 at the age of 78. He had previously entered the Buddhist priesthood.)

Minister of the Right: FUJIWARA Sanesuke [957–1046].[28] (Sanesuke was the real third son of Consultant Tadatoshi and the adopted son of Lord Seishin [Saneyori], Minister of the Right. Sanesuke was appointed Minister of the Right on the 25th day of the 7th month of 1021.)

Minister of the Center: FUJIWARA Norimichi [997–1075].

(Norimichi was appointed Senior Commander of the Imperial Bodyguards of the Left on the same 25th day of the 7th month of 1021.)

27. An early name of Hōjō-ji. Its first hall, the Amida Hall, was started in the 1st month of 1020, the year after Michinaga entered the priesthood. Other halls were built, and the entire temple was completed in 1022. Michinaga is commonly referred to as Midō (Grand Hall), another designation for the Amida Hall.

28. Sanesuke was grandson of Morosuke's brother Saneyori, and author of the famous diary, the *Chūyūki*.

The era name was changed to Kannin—which lasted four years [1017–21]—on the 23rd day of the 4th month of 1017. (The first year was *hinoto-mi.*) Retired Emperor Sanjō [67] died (at the age of 42) on the 9th day of the 5th month of Kannin 1 [1017]. On the 2nd day of the 2nd month of 1021, the era name was changed to Jian, which was an era of three years [1021–24]. (The first year was *kanoto-tori.*) On the 13th day of the 7th month of 1024, the era name was changed to Manju, which lasted four years [1024–28]. (The first year was *kinoe-ne.*) On the 25th day of the 7th month of 1028, the era name was changed to Chōgen, which lasted nine years [1028–37]. (The first year was *tsuchinoe-tatsu.*)

   Tendai Abbots:

   High Priest Myōgu [946–1020]. (Abbot of Jōdo-ji.)
   (Myōgu was appointed Tendai Abbot by an Imperial Mandate of the 20th day of the 10th month of 1019, when he was 74. He administered the affairs of Mt. Hiei one year and died on the 5th day of the 7th month of 1020 at the age of 75.)
   Priest First Grade Ingen [954–1028]. (Abbot of Saihō-in.)
   (Ingen became Buddhist Judge and Senior High Priest. He was appointed Tendai Abbot at the age of 70 by an Imperial Mandate issued on the 17th day of the 7th month of 1020. He administered the affairs of Mt. Hiei eight years and died on the 24th day of the 5th month of 1028 at the age of 78.)
   Provisional High Priest Kyōmyō [d. 1038]. (Abbot of Mudō-ji.)
   (Kyōmyō was appointed Tendai Abbot by an Imperial Mandate issued on the 19th day of the 6th month of 1028, when he was 64. He administered Mt. Hiei eleven years and died on the 7th day of the 9th month of Chōryaku 2 [1038] at the age of 75.)[29]

Emperor Go-Ichijō died (at the age of 29) on the 17th day of the 4th month of Chōgen 9 [1036]. He had one Empress and two Imperial daughters. Koichijō-in [son of Emperor Sanjō] had been appointed Crown Prince but resigned during this reign.

   (69) Emperor Go-Suzaku [1009–45]. A reign of nine years [1036–45].

   Go-Suzaku's personal name was Atsunaga. He received the throne (at the age of 28) on the 17th day *(kinoto-ushi)* of the 4th

---

29. When Kyōmyō died, it was rumored that Myōson, a disciple of Chishō and a member of the Church Order, was to be the next Tendai Abbot. But the Tendai priests of the Mountain Order went to Yorimichi's mansion to object, and Kyōen received the appointment. This is referred to as the Chōryaku (1037–40) Incident. [NKBT, 86.386, note 125.] But Myōson replaced Kyōen in 1048.

month of 1036. He had been appointed Crown Prince (at the age of nine) in 1017. Go-Suzaku was the third son of Emperor Ichijō [66]. He had celebrated his coming-of-age (at the age of 11) on the 28th day of the 8th month of 1019. His Imperial mother was Empress Jōtō-mon In.

> *Chancellor and Minister of the Left:* FUJIWARA Yorimichi [992–1074].[30]
>
> *Minister of the Right:* FUJIWARA Sanesuke [957–1046].
>
> (He [had been] Senior Commander of the Imperial Bodyguards of the Right.)
>
> *Minister of the Center:* FUJIWARA Norimichi [997–1075].
>
> (He [had been] Senior Commander of the Imperial Bodyguards of the Left.)

On the 21st day of the 4th month of 1037, the era name was changed to Chōryaku, which was an era of three years [1037–40]. (The first year was *hinoto-ushi.*) On the 10th day of the 11th month of 1040, the era name was changed to Chōkyū, which lasted four years [1040–44]. (The first year was *kanoe-tatsu.*) On the 24th day of the 11th month of 1044, the era name was changed to Kantoku, which was an era of two years [1044–46]. (The first year was *kinoe-saru.*) Emperor Go-Suzaku died on the 18th day of the 1st month of Kantoku 2 [1045] (at the age of 37).

> *Tendai Abbot:* Provisional Senior Vicar General Kyōen [d. 1047]. (Kyōen was appointed Tendai Abbot by an Imperial Mandate issued on the 12th day of the 3rd month of 1039, when he was 61. He administered the affairs of Mt. Hiei nine years and died on the 10th day of the 6th month of 1047 at the age of 70.)

Emperor Go-Suzaku abdicated on the 16th day of the 1st month of Kantoku (2) [1045]. He had five Empresses and seven Imperial sons.

(70) Emperor Go-Reizei [1025–68]. A reign of 23 years [1045–68].

Go-Reizei's personal name was Chikahito. He received the throne (at the age of 21) on the 16th day of the 1st month of 1045. He had been appointed Crown Prince (at the age of 13) on the 17th day of the 8th month of 1037. Go-Reizei was the first son of Emperor Go-Suzaku. He had celebrated his coming-of-age (at 13) on the 2nd day of the 7th month of 1037. His Imperial mother was FUJIWARA *Kishi* [1007–25], Head Mistress of the Court Ladies (she was a younger daughter of FUJIWARA Michinaga). Go-Reizei had three Empresses and no Imperial sons or daughters.

30. Yorimichi served as Regent or Chancellor continuously from 1017 to 1067.

Chancellor and Prime Minister: FUJIWARA Yorimichi [992–1074].[31]
(Yorimichi resigned as Prime Minister on the 2nd day of the 9th
month of 1062, and on the 13th day of the 12th month of 1064
he yielded the headship of the FUJIWARA clan to the Minister of
the Left [Norimichi]. He was still Chancellor and on the 7th day
of the 10th month of 1067 was granted an Empress's [privileges
of making a certain number of annual appointments and annual
advancements in court rank at certain levels]. On the 5th day of
the 12th month of 1067 Yorimichi resigned from his position as
Chancellor, and on the 29th day of the 1st month of 1072 he
entered the Buddhist priesthood at Uji when he was 81.[32] His
Buddhist name was Jakukaku. On the 2nd day of the 2nd
month of 1074 he died at the age of 83, fifty-six years after he
had become Minister.)
Chancellor and Minister of the Left: FUJIWARA Norimichi [997–
1075].
(Norimichi was appointed Minister of the Left in the 7th month
of 1060, and on the 13th day of the 12th month of 1064 he was
made head of the FUJIWARA clan. He was appointed Chancellor
on the 16th day of the 4th month of 1068.)
Ministers of the Right:
    FUJIWARA Sanesuke [957–1046.]
    (Sanesuke died on the 18th day of the 1st month of 1046 at
    the age of 90.)
    FUJIWARA Yorimune [993–1065].
    (Senior Commander of the Imperial Bodyguards of the Right.
    Yorimune was appointed Minister of the Right on the 17th
    day of the 7th month of 1060. Because of illness, he entered
    the Buddhist priesthood on the 5th day of the 1st month of

31. Emperor Go-Reizei's ministers were related to his Imperial mother
Yoshiko as follows:

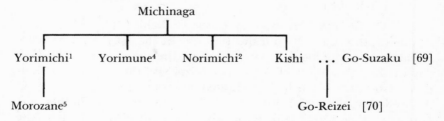

32. Shortly after Yorimichi's resignation and the appointment of his
brother Norimichi as Chancellor, relations between the two brothers became
somewhat strained (see Chapter 2). After Yorimichi entered the priesthood, he resided at the Byōdō-in.

1065 at the age of 73. He died on the 3rd day of the 2nd month of that year.)

FUJIWARA Morozane [1042–1101].

(Senior Commander of the Imperial Bodyguards of the Left. Morozane had been appointed Minister of the Center on the 17th day of the 7th month of 1060 at the age of 19. He was advanced to Minister of the Right on the 3rd day of the 6th month of 1065.)

Minister of the Center: MINAMOTO Morofusa [1009–77].

(Senior Commander of the Imperial Bodyguards of the Right. Morofusa was the third son of Prince Tomohira [son of Emperor Murakami]. He was appointed Minister of the Center on the 3rd day of the 6th month of 1065, when he was 58. On the 6th day of that same month he was concurrently appointed Senior Commander of the Imperial Bodyguards of the Right.)

On the 14th day of the 4th month of 1046, the era name was changed to Eishō, which was an era of seven years [1046–53]. (The first year was *hinoe-inu.*) On the 11th day of the 1st month of 1053, the era name was changed to Tenki, which was five years long [1053–58]. (The first year was *mizunoto-mi.*) On the 29th day of the 8th month of 1058, the era name was changed to Kōhei, which lasted seven years [1058–65]. (The first year was *tsuchinoe-inu.*) On the 2nd day of the 8th month of 1065, the era name was changed to Jiryaku, which was four years long [1065–69]. (The first year was *kinoto-mi.*) Emperor Go-Reizei died (at the age of 44) on the 19th day of the 4th month of Jiryaku 4 [1068].

Tendai Abbots:

Buddhist Judge and Senior High Priest Myōson [971–1063].[33] (Abbot of Shiga.)

(Myōson was appointed Tendai Abbot by an Imperial Mandate issued on the 11th day of the 8th month of 1048, when he was 78.)

Provisional Junior Vicar General Genshin [971–1053].[34] (Abbot of Saimyō-bō at Miidera.)

(Genshin became Provisional Senior Vicar General. He was appointed Tendai Abbot by an Imperial Mandate issued on the 21st day of the 8th month of 1048, when he was 78. He administered the affairs of Mt. Hiei five years and died on the 11th day of the 10th month of 1053 at the age of 83.)

33. Priest of the Church Order. Cf. note 29, above.

34. Not to be confused with the famous Genshin (942–1017) who wrote the *Ōjō yōshū* (Collection of Important Points about Rebirth in Paradise) in 985.

Provisional High Priest Gensen [977–1055]. (Abbot of Miidera.)

(Gensen was appointed Tendai Abbot by an Imperial Mandate issued on the 26th day of the 10th month of 1053, when he was 78.)

Provisional Senior Vicar General Myōkai [987–1070]. (Abbot of Nashimoto.)

(Myōkai became Senior High Priest. He was appointed Tendai Abbot by an Imperial Mandate issued on the 29th day of the 10th month of 1053, when he was 67. He administered Mt. Hiei 17 years.)

(71) Emperor Go-Sanjō [1034–73]. A reign of four years [1068–72].

Go-Sanjō's personal name was Takahito. He received the throne (at the age of 35) on the 19th day of the 4th month of 1068. He had been appointed Crown Prince (at the age of 12) in 1045. He was the second son of Go-Suzaku [69]. Go-Sanjō had celebrated his coming-of-age (at 13) on the 19th day of the 12th month of 1046. His Imperial mother was Teishi, Empress Yōmei-mon In [1012–94]. (She was the third daughter of Emperor Sanjō.)[35]

Chancellor and Prime Minister: FUJIWARA Norimichi [997–1075].[36]

Minister of the Left: FUJIWARA Morozane [1042–1101].

Tendai Abbot: Provisional Senior Vicar General Shōhan [996–1077].[37] (Abbot of Renjitsu-bō.)

(Shōhan became High Priest. He was appointed Tendai Abbot by an Imperial Mandate issued on the 9th day of the 5th month of 1070, when he was 75. He administered the affairs of Mt. Hiei seven years and died on the 27th day of the 1st month of 1077 at the age of 82.)

On the 13th day of the 4th month of 1069, the era name was changed to Enkyū, which ran for five years [1069–74]. (The first

35. Since Teishi's father was Emperor Sanjō, not a FUJIWARA, Go-Sanjō felt independent enough to think of administering state affairs as a Retired Emperor *(insei)*.

36. Although Norimichi had replaced Yorimichi as Chancellor at the beginning of the Go-Sanjō reign, the father of the Imperial mother was a former Emperor, not a FUJIWARA. So the year 1068 is thought of as the beginning point of a sharp decline in FUJIWARA power. Jien saw this (Chapter 2) as a "turning point" in Japanese history and concluded that Japan had entered the Final Age *(yo no sue)* when it was necessary for an Emperor to abdicate and to administer state affairs as a Retired Emperor.

37. The conflict between the Church Order and the Mountain Order became increasingly bitter during and after Shōhan's term.

year was *tsuchinoto-tori.*) It was during this reign that the Hachiman Animal-Freeing Rite *(hōjō-e)* was first held. Likewise it was during this reign that the Emperor first visited the Hie and Inari shrines.

Emperor Go-Sanjō abdicated on the 8th day of the 12th month of Enkyū 4 [1072] and entered the Buddhist priesthood on the 21st day of the 4th month of 1073. His Buddhist name was Kongō-gyō. He died (at the age of 40) on the 7th day of the 5th month of 1073. He had three Empresses and seven Imperial sons and daughters.

(72) Emperor Shirakawa [1053–1129]. A reign of 14 years [1072–86].

Shirakawa's personal name was Sadahito. He received the throne (at the age of 20) on the 8th day of the 12th month of 1072. He had been appointed Crown Prince (at the age of 17) in 1069. He was the first son of Go-Sanjō [71]. He had celebrated his coming-of-age (at 13) on the 9th day of the 12th month of 1065. Shirakawa's Imperial mother was FUJIWARA Moshi [d. 1062], who was post-humously granted the title of Empress Dowager. (She was the adopted daughter of Provisional Senior Counselor Yoshinobu and the real daughter of Middle Counselor Kinnari.)

Chancellor: FUJIWARA Norimichi [997–1075].

(Norimichi died on the 25th day of the 9th month of 1075 at the age of 80.)

Chancellor and Minister of the Left: FUJIWARA Morozane [1042–1101].

(Morozane was appointed Imperial Inspector on the 26th day of the 9th month of 1075 and made head of the FUJIWARA clan on the 3rd day of the 10th month of that same year.[38] On the 15th day of that month he was made Chancellor, and he resigned his position as Minister on the 19th day of the 1st month of 1083.)

Minister of the Center: FUJIWARA Moromichi [1062–99].[39]

(Moromichi was Senior Commander of the Imperial Body-guards of the Left. He was appointed Minister of the Center on the same day [that Morozane resigned as Minister], when he was 22 years old.)

On the 23rd day of the 8th month of 1074, the era name was changed to Shōhō, an era of three years [1074–77]. (The first year was *kinoe-tora.*) Empress Jōtō-mon In died on the 3rd day of the 10th

38. Morozane received these positions after Norimichi's death, although Norimichi had wanted his own son Nobunaga to succeed him. Morozane's advantage arose from having an adopted daughter Kenshi, who was Emperor Shirakawa's Principal Empress. Her son became the future Emperor Horikawa.

39. Morozane's eldest son.

month of Shōhō 1 [1074] at the age of 87. On the 17th day of the
11th month of 1077, the era name was changed to Shōryaku, an era
of four years [1077–81]. (The first year was *hinoto-mi.*) On the 10th
day of the 2nd month of 1081, the era name was changed to Eihō,
an era of three years [1081–84]. (The first year was *kanoto-tori.*) On
the 7th day of the 2nd month of 1084, the era name was changed to
Ōtoku, an era of three years [1084–87]. (The first year was *kinoe-ne.*)

    Tendai Abbots:

    Buddhist Judge and Senior High Priest Kakuen [1031–98].[40]
    (Abbot of Uji.)
    (Kakuen was appointed Tendai Abbot by an Imperial Man-
    date issued on the 5th day of the 2nd month of 1077, when he
    was 57.)
    Provisional Senior Vicar General Kakujin [1012–81]. (Abbot
    of Kongōju-in at Miidera.)
    (Kakujin became Provisional High Priest. He was appointed
    Tendai Abbot by an Imperial Mandate issued on the 7th day
    of the 2nd month of 1077, when he was 66. He administered
    Mt. Hiei four years and died on the 1st day of the 10th month
    of 1081 at the age of 70.)

On the 4th day of the 6th month of this year [1081] came the
burning of Miidera Temple by the monks of Mt. Hiei. Because of
this incident, Tendai Abbot [Kakujin] was rejected by Tendai monks.
The rejection of a Tendai Abbot occurred for the first time during
this reign. Later on, Tendai Abbots were frequently exiled. Details
about this are in another chapter.[41] The Miidera Temple was
burned on the 15th day of the 4th month of 1081.

    Provisional Senior Vicar General Ryōshin [1022–96].
    (Ryōshin became Provisional High Priest. He was appointed
    Tendai Abbot by an Imperial Mandate issued on the 25th day
    of the 10th month of 1081, and he died on the 13th day of
    the 15th month of 1096 at the age of 76.)[42]

Emperor Shirakawa abdicated on the 26th day of the 11th month
of 1086,[43] and he entered the Buddhist priesthood (at the age of 44)
on the 9th day of the 8th month of 1096. He died on the 7th day of
the 7th month of 1129 (at the age of 77). He governed the state

    40. Sixth son of Yorimichi and a disciple of Myōson. Like earlier Abbots
of the Church Order, Kakuen held the post only a few days.
    41. This sentence seems to refer to a secret chapter on the Mountain
Order that is not extant.
    42. At the end of Ryōshin's long term as Tendai Abbot he was chased
from the monastery by his monks, and he resigned two weeks later.
    43. This marks the beginning of the period of Retired Emperor rule
(insei).

more than 50 years. He had one Empress and one Imperial consort and nine Imperial sons and daughters.

Soon after Emperor Go-Sanjō had stepped down from the throne [in 1068], planning to govern the state [as a Retired Emperor], he died. After Shirakawa's abdication, the state was governed for a long time by Retired Emperors. The Hosshō Temple[44] was founded, and the Mahayana Mass and various Buddhist services were held there. This temple is still honored as a clan temple *(ujidera)* of our country's rulers. The disciples of Jikaku [of the Mountain Order] and the disciples of Chishō [of the Church Order] have served as lecturers at the Mahayana Mass in alternate years, whereas priests from the southern capital of Nara have been lecturers at the Imperial Communion *(gosai-e)* and the Yuima Mass.

Retired Emperor Shirakawa celebrated his 50th birthday in the Kōwa era [1099–1104]. And it was during [his administration as Retired Emperor] that Lower and Upper Guards were established at the palace of the Retired Emperor. The Upper Guards included men at the Master's level, and the Lower Guards included many officers *(shoshi* and *suke)* of the Guard Headquarters. Persons of the Lower Guards, armed with bows and arrows, guarded the rear of a Retired Emperor's procession. All later [Retired Emperors] followed this precedent.

(73) Emperor Horikawa [1079–1107]. A reign of 21 years [1086–1107].

Horikawa's personal name was Yoshihito. He received the throne on the 26th day of the 11th month of 1086. Prior to this, but on the same day, he was appointed Crown Prince. Horikawa died (at the age of 29) on the 19th day of the 7th month of 1107. He had two Empresses and three children. He was the second son of Shirakawa [72] and celebrated his coming-of-age (when 11 years old) on the 5th day of the 1st month of 1089. His Imperial mother was Principal Empress Kenshi [d. 1084], (adopted daughter of Great Lord

44. The six "superiority" temples were:

Temple Name	Founder	Date
1. Hosshō-ji (Superiority of Buddhist Law)	Emperor Shirakawa	1077
2. Sonshō-ji (Superiority of Worship)	Emperor Horikawa	1102
3. Saishō-ji (Most Superior)	Emperor Toba	1117
4. Enshō-ji (Superiority of Perfection)	Empress Taiken-mon In (daughter of Emperor Shirakawa)	1128
5. Jōshō-ji (Superiority of Becoming)	Emperor Sutoku	1139
6. Enshō-ji (Superiority of Duration)	Emperor Konoe	1149

Kyōgoku Morozane and the real daughter of Minister of the Right
Akifusa of Rokujō).

Regent and Prime Minister: FUJIWARA Morozane [1042–1101].[45]
(Morozane, who was later Chancellor, was appointed Prime
Minister on the 14th day of the 12th month of 1088. He resigned from his position as Chancellor on the 8th day of the 3rd
month of 1094 and entered the Buddhist priesthood on the
29th day of the 1st month of 1101. He died on the 13th day of
the 2nd month of that same year.)

Chancellor and Minister of the Center: FUJIWARA Moromichi
[1062–99].
(Moromichi was made Chancellor on the 9th day of the 3rd
month of 1094, when he was 33 years old.[46] On the 11th day of
that same month he was made head of the FUJIWARA clan. And
on the 23rd day of that month he was granted an official bodyguard. On the 5th day of the 1st month of 1096 he was advanced
to Junior First Rank. He died on the 28th day of the 6th month of
1099 at the age of 38.)

Minister of the Right: FUJIWARA Tadazane [1078–1162].
(On the 28th day of the 8th month of 1099, when Tadazane was
Senior Counselor, he became Imperial Inspector and head of
the FUJIWARA clan at the age of 22.[47] He was appointed Minister
of the Right on the 17th day of the 7th month of 1100 and was
made Chancellor on the 25th day of the 12th month of 1105,
when he was 28.)

45. Emperor Horikawa's ministers were related to his Imperial mother
Kenshi (adopted daughter of Morozane) as follows:

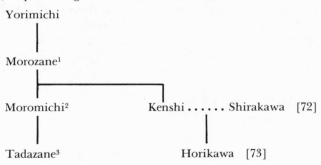

46. As Morozane's son and the adoptive brother of Horikawa's Imperial
mother, Moromichi was appointed Chancellor on the day that his father
Morozane resigned.

47. Tadazane was Moromichi's eldest son, but after the early death of his
father, he was made the adopted son of his grandfather Morozane, making
him the adoptive brother (rather than adoptive nephew) of the Imperial
mother Kenshi.

The era name was changed to Kanji, which lasted seven years [1087–94], on the 7th day of the 4th month of 1087. (The first year was *hinoto-u*). On the 15th day of the 12th month of 1094, the era name was changed to Kahō, an era of two years [1094–96]. (The first year was *kinoe-inu*.) On the 17th day of the 12th month of 1096, the era name was changed to Eichō, an era of one year [1096–97]. (The first year was *hinoe-ne*.) On the 21st day of the 11th month of 1097, the era name was changed to Shōtoku, lasting two years [1097–99]. (The first year was *hinoto-ushi*.) On the 28th day of the 8th month of 1099, the era name was changed to Kōwa, an era of five years [1099–1104]. (The first year was *tsuchinoto-u*.) On the 10th day of the 2nd month of 1104, the era name was changed to Chōji, which was two years long [1104–06]. (The first year was *kinoe-saru*.) On the 9th day of the 4th month, the era name was changed to Kashō, which lasted two years [1106–08]. (The first year was *hinoe-inu*.) Emperor Horikawa died (at the age of 29) on the 19th day of the 7th month of Kashō 2 [1107].

Tendai Abbots:

High Priest Ninkaku [1045–1102].[48] (Abbot of Ichijō-bō.)

(Ninkaku became Senior High Priest. He was appointed Tendai Abbot by an Imperial Mandate issued on the 11th day of the 9th month of 1093, when he was 50. He administered the affairs of Mt. Hiei for nine years and died on the 28th day of the 3rd month of 1102 at the age of 60.)

Priest First Grade, Provisional Senior Vicar General Kyōchō [d. 1107]. (Abbot of Jakujō-bō.)

(Kyōchō was appointed Tendai Abbot by an Imperial Mandate issued on the 13th day of the intercalary 5th month of 1102, when he was 76. He administered Mt. Hiei for three years and died on the 24th day of the 9th month of 1107 at the age of 81.)

High Priest Zōyo [1032–1116]. (Abbot of Ichijō-bō at Miidera.)

(Zōyo was appointed Tendai Abbot by an Imperial Mandate issued on the 14th day of the intercalary 2nd month of 1105, when he was 74.)

Priest First Grade Ningen [d. 1109]. (Abbot of Richi-bō.)

(Ningen became Provisional High Priest. He was appointed Tendai Abbot by an Imperial Mandate issued on the 17th day of the same intercalary 2nd month of 1105, when he was 48. He administered Mt. Hiei four years and died on the 9th day of the 3rd month of 1109 at the age of 52.)

The Sonshō Temple[49] was built [during this reign], and the Bap-

48. Son of MINAMOTO Morofusa.
49. Cf. note 44, above.

tismal Hall *(Kanjō Dō)* was built at which the Womb-store World Baptism and the Diamond World Baptism[50] were held in alternate years. Followers of Jikaku [of the Mountain Order] and of Chishō [of the Church Order] were designated Baptism Masters *(kanjō azari)*. Followers of Grand Preceptor Kōbō were designated [Baptism Masters for baptisms held at] the Kwannon Cloister of the Ninna Temple. After consultations, this arrangement was made.

On the 30th day of the 10th month of 1105, the priests of Mt. Hiei first took the portable shrine of the Hie Shrine and went down [to the foot of the mountain to make a protest. In the 6th month], Provisional Governor General FUJIWARA Suenaka and the Intendant Mitsukiyo of the Iwashimizu Hachiman Shrine, conspiring together, had shot at the portable shrine of the Kamado Shrine and killed Priest Entoku, a minor official *(sendō)* [on Mt. Hiei]. The priests came down to protest [the shooting of Entoku]. They went first to the Kyōgoku Temple and then brandished the portable shrine at the Taiken Gate of the Imperial Palace grounds. . . . Suenaka was sent into exile and Mitsukiyo was dismissed from his posts on the same 1st day. Since the Iwashimizu Hachiman Shrine also protested [the punishment of its priest], Mitsukiyo was reinstated on the 3rd day of the same month. It is heard that the first time priests of Mt. Hiei went down the mountain to make a protest was in 1092, but that is not so. The priests carried their portable shrine as far as the Central Hall [of the Enryaku Temple] in the 11th month of 1095,[51] but in that case too they did not go down to the capital. . . . In 1092 their complaint was against FUJIWARA Tamefusa [1049–1115], and in 1095 against MINAMOTO Yoshitsuna [d. 1134].

(74) Emperor Toba [1103–56]. A reign of 16 years [1107–23].

Toba's personal name was Munehito. He received the throne on the 19th day of the 7th month of 1107 (at the age of five). He had been appointed Crown Prince in the 8th month of 1103 (at the age of one). Toba abdicated (at the age of 21) on the 28th day of the 1st

50. In esoteric Buddhism, the Womb-store World *(taizō-kai)* mandala symbolized the principles *(ri)* of Dainichi Nyorai, and the Diamond World *(kongō-kai)* symbolized his knowledge *(chi)*.

51. The incident of 1095 arose out of a dispute with government officials that led to military conflict and bloodshed. The irate priests apparently did enter the capital but probably did not reach the palace because of military resistance. Some priests were killed and the current Tendai Abbot (Ninkaku) and his monks withdrew, taking the portable shrine to the Central Hall of Enryaku-ji, where a curse was put on Chancellor Moromichi. [NKBT, 32; *Heike Monogatari*, 1.129–130.]

month of 1123,⁵² and he died (at the age of 54) on the 2nd day of
the 7th month of 1156. Emperor Toba, the eldest son of Emperor
Horikawa, celebrated his coming of age (at the age of 11) on the 1st
day of the 1st month of 1113. He had three Empresses and 14 children. His Imperial mother was FUJIWARA Shishi [d. 1103], posthumously appointed Principal Empress. (She was the daughter of
Senior Counselor FUJIWARA Sanesue.)

> *Regent and Prime Minister:* FUJIWARA Tadazane [1078–1162].⁵³
> (Tadazane was appointed Regent on the 19th day of the 7th
> month of 1107 and Prime Minister on the 14th day of the 12th
> month of 1112. He resigned [as Prime Minister] on the 14th day
> of the 4th month of 1113, and on the 26th day of the 12th
> month [of 1113] he gave up his position as Regent and was
> made Chancellor. He resigned [as Chancellor]⁵⁴ on the 23rd day
> of the 2nd month of 1121.)
> *Chancellor and Minister of the Left:* FUJIWARA Tadamichi [1097–
> 1164].
> (Tadamichi was appointed Chancellor on the 5th day of the 3rd
> month of 1121 at the age of 25. He was granted the ox-drawn
> cart privileges and appointed Minister of the Left on the 17th
> day of the 12th month of 1122. Before that he had been Minis-
> ter of the Center.)

The era name was changed to Ten'nin, which lasted two years
[1108–10], on the 3rd day of the 8th month of 1108. (The first year
was *tsuchinoe-ne.*) On the 16th day of the 7th month of 1110, the era
name was changed to Ten'ei, an era of three years [1110–13]. (The
first year was *kanoe-tora.*) On the 13th day of the 7th month of 1113,
the era name was changed to Eikyū, which lasted five years [1113–
18]. (The first year was *mizunoto-mi.*) On the 3rd day of the 4th
month of 1118, the era name was changed to Gen'ei, an era of two
years [1118–20]. (The first year was *tsuchinoe-inu.*) On the 10th day
of the 4th month of 1120, the era name was changed to Hōan, an
era of four years [1120–24]. (The first year was *kanoe-ne.*)

> *Tendai Abbots:*
> Priest First Grade Kenzen [d. 1112]. (Abbot of Kyō-ō-bō.)
> (Kenzen was appointed Tendai Abbot by an Imperial Man-
> date issued on the 20th day of the 3rd month of 1109, when

52. Retired Emperor Shirakawa forced Toba to yield the throne to Toba's
five-year-old son Sutoku.
53. Tadazane was only distantly related to the Imperial mother but was
the eldest son of the previous Regent, Moromichi.
54. He was forced to resign because he had angered Retired Emperor
Shirakawa. The position of Chancellor was given to Tadazane's son
Tadamichi.

he was 81. He administered Mt. Hiei one year and died on the 23rd day of the 12th month of 1112 at the age of 85.)
Provisional Senior Vicar General Ningō [d. 1121]. (Abbot of Nanshō-bō.)
(Ningō became Provisional High Priest. He was appointed Tendai Abbot by an Imperial Mandate issued on the 12th day of the 5th month of 1110, when he was 60. He administered Mt. Hiei 11 years and died on the 4th day of the 10th month of 1121 at the age of 72. The Miidera Temple burned down in the 6th month of that year. This was the second time it had been burned.)[55]
Provisional High Priest Kankei. (Abbot of Daijō-bō.)
(Kankei was appointed Tendai Abbot by an Imperial Mandate issued on the 6th day of the 10th month of 1121, when he was 78. He administered Mt. Hiei two years.)

The Saishō Temple was founded [during this reign], and [it is said] that both types of baptisms were first held at the Sonshō Temple [then]. . . . The Emperor's 50th birthday was celebrated in the Ninbyō era [1151–54]. When Emperor Toba went on a pilgrimage to the Kumano Shrines, he was accompanied by Minister of the Right Naka-no-in (Munetada) and Minister of the Left (Arihito of) Hanazono.[56] There was the unspeakably [gay] affair of the Emperor himself playing the flute while he had the Minister of the Right perform the sake-drinking dance and the Minister of the Left play the *shō*. MINAMOTO Sukekata played the large hand-drum.

(75) Emperor Sutoku [1119–64]. A reign of 18 years [1123–41].

Sutoku's personal name was Akihito. He received the throne (at the age of five) on the 28th day of the 1st month of 1123. He had never been appointed Crown Prince, and he abdicated on the 7th day of the 12th month of 1141. Sutoku was the first son of Emperor Toba and celebrated his coming-of-age (at 11) on the 1st day of the 1st month of 1129. His Imperial mother was Shōshi, Empress Taiken-mon In [1101–45]. (She was the adopted daughter of Retired Emperor Shirakawa and the real daughter of Senior Counselor Kinzane.)
Former Chancellor: FUJIWARA Tadazane [1078–1162].
(By an Imperial edict issued on the 10th day of the 2nd month of 1140 Tadazane was granted the privilege of entering the middle palace gates by palanquin, and on the 5th day of the 6th

55. It was first burned in 1081.
56. Toba made 21 pilgrimages to the Kumano shrines. This one was made in 1134, 11 years after he abdicated.

month [of that same year] he was granted the privileges enjoyed by an Empress.[57] On the 2nd day of the 10th month [of that year] he entered the Buddhist priesthood—taking the Buddhist name of Enri—at the age of 63. He died on the 18th day of the 6th month of 1162 at the age of 85.)

Regent and Prime Minister: FUJIWARA Tadamichi [1097–1164].

(Tadamichi later became Chancellor.[58] He was appointed Prime Minister in the 12th month of 1128 and resigned on the 10th day of the 4th month of 1129.)

Minister of the Center: FUJIWARA Yorinaga [1120–56].[59]

(Yorinaga was Senior Commander of the Imperial Bodyguards of the Left. He was appointed Minister of the Center in the 12th month of 1136 at the age of 17.)

The era name was changed to Tenji, which was an era of two years [1124–26], on the 3rd day of the 4th month of 1124. (The first year was *kinoe-tatsu.*) On the 22nd day of the 1st month of 1126, the era name was changed to Daiji, which lasted five years [1126–31]. (The first year was *hinoe-uma.*) Retired Emperor Shirakawa [72] died (at the age of 77) on the 7th day of the 7th month of Daiji 4 [1129]. On the 29th day of the 1st month of 1131, the era name was changed to Tenshō, which was an era of one year [1131–32]. (The first year was *kanoto-i.*) On the 11th day of the 8th month of 1132, the era name was changed to Chōshō, which was three years long [1132–35]. (The first year was *mizunoe-ne.*) On the 27th day of the 4th month of 1135, the era name was changed to Hōen, which lasted six years [1135–41]. (The first year was *kinoto-u.*) On the 10th day of the 7th month of 1141, the era name was changed to Eiji, an era of one year [1141–42]. (The first year was *kanoto-tori.*)

Tendai Abbots:

High Priest Gyōson [1057–1135]. (Abbot of Byōdō-in of Miidera.)

(Gyōson was appointed Tendai Abbot by an Imperial Mandate issued on the 18th day of the 12th month of 1123, when he was 69. He paid his respects at the Imperial Court on the 23rd day of that month. . . . He resigned on that same day.)

Priest First Grade Ninjitsu [1090–1131]. (Abbot Second Grade.)

(Ninjitsu became High Priest. He was appointed Tendai Abbot by an Imperial Mandate issued on the 30th day of the

57. When Retired Emperor Shirakawa died in 1129, Tadazane was restored to favor.

58. Although Tadazane had been restored to favor, his son Tadamichi continued on as Chancellor for Emperor Sutoku, who celebrated his coming-of-age in 1129.

59. Young brother, and adopted son, of Tadamichi.

12th month of 1123, when he was 33. He administered Mt.
Hiei seven years and died on the 8th day of the 6th month of
1131 at the age of 41.)
Priest First Grade and Provisional Senior Vicar General Chū-
jin [1065–1138].
(Chūjin became Buddhist Judge and Senior High Priest. He
was appointed Tendai Abbot by an Imperial Mandate issued
on the 29th day of the 12th month of 1130, when he was 66.
He administered Mt. Hiei eight years and died on the 14th
day of the 10th month of 1138 at the age of 74.)
Senior High Priest Kakuyū. (Abbot of Toba.)
(Kakuyū became Buddhist Judge. He was appointed Tendai
Abbot by an Imperial Mandate issued on the 28th day of the
10th month of 1138, when he was 86.)
Buddhist Judge and Provisional High Priest Gyōgen [1097–
1155]. (Abbot of Mii Temple.)
(Gyōgen became Senior High Priest. He was appointed Tendai Abbot by an Imperial Mandate issued on the 29th day of
the 10th month of 1138, when he was 42, and he administered Mt. Hiei 17 years. He died on the 5th day of the 11th
month of 1155 at the age of 59.)
   Mii Temple was burned [by the priests of Enryaku Temple] a
third time on the 14th day of the 4th month of 1140. After Sutoku
abdicated on the 7th day of the 12th month of 1141, he seems not to
have done anything according to the wishes of Retired Emperor
Toba. Events following the death of Retired Emperor [Toba] are
detailed in [Chapter 2]. While Sutoku was on the throne, the Jōshō
Temple was built.

   (76) Emperor Konoe [1139–55]. A reign of 14 years [1141–
   55].

   Konoe's personal name was Narihito. He received the throne
on the 7th day of the 12th month of 1141 (at the age of three). He
had been appointed Crown Prince on the 17th day of the 8th month
of 1139 (at the age of one). He was the eighth son of Retired Emperor Toba and celebrated his coming-of-age (at 12) on the 4th day
of the 1st month of 1150. It is recorded that he was crowned by
Lord Hōshō-ji (Tadamichi), that his hair was cut by the Minister of
the Left of Uji (Yorinaga), and that preparations for crowning were
made by the provisional Controller of the Right, FUJIWARA Mitsuyori. . . . Konoe's Imperial mother was Tokushi [1117–60], Empress Bifuku-mon In (who was the daughter of Middle Counselor
Nagazane, posthumously promoted to Minister of the Left).[60] Em-

   60. Beginning with the Go-Sanjō reign in 1068, the Imperial mother was
no longer a sister or daughter of the current Regent or Chancellor. As Jien

peror Konoe died on the 23rd day of the 7th month of 1155 (at the age of 17).

Regent: FUJIWARA Tadamichi [1099–1164].

(Tadamichi later became Chancellor. He gave up the headship of the FUJIWARA clan on the 26th day of the 9th month of 1150, and on the 9th day of the 12th month was made Chancellor.)

Prime Minister: [SANJŌ] Saneyuki [1079–1162].⁶¹

(Saneyuki was the second son of Kinzane. He was appointed Minister of the Right on the 27th day of the 8th month of 1149, when he was 70, and was appointed Prime Minister on the 21st day of the 8th month of 1150.)

Minister of the Left: FUJIWARA Yorinaga [1120–56].

(Yorinaga was appointed Minister of the Left on the 28th day of the 7th month of 1149, when he was 30. He received the head-ship of the FUJIWARA clan on the 26th day of the 9th month of 1150, and on the 10th day of the 1st month of 1151 an Imperial decree was issued appointing him Imperial Inspector.)⁶²

Minister of the Left: MINAMOTO Arihito [1103–47].

(Arihito was a son of Prince Sukehito and was Senior Commander of the Imperial Bodyguards of the Right. He was later promoted to Senior Commander of the Imperial Bodyguards of the Left. On the 17th day of the 12th month of 1122 he was appointed Minister of the Center, and on the 22nd day of the 12th month of 1131 he was promoted to Minister of the Right. On the 9th day of the 12th month of 1136 he was advanced to Minister of the Left. Arihito entered the Buddhist priesthood on the 3rd day of the 2nd month of 1147, at the age of 45, and died on the 13th day of the same month.)

On the 28th day of the 4th month of 1142, the era name was changed to Kōji, which was an era two years long [1142–44]. (The first year was *mizunoe-inu*.) On the 22nd day of the 2nd month of 1144, the era name was changed to Tenyō, which lasted one year [1144–45]. (The first year was *kinoe-ne*.) On the 22nd day of the 7th

---

wrote (Chapter 2), the Imperial mother's relationship to the Regent/Chancellor house was a bit remote. But the relationship became more remote in later reigns. Konoe's Imperial mother Tokushi (Bifuku-mon In), was only the daughter of a Middle Counselor who is not considered important enough to be listed in biographical dictionaries. After the Hōgen Rebellion of 1156, the connection between the current Regent or Chancellor and the Imperial mother was more remote still.

61. Saneyuki was the Imperial mother's brother. That relationship no longer entitled a man to be Regent or Chancellor, but did entitle him to the honorary position of Prime Minister.

62. Tadamichi was removed from his position as head of the FUJIWARA clan in 1150 because of a falling out with his father, who favored the younger son Yorinaga.

month of 1145, the era name was changed to Kyūan, which lasted
six years [1145–51]. (The first year was *kinoto-ushi*.) On the 26th day
of the 1st month of 1151, the era name was changed to Ninbyō, an
era of three years [1151–54]. (The first year was *kanoto-hitsuji*.) On
the 28th day of the 10th month of 1154, the era name was changed
to Kyūju, which was two years long [1154–56]. (The first year was
kinoe-inu.) Emperor Konoe died on the 23rd day of the 7th month of
Kyūju 2 [1155].

The Enshō (Superiority of Duration) Temple was built [during
this reign]. After that, we do not hear of such Imperial-prayer temples being built by each new Emperor. With the addition of the
Enshō (Superiority of Perfection) Temple—built by Empress
Taiken-mon In—to the five *shō* (Superiority) Temples built by five
Emperors, we have "the six *shō* temples."[63] During this reign, there
emerged such incidents as the one in which Retired Emperor Toba
managed to have an Imperial decree issued appointing Minister of
the Left Yorinaga to the position of Imperial Inspector. Was not this
the beginning of what was to become a great disturbance? Events
following this reign are dealt with in detail in [Chapter 3].

(77) Emperor Go-Shirakawa [1127–92]. A reign of three
years [1155–58].

Go-Shirakawa's personal name was Masahito. He received
the throne on the 24th day *(tsuchinoto-mi)* of the 7th month of 1155
(at the age of 29). He had not been appointed Crown Prince. He
abdicated (at the age of 32) on the 11th day of the 8th month of
1158. He was the fourth son of Retired Emperor Toba and celebrated his coming-of-age ceremony (when 13 years old) on the 27th
day of the 12th month of 1139. His mother was the same as that of
Emperor Sutoku.

Chancellor: FUJIWARA Tadamichi [1097–1164].

(Tadamichi was [again] made head of the FUJIWARA clan on the
11th day of the 7th month of 1156.[64] He entered the Buddhist
priesthood at the age of 66 on the 8th day of the 6th month of
1162 and died on the 19th day of the 2nd month of 1164 at the
age of 68.)

Prime Minister: [SANJŌ] Saneyuki [1079–1162].

(Saneyuki resigned on the 9th day of the 8th month of 1157.)

Minister of the Left: FUJIWARA Yorinaga [1120–56].

(Yorinaga was Imperial Inspector and head of the FUJIWARA
clan. He met the Imperial army in battle on the 11th day of the

63. Cf. note 44, above.
64. He was reinstated after the Hōgen Rebellion of 1156, when the forces
of Retired Emperor Sutoku and Yorinaga were defeated.

7th month of 1156 and died on the 14th day of the same month
at the age of 37.)

On the 24th day of the 4th month of 1156, the era name was
changed to Hōgen, which was an era of three years [1156–59]. (The
first year was *hinoe-ne*.) Retired Emperor Toba died on the 2nd day
of the 7th month of Hōgen 1 [1156] (at the age of 54).

Tendai Abbot: Provisional High Priest Saiun [1105–62].

(Saiun was a Prince without a court rank. From the start [of his
priestly career] he was Priest First Grade. He was appointed
Tendai Abbot by an Imperial Mandate issued on the 30th day of
the 3rd month of 1156, when he was 53. He administered Mt.
Hiei six years. He died on the 16th day of the 2nd month of
1162.)

Emperor Go-Shirakawa entered the Buddhist priesthood (at the
age of 42) in the 6th month of 1169, taking the Buddhist name of
Gyōshin, and died (at the age of 66) on the 13th day of the 3rd
month of 1192.

By a request of this Emperor, 1000 statues of the Thousand-
armed Kwannon[65] were presented to the Hōjū Temple; and His
Majesty built a Great Hall *(midō)* called the Renge-ō Cloister. It is
written that there were such miracles as *argha* water gushing forth.
. . . During this entire reign the state was in constant turmoil. Details
are given in [Chapter 3]. This Emperor became a Master Teacher
for Life *(isshin azari)* and was eventually baptized. His Majesty's priest
was Senior High Priest Kōken, a follower of Grand Preceptor
Chishō.

(78) Emperor Nijō [1143–65]. A reign of seven years
[1158–65].

Nijō's personal name was Morihito. He received the throne
(at the age of 16) on the 11th day of the 8th month of 1158. He had
been appointed Crown Prince (at the age of 13) on the 23rd day of
the 9th month of 1155. Nijō was the eldest son of Go-Shirakawa and
celebrated his coming-of-age ceremony on the 9th day of the 12th
month of 1155. His mother was Imperial Consort Yoshiko (the
daughter of Senior Counselor [ŌIMIKADO] Tsunezane).

Chancellor and Minister of the Left: [KONOE] Motozane [1143–66].[66]
(Motozane received an Imperial edict of appointment as Chancellor on the day that Go-Shirakawa yielded the throne to Nijō,
when Motozane was 16 years old. He was appointed Minister of
the Left on the 11th day of the 8th month of 1160 and resigned

65. Actually the statue had only 40 arms, but each represented 25 measures of compassion.

66. Son of Tadamichi and founder of the KONOE house.

from the office of Minister of the Left on the 17th day of the
intercalary 10th month of 1164.)

On the 20th day of the 4th month of 1159, the era name was
changed to Heiji, an era of one year [1159–60]. (The first year was
tsuchinoto-u.) On the 10th day of the 1st month of 1160, the era name
was changed to Eiryaku, an era of one year [1160–61]. (The first
year was *kanoe-tatsu.*) On the 4th day of the 9th month of 1161, the
era name was changed to Ōho, which lasted two years [1161–63].
(The first year was *kanoto-mi.*) Lord Chishoku In (Tadazane) died on
the 18th day of the 6th month of Ōho 2 [1162]. On the 29th day of
the 3rd month of 1163, the era name was changed to Chōkan, an era
of two years [1162–64]. (The first year was *mizunoto-hitsuji.*) Lord
Hōshō-ji (Tadamichi) died on the 19th day of the 2nd month of
Chōkan 2 [1164] (at the age of 68). Retired Emperor Sutoku died on
the 26th day of the 8th month of Chōkan 2 [1164] (at the age of 46).
On the 5th day of the 6th month of 1164, the era name was changed
to Eiman, an era of one year [1164–65]. (The first year was *kinoto-
tori.*) Emperor Nijō died (at the age of 22) on the 28th day of the 7th
month of Eiman 1 [1165]. He had abdicated in the 6th month of that
year.

Tendai Abbots:

Provisional High Priest Kakuchū [1118–77]. (Abbot Hase of
Miidera.)

(Kakuchū became Buddhist Judge and Senior High Priest. He
was appointed Tendai Abbot by an Imperial Mandate issued
on the 30th day of the 2nd month of 1162, when he was 45.)

Provisional High Priest Jūyu [d. 1164]. (Abbot Zenchi-bō.)

(Jūyu was appointed Tendai Abbot by an Imperial Mandate
issued on the 3rd day of the intercalary 2nd month of 1162,
when he was 68. He administered Mt. Hiei one year and died
on the 13th day of the 1st month of 1164.)

Provisional High Priest Kaishū [d. 1172].[67] (Later Abbot of
Honkaku-in.)

(Kaishū became Buddhist Judge and Senior High Priest. He
was appointed Tendai Abbot by an Imperial Mandate issued
on the 25th day of the 5th month of 1162, when he was 65.
He administered Mt. Hiei two years. The Miidera burned, for
the fourth time, on the 2nd day of the 9th month of 1165.)

Provisional High Priest Shun'en [d. 1166].

(Shun'en was appointed Tendai Abbot by an Imperial Mandate issued on the 13th day of the intercalary 10th month of

67. He was chased from Mt. Hiei, and his residential hall destroyed, in
1164.

1164, when he was 56. He administered Mt. Hiei two years
and died on the 28th day of the 8th month of 1166.)

(79) Emperor Rokujō [1164–76]. A reign of three years
[1165–68].

Rokujō's personal name was Nobuhito. He received the
throne on the 25th day of the 6th month of 1165 and abdicated (at
the age of four) in 1168. He died on the 19th day of the 7th month
of 1176 (at the age of 13). He never celebrated his coming-of-age.
Rokujō was a son of Emperor Nijō. Who his Imperial mother was is
not clear. (It was Secondary Empress Ikushi [1146–73].[68] Another
account says that she was the daughter of Minister of the Right
FUJIWARA Kinyoshi.) Rokujō received the throne because he was said
to be the son of the Secondary Empress. We read that it was a con-
cealed fact that he was the son of a daughter of IKI Munetō, Vice
Minister of the Treasury. . . .
Regent: [KONOE] Motozane [1143–66].
(Motozane died on the 26th day of the 7th month of 1166 at the
age of 24.)
Regent: [MATSU] Motofusa [1144–1230].
(Motofusa became Regent on the 27th day of the 7th month of
1166[69] and resigned his position as Minister of the Left on the
4th day of the 11th month in that same year.)
Prime Minister: FUJIWARA Koremichi [1093–1165].[70]
(Koremichi resigned from [his position as Prime Minister] be-
cause of illness in the 2nd month of 1165. He entered the
Buddhist priesthood on the 11th day of that month and died on
the 15th at the age of 73.)
Prime Minister: TAIRA Kiyomori [1118–81].[71]
(Kiyomori was the eldest son of Tadamori, Minister of the Department of Justice. He was appointed Minister of the Center
on the 11th day of the 11th month of 1166 and Prime Minister

68. She had been adopted by FUJIWARA Tadamichi and made Emperor
Nijō's principal Empress.
69. KONOE Motozane's son Motomichi (1160–1233) was considered too
young for the position at the time. Motozane's young brother was therefore
given the post.
70. He had been named Prime Minister in 1160 during the Nijō reign.
He was not a direct descendant of Yorimichi but of Yorimichi's young
brother Yorimune.
71. Kiyomori had been head of the TAIRA clan since 1153, but only after
victories of the Heiji Uprising of 1159–60 did he receive high positions at
the Imperial Court.

on the 11th day of the 2nd month of 1167. He resigned in that
same year.)

Minister of the Left: [ŌIMIKADO] Tsunemune [1119–89].[72]

(Tsunemune was appointed on the 11th day of the 11th month
of 1166.)

Minister of the Right: [KUJŌ] Kanezane [1149–1207].[73]

(Kanezane was granted an official bodyguard and was appointed
Minister of the Right on the same day that Tsunemune was appointed Minister of the Left.)

Minister of the Center: FUJIWARA Tadamasa.

(Tadamasa was Senior Commander of the Imperial Bodyguards
of the Right. He was a grandson of Ietada and son of Middle
Counselor Tadaie, and he was appointed Minister of the Center
on the 11th day of the 2nd month of 1167.)

On the 27th day of the 8th month of 1166, the era name was
changed to Nin'an, an era of three years [1166–69]. (The first year
was *hinoe-inu.*)

Tendai Abbots:

High Priest Kaishū [d. 1172].

(Kaishū was the first man to be reappointed Tendai Abbot.
He was reappointed by an Imperial Mandate issued on the
2nd day of the 9th month of 1166, and he administered Mt.
Hiei [this time] one year. He died on the 12th day of the 6th
month of 1172, having lived six years after retirement.)

Priest First Grade Myōun [d. 1183].

(Myōun became Buddhist Judge and Senior High Priest. He
was appointed Tendai Abbot by an Imperial Mandate issued
on the 15th day of the 2nd month of 1167, when he was 52.
He administered Mt. Hiei 10 years. He was exiled in the 5th
month of 1177, but the priests of Mt. Hiei intercepted him at
Seta and took him back to Mt. Hiei.)

(80) Emperor Takakura [1161–81]. A reign of 12 years
[1168–80].

Takakura's personal name was Norihito. He received the
throne (at the age of eight) on the 19th day of the 2nd month of
1168. He had been appointed Crown Prince (at the age of seven) on

72. Brother of Nijō's Imperial mother Yoshiko. Although a maternal
uncle of Emperor Nijō, he was not made Regent or Chancellor.

73. Third son of Tadamichi and young brother of KONOE Motozane and
MATSU Motofusa. He was also the elder brother of Kanefusa and two famous priests: Shin'en and Jien (author of the *Gukanshō*). Kanezane was to become Regent in 1185 after the position was first held by sons of his elder
brothers (Motomichi and Moroie) and after he received the backing of
MINAMOTO Yoritomo.

the 10th day of the 10th month of 1167. (According to the *Hyakuren
Shō*, he was appointed Crown Prince in 1166.) Takakura was the
fifth son of Retired Emperor Go-Shirakawa [77] and celebrated his
coming-of-age (when he was eleven) on the 3rd day of the 1st month
of 1171. He abdicated on the 21st day of the 2nd month of 1180.
His Imperial mother was TAIRA Shigeko, Empress Kenshun-mon In
[1142–76].

Regent: [MATSU] Motofusa [1144–1230].

(Motofusa later became Chancellor, receiving the appointment
as Chancellor on the 27th day of the 12th month of 1172. His
appointments as Chancellor and head of the FUJIWARA clan
were cancelled on the 16th day of the 11th month of 1179. On
the 18th day of the same month he was demoted to Provisional
Governor General at Dazaifu. During that same month, while he
was sailing westward, he entered the Buddhist priesthood in the
neighborhood of Kawajiri when he was 35 years old. After that,
he stayed in the province of Bizen. In 1181, he received an Imperial order to return to the capital.)

Chancellor and Minister of the Center: [KONOE] Motomichi [1160–
1233].

(Motomichi was appointed Minister of the Center on the 14th
day of the 11th month of 1179.[74] Before that, he had been a
Middle Commander Second Rank. He was made Chancellor
and head of the FUJIWARA clan on the 16th day of that same
month, when he was 20 years old.)

Prime Minister: FUJIWARA Tadamasa.

(Tadamasa was appointed to this position on the 10th day of the
8th month of 1168 and resigned in the 6th month of 1170.)

Prime Minister: FUJIWARA Moronaga [1137–92].

(Moronaga had been appointed Minister of the Center on the
10th day of the 11th month of 1175. He was appointed Prime
Minister on the 5th day of the 3rd month of 1177 and resigned
from that post on the 17th day of the 11th month of 1179. He
was exiled to the province of Owari for his involvement in an
affair, and entered the Buddhist priesthood.)

Minister of the Left: [ŌIMIKADO] Tsunemune [1119–89].

Minister of the Right: [KUJŌ] Kanezane [1149–1207].

(Kanezane was granted an official bodyguard.)

Minister of the Center: MINAMOTO Masamichi [d. 1175].

(Masamichi was a Senior Commander of the Imperial Body-

74. This occurred after TAIRA Kiyomori entered the capital to put down
the anti-TAIRA forces that had gathered around Retired Emperor Go-
Shirakawa. After this victory, Kiyomori got the court to remove Motofusa
from his post as Chancellor and to appoint KONOE Motomichi (Motozane's
son).

guards of the Right and was the eldest son of Senior Counselor
Akimichi and the adopted son of Masasada. Masamichi was appointed Minister of the Center on the 10th day of the 8th
month of 1168. He died at the age of 58 on the 27th day of the
2nd month of 1175.)

Minister of the Center: TAIRA Shigemori [1138–79].[75]

(Shigemori was Senior Commander of the Imperial Bodyguards
of the Left and was appointed Minister of the Center on the 5th
day of the 3rd month of 1177. He resigned his position as
Senior Commander on the 5th day of the 6th month and resigned [his position as Minister of the Center] on the 11th day of
the 3rd month of 1179. Shigemori entered the Buddhist priesthood on the 25th day of the 5th month of that same year and
died on the 1st day of the 8th month.)

On the 8th day of the 4th month of 1169, the era name was
changed to Kaō, an era of two years [1169–71]. (The first year was
tsuchinoto-ushi.) On the 21st day of the 4th month of 1171, the era
name was changed to Shōan, an era of four years [1171–75]. (The
first year was *kanoto-u.*) On the 28th day of the 7th month of 1175,
the era name was changed to Angen, an era of two years [1175–77].
(The first year was *kinoto-hitsuji.*) On the 4th day of the 8th month of
1177, the era name was changed to Jishō, which lasted four years
[1177–81]. (The first year was *hinoto-tori.*)

Tendai Abbots:

Prince Master-Teacher Kakukai [1134–81].[76]

(Kakukai was appointed Tendai Abbot by an Imperial Mandate issued on the 11th day of the 5th month of 1177, when
he was 44 years old. He administered Mt. Hiei two years and
resigned on the 17th day of the 11th month of 1179. But it is
recorded that the date [of his resignation] was changed. . . . It
is also written that this matter is unclear. . . . Kakukai died on
the 6th day of the 11th month of 1181, living three years after
retirement.)

High Priest Myōun [d. 1183].[77]

(Myōun was [re]appointed Tendai Abbot by an Imperial
Mandate issued on the 16th day of the 11th month of 1179,
when he was 65 years old. He administered Mt. Hiei four
years [in this term] and died on the 19th day of the 11th

75. Eldest son of Kiyomori and hero of the *Heike monogatari.* Cf. Chapter 8.

76. Seventh son of Emperor Toba.

77. This was his second term. Myōun was reappointed because TAIRA
Kiyomori, who received the Buddhist precepts from Myōun, had regained
ascendancy at the Imperial Court.

month of 1183 at the age of 69. The circumstances of his
violent death are unspeakable.)

In 1173, Emperor Takakura's Imperial mother, Empress Kenshun-mon In, [participated in] a great mass for the dedication of
her Great Hall *(midō)* called the Saishōkō Cloister. The presiding
priest was Kakuchin, and the prayer chanter *(jugan)* was Myōun. In
1177, the Imperial Council Hall burned down. After it had been
built by the sage ruler *(seishu)* Go-Sanjō, it was repaired in the Hōgen
era [1156–59]. Now it was burned. The fire, which broke out at the
intersection of Higuchi and Kyōgoku, unexpectedly jumped to the
palace grounds. The area in between was not burned. After Takakura abdicated, he went to Itsukishima in the province of Aki.[78] It
was heard that Prime-Minister Lay-Priest TAIRA Kiyomori had seized
control of the state and had done such things as move the capital [to
Fukuhara],[79] and that when [he went to Itsukushima] he took
[Takakura] with him. [Takakura] wrote out a prayer in his own hand
and participated in a Buddhist rite. Takakura was a scholar who excelled in Chinese literature. He composed Chinese poems and had a
liking for miscellaneous writings *(zappitsu)*. He wrote many such
things as "petitions of Ladies in Waiting."

(81) Emperor Antoku [1178–85]. A reign of three years
[1180–83].

Antoku's personal name was Tokihito. He received the
throne (at the age of three) on the 21st day of the 2nd month of
1180. He had been appointed Crown Prince in the 12th month of
1178. Antoku was the eldest son of Emperor Takakura, and his Imperial mother was Secondary Empress TAIRA Tokuko [1155–1213],
(a daughter of Lay-Priest Prime-Minister TAIRA Kiyomori).[80]

Regent: [KONOE] Motomichi [1160–1233].

Minister of the Center: TAIRA Munemori [1147–85].

On the 14th day of the 7th month of 1181, the era name was
changed to Yōwa, an era of one year [1181–82]. (The first year was
kanoto-ushi.) On the 27th day of the 5th month of 1182, the era name

78. This Imperial visit was made in the 3rd month of 1180. The ancestral
Kami of the Imperial mother's clan, the TAIRA, was worshipped at the Itsukushima Shrine.

79. TAIRA Kiyomori moved Emperor Antoku to Fukuhara, where Kiyomori's headquarters were located, in the 6th month of 1180.

80. Since Antoku's Imperial mother was TAIRA Kiyomori's daughter To-
kuko, Kiyomori now enjoyed the same maternal relationship to the reigning
Emperor that had been traditionally enjoyed by heads of the FUJIWARA clan.
Tokuko first became the adopted daughter of Retired Emperor Go-
Shirakawa in 1171, and twelve days later became Emperor Takakura's con-
sort. At the time, she was 17 and Takakura 11.

was changed to Juei, an era of two years [1182–84]. (The first year was *mizunoe-tora.*)

The capital was moved during this reign. Details about it are in [Chapter 3]. After Emperor Antoku's maternal grandfather, Lay Priest TAIRA Kiyomori, had rebelled; and because soldiers of the MINAMOTO clan were attacking from the eastern and northern provinces, the Emperor's maternal uncle, Minister of the Center TAIRA Munemori, retreated from the capital and headed for the western provinces on the 25th day of the 7th month of 1183, taking Emperor Antoku with him. Finally, on the 24th day of the 3rd month of 1185, Antoku was drowned in the sea at Dan-no-ura, near the Moji Barrier in the province of Nagato. Antoku was seven years old at the time. The Imperial Sword sank into the water and was lost. The Sacred Jewel floated in its box and was recovered. The Sacred Mirror was recovered and returned by TAIRA Tokitada. These strange events are detailed in [Chapter 3].

(82) Emperor Go-Toba [1180–1239]. A reign of 15 years [1183–98].

Go-Toba's personal name was Takanari. He received the throne on the 20th day of the 8th month of 1183 (at the age of four). He abdicated on the 11th day of the 1st month of 1198.[81] Go-Toba was the fourth son of Emperor Takakura and celebrated his coming-of-age (when he was 11) on the 3rd day of the 1st month of 1190. He was crowned by the Regent and Prime Minister Kanezane; his hair cut for the occasion by Minister of the Left Sanesada; and preparations for crowning were made by the Director of the Bureau of Imperial Treasures, Noriyoshi.[82]

Regent: [KONOE] Motomichi [1160–1233].

(Motomichi's appointments as Regent and head of the FUJIWARA clan were cancelled on the 21st day of the 11th month of 1183, when he was 24 years old.)

Regent and Minister of the Center: [MATSU] Moroie [1172–1238].

(Moroie was made Minister of the Center on the 21st day of the

81. Go-Toba was only 13 in 1192 when Go-Shirakawa died, and therefore he was too young to abdicate and assume the responsibilities of administering state affairs as a Retired Emperor. But in 1198 he stepped down from the throne with that in mind. Apparently MINAMOTO Yoritomo was displeased by this abdication but died before he could do anything about it. In subsequent years, Go-Toba became the center of aristocratic resistance to the military government in Kamakura.

82. The chronology for this reign has two notable omissions: (1) nothing about Go-Toba's appointment as Crown Prince; and (2) nothing about his Imperial mother.

11th month of 1183; and he was also made Regent.[83] Originally he had been a Senior Counselor. Moroie was 12 years old at the time. His appointments as Regent and head of the FUJIWARA clan were cancelled on the 22nd day of the 1st month of 1184.)
Minister of the Center: [TOKUDAIJI] Sanesada [1139–91].
(Because he was in deep mourning [for a deceased parent], Sanesada had to be reappointed at a later date.)
Minister of the Center: [KONOE] Motomichi [1160–1233].
(Motomichi was made Regent [a second time] on the 22nd day of the 1st month of 1184, when he was 25 years old. His appointments as Regent and head of the FUJIWARA clan were cancelled [again] on the 12th day of the 3rd month of 1186.)
Regent and Prime Minister: [KUJŌ] Kanezane [1149–1207].
(Kanezane was appointed Imperial Inspector on the 28th day of the 12th month of 1185.[84] Though [Motomichi] was Regent, [Kanezane] still became Imperial Inspector. He was appointed Regent on the 12th day of the 3rd month of 1186. Kanezane was appointed Prime Minister on the 14th day of the 12th month of 1189 and was made Chancellor on the 17th day of the 12th month of 1191. His positions as Chancellor and head of the FUJIWARA clan were cancelled on the 25th day of the 11th month of 1196. Kanezane entered the Buddhist priesthood on the 28th day of the 1st month of 1202 at the age of 54 and died at the age of 59 on the 5th day of the 4th month of 1207.)
Minister of the Center: [KONOE] Motomichi [1160–1233].
(Motomichi was made Chancellor and head of the FUJIWARA clan [again] on the 25th day of the 11th month of 1196, when he was 37 years old.)
Prime Minister: [KUJŌ] Kanefusa [d. 1217].
(Kanefusa [brother of Jien] was appointed Minister of the Center on the 17th day of the 7th month of 1190 and Prime Minister on the 28th day of the 3rd month of 1191. He tendered [his resignation] to the throne in 1196.)
Minister of the Left: [ŌIMIKADO] Tsunemune [1119–89].
(Tsunemune was granted the privilege of entering the palace grounds by palanquin on the 17th day of the 11th month of 1184, and the ox-driven cart privilege on the 18th day of the same month. Precedents were unclear about granting the ox-driven privilege before the palanquin privilege, and so the latter

83. Since Moroie was only 12 at the time, obviously the Regent was no longer exercising control of court affairs.
84. Yoritomo arranged to have Motomichi replaced by Kanezane, Jien's brother. This MINAMOTO support of KUJŌ Kanezane is central to the *Gukanshō* view of recent history.

was granted first. This privilege had been granted because [persons of Tsunemune's rank] had to walk to the palace for the Great Thanksgiving Festival *(daijō-e)*, but the old man could not walk [that far].)

Minister of the Left: [TOKUDAIJI] Sanesada [1139–91].[85]

(Sanesada was appointed Minister of the Right in 1186 and Minister of the Left on the 10th day of the 7th month of 1189. He resigned from the position of Minister of the Left in 1190.)

Minister of the Left: [SANJŌ] Sanefusa [1147–1225].

(Sanefusa was a son of Kinnori. He was appointed Minister of the Right on the 10th day of the 7th month of 1189 and Minister of the Left on the 17th day of the 7th month of 1190. He resigned from the latter position on the 23rd day of the 3rd month of 1198 at the age of 50 and entered the Buddhist priesthood on the 25th day of the 4th month of that year.)

Minister of the Left: [KAZAN-IN] Kanemasa [d. 1199].

(Kanemasa, the first son of Tadamasa, was appointed Minister of the Center on the 10th day of the 7th month of 1189, Minister of the Right on the 17th day of the 7th month of 1190, and Minister of the Left on the 14th day of the 11th month of 1198.)

Minister of the Right: [ŌIMIKADO] Yorizane [1155–1225].

(Yorizane was Senior Commander of the Imperial Bodyguards of the Right and a son of Tsunemune. He was appointed Minister of the Right on the 14th day of the 11th month of 1198, passing Minister of the Center [KUJŌ Yoshitsune].)[86]

Minister of the Center: [KUJŌ] Yoshimichi [1167–88].[87]

(Yoshimichi was Senior Commander of the Imperial Bodyguards of the Left, but originally had been Senior Commander of the Imperial Bodyguards of the Right. Yoshimichi was appointed Minister of the Center on the 29th day of the 10th month of 1186 at the age of 20. He suddenly died on the 20th day of the 2nd month of 1188.)

Minister of the Center; FUJIWARA Tadachika [d. 1195].

(Tadachika was the young brother of [KAZAN-IN] Tadamasa and was appointed Minister of the Center on the 28th day of the 3rd month of 1191. He entered the Buddhist priesthood on the

85. He was a grandson of TOKUDAIJI Saneyoshi, Kinzane's son who founded the TOKUDAIJI house. Two other Kinzane sons founded houses: Saneyuki (1079–1162), the SANJŌ; and Michisue (1090–1128), the SAIONJI. All three Kinzane sons were brothers of Go-Shirakawa's Imperial mother, Taiken-mon In.

86. This was apparently a painful point for Jien, since Yoshitsune was his own nephew and Yorizane was a distant relative. But Yoshitsune was passed over after his father Kanezane lost the Chancellorship in 1196.

87. Eldest son of Kanezane.

15th day of the 12th month of 1194 and died on the 12th day of the 3rd month of 1195.)

Minister of the Center: [KUJŌ] Yoshitsune [1169–1206].

(Yoshitsune was Senior Commander of the Imperial Body-guards of the Left and was appointed Minister of the Center on the 10th day of the 11th month of 1195, when he was 27 years old. His appointment as Senior Commander was cancelled on the 19th day of the 1st month of 1198.)

Former Senior Commander of the Imperial Bodyguards of the Right: MINAMOTO Yoritomo [1147–99].

(Yoritomo was the son of Yoshitomo, Director of the Bureau of Horses, Left Division. As a reward for capturing and bringing in the former Minister of the Center [TAIRA Munemori], he was advanced to Junior Second Rank on the 27th day of the 4th month of 1185. Originally he had been Colonel of the Military Guards, Senior Fourth Rank lower rank. On the 9th day of the 11th month of 1190, Yoritomo was made provisional Senior Counselor. Originally he held a court rank but no office. On the 24th day of that same month, he was given an additional appointment as Senior Commander of the Imperial Body-guards of the Right. On the 3rd day of the 12th month of 1190, he resigned both positions.)

On the 16th day of the 4th month of 1184, the era name was changed to Genryaku, an era of one year [1184–85]. (The first year was *kinoe-tatsu.*) Emperor Antoku died on the 24th day of the 3rd month of Genryaku 2 [1185]. On the 14th day of the 8th month of 1185, the era name was changed to Bunji, an era that lasted five years [1185–90]. (The first year was *kinoto-mi.*) On the 11th day of the 4th month of 1190, the era name was changed to Kenkyū, which was an era of nine years [1190–99]. (The first year was *kanoe-inu.*) Retired Emperor Go-Shirakawa died on the 13th day of the 3rd month of Kenkyū 3 [1192] (at the age of 66).

Tendai Abbots:

Provisional High Priest Shungyō.[88] (Abbot of Taichi-in.)

(Shungyō was appointed Tendai Abbot by an Imperial Mandate issued on the 23rd day of the 11th month of 1183. He administered Mt. Hiei two months and was chased from Mt. Hiei on the 20th day of the 1st month of 1184.)

Former Provisional High Priest Zengen. (Abbot of Keirin-in.)

(Zengen became Buddhist Judge and Senior High Priest. He was appointed Tendai Abbot by an Imperial Mandate issued

---

88. Shungyō was appointed Tendai Abbot after KISO Yoshinaka entered the capital in 1183, and he was rejected by the monks of Mt. Hiei after Yoshinaka's defeat the following year.

on the 3rd day of the 2nd month of 1184, when he was 72
years old. He administered Mt. Hiei six years.)
Former Senior High Priest Kōken. (Abbot of Miidera.)
(Kōken became Buddhist Judge. He was appointed Tendai
Abbot by an Imperial Mandate issued on the 4th day of the
3rd month of 1190.)
Priest First Grade Kenshin [1131–92]. (Abbot of Ōhara.)
(Kenshin became provisional High Priest. He was appointed
Tendai Abbot at the age of 60 by an Imperial Mandate issued
on the 7th day of the 3rd month of 1190. He administered
Mt. Hiei for two years. He died in the 11th month of 1192 at
the age of 62.)
Provisional High Priest Jien [1155–1225].[89]
(Jien became Buddhist Judge and Senior High Priest. He was
appointed Tendai Abbot, at the age of 38, by an Imperial
Mandate issued on the 29th day of the 11th month of 1192.
He administered Mt. Hiei four years and resigned in the 11th
month of 1196.)
Prince Master-Teacher Shōnin [1169–97].[90] (Abbot of Kajii.)
(Prince Shōnin was appointed Tendai Abbot by an Imperial
Mandate issued on the 30th day of the 11th month of 1196,
when he was 28. He administered Mt. Hiei one year—actually
five months—and died on the 27th day of the 4th month of
1197.)
Priest First Grade Benga [d. 1201].
(Benga was appointed Tendai Abbot on the 21st day of the
5th month of 1197, when he was 63 years old. He administered Mt. Hiei four years and died on the 17th day of the 2nd
month of 1201 at the age of 67.)
After Emperor Antoku [81] drowned in the western seas, Go-Toba
[82] received the throne in accordance with an Imperial Mandate
issued by Retired Emperor Go-Shirakawa [77]. We hear that Toba's
[74] enthronement was not based upon an Imperial Mandate issued
by his predecessor, Emperor Horikawa [73], but by Retired Emperor
Shirakawa [72]. Later [Emperors also succeeded to the throne] in
this manner. After his abdication, Emperor Go-Toba participated in
the dedication of his Buddhist hall *(midō)* in 1207. This hall was
called The Saishō Shitennō Cloister. It was during this reign that

89. Jien received this first appointment as Tendai Abbot six years after
his brother Kanezane was appointed Regent and just a few months after the
death of Retired Emperor Go-Shirakawa. He was a disciple of Prince-Priest
Kakukai (56th Abbot) and was baptized by Zengen (the 59th Abbot). Jien
was forced to resign as Tendai Abbot in 1196 when his brother Kanezane
lost his position as Chancellor.
90. A son of Go-Shirakawa and disciple of Myōun.

there was instituted an arrangement in which the western guards (*saimen*) were added to the northern guards (*hokumen*), and many sons of soldiers served there. [Go-Toba] amused himself with archery and horseback riding; and many things were started during this reign that had not been done during or after the Medieval Age (*chūko*).

(83) Emperor Tsuchimikado [1195–1231]. A reign of 12 years [1198–1210].

Tsuchimikado's personal name was Tamehito. He received the throne (at the age of four) on the 11th day of the 1st month of 1198. He had not been appointed Crown Prince. He abdicated in the 11th month of 1210. Tsuchimikado was the eldest son of Go-Toba, and his coming-of-age was celebrated on the 3rd day of the 1st month of 1205. His Imperial mother was Empress Shōmei-mon In [1171–1257],[91] (an adopted daughter of Minister of the Center Michichika[92] and the real daughter of Nōen, Priest First Grade.)

Regent: [KONOE] Motomichi [1160–1233].

(Motomichi's positions were as before. He was dismissed as Regent and head of the FUJIWARA clan on the 25th day of the 12th month of 1202, when he was 43.[93] He entered the Buddhist priesthood on the 5th day of the 10th month of 1208 at the age of 49 and died on the 29th day of the 5th month of 1233 at the age of 74.)[94]

Regent and Prime Minister: [KUJŌ] Yoshitsune [1169–1206].

(Yoshitsune was appointed Regent on the 25th day of the 12th month of 1202 at the age of 34. He had been previously made [Imperial Inspector] and head of the FUJIWARA clan by an Imperial Mandate issued on the 27th day of the 11th month of

91. She received the name and title of Shōmei-mon In in 1202, four years after her son became Emperor.

92. Michichika was blamed for Kanezane's and Jien's dismissals in 1196. After his adoptive grandson became Emperor Tsuchimikado in 1198, Michichika enjoyed great influence at court, although members of the FUJIWARA clan continued to hold the major ministerial posts. He exerted his influence as Commissioner (*bettō*) for Retired Emperor Go-Toba and as Commissioner for Emperor Tsuchimikado. It appears that court rivalries after 1198 revolved around Michichika (the adoptive maternal grandfather of Emperor Tsuchimikado) and Kanezane (the former Regent). Jien, Kanezane's brother, does not list Michichika as a Minister of the Center, although Michichika was appointed to that position in 1199.

93. On this same day, these two positions were given to KUJŌ Yoshitsune, Jien's nephew.

94. At least the last part of this note was added by someone other than Jien, who died in 1225.

1202. . . . He died on the 7th day of the 3rd month of 1206 at
the age of 38.)

On the 27th day of the 4th month of 1199, the era name was
changed to Shōji, an era of two years [1199–1201]. (The first year
was *tsuchinoto-hitsuji.*) On the 13th day of the 2nd month of 1201, the
era name was changed to Kennin, which lasted three years [1201–
04]. (The first year was *kanoto-tori.*) On the 20th day of the 2nd
month of 1204, the era name was changed to Genkyū, an era of two
years [1204–06]. (The first year was *kinoe-ne.*) On the 27th day of the
4th month of 1206, the era name was changed to Ken'ei, which
lasted one year [1206–07]. (The first year was *hinoe-tora.*) On the 25th
day of the 10th month of 1207, the era name was changed to
Shōgen, an era of four years [1207–11]. (The first year was *hinoto-u.*)

Tendai Abbots:

Former Provisional High Priest Jien [1155–1225].

(Jien was reappointed Tendai Abbot by an Imperial Mandate
issued on the 19th day of the 2nd month of 1201, when he
was 47. He administered Mt. Hiei one year [this time] and
resigned on the 7th day of the 7th month of 1202.)[95]

Priest First Grade Jitsuzen [1140–1221].

(Jitsuzen became provisional High Priest. He was appointed
Tendai Abbot by an Imperial Mandate issued on the 13th day
of the 7th month of 1202, when he was 63. He administered
Mt. Hiei one year. He was removed because of fighting be-
tween the higher *(gakuto)* and lower *(dōshu)* ranking priests of
Mt. Hiei during the 8th month of 1203.)

High Priest Shinshō [1167–1230].

(Shinshō became Senior High Priest. He was appointed Tendai Abbot by an Imperial Mandate issued on the 28th day of
the 8th month of 1203, when he was 37. He administered Mt.
Hiei two years and resigned in the 12th month of 1205 probably because the Great Lecture Hall and other buildings of
Mt. Hiei burned down.)

Priest First Grade Shōen.

(Shōen became Buddhist Judge and High Priest. He was appointed Tendai Abbot by an Imperial Mandate issued on the
13th day of the 12th month of 1205, when he was 26. He
administered Mt. Hiei seven years and resigned in the 12th
month of 1211. It is said that the Sōji Cloister was destroyed

95. The fact that Jien was reappointed Tendai Abbot a year before
Michichika's death suggests that Michichika's influence was already waning.
But Jien's second term ended before Michichika's death. The chronology
gives reasons for the resignation of the next three Tendai Abbots, but says
nothing about the author's own resignation in 1202.

by fire and that the Hachiōji Shrine and other buildings in the Hiei Shrine complex were completely destroyed.... Was it not because of this [that Shōen resigned]?)

A comet, which had not been seen for a long time, appeared and did not disappear for several nights. After it disappeared, it soon appeared again. Consequently, the Emperor had various prayers offered up and stepped down from the throne. It was bruited about that there had never been another case such as this when those around the Imperial mother all died and a grandson of an ordinary priest occupied the throne.[96] Nevertheless, Emperor Tsuchimikado reigned more than ten years.

(84) Emperor Juntoku [1197–1242].[97] A reign of 11 years [1210–21].

Juntoku's personal name was Morinari. He received the throne (at the age of 14) on the 25th day of the 11th month of 1210. He had been appointed Crown Prince on the 15th day of the 4th month of 1200 (at the age of four). Juntoku was the second son of Retired Emperor Go-Toba, and he celebrated his coming-of-age on the 25th day of the 12th month of 1208 (at the age of 12). His Imperial mother was Empress Shūmei-mon In (the daughter of Norisue who was posthumously appointed Minister of the Left and who was, while alive, Junior Second Rank.)

Chancellor: [KONOE] Iezane [d. 1242].

(Iezane's appointments as Regent and head of the FUJIWARA clan were cancelled on the 20th day of the 4th month of 1221, when he was 43.)

On the 9th day of the 3rd month of 1211, the era name was changed to Kenryaku, which was an era of two years [1211–13]. (The first year was *kanoto-histsuji.*) On the 6th day of the 12th month of 1213, the era name was changed to Kempō, which was six years long [1213–19]. (The first year was *mizunoto-tori.*) On the 12th day of the 4th month of 1219, the era name was changed to Shōkyū, an era of three years [1219–21]. (The first year was *tsuchinoto-u.*)

Tendai Abbots:

Former Senior High Priest Jien [1155–1225].

(This was another reappointment for Jien. He was [re]-

96. Jien hints that the selection of Tsuchimikado as Emperor was a mistake, presumably because his Imperial mother was the daughter of a priest. The enthronement of Tsuchimikado certainly moved the throne farther from leaders of the FUJIWARA clan.

97. The name of Juntoku was given posthumously in 1249. It is therefore assumed that Jien originally referred to him in some such terms as "the current Emperor."

appointed Tendai Abbot by an Imperial Mandate issued on the 16th day of the 1st month of 1212, when he was 58. He administered Mt. Hiei [this time] for one year, yielding the position to Priest Kōen, First Grade, on the 11th day of the 1st month of 1213 and resigning. It is said that on that same day Kōen was first made provisional High Priest and that the Imperial Mandate of appointment as Tendai Abbot was issued afterward. . . .)

Provisional High Priest Kōen [d. 1235].

(Kōen was appointed Tendai Abbot by an Imperial Mandate issued on the same day that Jien resigned, when Kōen was 46 years old. He administered Mt. Hiei 10 months. In the 11th month of that same year, a dispute arose between the priests of the southern capital [Nara] and the priests of Mt. Hiei over Kiyomizu Temple.[98] This is why Kōen resigned. . . .)

Former Senior High Priest Jien [1155–1225].

(This was another reappointment for Jien, his fourth. He was appointed Tendai Abbot [again] by an Imperial Mandate issued on the 19th day of the 11th month of 1213, when he was 59. He administered Mt. Hiei one year and again resigned on the 10th day of the 6th month of 1214. The Miidera Temple was burned down [by the priests of Enryaku-ji] for the fifth time on the 16th day of the 4th month of 1214.)

Former Provisional High Priest Shōen [d. 1236].[99]

(This was a reappointment for Shōen. He was reappointed Tendai Abbot by an Imperial Mandate issued on the 12th day of the 6th month of 1214.)

As for ministers who were not Regents or Chancellors during the various reigns listed above, I have not listed them all—only important ones. The reader should understand this. Among those who held the post of Tendai Abbot, the former Senior High Priest Jien received that appointment four times. Such resignations as his were really strange and hard to understand. Why should His Majesty have appointed a man who had resigned so many times? And why should such a person who had resigned so many times have received reappointment after reappointment? There really ought to be some rea-

98. The trouble arose when Mt. Hiei monks responded to overtures from Kiyomizu Temple priests, suggesting to Nara Buddhists that Kiyomizu might be drifting into the Tendai camp. Consequently, armed monks from Nara were mobilized for an attack on Mt. Hiei. But government forces intervened and the Nara priests withdrew. This incident seems to have led to Kōen's resignation the following month.

99. Shōen, Jien's nephew, was apparently still Tendai Abbot when this portion of the chronology was compiled. He resigned on the 24th day of the 4th month of 1221.

son for this! Such developments seem to point to the truth of the Buddha Law—as understood in the Mountain Order—that there is a reciprocal relationship *(sōtai)* between Buddha Law and Imperial Law. Because I have become aware of the reasons why this Mountain Order was founded soon after the capital was moved to Heian [in 794], I am writing about the affairs of the Mountain Order at the back of this book.[100] That which is not clear will be clarified by that detailed account of those matters.

The Imperial Palace was destroyed by fire on the 13th day of the 7th month of 1219. This makes the 15th time that the Imperial Palace has been burned. It was set on fire by MINAMOTO Yorimochi during a battle that broke out when he—a provisional Director of the Bureau of Horses, Right Division, who was guarding the Imperial Palace as his ancestors had done—was called to the Imperial Court because there were rumors of a plot. . . . Yorimochi was immediately executed. The Emperor issued a special order that the palace be restored. . . . During the [administrations of Retired Emperors] Shirakawa and Toba [the Imperial Palace] was generally neglected. . . . These matters are not clear. . . .

In 1218, the priests of Mt. Hiei went down to the capital carrying the portable shrine of the Hie Shrine. This sort of thing occurred many times, reign after reign, and cannot be written up [in detail]. And since this is a very abbreviated account, [those demonstrations] will be dealt with in a summary fashion.

> *Note:*[101] This was written down in the 10th month of 1220. Later readers [of this book] should continue this account in accordance with this purpose.[102] A very abbreviated account is definitely the most valuable. That which is written in [a] separate chapter should not be shown to outsiders.[103]

(85) Current Emperor [Chūkyō][1218–34].[104]

[Chūkyō's] personal name is Kanenari. He received the throne on the 20th day *(kinoe-inu)* of the 4th month of 1221

---

100. This sentence, and others, indicate that Jien had written, or intended to write, a supplement to the *Gukanshō* that is not extant. The problem is discussed by MURAOKA Tsunetsugu in "Gukanshō no chosaku nendai hensei oyobi shahon," in *Zōtei Nihon shisō shi no kenkyū* (Tokyo, 1940), pp. 66–69. Cf. NKBT, 86.14–15 and 396–397, note 242.

101. It it thought that this note was appended to the chronology at a later time.

102. What follows this note was apparently added later, as Jien wanted.

103. Cf. note 100, above.

104. This section on the Chūkyō reign is thought to have been added sometime before the 9th day of the 7th month of 1221, when Go-Horikawa

(kanoto-mi) (at the age of four). He had been appointed Crown Prince on the 26th day of the 11th month of 1218 (when he was one year old). He was born at the *tora* hour of the 10th day of the 10th month. His Imperial mother is Secondary Empress Risshi (1192–1247), and he is the eldest son of Emperor Juntoku [84].

Regent and Minister of the Left: [KUJŌ] Michiie [1193–1252]. (Michiie was appointed Regent on the same day that Chūkyō received the throne, when Michiie was 29. He was the eldest son of [KUJŌ] Yoshitsune, Lord Go-Kyōgoku. An Imperial Mandate had been issued stating: "There is no precedent for *not* appointing a Minister to the position of Regent when he is a maternal grandfather or maternal uncle of the reigning Emperor. Making such an appointment is a requirement of Principle. . . ."[105] Michiie was made head of the FUJIWARA clan on the 26th day of the 4th month of 1221. He was given an official bodyguard. According to precedent, an Imperial order was handed down giving him the ox-drawn cart privilege. On that same day, he called on the Emperor to express his gratitude for the bestowal of an official bodyguard.)

On the 26th day [of the 4th month of 1221], the new Retired Emperor [Juntoku] proceeded, for the first time, to the Kaya-no-in palace of the senior Retired Emperor [Go-Toba]. On the 23rd day of that month [Juntoku] had been given the honorary title of Retired Emperor *(dajo tennō)*. . . . Another senior Retired Emperor was Emperor Tsuchimikado. . . . This was the first time that three Retired Emperors [had been alive at the same time]. . . .[106] There were many previous cases of [a previous Emperor receiving the title of] Priest-Emperor *(hō-ō)*. . . .

(86) Current Emperor [Go-Horikawa] [1212–34].[107]

[Go-Horikawa's] personal name is Yutahito. He received the throne on the 9th day *(kanoto-u)* of the 7th month of 1221 *(kanoto-mi)*, (when he was ten years old). He was enthroned at the palace office on the 1st day *(kanoe-tatsu)* of the 12th month of 1221. This

---

was enthroned. The posthumous name of Chūkyō was not granted until 1870. Before that, he was generally referred to as the "late dethroned Emperor" or as "the dethroned Emperor of KUJŌ." [NKBT, 86.123, note 35.]

105. Such an Imperial Mandate is not extant. With Michiie's appointment, the post of Regent was once more held by the brother of the Emperor's Imperial mother.

106. Actually, there was a previous case: after Kazan's abdication in 986. The three Retired Emperors alive then were: Reizei (950–1011), Enyū (959–991), and Kazan (968–1008).

107. The remainder of the chronology (except for the colophon) was probably written in 1224.

enthronement of a grandson of a previous Emperor is the first such
case since the enthronement of Emperor Kōnin [in 770]. . . .[108]
[Go-Horikawa] is a grandson of Emperor Takakura [80] and the son
of Princely Lay Priest Morisada (who was subsequently given the
honorary title of Retired Emperor). His Imperial mother is Empress
Kita Shirakawa In (1173–1238), (daughter of Middle Counselor
Motoie). Go-Horikawa celebrated his coming-of-age on the 3rd day
of the 1st month of 1222.

Regent: [KONOE] Iezane.

(Iezane was reappointed Regent by an Imperial edict issued by
the previous Emperor on the 8th day of the 7th month, the day
before Go-Horikawa received the throne. . . . No orders were
issued after that. . . .)

There was no Imperial banquet and no Imperial Mandate for
strengthening the guard or the barriers on the day that Go-
Horikawa received the throne. . . . Did not everyone consider this
strange? In the 8th or 9th month [of 1222], an order was handed
down stating that the Imperial edict issued by the previous Emperor
concerning the appointment of a Regent should be respected.[109]
Court Secretaries (*geki*) were surprised by the order. . . . Really
strange things happened on the night Emperor Kazan had abdicated
[back in 986], but on the next day an Imperial edict was handed
down appointing the Great Lord Lay Priest (Kaneie) to the position
of Regent. No Imperial banquet was held then, but the strengthening of barriers and such was carried out. People therefore said that
this way of doing things [at the time of Go-Horikawa's enthrone-
ment] was really terrible.

Minister of the Left: [KONOE] Iemichi [1204–24].

(Iemichi was the son and heir of Regent Iezane and Senior
Commander of the Imperial Bodyguards of the Left.)

Minister of the Right: [FUJIWARA] Kintsugu [1174–1227].

(This was the first time anyone had been reappointed Minister
of the Right. It was not like the case of Lord [TOKUDAIJI]
Sanesada's appointment [to the post]. . . . Kintsugu was concurrently a Senior Commander and was appointed Minister of the
Right on the 10th day of the intercalary 10th month of 1221.)

Minister of the Center: [SAIONJI] Kintsune [1171–1224].

(Kintsune was Senior Commander of the Imperial Bodyguards
of the Right. He was appointed Minister of the Center on the
same 10th day of the intercalary 10th month of 1221. A great
banquet [*daikyō*] was held on the night of that 10th day of the

108. The same point is made in a prayer that Jien wrote in 1224. [Aka-
matsu, *Kamakura Bukkyō no kenkyū*, 285.]

109. No reference to such an edict has been found in other sources.
[NKBT, 86.124, note 28.]

intercalary 10th month. It was customary to hold such a banquet on the night of a ministerial appointment. . . .)

The era name was changed to Jōō—which lasted two years [1222–24]—on the 13th day of the 4th month of 1222. (The first year of that era was *mizunoe-uma.*)

Tendai Abbot: Provisional High Priest Engi.

(Engi was appointed Tendai Abbot by an Imperial Mandate issued on the 27th day of the 8th month of 1221.)

It was heard that the eighteen-year-old Prince Lay Priest Sonkai [1204–46][110] was picked during the 4th month of 1221 to be the next Tendai Abbot, but since no precedent existed for handing down an Imperial Mandate of appointment before a Great Thanksgiving Festival *(daijō-e)* had been held, [the appointment was not formally made]. In the days of KISO Yoshinaka [1154–84], an Imperial Mandate appointing Shungyō to the position of Tendai Abbot was issued [before a Great Thanksgiving Festival had been held], but that was a good precedent. Before an Imperial Mandate had been handed down [for Prince Sonkai's appointment], the Shōkyū Rebellion broke out on the 15th day of the 5th month [of 1221]. In the 6th month, soldiers forced their way into [the capital] and this Tendai Abbot [designate] and his followers were forced to flee in confusion. Therefore people said: "[The selection of] this eighteen-year-old Prince as Tendai Abbot shows how Buddhist Law and Imperial Law have [deteriorated]." Then High Priest Engi, as the young brother of Regent [Iezane], had to be appointed Tendai Abbot. So this is probably why Prince Sonkai is not listed as a Tendai Abbot. Because the empire was involved in civil war during this year [of 1221], the Emperor and Regent were suddenly replaced, and the people were thrown into confusion. . . . The Senior Retired Emperor [Go-Toba] was exiled to the province of Oki. He entered the Buddhist priesthood at the Toba palace on the 8th day of the 7th month [of 1221] and left the capital on the 13th. . . . His departure was unceremonious. . . . He was accompanied only by Kiyonori, who had suddenly become a Lay Priest, and by two or three Ladies-in-Waiting. . . . Kiyonori, who was replaced by Priest Yoshishige, soon returned to the capital. . . . Retired Emperor Tsuchimikado, and new Retired Emperor [Juntoku], Prince Rokujō, and Prince Reizei were all sent into exile. . . . The new Retired Emperor [Juntoku] was exiled to the province of Sado on the 21st day of that [7th month of 1221]; Prince Reizei was exiled to Kojima in the province of Bizen on the 25th; Prince Rokujō[111] was exiled to the province of Tajima on the 24th; and after some time had passed—during the intercalary

110. Eighth son of Go-Toba.
111. These two princes were sons of Go-Toba.

10th month of that year—Retired Emperor Tsuchimikado was exiled to the province of Tosa. After that—in the 4th month of 1222—the era name was changed [to Jōō]. Around the 5th month, it was heard that [Retired Emperor Tsuchimikado] was moved to the province of Awa. Three Retired Emperors and two Imperial Princes had been sent into exile, and it was rumored that this had been done unceremoniously.

On the 16th day of the 8th month of 1221, the honorary title of Retired Emperor *(dajō tennō)* was granted to [Emperor Go-Horikawa's father], (who was called Retired Emperor Go-Takakura). There is no precedent in Japan [for such action]. There was talk that this was like the precedent set in China when the father of Kao Tsu (the founder of the Han Dynasty) was given the title of T'ai Kung. Emperor Go-Horikawa's Imperial mother was also given the title of *in* (Cloistered Empress), advanced to Junior Third Rank, and given the status of Empress on the 13th day of the 4th month of 1222. . . . Her name was Nobuko. She had entered the Buddhist priesthood in the spring of the previous year. There is no precedent [for granting such rank and privileges to a woman after she had entered the priesthood]. But the bestowal of the Third Rank on Masako of Kamakura (the widow of Yoritomo, who was Senior Commander of the Imperial Guards of the Right) may have been a precedent. But what was the precedent for giving it to Masako? Under conditions of the final reigns, such irregularities are not unusual. The Final Age is truly miserable. The era name was soon changed to Jōō on the 13th day [when the mother of the Emperor was given these honors]. Then, on the 11th day of the 7th month of that same year, it was decided that Nobuko, who now held the privileges of an Empress, should be given the title of Cloistered Empress. She was now called Empress Kita Shirakawa In. On the 14th day of the 5th month of 1223, the Retired Priest-Emperor *(dajō hōō)* (Go-Takakura) [Go-Horikawa's father] died. Everything was like a dream and the empire went into mourning *(ryōan)*. Then, on the 13th day of the 6th month of 1224, came the death of [HŌJŌ] Yoshitoki [1163–1224], who had served as guardian for several Shoguns in the eastern provinces. On the evening of the 17th day of that month, his son and heir Yasutoki [1183–1242], Governor of Musashi, left the capital for the eastern provinces; and he was followed, on the 19th, by his younger brother Tokifusa [1175–1240], Governor of Sagami.

Colophon.[112] In addition to these Imperial chronicles, I have written [other chapters] concerning the single course of Principles [that

---

112. Ishida concludes that this colophon was written in 1221, even though it appears after sections that were written later. Either a space was left in between or paper was inserted.

account for] worldly change from the time of Emperor Jimmu down to the year before last.[113]

Those who wish to understand well this [single course of Principle] should read what I have written. I have written only in Japanese because I was thinking of Principles. My main reason for writing in this way was to help those who have no understanding. In trying to find out about the conditions of these final reigns, [I reached the conclusion that] no person working with written sources *(bunbo)* — whether he be noble or mean, priest or layman—has any comprehension of right Principles *(giri)*, even though he reads a few things in Chinese with the purpose of producing a rare piece of scholarship. Even though laymen have access to a large number of Chinese histories, biographies, and classics, they are like people who look but do not understand what they see. And although priests have Buddhist sutras and commentaries, few study them. Books such as *Chronicles of Japan,* and other works on down to and including the penal civil codes, have been written in this country, but it is now difficult to find anyone who reads them with the slightest understanding. By writing in Japanese, one can get to the essence of Japanese words which are unrelated to Chinese characters. People will laugh at my writing in Japanese, saying that it is an absurd way to write and that Japanese words are still difficult to read. I have used such words as *hatato, muzuto, shakuto, dōto,* etc. They really lie at the heart of the Japanese language. Everyone knows their meaning. Even common laborers and watchmen understand many things through sentences written in this way. If I had considered such words ridiculous and not used them, I would have had to rely exclusively on Chinese characters. I have written this book as I think of particular Principles. Yet, people born in this country are not making distinctions—even to the extent that distinctions have been made in this book—in the evolving traditions of the country or the shifting trends of the age. Furthermore, even with respect to that which is destined to occur [in the future], people are really thinking that those events will not come to pass.

As for the many things I wanted to say but have left out, there is still much that remains in my heart. Since only a small part of what has become clear to me has been written, these [omissions] will be realized by anyone who has even a modicum of scholarly talent. But if I had written everything I wanted to say, the text would have become excessively long, and no one would have understood it. I have therefore refrained from writing that which could be left unsaid. Even [seemingly] unimportant items should all be thought about. I

113. This sentence supports the conclusion that the main body of the *Gukanshō* was written in 1219.

have written only those things which will arouse the heart and mind of a person and lead him to an understanding of Principles when he wants to understand and when his eye has been caught [by what I have written]. Persons who appear to have talent for scholarship and who have had their hearts and minds aroused by what has been written here should become more diligent in their pursuit of scholarship. Since not all reports passed on to us by word of mouth are accurate, and since there are many developments for which the really crucial points have not been subjected to critical review, I had to omit such questionable matters.

With such an understanding [of what I have written and why], you should read the following chapters[114] while consulting [this chronology], reign by reign.

> *Note:* Because I have left some space at the end [of the chronology] for four or five more reigns, what is written here [in this colophon] probably will not be noticed or read, because people will think [after coming to the end of the chronology] that there is nothing more. It is an age when people do not have enough ability to open a book and read page after page and to expect that there is probably something like this at the end. Human understanding has now become slight indeed. So my having written in this way should be regarded as another [manifestation of] Principle.

114. In all extant texts of the *Gukanshō* the chronology is followed by the narrative chapters. But the order has been reversed in this translation, following the modern practice of placing reference material at the back of the book.

Part III

Introductory Studies

8
Pre-Gukanshō
Historical Writing

by Delmer M. Brown

Three types of historical expression appeared in Japan during the five-century period that began with the presentation of the *Kojiki* in A.D. 712 and ended with the completion of the *Gukanshō* in 1219. First came the Six National Histories *(rikkokushi)* compiled by officials acting upon Imperial orders. Intended as Chinese-like reference works for the use of bureaucrats, these chronicles—submitted to the court between 720 and 901—were compiled when Japanese officials were paying close attention to Chinese administrative and educational models. The second type of historical expression, commonly referred to as Historical Tales *(rekishi monogatari)*, took the form of stories about the activities of distinguished aristocrats of the past. Written sometime between 1030 and 1130, when the Chinese bureaucratic system was being bypassed and when aristocratic attitudes were becoming increasingly pessimistic, these Tales—meant to interest and instruct the reader—were composed by individuals who were beginning to be influenced by Buddhist doctrines of continuous deterioration over time. The third type of historical work, Military Tales *(gunki monogatari)*, emerged after the Hōgen Rebellion of 1156 when military leaders were gaining dominance over the affairs of state. These later Tales, focused upon the rise and fall of military leaders, were also intended to be interesting and instructive but were more deeply influenced by Buddhist teachings and reflected a new preoccupation with military heroics and values.

Every one of these chronicles and Tales is colored by ideas and convictions found in earlier accounts, and the basic preoccupations of each are mirrored in the *Gukanshō*. These early historical works, and the *Gukanshō* as well, also show the effects of a powerful and persistent tension between foreign and native assumptions about such matters as the source and nature of Imperial authority, the selection and obligations of officials, and prospects for the future. Therefore this introductory chapter will have two interrelated objectives: to identify the core qualities of the three types of history that appeared before the *Gukanshō* was written; and to indicate something of the way these historical accounts were affected by interaction between ideas introduced from China and beliefs native to Japan.

Six National Histories, and the Kojiki

The *Nihongi* (Chronicles of Japan), the first of the Six National Histories and the one presented to the Imperial Court in A.D. 720, seems to have been based on written records and accounts that were at least a century old. The *Nihongi* covers events after about 600 in greater detail, and the information supplied in post-600 items is thought to be more reliable. Furthermore, two *Nihongi* entries refer specifically to chronicles that had been written at an earlier date but that are no longer extant.[1] We also know that after the days of Prince Shōtoku (574–622) Korean and Chinese immigrants, as well as Japanese who had studied on the continent, rose to positions of great influence in the Japanese government. It is therefore concluded that chronicles were compiled long before the *Nihongi* was submitted and that such historical work was undoubtedly done by persons who knew something about Chinese techniques of record keeping.

Chinese Historical Models

The most distinctive feature of the Six National Histories, and presumably of earlier chronicles which have been lost, is therefore their Chineseness. Written in Chinese and including many quota-

---

1. The first appears under the date of Suiko 28 (620) [NKBT, 68.203]; and the second is under Kōgyoku 4 (645)–6–13 [NKBT, 68.264–265]. Ishida thinks the accounts referred to in these references were something like grave records (*okutsuki no fumi*), a term that appears in an entry for Jitō 5 (691)–8–13 [NKBT, 68.510–511].

tions from Chinese classics, they stand rather close to the traditional pattern of an official Chinese history. Comparative study shows that the *Nihongi* is similar to two Han-Dynasty works: the *Hou-chi* (compiled by Hsün Yüeh, A.D. 148–209) and the *Hou-han-chi* (by Yuan Hang, 328–376). Like these two Han histories, the *Nihongi* has no biographies and no treatises on special subjects, although biographies and treatises are standard components of dynastic histories compiled after Ssu-ma Ch'ien put together his *Shih-chi* in about 100 B.C. Furthermore, the Chinese character for *gi* in *Nihongi* is the same as the one for *chi* in *Hou-han-chi*. The two Han histories and the *Nihongi* all have 30 chapters. The last five National Histories follow the Chinese pattern even more closely than the *Nihongi*. They are not only written in better Chinese but display greater familiarity with Chinese standards of record keeping and take on the character of Chinese Veritable Records (*shih-lu* in Chinese and *jitsuroku* in Japanese), which the Chinese considered to be the principal source for the next dynastic history. The last two National Histories (the *Nihon Montoku Tennō jitsuroku* and the *Nihon sandai jitsuroku*) are even called Veritable Records; and Minoru Shibata concludes that the gathering and selection of data were handled in somewhat the same way as in China.[2]

But as Chinese as the Six National Histories are, they still do not have the character of a Chinese dynastic history. In attempting to explain why this is so, Professor Robinson suggests that at first the Japanese simply did not have "enough material out of which to fashion a convincing replica of a Chinese dynastic history" and that later on it may have been "inertia or, possibly conscious conservativism" that kept them from following China's "illustrious example."[3] But it seems likely that the Japanese were also constrained by a definite cultural lag and by traditional assumptions concerning the sacred position of the Imperial family. As yet, the Japanese may not have become aware of social and economic problems about which they would have been impelled to write special treatises. An even more significant factor, however, was the effect of native belief in the sacred origins of an unbroken line of Imperial descent. Even though some ruptures had appeared in this line, notably with Emperor Keitai in the sixth century, the myth that it had been created by the Sun Goddess to last forever seems to have had a strong hold on the minds of aristocrats at the court, making them unreceptive to the Chinese idea that a Mandate of Heaven had ever established, or ever would establish, a new Japanese dynasty.

2. Cf. Shibata Minoru, "Heian jidai zenki no rekishi shisō: kidendō no seishin," *Nihon ni okeru rekishi shisō no tenkai* (Sendai, 1965), pp. 58–63.
3. *Historians of China and Japan* (Oxford, 1961), p. 220.

Chinese Ideas

If we look beyond the form of the Six National Histories to their thought, we will see several Chinese intellectual currents. Entries in these Histories provide incontestable evidence that Yin Yang occult arts, Confucianism, and Buddhism—all imported in the sixth century—were becoming increasingly important to Japan's ruling class during the two-hundred-year period in which National Histories were compiled. But Yin Yang occult arts were probably appreciated first, for Yin Yang principles of cosmological harmony were soon used to extend the functions and increase the power of the Emperor.

As early as 602, according to the *Nihongi*, envoys from the Korean state of Paekché presented books on calendar-making, astrology, geomancy, and the art of making oneself invisible. And in 607 an Imperial edict was issued that shows us how Yin Yang principles were utilized to strengthen the position of the Emperor:

> We hear that long ago, when our Imperial ancestors ruled, they—prostrating themselves before Heaven and walking quietly on earth—earnestly honored the Kami of Heaven and earth *(amatsukami kunitsukami)*, offered prayers to [the Kami of] the various mountains and rivers, and in mysterious ways were in communication with [the spirits of] Heaven and earth. Hence they developed and harmonized Yin and Yang and made ready to come together in procreation.[4]

After the Great Reforms of 645, when both Confucianism and Buddhism were beginning to receive offical support, the forces of Yin and Yang were still referred to in Imperial edicts which affirmed the sacred origin of Imperial rule, as can be seen in the opening lines of an edict issued in 646:

> Originally, Heaven and earth, Yin and Yang, and the four seasons were not in conflict with each other, and they created this Heaven and earth, and everything therein. Of the many things created, man was the most sacred. And the most sacred man was the sage *(hijiri)* ruler. Thus the sage-ruler Emperor or Empress finds his or her normative character in Heaven and rules the world below while considering the welfare of man, not forgetting it for a moment.[5]

Then when Emperor Temmu moved, between 673 and 686, to strengthen the Imperial system, he built an astrological observatory and established a Yin Yang Bureau within the Central Affairs Ministry. The Bureau was staffed with Yin Yang Masters *(onyōji)* who were

4. *Nihongi,* Suiko 15–2–9 [NKBT, 68.188–189].
5. *Nihongi,* Taika 2–8–14 [NKBT, 68.298–299].

to observe the movements of heavenly bodies, make the calendar, divine the future, and conduct occult rites. Temmu and his predecessors apparently were consciously attempting to make the Emperor—already a high priest for the worship of native Kami—into a ruler who could also assure peace and prosperity for the empire by taking steps—in the Chinese manner—to establish and maintain cosmic harmony.

Confucian "benevolent acts" of government (*jinsei*), as well as Buddhist rites, were thought to be actions that would re-establish cosmic harmony and thus eliminate—or alleviate the effects of—such disasters as epidemics, droughts, earthquakes, and floods. At the time of a particularly serious drought in 732, the Imperial Court first sent messengers to pray for rain at shrines in and around the capital; and when these were not answered, the reading of Buddhist scriptures and the performance of "benevolent acts" of government were ordered. The edict issued at the time reads in part as follows:

> There was a shortage of rain this spring, and because no rain has fallen during the summer, the water level in all the rivers has dropped and plants are withering. Certainly this is due to my lack of virtue, not because of any wrongs committed by the people. We have ordered that offerings be made at shrines located at famous mountains and large rivers in the capital and the various provinces. And [now] I order that a careful investigation be made to determine whether anyone has been placed in jail on false charges, that the dead be buried, that drinking *sake* and killing animals be prohibited, that welfare support (*shinkyū*) be increased for those who cannot sustain life on their own (because they are old or have been left without any support from others), and that an amnesty be declared throughout the country for the following types of persons. . . .[6]

Clearly the purpose was to remove disharmony, which was assumed to have been caused by human actions that were thought to be in conflict with the forces and movements of the cosmos.

Entries in the National Histories also reveal an increasing familiarity with Confucian principles. Clues to the nature and strength of that intellectual current emerge from a comparison of an Imperial edict issued in 697 (at the beginning of the Mommu reign) with one issued in 884 (at the beginning of the Kōkō reign). Although the former refers to the Emperor as a "manifest Kami" (*akitsumikami*) in an apparent attempt to transform the Japanese sovereign into an absolute ruler of the Chinese type, stress is placed on the Emperor's place in a divine and unbroken line of descent from the Sun God-

---

6. *Shoku Nihongi*, Tempyō 4–7–5 [KT, 2.128–129]. I have consulted, and used some sentences found in, Philip Thompson's unpublished translations of Imperial edicts found in the *Shoku Nihongi*.

dess, and no reference is made to Confucian virtue.[7] The latter, on the other hand, first reiterates the doctrine of "Heavenly sun-succession" but goes on to state that the Emperor has little virtue, refers to "good and wise ministers," proclaims that relief is to be given to the elderly, the widowed, and the poor, and announces that taxes not paid since the beginning of the previous reign are to be forgiven.[8]

During the intervening years, Japanese aristocrats had become more familiar with the Confucian classics. An Educational Bureau (*daigakuryō*) with a Confucian orientation had been made an integral part of the post-645 bureaucratic structure, and the sons of the principal clans were spending several years in the schools that had been established by the Educational Bureau and its provincial branches. Before the last National History had been compiled, *some* ambitious aristocrats were able to rise to inordinately high positions in government because of scholarly achievement in the study of Confucian literature and Chinese history. The whole of Japanese aristocratic culture, including the writing of history, had come to be affected by the ideas and principles expressed in the Confucian classics. Ever since that day, Japanese history writing has usually contained references to Confucian principles. And yet the case for the effect of Confucianism on early Japanese historical writing tends to be over-stated. No item in a National History carries the implication—even though there were Imperial edicts that claimed an Emperor had "little virtue"—that an Emperor's lack of virtue either justified his removal from the throne or the establishment of a new dynasty. Finally, it should be noted that the Japanese interest in Confucian thought was not associated, as it was in China, with the formation and power of a distinct literati class. So while the later National Histories contain an increasingly large number of Confucian terms and ideas, they never take on the exemplary character of a Chinese dynastic history.

The National Histories also reflect a growing interest in Buddhism, a foreign religion introduced from Korea and China. By the time the *Shoku Nihongi*—the second of the Six National Histories—was submitted to the court at the end of the eighth century, a system of government-supported Buddhist temples had made Buddhism into something like a state religion. Later National Histories therefore carry a vast amount of information about an increasingly active Buddhist movement. But, as in the case of Confucianism, this information leaves the impression that Buddhist symbols and ceremonies were valued above all for their magic power to prevent or

7. *Shoku Nihongi*, Mommu 1–8–17 [KT, 2.1].
8. *Nihon sandai jitsuroku*, Gangyō 8–2–23 [KT, 4.550–551].

alleviate calamity. Time after time an Emperor ordered Buddhist scriptures read or copied, Buddhist statues made, or temples built, for the purpose of stopping an epidemic or drought, curing the illness of an aristocratic dignitary, or bringing peace and prosperity to the state. In 741, after a succession of natural disasters, Emperor Shōmu decreed that Buddhist temples be constructed in every province of the land. At the beginning of his edict he states that an earlier edict had been followed by a good harvest, and then he justifies his decision to establish provincial temples in this way:

> In the [Ultimately Successful King *(saishō-ō)*] Sutra it is written that when a King shall cause this Sutra to be read, expounded devoutly, and propagated throughout the realm, the Four Deva Kings shall surely come to protect that country against all calamity, to avert sorrow and pestilence, and to cause the hearts of believers to be filled with joy forever. In view of this . . . it is my wish that the sacred Law of Buddha be made to flourish for so long as Heaven and earth shall last and that its protective blessings be bestowed upon the living and the dead forever.[9]

Emperor Shōmu and his daughter, Empress Kōken, were certainly ardent Buddhist believers; and by the middle of the eighth century Buddhist institutions had amassed considerable economic and political power. But Imperial edicts such as this suggest that magic—often focused on the mysterious power residing in a Buddha bone *(shari)* placed at the base of a pagoda—may have been the most basic ingredient of Japanese Buddhist faith until the establishment of the Tendai and Shingon sects at the beginning of the ninth century.[10]

Another important element in the early Buddhism of Japan—one reflected in the National Histories and one that has continued to be central to Buddhism in Japan—was the belief that Buddhist prayers and ceremonies were efficacious in quieting, consoling, and honoring souls of the dead. Until the sixth century, when Buddhism was probably first introduced to Japan, souls of deceased leaders were accorded special treatment at impressive burial mounds. But Japanese aristocrats came gradually to believe that conducting memorial services at impressive Buddhist temples was a superior way to honor and appease souls of the dead. As early as 606, according to the *Nihongi,* rites were held in all Buddhist temples on the 15th day of the 7th month, the traditional day for Festivals of the Dead; and later National Histories include numerous references to the reading of the Ullambana Sutra *(urabon-kyō),* the celebration of the Ullambana Festival *(urabon-e),* the presentation of Ullambana offer-

9. *Shoku Nihongi,* Tempyō 13–3–24 [KT, 2.163–164].
10. Cf. Kenko Futaba, *Kodai Bukkyō shisō shi kenkyū* (Tokyo, 1962), pp. 70–95.

ings *(urabon-gu)*, and the holding of Ullambana Entertainments *(urabon-sai)*—all of which were meant to please and honor the souls of deceased dignitaries.[11] Such evidence leads one to conclude that the traditional relationship between Buddhist worship and what is loosely called "ancestor worship" was beginning to emerge. Although the Festival of the Dead seems never to have been celebrated in India where the historic Buddha lived, and did not become popular in China until the sixth century, it clearly had an early and lasting appeal in Japan. But Ullambana rites were held only to honor the souls of Emperors, Empresses, and other prominent aristocrats.[12] Buddhist memorial rites for the ancestors of commoners did not come until much later.

In trying to assess the extent to which Buddhism had penetrated the historical consciousness of those who compiled the National Histories, one must pay close attention to references which suggest that the universalistic message of Buddhism was appealing. Of special interest are items about rites held at Tōdai Temple and its branch-like provincial temples, rites that were based upon teachings found in one or another of the "three protect-the-state sutras" *(chingo kokka sambukkyō)*: (1) the Golden Light Sutra *(konkōmyō-kyō)*; (2) the Benevolent Ruler Sutra *(ninnō-kyō)*; and (3) the Lotus Sutra *(hokke-kyō)*. The contents of those sutras, as well as the nature of the rites derived from them, leave no doubt but that they were appreciated—in Japan as well as in China—for their promise of Buddhist blessings for *any* state or ruler who would abide by their teachings. But probably the universalism of Buddhism was most clearly represented by Tōdai Temple's central object of worship, the fifty-foot statue of Vairocana which symbolized the twenty-five realms of existence. In spite of such representations of Buddhist universalism, it seems quite clear, however, that the *endless* power and authority of Buddha were valued most for the magic protection they provided one *particular* state and its ruler (Japan and the Japanese Emperor), and that the Buddhist message of salvation for all people at all times and places was not yet fully appreciated. To be sure, Saichō (767–822) and Kūkai (774–835) had both returned from China and founded the Tendai and Shingon sects before the last of the Six National Histories had been compiled, and these two religious thinkers based their teachings on the Buddhist message of universal salvation. But their thought cannot be detected in National Histories.

11. M. W. DeVisser, *Ancient Buddhism in Japan* (Leiden, 1935), 1.58–115. Ichirō Ishida thinks that these *urabon* rites were not merely for the ancestors of a particular clan but for deceased fathers and mothers generally.

12. Masao Maruyama notes that early Japanese chronicles do not speak of ceremonies held at burial mounds but pay considerable attention to what was done at the *mogari no miya,* the temporary place of interment.

Preoccupation with Divine Imperial Descent

Even though the National Histories have a strong Chinese flavor, native belief in the divine origin of the Imperial line made it impossible, as already noted, for the compilers of those chronicles to accept the Chinese doctrine that Heaven would ever hand down a mandate for the establishment of a new dynasty if rulers of the current dynasty were not virtuous. But more convincing evidence of preoccupation with divine origins and continuity of the Imperial line is found in the earliest extant chronicles, the *Kojiki* and the *Nihongi*. The very first chapters of both are devoted to the task of showing just how the earliest Kami were linked by successive generations of Kami descent to the first human Emperor.

The first two chapters of the *Nihongi*, entitled "Kami generations" *(Kami yo)*, begin with the first-generation Kami (Earth Eternal Standing Kami) and end with the birth of Japan's first Emperor, the son of a twelfth-generation Kami. Special attention is given to the creative acts of the seventh-generation couple (Izanagi and Izanami) to whom is attributed the creation (or procreation) of the islands, mountains, rivers, and plants of Japan, as well as the birth of an eight-generation Kami (the Sun Goddess) who is picked to rule over Izanagi's and Izanami's earthly creation. The second chapter on "Kami generations" opens with myths about the efforts of the Sun Goddess to get her son and then her grandson (Ninigi no Mikoto) to go down to earth and assume control over the Japanese islands. Then come myths that tell us of Ninigi no Mikoto's descent from Heaven to the islands of Japan and his marriage to the beautiful daughter of another Heavenly Kami. Later sections describe the exploits of their second son, married to a daughter of the Kami of the Sea, and end with Ninigi's grandson (a twelfth-generation Kami) producing a son who was to become Japan's first Emperor, a human being descended directly from the Sun Goddess.

The third *Nihongi* chapter moves to the reign of Emperor Jimmu, the first-generation human descendant of the Sun Goddess. It tells of his expedition to the east, the establishment of his control over the inhabitants of the islands, and his assumption of the throne as ruler of the Japanese islands. The remaining chapters, covering Imperial reigns through that of Jitō (690–702), detail the relationship of each Emperor or Express to his or her predecessor and successor, affirming over and over the belief that every sovereign stood in a direct line of descent from the Sun Goddess, a Heavenly Kami who had been produced by Izanagi and Izanami to reign over the Japanese islands. Although written in Chinese and influenced by Chinese ideas and beliefs, the *Nihongi* and the five other National Histories reflect an unwavering commitment to this native belief in the sacredness of the Imperial line.

While the power of this native belief seems to account for the basic form and intent of the National Histories, the imprint of that belief is deeper and sharper in the *Kojiki*, the chronicle thought to have been completed and presented to the court in 712. Although the *Nihongi* and the *Kojiki* were compiled at about the same time, and by men who seemed to have had access to the same body of sources, the Chinese flavor is much weaker, and the effects of native belief stronger, in the *Kojiki*. In the latter, Chinese characters are used phonetically for recording Japanese names and words, and the contents are not much influenced by Confucian ideas and principles. Since the *Kojiki* was finished eight years earlier than the *Nihongi*, and did not touch upon any reign after that of Empress Suiko (554–628), students of early Japanese history have tended to accept the Motoori Norinaga (1730–1801) view that the *Kojiki* provided a clearer picture of Japanese life before the wholesale importation of Chinese ideas and practices because it was the oldest chronicle. But Isezō Umezawa concludes that at least one Chinese-style chronicle preceded the *Nihongi* and that the compilation of the *Kojiki*—especially when seen in the light of the political and cultural situation that prevailed during the reign of Temmu (673–686)—resulted, in part at least, from a desire to counteract Chinese concepts of sovereignty which had seeped into earlier Chinese-like chronicles.[13]

While the reader may not be justified in concluding that the *Kojiki* was written by men who were simply reacting to Chinese ideas of sovereignty, he will readily admit that *Kojiki* treatments of past events reveal far less commitment to Confucian virtue than do *Nihongi* accounts of those same events. A notable example of the difference is found in the way the two chronicles handle the succession dispute which followed the death of Emperor Ōjin early in the fifth century. Both the *Nihongi* and the *Kojiki* say that Ōjin selected his younger son (Prince Uji) for the post of Crown Prince; that following the death of Ōjin, Prince Uji urged his elder brother (Prince Ōsazaki) to take the throne; that Prince Ōsazaki refused; and that no one occupied the throne until Prince Uji died and Prince Ōsazaki was enthroned as Emperor Nintoku. But there the similarities end.

According to the *Nihongi*, Prince Uji urged his elder brother to take the throne because Uji himself was stupid and lacked ability, whereas Ōsazaki was wise and able. The chronicle goes on to say that Prince Ōsazaki denied that he possessed wisdom and ability, pointed out that Ōjin had selected Uji as his successor, and insisted that Ōjin's wishes be respected. For three years, says the *Nihongi*, the two brothers deferred to each other and finally Uji decided to settle the

13. *Kojiki Nihon shoki* (Tokyo, 1971). Ichirō Ishida reports that Umezawa has revised his position somewhat.

matter by committing suicide. Prince Ōsazaki hastened to his dead
brother's side and, while "beating his breast and weeping aloud," Uji
came back to life. Ōsazaki then asked Uji why he had done such a
thing, and the reply—as recorded in the *Nihongi*—was: "It is the
command of Heaven. Who may stay it?"[14] In the *Nihongi's* treatment
of the incident, wisdom and ability seem to be more important than
the expressed will of the previous Emperor.

The *Kojiki* account of the same dispute, on the other hand, makes
no reference to wisdom, virtue, or commands of Heaven. It states
that "after the death of Ōjin, and in accordance with the command
of Ōjin, Prince Ōsazaki ceded the kingdom to Prince Uji." When Uji
urged his elder brother to take the throne, Ōsazaki refused. The
reasons given are not recorded in the *Kojiki,* but it is implied that
such action would have been contrary to Ōjin's expressed will. The
treatment of the affair is concluded with this brief statement: "However, Prince Uji died young and Prince Ōsazaki ruled the kingdom."[15] Here the decisive point seems to be the will of the previous
Emperor. The Imperial line of direct descent from the Sun Goddess
was to be maintained by expressions of sacred Imperial will, not by
foreign concepts of how an Emperor should behave.

Belief in the divine origins and descent of Japan's priestly rulers
made the compilers of the *Kojiki* far more interested than the compilers of the *Nihongi* in the country's creative Kami and in the
genealogical connection between those Kami and the Imperial line.
The following features of the *Kojiki* reveal the strength of that belief:
(1) it deals with five Kami generations that precede the earliest Kami
(Earth Eternal Standing Kami) discussed in the *Nihongi;* (2) its chapters in some cases contain only information on the genealogy of Emperors and Empresses; and (3) later chapters deal almost exclusively
with the predecessors, palaces, spouses, and children of a succession
of Japanese sovereigns, and with such matters as the selection of a
Crown Prince, the problems of establishing Imperial authority, and
the location of a deceased Emperor's or Empress's tomb. Although
not all entries are related directly to matters of Imperial descent—
Emperor Nintoku is even referred to as a "sage ruler" in the Confucian manner—the *Kojiki* draws a remarkably straight and clear line
between the first Heavenly Kami (Ame no minaka-nushi no Kami)
and Empress Suiko, who seems to have stood, in the minds of the
person or persons who compiled the *Kojiki,* at the end of Japan's
ancient past.

14. Nintoku reign [NKBT, 67.383–388].
15. Chapter 2, NKBT, 1.249–254. In making this and other translations
from the *Kojiki,* I have consulted Donald L. Philippi's *Kojiki: Translations
and Notes* (Princeton, and Tokyo, 1969).

Why the Kojiki Was Compiled

The order which Emperor Temmu issued in 681, and which is
quoted in the preface to the *Kojiki*, explains why the *Kojiki* (or something like it) was to be compiled:

> I hear that "Imperial records" *(teiki)* and "accounts of origin"
> *(honji)* handed down by the various houses have come to differ
> from the truth and that many falsehoods have been added. If
> these errors are not corrected at this time, the meaning of the
> records and accounts—the warp and woof of the Japanese state
> and the foundations of Imperial rule—will be lost before many
> years have passed. Therefore a study of the "Imperial records"
> for the purpose of selecting out and recording what is true, and
> an examination of the "ancient accounts" *(kyūji)* for the purpose of
> rejecting errors and determining truth, are commanded because I
> wish to have true records and accounts passed on to later genera-
> tions.[16]

Scholars are inclined to agree that the "Imperial records" included
genealogical information about Emperors and Empresses, but they
disagree about the character and content of the term "accounts of
origin" *(honji)*. Ishida feels that by equating *honji* with "ancient accounts" *(kyūji)*, earlier historians have missed the full significance
of "origins."[17] He points out that the first character of *honji* is the
one used for "origin" *(moto* when used alone) in a 612 *Nihongi* item
stating that a certain SOGA chieftain had had someone "eulogize"
(shinobigoto) the origins *(moto)* of his clan and hereditary title."[18] This
interpretation of the word *honji* indicates that Emperor Temmu,
when using the phrase "the warp and woof of the Japanese state and
the foundations of Imperial rule," was thinking not only of an accurate record of the Imperial line but of a "true account" of Kami
origins, helping us to understand why both the *Nihongi* and the
Kojiki were introduced by long chapters on "Kami generations."

The Roots and Power of the Preoccupation with Lineage

This close attention to successive generations of rulers who were in
turn descendants of successive generations of Kami seems to have
been rooted in ancient assumptions about the importance of a ruler's
divine origins and descent. The thousands of large burial mounds
erected for deceased rulers during the four centuries or so that preceded the compilations of the *Kojiki* and *Nihongi* suggest that such
assumptions had led one ruler after another to use much of his resources for building an impressive mound in which to bury his pre-

16. Chapter 1, NKBT, 1.44–47.
17. "Shinwa to rekishi," *Nihon bunka kenkyū* (Tokyo, 1960), pp. 18–22.
18. Suiko 19–2–20 [NKBT, 68.197].

decessor. Since most mounds were built before the keeping of written records, and before clan chieftains had taken to honoring their ancestors by building Buddhist temples and holding Buddhist memorial services, we have no written explanations of why rulers set such great store by mound building. Nor do we have descriptions of ceremonies conducted at these mounds. We do have, however, a third-century Chinese account that says Japanese kingdoms were governed by hereditary rulers.[19] Also, references to mound building found in the *Kojiki* and *Nihongi* leave no doubt that mounds were built by rulers in order to honor their deceased predecessors. A study of archaeological evidence suggests, in addition, that the richest and most powerful rulers built the largest and most impressive mounds, surrounded these mounds with the longest moats and fences *(haniwa)*, and inserted into mounds the largest number of valuable articles *(fukusōhin)*. Why should they have been willing to use so much of their resources in this way?

Since none of them has left a statement of his reasons for building a mound in which to bury his or her predecessor, scholars have held different and often contradictory views of what was intended. Realizing that the Japanese have always considered a corpse to be the most abhorent of all forms of pollution, and that they thought of the corpse of a powerful ruler as the most polluted of all corpses, many writers have concluded that a ruler of those early mound-building times must have had a very strong urge to cover and guard the corpse of a predecessor in a manner appropriate to his status. Knowing too that the Japanese have usually believed that a soul lives on after death, others have deduced that an ancient mound builder was trying, in a manner commensurate with the dignity of the deceased, to keep the soul quiet and peaceful. Undoubtedly these were elements in a complex motivational pattern, but it is submitted that the living ruler must have consciously or unconsciously wished to legitimize, sanction, and enhance his own new position—through the burial enterprise—by identifying himself with the divine origins and descent of this particular line of rulers. The current clan head or Emperor may have wanted to remove death pollution, to quiet the soul of his deceased predecessor, and to keep this soul contented in its life after death, but the head must also have had a deep urge to remind everyone, in the most impressive way possible, that he or she was the next link in a divine chain going back to the Kami which had created that particular line of succession.

If we knew more about the ceremonies conducted at mounds, we could be more certain about the ways in which a ruler affirmed his

19. *Wei Chih,* 30.25b–31a, as translated in Ryusaku Tsunoda, *Japan in Chinese Dynastic Histories* (South Pasadena, 1951), p. 9.

ties with his predecessor, and with his predecessor's predecessors, but neither archaeological investigations nor contemporary Chinese and Korean accounts tell us much about funerals held in Japan during the burial mound age (roughly A.D. 250–650). Ishida calls our attention, however, to three references in the *Nihongi* that refer to eulogies *(shinobigoto)* delivered at burial grounds. The latest and probably most reliable of the three is the one found in a 688 statement about ceremonies held at the tomb of Emperor Temmu, who had died in 686:

> On this occasion offerings of food were made and the "shield measure" dance was performed. Several Imperial Chieftains advanced in turn and presented eulogies which set forth the details of service rendered by ancestors.[20]

In another item added a few days later, we read that "Chitoko . . . eulogized the line of the Emperor's succession from the Sun Goddess."[21] Funeral services were certainly not limited to eulogies, but such references suggest that a funeral—like the *Kojiki* and the *Nihongi*—had a genealogical focus arising from belief in a lineal transmission of authority which, in the case of an Emperor, originated with the Sun Goddess and led directly to the current occupant of the throne. The "setting forth of the details of service rendered by ancestors" in a eulogy delivered at the time of burial must have been a verbal expression of lineage beliefs which justified the burial enterprise as a whole.

After the last half of the sixth century, as has been noted, huge and exotic Buddhist temples were also built by the heads of strong clans for the purpose of honoring and pleasing the souls of deceased predecessors. The *Nihongi* reports that the Asuka Temple (also known as the Hōkō-ji) was built by SOGA Umako, after his coup of 587, in order to fulfill a vow that he had taken. It is assumed that Umako had vowed to build a Buddhist temple if and when he succeeded in destroying the rival clan of MONONOBE. The *Nihongi* supplies no further information about Umako's motives for building the temple, but recent archaeological investigations carried out on the Asuka Temple site show that the central structure of the temple was a large pagoda *(tō)*, that a box enclosing a Buddha bone *(shari)* has been placed at the base of the pagoda, and that replicas of valuable articles customarily placed in burial mounds *(fukusōhin)* had been buried under or near the Buddha bone. Since *fukusōhin*-like objects were found in the most sacred place of the temple, it seems that Umako had consciously or unconsciously built the Asuka Tem-

20. Jitō 2–11–4 [NKBT, 68.492–493].
21. Jitō 2–11–11 [NKBT, 68.493].

ple for reasons akin to those that caused heads of great clans to bury deceased predecessors in huge earthen mounds. This deduction gains additional support from a 594 *Nihongi* statement that officials were beginning to vie with one another in building Buddhist temples "in appreciation for blessings *(on)* received from [deceased] sovereigns *(kimi)* and parents *(oya)*.²²

Further support for the view that early temples were built to honor deceased sovereigns—as burial mounds were—is obtained from two inscriptions carved on Buddhist statues made early in the seventh century. The earlier one reads:

> When Emperor Yōmei was ill in 586, prayers were offered and a vow was made for his recovery, but since the Emperor died before the vow was fulfilled, this statue of Yakushi Nyorai was completed during the year 607 in response to an order issued by Empress Suiko and Prince Shōtoku.²³

One purpose in having the statue made was to cure Emperor Yōmei's illness, but when Yōmei died the statue was completed in compliance with an order issued by Yōmei's sister (the reigning Empress) and his son (the Crown Prince). Another inscription on a statue made sixteen years later explains the circumstances under which this statue was completed:

> In 621, Princess Hishito, the mother of Prince Shōtoku, died. In the 1st month of the following year, the Prince and his consort, Princess Kashiwade no Kokikimi no Iratsume, also became ill. Then the Prince, his consort, and other princes vowed to have this statue made. In the 2nd month of that year [622], the Prince and his consort both died, but this statue was completed in 623 by the Buddhist priest Kuratsukuri no Obitotori.²⁴

This inscription, found on the back of the famous Buddhist Trinity at Hōryū-ji, reflects a preoccupation with the death of Imperial ancestors.

Ceremonies held at the earliest Buddhist temples also suggest that the practice of Buddhism by clans at clan temples *(ujidera)* was emerging from convictions and concerns not unlike those that were leading clan leaders to build burial mounds for deceased predecessors. A *Nihongi* entry for 659 reveals that the Urabon Sutra was being expounded at all temples of the capital "as an expression of gratitude to seven generations of ancestors."²⁵ It seems quite clear,

22. Suiko 2 (594)–2 [NKBT, 68.174–175].
23. Quoted in Inouye Mitsusada, *Nihon no rekishi: Asuka no chōtei* (Tokyo, 1965), 3.213.
24. Ibid., 3.214.
25. Saimei 5 (659)–7–15 [NKBT, 68.340–341].

therefore, that Japanese Buddhism was already assuming a character that has caused many to place the worship of Buddha at the core of what is termed "Japanese ancestor worship." With the seventh-century spread of clan temples, fewer burial mounds were constructed, suggesting that the building of exotic Buddhist temples was coming to be thought of as a more impressive (and therefore more appropriate) way to satisfy an urge that had led rulers at an earlier time to erect huge burial mounds. Thus all three of the endeavors discussed above—mound building, temple building, and chronicle compiling—were all rooted in a deep and persistent belief in the divine origins and descent of clan heads, especially of Emperors and Empresses who headed the dominant Imperial clan. And by all three, a succession of sovereigns for the emerging Japanese state were sanctifying and enhancing their authority as divine descendants of the Sun Goddess.

The seriousness of interest in lineage stands clearly revealed in an early *Nihongi* report, under an item for the year 415, that Emperor Ingyō had issued a decree saying:

> Ministers, functionaries, and provincial governors *(miyatsuko)* all claim that they are descendants of Emperors or various [Kami] who have miraculously come down from Heaven. . . . Ever since that time when the world was separated into three parts [Heaven, Earth and Man], thousands of years have passed and each clan has proliferated and received thousands of hereditary titles *(kabane)*. In order to determine the truth of what is difficult to know [about such claims], let all [heads of] clans and all holders of hereditary titles immerse [their hands] in boiling water, avoid pollution, and subject themselves to divine judgment *(kugatachi)*.[26]

The *Nihongi* goes on to say that tubs of boiling water were taken to a certain hill where everyone was told that if his claims were true he would not be harmed by placing his hands in the boiling water. Reporting that truthful persons were unharmed and that liars fled in terror, the item ends with the comment that "henceforth [claims about] clan [descent] and hereditary titles were automatically settled and no one told any more lies."[27]

It was undoubtedly such feelings about the importance of direct descent from a clan's creative Kami that had led the heads of clans to bury their deceased predecessors in huge mounds, that had led later Emperors and Empresses to erect Buddhist temples "as expressions of gratitude to seven generations of ancestors," that had led Emperor Temmu to order that "Imperial records" and "accounts of origin" be corrected and recorded, and that had finally led Empress

26. Ingyō 4–9–28 [NKBT, 67.438–439].
27. Idem.

Gemmei—who was appalled at the mistakes in the ancient accounts —to issue a command in 711 that ONO no Yasumaro record these "ancient accounts" that HIEDA no Are had practiced reading.[28]

Preoccupation with Imperial lineage had therefore colored the thoughts and actions of Japan's ruling class for a long time, affecting not only ancient burial practices and the introduction and spread of Buddhism but the use of imported techniques for compiling chronicles. Even though officials who compiled the *Nihongi* (and the other five National Histories) were influenced by Chinese models of record keeping—and were affected by Taoist, Confucian, and Buddhist ideas valued for their applicability to all peoples—their primary purpose was to affirm the uniqueness of Japan's line of priestly rulers. The marks of that purpose are much clearer, however, in the *Kojiki*. Thus Japan's first two extant chronicles—the more universalistic *Nihongi* and the more particularistic *Kojiki*—highlight a deep value tension in early historical expression.

The tension has persisted from that day to this. Whenever the Japanese have fallen under the spell of a foreign culture (Asian or Western), historical writing has been weighted by foreign ideas accepted and valued by the Japanese for their universal applicability. But at times of relative isolation from (or reaction to) foreign culture, historical works have been shaped by beliefs that are uniquely Japanese. At such times—especially in modern centuries—a deeper interest in the *Kojiki* has emerged as nationalistic writers have argued that the time had come for another restoration *(fukko)* of direct rule by the current descendant of the Sun Goddess.

As we shall see, the next two types of pre-*Gukanshō* historical writing are touched by the effects of an early drift from Chinese models to Japanese belief in sacred Imperial origins and descent. Although these two types, discussed in later sections of this chapter, reflect a somewhat deeper appreciation of Buddhist thought introduced from the continent, both stand somewhat closer to lineage beliefs (prominent in the *Kojiki*) than to universalistic ideas and principles (detected in the Six National Histories).

Historical Tales

The first thirty chapters of the *Eiga Monogatari*, the earliest work of Japan's second type of history, were not written until well over a century after the last National History had been presented to Emperor Daigo in 901. By that century, Japanese aristocrats had lost much of their old enthusiasm for Chinese political forms, and Emperors had stopped ordering the compilation of National Histories. Japanese officials had also come to permit the establishment of extra-

28. *Kojiki* preface [NKBT, 1.46–47].

legal organs of government which overshadowed the Chinese bureaucratic system built when Chinese methods were being used to
create and maintain a Chinese-like empire. And Japanese aristocrats,
especially women, were gaining a new appreciation of the Japanese
language and using it to write stories and compose poems. Even old
shrines for the worship of native Kami were becoming stronger and
contributing to the acceleration of Shinto-Buddhist fusion. By the
time the first thirty chapters of the *Eiga* had been written around
1030, Japanization was therefore well advanced. So it is not surprising that the *Eiga*, even though it was apparently intended to bring
the last National History up to date, should have strayed far from
the basic pattern of an official Chinese history. And yet, new Chinese
influences are detected. During the eleventh century, Japanese aristocrats were becoming more deeply interested in imported forms of
Buddhism associated with teachings concerning an inevitable and
continuous deterioration in Buddhist Law, in the abilities and life
expectancy of man, and in the conditions of the physical world.
Since Buddhism was to leave an increasingly deep imprint upon
later historical works (including the *Gukanshō*), this introductory section on Historical Tales will begin with an attempt to outline the
development of those strains of Buddhist thought that served to
make the Japanese believe in and write about continuous deterioration in history. Then an attempt will be made to identify central
qualities in the two principal Historical Tales (the *Eiga monogatari*
and the *Ōkagami*) to appear before the *Gukanshō* was completed in
1219.

Spread of Buddhist Doctrines of Continuous Decline

In reflecting upon Buddhist eschatology, Chinese Buddhists had
identified three forms of Buddhism that were felt to be appropriate
for three distinct stages of deterioration of Buddhist Law: (1) One
Vehicle Buddhism for the age of True Law; (2) Three Vehicle
Buddhism for the age of Imitation Law; and (3) "universally correct
and true Buddhism" for the age of Final Law. An early Japanese
interest in these "three teachings" *(sankai kyō)* is detected in the
Miraculous Exhibition of Virtue and Vice in Japan *(Nihon ryōiki)*,
written in about 820. The author (Keikai) not only identified the
length of the three ages of Buddhist Law but counted the number of
years that had elapsed since the death of Shakyamuni. As for the
sorry state of current affairs, he wrote: "We have already entered
the closing years of the present [deteriorating half of the present
small] kalpa. . . . I pray for birth in the western [Pure Land]
paradise."[29] But Saichō (767–822), the priest who introduced Tendai

29. Quoted in Tomio Ozawa, *Mappō to masse no shisō* (Tokyo, 1974), p. 30.

Buddhism to Japan, was the first Japanese priest to articulate the thesis that Tendai teachings and precepts should be accepted because they were more appropriate than other Buddhist teachings for the age of Final Law.

At the outset of Saichō's great debate with the Nara priests, which began when he wrote his *Ebyō Tendai shū* in 816, he argued that Tendai teachings were a synthesis of all that had been thought and written by famous Buddhist teachers of India and China. Because his arguments for the superiority of Tendai teachings were denounced by priests of the Nara temples, he wrote another book (the *Shō gonjitsu kyō*) in which he outlined the "ten points" of strength that continental Buddhists had identified. Then, in 818, as the debate became more intense, he wrote the *Shugo kokkai shō* in which his principal thesis was that Tendai Buddhism—or what he called the Great Vehicle of the Lotus Sutra—had special value for guarding the state. It was then that Saichō personally rejected the 250 precepts that all Nara priests accepted at the time of ordination—and that Saichō himself had accepted in 785—and moved to obtain Imperial sanction for the 58 precepts of Tendai *(endonkai)* and the establishment of a Tendai ordination hall *(endon kaidan)* so that the Great Vehicle of the Lotus Sutra could properly guard the Japanese state. In the *Shugo kokkai shō*, Saichō seems to have begun to think of his Great Vehicle as a message for the final age of Buddhist Law, since he writes there that "The ages of True Law and Imitation Law are gradually passing, and the age of Final Law is near." But the view is made more explicit in a memorial submitted to the throne in 819:

> It has come down to me from former Buddhist teachers that, for the purpose of protecting states and guarding houses, the Great Vehicle is very powerful and the assistance of the Bodhisattva very great. In these closing years of the age of Imitation Law, the "seven difficulties" emerge easily. And at this time the "five pollutions" and the "three disasters" cannot be avoided. So now we must turn away from the Small Vehicle and look to the Great Vehicle.[30]

His thoughts on the superiority of the Great Vehicle for an advanced stage of deterioration in Buddhist Law were more fully developed in his *Kenkai ron* of 820 and the *Hokke shūku* of 821. The whole last chapter of the *Hokke shūku* is focused upon that theme. The poem which he inserted at the end of that chapter shows that Saichō had come to think of the Great Vehicle not merely as a doctrinal synthesis which has the power to guard and protect the Japanese state, but as the vehicle of teachings particularly appropri-

---

30. *Dengyō daishi zenshū*, 1.590.

ate for the final age of Buddhist Law and the deteriorated "phase of
necessary conflict" in the abilities of man.[31]

Kūkai (744–835), a contemporary of Saichō, had also accepted the
Buddhist doctrine of continuous decline. He even counted the
number of years that would pass before the present small kalpa
would end. But it was not until En'nin (794–864) returned from
China in 847 that a Buddhist temple (the Jōgyō Sammai In) was built
for the worship of Amitābha, the Buddha to be worshipped in the
age of Final Law. At this new temple the name of Amitābha was
recited *(nembutsu)*, and the rite of "ceaselessly repeating the name of
Amitābha" *(fudan nembutsu)* was held before a statue of Amitābha
that is said to have emerged from the ocean on En'nin's way back
from China. En'nin also wrote a book, the *Jakkōdo ki* (Notes on
Paradise), which contains what is thought to be an early Japanese
expression of the Pure-Land idea that Amitābha was the Buddha to
be worshipped in the world's final age of deterioration. He writes
there that during the first one thousand years after the historic
Buddha's death (the age of True Law) this world was paradise; that
during the next thousand years (the age of Imitation Law) the two
worlds (paradise and this world) seemed to be distinct from each
other; but that thereafter (in the age of Final Law) they would be
actually separated. He added that in the final age people would find
it extremely difficult to enter paradise by practicing Buddhism in the
old ways, but fortunately they would still be able to gain rebirth in
the western Pure Land paradise by relying on the teachings of
Amitābha.[32]

The spread of Pure Land Buddhism during the next four centuries, after which it emerged as a popular Buddhist sect, was due to
many interrelated factors. At the beginning, the popularity of such
teachings in T'ang China certainly made them more attractive to
En'nin and his followers. And the association of Pure Land with "ancestor worship"—in Japan as well as in China—was obviously a
source of strength. But it cannot be denied that the simple message
of salvation by faith had a special appeal for people who were told
that they were living at a time when the Final Law was about to
begin, or had already begun; and that it provided the vocabulary,
and was a stimulus, for viewing history as a process of continuous
decline. In the introduction to his famous *Ōjō yōshū* (Collection of
Important Teachings about Rebirth), written in 985, Genshin (942–
1017) explains that Pure Land teachings and practices are for people
living in "these polluted final reigns" and that such teachings and

31. Cf. Ichirō Ishida, *Gukanshō no seiritsu to sono shisō* (Sendai, 1967), pp.
57–63, and his "Jiki sō-ō no ronri," *Nihon jōdo-kyō no kenkyū* (Kyoto, 1969),
pp. 131–146.

32. Ishida, "Jiki sō-ō no ronri," pp. 150–151.

practices can be followed by anyone, whether priest or layman, nobleman or commoner.[33] Japanese intellectuals of that day were becoming convinced that the age of Final Law would begin in 1052, not in 550 as the Chinese had at first claimed. So Genshin was propagating a faith for an age that was thought to be near at hand. More and more people were certain, as Keikai had felt more than a century before, that now a person could only "pray for rebirth in the western paradise." Even FUJIWARA Michinaga (966–1027), the most powerful aristocrat of Japan's aristocratic age, built a temple for the worship of Amitābha. Although Michinaga undoubtedly thought of his temple (the Hōjō-ji) as a monument to his greatness, it certainly drew men's minds—as did the Byōdō In erected by his son in 1053–to a form of Buddhism that was believed to be most suitable for that particular point in a continuous process of deterioration.

By 1086, when retired Emperor Shirakawa took over the control of state affairs as a Cloistered Emperor *(insei),* the major aristocratic clans and the principal Buddhist monasteries were torn by constant dissension and conflict, providing unmistakable evidence that the age of Final Law had arrived. Entries in extant diaries for dates before 1086 refer to the coming of the age of Final Law, but later ones prefer such secular equivalents as "final reigns" *(matsudai)* and Final Age *(sue no yo).* Of special significance is the diary (the *Chūyū ki)* of FUJIWARA Munetada (1032–1141), covering the period between 1087 and 1138. Until about 1094, Munetada reveals almost nothing of his own feelings and judgments, but the destruction of the Imperial Palace in 1094 brings a change of tone. After recording considerable detail about the disaster, Munetada lists the some twenty times that the palace had been burned since 960 and then adds this comment:

> Later on it was heard that [an official of] the Sacred Mirror Room was saying that she had had a dream on the night before the fire and that she had heard the bell of the Sacred Mirror Room ring out. While she was thinking that this was strange, the Emperor's residence was being burned down. These were omens of what was to happen! Although these are really the "final reigns," the Kami should be revered![34]

In later years, of greater tension and conflict, Munetada seems to have become more deeply aware of deterioration associated with the "final reigns."[35] In the early months of 1113, hostilities broke out again between armed monks of Enryaku Temple of Mt. Hiei and the Kōfuku Temple of Nara. As several hundred armed monks moved

33. Shinshō Hanayama, ed., *Ōjō yōshū,* (Tokyo, 1937), p. 1.
34. Kanji 8–10–29 [*Shiryō tsūran: Chūyū ki,* 1.193].
35. William McCullough reminds me that "final reigns" *(masse),* a word introduced from China, had an essentially political meaning, not a religious

toward the palace of Retired Emperor Shirakawa, troops were mobilized by the court, and an emergency conference was held at the
Imperial Palace. Munetada writes:

> The Emperor wishes to do something about the power of the
> priestly mob. The authority of the Imperial House is being slighted.
> Isn't it a time of Heaven's destruction? The Emperor is going
> to yield to the demands of the mob, thinking that this cannot be
> helped. While officials are conferring without coming to a deci-
> sion, the priests are becoming thunderously angry. No one can
> rectify the situation. It is simply the time for the destruction of
> Buddhist Law.[36]

Twenty-eight days later, when it was rumored that the priests of
Nara were about to invade the capital, Munetada strikes a deeper
note of despair:

> In general it is observed that the world is on the verge of conflict.
> It is truly lamentable! Just now we have arrived at a time when
> both Imperial Law and Buddhist Law are about to be destroyed.
> The situation cannot be corrected the least bit by the power of
> man. What can be done?[37]

Then, after Nara priests and government troops had actually become engaged in battle, Munetada reports the number of killed and
wounded and then makes this comment: "Nothing like this has ever
happened before. We have simply come to the time for the destruction of Buddhist Law!"[38]

The first two Historical Tales, the *Eiga Monogatari* and the
Ōkagami, were written after Genshin and his followers had succeeded
in making Pure Land Buddhism a strong ingredient of the Tendai
synthesis, and in giving currency to the view that the age of Final
Law would soon begin, leaving the impression that conditions in
Japan would henceforth deteriorate more rapidly than ever.
Nevertheless, the authors of these first two Historical Tales seem not
to have been as deeply affected by Final-Law thought as were some
of the aristocrats who were keeping diaries at the time, or as were
the authors of later Military Tales.

The Eiga Monogatari

The author of the *Eiga Monogatari* (Tales of Splendor)—probably
a woman by the name of Akazome Emon—was apparently a Bud-

---

one. Munetaka's references to the "destruction of Buddhist Law" suggest,
however, that his sense of political decline was rooted in Buddhist eschatological doctrine.

36. Ten'ei 4–4–28 [*Shiryō tsūran: Chūyū ki,* 7.274].
37. Ten'ei 4–4–28 [ibid., 7.279].
38. Ten'ei 4–4–30 [ibid., 7.279–280].

dhist nun who devoted much of her book to rites and ceremonies held at Michinaga's Pure Land temple (the Hōjō-ji), but she seems to have been far more interested in the visual and dramatic aspects of those activities than in their religious or historical meaning.[39] However, she does make this significant statement after telling about the palace fire of 1013:

> World affairs became quite disturbed and people died. Actually, the Emperor's feelings were just right, and the Minister was not bad. But it seems that such things [as this disastrous fire] had to occur because the world is in its Final Age (*yo no sue*). Epidemics break out every year and people die. Many things occur that are very disturbing.[40]

But clearly the author was too engrossed in the glories of aristocratic life at the time of Michinaga—a life about which she seems to have had first-hand knowledge—to be much interested in signs of social decay or the significance of an age of Final Law that was to begin in 1052, although later sections of the account (thought to have been written around 1092) were more gloomy and critical.

The *Eiga Monogatari* is a Tale—the first of the Historical Tales—that describes the glamor and splendor of aristocratic life in the days of FUJIWARA Michinaga. The author was apparently attempting to continue the chronicle of Japan's past beyond the point reached in the last of the National Histories. The very first sentence of the *Eiga* states: "Although this country has had more than sixty Emperors and Empresses since the state first came into existence, I will not be able to write exhaustively about conditions in all those reigns. Instead, I will concentrate on the events of recent reigns."[41] Mention is made of Emperor Uda, who is not dealt with in the sixth National History, and the first few pages provide a brief review of the Daigo and Suzaku reigns (897–946). But much fuller treatment is given to developments after 946, suggesting that the author may have thought of her work as a continuation of the *Shin kokushi,* a seventh National History (not now extant) that is thought to have covered the reigns of Uda, Daigo, and Suzaku. Two chapters are on the forty-year period between 946 and 986, while twenty-eight are devoted to the following 40-year period that begins with Michinaga's first major appointment in 987 and ends with his death in 1027. Whole chapters tell of events that take place within the time span of a few months, and one is concerned only with the dedication of the Hōjō Temple that lasted three days. But as uneven as the *Eiga's*

39. Introduction to the forthcoming translation of the *Eiga monogatari,* translated by William and Helen McCullough, from Stanford University Press.

40. Chapter 8, NKBT, 75.248.

41. Chapter 1, NKBT, 75.27.

coverage is, the chronological form of a National History is maintained throughout.

Even though the author of the *Eiga* may have felt she was writing a chronicle that would begin where the last National History had left off, her book is fundamentally different from a National History. To begin with, the *Eiga* is not a chronicle that was compiled by an official acting upon orders handed down in an Imperial edict, but by a woman wishing to tell about the activities of individual aristocrats, especially FUJIWARA Michinaga. The National Histories, having a public character, contain numerous Imperial pronouncements, appointment lists, and reports of action taken by the government; whereas the *Eiga,* being private in nature, is filled with narrative accounts of what noble men and women had done—stories about their marriages, attendance at ceremonies and rites, and rivalries for Imperial favor. While compilers of National Histories worked from official documents and records, the *Eiga* author seems to have written mostly from recollections of what she had personally witnessed or from what others had said or written down in diaries. The National Histories contain terse and uninteresting reports of bureaucratic action and political rivalry, but the *Eiga* is made up of vivid and lively descriptions of spectacular episodes and incidents that were centered on the life of Michinaga. Furthermore, the *Eiga* is not written in Chinese, as the National Histories are, but in Japanese. By Akazome's day, as the Professors McCullough have noted, written Japanese had been "moulded into a sensitive tool of expression through a century or more of use and experimentation by female authors."[42] Thus the *Eiga* was a new form of historical expression: it told stories in Japanese about actual events of the recent past.

The historical and tale-telling qualities of the *Eiga* cannot be disentangled from each other—the chronological form is filled with tales, and the Tales reveal preoccupation with the past. Akazome's interest in writing them may have been aroused by familiarity with the literary work of Murasaki Shikibu, who had completed her famous *Tale of Genji* a few years before. Both women had frequented the Imperial Court in the glorious days of Michinaga, and they knew of each other's literary activities: Murasaki commented in her diary on Akazome's poetry; and, as the McCulloughs have shown, Akazome made extensive use of material found in the Murasaki diary.[43]

Akazome—if she really was the author of the *Eiga*—may also have been influenced by Murasaki Shikibu's views concerning the historical value of Tales. In the Fireflies chapter of the *Genji*, Murasaki has Prince Genji calling on Lady Tamakazura and finding her engrossed

42. Introduction, McCulloughs' translation of the *Eiga monogatari.*
43. Idem.

in the reading of Tales. At first he chides her for spending her time in this way, saying that "in all these Tales there is very little truth," but he continues in this vein:

> Tales are written accounts of what has happened in this world since the age of Kami. Chronicles like the *Nihongi* tell us only a small part of the whole, but Tales fill in the details. . . . In a Tale, what a certain person says or does is not told just as it happened. But whether the conditions of a man living in this world have been actually observed, or whether those conditions are good or bad, an author of a Tale—having feelings that are difficult to express—will begin to write down what he or she wishes to pass on to later generations. When dealing with what is good, the extremes of good are selected; and when dealing with a person who is disobedient, the oddities of his wrongdoing will be brought together. But any aspect of any subject discussed is of this world and no other. Tales written in other countries are different; old Japanese Tales differ from those that are modern; and the deep differ from the shallow. But even that which is entirely imaginary does not stray from the heart of the subject. In this sense Tales are like the scriptures in which Shakyamuni has left us explanations of what was in his noble heart. These take the form of "convenient devices" *(hōben)* which *suggest* the truth of his teachings. An unenlightened person will therefore have doubts and objections about these scriptural explanations. Many "convenient devices" are found in the Mahayana sutras; but if we see their implications, we will realize that they all serve the same purpose: to help a person free himself from carnal desires *(bonnō)* and achieve enlightenment *(bodai)*. A Tale which concerns itself only with the good and bad of man is different, and yet nothing in it is empty or meaningless.[44]

Murasaki seems to be telling her reader that Tales point to deep levels of truth about the past that are not revealed or suggested in such chronicles as the *Nihongi*.

The author of the *Eiga* may have had similar views about the historical value of Tales, but her Tales are less imaginary and closer to what actually happened in the past than those found in the *Genji*. The difference between the two is clearly revealed in their treatments of the exile of FUJIWARA Korechika (974–1010) in the year 996. In the *Genji*, the incident is touched upon in the Suma chapter where we are told about Prince Genji's sorrow and misery over leaving the capital. While Genji is a composite historical figure who is not given the name of Korechika, and Genji's departure from the capital

---

44. Fireflies Chapter, *Nihon koten bunaku zenshū*, 14.204–205. Ivan Morris's *The World of the Shining Prince* (New York, 1964), and Edward Seidensticker's *The Tale of Genji* (New York, 1976) have been consulted in translating this and other excerpts from the *Genji*.

is not referred to as exile, scholars agree that Murasaki was writing about the Korechika incident, which occurred when she was about eighteen years old. She has Genji speaking to Murasaki (possibly the *Genji* author herself) in this way:

> If years pass and I have not been pardoned by this world, I will welcome you to my distant place among the rocks. But people would not like me to take you with me now. A person who is out of favor with those at court is not permitted to see even the sun or the moon. I am told that it would even be a serious crime for such a person to live comfortably. Although I have done nothing wrong, this has probably happened because of a karma created in a previous existence. There is no precedent that permits a person, in such a situation, to take his loved one with him. Since we are living in a world in which insanity invites insanity, to take you with me might cause an even worse disaster.[45]

Other parts of the chapter tell us what Genji said and felt as he talked with other members of his household before leaving, and about his loneliness and misery while away from the capital.

The *Eiga* treatment of the same episode, on the other hand, refers directly to Korechika and to a progression of events leading up to and following an Imperial Mandate which orders Korechika into exile:

> Then a formally dressed man worked his way through the unruly crowd and proceeded directly to the front of the main hall of the Imperial Palace. And as people were wondering what was going on, he read aloud from what he proclaimed to be an Imperial edict:
>
>> For the three crimes of attempting to kill the Retired Emperor, putting a curse on the Imperial mother, and secretly and privately holding a Daigen Mass—which has never before been held by persons outside the Imperial Court—Minister of the Center (Korechika) is hereby exiled from the capital as the Acting Governor General of Kyushu. And Senior Counselor (Takaie) is hereby exiled as the Provisional Governor of Izumo.
>
> While all persons at the palace, high and low alike, were wailing and crying, even the man who read the Imperial edict wept. The police too, wiping away their tears, thought keenly that this was a sad and miserable affair. Hearing the wailing, all persons in the neighboring mansions closed their gates, but, affected by the sounds that seeped through, they could not stop the flow of their own tears. The officer loudly urged the two brothers to "leave now," since it was getting dark, but there was no response whatever. When this was reported to the Emperor, His Majesty only

45. Suma Chapter, *Nihon koten bungaku zenshū*, 13.164.

said sternly: "Why is this? They shouldn't act that way! Get them moving!" Meanwhile, it had grown dark and the Lord Minister of the Center was wondering whether there would be an answer to his prayer that [the soul of his deceased father] leave with him, and large numbers of people were making a great noise. But in the middle of the night, after everyone had fortunately gone to sleep, the Lord Minister of the Center stole from the palace accompanied only by his uncle Akinobu and two or three others. He departed without mishap, probably because of some response to the many solemn prayers that were in his noble heart.[46]

The remainder of this section tells of Korechika's visit to his father's tomb, his pilgrimage to the Kitano Shrine, his return to the palace, his final departure from the capital, and his separation from loved ones.

As the McCulloughs state, the author of the *Eiga* tries to "add immediacy and realism to the narrative, and especially to convey the emotional quality of the occasion."[47] Since she wrote about events and episodes that had actually happened, and provided many details that are found in contemporary diaries, the work is justifiably classified as an Historical Tale. But since the author was also willing, at times, to distort the historical truth (or fill in imaginary detail) in order to sharpen the theme, deepen its emotional appeal, heighten its sense of drama, or add further glory to Michinaga's career, her work often retains the attributes of a fictional Tale.

The Ōkagami

The second Historical Tale to be written before 1219 was the *Ōkagami* (Great Mirror). On several counts this second Historical Tale stands closer to the universalistic pole of Japan's historical tradition than the *Eiga*. The *Eiga* was meant to be a continuation of the National Histories, which were like Chinese Veritable Records, but the author of the *Ōkagami* seems to have followed other Chinese models. Certain sections of his work remind one of three different parts of an official Chinese history. The first section, devoted to the 14 Emperors who reigned between 850 and 1025, corresponds to the "Imperial annals" *(pen-chi)*; the second, made up of biographical sketches of leading FUJIWARA aristocrats, is not unlike the "biographies" *(lieh-chuan)*; and the last two, containing miscellaneous tales about various clans, take the general form of "monographs" *(chih)*.[48]

46. Chapter 5, NKBT, 75.163–164.
47. Introduction, McCullough's translation of the *Eiga monogatari*.
48. Joseph K. Yamagiwa, *The Ōkagami: A Japanese Historical Tale* (London, (1967), p. 392.

But the similarity does not go much beyond form, for very little of the exemplary quality—so prominent in Chinese histories—is found in the *Ōkagami*. One of the variant titles for both the *Eiga* and the *Ōkagami* is "Succession Tales" *(Yotsugi no monogatari)*. As that title suggests, the authors of these first two Historical Tales were much more interested in descent than in weighing past deeds by Chinese standards of virtue and merit.

The *Ōkagami* was also more deeply influenced than the *Eiga* by a growing conviction that the age of Final Law had begun in 1052. Since the *Ōkagami* is thought to have been written around the turn of the twelfth century—well into the age of Final Law—and about 30 years after the power of FUJIWARA Regents and Chancellors had begun to be seriously undermined by the administrative control of Retired Emperor Shirakawa, the author was apparently beginning to assume—like other intellectuals of his day—that the affairs of state, as well as Buddhist Law, were being subjected to an inevitable process of decay. Although the *Ōkagami* seems to have been written some time around 1100, almost nothing is said there about developments after 1025, when Michinaga's career was coming to a close. As one of the *Ōkagami* raconteurs (Yotsugi) states, Michinaga was a great lord who can never be matched "now or in the future." Since the entire work is focused upon a succession of Imperial and FUJIWARA familial relationships that lead to the emergence of the incomparable Michinaga, the reader is left with the distinct impression that what happened after 1025 was marred by too much deterioration to be either absorbing or instructive. Although the author has Yotsugi saying, in the preface, that he wished to tell only about "recent times," the stress that is placed on a "golden age" in the immediate past surely arose from an assumption that the present, having been tarnished by considerable kalpic deterioration, ought to be disregarded. But the *Ōkagami* does not delineate a continuum of historical decline and contains no discussion of the connection between history and the Buddhist doctrine of continuous deterioration.

Two *Ōkagami* references do indicate, however, that the author was aware of this Buddhist doctrine and what it meant for Japanese history. In the last section, where Yotsugi is talking about his being 150 years old, he refers to the ancient idea that at the beginning of a kalpa an individual has a life expectancy of 80,000 years but that by the time of Buddha's appearance it had dropped to 100. (The average length of life was said to decrease by one year every century.) He goes on to say that Buddha died at the age of 80 and that, nowadays, a person rarely lives that long. Yotsugi even applies this theory to the longevity of Japanese Emperors, noting that while ten out of the first twenty or so Emperors lived to be 100 years old or more, very few have reached such an advanced age in the final reigns.[49] But the theory is not given a wider application to Japanese history.

The second reference appears in that same last section and comes at a point where Yotsugi is telling how Emperor Murakami was succeeded by Emperor Reizei in 969:

In various ways everything went well through the reign of Emperor Murakami, but at the beginning of the Reizei reign everyone felt that the world had somehow come to a time of darkness. And there has been deterioration in worldly affairs ever since.[50]

Yotsugi reports that in Reizei's time people became quite sad whenever they were reminded that Murakami was no longer alive, implying that they knew times would never be as splendid as they had once been. While these references, and certain implications of the *Ōkagami* account, show that the author was aware of, and possibly influenced by, the growing belief that the age of Final Law was at hand, this belief was not yet a decisive factor in Japanese historical writing.

The *Ōkagami* probably makes a more serious attempt to explain the past than does any earlier Tale or chronicle, even though its treatment is no more accurate than that of the *Eiga* and the author is not much influenced by Chinese ideas of what a history should be, or by imported Buddhist doctrines of inevitable decline. The work's historical strength is found in its two-layered account of the genealogy that gives Michinaga his exalted aristocratic stature. The first section of the *Ōkagami,* containing biographies of the 14 Emperors from Montoku (827–858) to Go-Ichijō (1008–36), presents the Imperial line; and the second, made up of biographies of great FUJI-WARA ministers, traces the FUJIWARA line. The relationship between the two lines is made clear in the opening sentences of the first Imperial biography: "The sovereign known as Emperor Montoku was the first son of Emperor Nimmyō; and his mother was Great Empress Dowager FUJIWARA Junshi, the daughter of Minister of the Left FUJIWARA Fuyutsugu. . . ."[51] The line of Emperors (section one) ends with Go-Ichijō, whose Imperial mother is Michinaga's daughter, and the line of FUJIWARA ministers (section two) ends with Michinaga himself.

49. Chapter 6, NKBT, 21.278. I have referred to and benefited from Yamagiwa's work (see note 48, above) when making translations from the *Ōkagami.*

50. Chapter 6, NKBT, 21.265.

51. Chapter 1, NKBT, 21.41.

The *Ōkagami*'s preface tells us, through the words of Yotsugi, what the author aims to do:

> In thinking seriously about what I want to say, I have come to feel that I should speak—here in the presence of priests and laymen, men and women—only about the circumstances and superiority of the present Lay Priest Michinaga. But there are many strands [to his greatness]. I propose to deal with them in terms of Michinaga's connections with Emperors and Empresses and with [FUJIWARA] ministers and noblemen. To the extent that I speak of the circumstances of the fortunate Michinaga, I will clarify the conditions of this world. According to what I have heard people say, before Shakyamuni expounded the Lotus Sutra he expounded other teachings. That is why we refer to the Lotus Sutra as "the fifth teaching." So in speaking about Lay Priest Michinaga, I will first tell about those who preceded him.[52]

In reading through the biographies which Yotsugi puts into story form, we find that the Imperial and FUJIWARA lines are joined by Imperial mothers who are daughters of FUJIWARA ministers. Thus an Imperial biography often includes stories about that Emperor's mother, particularly if her father was a FUJIWARA Regent or Chancellor. After stating that FUJIWARA Yasuko (927–964) was the Imperial mother of Emperors Reizei and Enyū, Yotsugi tells his listener that this was "an unavoidable consequence of karma."[53] And in the midst of his tales about Emperor Go-Ichijō, he interrupts himself with this comment:

> I might have gone on to [stories about Michinaga] without saying anything about our Emperors, but in dealing with the limitless glories of Michinaga I must tell you about previous Emperors and their Empresses. Only when the roots of a tree flourish does it produce limbs and bear fruit. So I will tell you about the succession of ministers after I have dealt with the succession of Emperors.[54]

The author is saying, through Yotsugi, that while the preeminence of a minister such as Michinaga is a product of his birth in a noble line of Imperial ministers, the position and power of that entire line is rooted in, and justified by, Imperial succession.

The second section on "the Succession of FUJIWARA ministers"—making up approximately two-thirds of the entire book—provides the principal thrust of the *Ōkagami* thesis. While the Imperial foundations of the first section could have been assumed, the FUJIWARA line of succession had not become firmly established—particularly

52. Preface, NKBT, 21.39.
53. Chapter 1, NKBT, 21.50.
54. Chapter 1, NKBT, 21.58.

in association with Imperial succession—until 930 when FUJIWARA Tadahira (880–949) was appointed Regent for his grandson, Emperor Suzaku. After that and until the succession of Sanjo in 1068, the affairs of state were always handled by a FUJIWARA minister who was either the father or brother of the reigning Emperor's mother. Thus, for the 95-year period from 930 to 1025, Yotsugi has no difficulty impressing his reader with the fact that each FUJIWARA minister was not simply a direct descendant of the great Fuyutsugu but a minister whose daughter or sister was the Emperor's mother. But the connection between the Imperial and FUJIWARA lines for the 95-year period *before* 930 is more tenuous. The three Emperors who reigned between 840 and 884 were all sons of a daughter or granddaughter of Fuyutsugu, but the next two (Kōkō and Uda) were not. Because the father of Kōkō's Imperial mother was not a direct descendant of Fuyutsugu, he is not even honored with a separate biography in the *Ōkagami*. The same is true of Emperor Uda's maternal grandfather, Prince Nakano. FUJIWARA Takafuji (838–900), Emperor Daigo's maternal grandfather, was descended from Fuyutsugu; but since he was never elevated to ministerial rank, he too has no biography. Even though the FUJIWARA line was at times poorly linked with the Imperial line before 930, Yotsugi makes an attempt, through stories about Fuyutsugu descendants who became ministers and who had familial ties to Imperial mothers, to convince his reader that the linkage was really there. The stress of section two is on an increasingly direct, and historically true, tie-up between the Imperial and FUJIWARA lines as history approaches the glorious days of Michinaga. Between 967 and 1025, Japan had six Emperors, two of whom were born to Michinaga's aunt (Yasuko), one to his cousin (Kaishi), two to his sisters (Akiko and Chōshi), and one to his daughter (Shōshi). So the seven FUJIWARA biographies for that 58-year period, requiring almost two-thirds of the entire section, contain numerous stories that come to a climax in a very long and laudatory biography of Michinaga.

As strong as the connection between Imperial and FUJIWARA succession is made in sections one and two, the rather short third section is designed to make the connection even stronger and more lustrous. First, FUJIWARA succession is pushed back to an earlier point in time, extending the eight generations of section two to thirteen generations that begin with FUJIWARA Kamatari (614–669). After completing a survey of these additional five generations of ministers, Yotsugi proceeds to name the leading minister in each of the thirteen generations, pointing out how each minister had served the throne and telling us what ministerial rank he had reached. More stories are then inserted to explain that the FUJIWARA line had prospered because its ministers had supported, and been supported by, famous FUJIWARA shrines (beginning with the Kashima and the Kasuga) and famous FUJIWARA temples (beginning with the Yamashina). Finally, this section adds information about 13 generations of ministers and their daughters who became Imperial consorts or, more important, Imperial mothers. Thus the theme of section one (Imperial succession) is tied more closely to that of section two (FUJIWARA succession) through Imperial mothers who were daughters of FUJIWARA ministers.

Section four is not just a cluster of "ancient tales" but an additional support for the Ōkagami view of what was important in Japan's past. First, there is an attempt to establish the veracity of Yotsugi's stories, trying in that way to make the point that these were not just interesting Tales but vehicles of truth about the very old, and increasingly strong, relationship between the Imperial House and the FUJIWARA clan. While the "ancient tales" of this section serve to make Emperors, Empresses, and ministers even more remarkable individuals, stress is placed on the accuracy of Yotsugi's memory. At the very beginning, Yotsugi tells about the first incident he remembers: the enthronement of Emperor Kōkō in 884, when he was nine years old. Although the account is embellished with considerable detail about what Yotsugi and his father did on that historic day, the main point is that Kōkō was enthroned in 884 and that Yotsugi, who claims he was 150 years old in 1025, really would have been nine years old at that time. All subsequent stories—told in chronological order—deal with events covered in existing diaries, chronologies, or other historical records; and most of the poems included can be found in well-known anthologies. Having told stories about events that had actually occurred, and having repeated poems that had really been composed by the persons to whom they were attributed, Yotsugi is then made to ask his listeners this question: "Am I not an old man who has really heard countless things—both sad and fortunate—about the affairs of this world?"[55] A few paragraphs later, Yotsugi insists—with the Three Treasures of Buddhism as his witness—that he had not added one word of "empty falseness."[56]

Modern scholars have been greatly impressed by the Ōkagami as literature, appreciating especially the author's technique of putting his work into the form of tales told by two old men attending a ceremony that was actually held in 1025. But the Ōkagami is also a remarkable piece of historical writing. The author obviously had two interrelated aims in writing this book: to please the reader with good stories well told, and to impress the reader with an historical process in which two lines of succession had been locked together, generation after generation, through Imperial mothers. The historical side

55. Chapter 6, NKBT, 21.276.
56. Chapter 6, NKBT, 21.277.

of the author's motivation accounts for a well-integrated thesis that is built up, step by step, and then capped with a final item concerning the occasion on which the Emperor visits his own Imperial mother.[57]

Japan's second form of historical writing, the Historical Tale, is therefore fundamentally different from the first. The earlier National Histories are shaped and colored, to some extent, by Chinese models of historical writing and by Chinese ideas and beliefs, but they also reflect a firm commitment to native belief in a sacred succession of Emperors that began when the Sun Goddess sent her grandson down to rule over the Japanese islands. The tension between Chinese ideas and native beliefs is quite different, however, in the Historical Tales. Since Japan's intellectuals were not so impressed, after 900, by China's cultural grandeur, these Tales are more Japanese in character: the imprint of Chinese historical models is not as sharp, and explanations of events in terms of Confucian virtue are virtually nonexistent, whereas the old Japanese preoccupation with clan lineage persists. To be sure, the influence of different Chinese historical forms, and of imported Buddhist ideas of kalpic deterioration, can still be detected. The most significant point, though, is that the ancient belief in the authority of the Imperial line is now used— implicitly in the *Eiga* and explicitly in the *Ōkagami*—to justify the authority and power of a succession of FUJIWARA ministers that reaches its highest pinnacle with Michinaga.

Military Tales

The third type of historical writing to appear before, or soon after, the *Gukanshō* was the Military Tale *(gunki monogatari)*, a form that arose out of an interest in the activities of military men at the beginning of Japan's military age. The wars fought in 1156, 1159–60, and 1180–85—about which the first three Military Tales were written—were struggles for political hegemony that propelled warriors and their clans into positions of control over state affairs. A separate military government (the *bakufu*) was formed in Kamakura after the last of those three wars had been fought. The head of the *bakufu* (the Shogun) gradually extended his control to outlying regions and even had a decisive voice in appointments and policy decisions made at the Imperial Court in Kyoto. The great monasteries, which had maintained their own private armies, were now forced to bow to the will of the *bakufu*. While the struggle for political supremacy between the old aristocratic clans and the new military ones continued until the Shōkyū War of 1221, the social and cultural life of Japan was already being transformed by military interests and values when these first three Military Tales, and the *Gukanshō*, were being written.

57. Chapter 6, NKBT, 21.284–285.

As accounts centered on military conflict, the Military Tales are similar to the old *Masakado ki,* a descriptive account of the TAIRA no Masakado revolt written in 940. In the sense that these Military Tales assume a story form, and are written in Japanese and deal with heroic figures of the past, they are also like the Historical Tales discussed above. And because many of the events dealt with in the Military Tales are infused with Buddhist ideas and beliefs, we are justified in concluding that they emerged, in part at least, from a tradition that goes back to the *Konjaku monogatari,* a collection of Buddhist tales probably assembled at the end of the eleventh century. Finally, the Military Tales are colored, as earlier forms of historical writing are, by a continuous interest in the way social and political relationships are—or can be—supported by proximity to the throne. But since the Military Tales assume a new form of historical expression, the following discussion will attempt to show how they differ from previous forms and are like the *Gukanshō.*

Before taking up qualities of Military Tales, it should be noted that textual study has produced no agreement as to when any one of them was written or who authored it. All three may have been known to the author of the *Gukanshō,* but the oldest extant texts are of a much later date. Popularly recited by blind priests to the accompaniment of the lute, they were frequently revised. Kenneth Dean Butler's study of the textual evolution of the *Heike Monogatari* (Tale of the Heike), the third and most distinguished Military Tale, has led him to conclude that later revisions added heroic detail concerning the activities of individual soldiers.[58] We cannot be certain, in any case, what part of the extant texts were written before 1219, or just how they were altered by later revisions. Nevertheless, a comparative study of existing editions of the first three Military Tales discloses changes of historical consciousness that help us to understand the thought of the *Gukanshō.*

Hōgen Monogatari

This first Military Tale is made up of three chapters: one each for events before, during, and after the Hōgen Rebellion of 1156. Chapter one aims to acquaint the reader with three interrelated levels of rivalry that led to the outbreak of that Rebellion. Rivalry at the highest level was between two Imperial sons of the powerful Retired Emperor Toba (1103–56): former Emperor Sutoku (1119–64); and Emperor Go-Shirakawa (1127–92), who was enthroned in 1155. We are told that the trouble began back in 1139 when Empress Bifuku-mon In, Toba's favorite, gave birth to an Imperial son

58. "The Textual Evolution of the Heike Monogatari," *Harvard Journal of Asiatic Studies* (1966), pp. 5–51.

(Konoe). Toba was then the most powerful man at court and could do as he pleased. Having decided to make Konoe the next Emperor, Toba and Bifuku-mon In arranged to have Konoe appointed Crown Prince; and two years later they forced Sutoku to abdicate so that Konoe could be placed on the throne. During the next 14 years Sutoku, the junior Retired Emperor, had almost no influence at court because his father, the senior Retired Emperor, had assumed full responsibility for the administration of state affairs. In 1155, following the early death of Emperor Konoe, Sutoku was disappointed to learn that his own son had been bypassed because Toba and Bifuku-mon In had decided that Go-Shirakawa, Sutoku's young brother, should ascend the throne as Konoe's successor. But Toba died in 1156. That event caused Sutoku to feel that at last he could, as the only surviving Retired Emperor, take over the administration of state affairs. But he was frustrated again—this time by his brother Go-Shirakawa (an adult sovereign who was apparently in no mood to be dominated by his resentful elder brother) and by his stepmother Empress Bifuku-mon In (who was convinced, according to the *Hōgen*, that Konoe had died early because of a Sutoku curse).

The rivalry between Retired Emperor Toba's two sons was paralleled and reinforced by a second-level rivalry between two sons of FUJIWARA Tadazane (1078–1162). Tadazane had not been on very good terms with his eldest son Tadamichi (1097–1164) since 1121, when Retired Emperor Shirakawa suddenly had Tadamichi replace Tadazane as Regent. Although Tadazane's relations with Toba were somewhat better than with Shirakawa, Tadamichi remained on as Regent. But in 1141, at the time that Konoe was made Emperor, Tadazane took it upon himself to make his young son Yorinaga (1120–56) head of the FUJIWARA clan. This made Tadamichi a Regent without the usual clan base, and Yorinaga head of the FUJIWARA clan without being Regent. Both brothers were therefore dissatisfied and on the alert for an opportunity to make their positions less ambiguous. The death of Toba in 1156 seemed to offer such an opportunity. When it was made clear that Go-Shirakawa preferred to keep Tadamichi in the position of Regent, Yorinaga began to associate himself with Sutoku's cause.

Young Emperor Go-Shirakawa, with the backing of Empress Bifuku-mon In and others who wished to carry out the wishes of the deceased Toba, was determined to prevent Sutoku and Yorinaga from seizing control. According to the *Hōgen*, Go-Shirakawa and his supporters soon detected signs of "rebellion" and took steps that seemed to have made Sutoku and Yorinaga more determined than ever to obtain what they thought were their rightful positions at court. Both those who sided with Emperor Go-Shirakawa and those who backed Retired Emperor Sutoku moved promptly to pick up what military support they could. Efforts to amass military forces soon created a split within the great military clan of MINAMOTO, placing the elder sons of MINAMOTO Tameyoshi on the side of Emperor Go-Shirakawa, and Tameyoshi and his younger sons on the side of the Retired Emperor Sutoku. So brother was pitted against brother, not only within the Imperial and FUJIWARA clans but within the military clan of MINAMOTO as well.

As the *Hōgen* moves into its historical story of how this three-level rivalry led to war, it takes up the main characters in the traditional status order: Emperors and former Emperors first, FUJIWARA ministers next, and MINAMOTO soldiers last. After outlining the basis of Sutoku's resentment, attention is given to Sutoku's FUJIWARA ally, Yorinaga, who is praised in terms of traditional aristocratic standards:

> Yorinaga did not appear to be incompetent in governing the empire. He excelled in both Chinese and Japanese ceremonies; he was not unacquainted with the records of his own house, and those of other houses; he probed into the strengths and weaknesses of various teachings; he considered the ups and downs of various developments; and in helping the Emperor to rule, he paid no attention to whether a person was or was not his friend. As Regent or Chancellor, he would take a back seat to no one, past or present. And yet he was jealous of his brother's beautiful calligraphy and proficiency in Chinese and Japanese literature, saying: "Poetry is an amusement for a time of leisure and is not needed for Court ceremony. Calligraphy, also one of the entertainments, is not necessarily an important accomplishment for a wise minister." [Yorinaga] studied, first of all, the Five Classics; he acted in strict accord with the principles of Benevolence, Righteousness, Wisdom, and Sincerity; and whenever he happened to make a mistake at Court banquets, appointment ceremonies, or in submitting memorials to the throne, he would immediately write out a letter of apology and hand it to the Director of the Imperial Secretariat or a Controller....[59]

Although the aristocratic taste for poetry and calligraphy is ridiculed, traditional standards of behavior for a Regent or Chancellor are not challenged.

But when *Hōgen* turns to actual preparations for military conflict and to its great military hero, MINAMOTO Tameyoshi's young son Tametomo (d. 1177), praise is presented in terms of the emerging military values of physical strength, bravery, and loyalty. We are told that Tametomo was seven feet tall, had a bow that took five men to

59. Chapter 1, NKBT, 31.64–65. For another version of this and subsequent translations from the *Hōgen*, see William R. Wilson's *Hōgen Monogatari: Tale of the Disorder in Hōgen* (Tokyo, 1971).

string, was so wild that he was sent off to Kyushu—at the age of thirteen—to keep him out of trouble, subjugated all nine provinces of Kyushu within three years, and was finally encouraged to return to the capital to support his father, who had decided to side with Retired Emperor Sutoku. When asked for his advice about how to oppose the Imperial forces, the *Hōgen* tells us that Tametomo spoke out as follows:

> I am Tametomo who, having lived in the western island since I was a boy, have already been engaged in about 30 battles. Whether one is defeating the enemy or taking territories held by him, no method is better than attacking at night. By advancing on the Imperial Palace before daybreak and setting fire to three sides of the palace while we advance on the fourth, we will create a situation in which those who flee from the fire will not be able to flee from our arrows, and those who avoid our arrows will not be able to avoid the fire. Probably my brother Yoshitomo will be the only one to put up a strong defense. Serving at the very center [of the attacking force], I will shoot arrows at the enemy and, dashing into their midst, will slash them down. Those I can get hold of will be thrown down, killed, and cast aside. I'll cut off their heads and tear out their arms. . . . The Emperor probably will move to some other position, and I will then shoot an arrow into his Imperial palanquin. Although released by me, the arrow will be one shot by the Sun Goddess and the true Hachiman. The Emperor's palanquin bearers, being frightened by the arrow, will drop the palanquin and flee. Then we can send the Emperor back to the Imperial Palace.[60]

Yorinaga, a true aristocrat, was not impressed by such bravado; and Tametomo's proposal was rejected. Although the *Hōgen* tells us that Tametomo yielded to the superior authority of Yorinaga, he is said to have made this parting comment:

> [Your way of dealing with this situation] is like the way of handling Imperial banquets, memorials to the Emperor, and Imperial appointments. I would have liked you to stand aside and leave battle plans to me. This situation is truly regrettable. Now you are simply frightened by the enemy. When the enemy appears, your soldiers will be thrown into confusion.[61]

Thus the aristocratic Yorinaga has his way, but, as the *Hōgen* makes clear in later sections, Sutoku's forces were defeated because Tametomo's advice had not been followed.

In chapter two, where the *Hōgen* turns to the course of the war, Tametomo first becomes involved in a dispute with his elder brother

60. Chapter 1, NKBT, 31.84.
61. Chapter 1, NKBT, 31.86.

Yorikata about the question of who should enter the fray first.
Yorikata insists on his right to be first, but Tametomo objects:

> What are you arguing about? On the battle field no distinctions
> should be made between elder and younger brother. Only ability
> matters then. Although I would like to be first, there is no point in
> arguing about it, for I will be called a bad fellow for not treating
> you as an elder brother. But you watch me attack—any number
> of times—where the enemy's position is strong![62]

And after the battle begins, Tametomo performs some truly remarkable feats. First he shoots an arrow that pierces the breast plate
of an enemy soldier (killing him instantly) and that lodges itself in
the sleeve of another enemy soldier. In the next foray, Tametomo
takes a shot at a particularly brave opponent, and his arrow not only
goes through the armor of the mounted soldier but pins his body to
the saddle. Against a third soldier who dares to challenge him,
Tametomo decides not to waste an arrow but to fight with his bare
hands, causing the enemy to flee. But in spite of such heroics,
Sutoku and his brave supporters are defeated by a vastly superior
force.

In the final section of chapter two, the *Hōgen* describes the humili-
ation of Sutoku (who becomes a monk) and Yorinaga (who finally
dies in disgrace from a wound caused by a wild arrow). The closing
paragraphs take up the tragic execution of MINAMOTO Tameyoshi,
carried out by his own son Yoshitomo. After stating that no one had
been executed in Japan for over three centuries, this chapter ends
with a comment that reveals an awareness of fundamental conflict
between aristocratic and military values: "Killing one's father under
the mask of 'loyalty' is the gravest perversion of filial piety, the extreme of unrighteousness."[63] In chapter three, we are told of the
most tragic consequences of the war: the execution of Tameyoshi's
young sons; the suicidal drowning of Tameyoshi's wife; the exile and
death of Sutoku; and finally the capture, exile, and suicide of
Tametomo—after he had sunk an enemy boat by shooting an arrow
through its hull. The *Hōgen's* last sentence, in at least one version,
stresses the main point of the Tale: "People say that from ancient
times to the present there has been no such high-spirited hero as
Tametomo."[64]

Heiji Monogatari

The second Military Tale covers the Heiji Rebellion of 1159–60
and, like the *Hōgen,* has three chapters: one each for the origins,

62. Chapter 1, NKBT, 31.98–99.
63. Chapter 2, *Nihon bungaku taikei,* 14.73.
64. Chapter 3, ibid., 14.108.

course, and results of that Rebellion. And just as the *Hōgen* relates the beginnings of the Hōgen Rebellion to the enthronement of Go-Shirakawa in 1155, the *Heiji Monogatari* relates the outbreak of the Heiji Rebellion to the 1158 enthronement of Go-Shirakawa's son, Emperor Nijō. Both Tales revolve about a three-layered struggle for power. In the *Heiji* it is between (1) Retired Emperor Go-Shirakawa and Emperor Nijō at the Imperial level; (2) FUJIWARA Michinori (known by his priestly name Shinzei) and FUJIWARA Nobuyori (1133–59) at the aristocratic level; and (3) TAIRA Kiyomori (1118–81) and MINAMOTO Yoshitomo (1123–60) at the military-clan level. Both Kiyomori and Yoshitomo had fought on the winning side in the Hōgen War, but they and their clans were opponents in the Heiji War: Yoshitomo siding with Emperor Nijō and Nobuyori, and Kiyomori backing Retired Emperor Go-Shirakawa and Shinzei. As in the *Hōgen*, the *Heiji's* sympathies are for the defeated military leader (MINAMOTO Yoshitomo) and his heroic son (Yoshihira). But the *Hōgen* and *Heiji* treatments of aristocrats and soldiers are quite different.

FUJIWARA Nobuyori is the most prominent aristocrat and is supported by the defeated MINAMOTO Yoshitomo and his heroic son Yoshihira, but he does not receive the kind of praise that is accorded Yorinaga in the *Hōgen*. Instead, Nobuyori is described as a man "versed neither in letters nor in military arts,"[65] a coward, a drunkard, and a man who takes on the airs of an Emperor. The aristocrat who receives the most favorable treatment is Shinzei, who is on the winning side but who is killed in an ignominious way before the issue is settled. Although Shinzei is depicted as a priestly bureaucrat who gets things done, he is a man honored primarily for his Buddhistic achievements. He is not only reputed to have an amazing knowledge of Buddhist scriptures but to have been recognized by a travelling Chinese priest as an incarnation of Kwannon.

The *Heiji's* military hero, MINAMOTO Yoshihira, seems to be just as strong and brave as the *Hōgen's* Tametomo. At the battle of the Taiken Gate, where Yoshihira is supported by only 17 mounted warriors, he drives back a TAIRA force of over 500. But he is more humane than Tametomo. As he is chasing the fleeing TAIRA, he has a chance to take on the great TAIRA Shigemori but elects to stop and save the life of a retainer. Like Tametomo in the *Hōgen*, Yoshihira is finally defeated. Eventually he is faced with a hopelessly superior force and, when challenged, shouts: "MINAMOTO Yoshihira is here!

65. Chapter 1, NKBT, 31.190. This and other translations from the *Heiji* differ somewhat from those in Edwin O. Reischauer, "The Heiji Monogatari," *Translations from Early Japanese Literature* (Cambridge, Mass., 1951), p. 398.

Come and see!" After a valiant battle in which he kills many worthy
opponents, he is captured and beheaded.

The *Heiji* reflects a deeper awareness of the emerging conflict between the old aristocratic and the new military elite. Opening paragraphs of the *Hōgen* are in the form of a traditional Imperial chronicle, but those of the *Heiji* turn immediately to the observation that in
China as well as in Japan a ruler has always needed both military
strength (generals) and learning (aristocratic bureaucrats):

> If we look at precedents followed in China and Japan, we will find
> that when rewarding subjects and ministers, rulers have always
> assigned high priority to both learning and military might. Learn-
> ing is helpful in various areas of administration; and military
> power enables rulers to suppress disturbances. So in his plans to
> preserve the empire and rule the land, a ruler seems to place
> learning at his left and military strength at his right—making
> them like a person's two hands. Neither can be dispensed with.[66]

These comments are followed by sentences which not only stress the
importance of Confucian principles in state administration but the
appropriateness—as time passes and the situation worsens—of according special recognition to military bravery:

> Benevolence and righteousness are quite important. With these
> principles the empire will achieve peace and prosperity. . . . As we
> approach the "final reigns," men become arrogant and have con-
> tempt for the dignity of the Imperial Court, and people become
> militarized and develop ambitions. Great care should be taken.
> Brave fellows should be appropriately recognized.[67]

Thus *Heiji* seems to have moved away from the rather simple narra-
tion of the *Hōgen* to the advocacy of principles and policies appropriate to these desperate times.

Heike Monogatari

The third and most famous of the Military Tales, and the one that
is most closely related to the *Gukanshō*, is the *Heike Monogatari*, a
work that provides a far more vivid portrayal of the emerging military ideal. Unlike the *Hōgen* and the *Heiji*, each of which is focused
on one tragic hero of one short war, the *Heike* takes up prominent
persons (men and women) engaged in a 20-year struggle between
two military clans: the TAIRA and the MINAMOTO. The whole is con-

66. Chapter 1, NKBT, 31.189.
67. Ibid.

structed around the rise and fall of three great military figures: TAIRA Kiyomori, KISO Yoshinaka, and MINAMOTO Yoshitsune (1159–89).

TAIRA Kiyomori, the most important political figure in Japan after his military victories of 1156, is pictured as a person who boasts of his descent from a former Emperor, who claims that his high position was a reward for service performed at the Imperial Court, and who takes pride in his knowledge of court ceremony and proper aristocratic behavior. But he is also shown as a cruel, arrogant, and unprincipled man who is interested first and foremost in the glory of his own TAIRA clan. The general outlines of that picture emerge from this deathbed pronoucement attributed to him:

> Since the Hōgen and Heiji eras [1156–60], I have frequently subdued enemies of the Imperial Court and obtained generous rewards. Although of humble origin, I have become the grandfather of an Emperor and been appointed Prime Minister, achieving glory and fame for my descendants. Not one thing more do I desire in this life. My only regret is that I have not yet seen the head of MINAMOTO Yoritomo, the former Major of the Left Guard who was exiled to the province of Izu. After I am dead, I want no temples or pagodas built and no Buddhist rites performed. Instead, I want to have Yoritomo attacked immediately and his head placed before my grave. That is the only rite I want performed.[68]

The person who wrote down that pronouncement added this condemnation: "So deep was his sin!"[69] Then the author went on to explain Kiyomori's early death:

> He cannot be said to have died of old age. Because his death was destined to occur [early], neither important nor mysterious rites could prevent it. Not even the power of Kami, nor the grace of the Three Buddhist Treasures, nor the various deities of Heaven could protect him. So what could be done by ordinary men? Even though tens of thousands of loyal soldiers willing to give their lives for him surrounded him, they could not drive away the unseen, extraordinary denizens of hell against whom the power of man is to no avail. So he simply went alone on that trip from which there is no return, across the mountains and river that separate the world of the living from the world of the dead. Probably the evils

68. Chapter 6, NKBT, 32.409. For this and other translations of the *Heike* the following translations have been studied: Arthur Lindsay Sadler's "Heike Monogatari," *Transactions of the Asiatic Society of Japan,* I (1918 and 1921); and Hiroshi Kitagawa and Bruce T. Tsuchida's *The Tale of the Heike* (Tokyo, 1975).

69. Chapter 6, NKBT, 32.409.

committed during his lifetime had become the denizens of hell
who welcomed him.[70]

The death of Kiyomori's sons and the destruction of the TAIRA
house were, according to the *Heike,* retribution for Kiyomori's "evil
deeds."

Kiyomori's eldest son Shigemori (1138–79), on the other hand, is
given all the desirable qualities that his father lacked. He becomes
the heroic equivalent of the young warriors who were the heroes of
the *Hōgen* and the *Heiji.* But instead of being described as a fierce
and ruthless soldier who was not particularly respectful to the Imperial throne or to divine beings, Shigemori comes across as a calm and
kind man with deep religious feelings who, above all, was loyal to the
Imperial Court. When a plot was uncovered in 1177, Kiyomori was
inclined, after arresting and exiling the ringleaders, to move against
Retired Emperor Go-Shirakawa. But at that crucial point, the *Heike*
tells us, Shigemori came forward calmly and with great dignity to
rebuke his father as follows:

> Hearing what you say, I conclude that you have already come to
> the end of your destiny. When the destiny of a person comes to an
> end, he necessarily thinks of committing evil deeds. Your appear-
> ance [in military garb] and moving again toward military action is
> something I cannot think is real. Although our country is only a
> peripheral land of small and scattered islands, the descendants of
> the Sun Goddess have been its rulers, and the descendants of
> Ame no Koyane Mikoto [the ancestral Kami of the FUJIWARA clan]
> have administered its affairs. Hasn't a person occupying the office
> of Prime Minister always violated the standards of what is right
> and proper by dressing himself in military attire? Since you are a
> lay priest, the violation is worse. By taking off the priestly robes
> which symbolize the various Buddhas (past, present, and future)
> and liberation from carnal passions, and by suddenly putting on
> armor and arming yourself with bow and arrow, you are commit-
> ting the shameless crime of breaking Buddhist commandments.
> Not only that, you will also violate the [Confucian] principles of
> Benevolence, Justice, Propriety, Wisdom, and Sincerity. No mat-
> ter how one looks at the situation, these are terrible things to say,
> but thoughts deep in my heart must be expressed. In this world
> there are four primary blessings: blessings received from [the
> deities of] Heaven and Earth; blessings received from the ruler of
> the country; blessings received from one's father and mother; and
> blessings received from living creatures. Among these, blessings
> received from the Imperial Court are the most important. There
> is no land in the empire that is not the Emperor's. . . . Somehow
> you have even risen to the highest office, that of Prime
> Minister—something never achieved by our ancestors. Even I, a

70. Chapter 6, NKBT, 32.410.

stupid man with no ability, have reached the position of minister. In addition, more than half of the districts and provinces of the country are possessions of our house, and all estates are disposed of as we wish. Are these not unusual blessings received from the current Emperor? By forgetting the great blessings received from the Emperor, and indecently moving to overthrow the Retired Emperor, you will be acting contrary to the will of the Sun Goddess and the true Hachiman. Japan is a Kami country, and the Kami will not permit impropriety. The thoughts of the Retired Emperor do not stand outside the bounds of Principle *(dōri)*. Although our house, in particular, has demonstrated incomparable loyalty by subjugating enemies of the court and putting down rebellions in all parts of the land, boasting about those accomplishments is unseemly. In his Seventeen Article Constitution, Prince Shōtoku said:

> Every man has a mind and every mind has its own opinions. He says it is good and I say it is bad; and I say it is good and he says it is bad. So who can say which position is really right? Wisdom and stupidity can not be separated one from the other—they are like a ring that has no end. So when one is angry, he must be fearful that he himself is to blame.

And yet, because your destiny has not run out, this plot has been exposed. Moreover, Narichika, who has consulted with the Emperor, has been arrested. So even if the Retired Emperor does have some strange thoughts, what is there to be afraid of? After meting out proper punishments you will be protected by the power of Kami—and not be opposing the divine will of Buddha—if you explain to the Retired Emperor the reasons for your actions and do your utmost to be a more loyal servant of His Highness and, for the sake of the people, give them more compassionate care. Because the Kami and the Buddhas will respond to your good deeds, you can expect that even the Retired Emperor's thoughts will be corrected. I am especially close to you and the Retired Emperor, but when there is both Principle and error, why should I not choose Principle?[71]

In setting the thoughts and beliefs of Shigemori against the bold and ruthless "evil deeds" of his father, the author of the *Heike* seems to be aware of conflict between the values of the old and new orders. While the author tells us how military leaders tended to act and think, sympathies are clearly with Shigemori, whose loyalties, attitudes, and beliefs are essentially aristocratic.

The *Heike* emphasizes—through tales about a heroic warrior—loyalty to an Emperor, the authority of ancestral Kami, the divine will of Buddhas, and the ethical values of Confucianism. Buddhist beliefs and activities are particularly prominent. The death of nearly

71. Chapter 2, NKBT, 32.171–173.

every important character is associated with thoughts of entering the Buddhist priesthood and with prayers and thoughts about life after death. Explanations of a particular death usually revolve about evil deeds, particularly those of Kiyomori, and refer to that late point in history (the age of Final Law) when disasters are destined to occur. Priests and nuns figure prominently in almost every episode, and the role of temples in major military-political crises is stressed. The Buddhist emphasis is especially striking in the large number of inter-related sections devoted to the slow but sure fate of TAIRA Shigehira (1157–85), the military leader who burned Nara temples. The *Heike* has Shigehira facing Amitābha in his last moments and praying as follows:

> It has come down to us that even though Devadatta committed the Three Transgressions and destroyed many sacred sutras, Shakyamuni swore that Devadatta would become Tennō Nyorai after death. Devadatta's sins were really serious, but because of the virtue of the sacred scriptures, his opposition to those scriptures became an Outer Cause *(en)* that was transformed into an Inner Cause *(in)* leading to enlightenment. . . . So my countless sins will be erased by reciting the name of Amitābha.[72]

Then, according to the *Heike*, Shigehira recited the name of Amitābha ten times in a loud voice, stuck out his neck, and was beheaded. Whereupon the thousands of commoners present, and the soldiers standing guard, wept, even though [Shigehira] "had recently done evil things." His head was nailed to the great *torii* at the Hannya Temple because it was there that he had destroyed temples during the Jisho War [of 1180].[73] Such prominence of Buddhist thought suggests that, as the *Tsurezuregusa* has stated, the *Heike* was actually written by a Buddhist lay-priest (Yukinaga) who taught his stories to a blind itinerant priest named Shōbutsu (living Buddha) and had him tell these stories to the accompaniment of a lute.[74]

Buddhist belief that the present is within the age of Final Law[75] is associated in the *Heike* with the assumption of continuous decline in worldly affairs. Shigehira is made to say, for example, that he is being executed simply because of a "Principle for the age."[76] The assumption that Japanese history has been subjected to an inevitable process of decline is made explicit in comments about the great earthquake of 1185, which occurred less than three months after the execution of Shigehira. After listing the temples that were destroyed

72. Chapter 17, NKBT, 33.377.
73. Idem.
74. No. 226, NKBT, 30.272.
75. For a discussion of Buddhist eschatology, see Chapter 10.
76. Chapter 11, NKBT, 33.377.

by the earthquake and highlighting the miseries that were caused by ensuing fires and floods, the *Heike* reflects on the meaning of that extraordinary event:

It is said that in ancient times—on the 8th day of the 3rd month of 856, when Montoku was on the throne—a great earthquake caused the head of Tōdai Temple's Buddha statue to fall off. Again we hear that, as a result of a great earthquake on the 5th day of the 4th month of 939, the Emperor was forced to leave his palace and to reside in a tent . . . erected for him in front of the Jonei Hall. Since these disasters occurred in ancient times, I am in no position to comment on them. But [just before this present earthquake] . . . an Emperor of the Ten Virtues left the capital [in 1181] and sank to the bottom of the sea [in 1185]. After that, ministers and nobles were brought back to the capital, where their heads were cut off at the jail gate. From ancient times to the present, vengeful souls have been terrifying. Therefore people of understanding could not but be saddened as they wondered what would become of this world.[77]

The *Heike* seems to be saying that although disasters had occurred in ancient times, and were connected with changes in the position of the Emperor, recent disasters affecting the position of the Emperor are much worse, because we are now living in the age of Final Law.

The assumption of continuous decline in both Buddhist Law and secular affairs is also reflected in comments about the relationship of Buddhist Law to Imperial Law *(ōhō)*.[78] As noted in the previous section, Saichō had maintained four centuries earlier that Buddhist Law was a "national treasure"; but he appears to have stressed only the point that Buddhist Law guarded and protected the state, not concerning himself with any special link between Buddhist Law and a sacred Imperial Law for Japan. But the *Heike*—written after four centuries of Buddho-Shinto fusion—contains passages that refer directly to connections between the two Laws. Especially significant are those found in sections dealing with the great debate of 1180 when priests of the great Buddhist monasteries were trying to decide whether to oppose TAIRA Kiyomori. After Prince Mochihito (second son of Go-Shirakawa) flees to the temple of Miidera, the priests there—according to the *Heike*—agree to the following statement:

In considering the recent state of world affairs, it becomes clear that there is now deterioration of Buddha Law and restraint on Imperial Law. If we do not now punish Lay Priest Kiyomori for his violence and evil actions, just when will we? Does not Prince Takakura's coming to Miidera indicate that we have the protec-

77. Chapter 12, NKBT, 33.380–381.
78. Imperial Law is discussed in the Introduction.

tion of the true Hachiman and the divine assistance of the Great Illuminating Kami of Shinra [who is the guardian Kami of Miidera]? The various deities of Heaven and Earth will come forth. Certainly with the power of Buddha and Kami, the enemy can be utterly destroyed.[79]

In letters that they send off to Mt. Hiei and Nara, the Miidera priests warn that both Buddhist Law and Imperial Law are in danger. One letter touches upon the interdependent relationship between the two in this way:

> The admirable thing about Buddhist Law is that it serves to up-hold Imperial Law. Furthermore, the duration of Imperial Law depends on Buddhist Law. Nowadays, Lord TAIRA no Ason Kiyomori (the lay priest and former Prime Minister who bears the priestly name of Jōkai) is arbitrarily making the prestige of the country *(koku-i)* his own private possession and confusing court affairs. While he was stirring up resentments and sorrow everywhere, the second son of Retired Emperor Go-Shirakawa suddenly came to Miidera on the 15th day of this month in order to avoid unexpected difficulties. . . . Both Buddhist Law and Imperial Law are about to be destroyed.[80]

In telling about the fire that destroyed the Zenkō Temple in 1177, the *Heike* concludes that it portends the eventual demise of Imperial Law, since "the end of Imperial Law is foreshadowed by the destruction of Buddhist Law."[81]

Such thoughts about the interrelated deterioration of Buddhist Law and Imperial Law seem to have been deepened by an increasingly bleak view of the future. Such pessimism—understandable for aristocrats whose positions were being threatened by the rise of a new military elite—is reflected in the consistency with which the main characters of the *Heike* conclude that, sooner or later, they will enter the priesthood and seek "rebirth" in the Pure Land paradise after death. Although the earliest versions of the *Heike* were probably written before Pure Land Buddhism became a separate sect, and before it was strengthened by the teachings of Shinran (1174–1268) and by the organizational activity of Rennyo (1415–99), almost every major episode draws our attention to activities believed to be appropriate for a person who has come to wish only for "rebirth" in the Pure Land. The *Heike* section on the last days of Kiyomori's grandson Koremori, for example, tells us about Koremori's decision to enter the priesthood, his pilgrimage to the Kumano Shrines (famous

79. Chapter 4, NKBT, 32.297.
80. Chapter 4, NKBT, 32.299–300.
81. Chapter 2, NKBT, 32.198.

for the worship of Amitābha), and his praise of Amitābha before drowning himself. In his last hours, a fellow priest consoled Koremori with these words:

> You should single-mindedly believe [in Amitābha's grace] and never have any doubts. If you recite the name of Amitābha ten times, or even once, Amitābha . . . will emerge instantly from the eastern gate of paradise to welcome you to the Pure Land. Therefore, even though your body may sink to the bottom of the deepest sea, [your soul] can ride on the purple clouds to paradise. And when you obtain enlightenment and achieve freedom [from further births and deaths], you can without the slightest doubt return to your native land of this world *(edo)* to lead your wife and children [to paradise].[82]

Such deep and pervasive preoccupation with Pure Land Buddhism—the form said to be most appropriate for the age of Final Law—becomes all the more significant in the light of the conclusion that the *Heike* was written for popular story-telling to the accompaniment of the lute. Apparently this form of Buddhism, believed to be particularly suitable when prospects for the future were bleak, was already beginning to spread from aristocratic circles into the lower reaches of Japanese society, causing more people to reject this polluted land *(edo)* and to affirm the glories of the Pure Land *(jōdo)*.

The *Heike* refers frequently to another form of thought about the future which, along with Pure Land thought, seems to have been rooted in the pessimism of the times: belief in the future coming of Maitreya *(Miroku)*, a future Buddha. The most telling *Heike* reference to the Maitreya faith is found in sections that describe Koremori's final days. Koremori's stopover at Mt. Kōya on his way to the Kumano Shrines was the occasion for touching on the special relationship between Grand Preceptor Kōbō (the founder of the Mt. Kōya monastery) and Maitreya. The account begins with a summary of a dream that Emperor Daigo had had about a century after Kōbō's death in 835. In Daigo's dream. Kōbō reportedly said that he wanted a certain kind of robe. Therefore the Emperor asked a messenger to take a robe of that description to Mt. Kōya where Kōbō had been buried. But when the messenger opened the door of the tomb, a mist appeared before his eyes, making it impossible for him to see the features of the great saint. The messenger was bitterly disappointed, but finally Kōbō appeared "like a moon coming from behind the clouds." Whereupon the messenger clothed Kōbō with the new robe and cut the deceased Kōbō's hair. According to the

82. Chapter 10, NKBT, 33.283.

Heike version of the tale, Kōbō then asked the messenger to convey
the following message to Emperor Daigo:

> A long time ago I met Fugen Bosatsu. He taught me all the magi-
> cal hand signs *(mudra)* and all the mystical formulas *(darani)*, and
> I took an unparalleled vow to save people in this distant and for-
> eign land and to have compassion for everyone, devoting myself
> to my vow with Fugen Bosatsu. So I now await the descent of
> Maitreya, exhibiting in my living body [the truth of] Samādhi.[83]

The *Heike* goes on to say that since Kōbō had died more than three
hundred years ago, he would have had to wait 5,670,000,000 more
years for Maitreya's birth in this world, as a second historic Buddha,
to save all sentient beings.[84]

Still another expression of Buddhist interest in the future
emerged from beliefs in the divinity and sacred power of Prince
Shōtoku, a distinguished patron of Buddhism who had died in 621.
Not long after his death, the belief spread among aristocrats that the
Prince had been born into this world as a reincarnation of the second patriarch of T'ien T'ai (Tendai) Buddhism. Saichō, who introduced Tendai Buddhism to Japan at the beginning of the ninth century, added his support to such belief. But toward the end of the
Heian Era, when social and political disintegration had convinced
more aristocrats that the age of Final Law had actually arrived, the
Prince was thought to have been an incarnation of Avalokiteśvara
and to have become, after death, a divine being that had the power
to lead a person, at the time of his own death, to the Avalokiteśvara
paradise. The Prince was also believed to have the power to predict
the future. His prophecies *(miraiki)*—like expressions of belief in the
birth of a second historic Buddha—appeared more frequently after
the eleventh century. The earlier ones predict future events in the
decline of Buddhism, but later ones predict secular decline. Thus
the *Heike* states, after listing the horrendous events that followed the
TAIRA retreat from the capital, that "Probably these developments
were included in the prophecies *(miraiki)* of Prince Shōtoku."[85]

The Military Tales, Japan's third type of early historical writing,
mix the old with the new. Although not shaped by efforts to follow
imported methods of writing history, as the National Histories had
been, they are still affected by the old belief in the uniqueness and
prestige of Japan's Imperial line. And although the Military Tales
are not primarily concerned with the splendor of the great FUJI-
WARA aristocrats, as the Historical Tales had been, the authors of the
later Military Tales provide more interesting stories of recent politi-

83. Chapter 10, NKBT, 33.272.
84. Chapter 10, NKBT, 33.272–273.
85. Chapter 8, NKBT, 33.119.

cal and military upheavals. What first makes them a new form of history is that they deal directly with, and are deeply affected by, fundamental change in the social and cultural life of twelfth-century Japan. Even though the authors did not attempt to identify the socioeconomic roots of that change, they did write in some detail about the conflict between aristocrats (whose political positions were based upon privileges accruing from noble birth and from advantages provided by education) and military dignitaries (whose positions of power had been obtained by the use of military force). Furthermore, these Military Tales describe, and reveal respect for, the tastes and values of the new military elite. The men who wrote the first Military Tales were probably closer to aristocrats than to military men and therefore could not avoid making an ideal military hero act and talk somewhat like an aristocrat. And yet their stories express excitement over the spectacular deeds of soldiers who were strong, brave, and loyal.

The Military Tales are different in other ways: they are informed by a better articulation of belief in the inevitability of historical decline, by reflection about the way Buddhist Law and Imperial Law are subjected to a process of inevitable decline, and by attention to prophecies from deities or the soul of Prince Shōtoku. While the earlier Historical Tales carry some marks of Final Law thought, the later Military Tales draw the reader's attention to deterioration that encompasses not merely Buddhist Law but the secular life of man. Final reigns *(matsudai)* and Final Age *(masse)*, terms which point to secular decline, appear with greater frequency in these later Tales. Use of the word Principle *(dōri)*[86] to explain crucial events in Japan's past provides further proof that Final Law belief had worked its way into Japanese thought about the passage of time.

While the *Heike* makes a number of references to the Buddhist doctrine of continuous decline, nothing is said about the relevance of this doctrine to future events. A future-oriented interpretation of past events appears first in the *Gukanshō*, a book written by a Buddhist priest who seemed to take prophecies seriously and who, feeling that able men had the power to bring about future improvement, delineated a process of change which was headed for a new political arrangement that had been willed and created by the ancestral Kami of Japan.

86. See the Introduction.

9
Jien and His Troubled Times
by Delmer M. Brown

For centuries, Japanese historians could reach no general agreement on either the authorship or the dating of the *Gukanshō,* but now they are inclined to accept (1) Hiroyuki Miura's (1871–1931) findings that the book was written by Jien (1155–1225) and (2) Tsunetsugu Muraoka's (1884–1946) conclusion that it was written prior to the Shōkyū War of 1221. Therefore a student who wishes to understand the basic character of the *Gukanshō's* historical interpretation should extend his study to the meaning of the convictions and concerns that led one particular Buddhist priest to write a history which would show why the secular affairs of the Japanese state had become so critical, and what must be done to achieve improvement.

In doing so, one will first note that Jien was not regarded by people of his own day as an original and interesting historian but as a well-connected aristocrat who had reached the highest levels of the Buddhist hierarchy and become known as a distinguished poet. It will also be easy to see significance in the known fact that Jien, living in the first decades of Japan's Military Age, was closely associated with a house (the KUJŌ) that had become ensnared in, and endangered by, a power struggle that erupted into open warfare a year or so after the *Gukanshō* was written. Recent studies also show that Jien believed future developments had been revealed to him in dreams. Turning our attention to Jien[1] and his times, let us therefore try to identify the relevance of (1) his aristocratic birth and Buddhist training, (2) the ups and downs of his KUJŌ house, and (3) his belief in dream revelations about the future.

Aristocratic Birth and Buddhist Training

Jien was born, at a time when birth was still the principle determinant of social and political position, into a house of the FUJIWARA clan from which Regents and Chancellors were selected. Three elder brothers followed their father in the office of Regent; three sisters became Empresses; and Jien himself was appointed Abbot of the Tendai Sect four times.

As high as the Regent-Chancellor house was,[2] its authority had long been subjected to erosion, especially after 1086 when retired Emperors began to assume responsibility for administering the affairs of state *(insei)*. Both Retired Emperor Shirakawa (1053–1129)

1. The major sources for a study of the life of Jien are: (1) the *Jichin kashō musō ki*, a dream interpretation written by Jien in 1209 and published in Toshihide Akamatsu's *Kamakura Bukkyō no kenkyū* (Kyoto: Heiraku-ji Shoten, 1957), pp. 318–322; (2) letters, prayers, poems, and other items written by Jien and included in his collected works: Munehaya Taga, ed., *Jien Zenshū* (Shichijō Shoin, 1945); (3) a prayer addressed by Jien to Prince Shōtoku on the 22nd day of the 1st month of 1224, published in Akamatsu, *Kamakura Bukkyō no kenkyū*, pp. 283–286; (4) previously unpublished letters written by Jien and having some connection with the *Gukanshō*, published in NKBT, 86.524–528; (5) the *Gukanshō;* (6) the diary of Jien's brother Kanezane covering the years 1164–1200: Kokusho Kankō Kai, ed., *Gyokuyō* (Tokyo, 1906–07), 3 vols.; and (7) the *Jichin kashō den,* an early biography of Jien published in the *Zenshū,* 763–772.

The most useful secondary studies of Jien's life are: (1) Tsunetsugu Muraoka's "Mappō shisō no tenkai to *Gukanshō* no shikan," *Nihon shisō shi kenkyū: Nihon shisōshi jō sho mondai* (Tokyo, 1964), 2.111–209; (2) Munehaya Taga, *Jien* (Vol. 15 of Kōbun Kan's *Jinbutsu sōsho* [Tokyo, 1959]); and (3) four articles by Toshihide Akamatsu: "*Gukanshō* ni tsuite," *Kamakura Bukkyō no kenkyū* (Kyoto, 1957), pp. 267–300; "*Jichin kashō musō ki* ni tsuite," ibid., pp. 317–335; "*Gukanshō* ni tsuite," *Zoku Kamakura Bukkyō no kenkyū* (Kyoto, 1966), pp. 373–389; and "Yoritomo to sono musume," ibid., pp. 390–409.

2. In attempting to glorify the KUJŌ as a Regent-Chancellor house, Jien traces its origins back to Morosuke, referring to Morosuke as Lord Kujō and emphasizing the importance of a patron pledge *(shidan no chigiri)* made between him and Grand Preceptor Ji'e, an incarnation of Avalokiteśvara (see Chapter 1). But Regent-Chancellor houses *(sekkan-ke)* are now thought to have developed in these stages: (1) the monopoly of Regent-Chancellor ap-

and Retired Emperor Toba (1103–56) held far more power than any Regent or Chancellor who was in office during those years. But political changes flowing from two short civil wars fought when Jien was still a child presented the Regent-Chancellor house with an even more serious threat: the rise of powerful military clans. Jien's father, Regent Tadamichi (1097–1164), had been associated with generals on the winning side of the first war (the Hōgen Rebellion of 1156) and was therefore able to retain the position of Regent. But for two decades after the second war (the Heiji Rebellion of 1159–60), every single Regent and Chancellor was dominated by the ruthless TAIRA no Kiyomori (1118–81), the victorious general.

During the 1160s, when Jien's brothers were little more than Kiyomori pawns, Jien was sent off to the Enryaku Temple on Mt. Hiei for Buddhist training under Prince-Priest Kakukai (1134–81), seventh son of Retired Emperor Toba. Jien was only ten years old at the time, and his father had just died. In attempting to explain Jien's early entrance into the Buddhist priesthood, biographers usually assign some significance to the prior death of both parents. But it was not uncommon in those days for younger sons of great clan leaders to be entrusted, at an early age, to some eminent priest for Buddhist training. And yet, poems composed by Jien suggest that he was indeed a lonely child and that he was attracted, quite soon, to Buddhist teachings of transience and impermanence. The first extant biography of Jien, the *Jichin kashō den,* tells us that when he was about twenty years old, he "secluded himself in the mountains for 1,000 days, carrying out a resolution to subject himself to religious austerities, enduring storms and snow, making offerings of water and flowers, observing the Buddhist commandments, and practicing Buddhist rites before the central object of worship."[3] Entries in his brother Kanezane's diary (the *Gyokuyō*) for those years refer frequently to Jien's desire to isolate himself in some remote temple for the worship of Buddha.[4] In 1180, according to the *Jichin kashō den,* Jien did seclude himself in the Zempō Temple located in the mountains to the west of the capital. And a few months later he went to

---

pointments by the northern house of FUJIWARA clan after Yoshifusa was named Regent in 858; (2) the monopoly of such appointments, in the northern house of FUJIWARA, by the descendants on Michinaga after Yorimichi was appointed Regent in 1017; (3) the division of the northern house into two houses, the KONOE and the KUJŌ, after KONOE Motozane was made Regent in 1166 and KUJŌ Kanezane received that appointment in 1186; and (4) the addition of the TAKATSUKASA house (a branch of the KONOE) and the ICHIJŌ and NIJŌ (branches of the KUJŌ) after the middle of the 13th century, accounting for the "five Regent-Chancellor houses" *(go-sekke).*

3. *Zenshū,* 767.

4. Cf. Toshihide Akamatsu, "*Gukanshō* ni tsuite," *Zoku Kamakura Bukkyō no kenkyū* (Kyoto, 1966), pp. 373–389.

another temple, the Myō-ō Cloister on the Katsura River, where he fasted for seven days and had a miraculous vision of a Buddhist deity (Fudō Myō-ō).[5]

Jien's pursuit of Buddhist enlightenment in some remote temple has been described as a second-stage escape from the secular world. Since the principal temples where sons of the leading aristocrats were customarily sent had collected vast land holdings and were deeply involved in the country's political and military struggles, their priests had assumed responsibilities that had very little connection with the worship of Buddha. Mt. Hiei has been referred to as a state within a state, not only controlling a great network of tax-free estates *(shōen)* but mobilizing armies of priestly soldiers *(sōhei)*. If an individual priest was sincerely interested in following the path of Buddha, he had to escape not only from the secular world but from the secular activities of Mt. Hiei. Thus Jien's desire to go into seclusion *(tonsei)* suggests that, at least until the age of 28, the practice of Buddhism was for him far more attractive than the secular life of his temple.

Turbulence in religious and political circles must have further strengthened his resolve to remain aloof from secular affairs. The great Tendai monastery on Mt. Hiei had long been disrupted by conflict between temples associated with Enryaku (the Mountain Order) and those associated with Miidera (the Temple Order) and also by rivalry, which often took the form of open warfare, with temples in the old capital of Nara. By the time Jien was seeking a life of seclusion, Mt. Hiei was also torn by internal strife. Temples of the Eastern Section were ranged against those of the Western Section, and in 1167 a battle broke out between them. Low-ranking priests *(doshū)* of all temples were beginning to resist the control of priests of high rank *(gakushō)*, who considered themselves to be true priests since they had spent many years in the study and worship of Buddha and held the highest positions in the Buddhist hierarchy. Traditionally the *doshū* helped the *gakushō* in ways that would give the latter more time and energy for religious activity, but as Mt. Hiei became embroiled in conflict that often resulted in the use of military force, the *doshū*—now more like soldiers than priests—became increasingly independent and frequently refused to follow orders handed down by their superiors. In 1178, TAIRA Kiyomori was even forced to send troops to Mt. Hiei to put down a *doshū* rebellion. The *gakushō* themselves were torn by dissension over political affiliation. One group at Mt. Hiei under the leadership of Abbot Myōun (d. 1183) allied itself with the TAIRA clan. Another group strongly backed by *doshū* was sympathetic with military forces that were moving against the TAIRA. And in between, a third group headed by Jien's teacher Kakukai tried to remain aloof from all political entanglements.

5. *Zenshū,* 767.

The situation at the Imperial Court, where close relatives of Jien held important posts, was also unsettled. On several occasions between 1156 and 1185, military action was followed by political changes that affected the throne itself. And in each case high-ranking members of the once-powerful FUJIWARA clan were arbitrarily moved in and out of offices and now had little more than nominal authority. TAIRA Kiyomori's use of military force against the Retired Emperor in 1179 was followed by very drastic political action: Retired Emperor Go-Shirakawa was placed under house arrest; a TAIRA-related child was enthroned as Emperor Antoku (1178–85); and Tadamichi's young grandson, KONOE Motomichi (1160–1233) was appointed Regent. Just four years later, when KISO Yoshinaka (1154–84) and his troops entered the capital and the TAIRA fled, another shakeup occurred: a child was enthroned as Emperor Go-Toba (1180–1239), and another Tadamichi grandson, MATSU Moroie (1172–1238), was named Chancellor. And after the four-year war of 1181–85 between the two great military clans, the TAIRA and the MINAMOTO, the victorious MINAMOTO Yoritomo (1147–99) not only removed his opponents from office but had an Imperial decree issued which authorized him to appoint military officials (*jitō* and *sōtsuibushi*)[6] at different locations around the country—an important step toward the establishment of an autonomous military government (*bakufu*).[7]

Although Jien's own teacher was caught between warring factions on Mt. Hiei, and several of his close relatives were involved in disturbances at and around the Imperial Court, Jien himself seems not to have permitted these political and military conflicts to divert him from a serious pursuit of Buddhahood. His practice of the austerities and the report that he had a miraculous vision of Fudō Myō-ō suggest that during these first three decades of his life he was a firm believer in, and student of, the Buddhist doctrines that lay at the base of his later historical reflections. But the appointment of his brother KUJŌ Kanezane (1149–1207) to the post of Regent in 1186 brought this non-political period of his life to a close.

The Golden Years of the KUJŌ House

For nearly a year after the TAIRA clan's defeat at Dan no Ura in 1185, the positions of Jien and his brother Kanezane were not much affected by the MINAMOTO clan's seizure of power. But in the 10th month of 1185 the Emperor issued an edict, upon the recommendation of MINAMOTO Yoshitsune (1159–89), that Yoshitsune's elder

---

6. The *sōtsuibushi* later became *shugo*.

7. The word *bakufu* did not come into use until later, but it is used here when referring to the military government structure that was built by MINAMOTO Yoritomo and his successors.

brother Yoritomo (1147–99) be attacked and killed. Within a few weeks, Yoritomo sent troops into the capital and forced the court to approve the appointment of military officials throughout the country—ostensibly to hunt down Yoshitsune and rebels supporting him, and to obtain supplies needed for such military operations—and demanded that Kanezane be appointed Imperial Inspector *(nairan)*. Then, in the 3rd month of 1186, Kanezane replaced KONOE Motomichi as Regent. During the hectic weeks of Yoritomo's moves against those who had supported Yoshitsune, Jien seems to have taken action against Tendai priests who had backed Yoshitsune. And having associated himself with Kanezane and Yoritomo, Jien soon received appointments as chief priest at several leading temples; and he was invited to the palace of Retired Emperor Go-Shirakawa (1127–92) to pray for His Majesty's health. But Kanezane was not yet the most powerful official at court, as was clearly demonstrated by Go-Shirakawa's refusal to transfer to Kanezane the estates that had been held by his predecessor.

Go-Shirakawa had abdicated in 1158, just before the outbreak of the Heiji Rebellion, with the intention of regaining the administrative power that had been enjoyed by Retired Emperors Shirakawa and Toba between 1086 and 1156. The victorious military general, TAIRA Kiyomori, stood in his way. But with the death of Kiyomori in 1181 and the destruction of the TAIRA forces in 1185, Go-Shirakawa's position was greatly strengthened, for MINAMOTO Yoritomo had opened up his campaigns against the TAIRA in response to a "Princely edict" issued by a Go-Shirakawa son and, furthermore, had elected to keep his military headquarters at Kamakura, far to the northeast of the Imperial capital in Kyoto. For these and other reasons, Go-Shirakawa had enough power and independence to keep both Kanezane and Yoritomo from obtaining everything they wanted. But in 1190 his control was weakened, and that of Kanezane and the KUJŌ house strengthened, when Yoritomo subjugated the military forces of Mutsu and made a grand entry into Kyoto. Then Kanezane's daughter, Gishū-mon In (1173–1238), was made Go-Toba's Empress, and everyone in the KUJŌ house looked forward to a time when there would be a reigning Emperor with a KUJŌ mother. And yet, Go-Shirakawa still had considerable influence. According to Kanezane's diary, Yoritomo told Kanezane, while Yoritomo was still in the capital, that the Retired Emperor's position was to be respected:

> I have unparalleled respect for the Emperor, but since the Retired Emperor is handling the administrative affairs of the empire, I will serve him. . . . After the Retired Emperor dies, I will serve the Emperor. . . . Eventually the empire will be straightened out. The Emperor is now a child and you too have many years ahead of you. If my good fortune holds out, administrative af-

fairs will probably be handed over to you. For the present, we
should leave everything to the Retired Emperor.[8]

Go-Shirakawa seems even to have prevented Yoritomo from realizing his wish for an appointment as Shogun.

Then, in the 3rd month of 1192, Go-Shirakawa died, leaving no
Retired Emperor to succeed him as head of the Retired Emperor's
semi-private administrative office (the *in no chō*). This left the
Kanezane-Yoritomo combination virtually unchallenged. Within a
few months, Yoritomo was granted the title of Shogun, and Jien was
given the two highest positions a Buddhist priest could hold: Tendai
Abbot *(zasu)* and Guardian Priest of the Emperor *(gojisō)*. The KUJŌ
house now entered its "golden age." Kanezane no longer complained
of not being a true Regent, and Jien no longer spoke of a desire to
isolate himself in some distant temple for the worship of Buddha. As
Jien later wrote, the Emperor was supported in those years by both
the learning of the KUJŌ house and the military might of the
MINAMOTO clan.

During his four-year first term as Tendai Abbot, Jien frequented
the Imperial Court and devoted much time to the conduct of
Buddhist rites that would benefit the Emperor, the Empress, or the
KUJŌ Regent. But he also built new temples, notably the Daijō Cloister at Mudō, and gave close attention to organized lectures for the
advancement of Buddhist studies *(kangaku kō)*. These lectures, made
possible by a large estate given to him by Yoritomo, were started in
1195, and a treatise on their history was written by Jien in 1208.
Thus Jien continued to be a devout Buddhist, but he was also preoccupied with that which would assure prosperity and power for the
KUJŌ house. Political concerns seem to have been as strong as his
belief in the teachings of Buddha.

Two Falls from Power

Having reached such dizzy heights, Kanezane and Jien were really
crushed, in 1196, when Kanezane was forced to resign as Regent,
Jien was ousted from his post as Tendai Abbot, and Gishū-mon In
was removed from the Imperial Palace. Their places were taken by
rivals and enemies: Motomichi (1160–1233) of the house of KONOE
was re-appointed Regent; Prince-Priest Shōnin (1169–97), a disciple
of Jien's rival Myōun, was made Tendai Abbot; and Shōmei-mon
In (1171–1257), an adopted daughter of the hated MINAMOTO
Michichika (1145–1202), became Emperor Go-Toba's senior Empress. When writing about this shift of power, Jien made Michichika
the villain, stating that this man, wishing to make his own daughter
the Emperor's senior consort, had conspired with other malcontents
to discredit Kanezane. Neither Kanezane's diary nor other contem-

8. *Gyokuyō* 1190–11–4 [*Dai Nihon shiryō*, Ser. IV, 3.278].

porary records explain the nature of the changes that led to Kanezane's downfall, but a resurgence of power among those who had been associated with the deceased Go-Shirakawa and his *in no chō* was undoubtedly an important factor. Although this semi-private bureaucratic structure had been greatly weakened by the death of Retired Emperor Go-Shirakawa in 1192, and Kanezane and Yoritomo had gained additional influence over political affairs during the period between 1192 and 1196, the Go-Shirakawa group led by MINAMOTO Michichika managed to marshal forces for a return to power.

Michichika was, however, not simply a wily conspirator, as Jien suggests, for he had some truly significant sources of strength. First of all, he was a member of the MINAMOTO clan that had contended, ever since the beginning of the *in no chō*, with the FUJIWARA for the highest appointments at court. During that period, men in this branch of the MINAMOTO had received many ministerial posts, even that of Prime Minister. Michichika had succeeded his father as Minister of the Center during the years of TAIRA no Kiyomori's control and, having cooperated with the TAIRA, gradually rose to a position of leadership within the Go-Shirakawa administrative structure. Secondly, Michichika had the backing of people who possessed or managed large or numerous tax-free estates. A particularly wealthy and influential landholder was TAKASHINA Eishi (d. 1216), who had been Go-Shirakawa's favorite consort after 1181. She may well have become the most powerful individual in Go-Shirakawa's palace in the years immediately preceding the Retired Emperor's death in 1192. Both she and her daughter, Empress Senyō-mon In (1181–1252), were able to retain their estates after Go-Shirakawa's death, and these women and their estate managers seem to have allied themselves with Michichika's cause.[9] A third support for Michichika was Emperor Go-Toba (1180–1239) who, like Go-Shirakawa before him, was interested in abdicating and restoring the *in no chō's* administrative control.

But probably the most decisive factor in the KUJŌ fall from power in 1196 was a change in Yoritomo's feelings about the situation at court. Neither Kanezane's diary nor other records of that day give us a full account of what Yoritomo was thinking and doing, but recent

9. Cf. Susumu Ishii, *Kamakura bakufu* (Vol. 7 of the Chūō Kōron Sha's *Nihon no rekishi* [Tokyo, 1974], pp. 226–230 and 353–356. One of the largest holdings, the *chōkōdō-ryō*, was made up of 112 estates *(shōen)*. It was apparently amassed by Retired Emperor Go-Shirakawa, and at the time of his death it was transferred to Empress Senyō-mon In, his favorite daughter by Eishi. Even in the 15th century this collection of estates produced a fabulous income, and Susumu Ishii concludes that it was an important factor in the strength of Michichika and Eishi at the time of the coup in 1196. [Ibid., pp. 354–355.]

studies reveal[10] that Yoritomo, while in Kyoto during the year 1195, spent more time with Michichika and Eishi than with Kanezane. He apparently was determined to control court affairs and decided that this objective could be most easily achieved by identifying himself with Imperial authority in the traditional way: by making his daughter the Emperor's senior consort and creating the possibility of becoming the maternal grandfather of a reigning Emperor. For such a plan he obviously could expect no support from Kanezane, whose daughter was already an Empress, and he therefore seems to have sought the backing of Michichika and Eishi. But when Kanezane was forced to resign and his daughter was removed from the palace, it was Michichika's daughter, not Yoritomo's, who became Go-Toba's senior consort. It has been suggested that Yoritomo's plans could not be implemented because his daughter had become seriously ill. Whatever the reason, Yoritomo apparently was not displeased to have Michichika replace Kanezane as the father of Go-Toba's senior Empress.

In 1198, Yoritomo became really upset, however, when he heard that Go-Toba had abdicated with the obvious intention of administering court affairs as Retired Emperor in the Go-Shirakawa manner. Yoritomo immediately sent off letters to both Kanezane and Jien asking for their advice. According to the *Gukanshō*, Yoritomo even planned another trip to Kyoto "in order to take care of some matters of state." But he died before such plans could be carried out. So Yoritomo failed to establish direct control over the court and, moreover, managed to undermine the position of his aristocratic allies in the KUJŌ house. Now the *bakufu* would come to face resistance from a Retired Emperor who wanted to handle political questions as previous Retired Emperors had, as well as from a KONOE Regent who had no familial ties with the MINAMOTO clan. These were disastrous developments for Kanezane, Jien, and the KUJŌ house. Even before Yoritomo's death in 1199, Kanezane had turned from politics to religion, becoming a convert to the Pure Land faith and entering the Buddhist priesthood in 1202. Jien returned to his secluded temple in the mountains and for roughly four years had little contact with the court. Such was the fate of the two brothers who had risen so high with the backing of the great MINAMOTO Yoritomo.

Tensions and rivalry within the *bakufu* after the death of Yoritomo encouraged Go-Toba to feel that the administration of court affairs by a Retired Emperor (*insei*) could now be re-established. Not only were military leaders less able to interfere in court politics, but Go-Toba was confident that he could obtain support from various clans

10. Toshihide Akamatsu, "Yoritomo to sono musume," *Zoku Kamakura Bukkyō no kenkyū* (Kyoto, 1966), pp. 390–409.

and temples. In moves that Go-Toba made to strengthen the *in no chō*, Jien thought he saw opportunities for a KUJŌ return to power, especially since he assumed that his personal friendship with Go-Toba, reinforced by a common interest in poetry, would enable him and the KUJŌ house to regain Imperial favor. Subsequent events surely made him more optimistic about the future: in 1200, Go-Toba arranged to have his own son, rather than the son of Emperor Tsuchimikado (1195–1231), appointed Crown Prince; at about that time, Jien was invited to conduct certain Buddhist rites at court; and a few months later he was reappointed Tendai Abbot and given a position in Go-Toba's Department of Poetry. But Michichika was still alive and powerful, apparently blocking Jien's endeavors to revive lectures for the advancement of Buddhist studies. Possibly it was because of Michichika's influence that Jien resigned, or was dismissed, from his post as Tendai Abbot in the 7th month of 1202.

The death of Michichika a few months after Jien's resignation or dismissal definitely brightened the political picture for members of the KUJŌ house. KONOE Motomichi was removed from his position as Regent, and KUJŌ Yoshitsune (1169–1206), Kanezane's son and Jien's nephew, was selected to replace Motomichi. Therefore the KUJŌ rose, once more, to the top of the aristocratic hierarchy. Although Jien was not immediately reappointed Tendai Abbot, he received an accelerated promotion to Senior High Priest and was permitted to build new temples, such as the Daisenpō Cloister. He also gained further fame as a poet during these years. The *Shin Kokin shū* anthology, compiled in 1205, contains 90 of Jien's poems, more than of any other poet except the great Saigyō (1118–90). So during the four years that Yoshitsune was Regent, Jien and the KUJŌ house were justifiably hopeful of regaining the power and prestige that had been enjoyed during the Kanezane Regency.

But on the 7th day of the 3rd month of 1206, Yoshitsune, still in his thirties, suddenly died. This was a brutal blow for the KUJŌ, particularly since the position of Regent was handed back to a man in the KONOE house. Ostensibly KONOE Iezane (d. 1242) was appointed because KUJŌ Michiie (1193–1252), Yoshitsune's son, was too young to assume the responsibilities of that high office. But Go-Toba may have decided that it would be easier for him to re-establish Retired Emperor control if the KUJŌ house was not allowed to gain additional strength. He certainly was aware of family ties between the KUJŌ and the MINAMOTO, and realized that the *bakufu* was the major obstacle to the realization of his plans. For the next 14 years the office of Regent was therefore held by KONOE Iezane (d. 1242), a man described by Jien as an individual who "knew, heard, saw, or learned absolutely nothing about either state administration or house customs." Thus the year 1206 marks the beginning of a 13-

year period—lasting until the *Gukanshō* was written in 1219—of
frustration for Jien and his KUJŌ relatives. There were a few hopeful developments during those years, but Jien seems to have been
plagued by a nagging fear of further disaster.

Searching for Supernatural and Historical Support

In the second year of KUJŌ Yoshitsune's term as Regent—in the
6th month of 1203—Jien had a dream about two of the three sacred
symbols of Imperial authority known as the Imperial Regalia. Not
long afterward, and again in 1204 and 1209, he wrote down his
thoughts about the meaning of that dream; and two copies of the
document, entitled the *Jichin kashō musō ki,* were recently found by
Toshihide Akamatsu.[11] Its contents provide interesting information
about the nature of Jien's early search for the supernatural and historical meaning of the KUJŌ role as a Regent/Chancellor house. The
various parts of the document were apparently written at crucial
points in an intellectual process by which Jien's religious convictions
were related historically to his deepest political concerns. The *Jichin
kashō musō ki* is therefore an important source for those who wish to
understand the evolution of Jien's historical thought.

Earlier parts of the document were apparently revised when the
last part was written in 1209, but it is deduced that the dream was
mainly about the Sacred Seal *(shinji)* appearing as a "jewel woman"
and being recognized by Jien as the Empress. In interpreting the
dream, Jien first concludes that seeing the Sacred Seal as the Empress meant that she is made pure *(shōjō)* by intercourse with the
Emperor. After further reflection, Jien also identifies the Imperial
Sword (symbolizing the Emperor) and the Sacred Seal (symbolizing
the Empress) with two symbols of esoteric Tendai Buddhism: the
"sword" and the "sheath." In this way Jien is consciously or unconsciously giving two levels of supernatural meaning to the position of
Empress: an ancestral-Kami one arising from her association with an
Emperor descended from the Sun Goddess, and an esoteric-
Buddhist one arising from the identification of the Sacred Seal with
the "sheath."

Jien further concludes, in this first interpretation of the 1203
dream, that two of the Imperial Regalia—the Sacred Seal and the
Imperial Sword—"complete the unity of the empire and are Regalia
which, by completing Buddha Law and Imperial Law, regulate the
state and benefit the people." The supreme deity of Imperial Law
(the Sun Goddess) and the highest deity of esoteric Buddhist Law
(Dainichi Nyorai) are related to the Emperor in the following way:
(1) the Emperor is the divine body *(gotai)* of the Sun Goddess, having

11. Toshihide Akamatsu, *"Jichin kashō musō ki* ni tsuite," *Kamakura Bukkyō
no kenkyū* (Kyoto, 1957), pp. 317–335.

been produced by an interaction between the three symbols of the Emperor's authority; (2) Dainichi Nyorai, having been manifested as the one essence *(ichiji konrin)* for the benefit of man, is the ruler of the Buddhist world; and (3) esoteric rites performed at the time of the Emperor's enthronement make the Emperor a manifestation of Dainichi Nyorai in this physical world. After further comment about the symbolic relationship between Fudō Myō-ō (a manifestation of Dainichi Nyorai) and the Emperor (an incarnation of the Sun Goddess), Jien closes this first interpretation of his 1203 dream with the comment that he has now come to understand what was previously "incomprehensible."

Jien's dream, and his first interpretation of it, came at a time when Regent KUJŌ Yoshitsune and Jien were obviously hoping that a Yoshitsune daughter would be made Emperor Tsuchimikado's Empress in 1205, when the Emperor was to come of age. Fifteen years later, Jien wrote about those hopes in considerable detail. In the light of Jien's wishes for the appointment of a KUJŌ Empress, one cannot but think of the 1203 dream as an unconscious, and of the early interpretations of that dream as a conscious, effort to give religious meaning to the position and role of the Empress.

Not long after the first dream interpretation had been written, Jien added a note reporting that after his interpretation was presented to Retired Emperor Go-Toba, Regent KUJŌ Yoshitsune sent Jien some material, including a copy of the *Nihongi*, that contained references relevant to the dream. Jien writes that in reading over the material he made two startling discoveries. First, that the *Nihongi* contained an item which stated that the Sacred Seal was a jewel. Second, that a document about the TAIRA–MINAMOTO War disclosed the fact that when soldiers recovered the Sacred-Seal box from the sea at the end of the 1185 battle of Dan no Ura, they opened it and saw that it contained a jewel. Such historical proof that the Sacred Seal was a jewel, as revealed in the 1203 dream, made Jien quite sure that he had obtained a marvelous revelation of divine truth. Professor Akamatsu expresses surprise that Jien, then approaching fifty and a man who would become a noted historian, had not yet read either the *Nihongi* or documents about the TAIRA–MINAMOTO War closely enough to see what they said about the Imperial Regalia. It may well be that Jien was just beginning to become a historian, just as he was just beginning to consciously relate his Buddho-Shinto beliefs to the position and role of the Empress.

In the 3rd month of 1209, a daughter of the deceased KUJŌ Yoshitsune was married to Crown Prince Juntoku, making it quite certain that she would soon become an Empress. And three months later, Jien wrote a longer interpretation of his 1203 dream. The first part reiterates what had been written in the earlier interpretation, and adds some further points about connections between Imperial and Buddhist symbols and deities, but it also contains sentences that reflect a growing interest in forces which account for historical change:

> The abilities *(kiryō)* of Emperors, whether bright or stupid, and nobility or meanness of the good or bad in Empresses, appear in accord with the ups and downs of time fate *(jiun)*. This means that everything deteriorates spontaneously *(hōni)*, something about which we should reflect deeply.[12]

In an attempt to clarify the relationship between time fate and the Japanese situation, Jien then raises some questions. In replying to the first question, he makes this statement:

> In the ancient past, wise rulers and intelligent ministers certainly had a clear understanding of the Imperial Regalia. But in the deteriorated age of the final reigns, people have not concerned themselves with such matters, and now there is absolutely no one who knows what the Imperial Regalia signify. In the *Masafusa kyō ki,* it is written that when an Emperor is enthroned he gives the "wisdom grasping *mudra*" *(chigen-in)* while sitting on the high throne. But it seems that no one else knew this. And even if someone had read the diary, he would not have inquired into the meaning of an Emperor giving this *mudra*. So in later enthronements it seems that this way of conducting the ceremony has been neglected. Usually there is improvement only when there is ability *(ki* of *kiryo)* in the study of divine and secular laws; and when there is no such ability, destruction occurs spontaneously *(hōni).*[13]

Clearly Jien was beginning to equate the "abilities" of man with a comprehension of "divine and secular laws," an ability that would enable a person to bring about improvement.

But at the very end of the 1209 interpretation, Jien shifts his attention to the meaning of the loss of the Imperial Sword, another of the three Imperial Regalia:

> After the Imperial Sword sank to the bottom of the sea, military Shoguns seized control of Japan and, doing as they pleased, placed Land Stewards in various provinces. . . . After the Imperial Sword was lost, was not its virtue *(toku)* pased to a human Shogun?[14]

By focusing his attention on the loss of the Imperial Sword and finding virtue *(toku)* in the power and position of the MINAMOTO Shogun, Jien finds metaphysical foundations for the KUJŌ's second pillar of support: its special relationship to the current Shogun. By

12. Ibid., p. 320.
13. Idem.
14. Ibid., p. 321.

that time, Jien is far more worried about growing tension between
Go-Toba and the *bakufu* than about the future appointment of a
KUJŌ Empress, an appointment which he now thinks will soon be
made.

Very little is known about the evolution of Jien's historical thought
between 1209 and 1216. In 1211, KUJŌ Yoshitsune's daughter, the
future Higashi Ichijō In (1192–1247), had become Empress. And
Jien was named Tendai Abbot twice more, once in 1212 and again in
1213. But Jien's last two terms as Tendai Abbot were short, and he
was no longer as close to Go-Toba as he had once been. Undoubtedly relations between them were becoming strained by Go-Toba's
determination to reduce or destroy *bakufu* control over state affairs.
Go-Toba might well have come to fear that members of the KUJŌ
house (and Jien) were too intimate with *bakufu* officials to be reliable
allies.

In 1216, Jien reportedly had another dream revelation that stimu-
lated further thought about the religious and historical meaning of
the KUJŌ position as a Regent-Chancellor house with special ties to
the MINAMOTO Shogun. What information we have about the 1216
dream comes from two prayers *(gammon)* that Jien wrote at a later
date, one in 1222 and another in 1224. Although the purpose of the
first was to seek relief from illness, it includes the following statements about the 1216 dream:

> I have been delighted—since receiving a "soul revelation" *(reikoku)*
> in the 1st month of 1216—that my wishes are in accord with di-
> vine will. I have been pleased with such a fusion of divine and
> secular truth *(shintai* and *zokutai).* One part [of the revelation] was
> hard to believe, and the other part I did believe. I could not stop
> [worrying] and prayed often. But for seven years there were no
> results, and I became exhausted by thinking about the beginning,
> middle, and end of things. After that, I wrote statements ad-
> dressed to the deities, the contents of which are all known to thee
> *(San-ō).* The Principles *(dōri)* which I have meanwhile been think-
> ing about will not be rejected by deities. The prediction that was
> revealed to me again the year before last [1220] was realized last
> year [1221]. A great rebellion broke out in the 5th and 6th
> months [of 1221], and in the 7th month there was another veering
> away [from what had been predicted]. I am now very confused,
> but the divine purpose is deep. . . .[15]

This prayer of 1222 indicates that the 1216 dream had prophesied
the coming of events that actually occurred in 1221. Since two de-

15. Jien prayer, judged to have been written in 1222 [*Dai Nihon shiryō*,
Ser. V, 2.736]. Akamatsu has edited and published another text in "*Gukanshō*
ni tsuite," pp. 298–299, and supplies his interpretation in ibid., pp. 274–276.

velopments of great importance to Jien and the KUJŌ house occurred at that time—the enthronement of KUJŌ Yoshitsune's grandson as Emperor Chūkyō (1218–34), and the appointment of KUJŌ
Michiie (1193–1252) as Regent—it is deduced that at least these two
events had been prophesied. The prayer also tells us that Jien had
been thinking about Principles.

The prayer of 1224, addressed to the spirit of Prince Shōtoku,
refers again to the 1216 dream:

> The unseen and the seen have become separated, and the hearts
> and minds of ordinary beings have become confused. Only
> through dreams do we know the future *(mirai)*. Since ancient times,
> there have been cases [of people knowing the future through
> dreams].
>   The divine soul of the Prince revealed to me—in a dream—a
> plaque that was the sacred body *(gotai)* of the "new shrine" and on
> which characters were written. This plaque indicated that Impe-
> rial Law and Buddhist Law would flourish. The "new shrine" is
> the shrine where the San-ō is worshipped. The plaque was re-
> vealed to me by Prince Shōtoku, and on it there was a Japanese
> poem written in Chinese characters. The poem was an oracle mes-
> sage from San-ō. The Chinese characters [told of] a vow that our
> Japanese Kami had made to bestow their blessings. It was indeed
> a miraculous dream!
>   After the lapse of some years, and while I was paying my re-
> spects to this temple [of Ten-ō], I prayed that I might be relieved
> of my official duties; but I had another dream, as a result of which
> I still have not been released from those duties. So I have always
> prayed to the San-ō about my uncertainties. Now once more, and
> in the closing years of my life, I pray to the Prince about what
> should and should not be done. This is the ninth year since the
> [1216] revelation. Meanwhile I have received many other dream
> revelations. These have been years of faith. After [I received that
> revelation nine years ago], several things happened that were
> predicted in it: the Shogun [Sanetomo] was cut down at the
> [Tsurugaoka Hachiman] Shrine; the Shogun was succeeded by
> the young [Yoritsune]; the Empress gave birth to an Imperial son;
> this Imperial son was enthroned; and the Emperor's maternal
> umcle was appointed Regent. Each of these events was in accord
> with the "soul revelation." And each deepened my faith in the
> divine will. But soon afterward, indescribable things happened
> that had not been predicted in the dream. . . .[16]

This prayer, written in the year before Jien's death, supplies further
detail about the 1216 dream. Three of the five events prophesied in
it had actually occurred before the *Gukanshō* was written in 1219: (1)

16. Jien prayer to Prince Shōtoku, 1224–1–22 [Akamatru, "*Gukanshō* ni
tsuite," pp. 283–284].

the assassination of Shogun Sanetomo in the 1st month of 1219; (2) the adoption of Yoritsune as Sanetomo's successor in the 6th month of 1219; and (3) the birth of an Imperial son to a KUJŌ Empress in 1218. The last two events were especially important to Jien and the KUJŌ house. They have much to do with Jien's decision to write the *Gukanshō,* and occupy a central position in its interpretation of Japanese history.

The first to occur was the birth of an Imperial son to a KUJŌ Empress in 1218. This son was appointed Crown Prince immediately, creating a situation in which KUJŌ Michiie (1193–1252), the Prince's maternal uncle, was sure to be made Regent as soon as this Prince was enthroned as Emperor. Jien and his KUJŌ relatives had been hoping, ever since KUJŌ Yoshitsune had been made Regent back in 1202, for just such a relationship to the throne. The *Gukanshō* reveals Jien's thoughts about the birth of an Imperial son to a KUJŌ woman:

> It is indeed a rare thing to have such an auspicious event in the Final Age! People at all levels of society—high, middle and low—has such thoughts as this: "Will not the age last a while longer?"

But the adoption of KUJŌ Michiie's son Yoritsune as Sanetomo's successor in 1219, just before Jien began writing the *Gukanshō,* probably had a more direct bearing upon Jien's decision to start writing his history of Japan.

Just what happened in Kyoto and Kamakura between the assassination of Sanetomo in the 1st month of 1219 and the departure of the two-year-old Yoritsune for Kamakura in the 6th month is not absolutely clear. Confusion certainly prevailed at both political centers. On the basis of what we are told in the *Gukanshō,* it seems that the principal figures in the negotiations between Kyoto and Kamakura during those months were: (1) HŌJŌ Masako (1157–1225), Yoritomo's widow and Sanetomo's mother; (2) Retired Emperor Go-Toba (1180–1229), the most powerful person in Kyoto at the time; and (3) Lady Second Rank (1155–1229), an extremely influential woman who had been Go-Toba's nurse. Masako apparently first proposed that an Imperial son be chosen to replace Sanetomo. Her aim, it seems, was to transform the position of Shogun into a source of authority for her father's military clan, the HŌJŌ, just as the Emperor had been the source of authority for power exercised by either a FUJIWARA Regent-Chancellor or a Retired Emperor. But since Go-Toba was intent upon increasing his power as a Retired Emperor, he was not willing to sanctify the power of the *bakufu* to that extent. He did agree to the adoption of a son from the KUJŌ house, which already had marriage ties with the MINAMOTO clan. While Go-Toba probably assigned no particular importance to the selection of Yoritsune as Sanetomo's successor, Jien did.

The appointment of a Crown Prince born to a KUJŌ mother had assured Jien that the KUJŌ, as a Regent-Chancellor house, would rise once more to a very high position in court affairs. But the selection of a KUJŌ son to be the next Shogun offered even more exciting possibilities. The KUJŌ had enjoyed a special relationship to the *bakufu* ever since the days of Kanezane and Yoritomo, but the prospect of having the military government headed by a person from the KUJŌ house fired Jien's imagination. Now he became convinced—in part because of earlier religious and historical reflection, and in part because of his understanding of current events—that the "single course" of Japanese history was leading directly to the establishment of an administrative arrangement in which the sacred role of a Regent-Chancellor and the sacred role of a Shogun would be played by the same person, KUJŌ Yoritsune, who would be Shogun *and* Regent.

But these hopes were mixed with fear that Go-Toba would challenge the *bakufu* and destroy all possibility of establishing a KUJŌ-centered form of cooperation between the Imperial Court and the *bakufu*. Go-Toba seems to have concluded that the complications attending the selection of Sanetomo's successor afforded excellent opportunities for destroying the autonomous power of the military. Even while negotiations were being carried on for an aristocratic successor to Sanetomo, Go-Toba was apparently gathering support and making plans for military action. Jien was not close enough to Go-Toba to know precisely what was being done, but he was surely aware that the situation was becoming increasingly tense and dangerous. And it was in such a state of mind, one in which high hopes were mixed with fears of disaster, that Jien began to write a book which would convince Go-Toba and his advisers that the "one course" of history, the divine will of ancestral Kami, and the Principles for the Final Age of history, all required organizational cooperation—under KUJŌ leadership—between the court and the *bakufu,* not confrontation. The denouement of the historical account is therefore found in the closing sections of his concluding chapter where he devotes several pages to specific advice for Go-Toba. The Retired Emperor is not only reminded of what the ancestral Kami had decided, what wonderful support a Regent-Shogun could provide, and where history was headed, but that (by implication) he might be removed from office—as Emperor Yōzei had been—if he does not comply with the will of the ancestral Kami, the requirements of Principles, and the demands of Japan's "true course" of history.

Jien could never completely divorce his position as a son and brother of Regents from his position as a priest who studied and practiced Buddhism within the great Tendai sect. For a time he tried to isolate himself completely from worldly affairs but was drawn deeply into current political rivalries by the appointment of his favorite brother as Regent after MINAMOTO Yoritomo's victories in 1185. And when the KUJŌ began to fall from power, especially after the death of Yoritomo in 1199 and while Go-Toba was pressing for greater control of the *in no chō*, Jien seems to have made a serious and conscious effort to relate his religious beliefs—both Shinto and Buddhist—to the changing fortunes of the KUJŌ house. And as recently discovered documents show, this effort was bound up with dreams and dream interpretations that deepened his faith in divine Principles which he believed were driving secular affairs toward a pattern of government the establishment of which had been foretold, in those dreams, by Buddhist and Shinto deities. Finally, after two young KUJŌ boys were placed (in 1218 and 1219) in extremely important positions, and when war was threatening to break out and to destroy the opportunity to realize cooperation between the Imperial Court and the *bakufu*, Jien started to work on a study of history that would show what the "single course" of history—moved by unseen Principles—required political leaders to do at that particular time of crisis.

10
Structure and Formation of Gukanshō Thought[1]

by Ichirō Ishida

As the younger brother of Regent KUJŌ Kanezane, Jien was deeply involved in the political affairs of the Imperial Court. And as a Buddhist priest who had been appointed Abbot of the Tendai Sect four times, he saw meaningful connections between political change and divine power. When he wrote that he "would like to write about Principles that have caused the world to change and deteriorate in a unilinear way," he was expressing the belief that political events had been moved along a "single course" by unseen forces and beings. Therefore I will try to show in the first part of this chapter how Jien's interpretation of history was structured by an interplay of concerns and commitments that were both political and religious. And in the second part, I will make some comments about the formation of his historical interpretation.

1. The first part of this chapter has been published in my "*Gukanshō no rekishi shisō*," *Nihon shisō shigaku* (September, 1969), 1–12; and the second part is taken from my "*Gukanshō to Jien*," *Fukui Hakase shōju kinen: Tōyō bunka ronshū* (Tokyo, 1969), pp. 55–72. A more detailed study has been made in my *Gukanshō no seiritsu to sono shisō: Tōhoku Daigaku Bungaku-bu kenkyū nempō*, No. 17 (Sendai, 1967).

Thought Structure

Let us think of *Gukanshō* thought as having a religious superstructure made up of two elements: Buddhist eschatological thought, and Shinto belief that ancestral Kami protect their descendants. (These two elements are represented as (1) and (2) in Figure 2.) The former is an imported element, having been introduced to Japan from India by way of China; but the second, inherited from the ancient past, is unique to Japan. The two elements have different origins and characteristics and in some ways are mutually contradictory. Yet they were joined together and made to complement each other by a mode of thought that had entered Mt. Hiei's intellectual heritage around the beginning of the Heian era, a mode that is revealed in thoughts about how ideals might be accommodated to the realities of a particular time, place, and level of human ability. (This binding force is represented as (X) in Figure 2.) Now let us think of this religious superstructure as being associated with an historical and political substructure with two additional elements: an historical awareness of modern times as the Final Age, and a political consciousness of the supremacy of the Regent-Chancellor houses. (These two elements are represented as (3) and (4) in Figure 2.) The former developed among aristocrats after the middle of the Heian era. The latter, affecting the thought of persons in the Regent-Chancellor houses after the middle of that era, was particularly strong in Jien, the young brother of Regent Kanezane of the KUJŌ house. In some respects these two elements are also mutually contradictory since they have different origins and characteristics, but they too were joined together and made to complement each other by Jien's thinking of what was appropriate to a particular time, place, and level of human ability (X).

While Buddhist eschatological thought (1) is supported, in Jien's thought structure, by a consciousness of modern times as the Final Age (3), the former provides metaphysical foundations for the latter. It is because of the strength of this metaphysically-grounded historical consciousness that the old idea of "one hundred reigns" *(hyaku-ō)* is transformed into a Japanese eschatological view. And while Shinto belief that ancestral Kami protect their descendants (2) is supported by a consciousness of the supremacy of the Regent-Chancellor houses (4), the former provides metaphysical foundations for the latter. And it is this metaphysically grounded consciousness of the supremacy of the Regent-Chancellor house that lies behind the emergence of the view that legitimate succession to the position of Regent or Chancellor exists only in the KUJŌ house. So thoughts about how ideals might be accommodated to the realities of a particular time, place, and human ability (X) not only joined elements in both the superstructure and the substructure but brought the two elements together on their two sides, creating a unified *Gukanshō* thought structure represented in Figure 2.

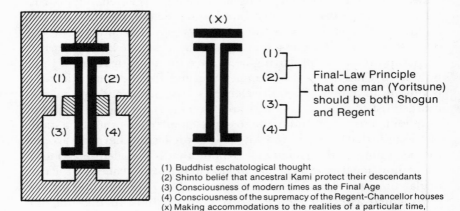

(1) Buddhist eschatological thought
(2) Shinto belief that ancestral Kami protect their descendants
(3) Consciousness of modern times as the Final Age
(4) Consciousness of the supremacy of the Regent-Chancellor houses
(x) Making accommodations to the realities of a particular time, place, and human ability.

Figure 2.

BUDDHIST ESCHATOLOGICAL THOUGHT (1) includes three important elements: the doctrine of the rotation of the four kalpas *(shikō junkan setsu)*; the doctrine of the three ages and the five periods *(sanji gokengo setsu)*; and the doctrine of the Mt. Sumera world view *(shumi seikai setsu)*. The last two were intertwined with each other in Jien's thought and built into the first. I summarize these three doctrines as they were apparently understood by Jien.

Theory of the Rotation of the Four Kalpas

Jien had read the *Abhidharma-kośa*[2] since the days of his youth and was greatly influenced by it. The doctrine of the rotation of the four kalpas is outlined in that Buddhist scripture as follows. At the beginning of a small kalpa, a person has a life expectancy of 80,000 years that decreases one year every century until it drops to 10 years. In this span of time, the deteriorating half of a small kalpa, the abilities and fortunes of man and his world gradually deteriorate. After this first half ends, man's life expectancy increases one year every century until it again reaches 80,000 years. During this span of time— the improving half of a small kalpa—the abilities and fortunes of man and his world improve. There are twenty small kalpas in one medium kalpa and four medium kalpas in one large kalpa. The four medium ones are: becoming *(jō)*, existing *(jū)*, destruction *(e)*, and emptiness *(kū)*. In the first, sentient beings and their world come into existence; in the second, they exist; in the third, they are destroyed and burned; and in the fourth, there is emptiness. The *Abhidharma-*

2. No. 1558 in *Taishō*, 29.62–63.

kośa goes on to say that time moves through these four medium kalpas forever, that the present stands near the end of the first half of the ninth small kalpa in the medium kalpa of existence, and that Shakyamuni was born when the average life span of man was 100 years. (See Figure 3.) Jien accepts this doctrine, concluding that deterioration would continue until the end of the first half of the current kalpa, that the present history of man (world history) is in its final stages of an unfolding process of inevitable decline, and that it is hard for man to check this decline, no matter what he does.

The Doctrine of the Three Ages and the Five Periods (Final Law Thought)

The *Abhidharma-kośa* identifies three distinct ages in the gradual deterioration of Buddhist Law after the death of Shakyamuni: True Law *(shōbō)*, Imitation Law *(zōhō)*, and Final Law *(mappō)*. And this scripture also sketches five periods in the deterioration of human abilities *(kengo)*: enlightenment *(gedatsu)*, meditation *(zenjō)*, listening *(tamon)*, temple and pagoda building *(zōtō)*, and conflict *(tōjō)*. Jien accepts these doctrines of continuing decline in Buddhist Law and human abilities following the death of Shakyamuni, and his periodization of Japanese history is affected by them.

The doctrine of the three Buddhist ages holds that the first age of True Law lasted 1,000 years after the death of Shakyamuni and that this was a time when sentient beings could understand and have Buddhist teachings *(kyō)*, practices *(gyō)*, and enlightenment *(shō)*. The second age of Imitation Law, it is said, would come during the next 1,000 years and would be a time when sentient beings no longer have or are capable of Buddhist enlightenment, retaining only Buddhist teachings and practices. And the third age of Final Law would begin in the 2,001st year following the death of Shakyamuni and continue for 10,000 years. This would be an age in which sentient beings would have and understand only Buddhist teachings, and even these are destined for ultimate destruction. The three-age doctrine provides, therefore, advance warning not only of continuing decline in Buddhist Law but of gradual deterioration in human abilities and the coming of the "five pollutions."

The doctrine of the five periods identifies five distinct stages of decline, in both Buddhist Law and human abilities, since the death of Shakyamuni—each period lasting 500 years. The first period was a time when man had the ability to achieve enlightenment by adhering to the teachings of Shakyamuni. During the second period he would no longer be able to achieve enlightenment, but could meditate; in the third he would still be able to listen to the reading of Buddhist scriptures; and in the fourth he would have the ability to build pagodas and temples. But in the last period his abilities would

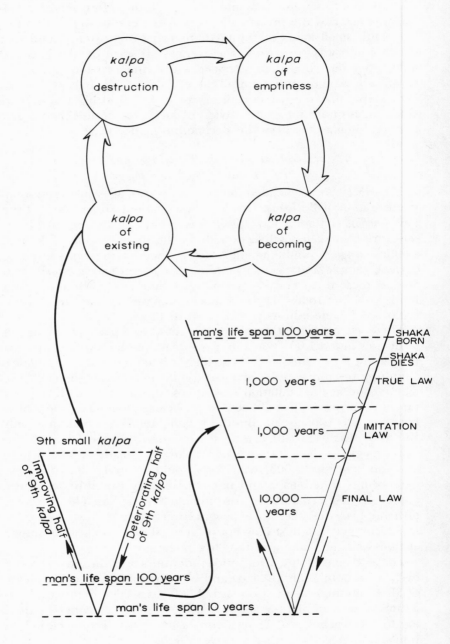

Figure 3.

be so deteriorated that he would simply be immersed in conflict and disagreement. As Buddhist Law would sink into oblivion, the world would also become polluted. In matching these five periods with the three ages outlined above, we see that the first two periods fall within the age of True Law, that the third and fourth come in the age of Imitation Law, and that the period of conflict and the age of Final Law both begin in the 2,001st year after the death of Shakyamuni.

Toward the end of the Heian era, the idea emerged that the age of Final Law and the period of conflict would begin in A.D. 1052. The increasingly violent wars of that day, involving both soldiers and soldier-monks, were thought of as indisputable evidence that the last Buddhist age and the last Buddhist period had indeed begun; and this view spread after the closing years of the Heian era. Jien writes in the *Gukanshō's* Imperial chronology that the first year of Emperor Jimmu's reign was the 290th year after the death of Shakyamuni, indicating that his calculation of the number of years that had passed since the death of Buddha was in accord with calculations which supported the conclusion that the age of Final Law had begun in 1052. Although Jien does not use the terms "Final Law" and "period of conflict" more than once in the *Gukanshō,* he certainly held an eschatological view based on Buddhist doctrines of continuous decline. Both "Final Law" and "period of conflict" appear frequently in poems and prayers written by him. For example, his "Confession on the Occasion of a Memorial Recitation of the *Sonsho Darani,*" written in 1213, reveals that he, like other intellectuals of his day, believed the age of Final Law had begun in 1052.

The Mt. Sumera World View and the View of Japan as a Peripheral Land

Ever since the introduction of Buddhism to Japan, Japanese Buddhists had considered the geographical and spiritual position of Japan in terms of the world view described in the *Abhidharma-kosá.* And Jien too had come to accept it.

According to the *Abhidharma-kosá,* a high mountain called Mt. Sumera stands majestically at the center of the world, rising 80,000 mythical miles above the level of the sea and reaching 80,000 mythical miles below. This great mountain is described as being equally wide. Its eastern slope is covered with silver, the western with crystal, the northern with gold, and the southern with lapis lazuli. The sun and moon revolve about the midsection of Mt. Sumera, causing the precious minerals on its four slopes to glisten and the sky in all four directions to be brightly colored. Mt. Sumera is circled by seven ranges of golden mountains, and between them lie seven perfumed seas (the inner seas) in concentric circles. Outside the golden mountains is a saltwater sea (the outer sea) surrounded by a range of iron

mountains called the "outer iron wall of the Mt. Sumera world."
Within the outer sea are four great continents: the eastern, western,
southern, and northern. The southern continent, called the Senbu
continent or *embudai,* is where the present history of man is evolving.
At the center of the southern continent is India. To the east of that
country lies China, and farther east, in the eastern seas, is the detached continent called Shamara. Near Shamara are the small islands
of Japan. And so Japan came to be referred to as a "peripheral land"
or as "millet scattered in a remote region." Of the four continents,
the southern one is described as the least fortunate; and regions
farthest from the southern continent's center are felt to be the least
fortunate places on this unfortunate continent. Therefore the small
country of Japan, the peripheral land, came to be thought of as the
most unfortunate place of all, one whose people had the least ability.
Of course the Chinese world view, described as "Heaven is round
and the earth is square" *(t'ien-yuan ti-fang),* was known to Japanese
intellectuals through Chinese books, but the Mt. Sumera world view
was generally accepted, particularly by Buddhists such as Jien.

The author of the *Gukanshō* therefore believed that the present
was close to the end of the deteriorating half of the ninth small kalpa
in the medium kalpa of existence, that the ages of True Law and
Imitation Law had passed, and that the age of Final Law had begun.
He also felt that the first four of the five periods had ended and that
the period of conflict had begun more than 160 years before he
started to write the *Gukanshō.* He assumed that the abilities of man
had reached a very low point and that the present, a time of the "five
pollutions," was on a downhill path leading to destruction at the end
of the first half of the present small kalpa. He was convinced that
even the center of the Mt. Sumera world was being subjected to pollution and evil, but that the situation in Japan, the peripheral land,
was much worse. By joining the Buddhist doctrines of the three ages
and the five periods with the conception of Japan as a peripheral
land, and building them into his idea of a time fate *(jiun)* of deterioration until the end of this half of the present small kalpa, Jien saw
the meaning and process of Japanese history in terms of laws of
deterioration in world history.

SHINTO BELIEF THAT ANCESTRAL KAMI PROTECT THEIR DESCEN-
DANTS (2) has ancient Japanese origins and traditions, and is one in
which an ancestral Kami *(soshin* or *ujigami)* is believed to protect all
of its clan descendants *(ujibito).* Therefore an incident affecting the
relations between two or three clans was thought of as having arisen
from an agreement reached between the ancestral Kami of those
particular clans. When Kanezane, Jien's brother, heard a rumor that
Shogun MINAMOTO Yoritomo's daughter was to be placed in the Im-

perial Palace as the Emperor's consort, and was afraid this would
complicate the realization of plans for his own daughter, he inserted
the following comment in his diary:

> Somebody says that Lord Yoritomo's daughter will be placed in
> the Imperial Palace on the 10th. Important events like this are
> simply the results of plans carried out by the ancestral Kami wor-
> shipped at the Ise, Hachiman, and Kasuga Shrines. Could they
> possibly have resulted from acts of human will?[3]

So when intimate relationships between two clans became permanent, it was concluded that this had been due to the power of an
agreement made in ancient times between the ancestral Kami of
those two clans, a power that penetrates the history of Japan.

Since Jien also believed in agreements between ancestral Kami, he
was convinced that the practice of having a Regent or Chancellor
administer the affairs of state had to come into existence because an
ancient agreement *(yakudaku)* had been made between the Sun Goddess (the ancestral Kami of the Imperial clan) and the Great Illuminating Kami worshipped at the Kasuga Shrine (the ancestral
Kami of the FUJIWARA clan). Likewise, when discussing the loss of
the Imperial Sword (one of the three Imperial Regalia) during the
naval engagement fought at Dan no Ura in 1185, Jien said this revealed a Kami decision that the time had come for the Imperial clan
to be guarded by soldiers, not by the Imperial Sword. He claimed
that the loss of the Sword had resulted from an agreement between
the Sun Goddess and the Great Hachiman Bodhisattva (the ancestral
Kami of the military clan of MINAMOTO). Then when the
MINAMOTO, which had seized control of the state after Dan no Ura,
was destroyed—after three generations—by the assassination of
Sanetomo in 1219, a young boy (Kanezane's grandson Yoritsune) of
the KUJŌ house was adopted as the MINAMOTO heir. In the *Gukanshō*,
Jien states that this was not the result of actions taken by man but of
an agreement between three ancestral Kami: the Sun Goddess of the
Imperial clan, the Great Illuminating Kami of the KUJŌ house of
FUJIWARA, and the Great Hachiman Boddhisattva of the MINAMOTO
clan. Shinto belief that ancestral Kami protect their descendants was
therefore like the eschatological thought of Buddhism, in that both
place the basic cause of an event outside history, not inside. But what
supported Shinto belief was a unique time-consciousness of eternal
return, not a consciousness of progress or deterioration. And yet, by
thinking of what was appropriate for particular times, places, and
human abilities (X)—thought that had become traditional in the

---

3. *Gyokuyō* 1191–4–5 [*Gyokuyō*, 3.676].

Tendai Sect—Jien linked belief in ancestral Kami who protect their descendants (2) to the originally unrelated eschatological thought of Buddhism (1).

THINKING OF HOW TO ADJUST IDEALS TO THE REALITIES OF A PARTICULAR TIME, PLACE, AND LEVEL OF HUMAN ABILITY (X). What I refer to as "making adjustments to time, place, and human ability" (ji-sho-ki sō-ō)[4] was a way of trying to relate ideals to the realities of temporal, spatial, and human deterioration—a mode of thought that had matured within Final Law thought at the time such thought (introduced from India) was developing in China. In the Pure Land movement of China, the idea spread that certain Buddhist teachings are appropriate to the age of Final Law. And there is no doubt that such ideas were introduced to Japan along with Pure Land teachings. But Pure Land Buddhism apparently did not prosper in Japan during the Nara era, and, as a result, neither Final Law thought nor thinking of what was appropriate to "time, place, and human ability" seem to have developed in this country during that era. Probably the first person to make this mode of thought a positive factor in Japanese intellectual life was Saichō, founder of the Enryaku Temple on Mt. Hiei at the beginning of the ninth century. From then on, this way of thinking was a traditional element in Tendai thought. Efforts were made to propagate belief in the Lotus Sutra as the Buddhist teaching most appropriate for that particular time (at a transition point between the age of Imitation Law and the age of Final Law), and Pure Land Buddhism matured as the teachings most appropriate to the age of Final Law.

After the Eishō era (1046–53), when it was thought that the age of Final Law had begun, there was a great surge in the Pure Land movement. And at that time the doctrine of "the essence being manifested" (honji suijaku)[5] was also developed. It maintained that a Buddha, being manifested as a Kami, was taking a form appropriate to the final reigns in the peripheral land of Japan. The fact that the rapid rise of Pure Land Buddhism coincided with the rapid spread of the "essence-being-manifested" doctrine has not been fully appreciated. Superficially the two developments may appear to have been parallel and unrelated phenomena, but they were actually bound together by thinking of what is "appropriate to a particular time, place, and human ability." Having been named Abbot of the

4. This subject has been explored more fully in my "Ji-ki sō-ō no ronri," Fujishima Hakase kanreki kinen ronshū: Nihon jōdokyō no kenkyū (Kyoto. Heiraku-ji Shoten, 1969), pp. 92–125.

5. Cf. Alicia Matsunaga, The Buddhist Philosophy of Assimilation (Tokyo, 1969).

Tendai Sect four times, Jien had inherited, and was committed to, Saichō's religious thought. And by faithfully inheriting ideas about what was "appropriate for a particular time, place, and human ability," he had become, while supporting Pure Land teachings, a firm believer in the doctrine of the "essence being manifested." Even in the *Gukanshō,* Jien ties Buddhist eschatological thought to Shinto belief in ancestral Kami by thinking of what is appropriate to a particular time, place, and human ability.

At about the time the *Gukanshō* was being written, priests at the Enryaku Temple on Mt. Hiei where Jien had served as Tendai Abbot four times were thinking that Shakyamuni had propounded Buddhist teachings appropriate to different times, places, and human abilities. We see this in the *Sanbō jūji shō.* While the three Buddhas (Shakyamuni, Yakushi, and Amitābha) were in essence one, it was believed that Buddha had appeared in forms suitable to the three Buddhist ages: Shakyamuni for the age of True Law, Yakushi for Imitation Law, and Amitābha for Final Law.

Jien seems to have made such thought the basis of his own view of history. While he felt that the ancestral Kami of the Imperial clan and of the FUJIWARA clan had always penetrated and moved Japanese history, he took the position that the Sun Goddess and the Great Illuminating Kami worshipped at the Kashima Shrine had guarded the country *in ancient times* by bestowing blessings upon their respective clans, and that the Great Hachiman Bodhisattva and the Great Illuminating Kami worshipped at the Kasuga Shrine were guarding this country *in modern times.* He theorized that the Sun Goddess and the Great Hachiman Bodhisattva were the same Kami, that the Great Illuminating Kami worshipped at Kashima and Kasuga were a single entity, and that both were manifestations of Buddha appropriate to a particular place: Japan. And he thought that just as Shakyamuni had propounded, in advance, teachings suitable for later ages, the ancestral Kami had provided, in advance, "unseen Principles" appropriate to successive ages of deterioration in, and successive stages of decline in the abilities of, their respective clans. In other words, the ancestral Kami had provided "unseen Principles" appropriate to time, place, and human ability. In Chapter 5 of the *Gukanshō,* Jien divides Japanese history into seven periods from the point of view of this connection between "unseen Principles" for successive ages of progressive deterioration, and for successive periods of deterioration in the abilities *(kiryō)* of man to understand "unseen Principles." Or, as Jien himself puts it, deterioration in the abilities of man to make "unseen Principles" into "seen Principles." His seven periods are related to the three Buddhist ages as follows:

Japanese periods	Years after the death of Shakyamuni (A.S.)	Buddhist age
1. Enthronement of Emperor Jimmu to death of Seimu	290 A.S. to 1140 A.S.	True Law
2. Enthronement of Emperor Chūai to death of Emperor Kimmei	1140 A.S. to 1518 A.S.	Imitation Law
3. Enthronement of Emperor Bidatsu in A.D. 572 to death of FUJIWARA Michinaga in 1027	1518 A.S. to 1974 A.S.	
4. Appointment of FUJIWARA Yorimichi as Regent in 1017 to death of Retired Emperor Toba in 1156	1974 A.S. to 2105 A.S.	
5. Military Age to death of MINA-MOTO Yoritomo in 1199	2105 A.S. to 2149 A.S.	Final Law
6. Beginning of Go-Shirakawa administration as Retired Emperor to abdication of Emperor Go-Toba in 1198	2108 A.S. to 2148 A.S.	
7. Beginning of Go-Toba's administration as Retired Emperor from 1198 on	2148 A.S. on	

If we read the *Gukanshō* carefully, we see that Jien divides his seven periods into three ages as shown above. He sees a sharp break after the reign of Seimu, writing that that was a time when "the spirit of the age of Kami" had been lost. And he sees another period of precipitous decline beginning with Go-Sanjō's administration as a Retired Emperor in 1072, stating that there was then "a sharp turn toward the Final Age" when "the state would now deteriorate rapidly." Noting that Jien places the first year of Emperor Jimmu's reign at the 290th year after the death of Shakyamuni, and that he believed the age of Final Law had begun in 1052, I have added to the above table the A.S. dates found in the *Teiō hennen ki*, which treats Japan's Imperial reigns in almost the same way the *Gukanshō's* Imperial chronology does.

If we compare Jien's seven periods of history with what has been said about Buddhist stages of deterioration in world history, the relationships shown in Figure 4 emerge.

Clearly the *Gukanshō's* periods of Japanese history correspond quite closely to Buddhist ages and periods of continuous decline in world history. This congruence (very much like that seen in the Buddhist history outlined in the chapter on "Conditions in the Southern Continent of the Mt. Sumera World" of the *Daihōtō daishu*

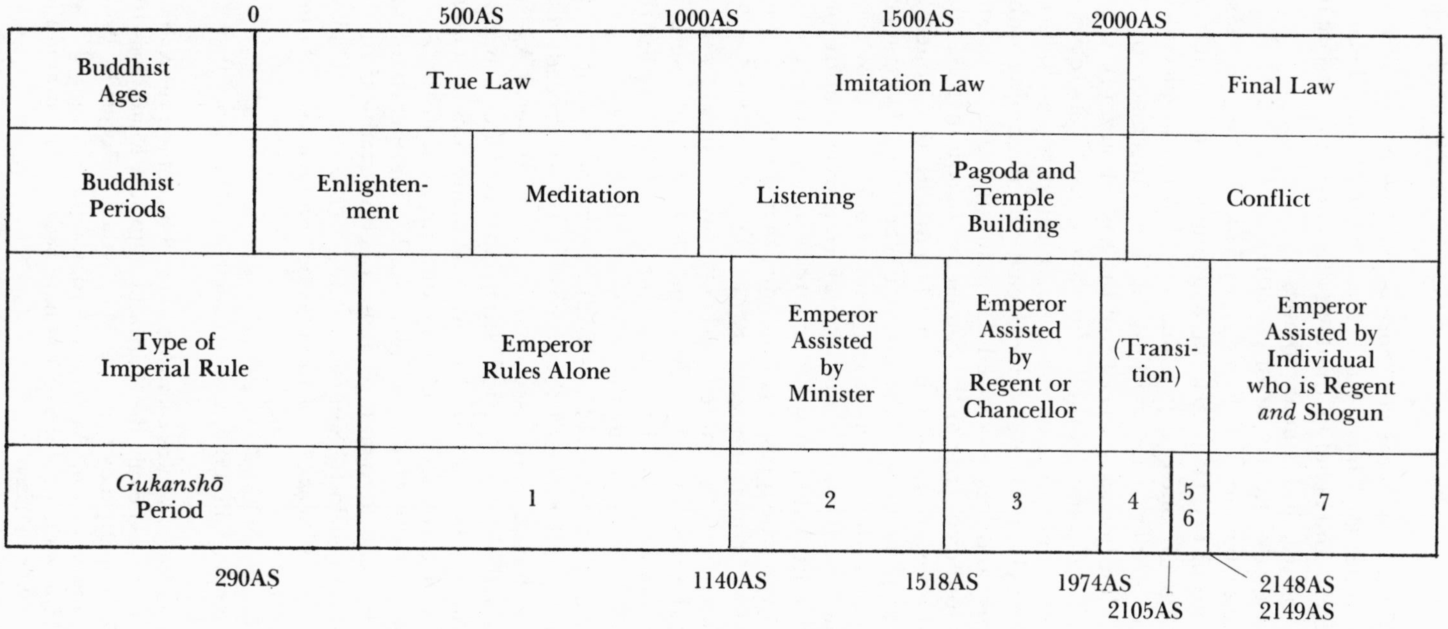

Buddhist Ages	True Law		Imitation Law		Final Law	
Buddhist Periods	Enlightenment	Meditation	Listening	Pagoda and Temple Building	Conflict	
Type of Imperial Rule	Emperor Rules Alone		Emperor Assisted by Minister	Emperor Assisted by Regent or Chancellor	(Transition)	Emperor Assisted by Individual who is Regent *and* Shogun
Gukanshō Period	1		2	3	4 / 5 6	7

Time scale: 0 — 500AS — 1000AS — 1500AS — 2000AS

290AS 1140AS 1518AS 1974AS 2105AS 2148AS 2149AS

Figure 4.

Sutra)[6] leads us to the very core of the *Gukanshō's* historical interpretation, one in which Final Law thought has been fused with ancestral-Kami belief by thinking of what is appropriate to particular times, places, and human abilities.

CONSCIOUSNESS OF MODERN TIMES AS THE FINAL AGE (3). Below the superstructure of Jien's historical thought lies a substructure made up of two elements: the consciousness of modern times as the Final Age (3), one that Jien shared with other intellectuals of his day; and a political consciousness of the supremacy of the Regent-Chancellor houses, especially of the KUJŌ house (4). Let us first take up the significance of the former and consider its relationship to the Japanese conception of the "one hundred reigns" *(hyaku-ō)*.

In the closing years of the Heian era, beginning with Go-Sanjō's administration as a Retired Emperor in 1072 and continuing on down to the collapse of the Kamakura *bakufu* in 1333, and especially with the series of civil wars that began with the Hōgen Rebellion of 1156 and ended with the Shōkyū War of 1221, aristocrats came to realize that their position was being undermined by the emergence of powerful military clans. Therefore a basic feature of intellectual movements within aristocratic circles at that time was an historical consciousness expressed in the idea that the present is in the age of Final Law. For example, FUJIWARA Toshinari (1114–1204) wrote in his *Korai fūtai shō* (Notes on Poetic Styles through the Ages)[7] that "First there was the *Manyōshū* anthology of Japanese poetry for the ancient past *(kami)*, then the *Kokinshū* and *Shūishū* for the Medieval Age *(chūko)*, and finally the *Go-Shūishū* for modern times *(kindai)*.[8] In Emperor Juntoku's (1197–1242) *Yakumo mishō* (Eight-Clouds Royal Treatise) and *Kimpishō* (Summary of Court Procedures),[9] the Emperor referred to the Ancient *(jōko)* and Medieval Ages *(chūko)* and concluded that the period after Emperor Shirakawa (1053–1129) was the modern age *(kindai)*. And he made such comments as these: "The sort of thing we see now did not exist in the Ancient Age; it began with the Medieval Age." And: "The hearts of modern man have become arrogant, and the openheartedness of the Medieval Age has been lost." Somewhat later, KITABATAKE Chikafusa (1292–1354), in his *Shokugen shō* (Notes on the Origins of Offices), also di-

6. No. 397 in *Taishō*, 13.298–351.

7. Compiled in 1197 and re-edited in 1201; No. 70 of *Gunsho ruijū*, 5.576–602.

8. The *Manyōshū* was compiled in the 8th century; the *Kokinshū* in 905 by Ki no Tsurayuki et al.; the *Shūishū* by FUJIWARA Kintō (966–1041); and the *Go-Shūishū* in 1086 by FUJIWARA Michitoshi. Cf. Robert H. Brower and Earl Miner, *Japanese Court Poetry* (Stanford, Calif., 1972), pp. 245 and 481–483.

9. Both works were thought to have been written around the time of the Shōkyū War of 1221.

vided Japanese history into three ages: Ancient, Medieval, and Modern. And in his *Jinnō shōtō ki* (Record of the Legitimate Succession of Divine Emperors),[10] he wrote that when we think of precedents, we refer to that which began after the reign of Kōkō (884–887). The period before that, he said, was the Ancient Age. He also states that the Medieval Age came after the reigns of Uda and Daigo (887–930), and he noted a sharp break after about the time of Emperor Shirakawa's reign (1072–86). Finally, he says that the Military Age began after the outbreak of the Hōgen Rebellion in 1156, and that the special characteristics of the modern age are: confusion in the empire, the rise of military men to positions of power, and a slighting of the Emperor's position.

Jien too has such an historical outlook. In the *Gukanshō* he writes that "the final years of the Ancient Age (*jōko*) and of [Japan's] True Law extended through the reign of Uda [887–889]," that the "tag end of that Age and the beginning of the Medieval Age" came during the reigns of Daigo (898–931) and Murakami (947–967), that the years from the reigns of Reizei and Enyū (967–984) down through Shirakawa and Toba (1072–86 and 1107–23) were in the Medieval Age, but that after Go-Sanjō's reign (1034–73) there was a "sharp turn toward the Final Age." Finally, he writes that after Toba's death "a great rebellion broke out [in 1156], and we came definitely to the Military Age." And with deep emotion he states that "since the close of the Go-Shirakawa reign (1155–58) there has been extreme deterioration; and the last 20 years [from the close of Go-Toba's reign in 1198] have been terrible."

The idea that "the present is the Final Age" provides spiritual foundations for: (a) the spread during the final years of the Heian era of Buddhist eschatological thought that took the form of doctrines about the three ages and the five periods; (b) the spread of the view among people of those times that the age of Final Law had begun in 1052; and (c) the tendency to count the numbers of years that had elapsed since the start of the Final Law age. At the same time, Buddhist eschatological thought provides metaphysical support for the view that "the present is the Final Age."

Buddhist eschatological doctrines together with the conviction that the present is the Final Age transformed the concept of "one hundred reigns"—which originally reflected belief in the permanence of the Imperial House—into a Japanese eschatological doctrine that Japan would be destroyed after one hundred reigns. Jien really believed in this transformed conception of "one hundred

10. The first of these works was written in 1341. The second, considered to be Japan's second great interpretive history, was written in 1339 and is published in NKBT, 87.

reigns." In prayers written by him, as well as in the *Gukanshō,* he calculated the number of reigns left, lamented that the destruction was near at hand, and warned that if people acted contrary to Principle, Japan might be destroyed before the advent of the 100th reign.

CONSCIOUSNESS OF THE SUPREMACY OF THE REGENT-CHANCELLOR HOUSES, ESPECIALLY OF THE KUJŌ (4). Consciousness of the supremacy of the Regent-Chancellor houses was particularly strong in Jien, who had been born into the KUJŌ house—one of the FUJIWARA houses from which a Regent or Chancellor could be appointed—as the brother of Regent KUJŌ Kanezane. Awareness of this superior position was reinforced by the fact that "house position" *(ie no sendo)*[11] had become firmly established in the world of court nobles around the middle of the Heian era, and also by the fact that appointments to the positions of Regent or Chancellor were limited to members of the northern branch of the FUJIWARA clan, and particularly to descendants of KUJO Morosuke (908–960). While consciousness of the supremacy of Regent-Chancellor houses (4) adds support to Shinto belief in ancestral Kami (2), the former is also given metaphysical foundations by the latter.

Shinto belief that ancestral Kami protect their descendants has a long tradition, but the idea that FUJIWARA Regents and Chancellors had assisted successive generations of Emperors and Empresses because of an agreement between the ancestral Kami of the Imperial clan and the FUJIWARA clan had not yet taken shape by the middle of the Heian era, when the Regent-Chancellor houses were flourishing. That idea emerged clearly after 1086, when Retired Emperors were handling the affairs of state, when the political position of Regents and Chancellors was being undermined by personal ministers *(kinshin)* who were serving cloistered Emperors, when Imperial sons (after the time of Yorimichi) were no longer being born to women from the Regent-Chancellor houses, and when the Regent-Chancellor houses (whose heads had maintained their positions by being the maternal grandfather or maternal uncle of a reigning Emperor) were trying to find a basis *only in historical tradition* for continuing to serve as Regents and Chancellors. ("House position" had already become an established historical fact, and the FUJIWARA clan had been monopolizing appointments to the positions of Regent and Chancellor for a long time.) The earliest reference to an agreement between the Sun Goddess of the Imperial clan and the Great Illuminating Kami of the FUJIWARA clan, so far as I know, is found in a memorial submitted to the throne by priests of the Yamashina Temple (the

11. A ranking of houses by the offices their members are entitled to hold.

FUJIWARA temple now known as the Kōfuku-ji) and recorded in an item of the *Fusō ryakki* for the 22nd day of the 8th month of 1093.[12]

But the idea that sacred agreements had been made between ancestral Kami, especially between three particular ancestral Kami, was more fully developed by Jien in the *Gukanshō*. There we can see clearly that consciousness of the supremacy of the Regent-Chancellor houses (4) reinforces the Shinto belief that ancestral Kami protect their descendants (2) and that this Shinto belief provides metaphysical foundations for the supremacy of the Regent-Chancellor houses. This bond between ancestral-Kami belief and consciousness of the supremacy of the Regent-Chancellor houses, particularly the KUJŌ, supports the theory of "legitimacy of succession to the position of Regent-Chancellor in the KUJŌ house" *(Kujō-ke shōtō ron)*. This theory held that while the male descendants of KUJŌ Morosuke were appointed to the position of Regent or Chancellor, and the sons of his female descendants became Emperors, after KUJŌ Kanezane it was Kanezane's male descendants who were legitimately appointed to the position of Regent or Chancellor, and the sons of Kanezane's female descendants who were legitimate occupants of the throne. On this point the *Gukanshō* is a forerunner of the *Jinnō shōtō ki,* which states that "both Emperors and ministers are descendants in the Emperor Murakami line." This theory of "legitimacy of succession to the position of Regent-Chancellor in the KUJŌ house" is clearly expressed in Jien's 1219 letter to SAIONJI Kintsune, and it penetrates the entire *Gukanshō* interpretation of history.

THINKING OF HOW TO ACCOMMODATE IDEAS TO THE REALITIES OF A PARTICULAR TIME, PLACE, AND HUMAN ABILITY (X). Originally, consciousness of modern times being in the Final Age (3) and consciousness of the supremacy of the Regent-Chancellor houses (4), having different origins and characteristics, were unrelated to each other. But Jien brings them together by thinking of both in terms of what is appropriate for a particular time, place, and human ability (X), developing the political attitude and idea that in creating an administration of Regents and Chancellors appropriate to the conditions of that particular time in history, the Regent-Chancellor house should cooperate with the emerging military house (the Kamakura Shogun) and establish a government of harmony between nobles and military leaders. A political consciousness had emerged within members of the Regent-Chancellor houses, especially the KUJŌ, that in Japanese political history there was first an age in which an Emperor ruled directly, then an age when Emperors were assisted by Regents or Chancellors, and finally a third age in which the military

12. *Shintei zōhō: Kokushi taikei,* 12.334.

had appeared and in which the state could not be governed at all well—and the Imperial House would not be safe—without military support. In reflecting about what was appropriate for that particular time, place, and human ability, it was felt that in this polluted and evil time people had to devise a political system of Imperial support that included the military. Regent KUJŌ Kanezane had established political cooperation with Shogun MINAMOTO Yoritomo soon after the emergence of military clans, but after Kanezane's death Jien came to realize that the Kamakura *bakufu* was firmly established and that the military clans were stronger than they had ever been during Kanezane's day. So after Kanezane's grandson Yoritsune was made heir to the headship of the Shogun house, Jien seems to have felt, more deeply than ever, that a government of cooperation between nobles and military men would be appropriate for the final reigns. He thought that, 20 years later, when the two-year-old Yoritsune would become an adult, Shogun Yoritsune should also be appointed Regent or Chancellor. (I have my doubts about the conclusion that Jien underestimated the power of the military and that he had a weak sense of current political realities.)

Jien's political attitudes coincided with those of FUJIWARA Teika (1162–1241), who felt that the *Manyōshū* anthology of Japanese poetry of the Ancient Age and the *Kokinshū* anthology of the Medieval Age were inappropriate for people living in the modern Final Age. Teika propounded a new theory of the beauty of mystery (*yūgen no bi*) and then compiled the *Shin Kokinshū* from that point of view. As noted above, court nobles of the Kamakura era had divided Japanese history into three ages: the Ancient, Medieval, and Modern. While they had a special yearning for the life of the Medieval Age, they had not yet lost their desire or capacity to accommodate Medieval ideals to the new age. Their nostalgia was not the weak thing that it became among members of the nobility in the later Muromachi era, but it had the strength to create a neo-classical culture. Jien's *Gukanshō* was a product of, and contributed to, that endeavor.

THE *GUKANSHŌ* ADVOCACY: *Final Age Principle of One Man Who Will Be Both Regent-Chancellor and Shogun.* As indicated in Figure 2, Jien's *Gukanshō* has a structure of five intellectual-history elements: (1), (2), (3), and (4) were brought together into a single thought structure by thinking of what was appropriate for particular times, places, and human abilities (X). Through such a mode of thought, the elements on each side of the structure were forged into clusters of thought and consciousness: Buddhist eschatological thought (1) was merged with an awareness of modern times as the Final Age (3), and belief that ancestral Kami protected their descendants (2) was merged with a consciousness of the supremacy of the Regent-

Chancellor houses (4). In sum, Jien thought of the meaning and process of Japanese history as existing within the context of deterioration in world history; he identified the unseen will *(meiryo)* of ancestral Kami (manifestations of Buddha) with "unseen Principles" that were appropriate to the three ages of True Law, Imitation Law, and Final Law; and he concluded that these "unseen Principles" were realized through different forms of government for those three ages. For the age of True Law, there was personal Imperial rule created by the Sun Goddess (the ancestral Kami of the Imperial House); for the age of Imitation Law, there was a Regent-Chancellor form of government created by an agreement between the Sun Goddess and the Great Illuminating Kami worshipped at the Kasuga Shrine (the ancestral Kami of the Imperial House and of the FUJI-WARA clan); and for the age of Final Law, there was a form of government in which one person would be both a Regent-Chancellor and Shogun, a form created by an agreement between the Sun Goddess, the Great Illuminating Kami worshipped at the Kasuga Shrine, and the Great Hachiman Bodhisattva—that is, between the ancestral Kami of the Imperial House, the FUJIWARA clan, and the MINAMOTO clan. Jien thought of these three forms of government as actualizations of "unseen Principles" for those three ages. Resolutely applying the logic of an accommodation to the realities of a particular time, place, and human ability, he came to believe that the establishment of a government in which the Emperor would be supported by a man who would be both a Regent-Chancellor and a Shogun was in accord with "the Principle of the final reigns." (See Figure 4.)

For Jien the task of subjectively grasping the thought structure (making it his own thought) and then moving toward its realization is the task of a statesman. A person who has that sort of historical sense and political capability is thought of as a person with "ability" *(kiryō)*, and Jien feels that the affairs of state should be taken over by a person of the Regent-Chancellor house who has such "ability." He says, however, that there are no persons of "ability" in the KONOE house, only in the KUJŌ. And just as certain Buddhist teachings are appropriate for the age of Final Law—bestowing the blessings of Buddha on depraved sentient beings living in the age of Final Law—Jien thinks that if a person of "ability" should take over the administration of affairs, the state will be peaceful. But if such a person does not assume control, Japan will be destroyed before the advent of the 100th reign. This is the *Gukanshō's* central thesis.

But Jien also assumes that vengeful souls *(onryō)*, demons *(tengu)*, and evil Kami are active in the process of deterioration, speeding it up by obstructing the endeavors of statesmen who have "ability." On the other hand, he believes that Buddhist rites—especially esoteric rites of the Tendai Sect—can help an able statesman to realize unseen Principles by oppressing those vengeful souls, demons, and bad Kami. So in advocating the Final Age Principle that one man should be both Shogun and Regent, Jien decorates the skeleton of his thought with an ancient form of Buddhism which held that Buddhist Law and Imperial Law are "like the two wheels of a cart," and with traditional thought held by priests serving at the Enryaku Temple on Mt. Hiei.

CONCLUSIONS: *Jien's Tenacity of Purpose and* Gukanshō *Thought.* The strongest element in Jien's thought arises from his consciousness of the supremacy of the Regent-Chancellor houses, especially the KUJŌ (4). This provides a tenacity of purpose that gives a devilish drive to his persistence. Although this tenacity is filtered through a penetrating mind, it still creates some disharmony of logic between elements in his thought, clouding his sharp historical insight. I would like to touch upon three such disharmonies, which are represented in Figure 5. (The four elements are represented by the same numbers given in Figure 2; and the arrows, pointing in opposite directions, suggest the nature of the disharmonies discussed below.)

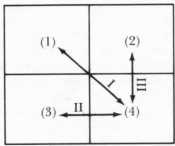

Figure 5.

I. Jien, a court nobleman, divides Japanese history into three ages: Ancient, Medieval, and Final. In placing the beginnings of the Regent-Chancellor administration in the Ancient Age, its flowering in the Medieval Age, and its deterioration in the Final Age, Jien comes to revere—from a preoccupation with the supremacy of the Regent-Chancellor houses (4)—the Medieval Age as an ideal period of history. But such an attitude is not consistent with Buddhist eschatological thought (1), which assumes an inevitable decline until the end of the deteriorating half of the current small kalpa.

II. While Jien thinks of different forms of government as being appropriate to the three Ages, he can not go so far as to say that a military government (which later became a reality) is appropriate for the age of Final Law. Instead, he writes that the form of government suitable for that Age is one which is headed by a man who is both a Regent-Chancellor and a Shogun (not later realized). Because of his strong belief in the ancestral Kami of the FUJIWARA clan (and of the

KUJŌ house), and the relationship of that belief to his consciousness of the supremacy of the Regent-Chancellor houses (4), he takes a position that is not wholly consistent with his thought that "the present is the Final Age" (3).

III. Also, Jien's commitment to the supremacy of the Regent-Chancellor houses, and particularly his ideas about the legitimacy of Regent-Chancellor appointments in the KUJŌ house (4), do not emerge solely from the Shinto belief that ancestral Kami protect their descendants (2). And so he uses belief in Grand Preceptor Ji'e as an incarnation of Buddha (a popular belief at that time) to provide a religious support for his idea of the legitimacy of Regent-Chancellor appointments in the KUJŌ house. He does this by exaggerating the master-patron vow that, he says, was made between Grand Preceptor Ji'e (912–985) and KUJŌ Morosuke (908–960), the founder of the KUJŌ house. And while drawing attention to KUJŌ Kanezane's devotion to his ancestral Kami *(shashoku no kokoro),* Jien (Kanezane's brother) also asserts that he himself is a disciple of the Ji'e school of Buddhism. In such ways does Jien develop the doctrine of the legitimacy of Regent-Chancellor appointments in the KUJŌ house. (Later on, the positions of Regent and Chancellor were not, as a matter of historical fact, monopolized by the KUJŌ house.)

In sum, the strongest element in Jien's historical thought is his preoccupation with the supremacy of the Regent-Chancellor houses, especially the KUJŌ. And because this is so, one of the intellectual characteristics of the *Gukanshō* is that the theoretical ordering of its structural elements is flawed, and the historical perspective distorted. This special quality of Jien's thought structure is due, I feel, to the fact that the *Gukanshō* was written in 1219—just after Kanezane's grandson Yoritsune had been made heir to the position of Shogun—with the political objective of opposing those enemies who objected to the selection of Yoritsune. Those who threatened the KUJŌ house—directly or indirectly, overtly or covertly—were: Retired Emperor Go-Toba of the Imperial House; the KONOE Regent-Chancellor house; the SAIONJI of the lower-ranking noble houses; and the military houses of the eastern provinces.

While the thought structure of the *Gukanshō* is very complex, the important point is that various old ideas about the course of human history being determined externally are now formed into a single organic structure by making "accommodations to particular times, places, and human abilities." While the same sort of historical meaning is seen in the achievements of FUJIWARA Teika in poetry, and Unkei in sculpture, probably the *Gukanshō* is a more imposing product of the neo-classical movement.

Such is the way I see the historical interpretation of the *Gukanshō,* a book written at a great turning point in history, just before the

Shōkyū War of 1221 which divided Japanese history into two great segments, and by a man whose tenacity of purpose was that of a very strong individual.

Thought Formation

In the opening sentence of the *Gukanshō's* first narrative chapter, Jien says that "with the passing of the years and days, I think only about the Principles of things." Apparently he had been reflecting about the "Principles of things" for a number of years, leading me to raise two interrelated questions: How did his historical thought develop during those years of reflection? And how did his changing political concerns affect that formative process?

Early Reflections about the Loss of the Imperial Sword

The earliest evidence we have of Jien's ideas about the passing of time is found in a short manuscript written by him between 1203 and 1209. Known as the *Jichin Kashō musō ki* (Record of Jien's Dream),[13] this manuscript is a three-stage report of the author's reflections about a dream he had had on the 22nd day of the 6th month of 1203. The dream was mainly about the Sacred Jewel and the Imperial Sword, two of the three sacred symbols of Imperial authority known as the Imperial Regalia. The first section of the manuscript, written shortly after the dream, and the second one, dated the 1st day of the 1st month of 1204, are focused upon mysterious connections between the Sacred Seal and the Empress. But the third section, written in the 6th month of 1209, is concerned with religious and historical connections between the loss of the Imperial Sword in 1185 and the subsequent rise of military power. The final paragraph of the last section reads as follows:

> How sad these final reigns are! The Sacred Mirror was at last melted down. . . . It has been in three fires. At the time of the first fire it mysteriously flew away; after the second it was found undamaged in the ashes; and in the third it was melted down, but the metal was retrieved and re-enshrined. The box of the Sacred Jewel has not been changed. Although revered, it has been opened and looked into. . . . The Imperial Sword finally sank to the bottom of the sea. It could not be found and has therefore been lost. After that, great military Shoguns seized control of Japan and, doing just as they pleased, had Land Stewards (*jitō*) appointed in various provinces, not permitting the Emperor to do anything. But with the formal acquiescence of the Emperor, Land

13. Published in Toshihide Akamatsu, "*Jichin kashō musō ki* ni tsuite," *Kamakura Bukkyō no kenkyū* (Kyoto, 1957), pp. 318–322.

Stewards were appointed by Imperial order. . . . After the Imperial Sword sank to the bottom of the sea, was not its virtue *(toku)* passed to human Shoguns? If there were a sage, would he not really understand why the Imperial Sword was lost, and reflect on the rise and fall of things? How sad! . . . Wisdom of this kind, however, is found only in the Storehouse of the Vairocana Buddha *(Birushana hizō-kai)*.[14]

Althought Jien had shared his brother Kanezane's views about the military, this passage—written two years after Kanezane's death—indicates that Jien was beginning to make a deeper search for the meaning of military power. Noting that the military had begun to seize control of state affairs only after the Imperial Sword was lost in 1185, Jien concludes that the Sword's protective function was then passed to military leaders.

It was just at this time that relations between the Imperial Court and the *bakufu* were becoming strained, an important development leading to the Shōkyū War of 1221.[15] In 1206, Retired Emperor Go-Toba had requested that a Land Steward, appointed to the Ōta Estate in the province of Bizen, be removed. This was not a perverse request. When Shogun Yoritomo had been alive, he had responded to such requests from the Retired Emperor by ordering Land Stewards removed, whether they had been assigned to property made into public land or to holdings previously held by rebels. But in 1206, Shogun Sanetomo personally sent a memorial to the Retired Emperor explaining that he could not revoke Land Steward appointments made by Yoritomo if the appointees had committed no serious crime. This was an historic decision. In taking such a position, the *bakufu* had changed its attitude toward the Imperial Court, publicly announcing—through the Shogun—that rights already gained by a military house were not to be challenged by aristocratic authority. Heretofore, military authority had been embedded in aristocratic authority, but now it had been moved one step toward independence.

Although the following poem by Retired Emperor Go-Toba was composed in 1208, two years after he had received Sanetomo's memorial, it reflects resentment toward the *bakufu:*

> Pushing through undergrowth
> Deep in the mountains
> Is the world's proper way.
> Shouldn't it be pointed out to man?

14. Ibid., pp. 321–322.

15. Cf. my "Genji no higeki," *Nihon no kaika* (Vol. 12 of the Bungei Shunjū's *Dai sekai shi,* [Tokyo, 1968]), pp. 74–90.

Go-Toba composed other poems reflecting such resentment. Verses
sent to him by Shogun Sanetomo include these three:

> Your Majesty's command
>   Stirs my heart.
> But how can this
>   Be made known to man?

> Mountains crumble and seas run dry.
>   Even at such times,
> How can I display to the sovereign
>   A rebellious heart?

> I reside in the eastern provinces
>   Resplendent in the morning sun.
> His Majesty's residence
>   Stands in my shadow.[16]

In the preface to these three verses, Sanetomo writes that he has
composed them after receiving a letter from Go-Toba. The usual
interpretation is that they reflect gratitude for the letter, but mine is
different. The message of the famous second verse is quite clear.
The first verse suggests that Sanetomo is perplexed by a situation in
which he can not comply with the Retired Emperor's request. And
the third verse is apparently an expression of sorrow that the Shogun is obstructing the Retired Emperor's attempts to gain control of
state affairs, an honest confession of agony over being caught between his powerful military retainers in Kamakura and the Retired
Emperor. From the tone of these verses one can deduce that Go-
Toba's letter had asked why the *bakufu* would not comply with his
earlier request.

Since Jien was something like a priestly Regent who was close to
Retired Emperor Go-Toba, he must have been well aware that relations between the Retired Emperor and the *bakufu* were becoming
strained. Conscious of the growing power of the military and familiar with the current situation in Kamakura, he had turned his attention from the meaning of connections between the Sacred Seal and
the Empress to the meaning of political and historical connections
between the loss of the Imperial Sword and the rise of *bakufu* power.
Taking the political stance inherited from his brother Kanezane, he
had become uneasy about the strong position Retired Emperor Go-
Toba was taking toward the *bakufu*. So he probably wished to warn
Go-Toba that while the military take-over was a sad feature of those
final reigns, the rise of military power was historically inevitable and
could not be prevented.

Jien's tenacity of purpose was rooted in deep feelings about the
supremacy of the Regent-Chancellor houses (4), feelings that were

16. *Kinkaishū*, NKBT, 29.421–422.

much stronger than his perception of the current reality or his consciousness of the present as the Final Age (3). Even though he had fallen heir to the logic of thinking about what is appropriate to particular times and human abilities (X)—a way of thinking that would have tied (4) and (3) together—there was as yet no sign that such a tie was being made. So Jien's historical thought had not yet been fully formed. All that he could do when he wrote his *Jichin Kashō musō ki* in 1209 was to recognize that Kanezane's type of cooperation between aristocrats and soldiers—the Go-Shirakawa–Yoritomo system—would no longer do.

The Incomprehensible Events of 1218 and 1219

In 1218, an unexpected event, the assassination of Shogun Sanetomo, induced Jien to use the strong word "incomprehensible" *(fukashigi)*. As a result of that assassination, the line of succession to the headship of the MINAMOTO clan had been broken after three generations. Shortly afterward, the young KUJŌ Yoritsune (grandson of Kanezane and son of Michiie) was made heir to the position of Shogun. Jien made the following comment in the *Gukanshō* about those remarkable developments:

> The present Crown Prince Chūkyō and Shogun Yoritsune are only two-year-old boys. Clearly they were created by the ancestral Kami of the Imperial House and the MINAMOTO clan *(sōbyō no kami)*. . . . The assassination of Shoguns, the complete destruction of the TAIRA and MINAMOTO clans, and the selection of this child to be the next Shogun *have not been ordinary events* [emphasis added].

And elsewhere in the *Gukanshō* he takes the same line:

> The recent selection of the Minister of the Left KUJŌ Michiie's son Yoritsune as the next great military Shogun was certainly *made by the great Hachiman Bodhisattva*. It is an *incomprehensible* development that seems certainly to have been *an act of Kami*, not the doing of man [emphasis added].

Go-Toba had not appointed Yoritsune directly to the position of Shogun, but it was assumed that the boy would be named Shogun when he grew up. So the possibility that Yoritsune might also become a Regent-Chancellor presented to Jien an unexpected solution to his problem of military power, and also to the problem of how to relate his convictions about the supremacy of the Regent-Chancellor houses (4) to his idea about modern times falling within the Final Age (3):

> It seems, in this connection, that we have probably come to the time when the state should be protected, and the sovereign

guarded, by uniting the Regent-Chancellor house of FUJIWARA with the military house of MINAMOTO, thereby combining learning with military might.

And in another place he attributes such an arrangement to the power and will of ancestral Kami:

> It was definitely a divine decision that it would be good for the sovereign to have the same person serve as Shogun and Regent. The reason for this decision has been made clear. The ancestral Kami decided to provide the sovereign with a guardian who would have no desire to follow a course of rebellion and who would also be powerful and prestigious.

Jien had come to believe that the sacred vows of the three ancestral Kami (the Sun Goddess, the Great Illuminating Kami, and the Great Hachiman Bodhisattva) had blessed the "one hundred reigns" by creating administrative forms appropriate to particular times, places, and abilities. (Jien referred to these self-limiting vows of response to particular times and human abilities—the internal bases of support for different administrative forms—as "Principles that created for Japan one form of administration after another.") And now he believed that the Kami had created an administrative structure that would usher in a time of stability. He was certain that the new Regent-Shogun system, created by the ancestral Kami of the Imperial House and of the FUJIWARA and MINAMOTO clans, was appropriate for the deteriorated abilities of man in the Final Age and that it would be established when Yoritsune became an adult twenty years hence.

A Later View of the Loss of the Imperial Sword

The following quotation from the *Gukanshō* shows how Jien's ideas about the loss of the Imperial Sword in 1185 had changed between 1209 and 1219:

> But then the Sun Goddess and the Great Hachiman Bodhisattva reached this agreement: "Clearly there is now a time fate (*jiun*) which makes it impossible, since great military Shoguns have definitely gained control of the state, for the country's ruler to survive if he openly opposes the wishes of those great military Shoguns." Consequently, the Imperial Sword no longer has a function to perform. Emperor Takakura was placed on the throne by the TAIRA clan in 1168, and the Imperial military talisman was finally and definitely lost in 1185. Understanding clearly why the Imperial military talisman was lost, I have come to feel deeply about conditions of the present age.

In Jien's 1209 thoughts about the connection between the loss of the Imperial Sword and the rise of the military he was moved only by his consciousness of the present as the Final Age. He had not yet related the coming of the Final Age to his belief that ancestral Kami protected their descendants, or to his deep convictions about the supremacy of the Regent-Chancellor houses. By then he had certainly internalized the five elements discussed above, but he had not yet brought them together into a unified organic structure. The later *Gukanshō* way of relating the loss of the Imperial Sword to the rise of military power is, on the other hand, quite different. There his interpretation of the loss of the Imperial Sword has the stamp of a fully developed thought structure. Therefore I do not see the *Gukanshō* interpretation simply as a bundle of miscellaneous chrysanthemums, but as a chrysanthemum doll. I do not think that the doll could have been put together before the elements of Jien's thought were united. And I do not picture him spending years in writing the book after he had developed an interest in history and while he was working out his thoughts about the movement of events through time. Rather, I picture him writing it quickly after the elements of his thought had become functionally fused. Motivated by the "incomprehensible" events of 1218 and 1219, and utilizing his ability to write and compose poems quickly, he must have written the manuscript in a very short time.

The Influence of the Shōkyū War of 1221

What did Jien think of the *Gukanshō* after the military forces of Go-Toba had been defeated in the Shōkyū War of 1221? Immediately after the War—on the 1st day of the 8th month of 1221—Jien wrote a will that contains the following article:

> After I worshipped at the "new shrine," I received a sacred message from the Kami. There are several scrolls *(maki)* that I have written [interpreting those messages]. Although they are read, do people understand them? So I request that they be burned in the presence of the Buddha.[17]

Toshihide Akamatsu has concluded that Jien wanted the *Gukanshō* burned,[18] although that work is not specifically mentioned in Jien's will. We know that Jien had received several dream messages and, from the existence of the *Jichin Kashō musō ki*, that he had written more than one dream interpretation. In his prayer to Prince

17. *Zenshū*, 869.
18. Toshihide Akamatsu, "*Gukanshō* ni tsuite," *Kamakura Bukkyō no kenkyū* (Kyoto, 1957), p. 290.

Shōtoku and the Jūzenji Shrine, Jien had in fact written that the Prince revealed to him a plaque on which a Japanese poem was written in Chinese characters, and that the plaque was revealed to him as the Kami body of the "new shrine" *(shingu)*.[19] Also it is quite certain that he had made an addition to the *Gukanshō's* Imperial chronology before the 8th month of 1222.[20] I doubt that he wanted to destroy the *Gukanshō* in 1221 and then made additions to it one year later. I am inclined to think, in any case, that Jien did not fundamentally alter his historical views as a result of the Shōkyū War.

On the 1st day of the 5th month of 1224, Jien wrote a letter to a priest by the name of Amyō in which he makes a specific reference to the *Gukanshō:*

> The one-hundred-day memorial mass before the central object of worship at the Jūzenji Shrine has been begun in a most reverent way. Surely the empire will be pacified by the great good *(daizen)* effected thereby. Your prayers are quite impressive. Please send the *Gukanshō* back to me. I want to take a look at it. Have it brought by some reliable priest.[21]

It was at about the time this letter was written that Jien made another addition to the *Gukanshō's* chronology (Chapter 7), the one which begins with comments about Emperor Go-Horikawa's father being given the honorary title of Retired Emperor Go-Takaura on the 16th day of the 8th month of 1221, and that ends with the sentence about the death of that same Retired Emperor on the 14th day of the 5th month of 1223. At about that time HŌJŌ Yoshitoki died, and so Jien seems to have made another addition in which he noted the death of Yoshitoki on the 13th day of the 6th month of 1224, the return of Yasutoki (the son of Yoshitoki) to Kamakura on the evening of the 17th, and the return of Tokifusa (brother of Yoshitoki) on the 19th.

The tone and content of the additions made after the Shōkyū War leave the distinct impression that Jien's outlook on history was substantially what it was when he wrote the *Gukanshō*. By stating in the Go-Horikawa section of the Imperial chronology that "this enthronement of a grandson of a previous Emperor is the first such case since the enthronement of Emperor Kōnin [in 770]," he was not simply recording an historical event but being critical. Later on in that same section, when commenting on the honorary title of Retired Emperor being given to Go-Horikawa's father, although the father had never occupied the throne, he was also critical: "There probably had been no precedent in Japan for such action." And he expressed

19. Jien prayer, 1224–1–22 [ibid., p. 284].
20. Cf. my *Gukanshō no seiritsu to sono shisō* (Sendai, 1967), pp. 2–11.
21. Jien [to Amyō], [1224]–5–1 [NKBT, 86.526].

the same attitude when commenting on the honors that had been bestowed upon Go-Horikawa's mother, a nun: "There probably was no precedent for this." And finally he wrote: "Under conditions of the final reigns such irregularities are not unusual. The Final Age is truly miserable!" Thus the enthronement of Go-Horikawa, who replaced the son of a KUJŌ mother, was seen as action that was not in accord with the will of ancestral Kami.

The Meaning of Go-Takakura's Death

The prayer that Jien made to the soul of Prince Shōtoku, and to Jūzen-ji of the Hie Shrine, in the 1st month of 1224 suggests a fateful connection between the death of Retired Emperor Go-Takakura the previous year and the appearance of a comet, and also a meaningful connection between those events and Jien's own wishes. What did he think the connections were? A clue is found in the way the *Gukanshō* deals with the appearance of a comet just before the glorious days of FUJIWARA Michinaga at the end of the tenth century:

> . . . a comet streaked across the sky in the last third of the 6th month of 989. The era name was changed to Eiso in the 8th month of that year. Then came the incomparable disaster known as the Eiso typhoon. And in the following year the era name was changed to Shōryaku.

Then Jien tells about the terrible epidemic of 994–995 in which many people died, including Chancellor Michitaka and seven other high-ranking noblemen. After stating that "not one of the above eight victims of the epidemic was a good man for that period," Jien speaks of the results: "Michinaga administered the state without mishap, and the state seemed definitely to settle down." As for the meaning of the appearance of the comet, followed by such disasters, Jien theorizes as follows:

> It is my general understanding that when there is to be improvement in state affairs, a comet (a heavenly change) reveals that disasters will occur, signifying future improvement. People who wish to deepen their understanding of changes in the heavens, or anything else, should reflect deeply about connections between the appearance of a comet and subsequent disasters and improvement.

Jien must have seen such meaning in the appearance of another comet: it would be followed first by disasters and then by improvement. And for Jien improvement could have come only with the rise of the KUJŌ to positions of power and influence at the Imperial Court and in the *bakufu,* and the disasters were the deaths of Cloistered Emperor Go-Takakura and HŌJŌ Yoshitoki.

The extant anthology of Jien's poems, the *Shūgyoku shū,* contains a group of poems sent to SAIONJI Kintsune on the 18th day of the 6th month of 1223,[22] poems that dealt with the death of Retired Emperor Go-Takakura the previous month. Seven of them are:

> Rain in the rainy season
>> Makes me think of
> The changeableness of life.

This suggests distress over the death of Retired Emperor Go-Takakura.

> Even if I die,
>> For the sake of man
> I think about
>> The future.

> The world is now calm,
>> But what does the omen
> Suggest will happen?

Here the death of the Retired Emperor is viewed as an omen, foretelling improvement in the affairs of state.

> Kami, listen!
>> Horses of the eastern provinces run
> Along a path, where pine trees rustle,
>> Toward the future.

This denotes expectancy, probably in anticipation of that day when Yoritsune will have grown up and become both Shogun and Regent.

> World affairs move in accord with
>> The light of a comet.
> So the Kami do not want us
>> To despair.

Here the appearance of the comet is associated with future improvement and Kami will.

> The light of the spring sun (Kasuga)
>> Shines on the clear rocky stream (Iwashimizu)
> Leading us to expect a time
>> When there will be a sparkling reign.

This verse clearly refers to the vow between the ancestral Kami of the FUJIWARA clan (worshipped at the Kasuga Shrine) and the ancestral Kami of the MINAMOTO clan (worshipped at the Iwashimizu Shrine). It supported Jien's belief that the time had come for an administration in which Yoritsune would become both Shogun and Regent.

22. *Zenshū,* 350–351.

> Revering the Kami of Hie Shrine,
> Who does not abandon the world?
> We rejoice that the Sun Goddess
> Is in the heavens.

Jien's joyful conclusion about the meaning of Retired Emperor Go-Takakura's death is clear.

Now let us return to the prayer that Jien offered to the soul of Prince Shōtoku and to a Buddhist incarnation worshipped at the Jūzenji Shrine of Hie in the 1st month of 1224, just a few months after Jien had sent the above poems to SAIONJI Kintsune. The prayer includes these sentences:

> The father of the present Emperor was granted the honorary title of Retired Emperor, and he administered the empire's affairs. Then another comet appeared in the heavens, and only two or three years later the Retired Emperor died. . . . We now frequently hear reports of heavenly and earthly changes, . . . and there also have been dream revelations. So we can expect that Retired Emperor Go-Toba will be returned from exile, that Regent Michiie will be reappointed Regent, and that Yoritsune will become an adult Shogun. It looks like all these expectations are about to be realized.[23]

On the basis of what Jien writes here about the comet portending the death of Retired Emperor Go-Takakura, it can be deduced that he felt Go-Takakura was not "a good man for that period" and that because of his death a time would come when, under the administration of KUJŌ Michiie and Retired Emperor Go-Toba, the state would settle down until Yoritsune should become both Shogun and Regent. Such beliefs are reflected in both the 1223 poems and the 1224 prayer.

Just three months after Jien had written the 1224 prayer to Prince Shōtoku and the Kami worshipped at the Jūzenji Shrine, a memorial mass was held before the Kami worshipped at the Jūzenji Shrine. And in the letter that Jien wrote to Amyō he refers to "the great good effected" by the mass, and states that "the empire will be pacified."[24] The word "pacified" (*ando*) as used in the 1224 prayer must have had somewhat the same meaning as "settling down" (*rakkyo*) had had in 1219.

Meaning of the Death of HŌJŌ Yoshitoki

After the Shōkyū War, HŌJŌ Yoshitoki had been prominent in decisions that forced the abdication of Emperor Chūkyō (son of a KUJŌ mother), the dismissal of KUJŌ Michiie from the post of Re-

---

23. Jien prayer to Prince Shōtoku, 1224–1–22 [Akamatsu, "*Gukanshō* ni tsuite," p. 285].

24. Jien [to Amyō], [1224]–5–1 [NKBT, 86.526].

gent, and the exile of three Emperors, including Go-Toba. Thus the death of HŌJŌ Yoshitoki in the 6th month of 1224 must have given Jien an additional reason for feeling that the predictions referred to in his prayer of the 1st month of 1224, and the hopes expressed in his letter to Amyō in the 5th month of 1224, were about to be realized. Immediately after Yoshitoki's death in the 6th month of 1224, Jien made his last addition to the *Gukanshō* chronology, recording Yoshitoki's death and the return of Yasutoki and Tokifusa to Kamakura.

I conclude, therefore, that Yoshitoki's death, as well as the appearance of the comet and the demise of Retired Emperor Go-Takakura, were thought of as signs that had a meaning like that associated with the strange events before the marvelous days of Michinaga, and again before the improvements anticipated when the *Gukanshō* was being written. This leads me to think that Jien's thought structure—formed over at least a decade before 1219, given unity by the logic of thinking about what was appropriate for particular stages of historical decline, and deeply colored by preoccupation with the supremacy of the KUJŌ house—was not altered at all by the defeat of Imperial forces in the Shōkyū War of 1221.

Glossary

Terms of importance to Jien's historical interpretation

Bō (蔀), cyclical unit of 60 years.

Bu (武), military might.

Bun (文), *learning*.

Buppō (仏法), Buddhist Law.

Bushi no yo (武士ノ世), Military Age.

Chingo kokka (鎮護国家), protection of the state.

Chūko (中古), Medieval Age.

Dōri (道理), Principle.

En (縁), Outer Cause.

Go-ichidaku (御一諾), divine agreement.

Gyakuma (逆魔), antagonistic demons.

Higagoto (ヒガ), wrongdoing.

Hijiri (ヒジリ), Holy Man.

Hitotsugime (一ツギメ), turning point.

Hōben kyōmon (方便教門), expedient teachings.

Hon'i (本意), basic intent [of deities].

Hōni (法爾), [occurring] spontaneously and naturally.

Hyaku-ō (百王), one hundred reigns.

Inga (因果), **cause and effect.**

Inga no dōri (因果ノ道理), causal Principle.

Itoku (威徳), prestige and virtue.

Jama (邪魔), evil demons.

Jisetsu (時節), point in time.

Jiun (時運), time fate.

Jōko (上古), Ancient Age.

Jumma (順魔), deceptive demons.

Kahō (果報), **causal effects.**

Ken (顕), visible.

Kiryō (器量), ability.

Kokumo (国母), Imperial mother.

Kōsho kōmatsu (劫初劫末), from the beginning to the end of the first half of the present small kalpa.

Kōtei nendai ki (皇帝年代記), Imperial chronology.

Kotowari (コトハリ), Principle.

Makoto no kokoro (誠ノ心), sincere heart.

Mappō (末法), age of Final Law.

Masse (末世), Final Age.

Matsudai (末代), final reigns.

Messō (滅相), deteriorating phase.

Mikokoro (御心), sacred will.

Miraiki (未来記), prophecy.

Mudō (無道), non-way.

Mukui (ムクイ), retribution.

Musa no yo (ムサノ世), Military Age.

Myō (冥), invisible.

Myōshū (冥衆), invisible beings.

Nihon koku no rangyabu (日本国ノ乱逆), rebellions of the country of Japan.

Nyonin jugan (女人入眼), women provide the finishing touches.

Ōbō (王法), Imperial Law.

Ōi no shōbō (王位ノ正法), True Law of Imperial succession.

Omobuki (趣), meaning.

Onryō (怨霊), vengeful soul.

Rishō hōben (利生方便), expedient blessings.

Shashoku (社稷), ancestral Kami.

Shidan no chigiri (師檀ノ契), patron pledge.

Shōbō (正法), age of True Law.

Shōdō (正道), correct way.

Shōnin (上人), Saint.

Sōbyō (宗廟), Sun Goddess and Hachiman.

Taiji no hō (対治ノ法), way of negating [deterioration].

Tendō (天道), Heaven Way.

Tengu (天狗), demons.

Un (運), destiny.

Ummei (運命), destiny.

Yo no sue (世ノスエ), Final Age.

Yotsugi no monogatari (世継物語), Succession Tales.

Zensei (善政), good government.

Bibliography

Sources and studies referred to in the text and notes. Items in the first four sections are listed chronologically. The location of Japanese publishers will be shown only if it is not Tokyo.

Gukanshō Texts and Commentaries

Kuroita Katsumi, ed. *Gukanshō*. In [*Shintei zōho*] *Kokushi taikei*. Yoshikawa Kōbunkan, 1930, vol. 19. [Hereafter, the [*Shintei zōho*] *Kokushi taikei* will be referred to as KT.] This edition, preceded by two editions published at the beginning of the twentieth century, is based upon the Bunmei text of 1476, which is thought to be the earliest of the extant texts.

Maruyama Jirō, ed. *Gukanshō*. In *Iwanami Bunko* series. Iwanami Shoten, 1949. Our translation is from this edition, which is based on texts discovered and studies made since the appearance of the Kuroita edition.

Okami Masao and Akamatsu Toshihide, eds. *Gukanshō*. In *Nihon koten bungaku taikei*. Iwanami Shoten, 1967, vol. 86. [Hereafter, the *Nihon koten bungaku taikei* will be referred to as NKBT.] The editors of this edition made use of the recently discovered Shimabara text and wrote voluminous notes that are very valuable.

Nakajima Etsuji. *Gukanshō hyōshaku*. Kokubun Kenkyū Kai, 1931. This commentary is limited largely to the *Gukanshō's* last narrative chapter (fascicle), the fifth chapter of the translation.

———. *Gukanshō zen chūkai*. Yūseidō, 1969. Here Nakajima includes explanatory notes for all seven chapters.

Other Writings by Jien

Taga Munehaya, ed. *Jien zenshū*. Kyoto: Shichijō Shoin, 1945. A complete collection of letters, poems, prayers, and manuscripts written by Jien.

Gammon (prayer of 1222). *Dai Nihon shiryō*, Series 5, 2.737. Also in: Akamatsu Toshihide. *Kamakura Bukkyō no kenkyū*. Kyoto: Heirakuji Shoten, 1957, pp. 298–299. This prayer tells of prophetic dreams that Jien had before writing the *Gukanshō*.

Jichin kashō musō ki. In Akamatsu Toshihide. *Kamakura Bukkyō no kenkyū*. Kyoto: Heirakuji Shoten, 1957, pp. 318–322. A dream interpretation written by Jien, in three stages, between 1203 and 1209, revealing the emergence of concerns that affected his later interpretation of Japanese history.

Gammon of Jōō 3 (1224)-1-22. In Akamatsu Toshihide. *Kamakura Bukkyō no Kenkyū*. Kyoto: Heirakuji Shoten, 1957, pp. 283–286. A long prayer written toward the end of Jien's life. It tells us much about Jien's view of history.

"*Gukanshō* kankei Jien jihitsu shōsoku." NKBT 86.524–528. Many of these items written by Jien are fragmentary and undated, but a few are helpful.

Chronicles, Historical and Military Tales, and Other Early Historical Accounts

Kojiki. Compiled by Ō no Yasumaro (d. 723). KT 7. Translation by Donald L. Philippi. *Kojiki*. Princeton University Press and University of Tokyo Press, 1969.

Nihon shoki. Compiled by Prince Toneri (676–735) et al. KT 67 and 68. Translation by W. G. Aston. *Nihongi: Chronicles of Japan from the Earliest Times to A.D. 697*. London: George Allen and Unwin, 1956 (reprint).

Shoku Nihongi. Compiled by Sugano Mamichi et al. KT 2. Partial translation by J. B. Snellen. "Shoku Nihongi (Chronicles of Japan)." *Transactions of the Asiatic Society of Japan*, 2nd Series, XI (1934), 151–239, and XIV (1937), 209–278.

Nihon kōki. Compiled by Fujiwara Otsugu (773–843) et al. KT 3.

Shoku Nihon kōki. Compiled by Fujiwara Yoshifusa (804–872) et al. KT 3.

Montoku jitsuroku. Compiled by Fujiwara Mototsune (835–891) et al. KT 3.

Nihon sandai jitsuroku. Compiled by Fujiwara Tokihira (871–909) et al. KT 4.

Nihon ryōi ki. By Keikai. NKBT 70.

Genji monogatari. By Murasaki Shikibu (987–1015). *Nihon koten bungaku zenshū*, vols. 12 to 17. Translated by (1) Arthur Waley. *The Tale of Genji: A Novel in Six Parts—The Tale of Genji, The Sacred Tree, A Wreath of Cloud, Blue Trousers, The Lady of the Boat, The Bridge of Dreams*. Modern Library, 1960. And (2) Edward G. Seidensticker. *Murasaki Shikibu: The Tale of Genji*. 2 vols. New York: Alfred A. Knopf, 1976.

Eiga monogatari. NKBT 75 and 76.

Ōkagami. NKBT 21. Translation by Joseph K. Yamagiwa. *The Okagami: A Japanese Historical Tale*. London: George Allen and Unwin, 1967.

Hōgen monogatari. NKBT 31. Translation by William R. Wilson. *Hōgen monogatari: Tale of Disorder of Hōgen*. Sophia University, 1971.

Heiji monogatari. NKBT 31. Partially translated by Edwin O. Reischauer. "The Heiji Monogatari." *Translations from Early Japanese Literature.* Cambridge, Mass.: Harvard University Press, 1951.
Heike monogatari. NKBT 32 and 33. Translated by (1) Arthur Lindsay Sadler. "Heiki Monogatari." *Transactions of the Asiatic Society of Japan,* I (1918), 1–278, and II (1921), 1–354. And (2) Hiroshi Kitagawa and Bruce T. Tsuchida. *The Tale of Heike: Heike Monogatari.* University of Tokyo Press, 1975.
Nihon kiryaku. KT 11.
Fusō ryakki. KT 12.
Mizukagami. [*Kōtei*] *Nihon bungaku taikei.* Kokumin Tosho, 1925–28, vol. 12.
Hyakurenshō. KT 11.
Azuma kagami. KT 32 and 33.
Shōkyū ki. [*Kōchū*] *Kokubun sōsho.* Hakubun Kan, 1912–15, vol. 15.
Jinnō shōtō ki. NKBT 87.

Diaries, Buddhist Writings, and Other Early Sources

Uda Tennō gyoki. By Emperor Uda (867–931). [*Zokuzoku*] *Gunsho ruijū.* Zoku Gunsho Ruijū Kansei Kai, 1969, 5.1–14.
Daigo Tennō gyoki. By Emperor Daigo (885–930). [*Zokuzoku*] *Gunsho ruijū.* Zoku Gunsho Ruijū Kansei Kai, 1969, 5.15–62.
Chūyū ki. By Fujiwara Munetada (d. 1141), Sasagawa Tanerō, and Yano Tarō, eds. *Shiryō taisei* (Naigai Shoseki Kabushiki Kaisha, 1934–39), vols. 8–14. [Hereafter the *Shiryō taisei* will be referred to as ST.]
Hyōhan ki. By Taira Nobumori (1112–87). ST 15–18.
Kikki. By Yoshida Tsunefusa (1143–1200). ST 22 and 23.
Gyokuyō. By Kujō Kanezane (1149–1207). In *Gyokuyō,* ed. Kokusho Kankō Kai. 3 vols. Tokyo Kappan Kabushiki Kaisha, 1906–07.
Meigetsu ki. By Fujiwara Sadaie (1162–1241). Kokusho Kankō Kai, ed. *Meigetsu ki.* 1911 reprint.
Myōhō renge kyō (S. Saddharma-pundarika-sūtra). *Taishō* [*shinshū*] *daizōkyō* (Daizō Shuppan, 1924–34), No. 264. [Hereafter the *Taishō* [*shinshū*] *daizōkyō* will be referred to as *Taishō.*] The Sanskrit text has been translated by H. Kern. *The Lotus of the True Law,* vol. 21 of the *Sacred Books of the East.* Oxford, 1885. Reprinted by Dover Publications in 1963. The Chinese text has been translated by Bunnō Katō and revised by W. E. Soothill and Wilhelm Schiffer. *Myōhō-renge-kyō: The Sutra of the Lotus Flower of the Wonderful Law.* Risshō Kōsei-kai, 1971.
Kusha ron (S. Abhidharma-kośa). *Taishō,* No. 1558.
Ninnō-kyō (S. Prajñāpāramitā-sūtra). *Taishō,* No. 246.
Daihōdō daijikkyō (C. Ta-fang-têng-ta-chi-ching). *Taishō,* No. 397.
Hieizan Gakuin, ed. *Dengyō daishi zenshū.* 5 vols. Hieizan Toshokan, 1927.
Hanayama Shinshō, ed. *Ojō yōshū.* Oyama Shoten, 1937.
Tendai zasu ki. In [*Zoku*] *Gunsho ruijū.* Keizai Zasshi Sha, 1902–12, vol. 4, section 3.
Engi shiki. KT 26. Partially translated by Felicia Gressitt Boch. *Engi-Shiki: Procedures of the Engi Era.* 2 vols. Sophia University, 1970 and 1972.
Kujō dono yuikai. By Fujiwara Morosuke (908–960). *Gunsho ruijū.* Keizai Zasshisha, 1959–60, vol. 27.
Korai fūtai shō. By Fujiwara Toshinari (1114–1204). [*Zoku*] *Gunsho ruijū,* vol. 16, section 3.

Renchū shō. By Fujiwara Suketaka. In [*Kaitei*] *Shiseki Shūran*. Kondō Shuppan Bu, 1882–1903, vol. 23.

Studies of the Gukanshō and Jien

Akamatsu Toshihide. "*Gukanshō* ni tsuite." *Kamakura Bukkyō no kenkyū*. Kyoto: Heirakuji Shoten, 1957, pp. 267–335.

———. "*Gukanshō* ni tsuite." *Zoku Kamakura Bukkyō no kenkyū*. Kyoto: Heirakuji Shoten, 1966, pp. 373–389.

———. "*Jichin kashō musō ki* ni tsuite." *Kamakura Bukkyō no kenkyū*, pp. 373–389.

———. "Yoritomo to sono musume." *Zoku Kamakura Bukkyō no kenkyū*, pp. 390–409.

Hambrick, Charles H. "Gukanshō: A Religious View of History." Unpublished Ph.D. dissertation. University of Chicago, 1971.

Harada Ryūkichi. "*Gukanshō* no dōri." *Bunka*, XXIV: 4 (1960), 25–53.

———. "*Gukanshō* no roni." *Bunka*, XX: 5 (1956), 807–818.

Inouye Mitsusada. "*Gukanshō* no rekishi kan." *Kokugo to Kokubungaku*, October, 1954, pp. 77–85.

Ishida Ichirō. "*Gukanshō*." In Maruyama Masao, ed. *Rekishi shisō shū* (Vol. 6 of *Nihon no shisō*; Chikuma Shobō, 1972), pp. 89–152.

———. "*Gukanshō* no rekishi shisō." *Nihon shisō shigaku*, September, 1969, pp. 1–12.

———. *Gukanshō no seiritsu to sono shisō*. No. 17 of the *Tōhoku Daigaku Bungakubu kenkyū nempō*. Sendai: Tōhoku University, 1967, pp. 1–108.

———. "*Gukanshō* to Jien." In *Fukui Hakase shōju kinen: Tōyō bunka ronshū*. Waseda Daigaku Shuppan Bu, 1969, pp. 55–72.

———. "Jiki sōō no ronri: Saichō to Hōnen Shinran wo tsunagumono." In *Fujishima Hakase kanreki kinen ronshu: Nihon jōdo-kyō no kenkyū* (Kyoto: Heirakuji Shoten, 1969), pp. 131–159.

Miura Hiroyuki. "*Gukanshō* no kenkyū." *Shirin*, VI: 1 (1921), 1–29.

Mochizuki Kenjirō. "*Gukanshō* no dōri ni tsuite." *Nihon Rekishi*, LI (August, 1952), 52–61.

Muraoka Tsunetsugu. "*Gukanshō* kō." In his [*Zōtei*] *Nihon shisō shi kenkyū*. *Iwanami Shoten*, 1940, pp. 21–61.

———. "*Gukanshō* no chosaku nendai hensei oyobi shahon." In his [*Zōtei*] *Nihon shisō shi kenkyū*. Iwanami Shoten, 1940, pp. 62–71.

———. "Mappō shisō no tenkai to *Gukanshō* no shikan." In his *Nihon shisō shi kenkyū*. Ōsaka: Sōgensha, 1957, 2.111–209.

Rhader, Johannes, trans. "Miscellany of Personal Views of an Ignorant Fool [Guk(w)anshō]." *Acta Orientalia*, XV: 3 (1936), 173–230.

Taga Munehaya. *Jien*. Vol. 15 of *Jimbutsu sōsho*. Yoshikawa Kōbunkan, 1959.

Tsuda Sōkichi. "*Gukanshō* no chosaku nendai ni tsuite no utagai." *Shisō*, XXXV (September, 1924), 1–16.

Studies Relating to Early Japanese Historiography

Beasley, William Gerald, and Edwin George Pulleyblank, eds. *Historians of China and Japan*. Oxford: Oxford University Press, 1961.

Brower, Robert H., and Earl Miner. *Japanese Court Poetry*. Stanford, Calif.: Stanford University Press, 1961.

Butler, Kenneth Dean. "The Textual Evolution of the *Heike Monogatari*." *Harvard Journal of Asiatic Studies* (1966), pp. 5–51.

Coates, Harper Havelock, and Ishizuka Ryūgaku. *Hōnen, the Buddhist Saint: His Life and Teaching.* 5 vols. Kyoto: Society for the Publication of Sacred Books of the World, 1949.

de Bary, William Theodore, et al., eds. *Sources of Japanese Tradition.* New York: Columbia University Press, 1958.

De Visser, Marinus Willem. *Ancient Buddhism in Japan.* 2 vols. Leiden: E. J. Brill, 1935.

Dubs, H. H. *History of the Former Han Dynasty.* 2 vols. Baltimore: Waverly Press, 1938–44.

Duyvendak, J. J. L. *The Book of Lord Shang: A Classic of the Chinese School of Law.* Chicago: University of Chicago Press, 1963.

Fung, Yu-lan. *History of Chinese Philosophy.* 2 vols. Derk Bodde, trans. Princeton: Princeton University Press, 1952.

———. *A Short History of Chinese Philosophy.* Derk Bodde, trans. New York: The Free Press, 1966.

Futaba Kenko. *Kodai Bukkyō shisō shi kenkyū.* Nagata Bunshō Dō, 1962.

Harada Ryūkichi. "Kamakura jidai no rekishi shisō: Mappō shisō no chōkoku." In Ichiro Ishida, ed. *Nihon ni okeru rekishi shisō shi no tenkai.* Sendai: Nihon Shisō Shi Kenkyū Kai, 1965, pp. 101–129. [Hereafter cited as *Rekishi shisō.*]

Holtom, D. C. *The Japanese Enthronement Ceremonies, with an Account of the Imperial Regalia.* Sophia University, 1972.

Hurst, G. Cameron, III. *Insei: Abdicated Sovereigns in the Politics of Late Heian Japan, 1086–1185.* Studies of the East Asian Institute. New York: Columbia University Press, 1976.

Inouye Mitsusada. *Shinwa kara rekishi e.* Vol. 1 of *Nihon no rekishi.* Chūō Kōron Sha, 1965.

Inouye Susumu. *Kamakura bakufu.* Vol. 7 of *Nihon no rekishi.* Chūō Kōron Sha, 1974.

Ishida Ichirō. "Kokka keisei jidai no rekishi shisō." *Rekishi shisō,* pp. 2–30.

———. *Nihon no kaika.* Vol. 12 of *Dai sekai shi.* Bungei Shunjū, 1968.

———. "Shinwa to rekishi: Shisei ritsuryō kokka to kasei rikken kokka no rinen." *Nihon bunka kenkyū,* No. 8. Shinchō Sha, 1960.

Ishida Takeshi. "*Gukanshō* to *Jinnō shōtōki* no rekishi shisō." In Maruyama Masao, ed. *Rekishi shisō shū* (Vol. 6 of *Nihon no shisō;* Chikuma Shobō, 1972), pp. 47–62.

Kazue Kyōichi. *Nihon no mappō shisō: Nihon chūsei shisō shi kenkyū.* Ōsaka: Kobundō, 1961.

Legge, James, trans. *The Chinese Classics.* 4 vols. London: John Alden, 1890.

Maruyama Masao. "Rekishi ishiki no kiso." In *Rekishi shisō shū.* (Chikuma Shobō, 1972), pp. 3–46.

Mass, Jeffrey P. *Warrior Government in Early Medieval Japan: A Study of the Kamakura Bakufu, Shugo and Jitō.* New Haven: Yale University Press, 1974.

Matsunaga, Alicia. *The Buddhist Philosophy of Assimilation.* Sophia University, 1969.

Miller, Richard. *Ancient Japanese Nobility.* Berkeley: University of California Press, 1974.

Morris, Ivan. *The World of the Shining Prince: Court Life in Ancient Japan.* New York: Columbia University Press, 1964.

Nishio Yōtaro. "Heian jidai kōki no rekishi shisō." *Redishi shisō,* pp. 75–99.

Ozawa Tomio. *Mappō to masse noi shisō.* Yūzankaku, 1974.

Reischauer, Edwin O. *Ennin's Travels in T'ang China.* New York: Ronald
    Press, 1955.
Sakamoto Tarō. *Nihon no shūshi to shigaku.* Vol. 42 of *Nihon rekishi shinsho.*
    Shibundō, 1958.
Shibata Minoru. "Heian jidai zenki no rekishi shisō: Kidendō no seishin."
    Rekishi shisō, pp. 55–73.
Tsunoda Ryūsaku, trans. *Japan in Chinese Dynastic Histories.* South Pasadena,
    Calif.: Perkins, 1951.
Umezawa, Isezō. "Asuka Nara jidai no rekishi shisō." *Rekishi shisō,* pp. 33–50.
——. *Kojiki Nihon shoki.* San'ichi Shobō, 1971.
Watson, Burton. *Early Chinese Literature.* New York: Columbia University
    Press, 1962.
——. *Records of the Grand Historian of China: Translated from the Shi Chi of
    Ssu-ma Ch'ien.* 2 vols. New York: Columbia University Press, 1961.

Index

Ability: is understanding Principles, 10, 22; subject to kalpic decline, 10, 208; alters history, 11; lack of justifies enforced abdication, 10–11, 235, 238, 240; will be possessed by KUJŌ Yoritsune, 11 and *n;* important in ministers, 47; lacking in Final-Age sovereigns, 47; lacking in Final-Age ministers, 65; causes strange developments, 83; lack of disqualifies man as Regent, 86; possessed by MINAMOTO Yoritomo, 154; demonstrated by KUJŌ Yoshitsune, 167; superior in KUJŌ Michiie, 173; in China, 203, 208; appropriate in FUJIWARA ministers, 213; enables person to avoid revenge of vengeful souls, 220; retained by few serving Go-Shirakawa, 233–34, 349; found only in KUJŌ house, 234–35

Accommodating ideals to realities of time, place, and human ability (element of G. thought structure): binds other elements together, 421, 422 Figure 2; developed in association with Final-Law thought, 428; binds Buddhist eschatological thought to ancestral-Kami belief, 428–32; associated with periods of decline in Japan, 429–32; binds Final-Law thought to convictions of Regent-Chancellor supremacy,

435–36; relationship to idea of KUJŌ-MINAMOTO cooperation in final reigns, 436

Amaterasu Ōmikami. *See* Sun Goddess

Ancestral-Kami belief (element of G. thought structure): relationship to other elements, 421, 422 Figure 2; protection of clan descendents, 426–27; agreements between ancestral Kami, 427; influenced by Buddhist eschatological thought, 427–28; focused on three ancestral Kami. *See also* Great Hachiman Bodhisattva; Great Illuminating Kami; Sun Goddess

Ancient Age: fine and noble events, 52; lasts until Daigo and Murakami, 52

Bifuku-mon In: Imperial mother of Konoe, 95, 324 and *n;* receives oath taken by Toba soldiers, 99; treated as Imperial mother of Go-Shirakawa, 99 and *n;* accompanies Go-Shirakawa to TAIRA Kiyomori mansion, 113; harbors Nijō, 116; backs Go-Shirakawa against Sutoku, 386–90

Buddha incarnations: associated with spread of Buddha Law and FUJIWARA prosperity, 5; emerge at turning points on single course of Japanese history, 8 and *n;* Prince Shōtoku, FUJIWARA Kamatari, SUGAWARA Michizane, Grand Preceptor Ji'e, 46

478

Index

Sun Goddess *(cont.)*
Illuminating Kami, 5, 29, 43, 211, and
n, 213 and *n*, 228 *n*, 429; makes
agreement with Great Illuminating
Kami and Great Hachiman
Bodhisattva, support Imperial rule
with learning and military might, 6,
228; divine force shaping secular
history, 9, 428–30; has plan for Final
Age, 29, 226, 228 and *n*, 429; decides
against more reigning Empresses, for
Imperial mothers who are FUJIWARA
daughters, 37; wishes to protect
FUJIWARA Michinaga, 59; can be relied
upon until end of one hundred reigns,
82–83; command equated with KUJŌ
Tadamichi advice, 98; agrees to
transfer function of Imperial Sword to
soldiers, 144; has Retired Emperors
administer state, 213; decides KUJŌ
Yoritsune shall be next Shogun, 214;
decides on improved relations between
sovereigns and Regent-Chancellors,
214; decisions respected by KUJŌ
Tadazane, 217; produces Chūkyō and
Yoritsune, 223; instructions revealed,
253, 276; shoots arrow for MINAMOTO
Tametomo, 389. *See* Ancestral-Kami
belief

Taiken-mon In: daughter of KAN'IN
Kinzane, 90, 322; Imperial mother of
Sutoku and Go-Shirakawa, 91, 98, 185,
322, 326; causes KAN'IN house to
prosper, 93
TAIRA Kiyomori: joins MINAMOTO
Yoshitomo in supporting
Go-Shirakawa, 102; opposes
MINAMOTO Yoshitomo, 107, 391;
Emperor Nijō moves to residence of,
111–12; has FUJIWARA Nobuyori
captured and beheaded, 115; marries
sister to KONOE Motozane, 117; hopes
wife's sister will become Imperial
mother, 118; Prime Minister, 120,
121–22, 329 and *n*; gives Motozane's
lands to Moriko, 120; has son of
Kenshun-mon In enthroned as
Takakura, 121; enters Buddhist
priesthood, 121; marries daughter to
Takakura, 122; prays to ancestral
Kami for Imperial grandson, 122;
Imperial grandson enthroned as
Antoku, 122; exiles Prince Mochihito
who flees to Miidera, 128; has Prince
caught and killed, 128; troops sent to
destroy MINAMOTO are defeated, 130;
destruction of descendants no doing of
man, 182; used destructive way to
select sovereign, 229; in *Heike*, 392–95

—Masakado: rebellion crushed, 295
and *n*
—Moriko: daughter of TAIRA Kiyomori
and wife of KONOE Motozane, 117–18
and *n;* receives land of deceased
Motozane, 120; land later given by
Go-Shirakawa to MATSU Motofusa, 126
—Munemori: adopted by Kenshun-mon
In, 122; succeeds Kiyomori, 131; flees
captial with Antoku, 132; moves to join
MINAMOTO Yoshinaka, 141; defeated
by MINAMOTO Yoshitsune, 141 and *n;*
captured and beheaded, 142, 145, 189;
Minister of the Center, 333
—Shigehira: burns Kōfuku and Tōdai
Temples of Nara, 128; captured by
MINAMOTO Yoshitsune, 141 and *n;*
beheaded in Nara to show that
enemies of Buddha Law are destroyed,
145; prominent in *Heike*, 396
—Shigeko. *See* Kenshun-mon In
—Shigemori: Kiyomori son, fine man,
121–22, 189; critical of father's
rebelliousness, 125; Minister of the
Center, 332 and *n;* hero of *Heike*,
393–94
—Tokiko: maternal grandmother of
Antoku, 142 *n;* jumps into sea with
Antoku and Imperial Regalia, 142
and *n*
—Tokitada: brother of Takakura's
Imperial mother, 117; worsens
relations between Nijō and
Go-Shirakawa, 117 and *n;* returns
Sacred Mirror, 334
—Yorimori: MINAMOTO Yoritomo saved
by mother of, 129; aided by
Go-Shirakawa, 132; seeks help from
MINAMOTO Yoritomo, 147; son serves
MINAMOTO Sanetomo, 190
TAKASHINA Eishi: attends Go-Shirakawa,
127 and *n;* meets KUJŌ Kanezane, 151
and *n;* plans to have daughter by
Go-Shirakawa made Go-Toba
Empress, 152; conspires with
MINAMOTO Michichika, 158–59, 410;
believes Go-Shirakawa soul vengeful,
169
TAKENOUCHI Sukune: first Imperial
minister, 22–23; allowed to serve as
proper minister by Empress Jingū, 37;
Chief Minister, 254; Great Imperial
Chieftain, 254, 255, 256
Tendai: introduced by Grand Preceptor
Dengyō, 34; priests make demands on
court, 88 and *n*, 320, 343; power
struggle between Abbots, 138; four
former Abbots after Kakujin are
frequently rejected by priests of, 316
and *n;* subject of additional G. chapter,

Designer	Dave Comstock
Composition	Typesetting Services of California
Lithography	Braun-Brumfield, Inc.
Binder	Braun-Brumfield, Inc.
Text	VIP Baskerville
Display	VIP Bembo
Paper	50 lb P&S Offset Vellum B32
Binding	Holliston Roxite B 53561 linen

DATE DUE